Advance Pr
Learning to Rea

D0348901

"A well-documented and thorough treatise on literacy development in infants and toddlers, *Learning to Read the World* will become a staple on the reading lists of early childhood faculty, administrators, consultants, and teachers working with young children."

— Pamela J. Winton, PhD, Senior Scientist and Director of Outreach, FPG Child Development Institute and Research Professor School of Education, University of North Carolina–Chapel Hill

"*Learning to Read the World* is masterful in its reach, thorough in its coverage, both wise and practical in its counsel, and exceptionally well written, chapter after chapter. This book, which provides essential background information about the earliest foundations of language and literacy development, is a must read for everyone who is interested in supporting literacy during the early years."

— Judith A. Schickedanz, PhD, Professor, Department of Literacy and Language, Counseling, and Developmental Studies, School of Education, Boston University

"This wonderful book links early language and literacy learning with caregiving experiences that promote social and emotional development in infancy and early childhood. Parents as well as professionals in the infant and family field will find this book enormously helpful in raising eager and successful readers who are ready to learn."

— Deborah J. Weatherston, PhD, Executive Director, Michigan Association for Infant Mental Health and Infant Mental Health Faculty, the Merrill-Palmer Institute, Wayne State University

"This book is a must have for those who work in early childhood. The strategies featured in many of the chapters in this book are valuable resources for everyone who touches the lives of children and their families."

— Rosa Milagros Santos, PhD, University of Illinois at Urbana-Champaign

Learning to Read the World

Language and Literacy in the First Three Years

Edited by Sharon E. Rosenkoetter and Joanne Knapp-Philo

ZERO TO THREE®

National Center for Infants,
Toddlers, and Families

Washington, DC

Published by

ZERO TO THREE

National Center for Infants,
Toddlers, and Families

ZERO TO THREE
Toll-free orders (800) 899-4301
Web: http://www.zerotothree.org

The mission of the ZERO TO THREE Press is to publish authoritative research, practical resources, and new ideas for those who work with and care about infants, toddlers, and their families. Books are selected for publication by an independent Editorial Board.

The views contained in this book are those of the authors and do not necessarily reflect those of ZERO TO THREE: National Center for Infants, Toddlers and Families, Inc.

Cover and text design: K Art and Design, Inc.

Library of Congress Cataloging-in-Publication Data

Learning to read the world : language and literacy in the first three years
/ [edited by] Sharon E. Rosenkoetter & Joann Knapp-Philo.
    p.   cm.
    Includes bibliographical references.
    ISBN 0-943657-86-5
    1. Language acquisition. 2. Literacy.   I. Rosenkoetter, Sharon E.,
    1944-   . II. Knapp-Philo, Joann.
    P118.L38993 2005
    401'.93--dc22   2005015804

10 9 8 7 6 5 4 3 2

ISBN 0-943657-86-5

Printed in the United States of America

Suggested citations:

Book citation: Rosenkoetter, S. E., & Knapp-Philo, J. (Eds.). (2006). *Learning to read the world: Language and literacy in the first three years.* Washington, DC: ZERO TO THREE Press.

Chapter citation: Barton, L. R., & Brophy-Herb. H. E. (2006). Developmental foundations for language and literacy from birth to 3 years. In S. E. Rosenkoetter & J. Knapp-Philo (Eds.), *Learning to read the world: Language and literacy in the first three years* (pp. 15–60). Washington, DC: ZERO TO THREE Press.

Dedication

To StoryQUEST teams, learning coaches, trainers, and partners,
who have taught us more than anyone knows,

and

To our children, our first teachers about early language and literacy.

and

To Larry and John, our partners in life.

In Memory of

Emily Fenichel, the heart of ZERO TO THREE Press and
the originator of this volume, enduring appreciation.

Table of Contents

The Foundations

The Family

Other Caregivers

The Program

The Community

Applications

Into the Future

List of Tables and Figures

Figures

Appendixes

Tables

Foreword

This lengthy, far-ranging, comprehensive volume is, paradoxically, focused like a laser beam on a single issue of major national importance: ensuring children's success in literacy by providing an adequate foundation in the first 3 years of life. The many chapters devoted to aspects of development from birth to 3 make clear that success in literacy builds on a foundation that includes much more than just exposure to books or early training in letters and sounds. The foundation for success in learning to read is high levels of cognition, language, and motivation. And infants can come to be motivated, cognitively competent, and linguistically skilled only through interactions with loving, caring adults. The relationships that adults forge with young children are the coffer in which opportunities for learning are delivered, enfolded in the protective bubblewrap of play, pleasure, curiosity, and joyful discovery.

Of course, parents have been providing their infants with love and care, with opportunities to play and chances to learn, forever. Why do we need a book alerting us to young children's need for such interactions? The reasons are many, but I will note only four:

- Preparation and support for parenting are inadequate.

- Out-of-home care is massively more common than it used to be.

- Stakes for achievement are higher than ever.

- The gap in achievement between middle class European-Americans and children from minority and immigrant groups is the civil rights agenda of the 21st century.

Parenting. Extended family contacts, access by first-time parents to older friends and relatives experienced with young children, easily accessible pediatricians and well-baby clinics, and other procedures for socializing and supporting parents are inadequate in the United States of the 21st century. Nuclear families, high family mobility, and the high cost of health care all play roles in their inaccessibility. Simultaneously, women's greatly increased role in the work force raises pressure on parents and threatens opportunities for parents to discover the joys of extensive interaction with their infants. Although parent education is often offered as part of prevention or intervention programs for low-income families, only a small proportion of the qualifying families are served, and the need for the information and the reassurance such programs offer may be just as great in less disadvantaged communities. This volume offers parents and prospective parents a wealth of ideas about how to maximize their enjoyment of their infants and toddlers, while simultaneously enhancing their children's development.

Out-of-home care. Out-of-home care is common, even for very young infants, and because the exigencies of families' lives make it inevitable, we must consider how to ensure such settings are optimal for children. Of course, the economics of child care in the U.S. constitutes a recurrent dilemma: Families of modest means can't really afford it because it is so expensive, and even so employees in child care settings receive poverty-level wages. Many of those employees have little professional preparation to care for children; clean hands and a warm heart are what they bring to the job. Yet their need for skill, knowledge, and expertise (in addition to the warm heart) is pressing, particularly given they are responsible for several young children at once. The chapters in this volume offer both them and their employers an understanding of the importance of their role, and great suggestions for activities to engage in, ways to interact, and things to notice about children.

High achievement stakes. The federal legislation No Child Left Behind has recently focused the country's attention on achievement in the domains of literacy and mathematics. It is clear that the worst possible response to the imposition of a test on third graders is to start test preparation in third grade. If the third grade literacy test is any good (and some of them are!), it will reflect knowledge and skills acquired throughout a child's life. The firm foundation that some children have established in the first 3 years, the opportunities to learn language, to learn about the world, to develop motivation to learn, and to read puts them in a much stronger position to pass the third grade test, as well as the tests that will come in the later grades. But the tests prescribed by this federal policy are not the most important reason to urge early attention to learning. Children without the firm foundation of learning during the first 3 years of life are more likely to struggle and be unhappy in kindergarten and first grade, are more likely to drop out of school without a high school diploma, and are less likely to have the literacy skills needed to get and keep a job. We can no longer let half those who enter high school drop out, as we did in 1950, because we no longer have jobs that will keep those dropouts off welfare, and furthermore we no longer have welfare. The importance of success in school goes far beyond the capacity to pass a set of accountability tests—it is crucial to survival in the knowledge economy.

The achievement gap. Programs focused on the groups most at risk of school failure—children growing up in poverty, children from homes where English is not spoken, children from homes where parents have low educational attainment—are key to closing the alarming gap in school performance associated with race, class, and home language. This gap reflects in part the greater vulnerability of those children to poor teaching, as well as their greater likelihood of ending up in schools where teaching is disrupted and classmates are low achievers. But particularly as the number of children from immigrant and non-English speaking families in our schools increases, we need to take steps to increase their chances of success. Early intervention, parental education, and improved quality of group care settings for infants and toddlers—all programs that could be massively improved if the rich information in this volume were available to them—constitute an important route to the prevention of school difficulties for such children.

Educational outcomes are not improved by fiat, nor do they show sudden advances as a result of novel programs, interventions, curricula, or professional development opportunities. Educational improvement is incremental, and all the topics represented in this volume (and more besides) must be addressed if it is to be achieved. Crucially, though, educational improvement rests on knowledge about children and their development, knowledge about adults and their learning, and knowledge about organizations that support children and how they can become more effective. All those topics are richly represented in this volume. Reading it is a good start.

Catherine Snow
Cambridge, MA

Preface

*"If a child is to keep his inborn sense of wonder, he needs
the companionship of at least one adult who can share it,
rediscovering with him the joy, excitement and mystery of the
world we live in."*
—Rachel Carson

*"Talk to your children while they are eating; what you say will
stay after you are gone."*
—Nez Perce Proverb

Infants and toddlers typically learn to read the world with the support of cherished adults in the course of day-to-day routines and interactions. Using research evidence from multiple fields, this volume explores infant–toddler learning related to beginning language and literacy. We pursue this exploration from numerous vantage points: scholarship, parenting, culture, leadership, policy, direct service, training, and community development. By addressing multiple perspectives, the authors provide a broad understanding of how very young children move toward literacy and suggest what readers can do to encourage young children's delight in words, shapes, sounds, symbols, concepts, and other facets of language and literacy development.

This volume begins with the presentation of an ecological approach toward how young children journey to language and literacy, surrounded by supports from families, caregivers, programs, and communities. In the first section of the book, authors explore the foundations of early language and literacy. Lauren Barton and Holly Brophy-Herb describe the incredible capacities for acquiring language and literacy that most infants bring into the world with them or develop in their earliest days. Angela Notari-Syverson illustrates the everyday tools of literacy that surround every child—tools that adults can readily use to support the development of symbolic behavior in infants and young children.

Citing research evidence, Sharon Rosenkoetter and Shannon Wanless assert that through caring relationships with family members and significant caregivers, young children begin to translate the mysteries of story and print into foundational understandings that underlie later school readiness. Patsy Pierce and Andrea Profio describe oral language development, one of the great miracles of the early years. From their perspectives on early literacy observed on three continents, Adriana Bus and Maria de Jong consider developmentally appropriate ways for families or caregivers to initiate literacy with babies and toddlers. Sounds form the basis of language and literacy, and Peg Griffin explains what is—and is not—known about the beginnings of phonological knowledge in the early years.

The second section of the book deals with family contributions as young children learn to read their world. The family is the primary teacher of early language and literacy, beginning with countless daily exchanges, as portrayed by Lorraine Kubicek. Culture and culture-driven family expectations guide young children as they learn to read their world. Wendy Jones and Isabella Lorenzo-Hubert share a framework for considering the role of culture in language and literacy development and provide practical suggestions for practitioners working with families from cultures different from their own. Given that infants and toddlers learn what they see adults doing and enjoying, Michael Gramling and Sharon E. Rosenkoetter support the practice of incorporating family literacy efforts as part of—not parallel to—child development programs. Finally, Linda Kimura describes how music supports early language and literacy in joyous and meaningful ways.

The book's third section explores the vital role of other caregivers and challenges every responsible adult to nurture the language and literacy development of infants and toddlers. Janet Gonzalez-Mena illustrates ways for all caregivers to infuse language and literacy into their daily caregiving routines. Susan B. Neuman shares her findings on literacy development, including print awareness, in the early years. Child-care researchers Chris Payne and Marion O'Brien contribute findings about promoting language and literacy with infants and toddlers in group settings, while Terry DeMartini discusses how group care environments can foster beginning language and literacy and provides numerous suggestions for providers interested in creating literacy-rich environments.

Program leadership is the focus of the book's fourth section. Leadership is essential to create the climate that celebrates early language and literacy for all children and encourages families and caregivers to nurture these important abilities through routine interactions hundreds of times each day. Patsy Pierce's chapter emphasizes the importance of holding and modeling high expectations for language and literacy for young children with significant disabilities. She also suggests strategies that leaders can share with family members and caregivers to support young children with disabilities in their development of beginning language and literacy skills. Joanne Knapp-Philo and Amy Flynn, both experienced program administrators, emphasize the importance of supervision in creating a supportive climate for early language and literacy and nurturing family members and staff as they develop new skills. Sharon Rosenkoetter outlines various approaches to mentoring to share the message, demonstrate new language and literacy facilitation skills to others, and provide feedback and encouragement to wider groups of family members and caregivers. Kimberly Stice and Tarima Levine discuss low-cost or no-cost resources that support early literacy efforts in child-care settings. Agencies need specific strategies that enable them to institutionalize their good ideas and prevent last year's priority from becoming this year's memory. Joanne Knapp-Philo, Jerry Hindman, Kimberly Stice, and Vicki Turbiville offer research-based, strategic efforts that help agencies sustain their innovations.

The fifth section, the Community, provides the larger context within which the literacy efforts of families, caregivers, and programs flourish. Infant–toddler personnel must act decisively to ensure that our youngest citizens are included in community efforts to support literacy. Ann Zukoski and Esminia Luluquisen offer evidence-based mobilization strategies to build community support for early language and literacy. Clara Pratt and Rebecca Hernandez emphasize social marketing strategies that share information about child development and build public and private commitment to early language and literacy efforts. In a current movement underway in many communities, libraries are becoming places that support families and infant–toddler learning. Kathleen Deerr, Sandra Feinberg, Elizabeth Gordon, and Diantha Schull provide suggestions to help libraries reach more citizens. Finally, Ronald Lally and Peter Mangione (with assistance from the ZERO TO THREE Policy Center staff) recommend public policies that will support the practices outlined throughout this volume.

In the sixth section, the authors exemplify the concepts of the previous chapters by sharing some specific approaches. Two chapters describe applications of the above themes. The first application in this section is StoryQUEST[1], a comprehensive training program for families, early care and education staff, programs, and communities that focuses on beginning language and literacy for infants and toddlers. Joanne Knapp-Philo and Linda Brekken present StoryQUEST, and about half of the other authors of this volume were involved in developing, implementing, and evaluating the program model. The second application in this section is Language Is the Key, a dialogic reading approach to early language and literacy that Kevin Cole, Young Sook Lim, and their colleagues adapted from work by Grover Whitehurst. StoryQUEST staff subsequently modified this approach, gearing it specifically toward infants and toddlers, and called it "Follow the CAR." Sally Anderson shares a set of strategies for selecting books for young children. Matthew Gollub, children's author and musician, ends this section by recommending techniques for using rhythm to help children learn.

The book concludes with a celebration of the joyous opportunities that families, caregivers, programs, and communities have to help young children learn to read the world. We hope that our discussion of these research-based approaches will stimulate more families, caregivers, programs, communities, policymakers, and scholars to engage in serious efforts to appreciate and foster language and literacy in the first 3 years.

Sharon E. Rosenkoetter and Joanne Knapp-Philo
January 2006

[1] StoryQUEST was developed under a 2002 grant from the U.S. Department of Education's Early Childhood Professional Development Program to the California Institute on Human Services at Sonoma State University (Award # S349A020002). The project developed, implemented, and evaluated in a comparison study a successful model to prepare 19 communities to celebrate and foster early language and literacy with infants and toddlers and their families, programs, and communities.

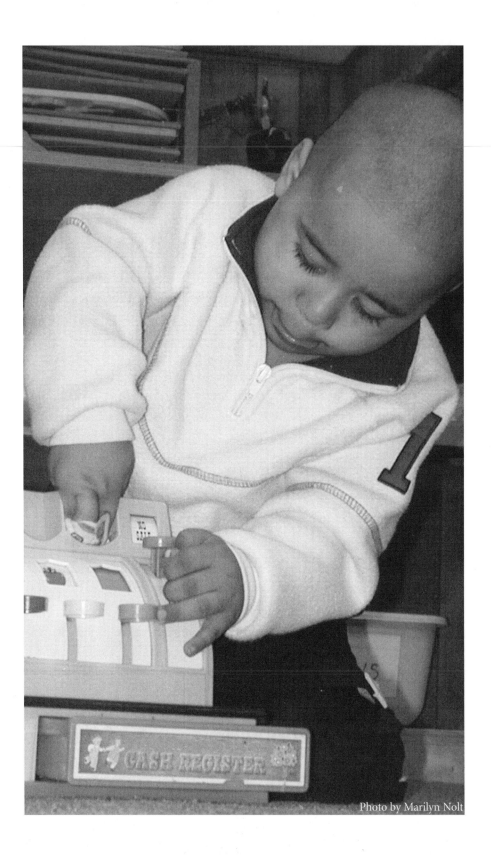

CHAPTER 1

Learning to Read the World: A Beginning

Sharon E. Rosenkoetter

Baby Isaac, age 6 weeks, hears a familiar male voice and struggles mightily to raise his head enough to turn toward the sound that he has heard often before.

Ali, age 26 months, scribbles on a grocery sack. Round and round and round go the circles, forerunners of "my name."

Larissa, age 16 months, bangs her cup on the high chair tray. After Mother fills it with water, Larissa snorts and points to the orange juice carton on the counter. "Duce!" Mother understands the message and responds by pouring juice into the cup.

Three-year-old Ibrihim cautiously ascends the climbing structure, turns, and gives his teacher a "high five." Both know what the sign means.

Alexis, whose body battled spinal meningitis at age 2 months, still does not speak at age 2 years, but, gripping two books, she teeters toward her mother, clearly communicating her powerful desire to "read."

During the first 3 years, young children begin to read their world. Initially without verbal labels, they discriminate self—that is, *me* from *not me*: "This is *my* hand." "That is what *I* want." "*Mine!*" They also define familiar caregivers—of course, wordlessly at first: "Mommy feeds me." "Nana likes that!" "Papa plays with me." Baby Isaac's head-lifting response, described above, acknowledges his father, an important person in Isaac's young life. Infants and toddlers begin early to discern familiar objects and to formulate the laws that systematically govern their properties: "When Mommy holds me in a certain way, it is time to eat." "Kicking this mobile makes something happen." "When I drop my spoon, people react." "When they put me in my bed, it is time to sleep." Ali (above) has learned, for example, that rubbing the marker across the paper makes colorful lines that are delightful to herself and others. As infants' random movements and utterances are interpreted to convey emotions and ideas, they learn that gestures and words share meanings among groups of people. Thereby young children take giant steps into the world of communication (Bloom & Lahey, 1978; De Boysson-Bardies, 1999): Hands out means "pick me up." Head shake means "no." "Dink" means "Give me water, please." Thus Larissa and Ibrihim (above) have already learned some conventional signs that communicate meaning to the important people in their worlds. Finally, young children learn that print carries meaning: "Books are for reading." "A yellow *M* means Happy Meals." "That is my name." Alexis (above) knows that her storybooks feature delightful tales that she and her caregiver can enjoy together. Further, she knows that squiggles on the pages carry words that her caregiver can read over and over and over again. Scribbling conveys messages: "I make my doggie's picture." "Here is Barney."

From this foundation of basic learnings and subsequent daily explorations with everyday people and objects, the young child builds many other understandings of self and others, as well as concepts of economics ("He has more; I have less."), politics ("The teacher is the 'boss' of the classroom."), geography ("This is my neighborhood; Grandma lives far away by an airplane ride."), philosophy ("Everybody has more fun when we share." "That's not fair!"), and physics ("When I let go of my toy car on a hill, it will go down."). Upon such simple notions about the way the world works, the child builds sophisticated understandings, elaborate vocabulary, complex reasoning, and a growing power to influence others by verbal and written arguments. Thus, young children begin to read their world and to have wider and greater impact upon it.

The Early Years Matter

As media attention and public policy increasingly focus on improving literacy for all the nation's children (U.S. Department of Education, 2002), it is astounding that so little attention has been paid to the first 3 years of life. The first thesis of this chapter is that the infant–toddler years are incredibly important in producing a nation of readers. Thought and language, from which all later understanding comes, begin and intertwine during the earliest years (Vygotsky, 1962, 1978). Basic understandings from the infant–toddler period contribute to symbol knowledge—this symbol represents that person, object, or idea—which forms the basis of later school learning and abstract thinking in adolescence and adulthood (Bloom, 2000).

This dynamic process is inherently a social one (Notari-Syverson, O'Connor, & Vadasy, 1998; Shatz, 1994). In the shelter of nurturing adults, the infant or toddler learns to read the world as safe or scary, fascinating or dull, responsive or threatening, caring or neglectful, colorful or bland. The baby learns which people are predictable, what objects do, and how "our family" lives and works and has fun. Further, young children come to realize that all of these learnings about the world have labels—words—and, eventually, children also grasp the signs that identify these words—print or other icons. Finally, they learn that words and print have unbelievable power to activate family members, caregivers, and even people who reside in other places who get our messages by telephone or mail. The concept that words carry power begins during the first 3 years of life. So also does the confidence that "I can read! I can read! I can read!" along with an awareness of how important (or unimportant) reading is to the people whom the child sees every day.

Families Are Critical in Early Literacy

The second thesis of this chapter is that every family can, in culturally appropriate ways, help infants and toddlers learn to read the world. Family members do not need a special degree, advanced training, a high IQ, or special creative talent. They do need *presence, time, words, print,* and *intention.* Infants and young children need adults who are *present,* who are there when the child reaches for a toy, smiles his first social smile, or opens a book, and who respond with acknowledgment, pleasure, and verbal labels. This takes *time*—time to notice, time to expand the child's efforts, time to explain the conditions and boundaries of actions and words, and time to share wonder in everyday miracles such as the cat's silent approach, the pigeon's chattering from the stoop railing, or waves hitting the beach with an unending rhythm. Helping children learn to read their world takes *words*, lots of words (Hart & Risley, 1995, 1999)—words well-chosen to encourage childish efforts (Shatz, 1994), words combined with expectant waiting for the child to offer tentative first communication attempts via whole-body movements, gestures, vocalizations, or pseudowords (McDonald & Mitchell, n.d.). Adults help children read their world when they acknowledge the surrounding *print*, from a cash register receipt to a billboard, a bus schedule to a restroom sign, a popular magazine, a novel, or a board book for baby. Finally, *intention* repeatedly and emphatically emphasizes the lifelong importance (for both adult and child) of words and print. Intention underscores the adult's commitment to cherishing these foundational forms of communication, enjoying them in culturally meaningful ways, explaining them to children in age-appropriate ways, and purposefully using them in mutually satisfying co-constructions countless times every day (Knapp-Philo & Stice, 2003a, 2003b). As the adult senses the child's interests and responds to the child's concerns with language and appropriate references to print, early literacy begins and flourishes during the first 3 years of life. The message is "Language works. Print is fun. They make my life better."

Families can learn simple research-based strategies for taking turns in speech with their infants and toddlers, sharing books, and providing vocabulary for the experiences of daily life. Adults can sing songs from their family's tradition; make up nonsensical ditties that celebrate sounds and rhythm; and repeat TV jingles, nursery rhymes, or fingerplays that match words with physical movements. They can encourage older children to read with infants and toddlers, thereby building sibling relationships, enhancing the older children's reading skills, and supporting the notion that high-quality care for young children always includes literacy. Families can put words to their routines of daily living and play word games during waiting times (Knapp-Philo & Stice, 2003a, 2003b, 2004). Because of the special family–child bond and the immediacy of current events, these brief interactions are invaluable for helping the child learn to read her world.

Caregivers Help Infants and Toddlers Read the World

The third thesis of this chapter is that every caregiver can, in culturally appropriate ways, help infants and toddlers grow in language and literacy. Caregivers, like parents, need *presence, time, words, print,* and *intention* to share language and literacy with infants and toddlers. All five qualities are important. But it is *intention* that turns the physical activity of diapering into a delightful exchange of sound play, a trip to the grocery store into a vocabulary lesson about colors and the names of fruit, or the retelling of a game on the playground into a description that teaches sequencing and narrative skills. Caregivers need knowledge of the cultural supports for the language and literacy learning of the children and families they are serving (Neuman & Roskos, 1992). Caregivers need to have sufficient skills in guiding small groups of children in order to give full attention to individual young children's language and literacy efforts. They need to draw out shy children while they help very talkative ones begin to listen to others as well as to speak. Caregivers need to arrange environments that are symbol rich and interesting without being overwhelming to infants and toddlers (Rosenkoetter, Notari-Syverson, & Knapp-Philo, 2005). Caregivers, like parents, can put words to their routines of daily living and play rhyming games during waiting times (Weitzman & Greenberg, 2002). Even the simplest exchange becomes a literacy lesson when it includes the warmth of a relationship coupled with words, their concepts, and perhaps a graphic symbol.

Programs Establish Expectations for Significant Adults

The fourth thesis of this chapter is that early childhood programs must intentionally and frequently support families and caregivers in helping infants and toddlers learn to read the world. What gets noted gets repeated (Peters, 1987). Program leaders bear significant responsibility for nurturing positive language and literacy practices among their infant–toddler staff members as well as for developing a staff culture in which supporting young children's language and literacy efforts is highly valued. For administrators, coordinators, board members, and other program leaders, *presence, time, words, print,* and *intention* are essential to leadership. These emphases are seen in the regular *presence* of the leader in group settings and on home visits, where the leader notes positive staff practices related to early language and literacy development and encourages additional ones. Key behaviors are observed (a) when program leaders provide *time* for one-to-one and group staff development related to early literacy; (b) when program leaders share personal *words* that frequently, concisely, and memorably reiterate the importance of everyday language and literacy interactions with infants and toddlers as well as model continuing learning with staff and family members; and (c) when program leaders establish *print* priorities that continually provide developmentally appropriate books for young children and families, and articles, videotapes, and on-site coaches with early literacy ideas for staff. Underlying all these emphases is *intentionality* that makes child and family literacy an agency priority.

In high-quality programs, professional development and family learning opportunities about research-based language and literacy strategies affirm current practices that are productive and introduce promising new ones (International Reading Association & National Association for the Education of Young Children, 1998; Knapp-Philo & Stice, 2003a, 2003b, 2004). Leadership creates a climate of experimentation and innovation in literacy efforts. An atmosphere of discovery and continual learning among adults promotes a setting in which young children can explore and gain language and literacy skills.

Program leaders are instrumental in encouraging family literacy: Adults who talk and read model the importance of language and literacy in their homes when they portray joy in words and stories and create a setting where books and print are abundant. In this kind of home, young children learn early that literacy matters. Many families have not had these kinds of experiences themselves and do not know how powerful such experiences are for their children. Leaders of programs for young children can provide families with needed information, share ideas and strategies, and create an environment that encourages regular experiences of adults and children learning and growing together.

Communities Recruit Attention, Provide Resources, and Encourage Families and Programs

The fifth thesis of this chapter is that communities must encourage infants and toddlers and their families, caregivers, and early childhood programs in efforts to foster early language and literacy. The entire human environment is critical in encouraging the relationships and strategies that make a difference for infants and toddlers as they learn to read their world. Words, stories, books, and print weave a fabric for everyday life that enfolds young children and nurtures them as talkers, readers, and writers (Regalado, Goldenberg, & Appel, 2001).

Communities encourage early literacy in many ways, including family literacy programs, social marketing of literacy themes, free books for infants and toddlers, library children's hours, storytelling festivals, story walks, religious story nights, puppet theaters, and much, much more. Billboards and bus signs encourage adults to talk and listen to babies, read books, and share stories. Public service announcements call families' attention to sounds, rhythms, and rhymes as building blocks for later literacy. Parenting education fosters adult–child book reading. Community leaders take time to read to toddlers and are photographed by the media doing so. Communities can create a climate in which children's capacity to use symbols is engaged by people who model and demonstrate their use, who involve children in symbol-using activities, who encourage children to use symbols in a variety of ways, and who give children materials with which to explore, experiment, and play (McLane & McNamee, 1990). The clear message is that early language and literacy matter!

On Apple Pies, School Readiness, and Support for Early Literacy

Carl Sagan, the noted astronomer, wrote, "If you wish to make an apple pie from scratch, you must first create the universe" (1980). The point of Sagan's comment is that causation of even simple phenomena is quite multifaceted and complex, and one needs to start early in the chain of relationships to begin to discern true cause and effect. School readiness is like that. So is literacy. Many thousands of interactions embedded in hundreds of meaningful relationships support a child in learning to read the world (Elicker, Fortner-Wood, & Noppe, 1999). Infants and toddlers successfully come to decode the words and print symbols that convey concepts when many ordinary people play their varied roles across the early years. Thus, the overriding thesis of this chapter is that it takes all of us to nurture infants and toddlers to become readers (see Figure 1.1, p. 8; see also Bronfenbrenner, 1977, 2002).

Figure 1.1.
Context for Infants' and Toddlers' Learning to Read Their World

Such a literacy-supportive world might look like this: Infants and toddlers, each in their individual ways, welcome or redirect initiatives from others. Families provide the thousands of experiences with events, words, and print every day that help young children read their world. Families also supply their own cultural messages and, by responding to young children's cues and providing loving attention from treasured people, they help infants and toddlers see patterns in multiple stimuli.

Caregivers share words and print with infants and toddlers all day long in ways that honor the cultures and languages of the families in their programs. Caregivers adapt the environment to encourage young children with special needs to participate in activities of their choice and label daily events in words, signs, and print. Through the contributions of all their caregivers, young children's worlds become larger and more interesting; objects gain names, attributes, and actions; books become friends and sources of information; and infants and toddlers acquire language as a tool for sharing desires, ideas, and fun through statements, rhymes, stories, and songs.

Program administrators, governing boards, home visitors, and continuing education providers support families and caregivers in knowing that language and literacy matter. They regularly model and offer strategies to enhance adult–child interactions.

Program policies and program leaders emphasize the modeling of literacy among all staff members, from bus driver to custodian, teacher to therapist, nurse to caseworker. The shared investment in early literacy goes beyond education as it is embraced by health, human services, business, and the arts.

When communities mobilize for literacy, they include the youngest children and their families in literacy initiatives. Early literacy is now marketed like soap or the latest toy. Board books can be found on buses, in restaurants, in doctors' and dentists' offices, and in play and religious venues. In every community setting, we are sending the message that early literacy matters!

Policymakers at local, state, and national levels emphasize a comprehensive view of early literacy—that is, adequate jobs, health care, housing, child care, schools, and recreation give families a solid base from which to help their young children learn to read their worlds (National Research Council & Institute of Medicine, 2000).

Finally, research continues to validate real-world literacy strategies that support the learning of infants and toddlers within a climate of acceptance and joy. Such research guides policymakers, program leaders, caregivers, and family members along paths that will produce readers once today's infants and toddlers reach school age.

Early Literacy: A Promise of Success

The promotion of early literacy is a work in progress, but the potential of our nation to foster early language and literacy is mighty—and it is increasing. Families, infant–family professionals, program leaders, and policymakers can employ an array of effective strategies to support early language and literacy in very young children. Research has clearly demonstrated that infants and toddlers learn in the context of everyday routines of families, programs, and communities. Proven strategies will move the quest for early language and literacy forward through comprehensive, developmentally responsive approaches that honor the diversity of the nation's people. Pursuing this quest is a worthwhile commitment—one that promises success for individuals, families, communities, and the nation.

References

Bloom, L. (2000). Pushing the limits on theories of word learning. *Monographs of the Society for Research in Child Development, 65*(3), 124–135.

Bloom, L., & Lahey, M. (1978). *Language development and language disorders.* New York: Wiley.

Bronfenbrenner, U. (1977). Toward an experimental ecology of human development. *American Psychologist, 32,* 513–531.

Bronfenbrenner, U. (2002). Preparing a world for the infant in the twenty-first century: The research challenge. In J. Gomes-Pedro & J. K. Nugent (Eds.), *The infant and family in the twenty-first century* (pp. 45–52). New York: Brunner-Routledge.

Campos, J. J., Barrett, K. C., Lamb, M. E., Goldsmith, H. H, & Stenberg, C. (1983). Socioemotional development. In P. H. Mussen (Ed.) *Handbook of child psychology, Vol. 12, infancy and developmental psychobiology.* New York: Wiley.

De Boysson-Bardies, B. (1999). *How language comes to children: From birth to two years.* Cambridge, MA: MIT Press.

Elicker, J., Fortner-Wood, C., & Noppe, I. C. (1999). The context of infant attachment in family child care. *Journal of Applied Developmental Psychology, 20*(2), 319–336.

Hart, B., & Risley, T. R. (1995). *Meaningful differences in the everyday experience of young American children.* Baltimore: Paul H. Brookes.

Hart, B., & Risley, T. R. (1999). *The social world of children learning to talk.* Baltimore: Paul H. Brookes.

International Reading Association, & National Association for the Education of Young Children. (1998). Learning to read and write: Developmentally appropriate practices for young children. *The Reading Teacher, 52,* 193–216.

Knapp-Philo, J., & Stice, K. (Eds.). (2003a). *StoryQUEST 1: Celebrating beginning language and literacy.* Rohnert Park: California Institute on Human Services at Sonoma State University.

Knapp-Philo, J., & Stice, K. (Eds.). (2003b). *StoryQUEST 2: Celebrating beginning language and literacy.* Rohnert Park: California Institute on Human Services at Sonoma State University.

Knapp-Philo, J., & Stice, K. (Eds.). (2004). *StoryQUEST 3: Celebrating beginning language and literacy.* Rohnert Park: California Institute on Human Services at Sonoma State University.

McDonald, J. D., & Mitchell, B. (n.d.). *Communicate with your child: Practical guide based on the ECO language programs.* Columbus, OH: Communicating Partners Center.

McLane, J. B., & McNamee, G. D. (1990). *Early literacy: The developing child.* Cambridge, MA: Harvard University Press.

National Research Council & Institute of Medicine. (2000). *From neurons to neighborhoods: The science of early childhood development.* Committee on Integrating the Science of Early Childhood Development. J. P. Shonkoff & D. A. Phillips (Eds.). Board on Children, Youth, and Families, Commission on Behavioral and Social Sciences and Education. Washington, DC: National Academy Press.

Neuman, S. B., & Roskos, K. (1992). Literacy objects as cultural tools: Effects of literacy-related activity in play. *Reading Research Quarterly, 27,* 202–225.

Notari-Syverson, A., O'Connor, R. E., & Vadasy, P. F. (1998). *Ladders to literacy*. Baltimore: Paul H. Brookes.

Peters, T. J. (1987). *Thriving on chaos: Handbook for a management revolution*. New York: Knopf.

Regalado, M., Goldenberg, C., & Appel, E. (2001). Reading and early literacy [report]. In N. Halfon, E. Shulman, & M. Hochstein (Eds.), *Building community systems for young children* [series]. Los Angeles: UCLA Center for Healthier Children, Families, and Communities.

Rosenkoetter, S. E., Notari-Syverson, A., & Knapp-Philo, J. (2005). *StoryQUEST Early Language and Literacy Environmental Assessment for Infants and Toddlers*. Corvallis: Oregon State University, Human Development and Family Sciences.

Sagan, C. (1980, November 23). *The world: Science. Cosmos, #3224*. Public Broadcasting System.

Shatz, M. (1994). *A toddler's life: Becoming a person*. New York: Oxford University Press.

U.S. Department of Education, Office of the Under Secretary. (2002). *No child left behind: A desktop reference*. Washington, DC: Author.

Vygotsky, L. S. (1962). *Thought and language*. Cambridge, MA: MIT Press.

Vygotsky, L. S. (1978). *Mind in society: The development of higher psychological processes*. Cambridge, MA: Harvard University Press.

Weitzman, E., & Greenberg, J. (2002). *Learning language and loving it*. Toronto, Ontario, Canada: The Hanen Centre.

Portions of this work were supported by grant #S349A02002 from the U.S. Department of Education, Office of Elementary and Secondary Education, to Sonoma State University, the StoryQUEST Project.

CHAPTER 2

Developmental Foundations for Language and Literacy From Birth to 3 Years

Lauren R. Barton and Holly E. Brophy-Herb

Anton, 2 minutes old, squints and cries as he emerges from his mother's womb into a new world of sights and sounds. He gazes about and is held close on his mother's chest. Soon, he finds his mother's breast and begins to nurse. A new journey of discovery has begun for Anton.

At first glance, a parent might assume that a newborn baby is completely helpless. However, when infants are first thrust into this strange new world, they are ready to learn. They investigate sounds by turning their heads, gaze intently at faces and objects, grasp on fingers and toys placed in their hands, and actively communicate their needs and experiences. Even from these earliest moments, infants are adept at extracting information from the environment and modifying their behavior to explore curiosities and to protect themselves from experiences that are overwhelming or dangerous to them. Like Anton, any newborn will turn away from bright lights and search diligently for the breast, even moving her body up toward the breast from her mother's abdomen (Klaus & Klaus, 1985).

Throughout the first 3 years of life, babies are undertaking new activities and acquiring new skills with amazing speed. Infants use their growing skills in increasingly sophisticated and intentional ways to engage the world and learn about it. Emerging abilities to use the senses to gain information about the environment and to coordinate incoming data increase infants' knowledge about their world. Rapidly advancing thinking skills prompt new discoveries during the first 3 years. The acquisition of milestones in motor development supports the infant's abilities to explore actively, play, and learn. New communication capabilities mean the infant is increasingly able to express thoughts, ideas, and wishes to caregivers and peers. Achieving healthy emotional development contributes to the infant's readiness for learning.

Taken together, these emerging abilities across developmental areas provide the foundations for later learning, including literacy and school success. By understanding typical developmental changes that occur, we can anticipate how best to support infants and toddlers in acquiring new skills and in preparing them for the learning to come. This chapter describes key developmental changes in children from birth to 3 that form critical foundations for language and literacy development. Of course, all of these developmental areas both reflect and influence rapid and significant changes in brain development. We will begin here.

Brain Development

The human brain is an exceptional organ with a great aptitude for adaptation. The brain houses a monumental amount of information, engineers connections and communications between bodily systems, processes environmental input for meaningful use, and governs emotion, rational thought, and problem-solving capabilities. Scientists are only beginning to understand how the central nervous system coordinates and achieves these considerable tasks. Brain development is driven partly by genetic, developmental processes. In recent decades, emerging evidence has identified numerous changes in the structure and functioning of the brain that coincide with considerable changes observed in the thoughts, feelings, and actions of infants and toddlers (Johnson, 1998). However, to a very great extent, brain development is shaped by environmental forces. Stimulation from the physical and social environments influences ongoing brain development (Greenough & Black, 1992; Nelson, 1999) as do more negative forces, such as malnutrition, heightened stress, and exposure to environmental toxins (Black, Jones, Nelson, & Greenough, 1998; Gunnar, 2000; Karns, 2001).

Scientists have observed a proliferation prenatally and postnatally of numerous synapses connecting neurons that transmit information to one another

(Huttenlocher, 1990, 1994). These connections allow nearly limitless possibilities for the brain to organize in various ways to integrate information. As children gain experience with the world and use some connections more than others, underused synapses are pruned to promote greater efficiency in the system. This pruning strengthens existing connections and frees energy and resources to expand connections in other areas where they are more likely to be valuable for the individual. Thus, as brain development proceeds, its organization influences not only how individuals interpret and respond to experiences but also the ways in which subsequent brain development occurs.

The brain has tremendous plasticity, which means that it can and does adapt to adverse circumstances. Plasticity seems to be greatest during the childhood years. For instance, some types of brain injuries, like unilateral brain lesions (i.e., tissue damage on one side of the brain), have few effects on language development if the injury occurs before the age of 5 or 6 years (Feldman, 1994; Gadian, Mishkin, & Vargha-Khadem, 1999). After that time, or if both hemispheres of the brain are injured, development is usually impaired and permanently affected.

Brain development continues throughout life, allowing individuals to continue to learn and adapt at any age. Although research has found periods when children display a greater readiness for the development of complex skills such as language, there are relatively few domains where critical stimuli must be encountered within a very specific window of opportunity for healthy brain development to occur (National Research Council & Institute of Medicine, 2000). One exception occurs in the case of necessary early visual stimulation to enable typical vision at later ages (Hubel, Wiesel, & Levay, 1977). Despite the considerable plasticity, or adaptability, of the brain and the gradual development of most systems within it, certain types of experiences foster brain development (Thompson, 2001). These include supportive, rich, early experiences in communication as well as interactions with objects and people. Experts note that although children's brains seem hardwired to develop language skills with relatively little environmental support, the *quality* of the language development and its specific features and characteristics depend to a very real extent on children's environments (National Research Council & Institute of Medicine, 2000). Of significant note, these recommendations do not indicate that children require a specific regimen of baby activity classes, videos, or prescribed music for optimal development. Rather, sensitive, interactive caregiving that relates to children's experiences and understandings of the world provides the critical catalyst for effective growth (Martin, 1989). For the infant and toddler, whether stopping to describe the bug on the sidewalk, watching the water swirl as the toilet flushes, or feeling the oranges in the grocery bag, everyday situations provide opportunities for stimulating experiences that support development.

Major Milestones in Sensory Capabilities

Much of what humans learn during the first 3 years of life comes from our physical interactions with the world. It is by seeing, hearing, touching, tasting, and feeling objects and people that babies begin to understand what those objects are, what they usually do, and how they are different from other objects and people (e.g., a toy car versus a block, a balloon versus a ball, mother versus a stranger). Developing this concrete understanding of the world is essential for understanding the ideas that words represent when children begin to speak and read. However, in learning about objects, some differences between items can be quite subtle (e.g., a blue block versus a purple block, a sad versus a confused facial expression). These differences require detailed information from the sensory systems to be distinguished. Thus, it is important to consider a child's sensory capabilities when selecting toys, drawing attention to object attributes (e.g., color, texture), or interacting during play.

At birth, all of the sensory systems function and are prepared to convey information about the environment to the baby. One of the first tasks the infant must master is learning to absorb and learn from all of the sensory information available in the environment without becoming overwhelmed by it (Greenspan, 1994; Greenspan & Lewis, 1990). Most healthy babies use a wide array of verbal and nonverbal cues to express their readiness to participate in more activity or to signal when the demands from the environment are too great (Sumner & Spietz, 1994). Whether stimulation comes from the bright light of a window or the overly enthusiastic voice of a well-meaning grandparent, babies tune out excessive stimulation by turning away, falling asleep, or crying to express their discomfort to receptive caregivers.

When children are actively engaged, they can learn much from the events and interactions that occur. Rapid improvement occurs in sensory functioning after repeated experiences associating sensory information with outcomes; for example, as a ball is thrown to the infant, the ball's image becomes larger in the center of his visual field, and then the ball bounces off his chest. Ongoing neural development also enhances the efficiency and capabilities of the sensory systems of infants (Johnson, 1998). Vision and hearing are two of the most important sensory systems for infant learning and development.

Vision

Significant changes occur in the visual system throughout the first 3 years. At birth, infants do not have the same visual acuity that most adults take for granted. Holding an object 20 feet away from a newborn provides her with an image that is comparable to images that adults see when objects are 600 feet (two football fields) away (Banks & Dannemiller, 1987). On the other hand, from about 12 inches (30 cm) away, neonates can discriminate lines that are 1/8th of an inch apart as separate images from each other (Hainline, 1998). As a result, young babies tend to focus on objects that are close to them, with an optimal distance of 4 to 30 inches away. The librarian reading a story 15 feet in front of a group of children will attract considerably less attention from the baby than will his mother's face, a striped purse, or another child moving in more immediate proximity.

Vision does improve considerably during the first year. Around the age of 4 months, infants can simultaneously focus both eyes on the same object (Held, 1985). This binocular vision gives infants the ability to perceive depth and motion, abilities that will continue to improve with experience. By the age of 8 to 9 months, infants display sufficiently refined binocular vision to engage in efficient hand–eye coordination with moving objects. By the age of 6 months, distance vision has improved markedly to nearly 20/20 acuity (Hamer, Norcia, Tyler, & Hsu-Winges, 1989). Yet, as children gain experience moving throughout their environments, they continue to acquire a richer understanding of relationships between changing visual images and their meanings for object properties, distance relationships, and dangerous events (e.g., crawling off the edge of a bed; Bertenthal & Campos, 1990; Bornstein, 1992).

Infants' visual abilities also influence the kinds of books and toys that attract the greatest interest. In the first several months, objects with low contrast (e.g., two solid patterns where one is navy blue and one is deep purple) may visually blur together and not be readily distinguishable. Thus, simple patterns with high contrast (e.g., toys with black and white designs; the hairline area on a face) attract the greatest interest early on (Slater, 2001). By about the age of 3 months, colors appear more intensely and become easier to distinguish, although simple pictures are still preferred (Bornstein, 1976). Throughout childhood, visual perception capabilities gradually improve with greater selective attention, visual integration of shape, and speed of visual information processing (Enns & Girgus, 1985, 1986; Nettlebeck & Wilson, 1985). In addition, as infants develop, their understanding about the people, objects, and images that they see also expands and provides greater meaning to visual experiences.

Hearing

Hearing is also critical for infant development because sounds contain important information about the movements and feelings of caregivers. Sounds also provide essential input for learning language and using it to communicate with others (Fernald, 2001; Sloutsky & Napolitano, 2003). Auditory information helps infants make sense of their social worlds. Studies suggest that babies reliably detect noises in the external environment around the sixth month of fetal life and continue to be highly responsive to sounds after birth (Cheour-Luhtanen et al., 1996; Kisilevsky, Muir, & Low, 1992; Lecanuet, Graniere-Deferre, Jacquet, & DeCasper, 2000). In fact, babies recognize familiar voices that were heard often in the womb and will increase specific behaviors to continue listening to them (DeCasper & Fifer, 1980).

Infants show a remarkable readiness for hearing language sounds and learning to communicate with other people. Studies suggest that, when presented at appropriate speeds, pitches, and volumes, infants can distinguish sounds found across a wide range of non-native languages (Trehub, 1976; Werker & Tees, 1984). Young babies will even discriminate between foreign language sounds that their parents can't vocalize or discriminate. However, over the course of the first year, infants become increasingly attuned to the specific language sounds used by their caregivers, and they become less capable of differentiating sounds not heard in their own environments (Werker, 2000; Werker & Tees, 1984). Children also exhibit strong preferences for language (even nonsense language) that follows the same rules of syllable emphasis, recurring patterns of syllable clusters, and word segmenting as the language spoken around them (Jusczyk, 1997; Saffran, Aslin, & Newport, 1996). As a result, children in France prefer to hear sounds with stress on the second syllable (e.g., *bonjour*) while infants in America prefer sounds with emphasis on the first syllable (e.g., *hello*), even when studies test with nonsense words rather than real ones. Bilingual children demonstrate preferences for sounds from both their languages and quickly discriminate which language to expect in various contexts and with specific caregivers as they skillfully learn the complex rules and vocabularies of both languages (Lanza, 1992; Pearson, Fernandez, & Oller, 1993). While infants demonstrate these remarkable capacities to hear and learn language, the emerging development of the auditory system also influences what babies hear.

Young infants are similar to adults in how well they detect sounds of varying pitches. Both infants and adults display greater auditory sensitivity when listening to higher pitched sounds. However, infants require a higher threshold of sound than adults to respond. This threshold is 15–30 dB[1] higher in 3-month-olds and 10–20 dB higher in 6-month-olds. It continues to decrease throughout the first 2 years (Olsho, Koch, Carter, Halpin, & Spetner, 1988). Likewise, infants' sensitivity to changes in frequency, intensity, and duration of sounds during speech is fairly close to adult levels by the age of 6 months although greater sensitivity continues to develop (Aslin, Jusczyk, & Pisoni, 1998). This sensitivity helps infants analyze complex sounds and discriminate inflection patterns, that is, the emphasis points in words. Of course, these abilities are precursors to early language and literacy development.

Distinguishing between the rapidly changing sounds that form words (e.g., /ba/ versus /pa/) requires babies to discriminate between variations in both the duration of the sounds themselves and the length of the silent gaps between sounds. Thresholds for making these distinctions are about twice as long at 6 months as they are for adults. They continue to decrease throughout early childhood (Trehub, Schneider, & Henderson, 1995). Taken together, these findings suggest that even young infants are equipped to take in extensive auditory and speech information from the environment. However, modifying speech directed at infants to be louder, higher pitched, slower, and exaggerated in tone and emphasis helps overcome babies' sensory challenges and facilitates communication with them (Fernald, 1984; Fernald et al., 1989). This pattern of speech, called *parentese, motherese,* or *child-directed speech,* is common in every culture worldwide (Cooper, 1993). In fact, as much as 80% of parents' speech to their

---

[1] A difference of 15 decibels is comparable to the difference in loudness between a typical washing machine and a hair dryer.

infants is in the form of parentese (Stern, Spieker, & MacKain, 1982). Parentese plays several important roles in helping infants lay the foundations for language and literacy development. With its unique intonation and rhythm, parentese contributes to infants' abilities to tune into and discriminate adults' words and sentence structures (Grieser & Kulh, 1988). When speaking parentese, adults often incorporate gestures in a playful manner. Matching visual cues by touching or pointing to objects while simultaneously using expressive, child-directed speech descriptions further facilitates understanding of relationships between objects and word symbols (Gogate, Bahrick, & Watson, 2000).

Major Milestones in Children's Attention

The ability to pay attention to an object or person in play is a crucial, but often overlooked, skill that influences children's exploratory experiences and cognitive development as well as communicative interactions. Although children's environments provide many different learning possibilities, infants learn the most about the objects that they attend to and interact with personally. When a parent says "See the doggie?" and points to the dog as the toddler passes by, the child is encouraged to focus her attention and interact with that particularly novel, or interesting, dog. This encounter also facilitates understanding of the meaning of the symbolic word *dog*. Situations like this, in which the infant and a caregiver jointly focus their attention, are vital. They support the development of shared realities, or perspective-taking if realities diverge, and they form the foundation for acquisition and use of language (Butterworth, 2001). Indeed, research has found that more frequent episodes of joint visual attention observed in parent–child interactions are associated with more advanced levels of language development in children (Rollins & Snow, 1998).

The emergence of joint attention is not haphazard. Instead, its development emerges over time in a common sequence (Adamson & MacArthur, 1995). At birth, shared attentiveness, an important precursor to later joint attention, often occurs between caregiver and child. The facial contrast patterns, movement, and familiar voices of parents attract infants' interest. However, the adult frequently monitors and provides most of the effort to maintain gaze and shared attentiveness episodes while interacting. By 6 to 8 weeks, more extensive interpersonal engagement appears, with mutual gaze and gaze avoidance regulating behavior. This involves a deeper emotional attunement and responsivity to one another in movement, sounds, or facial expressions. Such attunement (Stern, Hofer, Haft, & Dore, 1985) means that the parent is sensitively responding to the baby's vocalizations, expressions, and body movements. In turn, the baby responds to the parent's behaviors. Sometimes these types of interactions are called synchronous because the parent's and infant's responses to each other are so well-timed and well-matched (Isabella & Belsky, 1991). At about the age of 3 to 4 months, some fragile efforts at triadic joint attention emerge. These usually are initiated in situations with multiple caregivers where the baby interacts with one parent and, while maintaining current expressiveness or emotion, looks frequently to engage the other parent as well (Fivaz-Depeursinge & Corboz-Warnery, 1999). By 5 to 6 months, these early triadic episodes also begin to contain toys and objects as a focus.

Between 9 and 15 months, episodes of joint attention become much more robust and appear more regularly. Whereas earlier episodes required considerable parental support to maintain, the need for active adult efforts gradually diminishes. Episodes of joint attention to third party objects and events become clearly coordinated efforts involving reciprocity between two or three individuals with separate, though complementary and often shared, perspectives (Bakeman & Adamson, 1984). An infant follows the head movements and gaze of a parent to focus her own attention on the object of interest to the parent, thus shifting the image from the peripheral to the central area of her vision. With age, infants persist in seeking the object for shared attention longer before giving up, and they will even look behind themselves for objects outside of their own peripheral vision. Both parents and children also incorporate increasing use of pointing and vocalization or language (Butterworth, 2001).

In contrast to the earlier example of orienting joint attention to the dog, joint attention is not always the result of an adult directly leading or teaching the child about an event or object. Either the child or the adult may initiate or invite the gaze shift. Often, infants remain engaged longer and learn more when caregivers follow the child's lead in identifying objects or events that are of interest at that moment, rather than when adults dictate the focus. Moreover, these joint focusing episodes are built on the mutual understanding evident in the give and take of turntaking interactions. In the same way that parent and child involvement are balanced in turntaking, episodes of joint visual attention involve sensitivity to the cues and expressions of the other person about the event or object of shared interest. That is, neither the parent nor the child dominates.

During episodes of joint attention, parents often imitate the vocalizations and behaviors of young infants as a way to express their warm feelings toward the baby and to encourage the infant to continue the behavior. Later, between 9 and 12 months, many parents and babies show a high degree of attunement in their interactions (Stern, 1984; Stern et al., 1985). Now, instead of only imitating the infant's actions, the parent builds on the infant's activities by matching the baby's behavior using a corresponding behavior. For example, a 9-month-old boy reaches for a toy just outside of his grasp. He stretches his body and is working very hard to reach the toy. As he does, his mother says "Uuuh…uuuuh!" with a crescendo of vocal effort (Stern et al., 1985, p. 250). The mother shared her attention toward the toy, but she also matched her vocalization and its intensity to the increasing physical effort of her son.

While these ideas about joint visual attention apply to many objects, events, and environments, they clearly are applicable to reading interactions. In reading, both the caregiver and the child attend to the book. However, both are also sensitive to the items of interest to the other, with pointing, vocalizing, and talking about specific elements on pages that attract the other's gaze. Because the ability to maintain lengthy episodes of joint attention emerges over time, so too does the ability to sustain reading. Likewise, in the example above, the parent uses a type of verbal "scaffolding" (Bruner, 1983) to support and encourage the child's mastery of the task. These same scaffolding behaviors are important in supporting literacy, as the parent, for instance, says to her toddler, "Hickory, dickory dock, the mouse ran up the (pause)" as the toddler points to the picture and gleefully cries, "Clock!".

Major Milestones in Thinking and Understanding

Throughout the first 3 years, infants and toddlers master six major skills related to thinking and understanding (Lally, 1995). These skills are (a) learning about how objects and actions are alike and different, (b) learning about cause and effect, (c) learning to use tools, (d) learning that objects and people exist even if they cannot be seen, (e) developing symbolic thinking, and (f) learning to imitate (Lally, 1995).

Learning About Objects and Actions

One of the first actions that many infants discover is sucking a thumb or finger. This activity appears to be associated with the feeding system. Quite early, finger sucking becomes an organized, purposeful event that brings the infant much pleasure (Bertenthal & Clifton, 1998). Over time, babies discover many other objects and activities that also acquire meaning.

During the first 2 years, infants and toddlers learn about how objects are alike and different. This learning begins with basic perception about objects. Babies learn to differentiate where one object stops and another one starts, for example, discriminating an object from background visual images (Bremner, 2001). They identify core features or characteristics that distinguish between similar objects. Exploratory play through which infants touch, smell, taste, see, and listen, helps infants and toddlers learn the basic concepts related to an object's properties (e.g., hard, soft, wet, dry) as well as concepts related to its uses (e.g., eat with a spoon, talk into a telephone). Over time, infants and toddlers learn to combine information about objects and actions. For example, initially a fork and a spoon appear to be very much alike. Eventually, the toddler learns that each utensil has its own features and purposes. She learns to eat green beans with a fork and yogurt with a spoon.

Learning About Cause and Effect

Establishing relationships between events and subsequent actions is a major discovery of the first 3 years. Infants first learn cause and effect through their own actions on the world. A 4-month-old happens to bat at a wind chime, setting off an interesting sound. Soon he learns that he can repeat this action to maintain the sound of the chimes. Beginning at the age of 12 to 15 months, toddlers become very curious about toys that trigger physical or social reactions, such as a jack-in-the-box or room lights as they are switched off and on. Learning about cause and effect is, of course, essential to developing understanding of even a simple story or social script.

Learning to Use Tools

To return to the example of thumb sucking, an infant's own body, in this case, the thumb, serves as a first tool. A crying baby soon knows that sucking a thumb is comforting. Later the infant learns to use tools in the environment to make things happen. A 6-month-old uses her arms and fingers to reach and grasp an inviting toy. A 10-month-old pulls on the tablecloth, bringing the shiny spoon on the surface closer to his reach. A 15-month-old brings her father to the refrigerator and motions for a drink. Learning to use physical and mental tools is a critical skill that contributes to learning. For instance, a toddler might repeat a key phrase like "no touch, no touch" as he considers the stove and remembers its dangerous features (Dunn, 1985). Words become important tools for oneself and later also to convey messages to others through writing and reading.

Learning That Objects and People Exist Even Unseen

Up until about the age of 5 months, infants operate from an out-of-sight, out-of-mind viewpoint. Mother shakes a rattle in front of baby, hides the rattle behind her back, and then brings the rattle into view again. The baby does not know that the rattle continues to exist once it is out of sight. Games like peeka-boo or partially hiding a toy cat under a cloth and asking, "Where's the kitty?" help to promote infants' gradual acquisition of a sense of object permanence. Attaining object permanence also helps infants and toddlers feel more secure in their world and in their relationships with parents and caregivers (Lally, 1995). For example, over time, the toddler understands that the parent who takes him to child care in the morning will come back in the evening to pick him up. In the meantime, he can hold a mental image of his parent in his mind.

Developing Symbolic Thinking and Imitation

As toddlers, children make significant strides in understanding symbols. By their first birthdays, the set of sounds or sign language gestures so frequently associated with a particular person, object, or action begin to acquire meaning, and children start to understand words. Once sounds or signs represent objects, generating words is not far behind because toddlers want to communicate more fully with others around them (see Notari-Syverson, this volume, p. 61). Soon they realize that everything has a name, and toddlers eagerly seek out names for familiar items. Symbols come in many forms in addition to sounds. Pictures, like sounds, also gradually begin to have meaning, representing the actual person, object, or action that is not present (Suddendorf, 2003; Uttal et al., 1998). Children seek opportunities to show caregivers objects represented in clay, play dough, and scribbling as the world of symbols unfolds before them.

Between the ages of 2 and 3 years, children's understandings of concepts become much richer. For instance, 24-month-old Kaleel can look at a photograph of his father or visualize an image of him for comfort until he sees his father again. Kaleel also has learned concepts relating to everyday rituals, like saying "good-bye" when Daddy takes him to child care. He knows that the gesture of waving and saying the words "bye-bye" are part of the morning ritual. Through experiences like this, toddlers identify certain objects and actions that go together, and they begin imitating scripts that represent common sequences of activities (e.g., put food on pan on play stove, take food off, put on plate, and serve). Skills shift from watching an activity, to imitating and talking about the activity using representational objects (e.g., using a toy brush as a brush), to imitating the activity using a nonrepresentational object (e.g., pretending a block is a brush instead of using an actual toy brush), to pretending that the event happened either in the absence of toys or in response to a picture of an object or activity in the sequence (Bretherton, 1984). Watching children play provides a window to new growth in thinking skills, such as symbolic thinking. Table 2.1 illustrates the stages in play as children include more and more symbolic representation and imitation of common events in their play.

Table 2.1. Levels of Exploratory and Pretend Play

Approximate Age Range When Behaviors May First Appear	Stage	Description
Birth to 6 months	Mouthing	Indiscriminate mouthing of materials
	Simple Manipulation	Behaviors that involve looking at an object for at least 5 seconds while handling it and that cannot be categorized somewhere else
6–9 months	Functional	Looking at an object and handling it in a way that is particularly appropriate for that object and involves some unique piece of information about that object (e.g., turn the dial on a toy phone)
	Relational	Bringing together and integrating two objects in a manner not related to their intended functioning (e.g., setting a cup on a toy doll instead of setting a cup on a saucer or on a toy table)

continued

Table 2.1. Levels of Exploratory and Pretend Play continued

9–12 months	Functional-Relational	Bringing together and integrating two objects in an manner related to their intended functioning (e.g., setting a cup on a saucer or on a toy table)
	Enactive Naming	Carrying out play that borders on pretend play but without actually engaging in pretend actions (e.g., holding a cup to the mouth without pretending to drink)
12–15 months	Pretend Self	Pretend play directed toward the self with pretend actions (e.g., holding a cup to the mouth and pretending to drink)
	Pretend Other	Pretend play directed toward another person or object with pretend actions (e.g., pretending to feed a doll; pushing a car on the floor saying "vroom vroom")
	Substitution	Using a "meaningless" object in a creative way (e.g., using a block as telephone) or using an object in pretend play in a way that is different from how the child has previously used the object (e.g., pretending a spoon is a hairbrush after already using the spoon to feed a doll)
	Sequence Pretend	Repetition of a single pretend play act with little variation (e.g., drink from a bottle, feed the doll) or linking together different pretend play acts (e.g., put the doll in a cradle and then kiss good night)
15+ months	Sequence Pretend Substitution	Same as sequence pretend except using object substitution within the sequence (e.g., put doll in cradle and then cover the doll with piece of clothing as a blanket)
	Double Substitution	Pretend play in which two materials are transformed—within a single act—into something they are not in reality (e.g., treat peg as a doll and a piece of clothing as a blanket, cover the peg with the clothing and say "good night")

Source: From "From Exploration to Play: A Cross-Sectional Study of Infant Free Play Behavior" by J. Belsky & R. K. Most, 1981, *Developmental Psychology, 17,* p. 633. Copyright 1981 by the Authors. Adapted with permission.

Capabilities in symbolic thinking derive from understanding how different objects function and what words and other symbols represent those objects and their actions. These new understandings, reflected in imitative behavior, lay the foundations for later learning. For instance, later literacy skills require children to draw on this background to fathom that a collection of letters can be arranged into a symbol that represents an object. In addition, knowledge about sequences in which activities occur and which objects and actions frequently are described together will facilitate children's identification of words as they begin to read in later years (Bristow, 1985; Erwin, 1991).

Learning to Imitate

Many factors support the mastery of thinking and reasoning skills during the first 3 years of life, including caregivers' roles in providing a variety of materials and experiences for infants and toddlers. Characteristics of children themselves also influence development. For instance, memory becomes more advanced over time as the infant brain matures and develops. These enhanced memory skills allow the infant to better receive, store, and then recall information derived from interactions with the environment, increasing mastery of a variety of tasks. For instance, when discovering the ways in which objects are alike and different, infants and toddlers must be able to input, store, and then recall previous information about those objects or similar objects. Another skill, learning to imitate behaviors, also relies on memory. Consider the example of a toddler waving "bye-bye" when mommy leaves for work. This behavior is dependent on the toddler's abilities to take in and store information about waving bye, recall the setting and context in which mommy waves bye, and apply that memorized information the next time mommy leaves.

Infants' abilities to store and recall information increase over time (Rovee-Collier & Barr, 2001). Six-month-olds, for instance, can recall and imitate a behavior after a 24-hour delay (Barr, Dowden, & Hayne, 1996); 14-month-olds have been shown to recall and imitate a behavior after a 4-month delay (Meltzoff, 1995). Strategies, such as reminding infants and toddlers about previous experiences, either verbally (Lipsitt, 1990) or nonverbally, perhaps by showing the baby an object used during a particular experience (Barr, Marrott, & Rovee-Collier, 2003; Rovee-Collier, 1999), can boost recall skills. Such "priming" helps infants retrieve forgotten memories. These cuing strategies become even more effective as infants grow older (Joh, Sweeny, & Rovee-Collier, 2002; Rovee-Collier & Barr, 2001).

Major Milestones in Motor Development

During the first 3 years, children experience rapid changes in physical growth and in their abilities to coordinate their movements and maintain balance. While infants are growing at the fastest rate of their lives, they also are experiencing extensive changes in the proportions of their bodies (Mercer, 1998). Newborn clothes appear so tiny in part because the baby's head accounts for a considerable amount of the child's overall weight and mass. While the head does continue to grow, the extensive growth of the body and extremities eventually results in a much more balanced proportion, scaled similarly to adults by school age. In the midst of all these changes, children show remarkable abilities to adjust their actions to explore skillfully and maneuver in the world around them.

Movement forms a critical foundation for literacy because it enables children to investigate their environments, intentionally interact with objects and people, and eventually use tools and symbols to communicate with others (Gibson, 1988). Early in life, children move their heads and shift their gazes to observe and investigate their environments. However, countering gravity to maintain head control remains difficult, and most movements of arms and legs are not yet coordinated efforts to touch people or retrieve objects. Newborn movements are largely reflexive responses to stimulation (e.g., for protection or feeding) or repetitive movements that are rewarding because of the action rather than the outcome. Sometimes as babies kick their arms and legs in circles, they encounter and explore new objects. Their delight in these discoveries stimulates more efforts to interact with objects.

Infants gain control over balance and movements gradually, with initial control over the head, neck, and trunk extending downward and increasing control from the center of the body outward (see Table 2.2). As motor skills develop, the infant can use more intentional movement to see events at a slight distance from a caregiver's shoulder, to elevate the head and shoulders when lying outstretched on the stomach, and eventually to roll over (Goldberg, 1989). With continued experience and growth, children maintain their balance while sitting. Last to develop are more complex and coordinated skills involving their legs, like crawling and then standing and moving (e.g., walking, running, galloping, hopping; Bertenthal & Clifton, 1998).

Successful coordination of basic arm movements appears before babies demonstrate motor skills with their legs. First, they hone skills with large muscle groups to reach at objects, though they frequently miss them (Bertenthal & Clifton, 1998). Next, children's fine motor skills become more precise. As they gain control over using the small motor muscles, children become more adept at touching objects of interest and then grasping them, passing them from one hand to the other, and using more precise grips with their thumbs to pick up tinier objects (e.g., feeding oneself a pea; Smitsman, 2001). After 1 year, infants gradually acquire skills in balancing other objects as well as themselves. For instance, babies begin to stack blocks in small towers and exuberantly knock them over, or they practice putting objects in and out of spaces to see where they fit.

Table 2.2. Milestones of Gross and Fine Motor Development in the First Year of Life

Developmental Age (variation is typical)	Typical Action
Birth to 1 month	Sleeps in fetal position
1 month	Holds chin up while lying on stomach
2 months	Lifts chest while lying on stomach
3 months	Reaches for items while lying on back, but misses
4 months	Sits with support
5 months	Sits on lap and grasps objects
6 months	Sits and grasps dangling objects
7 months	Sits alone
8 months	Stands with help
9 months	Stands holding furniture
10 months	Begins crawling
11 months	Walks while holding a hand
12 months	Pulls self to stand by furniture
13 months	Climbs single steps
14 months	Stands alone
15 months	Walks alone

When given opportunity, toddlers also demonstrate emerging skills using large writing utensils. At first, large pencils are held from the far end and children only sporadically make marks on paper. But, by age 2, most toddlers steady the paper with the opposite hand, display a more coordinated grip of fingers near the pencil tip, and have sufficient control to scribble extensively. They also can differentiate their scribbling from a more intentional vertical or horizontal stroke and, if asked, will proudly tell you what their drawing represents (Smith, 1979). By age 3, children's fine motor movements and dexterity in their hands and fingers become even more adept, and they can imitate drawing circles or roughly tracing outlines of shapes (Matthews, 2003). Practice with seeing and drawing shapes provides an important foundation not only for toddlers to discriminate between the shapes in letters (e.g., *b* versus *d* or *p* versus *q*) when they later begin to read but also for them to assemble shapes to write letters in words and sentences in future years (Craig, Connor, & Washington, 2003). In addition, exposure to print-rich environments, with many opportunities to see, make, read, and hear how words and shapes are central in the world of grown-ups, enhances the motivation and learning of emerging literacy skills (Lenhart & Roskos, 2003).

Major Milestones in Exploratory and Play Behavior

One of the most exciting advancements during infancy and toddlerhood is the emergence of exploratory and play behaviors. Exploratory behaviors that involve manipulating and examining certain objects help children learn how things work, what their purposes are, and what properties are unique to them (Kostelnik, Whiren, Soderman, Stein, & Gregory, 2002). Exploratory behaviors are a reaction to new experiences. That is, the infant is on a fact-finding mission of sorts as she interacts with a novel object. She gathers information about the object through activities like mouthing, shaking, or dropping it. Armed with the "facts" about an object gained through exploration, the infant or toddler is free to move on to more advanced play behaviors that build on knowledge of the object's characteristics (Belsky & Most, 1981). Specifically, the child becomes able to *apply* the pre-existing knowledge about the object. Imagine, for example, a toy rattle. Through his exploratory behaviors, the baby has learned what the object is, how it can be moved, and what interesting sound it produces when moved. With that information in mind, he can use the toy in play by shaking it, giggling, and handing it to Grandpa for a turn. Over time, play eventually includes other children and complex themes like playing house. Table 2.3 describes types of exploratory and play behaviors during the first 3 years. Throughout childhood, children continue to demonstrate both exploratory behaviors and all levels of play. However, play generally becomes more associative and cooperative as children mature and gain skills.

Table 2.3. Types of Play in the First 3 Years

Type of Play	Description
Unoccupied Behavior	The child is not engaged in any task and spends most of the time looking around or moving around.
Onlooker Play	The child watches other children and is actively engaged in observing specific activities (e.g., watching other children play in the sandbox at the park).
Solitary Play	The child plays with toys alone and independently, without interacting with others (e.g., digging in the sandbox).
Parallel Play	The child plays independently, but the activity brings the child near other children who are playing with like materials (e.g., two children scribbling with chalk at the same table or digging separate holes in the same corner of the sandbox).
Associative Play	The child plays with other children and interacts with them using similar materials. The child may talk with the other children but is focused on his role in the play (e.g., While in the sandbox, Jose pretends to make soup, and Maria pretends to pour juice with her sand and cups; Jose says, "I hungry" and continues to stir his sand soup.).
Cooperative Play	The child plays in a group that is organized to make some product or achieve some common goal (e.g., playing ring-around-the-rosie; building a sandcastle together).

Source: From *Guiding Children's Social Development: Theory to Practice* (4th ed.) by M. Kostelnick, A. Whiren, A. Soderman, L. Stein, and K. Gregory, 2002, Albany, NY: Delmar Learning. Copyright 2002. Adapted with permission of Delmar Learning, a division of Thomson Learning.

Exploratory Behaviors

For infants and toddlers, even common household objects and routine tasks provide new and fascinating experiences, which is one reason why infants and toddlers spend so much time engaging in exploratory behaviors. Infants use a wide variety of exploratory behaviors to discriminate between objects and learn about their properties. Initially, infants use their senses to explore images and objects that come to them (e.g., a parent places the rattle in the baby's hand) or that the child accidentally encounters through spontaneous movement of his arms, legs, or head. Over time, however, babies gain greater control over their bodies. They begin to reach and grasp specific objects and eventually crawl, cruise, walk, or run to investigate items of interest. As they master each new motor skill, infants incorporate these new movements into their exploration of toys and objects.

The earliest type of exploratory behavior to appear is mouthing objects. Most parents observe that when given a toy, an infant will immediately put the toy in her mouth. By 3 months, infants are visually examining objects, staring intently at a mobile, for instance. In the second half of the first year, infants explore objects through shaking, dropping, and throwing (Uzigiris, 1967). From mouthing toys to discovering how they feel and taste to dropping them from the high chair and watching the speed with which they fall, babies use their developing skills to learn about the world. These experiences are central to understanding the features of objects, how things work, and how other people respond.

Exploratory behaviors offer considerable opportunities for repetition and the learning it promotes. As the infant delights in dropping the toy again, and again, and again, she learns what to expect from a falling object. She draws connections between cause and effect by associating dropping that particular toy with sounds, speed of falling, and changes in the object's size and shape at different points in the trajectory. She sees differences in what happens with the object when it is released from varied heights, dropped onto different surfaces, or let go in front of mom versus dad. She compares what happens, both to the object and in the responses of people watching, when she drops different kinds of items (e.g., toys, food, breakable objects). Thus, repeated explorations of the environment teach children a considerable amount about objects in the world and how people talk about and use them, as well as about social relationships with individuals. These experiences form an important foundation of knowledge needed to talk about and eventually read about objects and social interactions (Omanson, 1985). Indeed, a recent study found that infants high in manipulative exploration acquired language at a faster rate than those who explored their environments less (Karrass, Braungart-Rieker, Mullins, & Lefever, 2002).

Exploratory behaviors not only offer information about objects, but also provide the infant with information about people. Six-month-old SaRonn crawls to Joey, grasps his hair, and lowers her mouth to his head. Is this aggression? Not likely. These actions are very common exploratory behaviors as babies try to learn about one another. Even in the earliest months of life, infants show a social interest in other children. For instance, young babies show excitement at seeing other babies, as evidenced by their facial expressions, increased body activities, and staring behaviors (Eckerman, 1979). Between the ages of 6 and 9 months, infants babble to and respond to their peers and smile at other infants (Hay, Pederson, & Nasg, 1982; Vandell & Mueller, 1995; Vandell, Wilson, & Buchanan, 1980). Between the ages of 9 and 12 months, infants begin to imitate one another, a milestone in emerging social play behaviors (Mueller & Silverman, 1989; Vandell & Mueller, 1995).

More Advanced Forms of Play

Exploratory behaviors contribute to and are combined with play behaviors. In early infant play, called *onlooker play*, babies carefully watch others engaged in play. Other types of play common among infants and toddlers are called *solitary play* and *parallel play* (Kostelnik et al., 2002). Solitary play involves the child playing alone, typically engaged with an object. A 15-month-old carefully dropping clothes pins into a bucket and dumping the bucket is engaging in solitary play with exploratory dropping behaviors. Parallel play is similar to solitary play in that the child is focused independently on his task but is playing in close physical proximity to one or more other children.

Over time, infants and toddlers continue to engage in exploratory behaviors, but their play begins to reflect their advances in thinking and language skills (Power, 2000). Play themes become more organized and sophisticated. The focus moves away from simple exploratory behaviors and toward more imitative behaviors (e.g., pretending to cook supper) and imaginative behaviors (e.g., using a block as a hairbrush and then as a telephone). As play advances, infants and toddlers begin to include one another in their play (Kostelnik et al., 2002; Ross, Conant, Cheyne, & Alevizos, 1992). Cooperating with one another in play to achieve a common goal, like building a block tower together, is more characteristic of preschoolers. However, toddlers may begin to engage in cooperative play (Dunn & Dale, 1984). Common types of play in childhood are described in Table 2.3.

Play is important work for children. It allows them to integrate and practice their many developing skills in new and creative ways. As infants and toddlers play, they practice existing skills, acquire sensitivity to subtle features in objects or events, create unique combinations or reactions from familiar objects, identify ways to solve problems, imagine the world from someone else's point of view, and learn social skills from practice in peer interactions (Creasy, Jarvis, & Berk, 1998; Gibson, 1988; Kavanaugh & Engel, 1998). Children, quite literally, construct new knowledge and new understandings about people, objects, and events through play (Piaget, 1952). These more advanced behaviors reflect increased language capabilities, which allow children to include dialogue in their play, express their needs and wishes, and eventually conduct social problem solving. As children engage in pretend play, they use symbols in increasingly refined and complex ways. In play, children enact sequences of events and roles that they would be unable to undertake in "real" life; they reinterpret the objects, experiences, and perspectives of others to be personally meaningful, and they comprehend and use language to describe events independent of the immediate situation (Kavanaugh & Engel, 1998; Roskos & Neuman, 1998). Play experiences allow children to practice using the type of language found in books (i.e., decontextualized language) in addition to the kind they use more frequently in everyday conversations (McGee, 2003).

Major Milestones in Language Development

Effective communication is central to developing social interactions and organized play behaviors. Impressively, infants demonstrate extraordinary abilities to learn the complex system of symbols and rules embedded in the language around them. In the first 4 to 6 months of life, a baby demonstrates receptive language skills, or the ability to hear and understand language, when she turns toward a beloved caregiver calling her name. A 10-month-old shows receptive language when he complies with his mother's request to come to her, or even if he vehemently shakes his head "no." Receptive language skills are often more advanced than expressive language capabilities (i.e., speaking or producing language). In other words, infants and toddlers typically understand more language than they can produce themselves. Infants and toddlers learn a considerable amount of language in a short time. For instance, by age 3, most children know at least 1,000 words.

Parents and other caregivers play a tremendously important role in helping infants and toddlers acquire language. Playful games like peekaboo or imitating and responding to baby's sounds and gestures provide practice in turntaking behaviors. These early turntaking games are actually critical precursors to patterns of later conversational speech in which speech partners take turns listening and speaking (Bornstein & Tamis-LeMonda, 2001). When parents are highly responsive to their children's interests, behaviors, and communication attempts during infancy, their toddlers acquire language faster during the second year (Tamis-LeMonda, Bornstein, Kahana-Kalman, Baumwell, & Cyphers, 1998). In addition, the more language children hear as infants and toddlers from their parents, the larger their vocabularies and the higher their IQ test scores in the preschool years and beyond (Hart & Risley, 1995). Moreover, the type of language parents model for their children is key in infants' and toddlers' acquisition of language (Hart & Risley, 1995). For instance, when a parent uses language to richly describe the events of the moment, like making dinner, the child is exposed to diverse vocabulary and sophisticated sentence structures, much more so than if the parent uses language only to issue directives (e.g., "Sit down."). Exposing children to diverse vocabularies not only builds language skills but also other skills. Consider the fact that the more emotion words (e.g., *happy, sad, angry, frustrated*) a parent uses with his toddler, the more extensive the child's emotion vocabulary and the greater his social skills are likely to be in the preschool years (Dunn, Brown, & Beardsall, 1991).

Over time, infants and toddlers become skilled at communicating their observations, desires, feelings, responses, and experiences to others. In the span of only a few months, infants move from producing reflexive vocalizations at birth to purposeful cooing. This development is followed by babbling and jargoning speech, which possesses the same intonations and rhythm as adult speech but without meaningful words. Although normative ranges vary widely, many infants speak their first words between the ages of about 10 and 15 months. Toddlers' early speech is often accompanied by gestures, like pointing, as an additional tool to communicate. Such tools play an important role in language development. For instance, studies show that both children from families where parents point more while communicating with toddlers and children who begin pointing at earlier ages demonstrate greater speech production and language development at later ages than children with fewer of those pointing experiences (Camaioni, 1993; Fenson et al., 1994). Once children begin speaking, they learn at an incredible rate. Consider the child who at 18 months begins to learn an average of nine new words a day (Carey, 1978). One- and two-word utterances have developed into full sentences, with subjects, verbs, adjectives, and clauses, by the time children are about 3 years old (Hoff-Ginsberg, 1997). Chapter 5 (Pierce & Profio, this volume, p. 103) provides an overview of language in the first 3 years.

In the process of developing these abilities to communicate, children learn vital skills needed for literacy. They are sensitized to differentiating sounds and understand that subtle changes in sounds also alter meaning (e.g., *no* versus *go*; *dog* versus *dogs*; Invernizzi, 2003). Children identify relationships between symbols and the objects, events, and experiences that those symbols represent (Whitehead, 1997). Soon, they learn that each symbol frequently is associated with other core ideas, based on the context surrounding the object or the actions that the object undertakes. For example, dogs are likely to bark, run, walk, and fetch, but not talk. With language, children also eventually describe events and objects that are removed from their immediate surroundings in time or space (e.g., Yesterday I ran; played at Grandma's house). Handling these decontextualized narratives is a central ability necessary for later reading (McGee, 2003). Language permits young children to describe possible events that may be imagined but have never happened and to act out these experiences descriptively during pretend play. Skilled communication also requires children to take the perspectives of their listeners, understand what information they know, and adapt details to explain ideas further.

Children's future literacy expands on these language skills (Mayberry, Wodlinger-Cohen, & Goldin-Meadow, 1987). In reading and writing, children differentiate graphical symbols, attach them to ideas, use complex rules to assemble them, and place them in the context of other events and objects. This process allows them to understand or to communicate a meaningful idea to others who are removed from the experience. Thus, early language skills are important precursors to literacy. By nurturing and supporting children's developing language skills, adults provide an important foundation for literacy.

Major Milestones in Emotional Well-Being

During the first 3 years, infants and toddlers master an impressive array of emotional skills and social understandings. Some of these skills include building loving, emotional attachments to parents and other caregivers; developing a basic understanding of emotions; attaining a sense of themselves as separate individuals; and learning how to act as full partners in social exchanges. Healthy emotional development is an important foundation for learning.

Emotional Attachments in Relationships

For infants and toddlers, healthy emotional development unfolds within the contexts of relationships. Babies learn and develop within relationships with their parents, caregivers, and siblings. More advanced cognitive development and language acquisition are observed when caregivers effectively interpret infants' signals and experiences and provide responsive, contingent verbal and nonverbal feedback to children (Bornstein & Tamis-LeMonda, 1989; Tamis-LeMonda, Bornstein, & Baumwell, 2001).

Moreover, a trusting, nurturing caregiver–child relationship provides a secure base from which to learn about new things. Infants who are confident that support will be available if situations become anxiety-producing or overwhelming demonstrate more exploratory behavior in novel situations. Likewise, toddlers who are securely attached to their parents are less easily frustrated when engaging in challenging tasks, and they are more persistent. Toddlers' efforts at social pretend play are also dependent on a positive emotional relationship between the play partners (Dunn, 1991). As preschoolers, these toddlers have better social skills than toddlers with insecure attachments (Matas, Arend, & Sroufe, 1978). In addition to the learning that occurs within the caregiver–child relationship, this broader exposure to objects, events, and experiences that results from infant security contributes to an expanded understanding of the world.

Understanding Emotions

Part of understanding the world requires that infants gain a basic understanding of emotion. Certain basic emotions, such as anger, joy, and sadness, are thought to exist in infancy (Abe, & Izard, 1999; Campos, 1983; Izard, 1991). Through interactions with parents and caregivers, infants and toddlers come to understand these feeling states, and they gradually gain abilities to identify their feelings verbally. Specific characteristics of adult behaviors support these skills. For instance, most adults imitate infant emotional expressions without even thinking about it. When a baby coos, smiles, and wiggles her arms and legs as her aunt approaches her, the adult most likely smiles in return, uses the same intonation as the baby, and perhaps even labels the emotion for the baby, "Oh, you're happy today!" Over time, these types of behaviors in interactions teach infants and toddlers what types of emotions are linked with certain situations (e.g., baby feels sad when a parent leaves), what each emotion "feels" like, and what language terms represent each emotion (Rochat, 1995).

When surrounded by these types of sensitive interactions, infants and toddlers learn emotion skills, such as recognizing and decoding facial expressions. Six-month-olds, for instance, have been shown to recognize and decode facial expressions of anger, fear, and surprise (Serrano, Iglesias, & Loeches, 1992). By the age of 2 years, toddlers have a basic understanding of emotional expression and can recognize a wide range of emotional facial expressions (Nelson, 1987; Nelson & deHaan, 1997). Their skills and accuracy in recognizing emotions and identifying what types of situations elicit particular emotions continue to increase over time. Understanding about emotional states contributes to language development. Toddlers with more advanced understanding of emotion states and better emotion regulation skills (i.e., the ability to inhibit or increase emotional behaviors) demonstrate better social skills as preschoolers and in later classroom experiences. In social situations, they are better able to use a variety of skills, including language, to solve social problems, negotiate challenges, and communicate with teachers and peers.

Self-Esteem and Self-Understanding in Social Interactions

Strong self-esteem, so important for motivation and positive attitudes related to learning, is also dependent on the quality of the infant's relationship with her parents and other caregivers. Infants develop a sense of self that is reflective of their interactions with others (Fogel, 1993, 1995). If a baby is parented in a loving, responsive manner, she comes to view herself as a capable, lovable person. This self as a reflection of the interactions and beliefs of others continues throughout toddlerhood. When 3-year-old Isabelle cries "Look at me, Daddy" as she jumps off the step, she is, in part, seeking affirmation of herself as a courageous, smart, and capable child (Rochat, 2001).

When they have been cared for in responsive, loving ways, infants come to see themselves as social agents at a very early age. Consider the 3-month-old who engages in cooing turns with her caregiver. Quickly, babies learn to reciprocate behaviors, and they develop social expectations about such interactions (Rochat, Querido, & Striano, 1999; Rochat & Striano, 1999). New communication skills contribute to the infant's sense of competence and independence. In fact, toddlers are faced with the developmental task of attaining a sense of autonomy (Erikson, 1963); that is, they must develop a sense that they can be successful social agents in their world and that they can act independently. Sensitive parents and caregivers set up the environment in ways that provide opportunities for toddlers to try out their new skills in successful ways.

By the age of 18 months, toddlers can gaze at their own reflections and know that the image they see in the mirror is their own (Lewis & Brooks-Gunn, 1979). This time is also when toddlers begin to demonstrate self-referencing behaviors, such as pointing to themselves. Interestingly, the development of these self-referencing behaviors coincides with the explosion in language production. Toddlers' gestures, combined with their expanding vocabularies, afford toddlers' better abilities to express their thoughts, ideas, and feelings.

Around age 2, toddlers begin to express more emotions, particularly self-conscious emotions, such as embarrassment (Lewis & Brooks-Gunn, 1979). Toddlers at this age often glance at a parent to gauge the adult's reaction to a particular behavior. In fact, such social referencing plays an important role in helping infants and toddlers make sense of any given situation. By decoding the parent's facial expression, the infant identifies a situation or an object as being potentially fearful or pleasant (Feinman, 1982). Social referencing also aids infants and toddlers in learning socially appropriate behaviors, many of which address social rules for language. For instance, imagine a parent and toddler shopping in the grocery store when a family friend stops to talk. When the neighbor asks a question of the toddler, he shyly glances toward his father for some guidance about what to say or do. "Say hello," prompts his father.

Along with this new sense of self-identity, the toddler also comes to view herself as an intentional communicator (Tomasello, 1995). Of course, infants show intentional communication during the earliest months of life, but toddlers, for the first time, come to understand that others are also intentional communicators, and language can be used to communicate effectively about events and feelings (Tomasello & Akhtar, 1995). As toddlers learn the power of language to convey thoughts and feelings, to create reactions, and to accomplish goals, they become quite motivated to build their language skills. In situations where toddlers do not experience regular validation of themselves, their self-expressions, and their efforts to influence the world using language, children may not learn and use language as effectively. For example, in families with documented child maltreatment, toddlers displayed less expressive language at 31 months and especially less comfort in communicating about their own intentions, feelings, and thoughts than peers from similar neighborhoods reared in more nurturing environments (Cicchetti & Beeghly, 1987). Over time, learning to communicate about events and feelings enhances children's abilities to control and express their emotions in positive ways. During the preschool years, children become much more able to control their emotional responses, articulate their feelings (e.g., "I am so mad!"), and understand the feelings of others described verbally or in stories. It is noteworthy that the foundations for these skills begin in infancy and toddlerhood as children learn about themselves and their feelings in the context of nurturing relationships.

Individual Differences

This chapter has described a series of changes typically observed in infants and toddlers at different ages. However, individual children vary considerably. Babies acquire skills at different rates. For instance, learning to crawl to get toys may be particularly difficult for a chunky baby, but easier for a lighter one. Achieving this milestone also may be influenced by cultural beliefs, traditions, or safety concerns that affect the amount of time the child is free to move on the floor versus being held by caregivers (Roopnarine, Lasker, Sacks, & Stores, 1998).

An infant's existing developmental skills will influence which strategies support the most effective interaction with the child. If a child has a serious delay in one developmental domain, this may affect the child's development in other areas as well (Preisler, 2001). For example, if an infant exhibits mobility delays, he may not engage in typical levels of exploratory behavior which, in turn, could contribute to a delay in cognitive development. Even in cases with less extreme challenges, variations in children can be noticeable. Ear infections that cause pain and disrupt auditory information may contribute to discontent, reduced interaction, and slower speech development, particularly if they persist for long periods (Roberts, Wallace, & Henderson, 1997; Teele, Klein, & Rosner, 1984).

Understanding how developmental capabilities build on one another can help caregivers utilize strategies that incorporate existing skills in alternative ways to promote ongoing development. For instance, providing assistive technology that permits independent mobility for the child with delays or offering varied environments with considerable exploratory possibilities in close proximity to the child might support cognitive development for children with motor limitations. Or, intentionally incorporating gesture and sign language into interactions with children with hearing impairments may promote positive parent–child interactions and support the child's learning about symbolic representation and language development (MacTurk, Meadow-Orlans, Koester, & Spencer, 1993).

In addition to considering their individual capabilities when interacting with infants, it is also crucial for caregivers to understand their unique preferences and responses. Babies each have a personal style, or temperament, that influences how they interact and develop (Goldsmith et al., 1987). Some children have very high activity levels and want always to be moving whereas others' pace is more leisurely. Babies differ in how quickly and how intensely they react and adapt to new situations and in how easily they settle into routines. General quality of mood, length of attention span, and distractibility also vary among children. These individual characteristics influence the kinds of situations that parents expose children to and the ways that infants and toddlers respond within those settings (Lerner & Lerner, 1987). Efforts to promote positive interactions and learning experiences for children must be responsive to the unique characteristics of each child, to the individual's needs and preferences in approaching new situations, and to his or her growing readiness to engage with people or objects in the environment.

Environmental Differences

A host of cultural and socioeconomic factors inherent in children's environments interact with and contribute to their development.

Cultural Environment

Children's individual differences are interpreted within a cultural context. For instance, studies have shown significant variations in caregiver expectations, interactions, and developmental outcomes in deaf children born on Martha's Vineyard when a high proportion of children there were congenitally deaf relative to those living on the American mainland during the same period (McDermott & Varenne, 1996). Culture influences the competencies that are valued by a group as well as the opportunities and encouragement offered to facilitate skill development (Ogbu, 1988; Roopnarine et al., 1998). In the case of literacy, culture influences the types of talk addressed to young children, expectations for their responses, and appropriate uses for written and verbal communication styles (Brice-Heath, 1988).

Cultural traditions also influence a wide range of choices that parents make about raising children. For example, in the case of feeding infants, some mothers breast-feed their infants whereas other mothers nourish their babies with infant formula. Studies have shown that the special contents of breast milk provide immunity against infection (American Academy of Pediatrics, 1995; Karns, 2001; Newberg & Street, 1997), advantages in cognitive development (Rogan & Gladen, 1993), and greater visual acuity (Golding, Rogers, & Emmett, 1997) that contribute to language development and later literacy skills. As parents, neighbors, teachers, and friends naturally emphasize specific child-rearing strategies, display expectations, provide opportunities for children to practice skills, and reinforce behaviors that are valued within their culture, they shape child development. Understanding how and why such characteristics influence development is critical for identifying appropriate ways to support and nurture development, including early language and literacy.

Environmental Resources and Socioeconomic Status

Variations in the characteristics of children's environments also may dramatically affect development. For example, the economic status of the family influences characteristics of speech patterns in the home and the size of a child's subsequent vocabulary (Hart & Risley, 1995; Hoff, 2003). Children growing up in poverty are more likely to experience developmental delays than are those from more privileged backgrounds because they are disproportionately exposed to a wide range of risk factors that can hinder development (Bolig, Borkowski, & Brandenberger, 1999; Bradley & Corwyn, 2002; Brooks-

Gunn, 1995; Brooks-Gunn, Klebanov, Liaw, & Duncan, 1995). For example, children from low-income backgrounds are more likely to be exposed to the following risk factors:

- malnutrition (Guthrie & Morton, 1999; Monroe, O'Neil, Tiller, & Smith, 2002);

- substandard housing, or being homeless (Evans & English, 2002; Koch, Lewis, & Quinones, 1998);

- low-quality, out-of-home child care arrangements (Children's Defense Fund, 1992; Shonkoff, 1995);

- environmental hazards (e.g., lead paint exposure, second-hand smoke, rats/pests; Cohen et al., 2003; Jacobs et al., 2002; Wamboldt et al., 2002);

- less stimulating home environments with fewer developmentally appropriate toys and resources that promote learning (Bradley, Corwyn, McAdoo, & Garcia Coll, 2001; Brooks-Gunn, Leventhal, & Duncan, 2000);

- domestic and community violence (Brooks-Gunn et al., 2000; Hsieh & Pugh, 1999); and

- interactions with caregivers who have serious mental health concerns or whose nurturing interactions are diminished from chronic stress (Adler et al., 1994; Adler, Boyce, Chesney, Folkman, & Syme, 1993; Lorant et al., 2003).

The negative impact of these challenges on development appears to be cumulative and interacting. For instance, chronic undernutrition contributes to infant apathy and minimizes efforts by toddlers to seek out whatever cognitively stimulating toys and resources might be available in the environment (Lozoff et al., 1998). Malnutrition also contributes to diminished resistance to disease that compounds susceptibility to health and developmental problems associated with exposure to environmental hazards (Law, Carbonell-Estrany, & Simoes, 2002; Motarjemi, Kaferstein, Moy, & Quevedo, 1993).

Even so, it is important to note that many children display amazing resilience and thrive in the face of considerable environmental challenges. For instance, children growing up in impoverished, even violent, neighborhoods can fare well when their parents or other adults in the community believe that they have an active role in shaping and supporting their children's development (Luster,

Rhoades, & Haas, 1989) and are committed to monitoring their children's whereabouts, communicating with their caregivers and teachers, and regularly talking to and reading with their children (Jarrett, 1997). Likewise, socioeconomic privilege alone does not guarantee optimal child development (Eckersley & Dear, 2002; Goodman, 1999; Mathur & Freeman, 2002). Considering the specific features of the home, neighborhood, and community, the contexts in which infants and toddlers develop must inform understanding of their development and offer guidance about effective strategies to support language and literacy in each particular situation.

Conclusion

The foundation for literacy begins at least at birth. From their earliest days, infants are building and strengthening the capacities they will need to communicate with others through language and through the graphical symbols of literacy in our society. This chapter described some of the critical changes and developmental tasks that infants and toddlers evidence during the first 3 years of life that contribute to later language learning and literacy.

Children's transformation during this period involves enormous shifts in every domain of development. Moreover, these developmental domains are interconnected such that developmental advances in one area prompt or are prompted by developmental shifts in another area. Advances the child makes in abilities to gather information about the environment through the senses and by using emerging motor skills allow the child to engage in more exploratory behaviors. Such behaviors build language and thinking skills. Changes in thinking skills and advances in play behaviors create new understandings of the world that can be communicated to caregivers and peers through verbal, nonverbal, and eventually written means. Healthy emotional development provides the confidence for infants and toddlers to explore their worlds and develop new skills. Advances in language skills open the doors to new ways to explore the world and communicate effectively.

Although common sequences in development typically can be identified, wide variation between individual infants and toddlers underscores the necessity of individualizing interactions and interventions to the specific strengths, needs, experiences, and styles of each child. Nevertheless, by understanding the changing abilities of infants and toddlers during the first 3 years, parents and caregivers can more effectively recognize and facilitate actions that support emerging language and literacy in our youngest citizens.

References

Abe, J. A., & Izard, C. E. (1999). The developmental functions of emotions: An analysis in terms of differential emotions theory. *Cognition and Emotion, 13*(5), 523–549.

Adamson, L., & MacArthur, D. (1995). Joint attention, affect, and culture. In C. Moore & P. Dunham (Eds.), *Joint attention: Its origins and role in development* (pp. 189–204). Hillsdale, NJ: Erlbaum.

Adler, N. E., Boyce, T., Chesney, M. A., Cohen, S., Folkman, S., Kahn, R. L., & Syme, S. L. (1994). Socioeconomic status and health. The challenge of the gradient. *American Psychologist, 49*(1), 15–24.

Adler, N. E., Boyce, W. T., Chesney, M. A., Folkman, S., & Syme, S. L. (1993). Socioeconomic inequalities in health. No easy solution. *JAMA, 269*(24), 3140–3145.

American Academy of Pediatrics. (1995). Human milk, breastfeeding, and transmission of human immunodeficiency virus in the United States RE9542. *Pediatrics, 96*(5), 977–979.

Aslin, R. N., Jusczyk, P. W., & Pisoni, D. B. (1998). Speech and auditory processing during infancy: Constraints on and precursors to language. In D. Kuhn & R. S. Siegler (Eds.), *Cognition, perception, and language* (Vol. 2, pp. 147–198). New York: Wiley.

Bakeman, R., & Adamson, L. (1984). Coordinating attention to people and objects in mother-infant and peer-infant interaction. *Child Development, 55*, 1278–1289.

Banks, M. S., & Dannemiller, J. L. (1987). Infant visual psychophysics. In P. Salapatek & L. Cohen (Eds.), *Handbook of infant perception* (Vol. 2, pp. 115–184). New York: Academic Press.

Barr, R., Dowden, A., & Hayne, H. (1996). Developmental changes in deferred imitation in infancy: Practice makes perfect? *Infant Behavior and Development, 19*, 253–257.

Barr, R., Marrott, H., & Rovee-Collier, C. (2003). The role of sensory preconditioning in memory retrieval by preverbal infants. *Learning and Behavior, 31*(2), 111–123.

Belsky, J., & Most, R. K. (1981). From exploration to play: A cross-sectional study of infant free play behavior. *Developmental Psychology, 17*, 630–639.

Bertenthal, B. I., & Campos, J. J. (1990). A systems approach to the organizing effects of self-produced locomotion during infancy. In C. Rovee-Collier & L. P. Lipsitt (Eds.), *Advances in infancy research* (Vol. 6, pp. 1–60). Norwood: NJ: Ablex.

Bertenthal, B. I., & Clifton, R. K. (1998). Perception and action. In D. Kuhn & R. S. Siegler (Eds.), *Cognition, perception, and language* (5th ed., Vol. 2, pp. 51–102). New York: Wiley.

Black, J. E., Jones, T. A., Nelson, C. A., & Greenough, W. T. (1998). Neuronal plasticity and the developing brain. In N. Alessi, J. T. Coyle, S. I. Harrison, & S. Eth (Eds.), *Handbook of child and adolescent psychiatry: Basic psychiatric science and treatment* (Vol. 6, pp. 31–53). New York: Wiley.

Bolig, E. E., Borkowski, J., & Brandenberger, J. (1999). Poverty and health across the life span. In T. L. Whitman & T. V. Merluzzi (Eds.), *Life span perspectives on health and illness* (pp. 67–84). Mahwah, NJ: Erlbaum.

Bornstein, M. (1976). Infants are tricromats. *Journal of Experimental Child Psychology, 21*, 425–445.

Bornstein, M. H. (1992). Perception across the life span. In M. H. Bornstein & M. E. Lamb (Eds.), *Developmental psychology: An advanced textbook* (3rd ed., pp. 155–209). Hillsdale, NJ: Erlbaum.

Bornstein, M. H., & Tamis-LeMonda, C. S. (1989). Maternal responsiveness and cognitive development in children. In M. H. Bornstein (Ed.), *Maternal responsiveness: Characteristics and consequences* (Vol. 43, pp. 49–61). San Francisco: Jossey-Bass.

Bornstein, M. H., & Tamis-LeMonda, C. S. (2001). Mother-infant interaction. In G. Bremner & A. Fogel (Eds.), *Blackwell handbook of infant development* (pp. 269–295). Malden, MA: Blackwell.

Bradley, R. H., & Corwyn, R. F. (2002). Socioeconomic status and child development. *Annual Review of Psychology, 53,* 371–399.

Bradley, R. H., Corwyn, R. F., McAdoo, H. P., & Garcia Coll, C. (2001). The home environments of children in the United States, Part I: Variations by age, ethnicity, and poverty status. *Child Development, 72*(6), 1844–1867.

Bremner, J. G. (2001). Cognitive development: Knowledge of the physical world. In G. Bremner & A. Fogel (Eds.), *Blackwell handbook of infant development* (pp. 99–138). Malden, MA: Blackwell.

Bretherton, I. (1984). Representing the social world in symbolic play: Reality and fantasy. In I. Bretherton (Ed.), *Symbolic play: The development of social understanding.* Orlando, FL: Academic Press.

Brice-Heath, S. (1988). Language socialization. In D. T. Slaughter (Ed.), *Black children and poverty: A developmental perspective* (Vol. 42, pp. 29–41). San Francisco: Jossey-Bass.

Bristow, P. S. (1985). Are poor readers passive readers? Some evidence, possible explanations, and potential solutions. *Reading Teacher, 39*(3), 318–325.

Brooks-Gunn, J. (1995). Children in families in communities: Risk and intervention in the Bronfenbrenner tradition. In P. Moen & G. H. Elder, Jr. (Eds.), *Examining lives in context: Perspectives on the ecology of human development* (pp. 467–519). Washington, DC: American Psychological Association.

Brooks-Gunn, J., Klebanov, P., Liaw, F. R., & Duncan, G. J. (1995). Toward an understanding of the effects of poverty upon children. In H. E. Fitzgerald & B. M. Lester (Eds.), *Children of poverty: Research, health, and policy issues* (pp. 3–41). New York: Garland.

Brooks-Gunn, J., Leventhal, T., & Duncan, G. J. (2000). Why poverty matters for young children: Implications for policy. In J. D. Osofsky & H. E. Fitzgerald (Eds.), *Parenting and child care* (Vol. 3, pp. 89–131). New York: Wiley.

Bruner, J. (1983). *Child's talk: Learning to use language.* Oxford, UK: Oxford University Press.

Butterworth, G. (2001). Joint visual attention in infancy. In G. Bremner & A. Fogel (Eds.), *Blackwell handbook of infant development* (pp. 213–240). Malden, MA: Blackwell.

Camaioni, L. (1993). The development of intentional communication: A re-analysis. In J. Nadel & L. Camaioni (Eds.), *New perspectives in early communicative development* (pp. 82–96). London: Routledge.

Campos, J. J., Barrett, K. C., Lamb, M. E., Goldsmith, H. H, & Stenberg, C. (1983). Socioemotional development. In P. H. Mussen (Ed.) *Handbook of child psychology, Vol. 12, infancy and developmental psychobiology.* New York: Wiley.

Carey, S. (Ed.). (1978). *The child as a word learner.* Cambridge, MA: MIT Press.

Cheour-Luhtanen, M., Alho, K., Sainio, K., Rinne, T., Reinikainen, K., Pohjavuori, et al. (1996). The ontogenetically earliest discriminative response of the human brain. *Psychophysiology, 33*, 478–481.

Children's Defense Fund. (1992). *Child care under the Family Support Act: Early lessons from the states.* Washington, DC: Author.

Cicchetti, D., & Beeghly, M. (1987). Symbolic development in maltreated youngsters: An organizational perspective. *New Directions for Child Development, 36*, 47–67.

Cohen, D. A., Mason, K., Bedimo, A., Scribner, R., Basolo, V., & Farley, T. A. (2003). Neighborhood physical conditions and health. *American Journal of Public Health, 93*(3), 467–471.

Cooper, R. P. (1993). The effects of prosody in young infants' speech perception. In L. P. Lipsitt, & C. Rovee-Collier (Eds.), *Advances in infancy research* (Vol. 8, pp. 137–167). Norwood, NJ: Ablex.

Craig, H. K., Connor, C. M., & Washington, J. A. (2003). Early positive predictors of later reading comprehension for African American students: A preliminary investigation. *Language, Speech, and Hearing Services in Schools, 34*(1), 31–43.

Creasy, G. L., Jarvis, P. A., & Berk, L. E. (1998). Play and social competence. In O. N. Saracho & B. Spodek (Eds.), *Multiple perspectives on play in early childhood education* (pp. 116–143). Albany: State University of New York Press.

DeCasper, A., & Fifer, W. P. (1980). Of human bonding: Newborns prefer their mothers' voices. *Science, 208*, 1174–1176.

Dunn, J. (1985). The beginnings of moral understanding: Development in the second year. In J. K. S. Lamb (Ed.), *The emergence of morality in young children.* Chicago: University of Chicago Press.

Dunn, J. (1991). Understanding others: Evidence from naturalistic studies of children. In A. Whiten (Ed.), *Natural theories of mind: Evolution, development, and simulation of everyday mindreading.* Oxford: Blackwell.

Dunn, J., Brown, J., & Beardsall, L. (1991). Family talk about feeling states and children's later understanding of others' emotions. *Developmental Psychology, 31*, 649–659.

Dunn, J., & Dale, N. (1984). I a daddy: 2-year-olds' collaboration in joint pretend with sibling and with mother. In I. Bretherton (Ed.), *Symbolic play: The development of social understanding.* New York: Academic Press.

Eckerman, C. O. (1979). The human infant in social interaction. In R. B. Cairns (Ed.), *The analysis of social interactions: Methods, measures, and illustrations* (pp. 163–178). Hillsdale, NJ: Erlbaum.

Eckersley, R., & Dear, K. (2002). Cultural correlates of youth suicide. *Social Science and Medicine, 55*(11), 1891–1904.

Enns, J. T., & Girgus, J. S. (1985). Developmental changes in selective and integrative visual attention. *Journal of Experimental Child Psychology, 40*, 319–337.

Enns, J. T., & Girgus, J. S. (1986). A developmental study of shape integration over space and time. *Developmental Psychology, 22*, 491–499.

Erikson, E. H. (1963). *Childhood and society* (Rev. ed.) New York: W. W. Norton.

Erwin, B. (1991). The relationship between background experience and students' comprehension: A cross-cultural study. *Reading Psychology, 12*(1), 43–61.

Evans, G. W., & English, K. (2002). The environment of poverty: Multiple stressor exposure, psychophysiological stress, and socioemotional adjustment. *Child Development, 73*(4), 1238–1248.

Feinman, S. (1982). Social referencing in infancy. *Merrill-Palmer Quarterly, 28*, 445–470.

Feldman, H. N. (Ed.). (1994). *Language development after unilateral brain injury: A replication study*. Hillsdale, NJ: Erlbaum.

Fenson, L., Dale, P. S., Reznick, L., Bates, E., Thail, D., & Pethick, S. J. (1994). Variability in early communicative development. *Monographs of the Society for Research in Child Development, 59*(5).

Fernald, A. (1984). The perceptual and affective salience of mothers' speech to infants. In L. Feagans, C. Garvey, & R. Golinkoff (Eds.), *The origins and growth of communication* (pp. 5–29). Norwood, NJ: Ablex.

Fernald, A. (2001). Hearing, listening, and understanding: Auditory development in infancy. In G. Bremner & A. Fogel (Eds.), *Blackwell handbook of infant development* (pp. 35–70). Malden, MA: Blackwell.

Fernald, A., Taeschner, T., Dunn, J., Papousek, M., Boysson-Bardies, B., & Fukui, I. (1989). A cross-language study of prosodic modifications in mothers' and fathers' speech to preverbal infants. *Journal of Child Language, 16*, 477–501.

Fivaz-Depeursinge, E., & Corboz-Warnery, A. (1999). *The primary triangle*. New York: Basic Books.

Fogel, A. (1993). *Developing through relationships: Origins of communication, self, and culture*. Chicago: University of Chicago Press.

Fogel, A. (1995). Relational narratives of the prelinguistic self. In P. Rochat (Ed.), *The self in infancy: Theory and research* (pp. 117–140). Amsterdam: North-Holland/Elsevier.

Gadian, D. G., Mishkin, M., & Vargha-Khadem, F. (1999). Early brain pathology and its relation to cognitive impairment: The role of quantitative magnetic resonance techniques. *Advances in Neurology, 81*, 307–315.

Gibson, E. J. (1988). Exploratory behavior in the development of perceiving, acting, and the acquiring of knowledge. *Annual Review of Psychology, 39*, 1–41.

Gogate, L. J., Bahrick, L. E., & Watson, J. D. (2000). A study of multimodal motherese: The role of temporal synchrony between verbal labels and gestures. *Child Development, 71*(4), 878–894.

Goldberg, C. (1989). Normal motor development. In J. Tecklin (Ed.), *Pediatric physical therapy* (pp. 1–15). Philadelphia: Lippincott.

Golding, J., Rogers, I. S., & Emmett, P. M. (1997). Association between breast feeding, child development and behavior. *Early Human Development, 49*(Suppl), S175–184.

Goldsmith, H. H., Buss, A. H., Plomin, R., Rothbart, M. K., Thomas, A., Chess, S., et al. (1987). Roundtable: What is temperament? Four approaches. *Child Development, 58*, 505–529.

Goodman, E. (1999). The role of socioeconomic status gradients in explaining differences in U.S. adolescents' health. *American Journal of Public Health, 89*(10), 1522–1528.

Greenough, W. T., & Black, J. E. (1992). Induction of brain structure by experience: Substrates for cognitive development. In M. R. Gunnar & C. A. Nelson (Eds.), *Developmental behavior neuroscience* (Vol. 24, pp. 155–200). Hillsdale, NJ: Erlbaum.

Greenspan, S. I. (1994). *First feelings: Milestones in the emotional development of your baby and child.* New York: Penguin.

Greenspan, S. I., & Lewis, D. (1990). Emotional growth in infants and young children with communicative challenges. *Folia Phoniatrica, 42*(5), 251–259.

Grieser, D. L., & Kulh, P. K. (1988). Maternal speech to infants in a tonal language: Support for universal prosodic features in motherese. *Developmental Psychology, 24,* 14–20.

Gunnar, M. R. (2000). Early adversity and the development of stress reactivity and regulation. In C. A. Nelson (Ed.), *The effects of adversity on neurobehavioral development, Vol. 31* (pp. 163–200). Hillsdale, NJ: Erlbaum.

Guthrie, J. F., & Morton, J. F. (1999). Diet-related knowledge, attitudes, and practices of low-income households with children. *Journal of Early Education and Family Review, 6*(3), 26–33.

Hainline, L. (1998). The development of basic visual abilities. In A. Slater (Ed.), *Perceptual development: Visual, auditory, and speech perception in infancy* (pp. 37–44). Hove, UK: Psychology Press.

Hamer, R. D., Norcia, A. M., Tyler, C. W., & Hsu-Winges, C. (1989). The development of monocular and binocular VEP acuity. *Vision Research, 29,* 397–408.

Hart, B., & Risley, T. R. (1995). *Meaningful differences in the everyday experience of young American children.* Baltimore: Paul H. Brookes.

Hay, D. F., Pederson, J., & Nasg, A. (1982). Dyadic interaction in the first year of life. In H. K. H. Rubin & H. S. Ross (Eds.), *Peer relationships and social skills in childhood* (pp. 11–40). New York: Springer-Verlag.

Held, R. (1985). Binocular vision: Behavioral and neuronal development. In J. Mehler & R. Fox (Eds.), *Neonate cognition: Beyond the blooming, buzzing confusion* (pp. 37–44). Hillsdale, NJ: Erlbaum.

Hoff, E. (2003). The specificity of environmental influence: Socioeconomic status affects early vocabulary via maternal speech. *Child Development, 74*(5), 1368–1378.

Hoff-Ginsberg, E. (1997). *Language development.* Pacific Grove, CA: Brooks/Cole.

Hsieh, C.-C., & Pugh, M. D. (1999). Poverty, income inequality, and violent crime: A meta-analysis of recent aggregate data studies. In I. Kawachi, B. P. Kennedy, & R. G. Wilkinson (Eds.), *Income inequality and health* (Vol. 1, pp. 278–296). New York: The New Press.

Hubel, D. H., Wiesel, T. N., & Levay, S. (1977). Plasticity of ocular dominance columns in monkey striate cortex. *Philosophical Transactions of the Royal Society of London, B278,* 307–409.

Huttenlocher, P. R. (1990). Morphometric study of human cerebral cortex development. *Neuropsychologia, 28,* 517–527.

Huttenlocher, P. R. (1994). Synaptogenesis, synapse elimination, and neural plasticity in human cerebral cortex. In C. A. Nelson (Ed.), *Threats to optimal development* (Vol. 27, pp. 35–54). Hillsdale, NJ: Erlbaum.

Invernizzi, M. (2003). Concepts, sounds, and the ABCs: A diet for a very young reader. In D. M. Barone & L. M. Morrow (Eds.), *Literacy and young children: Research-based practices* (pp. 140–156). New York: Guilford Press.

Isabella, R., & Belsky, J. (1991). Interactional synchrony and the origins of infant-mother attachment: A replication study. *Child Development, 62*, 373–384.

Izard, C. E. (1991). *The psychology of emotions.* New York: Plenum.

Jacobs, D. E., Clickner, R. P., Zhou, J. Y., Viet, S. M., Marker, D. A., Rogers, J. W., et al. (2002). The prevalence of lead-based paint hazards in U.S. housing. *Environmental Health Perspectives, 110*(10), A599–606.

Jarrett, R. L. (1997). African American family and parenting strategies in impoverished neighborhoods. *Qualitative Sociology, 20*, 275–288.

Joh, A., Sweeny, B. & Rovee-Collier, C. (2002). Minimum duration of reactivation at 3 months of age. *Developmental Psychobiology, 41*(1), 23–32.

Johnson, M. H. (1998). The neural basis of cognitive development. In D. Kuhn & R. S. Siegler (Eds.), *Cognition, perception, and language* (5th ed., Vol. 2, pp. 1–49). New York: Wiley.

Jusczyk, P. W. (1997). *The discovery of spoken language.* Cambridge, MA: MIT Press.

Karns, J. T. (2001). Health, nutrition and safety. In G. Bremner & A. Fogel (Eds.), *Handbook of infant development* (pp. 693–725). Malden, MA: Blackwell.

Karrass, J., Braungart-Rieker, J. M., Mullins, J., & Lefever, J. B. (2002). Processes in language acquisition: The roles of gender, attention, and maternal encouragement of attention over time. *Journal of Child Language, 29*, 519–543.

Kavanaugh, R. D., & Engel, S. (1998). The development of pretense and narrative in early childhood. In O. N. Saracho & B. Spodek (Eds.), *Multiple perspectives on play in early childhood education* (pp. 80–99). Albany: State University of New York Press.

Kisilevsky, B. S., Muir, D. W., & Low, J. A. (1992). Maturation of human fetal responses to vibroacoustic stimulation. *Child Development, 63*, 1497–1508.

Klaus, M. H., & Klaus, P. (1985). *The amazing newborn.* Reading, MA: Addison-Wesley.

Koch, R., Lewis, M. T., & Quinones, W. (1998). Homeless: Mothering at rock bottom. In C. G. Coll & J. L. Surrey (Eds.), *Mothering against the odds: Diverse voices of contemporary mothers* (pp. 61–84). New York: Guilford.

Kostelnik, M. J., Whiren, A., Soderman, A. K., Stein, L.C, & Gregory, K. (2002). *Guiding children's social development: Theory and practice* (4th ed). Albany, NY: Delmar.

Lally, J. R. (1995). Discovery in infancy: How and what infants learn. In P. L. Mangione (Ed.), *Infant/toddler caregiving: A guide to cognitive development and learning.* Sacramento:: California Department of Education.

Lanza, E. (1992). Can bilingual two-year-olds code switch? *Journal of Child Language, 19*, 633–658.

Law, B. J., Carbonell-Estrany, X., & Simoes, E. A. (2002). An update on respiratory syncytial virus epidemiology: A developed country perspective. *Respiratory Medicine, 96*(Suppl B), S1–7.

Lecanuet, J. P., Graniere-Deferre, C., Jacquet, A. Y., & DeCasper, A. J. (2000). Fetal discrimination of low-pitched musical notes. *Developmental Psychobiology, 36*, 29–39.

Lenhart, L., & Roskos, K. (2003). What Hannah taught Emma and why it matters. In D. M. Barone & L. M. Morrow (Eds.), *Literacy and young children: Research-based practices* (pp. 83–100). New York: Guilford.

Lerner, R. M., & Lerner, J. V. (1987). Children in their contexts: A goodness-of-fit model. In J. B. Lancaster, A. S. Rossi, L. R. Sherrod (Ed.), *Parenting across the lifespan: Biosocial dimensions* (pp. 377–404). New York: Aldine de Gruyter.

Lewis, M., & Brooks-Gunn, J. (1979). *Social cognition and the acquisition of self.* New York: Plenum.

Lipsitt, L. P. (1990). Learning and memory in infants. *Merrill-Palmer Quarterly, 36,* 53–66.

Lorant, V., Deliege, D., Eaton, W., Robert, A., Philippot, P., & Ansseau, M. (2003). Socioeconomic inequalities in depression: A meta-analysis. *American Journal of Epidemiology, 157*(2), 98–112.

Lozoff, B., Klein, N. K., Nelson, E. C., McClish, D. K., Manuel, M., & Chacon, M. E. (1998). Behavior of infants with iron-deficiency anemia. *Child Development, 69,* 24–36.

Luster, T., Rhoades, K., & Haas, B. (1989). The relation between parental values and parenting behavior: A test of the Kohn hypothesis. *Journal of Marriage and the Family, 51,* 139–147.

MacTurk, R., Meadow-Orlans, K. P., Koester, L. S., & Spencer, P. E. (1993). Social support, motivation, language, and interaction. *American Annals of the Deaf, 138*(1), 19–25.

Martin, J. A. (1989). Personal and interpersonal components of responsiveness. In M. H. Bornstein (Ed.), *Maternal responsiveness: Characteristics and consequences* (Vol. 43, pp. 5–14). San Francisco: Jossey-Bass.

Matas, L., Arend, R., & Sroufe, L. A. (1978). Continuity of adaptation in the second year: The relationship between quality of attachment and later competence. *Child Development, 49,* 547–556.

Mathur, V. K., & Freeman, D. G. (2002). A theoretical model of adolescent suicide and some evidence from U.S. data. *Health Economics, 11*(8), 695–708.

Matthews, J. (2003). *Drawing and painting: Children and visual representation* (2nd ed.). London: Paul Chapman Publishing.

Mayberry, R., Wodlinger-Cohen, R., & Goldin-Meadow, S. (1987). Symbolic development in deaf children. In D. Cicchetti & M. Beeghly (Eds.), *Symbolic development in atypical children* (Vol. 36, pp. 109–125). San Francisco: Jossey-Bass.

McDermott, R. P., & Varenne, H. (1996). Culture, development, disability. In R. Jessor, A. Colby, & R. A. Shweder (Eds.), *Ethnography and human development: Context and meaning in social inquiry* (pp. 101–126). Chicago: University of Chicago Press.

McGee, L. M. (2003). Book acting: Storytelling and drama in the early childhood classroom. In D. M. Barone & L. M. Morrow (Eds.), *Literacy and young children: Research-based practices* (pp. 157–172). New York: Guilford.

Meltzoff, A. N. (1995). Understanding the intentions of others: Re-enactment of intended acts by 18 month-old children. *Developmental Psychology, 31,* 838–850.

Mercer, J. (1998). *Infant development: A multidisciplinary introduction.* New York: Brooks/Cole.

Monroe, P. A., O'Neil, C., Tiller, V. L., & Smith, J. (2002). *The challenge of compliance: Food security in rural households affected by welfare reform.* Mississippi State: Southern Rural Development Center, Mississippi State University.

Motarjemi, Y., Kaferstein, F., Moy, G., & Quevedo, F. (1993). Contaminated weaning food: A major risk factor for diarrhoea and associated malnutrition. *Bulletin of the World Health Organization, 71*(1), 79–92.

Mueller, E., & Silverman, N. (1989). Peer relations in maltreated children. In D. Cicchetti & V. K. Carlson (Ed.), *Child maltreatment: Theory and research on the causes and consequences of child abuse and neglect* (pp. 529–578). New York: Cambridge University Press.

National Research Council, & Institute of Medicine. (2000). *From neurons to neighborhoods: The science of early childhood development* (J. P. Shonkoff & D. A. Phillips, Eds.). Committee on Integrating the Science of Early Childhood Development; Board on Children, Youth, and Families; Commission on Behavioral and Social Sciences and Education. Washington, DC: National Academy Press.

Nelson, C. A. (1987). The recognition of facial expressions in the first two years of life: Mechanisms of development. *Child Development, 58*(4), 889–909.

Nelson, C. A. (1999). Neural plasticity and human development. *Current Directions in Psychological Science, 8,* 42–45.

Nelson, C. A., & deHaan, M. (1997). A neurobehavioral approach to the recognition of facial expressions in infancy. In J. A. Russell & J. M. Fernandez-Dols (Eds.), *The psychology of facial expression: Studies in emotion and social interactions* (pp. 176–204). New York: Cambridge University Press.

Nettlebeck, T., & Wilson, C. (1985). A cross-sequential analysis of developmental differences in speed of information processing. *Journal of Experimental Child Psychology, 40,* 1–22.

Newberg, D. S., & Street, J. M. (1997). Bioactive materials in human milk: Milk sugars sweeten the argument for breast-feeding. *Nutrition Today, 32*(5), 191–200.

Notari-Syverson, A. (2006). Everyday tools of literacy. In S. E. Rosenkoetter & J. Knapp-Philo (Eds.), *Learning to read the world: Language and literacy in the first three years* (pp. 61–80). Washington, DC: ZERO TO THREE Press.

Ogbu, J. U. (1988). Cultural diversity and human development. In D. T. Slaughter (Ed.), *Black children and poverty: A developmental perspective* (Vol. 42, pp. 11–28). San Francisco: Jossey-Bass.

Olsho, L. W., Koch, E. G., Carter, E. A., Halpin, C. F., & Spetner, N. B. (1988). Pure-tone sensitivity of human infants. *Journal of the Acoustical Society of America, 84,* 1316–1324.

Omanson, R. C. (1985). Knowing words and understanding texts. In T. H. Carr (Ed.), *The development of reading skills* (Vol. 27, pp. 35–53). San Francisco: Jossey-Bass.

Pearson, B. Z., Fernandez, S. C., & Oller, D. K. (1993). Lexical development in bilingual infants and toddlers: Comparison to monolingual norms. *Language Learning, 43,* 93–120.

Piaget, J. (1952). *The origins of intelligence in children.* New York: International University Press.

Pierce, P., & Profio, A. (2006). From cooing to conversation to *The Carrot Seed*: Oral and written language connections. In S. E. Rosenkoetter & J. Knapp-Philo (Eds.), *Learning to read the world: Language and literacy in the first three years* (pp. 103–122). Washington, DC: ZERO TO THREE Press.

Power, T. G. (2000). *Play and exploration in children and animals.* Mahwah, NJ: Erlbaum.

Preisler, G. (2001). Sensory deficits. In G. Bremner & A. Fogel (Eds.), *Handbook of infant development* (pp. 617–638). Malden, MA: Blackwell.

Roberts, J. E., Wallace, I. F., & Henderson, F. W. (1997). *Otitis media in young children.* Baltimore: Paul H. Brookes.

Rochat, P. (1995). Early objectivication of the self. In P. Rochat (Ed.), *The self in infancy: Theory and research* (pp. 53–71). Amsterdam: North-Holland/Elsevier.

Rochat, P. (Ed.). (2001). *Origins of self-concept.* Oxford: Blackwell.

Rochat, P., Querido, J. G., & Striano, T. (1999). Emerging sensitivity to the timing and structure of protoconversation in early infancy. *Developmental Psychology, 35,* 950–957.

Rochat, P., & Striano, T. (1999). Social cognitive development in the first year. In P. Rochat (Ed.), *Early social cognition: Understanding others in the first months of life* (pp. 3–34). Mahwah, NJ: Erlbaum.

Rogan, W. J., & Gladen, B. C. (1993). Breast-feeding and cognitive development. *Early Human Development, 31*(3), 181–193.

Rollins, P. R., & Snow, C. E. (1998). Shared attention and grammatical development in typical children and children with autism. *Journal of Child Language, 25,* 653–673.

Roopnarine, J. L., Lasker, J., Sacks, M., & Stores, M. (1998). The cultural contexts of children's play. In O. N. Saracho & B. Spodek (Eds.), *Multiple perspectives on play in early childhood education* (pp. 194–219). Albany: State University of New York Press.

Roskos, K., & Neuman, S. B. (1998). Play as an opportunity for literacy. In O. N. Saracho & B. Spodek (Eds.), *Multiple perspectives on play in early childhood education* (pp. 100–115). Albany: State University of New York Press.

Ross, H. S., Conant, C., Cheyne, J. A., & Alevizos, E. (1992). Relationships and alliances in the social interactions of Kibbutz toddlers. *Social Development, 1,* 1–17.

Rovee-Collier, C. (1999). The development of infant memory. *Current Directions in Psychological Science, 8,* 80–85.

Rovee-Collier, C., & Barr, R. (2001). Infant learning and memory. In G. Bremner & A. Fogel (Eds.), *Blackwell handbook of infant development.* Malden, MA: Blackwell.

Saffran, J. R., Aslin, R. N., & Newport, E. L. (1996). Statistical learning by 8-month-old infants. *Science, 274,* 1926–1928.

Serrano, J. M., Iglesias, J., & Loeches, A. (1992). Visual discrimination and recognition of facial expressions of anger, fear, and surprise in 4- to 6-month-old infants. *Developmental Psychobiology, 25*(6), 411–425.

Shonkoff, J. P. (1995). Childcare for low-income families. *Young Children, 50*(6), 63–65.

Slater, A. (2001). Visual perception. In G. Bremner & A. Fogel (Eds.), *Blackwell handbook of infant development* (pp. 5–34). Malden, MA: Blackwell.

Sloutsky, V. M., & Napolitano, A. C. (2003). Is a picture worth a thousand words? Preference for auditory modality in young children. *Child Development, 74*(3), 822–833.

Smith, N. R. (1979). How a picture means. In D. Wolf (Ed.), *Early symbolization* (Vol. 3, pp. 59–72). San Francisco: Jossey-Bass.

Smitsman, A. W. (2001). Action in infancy—perspectives, concepts, and challenges: The development of reaching and grasping. In G. Bremner & A. Fogel (Eds.), *Blackwell handbook of infant development* (pp. 71–98). Malden, MA: Blackwell.

Stern, D. N. (1984). Affect attunement. In J. D. Call, E. Galenson, & R. T. Tyson (Eds.), *Frontiers of infant psychiatry* (Vol. 2, pp. 3–14). New York: Basic Books.

Stern, D. N., Hofer, L., Haft, W., & Dore, J. (1985). Affect attunement: The sharing of feeling states between mother and infant by means of inter-modal fluency. In T. M. Fields & N. A. Fox (Eds.), *Social perception in infants.* Norwood, NJ: Ablex.

Stern, D. N., Spieker, S., & MacKain, K. (1982). Intonation contours as signals in maternal speech to prelinguistic infants. *Developmental Psychology, 18,* 727–735.

Suddendorf, T. (2003). Early representational insight: Twenty-four-month-olds can use a photo to find an object in the world. *Child Development, 74*(3), 896–904.

Sumner, G., & Spietz, A. (1994). *NCAST caregiver/parent-child interaction teaching manual.* Seattle: NCAST Publications, University of Washington, School of Nursing.

Tamis-LeMonda, C. S., Bornstein, M. H., & Baumwell, L. (2001). Maternal responsiveness and children's achievement of language milestones. *Child Development, 72*(3), 748–767.

Tamis-LeMonda, C. S., Bornstein, M. H., Kahana-Kalman, R., Baumwell, L., & Cyphers, L. (1998). Predicting variation in the timing of language milestones in the second year: An events history approach. *Journal of Child Language, 25,* 675–700.

Teele, D. W., Klein, J. O., & Rosner, B. A. (1984). Otitis media with effusion during the first three years of life and development of speech and language. *Pediatrics, 74,* 282–287.

Thompson, R. A. (2001). Development in the first years of life. *The Future of Children, 11*(1), 21–33.

Tomasello, M. (Ed.). (1995). *Joint attention as social cognition.* Hillsdale, NJ: Erlbaum.

Tomasello, M., & Akhtar, N. (1995). Two-year-olds use pragmatic cues to differentiate reference to objects and actions. *Cognitive Development, 10,* 201–224.

Trehub, S. E. (1976). The discrimination of foreign speech contrasts by infants and adults. *Child Development, 47,* 466–472.

Trehub, S. E., Schneider, B. A., & Henderson, J. L. (1995). Gap detection in infants, children, and adults. *Journal of the Acoustical Society of America, 98,* 2532–2541.

Uttal, D. H., Marzolf, D. P., Pierroutsakos, S. L., Smith, C. M., Troseth, G. L., Scudder, K. V., & DeLoache, J. S. (1998). Seeing through symbols: The development of children's understanding of symbolic relations. In O. N. Saracho & B. Spodek (Eds.), *Multiple perspectives on play in early childhood education* (pp. 59–79). Albany: State University of New York Press.

Uzigiris, I. C. (1967). Ordinality in the development of schemes for relating to objects. In J. Hellmuth (Ed.), *Exceptional infant* (Vol. 1, pp. 317–334). Seattle, WA: Special Child Publications.

Vandell, D. L., & Mueller, E. C. (1995). Peer play and friendships during the first two years. In H. C. Foot, A. J. Chapman, & J. R. Smith (Eds.), *Friendship and social relations in children* (pp. 181–208). New Brunswick, NJ: Transaction.

Vandell, D. L., Wilson, K. S., & Buchanan, N. R. (1980). Peer interaction in the first year of life: An examination of its structure, content and sensitivity to toys. *Child Development, 51,* 481–488.

Wamboldt, F. S., Ho, J., Milgrom, H., Wamboldt, M. Z., Sanders, B., Szefler, S. J., & Bender, B. G. (2002). Prevalence and correlates of household exposures to tobacco smoke and pets in children with asthma. *Journal of Pediatrics, 141*(1), 109–115.

Werker, J. F. (2000). Becoming a native listener. In D. W. Muir & A. Slater (Eds.), *Infant development: The essential readings* (pp. 149–162). Malden, MA: Blackwell.

Werker, J. F., & Tees, R. C. (1984). Cross-language speech perception: Evidence for perceptual reorganization during the first year of life. *Infant Behavior and Development, 7*, 49–63.

Whitehead, M. R. (1997). *Language and literacy in the early years.* London: Paul Chapman Publishing.

CHAPTER 3

Everyday Tools of Literacy

Angela Notari-Syverson

Twelve-month-old Yassine is playing on the beach with her older brother, Mawi. She touches the wet sand and notices the marks she left. She looks at her hand and looks at the image in the sand. She places her hand in the sand again several times. She vocalizes and gestures excitedly to get her brother's attention and points to the images in the sand. Mawi tells her, "That's your hand." Yassine looks at the sand, then at her hand and repeats: "An." Mawi also shows Yassine some dog prints left by the family pet and explains: "That's Rieka's hand!" "Riri," repeats Yassine.

Mastering the symbols of their culture is a central developmental task for young children (DeLoache, 1997). In her explorations with sand, we see Yassine discover how the image in the sand represents her hand. We also see how her brother provides her with a verbal symbol to signify her hand and shows her how to interpret other images in the sand (dog prints).

What does this situation have to do with literacy? Literacy does not consist merely of reading and writing; rather it is a multifaceted and complex process that is closely intertwined with knowledge of the world (Freire & Macedo, 1987). Literacy is an important mental tool we use to gain knowledge, to express ideas, and to make sense of our experiences. Children learn to read and interpret the world well before they learn to read words. As they explore their world in the context of reciprocal relationships with caregivers, young children assign meanings to their experiences. These meanings become more and more sophisticated as children develop and learn to use a variety of verbal, gestural, and graphic symbols to represent objects, ideas, and feelings.

This chapter discusses the early development of literacy in infants and toddlers from a social-constructivist perspective. In this perspective, caregivers play a critical role in supporting the development of early social, cognitive, and language behaviors that are the foundation for later literacy. One purpose of this chapter is to illustrate how adults use everyday objects, activities, and routines as tools of literacy in ways that are meaningful and responsive to the child's interests. To begin, we propose a broad definition of literacy that is inclusive of cultural diversity and individual variations in development. We then describe how infants and toddlers develop and use early language and literacy tools, beginning with early intentional behaviors and progressive mastery of symbols. Finally, we discuss specific ways for caregivers to facilitate early language and literacy in the context of everyday environments and activities.

Literacy as a Tool

The notion of literacy as a tool comes from the Vygotskian view of development that emphasizes the critical role of mental tools in human behavior. Mental tools help us think about and act on our world (Bodrova & Leong, 1996). Language and literacy are two primary mental tools (Vygotsky, 1978). Children learn and develop through a process of gradual appropriation of tools in the context of shared experiences with more knowledgeable others (Rogoff, 1993). For example, it is in the context of her relationship with Mawi that Yassine discovers that different types of symbols (images and sounds) can be used to represent the same object (her hand). Caregivers play a mediating role in supporting meaningful experiences for children as they gradually acquire the mental tools specific to their culture (Klein, 1996). In cultures that are print-based, children participate in daily experiences with tools of literacy such as picture books, signs and labels, drawing and writing utensils, and words and sounds that help build the foundations for formal reading and writing. Cultures based on oral traditions rely more on tools such as storytelling, music, and movement.

All Children Can Learn

Mara and Nando are looking at The Hungry Caterpillar *together. Mara, who does not yet communicate verbally, takes*

*the lead, turning the pages and pointing to pictures. Nando
names the pictures for Mara in Spanish, their native language.
Their friend Gabriele joins them, labeling the pictures in English
and starting an animated conversation about bugs and their
names in English and Spanish.*

* * *

*Nadia rarely uses oral language to communicate. When she talks
she usually just repeats what she heard or recites catchy songs
from TV advertisements. She enjoys looking at picture books
and has her very own book with pictures of daily activities and
favorite objects that she uses to communicate with her parents
and child-care provider. The pictures are especially useful during
transitions from one activity to another, a time when Nadia
tends to get very anxious and overwhelmed. By showing her the
pictures, the adults can let Nadia know ahead of time what will
come next and help her get prepared for the transition.*

These 2½-year-old children have very different language, social, and cognitive
skills, yet they are all using literacy tools to develop new skills. Mara, who
communicates mostly with gestures, learns new words and simple book conventions (e.g., turning pages from front to back). Nando, who recently came
to the United States from Mexico, expands his English vocabulary with
Gabriele, and Gabriele, a native English speaker, practices narrative skills and
sentence structure and learns words in a second language. For Nadia, visual
symbols are more meaningful than spoken language. Nadia uses pictures for
both pleasurable and functional purposes: to communicate, to learn, and to
gain understanding and control of her environment.

These vignettes illustrate the multifaceted nature of literacy. Literacy consists of
diverse tools and serves many purposes, enabling all children to participate in
literacy activities at some level.

Multiple Tools = Multiple Literacies

*Two-year-old Ken usually spends Saturday mornings with his
mother, sorting through all the mail that piled up during the*

week. Ken's mother has two piles: one for mail she will keep and the other for junk mail that she will recycle. Ken's task is to place the junk mail his mother hands him in the recycling pile. Ken enjoys this task. He likes to look at the colorful graphics and pictures and talk about them with his mother.

* * *

Two-and-a-half-year-old Clara often spends time with her grandfather in his workshop on the reservation. Her grandfather makes beautiful woodcarvings. As he works he tells Clara stories he heard from his mother and grandmother about Raven, Thunderbird, Twin Frogs, and other characters represented in his carvings.

* * *

On a rainy afternoon Lisa and Sue snuggle up with Lisa's 6-month-old baby and Sue's 18-month-old toddler on the couch to watch an old childhood video of Lisa's eighth birthday party. The two sisters share memories and stories and point out family members on the videos to their children. When they hear the Happy Birthday song on the video, they all start to sing along together.

Literacy is a way of representing and interpreting the world we live in. The notion of multiliteracies (New London Group, 1996) views literacy as multi-modal, including not only oral language and traditional print but also visual, audio, and digital media (e.g., television and the Internet). Tools of literacy differ according to culture and context and may include oral stories, songs, music, dances, paintings, and the popular culture of television shows, cartoons, video games, computer icons, and movies (Makin & Diaz, 2002). Cultural variations exist not only in the types of literacy tools but also in their functions or uses. In some cultures, reading and writing are important sources of pleasure and self-expression, while in others, print is mostly associated with religion (reading the Bible or the Koran) or used only for practical purposes (paying bills, reading sales advertisements).

Children growing up in bilingual settings experience different sets of literacy tools and practices across different sociocultural and linguistic contexts (e.g., home, child care, community; Diaz & Harvey, 2002). As long as children develop a strong foundation in their home language and are exposed to literacy activities, they develop skills that will transfer to English (Tabors & Snow, 2000). Experiences with different codes and symbols actually help children develop greater awareness of the representational nature of symbols.

Building the Foundations

Literacy is about using symbols to communicate and to assign meaning to the world. Infants and caregivers engage in social interactions where each partner reads and interprets each other's cues and behaviors and responds accordingly. An infant cries. His grandmother picks him up and rocks him gently in her arms. A toddler in tears points to her scraped knee, using a few words to explain what happen. Her father blows a kiss on his daughter's knee and pulls her onto his lap to read her favorite storybook. In both examples, the adults interpret and respond to the child's discomfort. The infant communicates through cries and facial expressions and responds to tactile and kinesthetic behaviors. The toddler uses and responds to more symbolic tools: gestures, words, and books. Levels of interpretation and specific tools gradually become more sophisticated during development as communication becomes more intentional and symbolic.

Intentional Communication and Goal-Directed Activity

An essential element to all communication is intentionality. Intentional communication first appears with gestures and prelinguistic vocalizations and later with language and literacy (Bates, 1979). Over the first year, children's behavior becomes increasingly more purposeful and goal-directed. As early as the age of 12 months, we see goal-directed, planful behavior in infants, around the same time as they learn to use language and represent the world through symbols (Lifter & Bloom, 1998). A 12-month-old asking for "juice" clearly has a specific result already in mind. Yassine's behavior also shows intentionality and goal-directed actions as she repeatedly places her hand in the sand to observe the resulting image and as she gestures and vocalizes to get her brother's attention.

Intentional behavior builds on the infant's awareness (a) that his or her behavior can have an effect on others and (b) that people and objects can be used as tools to solve problems (Bates, 1979; Bruner, 1981). Children as young as 8–12 months can demonstrate cause–effect and means–ends behavior. By creating associations between an action and its result, experiences with cause–effect toys and games help infants develop goal-directed behaviors. Gradually the child will go beyond the here and now and learn to anticipate events before they occur (Berk & Winsler, 1995; Bloom, 1994).

Means–ends behavior or tool use also implies intentional, goal-directed behavior. The choice of a tool depends upon a predetermined goal (Inhelder & Cellerier, 1992). A cup is the best choice for transporting water for drinking, but a bucket is better for filling a plastic swimming pool. A crayon or pen works best for writing messages, but a paintbrush may be a better tool for exploring colors and expressing emotions. Gestures are tools used by infants and toddlers to convey different communicative intentions. For example, a toddler uses a pointing gesture to draw attention to the appearance of a favorite person but raises his arms to ask to be picked up.

Symbolic Communication

A major achievement for young children is the development of symbolic communication, or the capacity to use symbols such as words and signs to communicate (Wetherby, Reichle, & Pierce, 1998). A symbol is an object, word, gesture, sound, or image that stands for something else. The capacity to use symbols corresponds to the cognitive achievement of mental representations (Piaget, 1970)—that is, the ability to represent things that are not physically present. Mental representation is a powerful tool that enables children to access objects and events from memory and to link present actions to a future goal (Bloom, 1994; Kopp, 1997). The acquisition of symbolic communication leads the way to rule-governed communication systems based on verbal, gestural, and graphic modalities such as spoken English, American Sign Language (ASL), and written text (Wetherby et al., 1998).

Language and Literacy-Rich Environments

Well before their first birthday, young children are experimenting with the use and functions of tools specific to literacy. The tools of literacy are many and varied and include signs, pictures, photographs, catalogs, newspapers, bill-boards, calendars, receipts, bus tickets, coins, stickers, picture books, magnetic letters, drawing and writing utensils, and computers (Rosenkoetter & Barton, 2002). Infants and toddlers first learn about tools and literacy during everyday routines with their caregivers as illustrated by the following example of an infant learning about the representational nature of pictures and sounds. The infant is looking at a photograph of a watch in a magazine and notices the real watch on the caregiver's wrist. The caregiver lets him listen to the ticking sound of the watch. The infant then places his ear on the photograph expecting to hear a similar sound (Edwards, Gandini, & Forman, 1998).

Tools of literacy are part of everyday environments. Everyday routines in the home, in child care, and in the neighborhood afford many opportunities for infants and young children to engage in experiences with different tools of literacy (Orellana & Hernandez, 1999). Adults can use virtually everything in the environment that the child shows an interest in as a tool of literacy: a photograph on the refrigerator, a logo on a paper bag, a label or design on a piece of clothing, a stick in the sand. The possibilities are infinite! While riding the bus, adults can talk about what the child sees through the window, or they can play at hiding and seeking a child's favorite toy in a bag or backpack. They can look at picture books together or trace figures on a fogged window. A trip to the grocery store is full of opportunities for literacy experiences. Children as young as 12 months learn to recognize and anticipate familiar landmarks (e.g., a relative's house) and signs on the way to the store. In the store, they are surrounded by labels, signs, numbers, colors, and foods as well as other interesting topics of conversation.

It is important that caregivers expose children to a range of different types of symbols to help them understand that there are multiple tools and modalities for representing objects and ideas. A variety of symbols and literacy tools such as photos, pictures, signs, magazines, newspapers, books, calendars, menus, soft toys, puppets, miniature objects, and visual icons from electronic media as well as art and drawing tools, including sand, textures, finger paint, and markers, should be present and used throughout the home and in child-care environments, not only in library and art areas but also in block construction, pretend play, eating, toileting, and outdoor areas. Materials should be meaningful to infants and toddlers and easily accessible to encourage active exploration and problem solving.

Literacy tools can be used for multiple functions: communicating, expressing ideas, and obtaining information. Caregivers can make these functions explicit by talking about how signs, icons, and pictures are used for a purpose (e.g., children's photographs and names to indicate personal belongings; simple icons on drawers representing inside contents, photos of children in home and child-care activities to share information among the child's different caregivers).

Tools of literacy and social relationships. Children learn the forms, signs, and functions of literacy in the context of dynamic relationships with adults (Bruner, 1981; Klein, 1996; Rogoff, 1993). During daily activities, caregivers scaffold (i.e., support or co-construct with) infants and toddlers in numerous ways. They model, encourage, provide meaning to activities, and offer directions for tasks or adaptations for materials to make them appropriate for the child's interests and developmental levels (Klein, 1996). For example, when Yassine's grandmother reads to her, she selects a quiet, comfortable place. She makes sure that Yassine is interested in the book. They usually look at picture books with simple, colorful illustrations. These are board books that are sturdy enough to allow Yassine to turn the pages easily and touch the pictures. As her grandmother talks about the pictures that interest Yassine, the adult uses an expressive voice and simple language that she knows Yassine will understand.

Facilitating Experiences With Tools of Literacy

Following are a number of suggestions of ways to support and facilitate emergent literacy skills in infants and toddlers. All children can be involved at some level in experiences with tools of literacy (Koppenhaver, Pierce-Colman, Kalman, & Yoder, 1991; McNaught, 2002; Notari-Syverson, 2004). Given the opportunity and appropriate support, children with disabilities can learn from experiences that are similar to those of other children (Berk & Winsler, 1995; Pierce, this volume, p. 335; Saint-Laurent, Giasson, & Couture, 1997; Snow, Burns, & Griffin, 1998). Even children who are nonverbal and have significant physical disabilities can access literacy activities through assistive technology devices and alternative communication tools such as Picture Communication Symbols, eye gaze boards, and electronic books (Beck, 2002; Downing & Peckham-Hardin, 2002).

"Quack-quack!" says 15-month-old Tim as he tells his mother
what he saw on his walk with his aunt. "Ducks. Yes, we fed the
ducks," confirms his aunt. "Look, duck!" adds his mother hold-
ing up Tim's favorite bath toy. "Tim has a book about ducks.
Let's go read the book."

The notion of scaffolding refers to adult–child interactions in which adults
guide and support the child's learning by building on what the child is able to
do (Wood, Bruner, & Ross, 1976). In the vignette above, Tim's mother and
aunt expand on Tim's verbalization by modeling new words and making
connections with other types of symbols and experiences. Scaffolding implies
responsiveness to an individual child and takes into account different ways
of learning, not only by interacting orally but also by observing and doing.
Scaffolding can involve minimal adult assistance (e.g. providing encouragement, asking questions to help children discover their own solutions) or more
explicit instruction (modeling, giving directions). No one strategy works for all
children. It is important to keep in mind that wide variations occur in
adult–child interactions and scaffolding (e.g., linguistic and nonlinguistic;
directiveness or cooperation) both among and within cultures (Chavajoy &
Rogoff, 2002; Yoder, Warren, McCathren, & Leew, 1998). When children experience caregiving in multiple cultural settings, it is important for caregivers and
families to establish two-way communication and share information about language and literacy practices and cultural values (Diaz & Harvey, 2002; Orellana,
Monkman, & MacGillivray, 2002; Tabors & Snow, 2000).

Facilitating Intentional Communication and Goal-Directed Behaviors

Adult social responsiveness to infants' early communicative attempts helps
infants develop intentional communication, create secure attachments, and
promote the expectation that their behavior has an effect on the world. Adult
responses should be semantically related to and occur immediately after the
infant's behavior (Yoder et al., 1998). Responses can be linguistic (e.g., commenting on what the child is doing) and nonlinguistic (e.g., imitating the
child's expressions or gestures, smiling, looking). They vary across cultures.

Two types of facilitative adult–child interaction are joint attention and joint
problem solving. Joint attention, which occurs when adults focus on what the

infant is interested in and talk about what the baby sees, fosters the association between an object and its linguistic symbol (Tomasello & Farrar, 1986). In joint problem solving, caregivers help infants and toddlers organize activities toward achieving goals. Adults can help children select appropriate problem-solving tools and strategies for checking out the effects of their actions (Musatti & Mayer, 2002). "Use your words," suggests a father to his toddler who is gesturing for an object out of reach. Caregivers can help children create associations between an action and its result by encouraging them to use cause–effect toys and games (e.g., rattles, mechanical toys, string toys). Interactive games with predictable and repetitive actions and language, for example, peekaboo and pat-a-cake, are ideal for helping infants and toddlers build language, anticipate events, and develop expectations that lead to later mental representations and use of symbols.

Mastering Symbols

Symbols are tools used to represent meaning. The special blanket or teddy bear a child may bring to child care has a personal emotional meaning for the child. It is also a powerful tool to help the child master the anxiety of being separated from his mother as he transitions to greater independence. Symbols play an important role in both cognitive and emotional development. Caregivers can encourage children to learn about the representational nature of symbols. They can encourage infants to explore mirrors and make the connection between themselves and the reflection in the mirror. They can take photos of children and help them recognize themselves and their peers. They can make tactile books of personal memories by placing into plastic bags some objects gathered during a walk in the park and then tying the bags together for children to examine and talk about later. Play is an ideal context for children to learn about symbols, especially with toys, puppets, and other pretend play materials that stimulate children to create imaginary worlds and express personal meanings.

Symbols also are a source of information. Caregivers can demonstrate and encourage the use of symbols (pictures, icons, signs, and print) to gain information. For example, they can show how different colors or icons on containers and drawers signify their contents. They can help children understand the meaning of signs in the environment (e.g., "Look at the picture on the door. See, it's the girl's room."). They can explain how pictures tell us about something and help us remember or share events with others who were not present at an event. Caregivers can model reading, writing, and using computers and other technologies and explain their purposes (e.g., "I'm looking at the menu to decide what to order for lunch"; "I'm writing Auntie's new phone number so I'll know what numbers to dial"; "I'm e-mailing Grandma these pictures so she can see what we did on your birthday").

Learning About Books and Print

Early shared picture book reading experiences help children develop emergent literacy and later reading skills (Bus, van Ijzendoorn, & Pellegrini, 1995; DeLoache & Mendoza, 1987). Looking at books and other print materials together is an activity that is enjoyed by many children and adults across a diversity of cultures. Picture book reading provides a collaborative context where adults can support children's learning and motivation. It has been used in many early interventions with young children who are at risk and those with disabilities (Cole & Lim, this volume, p. 537; Justice & Kaderavek, 2002; McCathren & Allor, 2002; Saint-Laurent et al., 1997).

Infants often take pleasure in manipulating and exploring books—reaching, grasping, chewing, and touching. It is best to use sturdy books at early ages. Books made of plastic or cloth and books that are fun to touch such as those with tactile pages, pop-ups, and flaps are likely to be much appreciated (Child Care Action Campaign, 2001). Toddlers are generally more interested in the pictures than the words. Through exploring books, toddlers learn new words and sentences and how pictures represent real objects and events. They become familiar with important literacy conventions (a book is held upright; reading text goes from left to right in English or Spanish or many other, but not all, languages). Toddlers like turning pages, pointing to pictures, labeling, and making comments and gestures.

Caregivers can help infants and toddlers build language and emergent literacy skills by focusing on and expanding on what the child is interested in. They can label and make comments about pictures, talk about children's own experiences related to the pictures; make pretend gestures related to the pictures (e.g., pretend to eat; move fingers, pretending a mouse is running across a page; make animal sounds). With toddlers, caregivers can introduce symbols such as numbers, letter names, and sounds (*A* is for *apple*); point to printed words; and direct reading of text from left to right. They can talk with children about the title, author, and illustrator of the book (Knapp-Philo & Stice, 2003). Adults also can make story boxes with props and objects that are related to picture books.

Families and professionals can obtain books and other literacy-related materials from libraries as well as access computers and the Internet (Deerr, Feinberg, Gordon, & Schull, this volume, p. 477; Saint-Laurent et al., 1997). Many families may not be aware that libraries also offer interactive literacy activities such as storytelling and family literacy programs that are appropriate for babies, toddlers, and older children with special needs (Deerr, 2000). It is important to help caregivers get a library card and feel comfortable in going to the library, especially those who may not be using books and print-related materials in the home (Birckmayer, 2000; Rosenkoetter & Barton, 2002).

Learning About Graphic Symbols

Graphic symbols such as pictures, signs, printed words, and visual icons from electronic media are important tools for communication and self-expression. They have proven to be especially useful in facilitating communication with children who have severe communication impairments (Wetherby et al., 1998). Experiences with artistic media can help young children begin to understand and use graphic symbols to express meaning (Dyson, 2000). Children who learn how to hold crayons, markers, and paintbrushes become aware that their marks can be used to represent something. They become more skilled in their control of movement. Infants begin with sensorimotor exploration of materials, using their fingers to make marks on paper with fingerpaint and to trace lines and circles in sand or in their food. Some may get interested in crayons and paper, crumpling or tearing up paper and exploring with a crayon by banging it on the paper or making accidental marks. Toddlers learn how to use crayons, pencils, and paintbrushes and begin to give meaning to their marks or scribbles. They may begin with scribbling over the page; then making dots, lines, and circles; and perhaps even drawing simple figures and letter-like forms (Dyson, 2000; Ferreiro & Teberosky, 1982). Caregivers can encourage infants and toddlers to explore a variety of graphic and artistic media by drawing, writing, and painting themselves; can display children's creations; and can talk about children's productions to help children understand that their scribbling can have meaning (Knapp-Philo & Stice, 2003).

Sharing Games, Songs, Lullabies, and Nursery Rhymes

Songs and early games with actions and language play are also important, culturally specific tools that help develop later literacy. Singing songs, playing with words and sounds, and reciting nursery rhymes all help children develop phonological sensitivity, or sensitivity to the sounds of language, important skills that are related to later reading (Gollub, this volume, p. 563; Kimura, this volume, p. 235; Maclean, Bryant, & Bradley, 1987). Children also develop listening skills and memory from rhythmic play. As they play with words and sounds, infants and toddlers discover how words are made up of individual sounds and how changing a sound in the word may change its meaning (e.g., *Row, row, row your boat* becomes *Bow, bow, bow your coat*). Caregivers can imitate children's babbling and can introduce new sounds, sing songs and nursery rhymes, encourage children to sing along or fill in parts, play with words, add sounds to make words longer, change sounds, invent silly words, and talk about how some words sound almost the same (i.e., rhyme; Knapp-Philo & Stice, 2003).

A Comprehensive Approach to Literacy

The early years of life set the stage for later learning. "Early environments matter, and nurturing relationships are essential" (National Research Council & Institute of Medicine, 2000, p. 6; see also Barton & Herb-Brophy, this volume, p. 15). Literacy is a complex activity that builds on early language, print, and phonological sensitivity skills that are interrelated and that mutually influence one another (Dickinson, McCabe, Anastasopoulos, Peisner-Feinberg, & Poe, 2003). Learning about literacy begins at birth with the development of intentional and goal-directed behaviors that lead ultimately to intentional and symbolic communication (Wetherby et al., 1998). With symbolic communication, dramatic changes occur as children go on to develop early print knowledge, oral language, and phonological sensitivity skills that form the basis for later reading and writing (e.g., Senechal & LeFevre, 2002; Whitehurst & Lonigan, 1998).

Young children learn best about literacy through everyday life activities that integrate different developmental areas including cognitive, language, socioemotional, and fine and gross motor development (Burns, Griffin, &

Snow, 1999). From birth, children interact with the visual, verbal, digital, and other representational tools in their environments and learn to use the everyday tools of their culture to think and communicate. New tools and technologies open new pathways for broader participation in literacy activities, especially for children and adults who have limited access to traditionally print-based activities because of physical and language limitations or cultural differences. Everyday tools of literacy are primary tools of learning and expressing meaning. The challenge is to ensure that all children *from birth* have access to supportive environments and culturally appropriate literacy tools to develop and learn to their full potential.

References

Barton, L. R., & Brophy-Herb, H. E. (2006). Developmental foundations for language and literacy from birth to 3 years. In S. E. Rosenkoetter & J. Knapp-Philo (Eds.), *Learning to read the world: Language and literacy in the first three years* (pp. 15–60). Washington, DC: ZERO TO THREE Press.

Bates, E. (1979). *The emergence of symbols: Cognition and communication in infancy.* New York: Academic Press.

Beck, J. (2002). Emerging literacy through assistive technology. *TEACHING Exceptional Children, 35*(2), 44–48.

Berk, L., & Winsler, A. (1995). *Scaffolding children's learning: Vygotsky and early childhood education.* Washington, DC: National Association for the Education of Young Children.

Birckmayer, J. (2000). The role of public libraries in emergent and family literacy. *Zero to Three, 21*(3), 24–29.

Bloom, L. (1994). Meaning and expression. In W. Overton & D. Palermo (Eds.), *The ontogenesis of meaning* (pp. 215–235). Hillsdale, NJ: Erlbaum.

Bodrova, E., & Leong, D. (1996). *Tools of the mind. The Vygotskian approach to early childhood education.* Englewood Cliffs, NJ: Prentice Hall.

Bruner, J. (1981). The social context of language acquisition. *Language and Communication, 1,* 155–178.

Burns, S., Griffin, P., & Snow, C. (Eds.). (1999). *Starting out right: A guide to promoting children's reading success.* Committee on the Prevention of Reading Difficulties in Young Children, National Research Council. Washington, DC: National Academy Press.

Bus, A. G., van Ijzendoorn, M. H., & Pellegrini, A. D. (1995). Joint book reading makes for success in learning to read: A meta-analysis on intergenerational transmission of literacy. *Review of Educational Research, 65,* 1–21.

Chavajoy, P., & Rogoff, B. (2002). Schooling and traditional collaborative social organization of problem solving by Mayan mothers and children. *Developmental Psychology, 38*(1), 55–66.

Child Care Action Campaign. (2001). *Talk, reach, read.* New York: Child Care Action Campaign.

Cole, K. N., & Lim, Y. S. (2006). Language is the key: A proven approach to early language and literacy. In S. E. Rosenkoetter & J. Knapp-Philo (Eds.), *Learning to read the world: Language and literacy in the first three years* (pp. 537–552). Washington, DC: ZERO TO THREE Press.

Deerr, K. (2000). Journey toward inclusion: One library's experience. *Zero to Three, 21*(3), 19–23.

Deerr, K., Feinberg, S., Gordon, E., & Schull, D. (2006). Libraries are family places for literacy and learning. In S. E. Rosenkoetter & J. Knapp-Philo (Eds.), *Learning to read the world: Language and literacy in the first three years* (pp. 477–498). Washington, DC: ZERO TO THREE Press.

DeLoache, J. (1997). Shrinking trolls and expanding minds: How very young children learn to understand and use symbols. *Zero to Three, 17*(3), 10–16.

DeLoache, J. S., & Mendoza, O. (1987). Joint picturebook interactions of mothers and 1-year-old children. *British Journal of Developmental Psychology, 5,* 111–123.

Diaz, C. J., & Harvey, N. (2002). Other words, other worlds: Bilingual identities and literacy. In L. Makin & C. J. Diaz (Eds.), *Literacies in early childhood: Changing views, challenging practices* (pp. 175–195). Baltimore: Paul H. Brookes; Sydney, Australia: MacLennan & Petty.

Dickinson, D., McCabe, A., Anastasopoulos, L., Peisner-Feinberg, E., & Poe, M. (2003). The comprehensive language approach to early literacy: The interrelationships among vocabulary, phonological sensitivity, and print knowledge among preschool-aged children. *Journal of Educational Psychology, 95*(3), 465–481.

Downing, J., & Peckham-Hardin, K. (2002). Daily schedules: A helpful learning tool. *TEACHING Exceptional Children, 33*(3), 62–68.

Dyson, A. H. (2000). Writing and children's symbolic repertoires: Development unhinged. In S. B. Neuman & D. K. Dickinson (Eds.), *Handbook of early literacy research* (pp. 126–141). New York: Guilford.

Edwards, C., Gandini, L., & Forman, G. (Eds.). (1998). *The hundred languages of children. The Reggio Emilia approach—Advanced reflections* (2nd ed.). Greenwich, CT: Ablex.

Ferreiro, E., & Teberosky, A. (1982). *Literacy before schooling.* Exeter, NH: Heinemann.

Freire, P., & Macedo, D. (1987). *Literacy: Reading the word and reading the world.* Westport, CT: Bergin & Garvey.

Gollub, M. (2006). Thoughts from a children's author (and jazz drummer): Going through the day with snap, crackle, and jazz. In S. E. Rosenkoetter & J. Knapp-Philo (Eds.), *Learning to read the world: Language and literacy in the first three years* (pp. 563–570). Washington, DC: ZERO TO THREE Press.

Inhelder, B., & Cellerier, G. (1992). *Le cheminement des decouvertes de l'enfant: Recherches sur les microgeneses cognitives.* [The path of the infant's discoveries: Research on cognitive microgeneneses]. Neuchatel, Switzerland: Delachaux and Niestle.

Kimura, L. (2006). Music: The great organizer for early language and literacy. In S. E. Rosenkoetter & J. Knapp-Philo (Eds.), *Learning to read the world: Language and literacy in the first three years* (pp. 235–254). Washington, DC: ZERO TO THREE Press.

Klein, P. S. (1996). *Early intervention: Cross-cultural experiences with a mediational approach.* New York: Garland.

Knapp-Philo, J., & Stice, K. (Eds.). (2003). *StoryQUEST 1: Celebrating early language and literacy.* Rohnert Park: California Institute on Human Services at Sonoma State University.

Kopp, C. B. (1997). Young children: Emotion management, instrumental control and plans. In S. L. Friedman & E. K. Scholnick (Eds.), *The developmental psychology of planning: Why, how and when do we plan?* (pp. 103–124). Mahwah, NJ: Erlbaum.

Koppenhaver, D., Pierce-Coleman, P., Kalman, S., & Yoder, D. (1991). The implications of emergent literacy research for children with developmental disabilities. *American Journal of Speech-Language Pathology, 1*(1), 20–33.

Justice, L., & Kaderavek, J. (2002). Using shared storybook reading to promote emergent literacy. *TEACHING Exceptional Children, 34*(4), 8–13.

Lifter, K., & Bloom, L. (1998). Intentionality and the role of play in the transition to language. In A. Wetherby, S. Warren, & J. Reichle (Eds.), *Transitions in prelinguistic communication* (pp. 161–195). Baltimore: Paul H. Brookes.

Maclean, M., Bryant, P., & Bradley, L. (1987). Rhymes, nursery rhymes and reading in early childhood. *Merrill-Palmer Quarterly, 33*, 255–281.

Makin, L., & Diaz, C. J. (2002). *Literacies in early childhood: Changing views, challenging practices.* Baltimore: Paul H. Brookes & Sydney, Australia: MacLennan & Petty.

McCathren, R., & Allor, J. H. (2002). Using storybooks with preschool children: Enhancing language and emergent literacy. *Young Exceptional Children, 5*(4), 3–10

McNaught, M. (2002). Literacy for all? Young children and special literacy learning needs. In L. Makin, & C. J. Diaz (Eds.), *Literacies in early childhood: Changing views, challenging practices* (pp. 233–249). Baltimore: Paul H. Brookes & Sydney, Australia: MacLennan & Petty.

Musatti, T., & Mayer, S. (2002). Knowing and learning in an educational context: A study in the infant-toddler centers of the city of Pistoia. In L. Gandini & C. P. Edwards (Eds.), *Bambini: The Italian approach to infant/toddler care* (pp. 167–180). New York: Teachers College Press.

National Research Council, & Institute of Medicine. (2000). *From neurons to neighborhoods: The science of early childhood development* (J. P. Shonkoff & D. A. Phillips, Eds.). Committee on Integrating the Science of Early Childhood Development; Board on Children, Youth, and Families; Commission on Behavioral and Social Sciences and Education. Washington, DC: National Academy Press.

New London Group. (1996). A pedagogy of multiliteracies: Designing social futures. *Harvard Educational Review, 66*(1), 60–92.

Notari-Syverson, A. (2004). Literacy for all children: Scaffolding early language and literacy in young children with special needs. *Children and Families, 28*(1), 48–52.

Orellana, M., & Hernandez, A. (1999). Talking the walk: Children reading urban environmental print. *The Reading Teacher, 52*(6), 612–619.

Orellana, M., Monkman, K., & MacGillivray, L. (2002). *Parents and teachers talk about literacy and success.* Center for the Improvement of Early Reading Achievement, University of Michigan, Ann Arbor. Retrieved September 2, 2003, from http: www.ciera.org

Piaget, J. (1970). *Genetic epistemology.* New York: Norton.

Pierce, P. (2006). High expectations for language and literacy with infants and toddlers who have significant disabilities. In S. E. Rosenkoetter & J. Knapp-Philo (Eds.), *Learning to read the world: Language and literacy in the first three years* (pp. 335–352). Washington, DC: ZERO TO THREE Press.

Rogoff, B. (1993). Children's guided participation and participatory appropriation in socio-cultural activity. In R. H. Wozniak & K. W. Fischer (Eds.), *Development in context: Acting and thinking in specific environments* (pp. 121–153). Hillsdale, NJ: Erlbaum.

Rosenkoetter, S., & Barton, L. (2002). Bridges to literacy: Early routines that promote later school success. *Zero to Three, 22*(4), 33–38.

Saint-Laurent, L., Giasson, J., & Couture, C. (1997). Parents + Children + Reading activities = Emergent literacy. *TEACHING Exceptional Children, 30*(2), 52–56.

Senechal, M., & LeFevre, J. (2002). Parental involvement in the development of children's reading skill: A five-year longitudinal study. *Child Development, 73*(2), 445–460.

Snow, C., Burns, S., & Griffin P. (1998). *Preventing reading difficulties in young children.* Washington, DC: Committee on the Prevention of Reading Difficulties in Young Children, National Research Council and National Academy of Sciences.

Tabors, P. O., & Snow, C. E. (2000). Young bilingual children and early literacy development. In S. B. Neuman & D. K. Dickinson (Eds.), *Handbook of early literacy research* (pp. 159–178). New York: Guilford.

Tomasello, M., & Farrar, M. J. (1986). Joint attention and early language. *Child Development, 57,* 1454–1463.

Vygotsky, L. S. (1978). *Mind in society: The development of higher psychological processes.* Cambridge, MA: Harvard University Press.

Wetherby, A., Reichle, J., & Pierce, P. (1998). Transition to symbolic communication. In A. Wetherby, S. Warren, & J. Reichle (Eds.), *Transitions in prelinguistic communication* (pp. 197–230). Baltimore: Paul H. Brookes.

Whitehurst, G., & Lonigan, C. (1998). Child development and emergent literacy. *Child Development, 69,* 848–872.

Wood, D., Bruner, J. S., & Ross, G. (1976). The role of tutoring in problem-solving. *Journal of Child Psychology and Psychiatry, 17,* 89–100.

Yoder, P., Warren, S., McCathren, R., & Leew, S. (1998). Does adult responsivity to child behavior facilitate communication development? In A. Wetherby, S. Warren, & J. Reichle (Eds.), *Transitions in prelinguistic communication* (pp. 39–58). Baltimore: Paul H. Brookes.

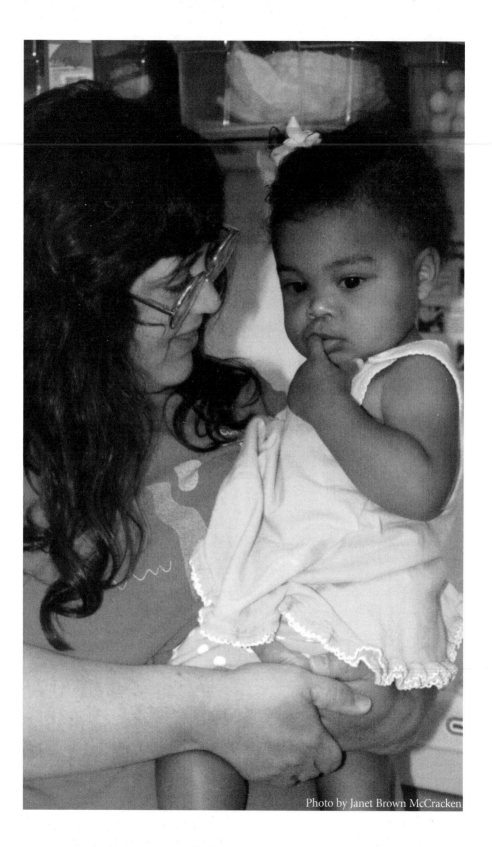

CHAPTER 4

Relationships: At the Heart of Early Language and Literacy

Sharon E. Rosenkoetter and Shannon B. Wanless

Children learn to talk and eventually to read through a relationship with a beloved parent or grandparent, an admired older sibling or cousin, a respected caregiver or teacher, or some other special person in their lives (Bruner, 1983; Hall, 1987; Snow & Ninio, 1986). Readers may recall with fondness beloved childhood stories or books repeatedly requested of favorite adults. Some may remember being cradled by caring arms while saying evening prayers or hearing a lullaby. Some can hum rhymes or raps or jump rope chants that older children taught. Some may remember spending time with a special adult, baking cookies, enjoying Sunday dinner, catching a fish, riding a merry-go-round, or riding in a grocery cart at the neighborhood market. Sometimes the best part of these experiences was coming home and describing to others "what we did." Basic concepts for life—and literacy—may be embedded among a family's most meaningful shared memories, retold at odd moments or preserved in a family photo album, scrapbook, or "memory box" of often reviewed mementoes. Sharing recollections and symbols of past events may bring smiles, tears, or perhaps even additions to the stories, to be reiterated in future retellings. When adults recall treasured memories and retell stories, toddlers and young children imagine the scenes, gradually producing more and more of the narratives themselves and absorbing the stories' main ideas into their developing sense of who they are as people. Through secure early experiences of hearing and observing communication and attempting to talk or read with a special person, young children build a strong foundation for later language and literacy development (Bus, van Ijzendoorn, & Pellegrini, 1995; Sulzby & Teale, 1991; Whitmore & Goodman, 1995).

The Importance of Relationships

Through many thousands of language-rich and print-rich experiences in daily living during the earliest years, children begin to develop readiness for school (Dickinson & Tabors, 2001; Hart & Risley, 1999; Lonigan, 1994). This chapter argues that building a love for words, writing, stories, and books within special adult–child relationships is at the heart of developing school readiness skills. As infants and toddlers learn from their favorite people to love language and stories and begin to grasp the essence of oral and written communication, they develop the capacity to learn to read when they get to school (Neuman, this volume, p. 275; Schickedanz, 1999; Whitehurst & Lonigan, 1997, 2001).

The most significant adults from the child's early years are influential in the development of language and literacy skills precisely because of the positive relationship they share. During the first 3 years of life, family members and caregivers focus the child's attention and label elements of daily experiences in ways that emphasize the priorities of their own worldviews (Ahktar, Dunham, & Dunham, 1991; Hart & Risley, 1995). By the child's second birthday, the process of observational and participatory learning is well underway (Wells, 1986). Consciously or not, adults make decisions every day about how they will interact with their children. These everyday interactions help the toddler learn when to speak and when to be still; whether facial expressions indicate confidence or uncertainty; whether loved ones feel safe, threatened, or cautious; whether to use brief or extended utterances and formal or informal, polite or casual language; when "inside voices" or "outside voices" are appropriate to communicate desires; and whether print is a regular and useful part of life or an insignificant element in a far off place called school. By age 34–36 months, young children are using the language styles and interaction patterns of the culture of their primary caregivers (Hart & Risley, 1999). Young children imitate the people they love and whom they sense love them.

The Complexity of Early Language and Literacy Development

Various types of communication, such as listening, talking, reading, and writing, develop simultaneously and interrelatedly (Teale & Sulzby, 1986). The timeline for this process, however, varies for each child (Hoff, 2001; IRA & NAEYC, 1998). Infants and toddlers have idiosyncratic rates and patterns of development (Garton & Pratt, 1989). When children have rich opportunities for warm and facilitative interactions with caring adults, the foundations of spoken and written communication begin early (De Boysson-Bardies, 1999; Shatz, 1994). Through relationships, infants and toddlers can begin to develop a love for language, stories, and books as well as many specific language and literacy skills.

During the past 25 years, research has begun to examine language and literacy development processes across cultures (Anderson, Anderson, Lynch, & Shapiro, 2003). Much of the earliest research on language and literacy development was conducted in university towns with middle-class families (e.g., Brown, 1973). These populations were unrepresentative of the United States as a whole and even more atypical of much of the rest of the globe. In recent years there have been deliberate efforts to gather broader samples for research (Anderson et al., 2003).

Scholars have demonstrated major differences in the amounts of language (Hart & Risley, 1995, 1999) and the types of language (Bernstein, 1981; Heath, 1983) that infants and toddlers in different families hear. In some cases, those differences precede ongoing disparities in the performance of children as they advance in the United States' educational system that rewards certain types of communication over others. Data collected by the National Education Goals Panel (2004) and the Head Start Bureau's (2002) FACES study show that families and other caregivers in different parts of the country and in various cultural groups read to their children at frequencies from not at all to multiple times per day. Family book reading itself varies in its patterns of interactions (Bus, 2003; Bus & de Jong, this volume, p. 123; Hammett, van Kleeck, & Huberty, 2003), with some parents responding to their children's interests and others following closely along with the words printed in the book. Rich language interactions promote numerous benefits for young children.

Benefits of Sharing Language and Literacy Experiences

Within nurturing relationships, the process of sharing language during singing, cooking, playing, reading, traveling, and other routine activities supports the development of infants' and toddlers' language and literacy foundations. This process has numerous and powerful benefits, eight of which are discussed here.

1. The family's everyday experiences with language and literacy provide opportunities to pass on the family's heritage, interests, and values (Bowman, 2002; Bus, 2001; Heath, 1983; Jones Diaz, & Harvey, 2002). Sharing language, play, stories, folk songs, environmental print, and favored books communicates to young children who their family is and what their family values. It provides opportunities to transmit the family's heritage; for example, parents and infants or toddlers may communicate in sign language, light candles on Sabbat, try on a Korean birthday gown, or sing the "Happy Birthday" song and blow out candles on a cake. Performing these activities together and talking about them conveys to the family's infants and toddlers that the family values these customs and the traditions from the past that they represent.

Shared leisure activities with their related vocabulary and language styles allow families to demonstrate their favored pastimes, which may be car races, Frisbee contests, stories from the heritage of the Koran, astronomy, baseball games, vegetarian cooking, or other personally meaningful activities. Talking and sharing books about these interests also help young children to enjoy them, just as their special people do.

Discussing the family's history, dreams, and challenges gives families ways to pass on their values. The Migrant and Seasonal Head Start Quality Improvement Center and the Head Start Bureau published a series of first-person stories in English and Spanish by parents who have lived as migrant farm workers in America (2001, 2003). These stories (to be greatly simplified for toddlers and young children) show pride in the authors' families and respect for hard work. Both virtues are strong values for many families who support themselves as migrant workers. Apart from storytelling, these family values might also be reiterated with infants and young children through comments (self-talk) throughout the day as a parent gets ready for work, cooks dinner, packs a lunch for the next day, or helps a toddler get ready for child care.

2. Sharing words, stories, songs, and books with infants and toddlers builds the adult–child bond (Bowman, 2002; Bus, 2003; Butler, 1998; Sulzby & Teale, 1991; Taylor & Strickland, 1986). As parents and other caregivers share word play, stories, and books with children, they learn to like each other, trust each other, and enjoy being together. Experiences such as reading or singing together and cuddling daily before naptime or bedtime, communicate nonverbally the affection of adults and children for one another (Rosenkoetter & Barton, 2002). Repeated, positive routines—rituals—accompanied by language offer the foundation for parents and children both to trust each other and to use language to describe their positive regard. For example, Antonio and his father milk the cow every morning and evening, Mai puts spoons in one tray and forks in another each time the dishes are washed, and Karisha and her mother play each day with a sticker book after the toddler awakens from her nap. Research repeatedly demonstrates that children learn well in routine situations where there is a relationship of acceptance and trust (Kubicek, 2002, this volume, p. 163). Thus, rituals and ritualistic language build trust and language learning, which, in turn, build the adult–child bond and foster yet more mature rituals. Bus (2003) found that mother–child attachment security predicts the quantity and quality of later book reading. When efforts to talk, tell stories, and read are supported, then the child becomes ready to try new ways of communicating.

One strategy that some families and other caregivers use to emphasize routines and the language of routines is to make personal books that show the child and other family members having fun together. These special books tend to become favorites, and their contents become family lore: *Lola's Birthday Party*, *Sam and Lisa Walk in the Park*, and *JoonKoo Helps To Make Dinner*. Other families have serious or goofy songs, rhymes, slogans, or aphorisms that they have made up or repeated to communicate family experiences and feelings. Regularly reiterating these words strengthens the adult–child bond.

3. Sharing developmentally appropriate books and modeling the use of text in everyday situations with infants and toddlers increases print motivation (Arnold, Lonigan, Whitehurst, & Epstein, 1994; IRA & NAEYC, 1998; Lyytinen, Laaksol, & Poikkeus, 1998; Neuman & Dickinson, 2001). At a time when many infants and toddlers spend long hours in child care, providers share responsibility with family members for introducing young children to the delights and usefulness of early language and literacy. Of course, this introduction happens within the warmth of their positive relationships (McLane & McNamee, 1990).

Having *print motivation* means that infants, toddlers, and young children like to read, initiate reading, and come to know that reading is useful. Sharing stories and books with the special people in their lives increases the likelihood that children will like to read: Lonigan (1994) found that parents who begin reading to their children before the age of 6 months have children who are more interested in reading and enjoy reading sessions more than children who were not read to in early infancy. Sharing books also leads children to initiate reading activities. For example, parents who begin reading to their children before the age of 6 months have children who are more likely to initiate reading sessions than those for whom reading began later (Lonigan, 1994). Research shows that children who like to read, read more (McLane & McNamee, 1990). And, children who have developed print motivation, as a rule, do better in school than those who read less (Burns, Griffin, & Snow, 1999).

Authentic text is print material that is "representative of the real world; nonacademic text; as bus schedules, directions for assembling a computer, etc." (Harris & Hodges, 1995, p. 15). Infants and toddlers who see their parents and other caregivers consulting authentic text to cope with daily activities come to realize the usefulness of learning to read and are motivated to gain this skill in the future (Heath, 1983). Thus, on occasion, a toddler will attempt to read a volume that is much too difficult or try to discern the meaning of a sign that contains information that appears to be interesting or important for what he or she wants to do. Lonigan (1994) argued that small differences in early literacy experiences may be magnified over time and, as a result, they may contribute significantly to later school success.

4. Sharing sound play, words, stories, songs, and books with infants and toddlers promotes phonological awareness (Burns et al., 1999; Griffin, this volume, p. 145; Snow, Burns, & Griffin, 1998; Whitehurst, 2001). *Phonological awareness* involves attending to and appreciating the sounds and the rhythms of the language. Children with phonological awareness enter school with readiness to link sounds with written symbols to get meaning and thus are more equipped to learn to read (National Early Literacy Panel, in press). Vocal play with adult imitation, finger plays, folk songs, and nonsense rhymes, as well as poems and traditional nursery rhymes, promotes such learning for infants and toddlers. Sound play in isolation isn't nearly so much fun as reciprocal sound play with an adult or peer sound play with siblings or classmates (Prelutsky,

1986; Rosen, 1993). Again, relationships appear to be very important in the child's developing language and literacy skills.

5. Sharing words, stories, songs, and books with infants and toddlers builds vocabulary (Metsala & Walley, 1998; Tabors, Beals, & Weizman, 2001). Vocabulary defines the words a culture uses, the ideas it shares, and the concepts that help young children develop as they increasingly learn to read their world. The contents of children's vocabularies differ according to the experiences they have, but children with larger vocabularies usually have higher scores on intelligence tests and do better in school than children with more limited vocabularies (Hart & Risley, 1995). Burns, Griffin, and Snow chose the phrase "falling in love with words" (1999, p. 23) to describe the interest in acquiring new vocabulary. It may very well stimulate the perseverance in unlocking words that is required later in learning to decode alphabetic symbols. DeTemple and Snow (2003) noted that vocabulary acquisition is one of the major learning challenges of the early years. Vocabularies grow during conversations with extended discourse, talk about nonpresent events, fantasy play (Owocki, 1999, 2001), and other types of verbal interactions with the child's important people. As adults introduce new words in meaningful situations, they are significantly helping to build the child's listening and speaking (receptive and expressive) vocabularies. Book reading is one "particularly efficient and effective context" for vocabulary development (DeTemple & Snow, 2003, p. 29). In the first 18 months of life, perhaps even before infants are speaking words, they are building their receptive vocabularies. For example, infants learn that *Mama* is a source of food and comfort; *drink* produces liquid that satisfies thirst; *Rufus* (dog) is a bounding, loving creature that likes to lick faces; and *kaku* means a crunchy cracker. Toddlers learn that some of these words (*Mama* and *drink*) are vocabulary generally used in the culture while others (such as *Rufus*) have meaning only in a particular context, the family, or as with *kaku*, within just the caregiver–child relationship. When babies produce their first sounds, significant adults are eager to shape those utterances into meaningful speaking vocabulary, and expressive vocabulary begins (Hoff, 2001).

6. Sharing books and talking about environmental print with infants and toddlers increases their print awareness (Adams, 1990; Dyson, 2001). *Print awareness* includes knowing that writing has rules; for example, print in English or Spanish "reads" left to right and top to bottom. Other languages may have different rules for a child to master. Toddlers may begin to develop print awareness from their everyday encounters with print in their homes, child-care centers, or neighborhoods; for example, they may come to associate their names or name symbols with themselves. Children begin to connect significant environmental print with a meaningful place or object, such as the logo of the local grocery store, the name of a favorite cereal, or the print on a sign for a popular restaurant or discount store.

Print awareness also develops when the child realizes that the squiggles on the page are related to the words the adult is saying and to the pictures on the page. The child learns that a book "reads" from front to back and one page at a time. Later the child learns that books have authors who make the words and illustrators who make the pictures. Another name for this kind of knowledge is the *conventions of print.* Relationships are important for learning the conventions of print because the child must remain engaged in a three-way interaction with adult and text long enough and frequently enough to encounter repeatedly the basic concepts such as "read from left to right," "turn the page," and "start reading the words here."

Snow and Ninio described how infants, toddlers, and young children are "inducted into the contracts of literacy" (1986, p. 121). Shared picture book reading, a relational activity with joint focus, exposes even young infants to those contracts, which help the child bridge from speaking to reading during the first 6 years of life. The few simple but monumental contracts for the early years include the following (Snow & Ninio, 1986):

- Books are for reading, not for manipulating (though reading during the early years may include manipulations to keep the child involved in the three-way relationship).

- In book reading, the book is in control; the reader is led by the book's contents.

- Pictures are not things but representatives of things.

- Pictures call for naming.

- Pictures, though static, can represent events.

- Book events occur outside real time.

- Books often report an autonomous fictional world.

In the three-way relationship among child, caregiver, and book, the child gradually develops print awareness, learns the conventions of print, and is inducted into the contracts of literacy.

7. Sharing stories, songs, and books teaches infants and toddlers about narrative skills (Rosenkoetter & Barton, 2002). Narratives are communications that extend beyond a brief interaction. Narratives require a story (oral or printed), storyteller (narrator), and audience (Van Dongen & Westby, 1986). Understanding narratives is a primary form of thought (Bruner, 1985), a basic act of mind (Hardy, 1978), and a primary form for communication within many cultures, though cultures differ in how they construct and share their narratives (Heath, 1986a). Infants and toddlers are learning their own culture's narrative patterns as they hear them and begin to speak. Heath (1986b) describes four types of narratives, all of which it appears may occur during relationships of the infant–toddler period. First, the *recount* brings into present discussion a past experience ("Tell Nana what you saw at the park today."). Second, the *eventcast* is a verbal replay, parallel description, or anticipatory discussion of an action or activity ("The little bear came into the forest and saw her mama." "You be the mommy, and I'll be the baby."). Third, *accounts* are stories initiated by the teller and often interspersed with questions ("You know what?..." "Guess what?..."). Adults don't directly teach children to share accounts. Rather, toddlers observe others delivering them and then make their own attempts. Accounts can be challenging to share because the speaker must gain and hold the attention of others as well as produce a coherent narrative. Toddlers are just beginning to have small successes with accounts, provided adults support their efforts. Fourth, *stories* have a known structure that both speaker (and later, writer) and audience anticipate. Within relationships, toddlers and young children can build all these types of narrative skills, depending on what they hear and see in their daily interactions.

Learning narrative skills commonly includes awareness of the sequence of a story. Initially the "story" may be a simple chronology, possibly only two steps: "First we'll get the diaper, and then we'll put it on." Over time and continuing into the school years, the young child learns not only to sequence events but also to differentiate and predict setting, protagonist, challenge, action, resolution, and moral or lesson, eventually for subplots as well as the main plot (Hedberg & Westby, 1993; Stein, 1988). The toddler becomes able to recount what happened after a simple event, usually with help from a supportive adult

(Cazden, 1983). This capacity becomes essential for effective communication, both oral and written, of actual events and fantasy. Awareness of narrative structures contributes to *comprehension skills* in conventional reading instruction.

Toddlers begin to recognize cues for understanding stories. "Once upon a time" starts some stories, and "they lived happily ever after" ends many others. Toddlers also begin to learn sequences, both in internal scripts for daily routines (Nelson & Gruendel, 1979) and in stories, and they start to predict proximal upcoming events. Children develop the ability to retell stories (Rosenkoetter, 1991). Eventually they learn to use different narrative structures for different genres (e.g., chronological accounts, descriptions, or fairy tales). Narrative skills are necessary for children and adults to make sense of what is heard or read (Wells, 1986).

8. Sharing conversation and books provides many opportunities for developing letter knowledge (Rosenkoetter & Barton, 2002; van Kleeck, Stahl, & Bauer, 2003). Children learn first that letters are important to their significant adults, that letters are different from one another, and that every letter has a name and makes one or more sounds. Then they begin to differentiate among letters and among sound units also known as *phonemes* (Adams, 1990; Burns et al., 1999). Children below kindergarten age may sing or otherwise rehearse the names and various sounds of alphabet letters as they strive to make the associations that matter to their significant people. Young children learn, sometimes as early as the toddler years, that parents and other caregivers know the meaning of a "secret" code of letters and words that they are just beginning to translate. Asking to be read to becomes a search for clues to the special adult's language and literacy knowledge.

How to Facilitate the Development of Early Language and Literacy Skills

Certain lifeways and interaction styles of adults are more likely to encourage language and literacy development (Cole & Lim, this volume, p. 537; Hart & Risley, 1995, 1999; Whitehurst, 2001; Whitehurst & Lonigan, 1997, 2001), though strategies proven to date are almost certainly not the only efficacious approaches. Loughlin and Martin (1987) identified five elements of adult–child sharing that promote language learning, whether the mode is talking, listening, writing, or reading. Many literacy interaction strategies that have been tested, including several described in this book, incorporate these five components of language and literacy learning. All of these five components can readily occur within daily activities when adults and children spend time together.

1. Environmental Stimulation and Modeling

Parents and other caregivers may themselves read and verbalize to infants and toddlers the importance of reading and writing to solve challenges and cope with everyday issues. Books, signs, bills, posters, recipes, instructions, newspapers, poetry, notes, billboards, entertainment guides, advertisements, schedules, and many other formats can be ostentatiously perused, signaling to toddlers that this activity is one that they, too, will be able to do successfully some day. Further, caregivers can call the infant or toddler's attention to the reading act and, perhaps, point to the text of the message (Heath, 1983; Schickedanz, 1999). In addition, adults in every setting can make books and other print readily available to infants and toddlers (IRA & NAEYC, 1998). Caregivers can repeat sounds that an infant or toddler makes ("wah wah wah wa-a-ah"; "bumpity bumpity bump") and show by smiles and imitation their delight when infants or toddlers play with sounds (Burns et al., 1999). When a child asks for the name or sound of a letter or word, it should be provided (Schickedanz, 1999). When adults emphasize their own daily interactions with language and literacy, they help initiate infants and toddlers into literate lifeways.

Families and caregivers help infants and toddlers learn the rules of print when they point to letters, words, and other symbols in the child's environment and when they emphasize the careful use of books while handling them. Pointing out the first letter in the child's name along with a few other personally meaningful letters and calling attention to these letters frequently facilitates literacy learning. Creating a "Me" book for each child draws attention to letters as well as to the special adult–child relationship, most notably when the special book includes the toddler's name in big letters. Making writing tools available daily is another way to expose infants and toddlers to print. Accessible and child-sized materials allow toddlers to experiment with scribbling, drawing, and writing. Supporting all writing efforts pays off as children experiment at length and, over several years, move closer to the socially approved ways to communicate through written symbols (Ferreiro & Teberosky, 1985).

2. Opportunities for Interaction

The give and take of everyday interactions teaches nonverbal and verbal turn taking as well as initiating and responding (Knapp-Philo & Stice, 2003). It focuses joint attention and teaches vocabulary in the context of meaningful relationships (Ahktar et al., 1991). Intentional back and forth interactions also increase the quantities of language that infants and toddlers hear, a predictor of later school success (Hart & Risley, 1995, 1999). Instituting at least some structured routines each day in home and child care provides a familiar setting (Dickinson & Tabors, 2001; Kubicek, 2002) and vocabulary and allows children to begin to formulate personal scripts for sequences of action for everyday activities (Nelson & Gruendel, 1979).

3. Purpose and Meaning for Communication

Children are inherently meaning seekers (Allen & Mason, 1989; Pinker, 1994; Wells, 1986). Helping children connect disparate pieces of a language mystery helps them achieve both meaning and new tools to use in other situations. Consider, for example, the following adult comments, spoken slowly to an 18-month-old: "Sally is sick. She is not here. Play with Tanya." The short sentences are aimed at the toddler's receptive language level. Accompanied by a head shake and a point at Tanya, these words communicate meaning. They show cause and effect and logical sequence. They guide behavior. They provide the toddler with a brief script of actions for the present and potentially for the future. In short, language is powerful!

It is wise to arrange the child-care or home environment and schedule to provide many times in the day when there is a need for the child to communicate (Hart & Rogers-Warren, 1978). Materials may be placed just out of reach, an item needed for an activity may be missing, or the adult can purposefully make a small "mistake" that the child will delight in correcting. Sometimes appropriate words also may need to be modeled ("Say, 'Help me, please.'" "Would you like the truck or the car? Use words please!").

4. Practice

In a trusting relationship with an adult, an infant or toddler can safely rehearse new behaviors, including those involved with early language and literacy (De Boysson-Bardies, 1999). This high level of comfort is seen when adults exchange thousands of messages in a day with a young child (Hart & Risley, 1995). It is seen when the adult prepares a situation for the child, making it easy for him or her to communicate needs or desires or successfully transmit a message (Shatz, 1994). It is seen when caregivers sing, chant, or hum to children from their earliest days. Caregivers encourage practice when they share rhymes and poetry (even TV jingles, homespun ditties, or sequences of nonsense syllables) many times each day and show delight when their children join in (Burns et al., 1999). When caring adults read picture books every day at the same time and same place (and, preferably, more than once), they are encouraging young children to practice foundational skills for literacy.

Valuable practice occurs when adults urge toddlers to recall and retell events just experienced, either as rehearsal ("Let's try to remember what happened.") or to a person who has just entered the scene ("Let's tell Mama what we made."; Heath, 1986b). Toddlers and children of preschool age typically need support in their retellings, but gradually they learn to recount events from a simple stimulus (Cazden, 1983).

Young children are known for requesting the same picture book over and over—a practice behavior—until they can actually recite the text from memory. When young children are attempting so many new and different elements of literacy at once, they need many opportunities to learn the lessons that reading the story can teach (Heath, 1986b). They may also appreciate the sense of mastery that comes from anticipating the next phrase in a familiar story. It is appropriate for adults sharing books to talk about the pictures rather than simply read the words of the text, just as it is for them to make mistakes, change the words, make the reading time very brief, and re-read favorite books day after day. The nature of the reading experience should fit the child, not, research shows, require that the expectations for the child be conformed to the text (Bus, 2003). That way, the familiar book in the familiar setting becomes a part of the familiar relationship with a caring adult, a routine part of a special relationship.

All of the activities described so far provide young children with opportunities to practice new skills and build confidence in using them. Principles of generalization suggest that the child should be supported to demonstrate new learnings in different settings, with different people, and within different kinds of activities (Wolery, Bailey, & Sugai, 1988). The support of a caring and familiar adult provides the security that allows the child to venture into unknown territory. In considering practice in language and literacy for infants and toddlers, avoid phonics drills, alphabet cards, or structured "literacy lessons" (Rosenkoetter & Barton, 2002). Literacy experts advise against isolated drill of toddlers on reciting the alphabet or naming letters apart from a meaningful context (IRA & NAEYC, 1998).

5. Adult Tolerance for Experimentation

In language and literacy interactions with infants and toddlers, it is adult support for the process, not accuracy or correctness, that matters. Experts advise against directly correcting a child's mis-speaking, but rather they suggest using the appropriate form of the word in a subsequent interaction to enable the child to hear the word or phrase spoken appropriately (Weitzman & Greenberg, 2002). When a child becomes comfortable with a language form or literacy behavior, then adults can "up the ante" (Bruner, 1983), that is, use a higher level of communication in their own future comments and anticipate more sophisticated responses from the child. Within secure relationships with family and caregivers, toddlers are likely to risk experimenting with new words, letters, writing attempts, storytelling, reenactments, and even reading from memory (Paley, 1986). It helps such explorations if the adult shows affection for the child and playfulness with new words and sound combinations, including admiration of the child's efforts to use them.

Handling of books is another area for tolerance and patience. Begin with books that are appropriate for the age (see Anderson, this volume, p. 553). Let an infant chew on board books or explore them in any other way, while the adult models appropriate book care. When a child is old enough for paper books, however, teach good habits and insist that books be handled with care or used with supervision. Repeated phrases may help ("Books are for reading. Paper is for writing.") Expect considerable damage to books, however, when young children use them because here, as in all other developmental areas, children learn by trial and error.

Conclusion

It is said that Dr. Albert Einstein, the noted physicist, was asked how to make children intelligent. His response was "Read them fairy tales." And how to make them more brilliant? Dr. Einstein allegedly replied, "Read them even more fairy tales!" (Einstein, 1933). Is there something magical about fairly tales then? Of course not! Fairy tales may not even be shared in many cultures that differ from that of Dr. Einstein. The not-so-secret ingredients in this recommendation are (a) the relationship of a caring adult with a curious child and (b) the sharing of language and stories that transport the participants to a world of stimulating events, sequential actions, imaginary scenes, and rich vocabulary. From this delightful mix come foundational attitudes and skills for the young child to build on in future academic life.

References

Adams, M. J. (1990). *Learning to read: Thinking and learning about print.* Cambridge, MA: MIT Press.

Ahktar, N., Dunham, F., & Dunham, P. (1991). Directive interactions and early vocabulary development: The role of joint attentional focus. *Journal of Child Language, 18,* 41–49.

Allen, J. B., & Mason, J. M. (1989). *Risk makers, risk takers, risk breakers: Reducing the risks for young literacy learners.* Portsmouth, NH: Heinemann.

Anderson, J., Anderson, A., Lynch, J., & Shapiro, J. (2003). Storybook reading in a multicultural society: Critical perspectives. In A. van Kleeck, S. A. Stahl, & E. B. Bauer (Eds.), *On reading books to children: Parents and teachers* (pp. 203–230). Mahwah, NJ: Erlbaum.

Anderson, S. (2006). Books for very young children. In S. E. Rosenkoetter & J. Knapp-Philo (Eds.), *Learning to read the world: Language and literacy in the first three years* (pp. 553–562). Washington, DC: ZERO TO THREE Press.

Arnold, D. S., Lonigan, C. J., Whitehurst, G. J., & Epstein, J. N. (1994). Accelerating language development through picture book reading: Replication and extension to a videotape training format. *Journal of Educational Psychology, 86,* 235–243.

Bernstein, B. B. (1981). Elaborated and restricted codes: Their social origins and some consequences. In K. Danziger (Ed.), *Readings in child socialization* (pp. 165–186). Oxford, UK: Pergamon Press.

Bowman, B. (Ed.). (2002). *Love to read: Essays in developing and enhancing early literacy skills of African American children.* Washington, DC: National Black Child Development Institute.

Brown, R. (1973). Development of a first language in the human species. *American Psychologist, 28,* 97–106.

Bruner, J. S. (1983). *Child's talk: Learning to use language.* Oxford, UK: Oxford University Press.

Bruner, J. S. (1985). Narrative and paradigmatic modes of thought. In E. Eisner (Ed.), *Learning and teaching the ways of knowing: Eighty-fourth yearbook of the National Society for the Study of Education* (pp. 97–115). Chicago: University of Chicago Press.

Burns, M. S., Griffin, P., & Snow, C. E. (Eds.). (1999) *Starting out right: A guide to promoting children's reading success.* Committee on the Prevention of Reading Difficulties in Young Children, National Research Council. Washington, DC: National Academy Press.

Bus, A. G. (2001). Joint caregiver-child storybook reading: A route to literacy development. In S. B. Neuman & D. K. Dickinson (Eds.), *Handbook of early literacy research* (pp. 179–191). New York: Guilford.

Bus, A. G. (2003). Social-emotional requisites for learning to read. In A. van Kleeck, S. A. Stahl, & E. B. Bauer (Eds.), *On reading books to children: Parents and teachers* (pp. 3–15). Mahwah, NJ: Erlbaum.

Bus, A., & de Jong, M. (2006). Book-sharing: A developmentally appropriate way to foster preacademic growth. In S. E. Rosenkoetter & J. Knapp-Philo (Eds.), *Learning to read the world: Language and literacy in the first three years* (pp. 123–144). Washington, DC: ZERO TO THREE Press.

Bus, A. G., van Ijzendoorn, M. H., & Pellegrini, A. D. (1995). Joint book reading makes for success in learning to read: A meta-analysis on intergenerational transmission of literature. *Review of Educational Research, 65,* 1–21.

Butler, D. (1998). *Babies need books: Sharing the joy of books with children from birth to six.* Portsmouth, NH: Heinemann.

Cazden, C. (1983). Adult assistance to language development: Scaffolds, models, and direct instruction. In R. P. Parker & F. A. Davis (Eds.), *Developing literacy* (pp. 3–18). Newark, DE: International Reading Association.

Cole, K. N., & Lim, Y. S. (2006). Language is the key: A proven approach to early language and literacy. In S. E. Rosenkoetter & J. Knapp-Philo (Eds.), *Learning to read the world: Language and literacy in the first three years* (pp. 537–552). Washington, DC: ZERO TO THREE Press.

De Boysson-Bardies, B. (1999). *How language comes to children: From birth to two years.* Cambridge, MA: MIT Press.

DeTemple, J., & Snow, C. E. (2003). Learning words from books. In A. van Kleeck, S. A. Stahl, & E. B. Bauer (Eds.), *On reading books to children: Parents and teachers* (pp. 16–36). Mahwah, NJ: Erlbaum.

Dickinson, D. K., & Tabors, P. O. (2001). *Beginning literacy with language.* Baltimore: Paul H. Brookes.

Dyson, A. H. (2001). Writing and children's symbolic repertoires: Development unhinged. In S. B. Neuman & D. K. Dickinson (Eds.), *Handbook of early literacy research* (pp. 126–141). New York: Guilford.

Einstein, A. (1933). *The world as I see it.* Reprinted from *Mein Weltbild.* Amsterdam: Querido Verlag.

Ferreiro, E., & Teberosky, A. (1985). *Literacy before schooling.* Portsmouth, NH: Heinemann.

Garton, A., & Pratt, C. (1989). *Learning to be literate: The development of spoken and written language.* Oxford: Blackwell.

Griffin, P. (2006). Sound steps in phonological form for later literacy. In S. E. Rosenkoetter & J. Knapp-Philo (Eds.), *Learning to read the world: Language and literacy in the first three years* (pp. 145–162). Washington, DC: ZERO TO THREE Press.

Hall, N. (1987). *The emergence of literacy.* Portsmouth, NH: Heinemann.

Hammett, L. A., van Kleeck, A., & Huberty, C. J. (2003). Patterns of parents' extratextual interactions during book sharing with preschool children: A cluster analysis study. *Reading Research Quarterly, 38*(4), 442–467.

Hardy, B. (1978). Narrative as a primary act of mind. In M. Meek, A. Warlow, & G. Barton (Eds.), *The cool web* (pp. 12–23). London: The Bodley Head.

Harris, T. L., & Hodges, R. E. (Eds.). (1995). *The literacy dictionary: The vocabulary of reading and writing.* Newark, DE: International Reading Association.

Hart, B., & Risley, T. R. (1995). *Meaningful differences in the everyday experiences of young American children.* Baltimore: Paul H. Brookes.

Hart, B., & Risley, T. R. (1999). *The social world of children learning to talk.* Baltimore: Paul H. Brookes.

Hart, B., & Rogers-Warren, A. (1978). A milieu approach to teaching language. In R. Schiefelbusch (Ed.), *Language intervention strategies* (pp. 193–235). Baltimore: University Park Press.

Head Start Bureau. (2002). *Head Start FACES 2000: A whole child perspective on program performance.* Prepared for the U. S. Department of Health and Human Services, the Administration for Children and Families by the Head Start Quality Research Consortium. Washington, DC: Author.

Heath, S. B. (1983). *Ways with words: Language, life and work in communities and classrooms.* Cambridge, UK: Cambridge University Press.

Heath, S. B. (1986a). Taking a cross-cultural look at narratives. *Topics in Language Disorders, 7*(1), 84–95.

Heath, S. B. (1986b). What no bedtime story means: Narrative skills at home and school. In B. B. Schieffelin & E. Ochs (Eds.), *Language socialization across cultures: Studies in the social and cultural foundations of language, No. 3* (pp. 97–124). New York: Cambridge University Press.

Hedberg, N. L., & Westby, C. E. (1993). *Analyzing storytelling skills: Theory to practice.* Tucson, AZ: Communication Skill Builders.

Hoff, E. (2001). *Language development.* Belmont, CA: Wadsworth.

IRA (International Reading Association) & NAEYC (National Association for the Education of Young Children). (1998). *Overview of learning to read and write: Developmentally appropriate practices for young children.* Retrieved July 28, 2003, from http://www.naeyc.org/about/positions/PSREAD0.asp

Jones Diaz, C., & Harvey, N. (2002). Other words, other worlds: Bilingual identities and literacy. In L. Makin & C. Jones Diaz (Eds.), *Literacies in early childhood: Changing views, challenging practice* (pp. 175–196). Sydney, Australia: Maclennan & Petty.

Knapp-Philo, J., & Stice, K. (Eds.). (2003). *StoryQUEST 1: Celebrating beginning language and literacy.* Rohnert Park: California Institute on Human Services at Sonoma State University.

Kubicek, L. F. (2002). Fresh perspectives on young children and family routines. *Zero to Three, 22*(4), 4–9.

Kubicek, L. F. (2006). Encouraging language and literacy through family routines. In S. E. Rosenkoetter & J. Knapp-Philo (Eds.), *Learning to read the world: Language and literacy in the first three years* (pp. 163–186). Washington, DC: ZERO TO THREE Press.

Lonigan, C. J. (1994). Reading to preschoolers exposed: Is the emperor really naked? *Developmental Review, 14,* 303–323.

Loughlin, C. E., & Martin, M. D. (1987). *Supporting literacy: Developing effective learning environments.* New York: Teachers College Press.

Lyytinen, P., Laaksol, M. L., & Poikkeus, A. M. (1998). Parental contributions to child's early language and interest in books. *European Journal of Psychology of Education, 13,* 297–308.

McLane, J. B., & McNamee, G. D. (1990). *Early literacy.* Cambridge, MA: Harvard University Press.

Metsala, J. L., & Walley, A. C. (1998). Spoken vocabulary growth and the segmental restructuring of lexical representations: Precursors to phonemic awareness and early reading ability. In J. C. Metsala & L. C. Ehri (Eds.), *Word recognition in beginning literacy* (pp. 89–120). Mahwah, NJ: Erlbaum.

Migrant Head Start Quality Improvement Center, the Academy for Educational Development, & the U.S. Department of Health and Human Services, Administration for Children and Families, Head Start Bureau. (Eds.). (2001). *Migrant Head Start success stories.* Washington, DC: Authors.

Migrant/Seasonal Head Start Quality Improvement Center, the Academy for Educational Development, & the U.S. Department of Health and Human Services, Administration for Children, Youth, and Families, Head Start Bureau. (Eds.). (2003). *Success stories: 2003.* Washington, DC: Authors.

National Early Literacy Panel. (in press). *National Early Literacy Panel Report.* Washington, DC: National Institute for Literacy.

National Educational Goals Panel. (2004). *Goal 1: Ready to learn.* Retrieved April 13, 2005, from http://govinfo.library.unt.edu/negp/page3-3.htm

Nelson, K., & Gruendel, J. M. (1979). At morning it's lunchtime: A scriptal view of children's dialogues. *Discourse Processes, 2,* 73–94.

Neuman, S. B., & Dickinson, D. K. (2001). *Handbook of early literacy research.* New York: Guilford Press.

Neuman, S. B. (2006). Literacy development for infants and toddlers. In S. E. Rosenkoetter & J. Knapp-Philo (Eds.), *Learning to read the world: Language and literacy in the first three years* (pp. 275–290). Washington, DC: ZERO TO THREE Press.

Owocki, G. (1999). *Literacy through play.* Portsmouth, NH: Heinemann.

Owocki, G. (2001), *Make way for literacy: Teaching the way young children learn.* Portsmouth, NH: Heinemann.

Paley, V. G. (1986). *Mollie is three: Growing up in school.* Chicago: University of Chicago Press.

Pinker, S. (1994). *The language instinct.* New York: HarperCollins.

Prelutsky, J. (Ed.). (1986). *Read aloud rhymes for the very young.* New York: Alfred A. Knopf.

Rosen, M. (Ed.). (1993). *Poems for the very young.* New York: Kingfisher Books.

Rosenkoetter, S. E. (1991). Recall of stories and descriptive passages by prekindergarten children: Analysis and intervention. *Dissertation Abstracts International, 53*(12A), 4259.

Rosenkoetter, S. E., & Barton, L. R. (2002). Bridges to literacy: Early routines that promote later school success. *Zero to Three, 22*(4), 33–38.

Schickedanz, J. A. (1999). *Much more than the ABCs: The early stages of reading and writing.* Washington, DC: National Association for the Education of Young Children.

Shatz, M. (1994). *A toddler's life: Becoming a person.* New York: Oxford University Press.

Snow, C., & Ninio, A. (1986). The contracts of literacy: What children learn from learning to read books. In W. H. Teale & E. Sulzby (Eds.), *Emergent literacy: Writing and reading* (pp. 116–138). Norwood, NJ: Ablex.

Snow, D. E., Burns, M. S., & Griffin, P. (Eds.). (1998). *Preventing reading difficulties in young children.* National Research Council, Committee on the Prevention of Reading Difficulties. Washington, DC: National Academy Press.

Stein, N. L. (1988). The development of children's storytelling skill. In M. B. Franklin & S. S. Barten (Eds.), *Child language* (pp. 282–298). New York: Oxford University Press.

Sulzby, E., & Teale, W. (1991). Emergent literacy. In R. Barr, M. Kamil, P. Mosenthal, & P. D. Pearson (Eds.), *Handbook of reading research* (Vol. 2, pp. 727–758). New York: Longman.

Tabors, P. O., Beals, D. E., & Weizman, Z. O. (2001). "You know what oxygen is?" Learning new words at home. In D. K. Dickinson & P. O. Tabors (Eds.), *Beginning literacy with language* (pp. 93–110). Baltimore: Paul H. Brookes.

Taylor, D., & Strickland, D. S. (1986). *Family storybook reading.* Portsmouth, NH: Heinemann.

Teale, W. H., & Sulzby, E. (1986). Introduction: Emergent literacy as a perspective for examining how young children become writers and readers. In W. H. Teale & E. Sulzby (Eds.), *Emergent literacy: Writing and reading* (pp. vii–xxv). Norwood, NJ: Ablex.

Van Dongen, R., & Westby, C. E. (1986). Building the narrative mode of thought through children's literature. *Topics in Language Disorders, 7*(1), 70–83.

van Kleeck, A., Stahl, S. A., & Bauer, E. B. (2003). *On reading books to children: Parents and teachers.* Mahwah, NJ: Erlbaum.

Weitzman, E., & Greenberg, J. (2002). *Learning language and loving it.* Toronto, Ontario, Canada: The Hanen Centre.

Wells, G. (1986). *The meaning makers: Children learning language and using language to learn.* Portsmouth, NH: Heinemann.

Whitehurst, G. J. (2001). *Address to the White House Summit on Early Childhood Cognitive Development,* July 26, Washington, DC.

Whitehurst, G. J., & Lonigan, C. J. (1997). Child development and emergent literacy. *Child Development, 68,* 848–872.

Whitehurst, G. J., & Lonigan, C. J. (2001). Emergent literacy: Development from prereaders to readers. In S. B. Neuman & D. K. Dickinson (Eds.), *Handbook of early literacy research* (pp. 11–29). New York: Guilford.

Whitmore, K., & Goodman, Y. (1995). Transforming curriculum in language and literacy. In S. Bredekamp & T. Rosegrant, *Reaching potentials: Transforming early childhood curriculum and assessment* (Vol. 2, pp. 145–166). Washington, DC: National Association for the Education of Young Children.

Wolery, M., Bailey, D. B., & Sugai, G. M. (1988). *Effective teaching: Principles and procedures of applied behavior analysis with exceptional students.* Boston: Allyn and Bacon.

CHAPTER 5

From Cooing to Conversation to *The Carrot Seed*: Oral and Written Language Connections

Patsy Pierce and Andrea Profio

"The basic need to communicate coupled with a rich and stimulating language environment seem to be the main factors that propel children's early language learning. Parents, grandparents, and early education caregivers need to know that child language development begins in infancy and is an ongoing process in which young children expand and refine their knowledge and use of language largely with the help of facilitating adults."

—Dorothy S. Strickland, quoted in North Carolina Department of Public Instruction (2004), p. 38

Whenever you stroll through a child-care center, stop and listen to the sounds of language development. In the infant room, you will hear crying children telling us that they are hungry, sleepy, or possibly wet. You will also hear happy, cooing sounds indicating that these babies are awake and ready to touch, look, eat, and move. Next door in the toddler room, listen to children making one- and two-word comments about what they see and about how they feel. Hear them ask simple questions such as "What that?" and respond to simple questions that their caregivers ask them. Move on to the older toddler and preschool classrooms and you may hear children still using sounds and words to communicate their wants, needs, and feelings, but you will also hear and see them using words, gestures, and other ways to tell us their ideas. You may even hear them using language from familiar storybooks, words they have heard over and over—for example, "It won't come up" in the children's book, *The Carrot Seed* (Krauss, 1945). From cooing to conversation to using storybook language, children learn to understand and use the language, or languages, of their different environments.

Language is used in social exchanges every day, vocally and silently, for everything from saying "hello" to a neighbor to creating the laws that govern the country. "Language is an organized system of symbols that humans use to express and receive meaning" (Kirk, Gallager, & Anastasiow, 2003, p. 301). Comprehending the components of this definition is the first step in understanding what language is in order to provide environments for children to develop effective oral and written language.

All forms of human language have certain features. Language is communicative, enabling humans to send and receive messages such as thoughts, emotions, and ideas. Language is abstract, consisting of signs or symbols that represent meaning. Language is also rule governed; that is, it encompasses a system of conventions, of agreed-upon guidelines, that determine word formation, word order, and word and phrase meaning. Language is social: Its main purpose is to support interaction among people. Language is versatile: It can be combined in unlimited ways (Jalongo, 2003). Language makes possible the complexity of modern life.

Often *language* and *speech* are used interchangeably; however, these two words and their meanings are quite different. Language involves words and phrases that convey meaning, whereas speech is the sound produced to make spoken words (Nilsen, 2001, p. 132). Speech can exist without language, but for audible language, there must be speech. Even so, non-aural language can occur without speech, as in the use of sign language, Braille, body language, and facial expressions. American Sign Language is second only to English and Spanish in amount of use in the United States (Lapiak, 2004). Graphic symbols also offer unspoken language. Visualizations of ideas, such as logos, photographs, or drawings, represent thoughts to be given and received.

Theories of Oral and Written Language Development

Linguist Noam Chomsky (1957) is best known as the creator of the theory of generative grammar. He explained how young children begin to learn language, using rules different from those of an adult learner. Chomsky approached language development as an *innatist*; that is, he posited that language acquisition stems from natural human functions and that the sequence of learning is the same for every child because of an inborn "language acquisition device."

A very different conception is the explanation for language acquisition proposed by B. F. Skinner (1953, 1957), a behaviorist who believed that all human and animal behaviors were determined by learning and reinforcement. Skinner noted that if a behavior produces a desirable outcome, it is likely to be repeated. Thus he emphasized the power that the environment has on language development: "The child makes random sounds, certain sounds are reinforced, and after thousands of such experiences, the child begins to talk" (Jalongo, 2003, p. 63).

A third theorist, Lev Vygotsky (1962), proposed that both thought and language develop through social interactions in which more knowledgeable adults support young children's attempts to reason and speak. Thus language is the means that cultures use to transmit their values (Vygotsky, 1978). Vygotsky's work has had a tremendous impact on the study of child language (Bruner, 1983). It is obvious that teaching children to use language is a major focus of many literate cultures.

A fourth explanation for language development, Jerome Bruner's constructivist theory (1983), builds on Jean Piaget's ideas of human development. In Bruner's theoretical framework, children actively create their own language, constructing personal concepts and new language forms based on their present and past encounters with things, ideas, and language—and, of course, other people. For instance, a child may see a four-legged animal with fur walk into her yard and then hear her mother explain, "This is a dog." The following day, when the child sees a cat, which is another four-legged animal with fur, she also calls this creature a dog. Based on what she has learned in the past, the child constructs an understanding of what she sees now.

Approaches to Literacy Development

Current developmental perspectives on written language agree on the importance of stimulating the child's motivation to read (Smith, Dickinson, Sangeorge, & Anastasopoulos, 2002) as well as the necessity after the infant–toddler years of every child learning to decode and comprehend print (Adams, 1990). Current scholars and practitioners emphasize a continuum of supports for a child's journey into understanding and using oral and written language. Clay (1966) originated the *emergent literacy* perspective, which stresses that children need to see adults using written language for real purposes. Children who observe and interact with literate adults who are writing and using shopping lists or recipes learn the power and function of print. This knowledge is a foundation for later literacy learning. Children "try out" their beginning understanding of the functions and forms of print through their earliest drawings and scribbles. Adults who offer, support, model, and respond to early literacy-related interactions (e.g., storybook reading, storytelling, singing songs, pretend play involving print, and real uses of print) help children to become literate, according to the emergent literacy perspective (Morrow, 2005; Sulzby & Teale, 1991; Vukelich & Christie, 2004). An example of this perspective's "language experience approach" strategy with very young children appears in *Molly Is Three* by Vivian Gussin Paley (1986), an illustrative description of a young girl learning to read her world by dictating brief stories that she later acts out with her classmates.

Children also need exposure to letter names, letter sounds, and rules for combining and segmenting words into sounds as well as guidance in understanding and using them. Approaches to addressing specific skills such as phonological and phonemic awareness, alphabet knowledge, and vocabulary growth began to be featured in 1990 with Adams's book, *Beginning to Read: Thinking and Learning About Print*; they continue today with the National Research Council's early literacy publications (Burns, Griffin, & Snow, 1999; Snow, Burns, & Griffin, 1998) and provide the foundation for curricula and strategies in the Federal Good Start, Grow Smart, Early Reading First, and Early Childhood Professional Development programs (Vukelich & Christie, 2004).

Exposure to the continuum of rich oral and written language experiences and fostering of their use must be integrated during the early childhood years to help all children develop their listening, speaking, reading, and writing abilities. This continuum of approaches to early literacy facilitation identifies oral language—input from adults and output from children—as extremely important for success in later literacy learning. Adults are intentional about communicating the importance of print and demonstrating the recurrent behaviors of literate people.

Oral and Written Language Connection

Adherents of both perspectives on literacy learning—oral approaches and written approaches—agree on the importance of the connection between the infant's first attempts to talk and the later emergence of reading and writing (Roth, Speece, & Cooper, 2002). They agree that oral language abilities provide foundations for later written language development and use. A young child's success at hearing and understanding the sounds of language, how the sounds are put together to make a large and diverse variety of words, and how to bring words together and use them meaningfully directly correlate with the child's success in exhibiting these same abilities in written form (Roskos, Tabors, & Lenhart, 2004). The initial findings of the meta-analysis of evidence-based emergent literacy research conducted by the National Early Literacy Panel indicate that receptive and expressive vocabulary, syntax, and the ability to retell narratives have significant positive effects on later written language comprehension. Oral vocabulary may also have a positive impact on phonological awareness, which is a positive predictor of written language decoding ability. Letter naming and phonological awareness are seen to be the greatest predictors of decoding ability (Lonigan, 2004).

One has only to look at the literacy learning difficulties of children who have problems understanding and using oral language to see the relevance and understand the importance of the link between oral and written language. For example, approximately 90% of children who have severe speech and physical impairments have significant literacy learning difficulties (Koppenhaver, Evans, & Yoder, 1991). Approximately 40% of preschool-age children with moderate to severe language impairments develop significant reading and writing problems, even if their delays appear to have been resolved by age 5 (Scarborough, 2002). In several studies of children who were born prematurely and with low birth weight, Fewell and Deutscher (2002, 2004) found that maternal responsiveness and interaction styles significantly contribute to child outcomes in both oral and written language development. Hart and Risley (2003) observed that children whose families communicated with them less had greater difficulty learning to read and write than did children who were exposed to more communication. And similarly, typically developing kindergarten children who can orally define words are significantly better readers by the end of third grade than are children who are weak on that skill (Gambrell, 2004). Young children who hear little conversation and who are not encouraged to talk themselves often face major obstacles in learning to read (Armbruster, Lehr, & Osborn, 2003).

The important connection between oral language and later literacy learning lies in the concept of communication. Human beings communicate in many ways, with the four primary media for communication being listening, speaking, reading, and writing. Form, content, and function are particular aspects of language, and each has its own conventions in the different media (i.e., in listening, speaking, reading, and writing). In the following paragraphs, we define each of these elements of language.

Form

Form is what the language looks like or sounds like. It has several different components. The first component of form in spoken language is *phonology*, or the rules that govern sound combinations. For instance, in the English language, when *p* and *h* appear together, speakers agree that the pronunciation will be the sound of /f/. Because of the phonology of spoken English, /sh/ has a different sound from that of either /s/ or /h/ or their individual sounds combined. A second form of language is *morphology*, the rules for the structure of words and the construction of word forms. *Syntax*, or grammar, is a third form of language, providing rules that govern the order and combination of words to form sentences as well as the relationships among the elements within a sentence. Syntax tells speakers or writers to say "She went to the store" instead of "She goed to the store" (Kirk et al., 2003). Deriving from the components of language are the two units of speech called *phonemes* and *morphemes*. Phonemes are the smallest units that make the sounds that are later assembled to make words. Some examples are /d/, /m/, and /p/. If speakers add vowels to phonemes to link them together in a meaningful way, they are then called morphemes, which are the smallest units of sound that have meaning (Nilsen, 2001). When sounds are combined to make words and then words are ordered appropriately to make meaningful sentences, the speaker produces language that enables people to communicate. Acquiring the knowledge and skills to combine sounds and words into meaningful combinations to produce language often takes at least 7 years of practice for typically developing children and perhaps even longer for children with disabilities. Children must attempt, receive feedback, refine their attempts, and try again to develop their communication abilities. (For a more in-depth discussion of the phonological terms used above, see also Griffin, this volume, p. 145.)

Content

The content of language is also called *semantics*. This element of language is the system that governs the meanings of words and sentences. Vocabulary development is now viewed as being of utmost importance in helping young children become readers and writers. Family members and caregivers must help young children to know the meaning of many words so they can develop the necessary background knowledge to understand oral and written stories and informational text (Roskos et al., 2004). Without semantics, a child might form words and sentences, but their meaning would be confused or missing, and no ideas or thoughts could be conveyed or understood (see also Barton & Brophy-Herb, this volume, p. 15; Kirk et al., 2003; Notari-Syverson, this volume, p. 61). In developing vocabulary, young children typically make two kinds of errors: overextensions and underextensions (Bloom & Lahey, 1978). The example above of a child calling all four-legged furry animals *dog* is an example of an overextension. Conversely, if a child fails to realize (quite rationally!) that a Chihuahua and a Great Dane are both dogs, then her vocabulary shows underextension.

Function

The rules for the functions of language are called *pragmatics*. This element of language is the system that combines phonology, morphology, syntax, and semantics into useful and socially appropriate communication (see also Kirk et al., 2003; Kubicek, this volume, p. 163; Rosenkoetter & Wanless, this volume, p. 81). Adults must expose children to the many uses of language and support their attempts to use language for purposes such as social interaction, giving and gaining information, sharing humor, and expressing emotion. A child's pragmatic ability also includes his use of the appropriate greetings, tone of voice, and other social conventions that are expected at home and at school

(Justice, 2004). At an early age, children should come to realize that they can interact; request; share information, ideas, and feelings; predict; and summarize by using printed and spoken words.

Spoken and written language share much of the same vocabulary, sounds, and rules for combining sounds and words. The two media develop from birth, and they support one another's growth. Therefore, if a child early in life has limited exposure to or difficulty with hearing, understanding, and using the words of the language or languages spoken in his or her environment, then the child is at great risk for problems with reading and writing these same words, phrases, and sentences (Butler, 1998; Hart & Risley, 2003 ; Koppenhaver, Coleman-Pierce, Kalman, & Yoder, 1991; Kupetz & Green, 1997; Morrow, 1997; see also Pierce, this volume, p. 335). Figure 5.1 indicates the ongoing, interrelated nature of communication development.

Figure 5.1. Interrelationship Among the Four Major Media of Human Communication

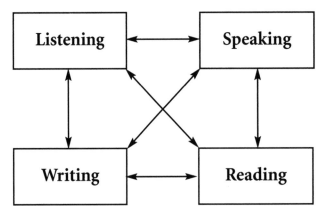

All four ways of communicating share the same basic sounds and rules for combining the sounds into words and words into sentences. We use each of these methods to learn and to communicate from birth, and throughout life. Each of these ways of communicating helps the other to develop.

All four of these ways of communicating can be accomplished or assisted by means of sign language and with the addition of technologies such as cochlear implants, hearing aids, augmentative communication devices, and computers. *All* children can communicate!

Table 5.1. Stages in Oral and Written Language Development

Stage One: Prelinguistic—Speech-Type Sounds but No Words (approximately birth to 11 months)	
Age Range	**Behaviors**
2 weeks	Less crying, random gestures and vocalizations
6 weeks	Squeals, gurgles, and *coos* (makes vowel sounds such as "uhh")
1 month to 2 months	Uses smile to communicate; likes to look at patterns more than solids
3 months to 6 months	Child babbles (makes consonant–vowel syllable sounds such as *ma, de, da*); can focus on large and bright pictures in a book; likes to chew and pat books
6 months to 9 months	Accidentally imitates sounds, more repetition of syllables (such as *ah ba ba*); utterances express emotions; can reach for books, often drops them and picks them up again
9 months to 11 months	Deliberately imitates sounds, shows definite signs of understanding some words and simple commands; uses expressive jargon, a flow of gibberish that has the intonation of real speech; listens to books, stories, and tries to turn pages
Stage Two: One-Word Utterances (approximately 1–2 years)	
12 months	Uses holophrases (one-word utterances): complex meanings can underlie one word; vocabulary of 3–6 words
12 months to 18 months	Intonation is complex and speech-like; extensive use of nouns
	Vocabulary: 3–50 words
	Social: Does not attempt to convey additional information or show frustration when not understood
	Literacy: Likes to turn pages, point to, and label pictures on his/her own
Stage Three: Words Extended Into Phrases (approximately 2–3 years)	
Approximately 2 years	Great strides in receptive language; child uses telegraphic speech, two- or three-word utterances
	Vocabulary: 50–200 words
	Social: Definite increase in communicative efforts, beginnings of conversation, although toddlers rarely extend conversations beyond two turns or sustain topics
	Literacy: Likes to listen to books, stories for longer periods of time and can hold the book correctly; begins to recognize logos (e.g., "golden arches" for McDonald's); begins to show differences in writing versus drawing

continued

Table 5.1. Stages in oral and written language development continued

3 years to 4 years	Often considered to be the most rapid period of language growth
	Vocabulary: Acquires many new words daily; 200–300 word vocabulary
	Social: Strives to communicate and shows frustration if not understood; ability of unfamiliar adults to understand the child increases
	Literacy: Likes to "read" stories to self and others; will protest if adult changes story; recognizes more logos and other environmental print; begins to show disconnected scribble and some letter-like forms

Stage Four: Use of Complete Sentences (approximately 4–6 years)

4 years to 5 years	Makes improvements in pronunciation and grammar
	Vocabulary: 1,400 to 1,600 words
	Social: Seeks way to correct misunderstanding; begins to adjust speech to listener's information needs; can resolve disputes with peers using words; makes more invitations to play
	Literacy: Understands story sequence and the functions and purposes of print; Produces more letter-like forms in scribbling; knows many letter names
5 years to 6 years	Generates complex, grammatically correct sentences; uses pronouns; uses past, present, and future tenses; increases average sentence length per oral sentence to 6.8 words
	Vocabulary: Uses approximately 2,500 words; understands about 6,000; responds to 25,000
	Social: Has good control of elements of conversation
	Literacy: Pays more attention to print; knows some words and is making some letter-sound associations; tries to spell words when writing

Stage Five: Symbolic Use of Language (reading and writing) (approximately 6 years and up)

6 years to 7 years	Uses more complex sentences more adjectives; uses If … then conditional clauses; average number of words per sentence, 7.6
	Vocabulary: Speaking vocabulary of about 3,000 words
	Literacy: Begins to decode new words independently
7 years to 8 years	*Social:* Uses adjectival clauses with which, more gerunds, subordinate clauses
	Literacy: Is beginning reading and writing with comprehension by having a sight word vocabulary and decoding strategies

Source: Adapted with permission of Allyn and Bacon from *Early Childhood Language Arts* by M. R. Jalongo, 2003, p. 64.

Becoming familiar with major oral and written language milestones (see Table 5.1) allows family members and other caregivers to understand what characteristics they should be looking for at certain ages. However, these expectations represent an age range, not an exact point when skills should be achieved (Allen & Marotz, 2003). Variations in development are common and expected because of the wide range in abilities in young children as well as the diversity in the settings and homes in which children are learning.

Developing Oral and Written Language Abilities

In promoting oral and written language development in young children, the National Association for the Education of Young Children says, "No one teaching method or approach is likely to be the most effective for all children" (National Association for the Education of Young Children & International Reading Association, 1998, p. 3). A common strategy among approaches to teaching children is providing language-rich environments—that is, surrounding young learners with language and a combination of meaningful reading, writing, and speaking models and activities.

The importance of language-rich environments can be seen in the landmark longitudinal study conducted by Hart and Risley (2003). The authors found that the adults in their sample of 42 families who spoke more to their children had children who produced more comments than those families with fewer communicative exchanges. Average utterances per hour of a child whose family produced 487 utterances per hour was 310. In comparison, a family that spoke 176 times per hour had children who produced only 168 utterances per hour. The more a child hears language, the more the child will speak (Hart & Risley, 2003). Language-rich learning environments have four major characteristics: (a) meaningful conversations; (b) frequent use of open-ended, descriptive, and structured questions; (c) modeling and expansion; and (d) storytelling and book reading.

The first characteristic of a language-rich learning environment is meaningful conversations. "When talking with children, use rare words, words that children are unlikely to encounter in everyday conversations" (Roskos, Christie, & Richgels, 2003, p. 53). Toy play provides many ways to introduce new, rare words in conversation because there are many objects to describe and there is usually only one adult and one or a few children close by (Dickinson & Tabors, 2001). Other times to introduce new words are during mealtimes and book readings. To make conversation more nurturing to language development, adults should summarize what they are saying, using specific names and helping children to realize that the caregiver is listening and interested in what they are saying (Tabors, 1997).

Another feature of language-rich settings is the type of questions that caregivers use when speaking with children. Open-ended questions are ideal because they do not trigger a yes or no response and they allow the child to create a personal response. Descriptive questions are broad and general. In responding to them, children are encouraged to describe their daily activities and experiences as well as the objects and people in their lives (Westby, Burda, & Mehta, 2003). Descriptive questions, such as "Tell me about your picture," allow the adult to discover what is important to the child by noting which words and ideas are chosen. Structural questions, on the other hand, are used to investigate the child's answer to a descriptive question, for example, "Tell me how you made the green on your paper." A subsequent helpful tactic when addressing children is to summarize what they have said aloud to enable the child and adult to agree on answers to the descriptive question (Westby et al., 2003).

Modeling and expansion are essential characteristics of language-rich environments. These two strategies allow children to learn correct methods of performing tasks and gain new ways to say what they thinking and seeing. Modeling involves demonstrating how to perform a certain activity (McGee & Richgels, 1996). Modeling can be performed directly, for example, by telling a child, "This is how you turn the pages of a book," or it can be done indirectly, for example, while reading a book to a child and turning the pages from right to left. Expansion involves responding to a child's speech with an elaborated version of what the child has already said (Jalongo, 2003); for example, if a child says, "It windy," the adult can reply, "It *is* windy outside. This would be a great day to fly a kite."

Of course, storytelling and book reading are also features of language-rich environments. The maximum potential for learning can be reached when children have the opportunity to participate actively during storytelling or reading. Predictable stories allow young children to rely on repetition to cue their language participation (Rog, 2001). Other print materials such as directions, recipes, toys, signs, cards, and food containers with labels can help to cue naming and also aid children in connecting spoken language to print (Pierce & DiLeone, 2003).

Positive Talk Environments

Current research outlining the connection between oral and written language development is plentiful. To facilitate both oral and written language development, adults can create positive talk environments in the following ways:

- **Regularly ascribe communicative meaning to infants' and toddlers' utterances, and consider all behavior meaningful.** For example, if one child hits another child, the hitter is seeking something that he wants or is trying to make something happen or stop happening, but he just does not have the words to communicate his message. The adults must provide words and urge the young child to use them.

- **Use positive, specific comments.** For example, say "You really spent a lot of time on this picture," not "What a pretty picture!" Similarly, say "I see two trees here," not "I like what you drew."

- **Model and expand frequently.** Adults model appropriate language structures and teach new vocabulary words by adding on to what a child has said: For example, in response to a child saying, "Dog," an adult might say, "It is a *big* dog."

- **Be sure that meaningful conversations occur regularly.** Caregivers or family members ask every child in the group about things the child is interested in and then truly listen to the answers. For example, "Jonah got a new puppy. Isaac, tell him about your puppy."

- **Share information.** Adults label feelings, actions, and objects in the child's environment and relate new ideas to the child's experiences to build vocabulary and understanding. For example, in the grocery store, an adult might say, "We chose some nice yellow bananas. Now I'm going to put the bananas on the scale. Let's see how heavy they are. Look, the needle is moving!"

• **Ask real questions.** Adults show true interest, asking children to describe what they are playing, how they are making constructions or artwork, and how they feel about their creations. For example, "It scared me when the blocks fell down. What did you think?"

• **Use open-ended questions and statements.** For example, "Tell me about your city." "What is the story in this book?" These types of questions cannot be answered with single words.

• **Encourage children's choices and decision making.** Give children ways to exercise their minds and voices by allowing them to select among alternatives. For example, "Which of these books shall we read?"

Positive Talk Environments

Environmental rating scales (e.g., Harms, Cryer, & Clifford, 1990) emphasize the importance of language development elements. In positive talk times or positive talk environments for infants and toddlers,

Children talk more than adults.

All children have multiple ways to communicate.

Adults show true interest in what children are doing and listen attentively to what children have to say.

Adults use children's interests as a basis for conversation.

Adults speak courteously to children.

Adults plan or use spontaneous opportunities to talk with each child informally.

Adults refrain from talking judgmentally about any children in their presence.

Adults show affection and sincere interest in children.

Adults send congruent verbal and nonverbal messages.

Adults invite children into extended conversations with peers and adults.

Conclusion

One cannot overemphasize the connection between oral and written language development and use. Effectively using all forms of communicating—listening, speaking, reading, and writing—has a favorable effect on young children's continuing development. Language-rich, positive talk environments that expose children to, and foster their awareness of, the content (semantics), form (phonology, morphology, syntax), and function (pragmatics) of language from birth onward will help children to be successful in the many aspects of life that require communication. Using and responding to cooing, talking, and print-related communication help children do the same. In *The Carrot Seed* (Krauss, 1945), the planted seed really did come up, "just as the little boy had known it would" (pages not numbered). In a nurturing, language-rich environment, young children's communication will also develop—from cooing to conversation and, finally, to understanding and using written language.

References

Adams, M. J. (1990). *Learning to read: Thinking and learning about print.* Cambridge, MA: MIT Press.

Allen, E. K., & Marotz, L. R. (2003). *Developmental profiles: Pre-birth through twelve.* (4th ed.). Clifton Park, NY: Delmar.

Armbruster, B. B., Lehr, F., & Osborn, J. (2003). *A child becomes a reader: Birth through preschool.* Portsmouth, NH: RMC Research Corporation.

Barton, L. R., & Brophy-Herb, H. E. (2006). Developmental foundations for language and literacy from birth to 3 years. In S. E. Rosenkoetter & J. Knapp-Philo (Eds.), *Learning to read the world: Language and literacy in the first three years* (pp. 15–60). Washington, DC: ZERO TO THREE Press.

Bloom, L., & Lahey, M. (1978). *Language development and language disorders.* New York: Wiley.

Bruner, J. S. (1983). *Child's talk: Learning to use language.* Oxford, UK: Oxford University Press.

Burns, S., Griffin, P., & Snow, C. (1999). *Starting out right: A guide to promoting children's reading success.* Washington, DC: National Academy Press.

Butler, D. (1998). *Babies need books.* Portsmouth, NH: Heinemann.

Chomsky, N. (1957). *Syntactic structures.* The Hague, The Netherlands: Mouton.

Clay, M. (1966). *Emergent reading behavior.* Unpublished doctoral dissertation, University of Auckland, New Zealand.

Dickinson, D. K., & Tabors, P. O. (2001). *Young children learning at home and school: Beginning literacy with language.* Baltimore: Paul H. Brookes.

Fewell, R., & Deutscher, B. (2002). Contributions of receptive vocabulary and maternal style: Variables to later verbal ability and reading in low-birthweight children. *Topics in Early Childhood Special Education, 22,* 179-188.

Fewell, R., & Deutscher, B. (2004). Contributions of early language and maternal facilitation variables to later reading abilities. *Journal of Early Intervention, 26*(2), 132–145.

Gambrell, L. (2004). Exploring the connection between oral language and early reading. *The Reading Teacher, 57*(5), 490–492.

Griffin, P. (2006). Sound steps in phonological form for later literacy. In S. E. Rosenkoetter & J. Knapp-Philo (Eds.), *Learning to read the world: Language and literacy in the first three years* (pp. 145–162). Washington, DC: ZERO TO THREE Press.

Harms, T., Cryer, D., & Clifford, R. (1990). *Infant/Toddler Environment Rating Scale.* New York: Teachers College Press.

Hart, B., & Risley, T. R. (2003). The early catastrophe: The 30 million word gap by age 3. *American Educator, 27*(1, Spring), 4–9.

Jalongo, M. R. (2003). *Early childhood language arts.* (3rd ed.). Boston: Allyn and Bacon.

Justice, L. (2004). Creating language-rich preschool classroom environments. *Teaching Exceptional Children, 37*(2), 36–44.

Kirk, S. A., Gallager, J. J., & Anastasiow, N. J. (2003). *Educating exceptional children.* (10th ed.). Boston: Houghton Mifflin.

Koppenhaver, D., Coleman-Pierce, P., Kalman, S., & Yoder, D. (1991). The implications of emergent literacy research for children with developmental disabilities. *American Journal of Speech-Language Pathology, 1*(1), 10–25.

Koppenhaver, D., Evans, D., & Yoder, D. (1991). Childhood reading and writing experiences of literate adults with severe speech and motor impairments. *Augmentative and Alternative Communication, 7*(1), 20–33.

Krauss, R. (1945). *The carrot seed.* New York: Harper.

Kubicek, L. F. (2006). Encouraging language and literacy through family routines. In S. E. Rosenkoetter & J. Knapp-Philo (Eds.), *Learning to read the world: Language and literacy in the first three years* (pp. 163–186). Washington, DC: ZERO TO THREE Press.

Kupetz, B., & Green, E. (1997). Sharing books with infants and toddlers: Facing the challenges. *Young Children, 52*(2), 22–27.

Lapiak, J. (2004). Visual languages. Retrieved March 27, 2004, from http://www.handspeak.com/

Lonigan, C. (2004, December). Findings of the National Early Literacy Panel. Presentation at the School Readiness Conference, University of North Carolina at Chapel Hill.

McGee, L. M., & Richgels, D. J. (1996). *Literacy beginnings: Supporting young readers and writers.* (2nd ed.). Boston: Allyn and Bacon.

Morrow, L. M. (1997). *Literacy development in the early years.* (3rd ed.). Boston: Allyn & Bacon

Morrow, L. M. (2005). *Literacy development in the early years: Helping children read and write* (5th ed.). Boston: Allyn & Bacon.

National Association for the Education of Young Children & International Reading Association. (1998). *Learning to read and write: Developmentally appropriate practices for young children.* Washington, DC: Author.

Nilsen, B. (2001). *Week by week: Plans for observing and recording young children.* (2nd ed.). Albany, New York: Delmar.

North Carolina Department of Public Instruction. (2004). *Foundations: Early learning standards for North Carolina preschoolers and strategies for guiding their success.* Raleigh, NC: Author.

Notari-Syverson, A. (2006). Everyday tools of literacy. In S. E. Rosenkoetter & J. Knapp-Philo (Eds.), *Learning to read the world: Language and literacy in the first three years* (pp. 61–80). Washington, DC: ZERO TO THREE Press.

Paley, V. G. (1986). *Molly is three: Growing up in school.* Chicago: University of Chicago.

Pierce, P., & DiLeone, B. (2003). *What to look for in a quality literacy-rich classroom: A guide for administrators, teachers, and parents.* Raleigh, NC: North Carolina Department of Public Instruction, Exceptional Children Division.

Pierce, P. (2006) High expectations for language and literacy with infants and toddlers who have significant disabilities. In S. E. Rosenkoetter & J. Knapp-Philo (Eds.), *Learning to read the world: Language and literacy in the first three years* (pp. 335–352). Washington, DC: ZERO TO THREE Press.

Rog, L. J. (2001). *Early literacy instruction in kindergarten.* Newark, DE: International Reading Association.

Rosenkoetter, S. E., & Wanless, S. B. (2006). Relationships: At the heart of early language and literacy. In S. E. Rosenkoetter & J. Knapp-Philo (Eds.), *Learning to read the world: Language and literacy in the first three years* (pp. 81–102). Washington, DC: ZERO TO THREE Press.

Roskos, K. A., Christie, J. F., & Richgels, D. J. (2003, March). The essentials of early literacy instruction. *Young Children, 58*(2), pp.52–62.

Roskos, K. A., Tabors, P. O., & Lenhart, L. A. (2004). *Oral language and early literacy in preschool.* Newark, DE: International Reading Association.

Roth, F., Speece, D., & Cooper, D. (2002). A longitudinal analysis of the connection between oral language and early reading. *The Journal of Educational Research, 95*(5), 259–272.

Scarborough, H. (2002). Connecting early language and literacy to later language reading (dis)abilities: Evidence, theory, and practice. In S. Neuman & D. Dickinson (Eds.), *The handbook of early literacy research* (pp. 97–111). New York: Guilford.

Skinner, B. F. (1953). *Science and human behavior.* New York: Macmillan.

Skinner, B. F. (1957). *Verbal behavior.* New York: Appleton-Century Crofts.

Smith, M. W., Dickinson, D. K., Sangeorge, A., & Anastasopoulos, L. (2002). *Early language and literacy classroom observation.* Baltimore: Paul H. Brookes.

Snow, C., Burns, S., & Griffin, P. (1998). *Preventing reading difficulties in young children.* Washington, DC: Committee on the Prevention of Reading Difficulties in Young Children. National Research Council. National Academy of Sciences.

Sulzby. E., & Teale, W. (1991). Emergent literacy. In R. Barr, M. L. Kamil, P. Mosenthal, & P. D. Pearson (Eds.), *Handbook of reading research* (Vol. 2, pp. 727–757). White Plains, NY: Longman.

Tabors, P. O. (1997). *One child, two languages: A guide for preschool educators of children learning English as a second language.* Baltimore: Paul H. Brookes.

Vukelich, C., & Christie, J. (2004). *Building a foundation for preschool literacy: Effective instruction for children's reading and writing development.* Newark, DE: International Reading Association.

Vygotsky, L. S. (1962). *Thought and language.* Cambridge, MA: MIT Press.

Vygotsky, L. S. (1978). *Mind in society: The development of higher mental processes* (M. Cole, V. John-Steiner, S. Scribner, & E. Souberman, Eds.). Cambridge, MA: Harvard University Press. (Original work published in Russian 1930, 1933, 1935)

Westby, C., Burda, A., & Mehta, Z. (April, 2003). Asking the right questions in the right ways: Strategies for ethnographic interviewing. *The ASHA Leader, 8*(8), 4–5, 16–17.

CHAPTER 6

Book Sharing: A Developmentally Appropriate Way to Foster Preacademic Growth

Adriana Bus and Maria de Jong

Eleven-month-old Johann is playing with his toys. His father sits next to him and picks a book from a nearby pile. "Shall we read about Max?" the father asks. The little boy takes the book from his father and starts to turn the page. When he sees the page with a picture of a crying child (the story's climax), Johann tries to make a face as if he were starting to cry. Then he lays his hand on his father's arm and looks at him to indicate that he wants him to read the book. His father points at the pictures and starts telling the story about two children playing with a car: "Max and Lisa are playing. With a car." When he notices that Johann is losing interest, his father skips a few pages and goes directly to the climax: "Lisa takes the car, and Max starts to cry." The father then imitates the crying child in the picture. Johann begins to pay attention to the story again and tries to imitate his father's sad face. The father points to the picture. Johann follows the pointing finger but continues to look at his father's face, apparently struggling to understand the meaning of his father's "crying." The child takes the book again and pages through it, apparently searching for something. He moves his finger over pictures; sometimes he makes sounds. When he gets to one page he makes a "crying" face. As Johann moves his finger over the pictures, his father names them: "Max, gate, car."

Books provide a rich source of language and literacy stimulation for young children. Even though Johann is far from a conventional reader, his approach suggests that he has already acquired knowledge relevant for reading. He has grasped structures and cadences found in the picture books. He shows book-handling behavior by turning the pages, and he demonstrates that he is able to reference concepts from one context to another by pretending to cry at one of the pictures. His facial expressions show that he is aware of main events of the story. This scenario also illustrates that referencing is a social act that is started and maintained by intimate caregivers; for example, when his father began to "cry," Johann looked back and forth from the book to his father's face as he tried to understand.

In this chapter, we will discuss how familiarizing infants and toddlers with books is a sustained process that depends on continuous efforts by the adults who care for them. We will also examine differences in how caregivers of young children from different cultural groups look at the activity of book reading to young children. Finally, we will discuss findings from a Dutch program intended to stimulate book reading specifically to babies.

Early Learning From Experiences With Books

Reading books to babies and toddlers familiarizes them with stories and written language. Moreover, book reading exposes young children to complex language that they might not encounter elsewhere. For example, simple picture story-books provide novel vocabulary, grammar, and colloquialisms, especially when they discuss situations that are unfamiliar to the young listener (Hayes & Ahrens, 1988). The authors of this chapter were surprised by the results of a recent pilot study they conducted to test the complexity of sentences in story-books for 4- to 5-year-olds. The findings indicate that plain sentences such as *That cures every ailment* and *It won't do any harm* were difficult to understand, even for an advanced 5-year-old.

We believe that picture books help infants and toddlers begin to understand symbols. The pictures in the book may be considered the earliest form of symbol, known as protosymbols because they present meaning directly. Even though the picture of the crying child in Johann's storybook may be a one-color, two-dimensional, 3- by 5-inch line drawing, Johann apparently recognizes the image, endows it with considerable meaning, and responds empathically. Actual symbols (e.g., a valentine heart, a hexagonal red stop sign, or a word) represent meaning (Werner & Kaplan, 1963). Reading books to babies familiarizes them with the representational function of pictures as symbols for events and stories. They begin to understand the representative meaning of pictures as they touch, look at, and share feelings about the pictures with an adult. Eventually gestures, particularly pointing to pictures, become a way for children and adults to share the meaning they find in those pictures. Indeed, a child's pointing involves not only an invitation to look but also an expectation that the adult will perceive the object as the child does. This understanding of representational function, then, emerges as a social interaction between child and adult.

When adults read to preverbal infants and toddlers frequently, the children gradually progress from behaviors such as hitting pages and grabbing at books to higher levels of referencing such as pointing and using protosymbols (Murphy, 1978). Bus and van IJzendoorn (1997) studied infants from the ages of 11 to 14 months as they shared a simple, developmentally appropriate picture book with their mothers and demonstrated that reading development starts at this early preverbal stage. Each page of the book showed a picture of an object found on a farm, accompanied by one sentence of text that described the pictured object. The younger children in the sample (11- to 13-month-olds) grasped, touched, reached for, and mouthed the book. However, soon, near their first birthday, the children shifted from acting on the book to higher levels of referencing. Toddlers who were the ages of 14 to 15 months pointed, made other gestures, vocalized, looked at, and laughed at the pictures. The older children were more responsive than the younger ones to their mothers' questions and comments. The following examples are typical of observations that were made in Bus and van IJzendoorn's (1997) study.

> *Anne, age 46 weeks, explored the book primarily by grabbing it, putting it in her mouth, and biting it. Her mother did not inhibit her actions. Anne showed hardly any sign that she recognized illustrations in the book (e.g., looking at pictures or touching them). Her mother was supportive. When she could see the pages of the book, she would make comments such as "Are you going to eat Bambi?" or "Look! A nice kitty. Meow." She continued to make such comments even though Anne did not respond*

to her mother's referencing (Bus & Van IJzendorn, 1997, pp. 55–56).

* * *

Frans, age 60 weeks, made animal sounds and gestures that fit the pictures in his book. When his mother responded to the picture of a pig by saying: "Gnr, gnr, gnr, little pig, little pig," Frans, looking at the book, answered, "Grrr." The child also responded to his mother's questions. For example, looking at the picture of a horse, the mother asked, "Do you see? Oh, horsey. Daddy rides on a horse." In response to the picture and his mother's comments, the child pantomimed riding on horseback. His mother then responded, "Yes, we are going to ride, yes. This is a horse" (pointing to the picture). *Frans also elicited responses from his mother. Later in the session, he repeated the horseback-riding movements. His mother responded by looking in the book for the picture of the horse while asking, "Do you want to see the horse again?"* (Bus & Van IJzendorn, 1997, pp. 55–56).

According to results of Bus and van IJzendoorn's (1997) study, page turning is not significantly related to age, although this type of behavior seems to increase slightly as children grow older. A few children in the sample focused mainly on page turning, only occasionally looking at or responding to the pictures.

Margereta, age 56 weeks, turned pages during the whole session. Her mother allowed her to do so and offered help when the child had difficulty turning a page. As the child turned pages, her mother responded to the pictures that became visible when a page was turned. She would ask, for example, "Where is quack quack? There is the little duck." She would then turn the page and say, "Ah there it is, give a kiss, give quack quack a kiss." Sometimes Margereta seemed to follow her mother's lead, but her attention span was quite brief. Sometimes her mother encouraged the child to find a specific picture (e.g., "Where is quack quack?") and responded enthusiastically when Margereta opened the book (even though perhaps accidentally) to the page with the picture of a duck (Bus & Van IJzendorn, 1997, p. 56).

Although the age range of the toddlers in this study was small and the study was not longitudinal, observations of the differences in behavior in children of different ages document the growth over time of very young children's under- standing that books are referential media. They recognize that books contain pictures and symbols that stand for people, animals, objects, and actions. The toddlers in the study behaved in ways that suggest that they were beginning to appreciate the symbolic features of picture books. It appears, then, that reading is developing even at this early, preverbal stage. Reading books with very young children may offer a main route to their becoming literate because it familiar- izes them with the representational function of pictures.

Engaging the Infant in the World of the Book

We believe that a child's interest in reading books is a result of sharing books and stories with adults and that it is not a factor of her temperament or per- sonality. The infant's or toddler's repertoire of behaviors related to books expands as a result of a caring adult investing numerous hours in attempts to alert the baby to the interesting facets of books.

We promote this hypothesis because anyone who has attempted to read to a very young child knows that simply reading the text is inadequate to maintain her attention. We have observed that for most children between the ages of 1 and 3 years, books are attractive only if the activity of reading a book includes more than the adult reading the words verbatim. Parents and other adults make books accessible to toddlers by skipping difficult parts, adding appropriate sound effects, adapting text to the child's level of understanding, creating new stories, and so forth.

It is our impression (untested as yet) that young children's active participation in and learning through book reading depends strongly on the caregiver's abili- ty to create a bridge between the child's world and the setting of the book. The adult accomplishes this feat through language, gestures, and careful choice of the pictorial images in the book itself. Only as children approach school age do their mothers tend to read more and talk less about the books that they are sharing with their children (van Kleeck, 2003). We have concluded that very young children need support to stay attentive, understand the pictures, and discover the interesting and exciting parts in the story. When an adult approaches book-reading interactions with flexibility and an understanding of the child's developmental stage, then the child responds with sustained interest and an increasing ability to understand the pictures and the story line.

To bridge the gap between the everyday world of the child and the world of the book, an adult has to become both reader (of the original written text) and creator (of the story she actually tells). It is essential that adults capitalize on their intimate knowledge of each child's personal world, including meaningful settings, possessions, and sensations, and that they use familiar language as they explore books, name concepts, and so forth (Jones, 1996). Typically, caregivers "read" the pictorial contents of an illustrated story and its accompanying text more idiosyncratically to younger or less experienced children than to older or more experienced ones. Jones's ethnographic study found that caregivers are more successful in engaging infants with books when they find cues that give a child pleasure and that narrow the gap between book and the child's experience. Adults interact more successfully when they identify a large number of pictorial details for the child and when they point out pictures and use words that communicate strong emotion to the child. Instead of reading a story exactly as it is written, most parents individualize a story for their child. For example, an adult may adapt a story by discussing details of pictures that interest his or her own child but that have little to do with the printed version of the story. The child may enjoy the illustrations for reasons that are not at all related to the story as written.

Research has revealed numerous examples of caregivers altering the text during book reading to make it more attractive to the child (e.g., Martin & Reutzel, 1999; van Kleeck, Alexander, Vigil, & Templeton, 1996). The following observation illustrates how such adaptations can drive the "official version" of the story into the background (Bus & Sulzby, unpublished data):

> *A mother was reading* Sam Vole and His Brothers *(Waddell & Firth, 1992). She started reading the text to her 28-month-old child, but when she noticed that the child had become more interested in a picture of a bumblebee (not mentioned in the text) than in the official story, she let him make up his own story about a bumblebee. The child asked: "What's that?" and "What is he (Sam) looking at?" After Mom explained that this was a*

> *bumblebee, the child concluded that Sam saw the bumblebee. Mother and child then discussed whether Sam might be frightened.*

The bumblebee was not part of the official story, but it was part of the child's story. The themes that an adult and a child discuss but that are not part of the official story may reflect closely the child's current real-life interests. These discussions serve as bridges between the world of the child and the world of the book and seem to be highly motivating and engaging to the child.

Maintaining the Conversation Matters

When reading to very young children, adults seem to give higher priority to maintaining the communicative relationship than to teaching infants by pointing at the pictures and evoking referencing behaviors. For example, in a study of 11- to 14-month-old infants (Bus & van IJzendoorn, 1997), it appeared that mothers did not make attempts to elicit referencing from children who had not yet started to use protosymbols spontaneously. The more children were still acting on books (e.g., banging on the book, hitting pages, touching pictures, reaching for the book, grasping the book, and pointing randomly), the less mothers attempted to elicit referencing. After the children exhibited referencing behavior, mothers then extended the infants' behavior by pointing to the pictures and evoking responses (e.g., "Pat the baa-lamb"). The mothers' behaviors of pointing and evoking responses were positively correlated with the child's responding (rs were .38 and .34, respectively) and referencing (rs were .47 and .35). Adult expansions of children's referencing behavior are a consequence of children's level of responding and are not present from an early age. These findings do not confirm Ninio and Bruner's (1976) suggestion that adults try to elicit referencing from babies at a very early age.

Additional research findings indicate that, with very young children, adults focus primarily on maintaining the adult–child relationship around the picture book. Instances in which the adults challenged children to develop referencing behaviors (by asking, for example, "Where is the duck?") were much less frequent. Indeed, caregivers focus primarily on selecting opportunities for infants and toddlers to display what they already know (van Kleeck, 2003). DeLoache and DeMendoza (1987) found that mothers offered a high proportion of nonchallenging input when reading with their 12-, 15-, and 18-month-old children. Mothers were significantly more likely to skip over pictures when they thought their children did not know the word for that picture, asking about such pictures only 8% of the time. Mothers were also much more likely to ask the child for words they thought the child could produce (49% of label requests) than for words they believed the child could only comprehend (18% of label requests). It appears, then, that mothers engage their young children in books by capitalizing on what is familiar to the child.

Even if they are not interested in a particular story, very young children may enjoy the intimacy of book reading (Bus, 2001, 2003). Adults who are sensitive to very young children's needs respond to them through dialogue rather than through direct teaching or the eliciting of referencing behaviors with *what* and *who* questions. Caregivers point at pictures and evoke responses, thereby adding to children's vocabulary, but they apply these types of strategies sparsely when the children are not very interested in the topic of the story. These findings lead us to doubt the appropriateness of the assumption that the positive effects of book reading depend on adults expecting very young children to actively participate in the beginning stages of sharing books (e.g., Whitehurst et al., 1988).

Affective Dimensions of Book Reading With Very Young Children

As described above, caregivers have a central role in making books interesting and relevant to the very young child. Bus and colleagues' idea that children's interest in books results from sensitive support by caregivers was affirmed in a series of studies (see for reviews: Bus, 2001, 2003). Bus and colleagues tested the hypothesis that a negative history of parent–child interaction inhibits not only the first stages of the child's book-sharing experiences but also the child's continuing interest in books and literacy throughout subsequent years. They compared groups of parent–child pairs who differed in levels of attachment security. A main characteristic of an insecure caregiver–child relationship is that the caregiver is less sensitive to her child's (or children's) needs. We expected the caregivers of insecurely attached children to be less sensitive and supportive while sharing books than caregivers of more securely attached children.

Using Ainsworth's well-known Strange Situation (Ainsworth, Blehar, Waters, & Wall, 1978), Bus and colleagues observed how children responded to an unexpected and unpleasant separation from the parent. A child's response to separation from the parent is assumed to be a valid indicator of the security of the parent–child relationship. Secure children seek proximity when the parent returns; however, after their parent cuddles them briefly, they move away and explore the environment again. Insecure–avoidant children avoid the parent when he or she returns after a separation. Typically, these children do not look at the parent in the face and often turn their backs on them. Insecure–resistant children seek proximity but are at the same time resistant to contact. These children do not let themselves be enticed into playing after the parent returns, but they also try to control the parent's behavior (e.g., demanding, "Take my bear").

Bus and van IJzendorn (1997) studied the atmosphere during book reading and mothers' successful use of scaffolding (i.e., adapting interactions to support the child in being a successful respondent) as a function of parent–child attachment security. The findings were similar to those of van Kleeck et al. (1996) in that they found mothers devoting most of their energy to getting and keeping their baby's attention and to encouraging the child's participation in the reading routine. Insecurely attached children were less attentive than secure ones and were more likely to look at objects in the environment or to make attempts to escape from their mothers' laps. Insecurely attached children responded to book content by referencing less frequently than securely attached infants and toddlers. Insecurely attached infants and toddlers were less inclined than securely attached children to respond to animal pictures by patting the picture, making animal sounds, or imitating the movements of the pictured animals (e.g., making horse-riding motions in response to a picture of a horse). Mothers of insecurely attached children seemed preoccupied with controlling their children's negative behaviors (e.g., by putting an arm around a child to restrict her movements or by holding the book out of reach).

In a study involving a sample of 18-month-old Caucasian American boys (Bus, Belsky, van IJzendoorn, & Crnik, 1997), mothers read from an expository book that included a series of pictures of babies making faces, crawling, sitting still, walking, playing, eating, drinking, being dressed or bathed, and sleeping. Each two-page spread also contained a few brief sentences. Bus and colleagues conducted a microanalysis of the strategies that mothers used to make the books understandable to their toddlers. As anticipated, most toddlers participating in this study (Bus et al., 1997) mainly responded to pictures in the book by pointing and labeling. Most mothers tried to initiate such actions by following predictable routines as described by Ninio and Bruner (1976). Typically, mothers initiated interactions with motivating statements (e.g., "Look here!"), pointing to pictures, questioning (e.g., "Look, what's that?"), and labeling (e.g., "See, a rabbit."). Children initiated interactions and responded to parental questions and comments by pointing, labeling, commenting, and responding nonverbally.

One group of insecure mother–child pairs seemed unable to merge their unique styles into a contingent and reciprocal relationship. These mothers did not succeed in creating an age-appropriate interaction with their children. Instead of using pictures as a way of evoking interactive routines with their toddlers, these mothers often simply read the text, ignoring the children's limited ability to understand the story and pictures independently. The children in this group tended to be unresponsive to the book's content as it was presented by their mothers and tended to be more distractible than securely attached children.

In this same study (Bus et al., 1997), a somewhat different picture emerged for another group of insecurely attached toddlers and their mothers. The toddlers were superficially more engaged in book reading than those previously discussed, but an in-depth analysis of the sessions revealed several problems. The mothers in this group tried repeatedly to motivate their children to become engaged with books (saying, for example, "Look at that!") and to correct their children's behavior more than other mothers. A number of studies (e.g., Cornell, Sénéchal, & Broda, 1988) have suggested that very young children need opportunities for active participation (e.g., pointing, manipulating, and vocalizing) in book sharing so they can maintain their engagement. Those observations would suggest, then, that the overstimulating and controlling behavior of these mothers seemed to covary with ambivalence in their children. The children in this group were not obviously disengaged, but they responded to the pictures and to their mothers' comments and questions less frequently than other children in the sample. In addition, they responded to books at somewhat lower developmental levels, for example, by hitting the book, and showed aggression toward their mothers by pushing and hitting them.

These and other studies clearly point to the conclusion that caregiver–child book reading is a profoundly social process, embedded in the adult–child affective relationship. Our conviction, in line with such results, is that family literacy programs should support caregivers to develop nurturing, appropriately stimulating responses. Programs that focus on the intimacy of sharing books may help adults to adopt new reading habits that are likely to foster their children's engagement in book reading and enjoyment of shared literacy. Further, improved parental interactive book reading may also build close, trusting relationships and strengthen the emotional bond between caregiver and child.

Adult–Child Book Reading Across Cultures

Although adult–child book reading has proven to be a major contributor to stimulating young children's language and reading development in some cultures (Bus, van IJzendoorn, & Pellegrini, 1995), we do not know the degree to which this finding can be generalized across cultures (Serpell, 1997). Adults in various cultures may differ in their beliefs about education and may have different ways of responding to and supporting their children's literacy (Sonnenschein et al., 1996). For example, when adults do not find reading books to be a source of pleasure for themselves, then activities such as book reading may not be embedded in family practice, and parents may not know how to engage children in reading sessions (Bus & Sulzby, 1996). As a consequence, numerous children around the world may be coming to school without this family preparation for reading.

De Groot and Bus (1995) tested the hypothesis that mothers' own interest in reading for enjoyment is a decisive factor for the opportunities that they as well as their babies and toddlers have to become involved with books. The researchers worked with a group of 30 Dutch mothers, born in The Netherlands, who had low levels of education. They asked the mothers what they thought about reading books to very young children and tested the mothers' own familiarity with reading by asking them to identify authors or magazine titles from checklists that contained plausible foils. These checklists were similar to those used by Stanovich and colleagues (e.g., Cunningham & Stanovich, 1990). The results of this study strongly supported the hypothesis that parents who did not consider reading to be an important source of personal enjoyment were not likely to think of reading as a source of pleasure and learning for their babies and toddlers. The mothers who tended to favor sharing books with their young children were those who were more familiar with authors and magazine titles than were other mothers (rs were .56 and .68, respectively).

In addition to the 30 native-born Dutch mothers studied by de Groot and Bus (1995), these same researchers interviewed 20 mothers who immigrated to the Netherlands from Morocco, Turkey, and Surinam. The mothers identified which of two contrasting statements best described them: "My caregiver read to me" or "I cannot remember being read to as a child." They were then asked to choose from other contrasting statements that described views on reading to babies soon after their birth. Most immigrant mothers (88%) agreed with the statement that reading books to young children is important preparation for school. Furthermore, 80% agreed with the statement that children learn from book reading and 95% with the statement that children who are read to will become better readers at school age (95%). However, the mothers did not agree with statements emphasizing that an early start is desirable: Only 25% agreed that book reading to infants or toddlers is worthwhile, and just 35% believed that book-reading routines give a boost to babies' and toddlers' reading development. Therefore, it is important to negotiate different cultural practices with parents in a way that not only honors their own experiences and values but also supports each child's optimal literacy development (also see Jones & Lorenzo-Hubert, this volume, p. 187).

Book Reading in Families Having a Genetic Disposition for Reading Problems

Parents who have reading problems themselves are less likely to provide their children with a rich and stimulating linguistic environment (Lyytinen, Laakso, & Poikkeus, 1998). Indeed, we might expect that children in families having a genetic disposition for reading problems may face increased risk for reading problems because the frequency and quality of parent–child book reading in their homes are not high. Although certainly no causal connections can be made, findings from longitudinal research suggest that children with dyslexia, whose parents also had dyslexia, had less frequent exposure to books than did children who became typical readers (Scarborough, Dobrich, & Hager, 1991). The Jyväskylä Longitudinal Study of Dyslexia (Laakso, 1999) explored parent–child book reading in a group of children having genetic risks to develop serious reading and writing problems. They were followed beginning at birth and compared with a normal control group. This Finnish study included 39 mothers who were diagnosed as reading disabled and who had a familial background of reading difficulties, 89 typically reading mothers, and the children of both groups of mothers. Data gathered when the children were approximately 1 year old suggested that joint storybook reading occurred less frequently in families with reading difficulties than in families with typically reading parents (Laakso, Poikkeus, & Lyytinen, 1997).

Considering these results, we may question whether providing books to families and encouraging them to read together will actually produce meaningful conversations in the context of homes and cultures in which reading is not intrinsically embedded in the parents' daily activities and entertainment. Parents who are not used to reading storybooks and who do not consider reading a source of enjoyment may need ongoing support in selecting appropriate books; in scaffolding interactions with their children during book reading; and in experiencing many pleasurable, nonthreatening interactions around print. Programs should consider these findings as they plan interventions with families.

Two Case Studies of Family Literacy Intervention

Two case studies by de Groot and Bus (1995) were embedded within a larger Dutch family literacy project (*Boekenpret*) that was designed to support book-sharing activities by Dutch and immigrant caregivers with low education and for whom reading is not part of daily life. Investigators hypothesized that the mothers, who were the primary caregivers of the young children in the two families studied, would be unlikely to build book-reading routines with their baby or toddler.

De Groot and Bus (1995) visited the two mother–child pairs, one Dutch and the other Surinamese, once a month during the first 6 months of their participation in the literacy intervention project. When the babies were about 6 months old, the researchers provided the mothers with books suitable for babies. In addition, home visitors whose ethnicity was similar to that of the mothers' visited them to discuss their experiences with child rearing. The home visitors offered mothers, fathers, grandparents, and other caregivers suggestions about reading to babies. The two case-study mothers gradually adopted many of these suggestions. Both mothers noted that they would not have started reading to a child this young without incentives from the project. Observations of the book-sharing interactions between these two mothers and their infants indicated that both children appeared to enjoy book reading more and more over time. Their responses gradually progressed to touching pages, touching details of pictures, pointing, and babbling. Mothers became more supportive of their infants' participation while sharing books with them.

The researchers found that book reading evolved in these two families from incidental events into a regular, but not daily, routine. In the beginning, when the children were 6 months old, both mothers reported that they did not share books with their child every day. One mother explained that it took effort to interest her baby in a book. When asked about reading, she said, "I don't read every day; after shopping I am too tired."

When the children reached the age of about 11 months, both mothers reported that they read almost every day because their children invited them to do so. The presence of books suitable for young children and the encouragement of the home visitors provided additional incentives to share books. Even more supportive may have been the growing evidence of interest from the children. Most stimulating of all, quite likely, was the parents' empathy for their children's interests, knowledge, motives, and understanding of the world, which not only encouraged the children but also enabled a balance in the adult–child conversation.

During the study with these two families, mother–child interactions moved from abstract–cognitive to affective–interpersonal communications. At the start of the literacy project, the mothers' focus on expanding their children's receptive vocabulary seemed to inhibit productive mother–child interactions. The mothers, concerned that they would not succeed in explaining the meaning of pictures or words, spontaneously used playthings to back up their verbal explanations. One mother, for example, used a toy that produced lifelike animal sounds to explain the meaning of the animal pictures in the book. (This strategy failed because the toy distracted the child's attention from the book.) With the passage of time and continued participation in the intervention group, the mothers became less "results-oriented." They shared reciprocally with their infants rather than communicated one-way messages. As the mothers placed fewer demands on their children to listen and respond, the interactions became more fruitful and rewarding for both mothers and children. Mothers, for instance, were less likely to insist on a particular order of responses and were more apt to wait for the child to communicate. This change is exemplified by the following interaction between the Surinamese mother and her 11-month-old child:

M: She has a shawl. *(points at it)*

C: *(laughs)*

M: And beautiful clothes, a sweater, pants, and boots, to wear outside in the snow. *(rubs the page)*

C: *(hits with two hands on the book and makes noises, then touches something on the page)*

M: Yes, nice shoes, nice pants. You have nice pants, too. *(touches the child's pants)*.

C: *(looks at his pants)*

M: Here are pants *(rubs over the page)* and a sweater *(rubs over the page and touches the child's sweater)*.

C: *(looks around)*

M: You see, sweater.

M: Nice, isn't it?

C: *(looks in the book, touches the page, rubs over the page)*

Why It Is Important to Share Books With Infants and Toddlers

The effects of book reading with infants and toddlers remain unclear. Although research findings are in line with the assumption that book reading is a precursor to literacy, whether or not book reading is actually a necessary ingredient of young children's daily experiences is still a matter of debate. A meta-analysis of 29 studies compared children who were read to *more* with children who were read to *less* (Bus et al., 1995). Results indicated a rather modest correlation between early storybook reading and later literacy ($r = .28$). However, the effect that book reading has in terms of predicting reading accomplishment in school-age children is sizable (Bus & van IJzendoorn, 2004). Figure 6.1 shows the extent to which prediction is enhanced as a result of the intervention (i.e., the percentage increase in prediction) with the use of intervention X (being read to in preschool age) to predict reading skill Y (reading accomplishment in school age). As shown in Figure 6.1, this correlation indicates that 64% of the more-read-to children would be successful in learning to read, whereas the success ratio in the less-read-to group would be 36%.

Figure 6.1. Predictive effects of book reading according to a meta-analysis including 29 studies and 2,248 participants.

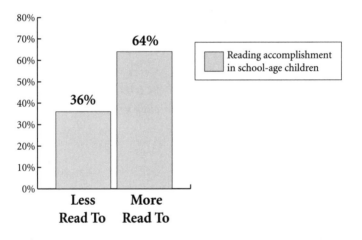

From Bus, van IJzendoorn, and Pellegrini (1995), "Joint Book Reading Makes for Success in Learning to Read. A Meta-Analysis on Intergenerational Transmission of Literacy."

It should be noted, therefore, that book sharing from a young age certainly can make a tremendous difference in the lives of young children. The difference in book-reading experiences would amount to a substantial difference in success rate in reading if we translate the outcome of the synthesis of research to the thousands of children who may profit from book reading. In a small country such as the Netherlands with about 17 million inhabitants, an estimated

100,000 children in the age range of 2 to 5 years are at serious risk for developing language and literacy problems.[1] Combining these data with the results of the synthesis of research, we estimate that 64,000 children (64% of the 2- to 5-year-old children at risk) run the risk of developing reading problems if they do not receive intervention to promote book reading in home or child care; with interventions that stimulate the frequency of book reading, the number of children at risk would decrease to 36,000 (36%).

Conclusion

Clearly, infants and toddlers develop many early literacy behaviors as early as the first year of life. Even before they learn to talk, infants shift gradually from acting on books as objects toward taking an interest in the book's content. They begin to point and to recognize protosymbols (illustrations) while looking at books. All these behaviors occur within the context of a social interaction with a caregiver.

A child's interest in a book's content reflects her early experiences and joint engagement with adults and books. Indeed, there is support for the assumption that infants' and toddlers' interest in books emerges from early interactions in which adults reciprocally share books with them rather than communicate messages unidirectionally. The important adult skill of book sharing requires the caregiver to be able to create a close and intimate atmosphere in which this kind of reading can occur. Indeed, shared book reading speaks of love and parental commitment (Whitehurst & Lonigan, 1998).

The data presented here provide clear indication for sensitive and well-placed family literacy interventions. Cultural and social variables influence the quality and frequency of book reading. When reading is not a source of enjoyment for parents and when parents are not used to reading books to children, then parents may need support in selecting appropriate books and in sharing those books with young children (cf. Neuman, 1997). Successfully stimulating young children's interest in books in the early stages of reading development strongly depends on the quality of caregiver–child interaction. Some family members and caregivers may also need long-term support in selecting appropriate books and in scaffolding interactions. Providing this kind of support is worthwhile

[1] Numbers provided by the Dutch Department of Education (www.minocw.nl/vve).

and important because, although no causal relationship has been established between shared book reading with infants and toddlers and reading success in school, the data clearly show that children who have more exposure to books before entering school are more likely to have successful reading accomplishments in school than those who have less exposure to books (see Figure 6.1).

References

Ainsworth, M. D. S., Blehar, M. C., Waters, E., & Wall, S. (1978). *Patterns of attachment: A psychological study of the Strange Situation.* Hillsdale, NJ: Erlbaum.

Bus, A. G. (2001). Early book reading experience in the family: A route to literacy. In S. Neuman & D. Dickinson (Eds.), *Handbook of research in early literacy* (pp. 179–191). New York: Guilford Press.

Bus, A. G. (2003). Social-emotional requisites for learning to read. In A. van Kleeck, S. A. Stahl, & E. B. Bauer (Eds.), *On reading books to children: Parents and teachers* (pp. 3–15). Mahwah, NJ: Erlbaum.

Bus, A. G., Belsky, J., van IJzendoorn, M. H., & Crnik, K. (1997). Attachment and book reading patterns: A study of mothers, fathers, and their toddlers. *Early Childhood Research Quarterly, 12,* 81–98.

Bus, A. G., & Sulzby, E. (1996). Becoming literate in a multicultural society. In J. Shimron (Ed.), *Literacy and education* (pp. 17–32). Cresskill, NJ: Hampton Press.

Bus, A. G., & van IJzendoorn, M. H. (1997). Affective dimension of mother-infant picturebook reading. *Journal of School Psychology, 35,* 47–60.

Bus, A. G., & van IJzendoorn, M. H. (2004). Meta-analysis in reading research. In N. K. Duke & M. H. Mallette (Eds.), *Literacy research methodologies* (227–251). New York: Guilford Press.

Bus, A. G., van IJzendoorn, M. H., & Pellegrini, A. D. (1995). Joint book reading makes for success in learning to read. A meta-analysis on intergenerational transmission of literacy. *Review of Educational Research, 65,* 1–21.

Cornell, E. H., Sénéchal, M., & Broda, L. S. (1988). Recall of picture books by 3-year-old children: Testing and repetition effects in joint reading activities. *Journal of Educational Psychology, 80,* 537–542.

Cunningham, A. E., & Stanovich, K. E. (1990). Tracking the unique effects of print exposure in children: Associations with vocabulary, general knowledge, and spelling. *Journal of Educational Psychology, 83,* 264–274.

De Groot, I. M., & Bus, A. G. (1995). *Boekenpret voor baby's. Ervaringen met het opgroeiboek* [Book-fun for babies. Final report on a project to stimulate emergent literacy.] Leiden/The Hague: Leiden University/Sardes.

DeLoache, J. S., & DeMendoza, O. A. P. (1987). Joint picturebook interactions of mothers and one-year-old children. *British Journal of Developmental Psychology, 5,* 111–123.

Hayes, D. P., & Ahrens, M. G. (1988). Vocabulary simplification for children: A special case of "motherese." *Journal of Child Language, 15,* 395–410.

Jones, R. (1996). *Emerging patterns of literacy. A multi-disciplinary perspective.* London: Routledge.

Jones, W., & Lorenzo-Hubert, I. (2006). Culture and parental expectations for child development: Concerns for language development and early learning. In S. E. Rosenkoetter & J. Knapp-Philo (Eds.), *Learning to read the world: Language and literacy in the first three years* (pp. 187–214). Washington, DC: ZERO TO THREE Press.

Laakso, M. L. (1999). *Prelinguistic skills and early interactional context as predictors of children's language development.* Unpublished doctoral dissertation, University of Jyväskylä, Finland.

Laakso, M. L., Poikkeus, A. -M., & Lyytinen, P. (1997, April). *The role of parent-child interaction in the early development of children's cognitive and linguistic skills.* Paper presented at the biennial meeting of the Society for Research in Child Development, Washington, DC.

Lyytinen, P., Laakso, M. -L., & Poikkeus, A. -M. (1998). Parental contribution to child's early language and interest in books. *European Journal of Psychology of Education, 13,* 297–308.

Martin, L. E., & Reutzel, D. R. (1999). Sharing books: Examining how and why mothers deviate from the print. *Reading Research and Instruction, 39,* 39–70.

Murphy, C. M. (1978). Pointing in the context of a shared activity. *Child Development, 49,* 371–390.

Neuman, S. B. (1997). Children engaging in storybook reading: The influence of access to print resources, opportunity, and parental interaction. *Early Childhood Research Quarterly, 11,* 495–514.

Ninio, A., & Bruner, J. S. (1976). The achievement and antecedents of labeling. *Journal of Child Language, 5,* 1–15.

Scarborough, H. S., Dobrich, W., & Hager, M. (1991). Preschool literacy experience and later reading achievement. *Journal of Learning Disabilities, 24,* 508–511.

Serpell, R. (1997). Literacy connections between school and home: How should we evaluate them? *Journal of Literacy Research, 29,* 587–616.

Sonnenschein, S., Baker, L., Serpell, R., Scher, D., Fernandez-Fein, S., & Munsterman, K. (1996). *Strands of emergent literacy and their antecedents in the home: Urban preschoolers' early literacy development* (Reading Research Rep. No. 48). Athens, GA: National Reading Research Center.

van Kleeck, A. (2003). Research on book sharing: Another critical look. In A. van Kleeck, S. A. Stahl, & E. B. Bauer (Eds.), *On reading books to children. Parents and teachers* (pp. 271–320). Mahwah, NJ: Erlbaum.

van Kleeck, A., Alexander, E. I., Vigil, A., & Templeton, D. E. (1996). Verbally modeling thinking for infants: Middle-class mothers' presentation of information structures during book sharing. *Journal of Research in Childhood Education, 10,* 101–113.

Waddell, M., & Firth, B. (1992). *Sam Vole and his brothers.* Cambridge, UK: Camblewick Press.

Werner, H., & Kaplan, B. (1963). *Symbol formation. An organismic-developmental approach to language and the expression of thought.* New York: Wiley.

Whitehurst, G. J., Falco, F. L., Lonigan, C., Fischel, J. E., DeBaryshe, B. D., Valdez-Menchaca, M. C., & Caulfiels, M. (1988). Accelerating language development through picture-book reading. *Developmental Psychology, 24,* 552–558.

Whitehurst, G. J., & Lonigan, C. J. (1998). Child development and emergent literacy. *Child Development, 69,* 848–872.

CHAPTER 7

Sound Steps in Phonological Form for Later Literacy

Peg Griffin

When babies coo and babble, grown-ups are enchanted. We make eye contact, stroke the babies, lift them up, and hug, kiss, and cuddle them. We respond vocally, too. We match the baby's "naanaanaa" with a "naanaanaa" or rhyme it with "baabaabaa." It makes our day when the baby matches or rhymes back. These conversations can last for quite some time. They can be the main focus of the interaction or just a way to pass the time of day while diapers are changed or little fingers are washed, a baby version of cocktail party chatter or clichés about the weather.

Adults can start these word defying sessions. "I love you, boo" can lead to a stream of "you boo doo boo" and so on. Sometimes real words are used but without regard for the meaning. For instance, a toddler may fill in the blank when a grown-up recites for the umpteenth time "Jack and Jill went up the hill. Jack fell down and broke his _____," even though neither grown-up nor child knows what the anticipated word *crown* means in the nursery rhyme. The chant "marezy dotes and doughzy dotes" is another example: Many a 10-year-old, familiar with the rhyme since infancy, is surprised to find that there are sensible sentences in it: "Mares eat oats and does eat oats, and little lambs eat ivy. A kid'll eat ivy, too, wouldn't you?" We laugh about the way children supply words that match the rhyme and rhythm of a piece even though the original words and meaning disappear: "where the great giraffes are stored," for "where the grapes of wrath are stored"; "a desk full of daisies" for "Adeste Fidelis"; "with liver tea and just us for all" for "with liberty and justice for all"; and "Jose, can you see" for "oh, say, can you see."

In babbling games, it does not matter what "naanaa" means; it is the form of the utterance that matters. Later, the same form may be a meaningful word: One child may use "naanaa" for "banana" while another means "grandmother" when he says it. In our society, many a family has some special baby word that becomes a part of family lore. Brennan, at about 9 months, filled gaps after an adult comment with a sound between "ooee" and "why." Grown-ups could not resist answering with "because" clauses, then Brennan would again say "ooee/why?" and so on. The baby was credited with being curious and an indefatigable conversationalist.

The development of language with meaningful words is very important and central to the other chapters in this book. Infants and toddlers who are growing in language and literacy communicate about the world and share perceptions, feelings, and ideas. Language functions to establish and maintain relations, working out the turntaking and joint attention that lead to ever more sophisticated language meanings and functions. The early "naanaa" episodes perform some of those functions, but they also highlight the *form* of language over word meaning.

Language form is important to the independent and accomplished use of written language. Written language expresses meaning *indirectly*; that is, reading and writing go through spoken language to get at meaning. The smallest unit of form in written language is easy to see, touch, even to put on the refrigerator as a magnet: For written English, those units are the 26 letters from the Latin alphabet. The smallest unit of form in spoken language, however, the one that links to letters, is not so tangible: For American English, the linked sounds are 40 or more small units called *phonemes*. This chapter is about (a) phonology—the language subsystem in which phonemes operate, (b) phonemic awareness in literacy development, (c) the limited knowledge base about developing children's phonological awareness, and (d) relevant activities that can be done with infants and toddlers.

Phonology: Units and Uses of Sounds

Phonology is one of several systems of language structure or form. It has to do with the sounds of the language. (Note the same root word as in "tele*phone*" and "*phon*ograph.") Other language systems are morphology and syntax (commonly thought of as grammar) and semantics and pragmatics (issues of meaning and use). As they develop language, children gain receptive and productive control of these systems, working within them to understand others and express themselves. To do this, children need not be knowledgeable about or even aware of the units and rules of language systems, but they must develop deep enough knowledge so brand new utterances can be understood and produced. (For views of language development, see Barton & Brophy-Herb, this volume, p. 15; Ninio & Snow, 1996; Pierce, this volume, p. 335; Pinker, 1999; Tomasello & Bates, 2001.)

Research on the development of sounds has revealed both broad common patterns and significant individual differences (see, for example, Bates, Thal, Finlay, & Clancy, in press; MacWhinney, 1999). Vocalizations in the first 2 months reflect the baby's physical needs. Caregivers in our society interpret and respond to the sounds, weaving them into the pragmatics of the language. By the third month, babies coo, especially when adults coo back. Children begin with vowels or simple consonant and vowel strings (such as *coo*), even using sounds that do not occur in the language used around them. Between 6 and 8 months, babbling (long sequences of repeated consonants and vowels such as *naanaanaa*) begins and continues for some time unless severe neglect occurs in which adults do not respond. At about 9 months, a baby's babbling starts to favor sounds found in the language used around the baby. In the next few years, children acquire the essence of the phonology—the sound system—of their native language. Some phonemes and phonological patterns are likely to be still developing when children begin kindergarten, but the bulk of phonology is in place by the time children are 3 years old.

Phonemes (pronounced to rhyme with *lone teams*) are the basic units of phonology. Phonemes make words different from one another, but they do not make up the meaning of words, just the sound form. A substitution of one phoneme turns *cat* into *hat*, and a change in the order of the phonemes turns *cats* into *scat*. A word such as *six* is written as /sIks/[1] in studies of the sounds, the phonology of the word. A phoneme can be described as a sound wave in the air or movements in the mouth, throat, and nose, but its real identity is found in the phonological system, a matter of contrasts. For example, a /p/ is not /b/, not /m/, not /k/, not /I/, and so on—not any of the other 40 or so phonemes of English. What makes a /p/ in English is different than what makes

---

[1] Slashes are used to set off transcriptions that linguists use for phonemes as they study spoken language.

a /p/ in Korean. Phonemes are defined the way a concept like "middle child" is: It depends on the structure of the whole family.

Finding phonemes in isolation is not necessary during everyday speaking and listening. Indeed, phonemes are hard to isolate. Syllables are more accessible sound units than phonemes. Machine analysis of sound waves shows syllable boundaries, but not phoneme boundaries, within a syllable. When we try to produce a phoneme like /k/ in isolation, we usually unknowingly add an extra phoneme, a vowel like the one in *cut*. It is not hard to say the syllable *cut*, just difficult to say some of the phonemes separately. But separate phonemes are important for the written forms of some languages—English, for example.

A Caution About Phonology

Related to phonology, a strong warning must be issued about dialect differences in American English. This writer, from working class southeastern New England, does not pronounce *dog* and *frog* as if they rhyme. *Log* and *frog* rhyme in my dialect, but not *dog*. I also recognize that *history* and *ham* are alliterative (have the same initial phoneme), but that *human* is not like those words and instead starts like the word *you*. In addition, unlike friends from California, I use different vowel phonemes in *don* and *dawn*. Some people use the the same vowel phonemes in all of the following words whereas they each are distinct in my dialect: *merry, Mary, marry, Murray*. Dialects vary by region of the country, by urban–rural distinctions, and by social groupings based on characteristics such as ethnicity, socioeconomic status, and gender. The pronunciation of a word in one dialect can be misunderstood as a different word in another: One person's "cod" may be heard as another's "cad," "balance" as "bounce," and "jail" as "gel." For some who are influential in our society, the word "nuclear" has a "cue" in the middle, and for others it is merely a combination of "new" and "clear." Each dialect system is as sophisticated, complete, and developed as another. In our country we have no King and no King's English (Strickland, Snow, Griffin, Burns, & MacNamara, 2002, pp. 90–91). Materials, professional development experiences, and parent information concerning phonological awareness make little sense—and can do harm—if they are not responsive to dialect differences in the community of practice.

Integrated Support for Becoming a Skilled Reader[2]

Reading and writing are soundless activities; we have a special expression "read aloud" for occasions when we add sounds. But, sounds—phonology—are involved whenever written language is used; attention to how phonology is involved in reading is a part of preparing children for membership in our literate society. There is a good deal of agreement about how children become skilled readers (e.g., Ehri & Snowling, in press; Kamil, Mosenthal, Pearson, & Barr, 2000; National Reading Panel, 2000; Snow, Burns, & Griffin, 1998). There are some disagreements about research methods and implementation, often overplayed in politics and policy. (See efforts to mitigate this disagreement, as in Camilli, Vargas, & Yurecko, 2003.)

Researchers usually study one of the three aspects of skilled reading—identifying printed words, constructing meaning, or developing fluency—but they agree that focusing on any one of these exclusively is not sufficient to develop reading expertise. Publications for practice and policy audiences (Burns, Snow, & Griffin, 1999; Strickland et al., 2002) have emphasized the integration of the three aspects of skilled reading. These works use a pillar as metaphor rather than, say, a tripod because, like rings used for betrothal and marriage, a pillar emphasizes the united, seamless functioning of the different aspects of becoming a reader (see Figure 7.1).

The foundation of the pillar is most important for the youngest children. (See the articles in Dickinson & Tabors, 2001, for elaboration.) The first line on it describes familiar activities: conversations, play, being read to, and trying to write. The second line refers to the mental outcomes of a child's participation in our literate society: print concepts, letter knowledge, and motivation to read. The third line describes the range of literacy genres and uses that children meet and master: narrative for stories, both fiction and true reports; expository for lists, procedures, and explanations; and, of course, poetry in speech and song. Elsewhere and in other chapters of this book these matters are explored in detail. The less familiar terms in the last line of the foundation—phonemic and phonological awareness—are the focus in this chapter.

---

[2] For background and details about this section, see Snow, Burns, & Griffin, (1998); Burns, Snow, & Griffin. (1999); Strickland et al. (2002).

Figure 7.1. Supported Skilled Reading

SUPPORTED SKILLED READING

Developing Fluency
Speedy, accurate, and coordinated
word identification and comprehension

Identifying Printed Words
Sound and spelling patterns;
(Alphabetic principle/phonics);
Automaticity;
Sight word repertoire

Constructing Meaning
Conceptual knowledge (background);
Vocabulary depth and breadth;
Comprehension strategy use;
Specific forms and domains

Foundations
Conversations, play, being read to, trying to write;
Print concepts, letter knowledge, motivation to read;
Explore purpose and form (narrative, expository, poetry);
Language Development, including phonemic and phonological awareness

Source: From *Preparing Our Teachers: Opportunities for Better Reading Instruction*, by
D. Strickland, C. E. Snow, P. Griffin, M. S. Burns, and P. MacNamara, 2002. Washington, DC:
National Academies Press. Copyright 2002 by the Publisher. Reprinted with permission.

Phonology and Written Language

Not every meaningful thing produced on paper, generated on computer screen,
carved in clay, or painted on walls is written language, of course. There are also
drawings and notational systems. In a drawing, one might figure out that # # #
stands for *six*; in mathematics notation, there are numerals and operation
signs and conventions for combining them. For writing, a word like *six* represents the spoken word /sIks/; the reader and writer rely on shared convention
to link the grapheme *s* (written) with the phoneme /s/ (pronounced), the
grapheme *i* with the phoneme /I/, and the grapheme *x* with the two phonemes
/k/ and /s/. The reader uses the graphemes, the spoken word, and a good deal of
background knowledge to work out the intention of the writer, the meaning of
the written piece.

English written language is organized around the alphabetic principle. It links units of phonology, called phonemes, with units of orthography, called graphemes or letters. Writing in many languages is governed by the alphabetic principle. Some languages such as Spanish use the same alphabet that English does; others such as Russian and Vietnamese use different alphabets. The symbols for some written languages represent whole syllables, not just phonemes (for example, the kana that is part of Japanese writing). Still other writing systems link units of morphology (for example, words) to logographic symbols.

Grapheme–phoneme conventions (GPCs) are not just one-to-one links. The *x* in *six* links to more than one phoneme; the word /sɪk/, with three phonemes, is written as *sick*, with four graphemes. Any GPC, by definition, applies in many words, but the conventions can be conditional. The grapheme *ck* is used for /k/ at the end but not the beginning of a syllable, and the grapheme *c* stands for /s/ or for /k/ depending on which vowel follows. Some GPCs are discontinuous; for example, long vowels (diphthongs) in words such as *take* or *kite* use two graphemes separated by an intervening consonant.

When kindergartners or first graders learn to apply GPCs and blend the resulting phonemes into words, we say they are "sounding out" words. Instruction about GPCs and how to blend them is called *phonics*. Success in phonics lessons depends on the ability to recognize and discriminate among the 26 letters, but success also requires surmounting less obvious hurdles. One involves *phonemic awareness*, a term that is widely used nowadays but sometimes in misleading ways.

Metacognition, Phonological Awareness, and Phonemic Awareness

Metacognition means thinking about thinking—about mental objects and processes. The term is familiar from discussions of strategies for comprehension of spoken and written language. Metacognitive monitoring of a passage being read, for example, can reveal misunderstandings and invoke re-reading to solve the problem that has been noticed. Table 7.1 presents examples of metacognition focused on different subsystems of language.

Table 7.1. Examples of Metacognition

Example	Alternate	Language System	Metacognitive Note
Ma bought the house	Irene Griffin bought the house	Pragmatics	Change reference term outside of informal family settings.
John walked home	John trudged home	Semantics	Imply *walk* but refer to mental state as well as action details.
He might do	He might or He might do it	Syntax	Switch from British to American English ellipsis for a proposition like "He might run the marathon."
Teach	Teacher	Morphology	Derive noun from verb with *er* suffix.

Phonological awareness means metacognition within the phonological system. Some types of phonological awareness cover units larger than words, including intonation contours; emphatic stress; and word, phrase, and clause boundaries. For example, jokes about "paper view TV" play with phonologcal awareness ranging over the phrase "pay per view."

Other types of phonological awareness operate within a word. Word-level phonological units include syllables, onsets, rimes, and the phonemes discussed above. Syllables are familiar units. *Sick* has one syllable; *sickly* has two. Onsets and rimes are units within syllables. The onset is the sound before the vowel (/s/ in /sIk/ and /st/ in /stIk/), while the rime starts at the vowel nucleus and goes to the syllable end (/Ik/ in /stIk/ or /sIk/ and in /Ilk/ in /sIlk/).

Phonemic awareness is metacognitive control over phonemes. Anyone who speaks and listens knows how to use phonemes. But, not everyone knows about phonemes enough to identify them or manipulate them. If they do, they are phonemically aware. Phonemic awareness is the only kind of phonological awareness tied to GPCs and the alphabetic principle. Phonemic awareness and reading influence each other: They have a reciprocal relation. Phonemic awareness of spoken words brings what is well known from everyday speaking and listening into service for the new challenges of reading and writing when children get to kindergarten and first grade. Reciprocally, learning to read brings more phonemic awareness.

Individual differences in phonological awareness have been related to the rate of acquisition of reading, regardless of a child's intelligence, receptive vocabulary, memory skills, or home and school background. Phonological awareness is an important part of the widely accepted model (Share, 1999) developed to explain how children self-teach the many words that are never "covered" in a reading syllabus. Phonemic awareness improvement, namely, attention to individual sounds, appears to matter most between kindergarten entry and second grade.

Phonological awareness at the onset-rime level is particularly intriguing for those who work with infants and toddlers. The rime is what matches in rhyming words, which are a big part of daily life with very young children in songs, poems, nursery rhymes, books, and play with rhyming syllables that may or may not be actual words. More experience with rhymes appears to be related to success with some phonological awareness tasks and with learning to read (Bradley & Bryant, 1985; Bryant, Bradley, MacLean, & Crossland, 1989; Bryant, MacLean, Bradley, & Crossland, 1990; Goswami & East, 2000). Phonological awareness of onsets and rimes plays a part in reading by analogy and instruction that uses word families (e.g., *pan, man, fan*), but there is current controversy about the role of analogy in early reading (Bryant, 1998; Hulme, Muter, & Snowling, 1998; Macmillan, 2002; Muter, Hulme, Snowling, & Taylor, 1997; Walton & Walton, 2002). Questions about analogy and rimes for 5- and 6-year-olds and other controversies about metacognition and phological awareness are important for professionals working with infants and toddlers because of consequences for understanding and enacting practices like reciting and playing with nursery rhymes.

Phonological Awareness Development in Young Children?

Oddly enough, given the recent popularity of calls for improving phonemic awareness, little definitive information exists about the origin and growth of phonological awareness. Studies of phonological development do not extend to phonological awareness. A review of emergent literacy studies (Whitehurst & Lonigan, 1998) points out that little is known about the origins of phonological awareness except that experiences like storybook reading, which support language and cognitive growth in general, do not appear to contribute to phonological awareness (see also Sénéchal, LeFevre, Thomas, & Daley, 1998). It appears that some aspects of phonemic awareness may be accessible to children before other aspects: alliteration (identifying or manipulating initial sounds) before rhyme and single consonant onsets before consonant clusters. There is, however, no evidence that competence with one aspect is a necessary precursor of any other or that one is a key to phonemic awareness in general.

It is not unusual for misconceptions to accrue when definitive information is not available. There are at least four issues that those dealing with very young children should be careful about. First, auditory discrimination and speech perception are not the same as phonological awareness. Auditory discrimination or speech perception may be assessed when a child is asked whether *pig* and *peg* sound the same. Such tasks do not call for phonemic or phonological awareness, though. Children who perform poorly on these tasks may have problems with speech perception, which may contribute to later difficulty with phonological awareness. Performing well on these tasks, however, does not guarantee phonological awareness. Like anyone else, children use phonology to tell that words are different without being aware of the phoneme that makes the difference or being able to manipulate it on demand and apart from attention to units of meaning. Phonology is one of the many things we can use without being explicitly aware of it: Who can say what goes into a simple action like walking, for instance?

Second, for many reasons, those dealing with infants and toddlers need to consider the languages children use at home. Phonological awareness is no exception. Studies suggest that specific characteristics of the language children are exposed to have an effect not only on the child's phonology but also on performance on certain types of phonological awareness tasks. See, for example, Silvén, Niemi, and Voeten (2002) about Finnish and Silva and Alves-Marins (2002) about Portuguese. Hence, special care must be taken when drawing conclusions about the phonological awareness of children who are learning English as a second or third language.

Third, there is no evidence that it is necessary for a child to master all types of tasks nor to practice on all the phonemes of a language before reading lessons begin. Appeals to begin very early in the child's life to cover all the territory are not warranted. On the other hand, it does not appear that phonological awareness is an all or nothing phenomenon, so one "ah-hah" is not necessarily enough; that is, a child may be aware of syllables but not onset phonemes, of initial phonemes but not final ones, of initial consonants but not if they are a part of a consonant cluster.

Fourth, some writers hint that phonemic awareness can be developed by practicing with units of decreasing size. They begin with a sentence divided in word parts, then parts of a compound word (e.g., cowboy), then syllables in a word (e.g., el-e-phant), then onset and rimes in a syllable (e.g., s-in), and finally phonemes (e.g., /s/ /I/ /n/). Sometimes the suggestion is that work on segmenting large-size units (e.g., sentences broken into words, compound words, words into syllables) had best begin even before children are 3 years old. Work with these larger units may be helpful for communicating what is required in tasks. It has not been shown, however, that phonemic awareness grows from prior work with larger phonological units. This lack of evidence is probably not an accident awaiting more research. Units of meaning are highlighted in tasks with sentences and compound words. Even syllable tasks often involve divisions between meaningful roots and suffixes, as in words like *hopeful* and *undo*. As children work with the larger units, they may well rely on meaning rather than the sound form and so miss the real point of phonological awareness. Only tasks concerning within-syllable units (onset, rime, or phoneme) require that sound be dealt with apart from meaning. Starting with large-sized units is unlikely to be a key to the growth of phonological awareness.

Four Promising Activities to Encourage the Development of Phonological Awareness

There is no doubt that the links between early language and early literacy involve all the subsystems of language (Chaney, 1992; Snow, 1991). However, few specific studies have been done to explore precursors to phonological awareness. Research suggests, though, that four topics hold promise about what might be good to do with babies to foster later phonological awareness: vocabulary, caregiver sensitivity, epilinguistic patterns, and sound play.

First, as a toddler's vocabulary grows, the structure in memory for the words he or she knows undergoes a transformation (Jusczyk, 1997; Metsala & Walley, 1998; Plaut & Kello, 1999). The mental representation for old words comes to be subdivided into smaller connected units as new words are learned; relations among words in the growing vocabulary, then, are relations among these smaller units. Sound similarities and differences, even at the phonemic unit level, are prominent. This focus suggests that one route to phonological awareness is by way of vocabulary growth. In fact, a recent longitudinal study in Finland shows just such a route: Vocabulary size at the age of 1 year predicts phonological awareness at 3 years (Silvén et al., 2002). Whatever promotes vocabulary growth may well have a side effect on phonological awareness. Thus, there is another reason for undertaking the kinds of conversations, active experiences, and book reading that support a baby's vocabulary growth!

Second, caregiver conversational input has been mentioned as a possible con-tributor to the growth of phonological awareness (Caravolas & Bruck, 1993; Whitehurst, 1996). Even though storybook reading does not appear to promote phonological awareness, there is some evidence that use of alphabet books (Murray, Stahl, & Ivey, 1996) and the sheer amount of caregiver engagement in literacy activities (Lonigan, Dyer, & Anthony, 1996) do have an effect on a child's phonological awareness. The longitudinal study from Finland that indicates the vocabulary route to phonological awareness also shows a comple-mentary route through caregiver sensitivity in verbal interactions during play with objects: Mothers who are more attuned to their baby's interests, more able to regulate and sustain the baby's attention, and more prone to support gradu-ally more independent play at the age of 1 and 2 years have an effect on the phonological awareness that children show at the age of 3 and 4 years (Silvén et al., 2002). Once again, the call is for conversations, engagement, and sensitive caregiver–baby interactions during play.

The third potential contributor to developing phonological awareness is the epilinguistic patterning of the language. As people speak and listen, the implicit patterns of language systems, including phonology, are shown. This is called *epilinguistics*. It takes a wide expanse of time and many diverse situations to reveal some epilinguistic patterns—like the structure and meaning of subjunc-tives in English. Phonological patterns within syllables, though, are displayed in even short snatches of discourse. Children show sensitivity to the epilinguistic patterning of onsets, rimes, and phonemes (see also Gombert, 1992; Goswami, 1999). *Phonological sensitivity* is shown and exercised as children remember better when the items in a list rhyme or are alliterative and when they find it easy to fill in the rhyming blank in a couplet or to add new items to a chain of alliterations. At the same time, though, they might not be able to say what part of a word rhymes or to substitute a word's onset with a different one.

Phonological sensitivity is like phonological awareness in that the child separates sound and meaning. Unlike awareness, though, sensitivity does not imply an ability to control performance on tasks like segmenting and blending the sounds in a word. It appears that more experience with the epilinguistic phonological patterns of a language promotes phonological sensitivity (Bryant et al., 1989) and that such growth is yet another route to phonological awareness. By the time they are 3 years old, many children have begun to develop enjoyment and expertise with cultural artifacts that highlight phonological patterns: songs, chants, nursery rhymes, poems, and finger plays. Adults, then, may help to promote phonological awareness as they sing and speak the children's favorite rhymes, as they help them learn new ones, and as they call attention to rhymes and alliteration in books they read aloud to the children.

Fourth, play with sounds is the final topic to explore in the search for origins of phonological awareness. Cooing and babbling have characteristics of play; they are voluntary, self-initiated, not instrumental to a specific goal, and pleasurable. Different types of language play, including sound play, have been identified (Cook, 2000; Garvey, 1977), but research has not been undertaken to show that any of these activities contributes to the development of phonological awareness. Ongoing research on language and literacy development during or through play is often in the Vygotskian tradition, focusing on the conditions and consequences of symbolic dramatic play (Vygotsky, 1978).

We do know, however, that babies can engage in some kinds of joint sound play with adults. Turntaking and some imitation occur early and, by approximately 9 months, babies begin to match adults' new vocalizations and gestures, such as "bye-bye." Caregivers' comments that are sensitive to the child's focus of attention sustain a 9-month-old's engagement, but coordinated joint attention to a third entity (like a toy) is not yet typical at 9 months. Sound play gets around the problem. It collapses two otherwise separate focal points: whom to coordinate with and what to coordinate about. For sound play, the play partner to coordinate with is also the source of the play object; that is, the play partner makes the sounds. (For more on joint activity with babies, see Bergen & Mauer, 2000; Carpenter, Nagell, & Tomasello, 1998; Moore, 1998; Ninio & Snow, 1996; Rollins & Snow, 1998.) One-year-olds have been observed to enjoy joint sound play, whether child or adult initiated. Two-and-a-half-year-olds play with sounds when they are alone and waiting for sleep (Weir, 1962), and 3- and 4-year-olds respond to prompts to sound play in a test situation (Chaney, 1992).

Sound play may turn out to be a long-lasting part of the adult–child repertoire for promoting later phonological awareness. To start, sound play helps the child to elaborate on some of the songs and rhymes that highlight epilinguistic patterning. "Willoughby, wallaby wonnie, an elephant sat on Bonnie" from Raffi's CD (1997) can lead a child to more play with rhyme and alliteration, drawing attention to the sounds that make up the child's own name and the names of objects in everyday life. It is a chance for Moesha to be Woesha, for a chair to be a ware, and a table to be a wable. Sound play provides the combination of familiar and novel that makes play safe but exciting. As everyone knows, children initiate repeated practice on these sorts of tasks, even when adults would rather they stop!

These are the four activities that may pave the way for later phonemic awareness: conversations to support vocabulary growth, sensitive caregiver interactions, efforts to develop sensitivity to epilinguistic sound patterns, and sound play. No experiments have been run to show that increasing attention to these matters paves the way for developing phonemic awareness. Nevertheless, while waiting for well-proven theories about the origins and growth of phonological awareness, we at least know that these activities are fun both for children and for their favorite adults.

References

Barton, L. R., & Brophy-Herb, H. E. (2006). Developmental foundations for language and literacy from birth to three years. In S. E. Rosenkoetter & J. Knapp-Philo (Eds.), *Learning to read the world: Language and literacy in the first three years* (pp. 15–60). Washington, DC: ZERO TO THREE Press.

Bates, E., Thal, D., Finlay, B., & Clancy, B. (in press). Early language development and its neural correlates. In F. Boller & J. Grafman (Series Eds.) & I. Rapin & S. Segalowitz (Vol. Eds.), *Handbook of neuropsychology, Volume 7. Child neurology* (2nd ed.). Amsterdam: Elsevier.

Bergen, D., & Mauer, D. (2000). Symbolic play, phonological awareness, and literacy skills at three age levels. In K. A. Roskos & J. F. Christie (Eds.), *Play and literacy in early childhood* (pp. 45–62). Mahwah, NJ: Erlbaum.

Bradley, L., & Bryant, P. (1985). Rhyme and reason in reading and spelling. Ann Arbor: University of Michigan Press.

Bryant, P. (1998). Sensitivity to onset and rhyme does predict young children's reading: A comment on Muter, Hulme, Snowling and Taylor (1997). *Journal of Experimental Child Psychology, 71*, 29–37.

Bryant, P., Bradley, L., MacLean, M., & Crossland, J. (1989). Nursery rhymes, phonological skills and reading. *Journal of Child Language, 16*, 407–428.

Bryant, P., MacLean, M., Bradley, L., & Crossland, J. (1990). Rhyme and alliteration, phoneme detection, and learning to read. *Developmental Psychology, 26*, 429–438.

Burns, M. S., Snow, C. E., & Griffin, P. (Eds.). (1999). *Starting out right: A guide to promoting children's reading success.* Washington DC: National Academy Press.

Camilli, G., Vargas, S., & Yurecko, M. (2003). Teaching children to read: The fragile link between science and federal education policy. *Education Policy Analysis Archives, 11*, 15. Available online: http://epaa.asu.edu/epaa/v11n15

Caravolas, M., & Bruck, M. (1993). The effect of oral and written language input on children's phonological awareness: A cross-linguistic study. *Journal of Experimental Child Psychology, 55*, 1–30.

Carpenter, M., Nagell, K., & Tomasello, M. (1998). Social cognition, joint attention, and communicative competence from 9–15 months. *Monographs of the Society for Research in Child Development, 63*.

Chaney, C. (1992). Language development, metalinguistic skills, and print awareness in 3-year-old children. *Applied Psycholinguistics, 13*, 485–514.

Cook, G. (2000). *Language play, language learning.* Oxford, UK: Oxford University Press.

Dickinson, D. K., & Tabors, P. O. (Eds.). (2001). *Beginning literacy with language: Young children learning at home and in school.* Baltimore: Paul H. Brookes.

Ehri, L., & Snowling, M. (in press). Developmental variation in word recognition. In B. Shulman, K. Apel, B. Ehren, E. Silliman, & C. Stone (Eds.), *Handbook of language and literacy development and disorders.* New York: Guilford.

Garvey, C. (1977). Play with language and speech. In C. Mitchell-Kernan & S. Ervin-Tripp (Eds.), *Child discourse* (pp. 27–47). New York: Academic Press.

Gombert, J. E. (1992). *Metalinguistic development.* London: Harvester Wheatsheaf.

Goswami, U. (1999). Phonological development and reading by analogy: Epilinguistic and metalinguistic issues. In J. Oakhill & R. Beard (Eds.), *Reading development and the teaching of reading: A psychological perspective* (pp. 174–200). Malden, MA: Blackwell.

Goswami, U., & East, M. (2000). Rhyme and analogy in beginning reading: Conceptual and methodological issues. *Applied Psycholinguistics, 21,* 63–93.

Hulme, C., Muter, V., & Snowling, M. J. (1998). Segmentation does predict early progress in learning to read better than rhyme: A reply to Bryant. *Journal of Experimental Child Psychology, 71,* 39–44.

Jusczyk, P. W. (1997). *The discovery of spoken language.* Cambridge, MA: MIT Press.

Kamil, M. L., Mosenthal, P. B., Pearson, P. D., & Barr, R. (Eds.). (2000). *Handbook of reading research: Volume III.* Mahwah, NJ: Erlbaum.

Lonigan, C. J., Dyer, S. M., & Anthony, J. L. (1996, April). *The influence of the home literacy environment on the development of literacy skills in children from diverse racial and economic backgrounds.* Paper presented at the annual convention of the American Educational Research Association, New York.

Macmillan, B. M. (2002). Rhyme and reading: A critical review of the research methodology. *Journal of Research in Reading, 25*(1), 4–42.

MacWhinney, B. (Ed.). (1999). *The emergence of language.* Mahwah, NJ: Erlbaum.

Metsala, J. L., & Walley, A. C. (1998). Spoken vocabulary growth and the segmental restructuring of lexical representations: Precursors to phonemic awareness and early reading ability. In J. L. Metsala & L. C. Ehri (Eds.), *Word recognition in beginning literacy* (pp. 89–120). Mahwah, NJ: Erlbaum.

Moore, C. (1998). Commentary, social cognition in infancy. *Monographs of the Society for Research in Child Development, 63,* 167–174.

Murray, B. A., Stahl, S. A., & Ivey, M. G. (1996). Developing phoneme awareness through alphabet books. *Reading and Writing, 8,* 307–322.

Muter, V., Hulme, C., Snowling, M. J., & Taylor, S. (1997). Segmentation, not rhyming, predicts early progress in learning to read. *Journal of Experimental Child Psychology, 65,* 370–396.

National Reading Panel. (2000). *Teaching children to read: An evidence-based assessment of the scientific research literature on reading and its implications for reading instruction.* Washington, DC: National Institute of Child Health and Human Development.

Ninio, A., & Snow, C. E. (1996). *Pragmatic development.* Boulder, CO: Westview.

Pierce, P. (2006). High expectations for language and literacy with infants and toddlers who have significant disabilities. In S. E. Rosenkoetter & J. Knapp-Philo (Eds.), *Learning to read the world: Language and literacy in the first three years* (pp. 335–352). Washington, DC: ZERO TO THREE Press.

Pinker, S. (1999). *Words and rules: The ingredients of language.* New York: Basic Books.

Plaut, D. C., & Kello, C. T. (1999). The interplay of speech comprehension and production in phonological development: A forward modeling approach. In B. MacWhinney (Ed.), *The emergence of language* (pp. 381–415). Mahwah, NJ: Erlbaum.

Raffi. (1997). *The singable songs collection.* [CD]. Montpelier, VT: Rounder Kids.

Rollins, P. R., & Snow, C. E. (1998). Shared attention and grammatical skills in typical children and children with autism. *Journal of Child Language, 25,* 653–674.

Sénéchal, M., LeFevre, J., Thomas, E. M., & Daley, K. E. (1998). Differential effects of home literacy experiences on the development of oral and written language. *Reading Research Quarterly, 13*, 96–116.

Share, D. L. (1999). Phonological recoding and orthographic learning: A direct test of the self-teaching hypothesis. *Journal of Experimental Child Psychology, 72*, 95–129.

Silva, C., & Alves-Marins, M. (2002). Phonological skills and writing of presyllabic children. *Reading Research Quarterly, 37*(4), 466–483.

Silvén, M., Niemi, P., & Voeten, M. J. M. (2002). Do maternal interaction and early language predict phonological awareness in 3- to 4-year olds? *Cognitive Development, 17*, 1133–1155.

Snow, C. E. (1991). The theoretical basis for relationships between language and literacy in development. *Journal of Research in Childhood Education, 6*(1), 5–10.

Snow, C. E., Burns, M. S., & Griffin, P. (Eds.). (1998). *Preventing reading difficulties in young children.* Washington, DC: National Academy Press.

Strickland, D., Snow, C. E., Griffin, P., Burns, M. S., & MacNamara, P. (2002). *Preparing our teachers: Opportunities for better reading instruction.* Washington, DC: Joseph Henry Press (National Academy Press).

Tomasello, M., & Bates, E. (Eds.). (2001). *Language development: The essential readings.* Oxford: Blackwell.

Vygotsky, L. S. (1978). The role of play in development. In M. Cole, V. John-Steiner, S. Scribner, & E. Souberman (Eds.), *Mind in society: The development of higher psychological processes* (Chap. 7). Cambridge, MA: Harvard University Press.

Walton, P. D., & Walton, L. M. (2002). Beginning reading by teaching in rime analogy: Effects on phonological skills, letter-sound knowledge, working memory, and word-reading strategies. *Scientific Studies of Reading, 6*(1), 79–115.

Weir, R. (1962). *Language in the crib.* The Hague, The Netherlands: Mouton.

Whitehurst, G. J. (1996, April). *A structural equation model of the role of home literacy environment in the development of emergent literacy skills in children from low-income backgrounds.* Paper presented at the annual convention of the American Educational Research Association, New York.

Whitehurst, G. J., & Lonigan, C. J. (1998). Child development and emergent literacy. *Child Development, 69*, 848–872.

CHAPTER 8

Encouraging Language and Literacy Through Family Routines

Lorraine F. Kubicek

For infants and toddlers, learning is best when embedded in nurturing relationships with parents and other important caregivers. These early relationships are founded on the recurring interactions in which children and caregivers engage, often as part of family routines like the one described below.

> *Erin's mom is standing by the kitchen sink, getting ready to wash some potatoes for supper. She calls out to invite 21-month-old Erin, who is playing in the next room, to come and help her. Erin enters the kitchen carrying a child-sized chair. Mom sees her and suggests that she get a bigger chair, and then she helps Erin pull one from the kitchen table over to the sink. The following vignette begins as Mom helps Erin onto the chair.*

E: Thank you.

M: You're welcome.

E: xxx[1] *(looks into the sink)*

M: I'm going to wash potatoes. You want to help?

E: Okay. *(holds one potato under the running water)*

---

[1] Throughout this chapter, "xxx" is used to indicate babbling.

M: Okay, you hold it under there. Want to scrub it, with a sponge? (hands her the sponge) Scrub it with your other hand—you can wash the dirt off.

E: *(continues to hold the potato under the water and squeezes the sponge)*

M: See all the soap coming out of the sponge?

E: Clean it, Mommy. *(squeezes the sponge)*

M: You clean it? Oh, look at all of the soap coming out of that sponge. Why don't you scrub your potato with that. These are dirty!

E: *(squeezes the sponge and then holds her hand under the running water)*

M: Are your hands dirty?

E: Yeah.

M: Yeah?

E: Soap.

M: Want to put soap on them, too? How many potatoes? *(shuts the water off)*

E: *(puts potato to her mouth and begins to take a bite)*

M: Ooh, eh. Don't put them in your mouth yet. They're not cooked yet.

E: Dry. *(puts her hand under the water spout which is now off)*

M: How many potatoes?

E: Five, two.

M: There's five. Watch me. *(counts as she picks up each potato)* 1-2-3-4-5!

As Erin's mom begins her regular routine of preparing supper, she invites Erin to help her. For the next few minutes, the two stand side by side at the sink, washing potatoes and talking mostly about the task at hand. Although there is nothing extraordinary about the content of their conversation or their task of preparing supper, this shared activity represents an important time for Erin and her mom to be close together and for her mom to encourage Erin's emerging language. Mom does this as she names things and counts, asks Erin questions and waits for her to respond, and expands and clarifies Erin's own comments and responses.

This chapter will show how family routines can be a ready context for enriching children's language learning and beginning literacy. Family routines provide countless opportunities to make language interesting through talking, as well as through singing and reading together, and to make language an integral part of all that children do each day, starting in infancy.

Family Routines

Family routines are patterned interactions that occur with predictable regularity in the course of everyday living. Routines help to organize family life, define roles and responsibilities, reinforce family identity, and provide members with a shared and necessary sense of belonging (Wolin & Bennett, 1984).

At least one reason why adherence to family routines may be associated with these positive outcomes is that they provide an ongoing context for strengthening the caregiver–child relationship (Emde, Korfmacher, & Kubicek, 2000). Each day, caregiver and child come together around common goals and develop patterns of interaction that are adaptive and likely to enhance development. That is to say, routines provide the context for much of early socialization. Through repeated participation in shared, meaningful activities such as greetings, mealtimes, social games, and reading stories, children learn the beliefs, values, and practices of their family and culture (Bossard & Boll, 1950; Fiese, Hooker, Kotary, & Schwagler, 1993; Reiss, 1981; Rogoff, Mistry, Goncu, & Mosier, 1993). Important among these values and practices, of course, are attitudes toward language and literacy (Kubicek, 2002; Rosenkoetter & Barton, 2002).

Early Communication and Language Development

Infants and toddlers learn best when learning is embedded in meaningful relationships. This condition is especially true for learning language, which is rooted in social interaction and nurtured there (Kubicek, 1992, 1996).

As we consider ways to encourage learning language and beginning literacy, it is important to remember that although most children do not utter their first words until sometime close to their first birthday or even later in their second year, the development of communication and language begins early in infancy (Bates, O'Connell, & Shore, 1987). During the first year, an infant communicates with her caregivers through a varied repertoire of emotion-based signals such as gaze, facial expressions, cries, and other vocalizations. When sensitive caregivers attend to these signals and respond to her needs, she begins to learn important lessons about how communication works that provide the foundation for further development. For example, she learns about turntaking and social reciprocity and about how to repair errors or misunderstandings in communication when they occur. She also learns that her expressions and vocalizations have meaning for others, an understanding that is essential for learning to use language to communicate.

Young children understand words before they say words themselves. Typically, a child begins to comprehend spoken language at approximately the age of 9 months. She responds to her name, complies with a simple request like waving good-bye, or looks at favorite people or things, such as Mommy or a book, when someone says their names. As noted above, it is often several months later, around her first birthday, when the infant actually produces her first single words. These are often, but not always, names of familiar people or pets (e.g., *Daddy*), objects (e.g., *ball*), actions (e.g., *see*), or qualities (e.g., *hot*).

In the coming months, a toddler spends much effort expanding her vocabulary of individual words, leading to the next major milestone in language development, the transition from single- to two-word speech at about the age of 20 months. During this time, she begins to say simple word combinations like *me do, big dog, all gone,* and *see kitty*. Approximately 6 months later, at about the age of 26 months, grammar takes off, with most children mastering the basic word and sentence structures of their native language by the age of 3 years.

Individual Differences in Early Language Development

It is important to point to the enormous variability there is among young children in the age at which they reach the language milestones outlined above (Fenson et al., 1994). Research demonstrates that at least some of this variation is linked to differences in children's language learning environments. A number of studies have found a substantial positive relation between overall amount of parent-to-child talk and the size of children's productive vocabularies as well as other measures of language development (Hart & Risley, 1995; Huttenlocher, Haight, Bryk, Seltzer, & Lyons, 1991; Huttenlocher, Vasilyeva, Cymerman, & Levine, 2002; Tomasello, Mannle, & Kruger, 1986). "Extra talk," that is, talk that goes beyond simple directives and engages a child by highlighting and expanding on his experiences (Hart & Risley, 1995), seems to be especially important in supporting language development. So does repetition. Huttenlocher and her colleagues (1991) found that children learned those words that they heard most often earlier than those words that they heard least often.

These findings are significant because a child's competence in communicating with others is linked to competence in other areas of development. In fact, a child's ability to communicate effectively has a strong positive influence on his social, emotional, and cognitive development. A child with good language skills is better able to engage others and make friends and solve problems without resorting to tantrums and aggressive behavior than is a child with weak language skills. He is also better able to express his likes and dislikes, ask for help when he needs it, and follow simple requests. Moreover, language provides the foundation for beginning literacy.

Family Routines as a Context for Encouraging Early Language and Literacy

Talking with young children and singing together stimulate their understanding and use of language and help prepare them for later success in reading. The Partnership for Reading (2003) recommends that caregivers (a) talk and sing to children from birth, (b) respond to their babbles and coos, (c) play touching and talking games to teach parts of the body, (d) point to and name familiar objects, (e) expand on their early language, (f) encourage talk by asking questions, and (g) listen to children's questions and answer them patiently. In addition, the Partnership for Reading (2003) recommends reading together, which is detailed later.

Talking

The following examples of talking are taken from home visits with families participating in a longitudinal study of toddler language and emotional development (Kubicek & Emde, 2004) and a longitudinal study of infant and toddler social and emotional development (Kubicek, Riley, Miller, & Stokka, 2003). These examples clearly illustrate how the recommendations from the Partnership for Reading can be incorporated into familiar routines that children and caregivers are likely to engage in from day to day.

Example 1. The following exchange took place as Kate was lying on her blanket on the floor and her mother was sitting nearby. Kate was 4 months old.

> M: Go baby go. Go baby go.

> K: *(begins to kick her feet)*

> M: Go kicker. Go kicker.

> K: *(pushes up, raising her chest off the rug)*

> M: *(smiles)* You pushing up? That's nice. That's nice pushing, Kate. That's some nice pushing.

> K: xxx *(smiles)*

Example 2. The following exchange took place as Brendan and his mother were playing on the floor. Brendan was 11 months old.

> B: Ah *(reaches for clown-faced musical toy)*

> M: You want that? *(hands toy to Brendan)*

> B: *(smiles and takes toy from Mother)*

> M: That make you laugh? That make you a happy boy? You like that, huh, because his red nose lights up. There goes his red nose. *(points to clown nose)* Yeah. There goes his red nose.

B: *(smiles and points to clown nose)*

M: What do you think?

B: *(pats toy)*

M: The music is coming.

B: *(smiles, then begins to vocalize and bounce along with the music)* ah, ah, ah, ah.

M: *(smiles)* You want to dance? *(nods)* Is that what you want to do?

Example 3. The following exchange took place as Anna and her mother prepared to cook dinner. Anna was 21 months old.

M: 1-2-3! *(picks Anna up off the chair and walks with her to the kitchen)* Let's go cook supper. Want to . . . ? Want to make some noodles? *(takes pot out of cabinet)* Noodles?

A: Noodles.

M: *(opens refrigerator door and watermelon falls out and onto the floor)* Oh my goodness. Mommy just dropped the watermelon all over the floor. Look, look, Anna, oh my goodness.

A: Dropped it. *(points to watermelon)*

M: Yeah, I dropped it. Gotta clean it up. Ick! Ick!

A: *(Anna picks up the watermelon and hands it to Mom)*

M: Oh, thank you, sweetie. *(takes melon from Anna)*

A: Welcome. Dropped it. *(reaches up on to counter and takes a piece of watermelon Mom had put there)*

Example 4. The following exchange took place after Mom finished changing Nate's diaper. Nate was 15 months old.

M: Want to get your jammies on while you're up there?

N: Sure.

M: Sure? You say sure?

N: xxx

M: Oh, your shirt. Yeah, yeah, your pajamas. *(takes one sock off)* I'm going to tickle your feet. *(tickles Nate's feet)* I'm going to tickle 'em.

N: xxx

M: Sit up *(helps Nate sit up)*, and we'll put your pajama shirt on, okay? Arm? *(as she takes his right arm out of its sleeve)*

N: xxx

M: What about this arm? Just a minute. I'll give it back. *(takes left arm out of its sleeve)*

N: *(fusses)*

M: Over the head. *(takes shirt over Nate's head)*

N: xxx *(points to his stomach and looks up at Mom)*

M: Tummy? I'm gonna eat it. *(leans over and kisses his stomach)*

N: xxx *(puts head down as if trying to kiss his own stomach; takes wash cloth and rubs his stomach)*

M: Wanna wash it?

N: *(looks at Mom and smiles)*

As noted earlier, a child can communicate long before she can understand and use language. Despite these early developments, conversations between a caregiver and a child in the early stages of language learning involve partners of unequal status. Yet, as these vignettes illustrate, caregivers encourage their child's language by responding "as though" he or she were a more equal conversational partner. They attribute meaning to their child's gestures and pre-language utterances, repeat and expand their single-word and early sentence responses, ask questions "as if" their child could respond more fully, and answer their child's questions. They also supply names for objects and actions.

As the next two vignettes illustrate, caregivers do not simply limit conversations to the here and now. Through language, they help their child remember and reflect on events and experiences in the past as well as think about and look forward to events and experiences in the future.

Example 5. The next vignette took place while Bryan and his mother and father were eating dinner. Bryan was 24 months old.

> B: Happy Birthday, Momma.

> M: *(laughs)*

> B: xxx

> M: Well, it's not my birthday for a while, but it was just your birthday. And what did we do at your birthday?

> B: I blow candles out.

> M: Blow candles out. *(nodding)*

> B: Is my birthday? Today my birthday?

> M: No, today's not your birthday. *(shaking her head)*

> D: Not for another year yet.

> M: You already had your birthday. But we had a lot of fun.

> B: xxx

> D: How old are you, Bryan?

> B: Poppa was here on my birthday?

> M: Poppa was here on your birthday. *(nods)* Who else was here?

B: Gram.

M: Gram.

D: Who else? . . .

Example 6. The next vignette occurred just as Erin and her mother and father were finishing dinner. Erin was 21 months old at the time.

M: Want to go to the library tonight with Mommy?

E: Mommy. Library. Library Mommy. Library Daddy. *(looking from one to the other)*

M: Want to go to the library or go swimming?

E: Library.

M: Library. Okay.

In the first example, through their questions to Bryan and their answers to his questions, Bryan's parents help him remember his recent birthday and the many people who came to celebrate with him. In this way, they support him in creating a rudimentary narrative of this special event. In the second example, Erin's mother offers her a choice about how they will spend some time together later that evening.

Throughout the day, caregivers find ways to support young children's developing language not only through talk about real events and experiences in the past, present, and future but also about pretend and imagined events and experiences. The following vignette began shortly after Lori's mother answered the phone and began to talk with the caller.

Example 7. As Lori's mother talked on the phone, Lori found her toy phone and put the receiver to her ear. She was 18 months old at the time.

L: Mom. It's Mom. *(pause)* It's Mom. *(turns and looks at Mom)* xxx xxx Momma. Call Momma. We can, Lori, Lori can call Momma. Lori can call Momma.

M: *(ends her phone conversation)*

L: Lori can call Momma.

M: Lori can call Momma. Hello, Lori. Hello, Lori. *(picks up the phone again)* Telephone for Lori.

L: xxx

M: Telephone for Lori.

L: I got to talk little bit.

M: You're going to talk a little bit? Okay. Telephone for George? Can George talk? *(referring to Curious George doll)*

L: No.

M: No, no telephone for George, huh?

L: xxx what have walking xxx. *(while holding her phone and walking around living room)*

M: What, Honey? Who is on the telephone, Sweet Pea?

L: Mom.

M: Mom? Oh, Mom calling Lori. Hello, Lori. How are you today?

L: Good.

M: Good. *(smiles and touches Lori's head)*

L: xxx

M: Momma's going to the kitchen now. I'll talk to you later. *(bends over, closer to Lori's face)* See you soon. See you soon. Bye, bye.

Example 8. The next vignette took place after dinner when Bryan and his parents went into the living room. Bryan requested that they play his favorite family game, "Swimming Pool." His parents sat on the floor opposite each other and opened their legs to form a "pool." Bryan was 24 months old at the time.

B: Cold out xxx cold out.

M: Oh, is it cold?

B: It's warm in.

M: Oh, is it warm?

B: Yeah.

M: Where is it warm?

B: In, in here.

M: Is it warm in, is that warm water?

B: Yeah.

D: And where is it cold?

M: Is it cold in there too, or just warm?

B: Just warm.

M: Just warm.

B: Aah. *(pretends to splash around in the "pool")*

M: Aah.

B: Nice water.

M: Nice water. *(simultaneously with Dad)*

D: Nice water.

B: Fishies in here. Fishies! *(jumps out of the "pool")*

M: Oh, are there fishies in there?

D: You wanna feed them? *(puts hands out like holding fish food)*

B: Yeah. *(pretends to take food from Dad and to sprinkle it over the water)*

M: Oh, oh, oh! Look at all those fishies!

B: Let's pick 'em up.

M: Oh, you can pick them up.

B: *(pretends to show Mom fish in his cupped hands)*

M: What a nice fish. What color is it?

B: I love it!

M: You love it? What color is it?

B: Orange.

In both of these examples, caregivers encourage and participate with their children in using language to create pretend scenarios that most likely reflect or mimic real events from the past. These conversations are the products of adults' and children's shared imaginations. Language gives meaning to their behavior and makes such pretend play possible.

Singing

Talk about both real and imagined events and experiences provides children with invaluable experiences that support their understanding and use of language. Singing together can do the same. As the following examples illustrate, singing, like talking, also can easily be made a part of everyday routines.

Example 9. After getting dressed for bed, Nate goes over and stands by the rocking chair in his room. Mom asks if he would like to go in the chair, and when he says yes, she lifts him up and sits him down in the rocker. Nate is 15 months old.

M: Rock-a-bye baby in the treetop, when the wind blows, the cradle will rock *(sings while she rocks the chair)* You in the big chair? You like that?

N: xxx *(nods)*

M: Can you make it go yourself? Here, what's this? *(gives him his blanket)*

N: *(laughs, holds on to blanket and sucks his thumb)*

M: *(continues to sing while she rocks the chair)* When the bough breaks, the baby will fall, and down will come baby.

N: Baby, baby, baby. *(rocks side to side)*

M: You singing about the baby?

N: Baby, baby, baby.

M: Yeah, and down will come baby. . . .

Example 10. Bryan lies on the floor as Mom starts to put his overalls back on following a diaper change. Bryan is 24 months old.

M: Put your right foot in *(singing as she puts Bryan's foot into right leg of his overalls)*

B: Frankie get down. Frankie get down. *(pointing to something off camera)*

M: Frankie? Did she play with them when she was here? Put your left foot in. *(singing as she puts Bryan's foot into left leg of his overalls)*

B: Yeah.

M: Now both feet in. Then shake 'em all about. *(shakes Bryan's feet)*

B: About. *(smiles)* Hokey Pokey.

M: Do the Hokey Pokey. *(stands Bryan up)*

B: *(claps hands together)*

M: Clap your little hands.

B: *(rests head on Mom)* hands xxx

M: Oh. *(kisses Bryan's head)*

B: Oh.

M: That's what it's all about.

Singing together, like talking together, often brings caregivers and children physically close. Singing also exposes children to new words and, as these examples illustrate, provides them with opportunities to practice what they have learned and to have fun while they do.

Reading

Reading together is another way to stimulate children's understanding and use of language and to prepare them for later success in reading. The Partnership for Reading (2003) recommends that caregivers (a) make reading a pleasure, (b) show enthusiasm as they read with the child, (c) read often, and (d) talk with the child as reading goes forward.

Example 11 models the general recommendations of the Partnership for Reading. The remaining examples (Examples 12–15) are all from the first hour of a home visit with Tyler and her parents. What is interesting and important about these examples is how Tyler's parents not only take time to read story-books with her but also highlight reading as they go about their regular routines such as cooking dinner and looking through the day's mail. They are enthusiastic and talk with Tyler about the pictures and text as well as relate what they read and see to her own experiences. She, in turn, is as interested to sit on Dad's lap and look through a tool catalog as she is to sit and read a Dr. Seuss book with him.

Tyler's parents fit reading in wherever they can. They read not only storybooks with her but also food cartons and catalogs and magazines. No matter what they read, they are enthusiastic and talk with Tyler about the pictures and the print and try to relate them to her own experiences. Reading provides a time for the family to be close and to share positive emotions. Tyler was 15 months old at the time and, as the vignettes show, was at the early stages of using words to express herself.

Example 11. The following example occurred while Beth was sitting on her mother's lap as they relaxed on the living room floor. Beth was 4 months old.

> M: A hog and a frog do a dance in the bog, but not the hippopotamus. *(points on page)* Look at the hippo, standing there with no friends.

> B: *(looks at the book and holds on to the cardboard page, moving it back and forth)*

> M: You gonna help? You gonna help?

> B: xxx *(turns page)*

> M: You open it? There you go.

> B: xxx *(smiles)*

> M: Look at the hippo looking in the window. That's sad.

> B: xxx *(turns page)*

> M: Thank you. Thanks for your help.

> B: *(chews on book)*

> M: It's delicious. That was a good book for you. That was nice.

Example 12. Dad had just put some frozen rolls in the oven to bake. Mom and Tyler were nearby, sitting at the kitchen table.

D: How long is it going to take for these to cook?

M: Eight to 10 minutes. *(without looking at the wrapper)* We have to read it, Tyler. *(picking up carton)* Eight to 10 minutes until golden brown. That will be absolutely perfect!

Example 13. After dinner, Mom and Dad were sitting at the kitchen table looking through the mail. Tyler was seated on Mom's lap while they looked at a magazine.

M: Could you read that book to me?

T: Oh, boy.

M: Oh, boy. I see some trees. Do you see some trees?

T: No. *(shakes head)*

M: No? *(laughs)* Look at it. What are those? *(points to page)*

T: Bxxx

M: Bushes?

T: Bxxx *(turns magazine page)*

M: Trees. Some people. Snow! There's snow! Snow. Remember snow?

T: Momma. *(point on page)*

M: Remember when Dad and you built a snowman? Where's the sun? *(points on page)* Sun and a boat. Where's the doggies?

Example 14. A little later, Tyler was seated on Dad's lap, and they were looking through a tool catalog.

D: Router accessories.

T: Rxxx *(points on page)*

D: Router. Here's a worm drive. Would you like that?

T: xxx *(looks at catalog)*

D: Worm drive. We haven't seen any worms yet. Maybe this spring we'll find some in the garden, huh?

T: xxx

Example 15. Tyler ran to get a book and then turned toward Dad with her arms outstretched, holding the book out to him.

D: Do you want to read it?

T: Yeah.

D: Read it? Let's read.

T: Read. *(while walking toward Dad and holding the book out to him)*

D: I'll read it *(picks Tyler up and sits her on his lap)*

T: *(laughs as she settles in)*

D: Big A, little a, what begins with a?

T: xxx *(turns page)*

D: Ant and alligator, AAA.

T: xxx *(smiles, points to page, then turns it)*

D: Big B, little b, what begins with b?

T: Babababa. *(while turning page)*

D: Barber, baby, bubbles, and a bumblebee.

T: Bee.

D: What's a bee say?

T: Bee.

D: Buzz, buzz, buzz. . . . Big M, little m, many mumbly mice are making midnight music in the moonlight mighty mice. Where's the moon?

T: Mo. *(points to picture of the moon)*

D: Moon, that's the moon. Where are the mice?

T: Mi. *(points to picture of the mice)*

D: Yeah, okay, they're making music.

T: Da.

D: Midnight music. What do you do with music? *(bounces Tyler on his lap)* Do you dance? *(rhythmically moves his shoulders up and down)* Do you like music? Big N, little n, what begins with those, nine new neckties and a nightshirt and a nose? Where's a nose? Show me a nose.

T: *(points to picture of a nightshirt)*

D: That's a nightshirt. Here. *(points to picture of a nose)*

T: Na.

D: That's a nose.

T: *(points to her nose)*

D: Where's your nose? Yeah!

Summary and Discussion

Language provides the foundation for literacy, and one of the most important ways caregivers can encourage language and literacy is by providing their children with rich and exciting language environments during their infancy and early childhood years (Burns, Griffin, & Snow, 1999; Dickinson & Tabors, 2001; Parlakian, 2003; Snow, 1993). The goal of this chapter has been to show how family routines can provide a ready context to do just that. The numerous examples highlighted in the chapter illustrate how caregivers, in the midst of daily routines, talk with, sing with, and read with their children in ways that encourage their learning language and beginning literacy. They do this by listening to their children and by playing games that teach parts of the body, naming familiar objects and actions, asking and answering questions, and elaborating on what their children say. Through language, they help their children not only focus on the present but also remember and reflect on events and experiences in the past as well as think about and look forward to events and experiences in the future. They also help them pretend and create imagined worlds in play. What is so interesting and exciting is that they manage to do all of these things as well as express affection and share positive emotions with their children as they go through the day, changing diapers, sorting the mail, preparing dinner, and getting their children ready for bed.

References

Bates, E., O'Connell, B., & Shore, C. (1987). Language and communication in infancy. In J. D. Osofsky (Ed.), *Handbook of infant development* (2nd ed., pp. 149–203). New York: Wiley.

Bossard, W. T., & Boll, E. (1950). *Rituals in family living.* Philadelphia: University of Pennsylvania Press.

Burns, M. S., Griffin, P., & Snow, C. E. (Eds.). (1999). *Starting out right: A guide to promoting children's reading success.* Washington, DC: National Academy Press.

Dickinson, D. K., & Tabors, P. O. (Eds.). (2001). *Beginning literacy with language.* Baltimore: Paul H. Brookes.

Emde, R. N., Korfmacher, J., & Kubicek, L. F. (2000). Toward a theory of early relationship-based intervention. In J. D. Osofsky & H. E. Fitzgerald (Eds.), *Early intervention, evaluation, & assessment: Vol. 2. World Association of Infant Mental Health handbook of infant mental health* (pp. 2–32). New York: Wiley.

Fenson, L., Dale, P. S., Reznick, J. S., Bates, E., Thal, D. J., & Pethick, S. J. (1994). Variability in early communicative development. *Monographs of the Society for Research in Child Development, 59*(5, Serial No. 242).

Fiese, B. H., Hooker, K. A., Kotary, L., & Schwagler, J. (1993). Family routines in the early stages of parenthood. *Journal of Marriage and the Family, 55,* 633–642.

Hart, B., & Risley, T. R. (1995). *Meaningful differences in the everyday experiences of young American children.* Baltimore: Paul H. Brookes.

Huttenlocher, J., Haight, W., Bryk, A., Seltzer, M., & Lyons, T. (1991). Early vocabulary growth: Relation to language input and gender. *Developmental Psychology, 27,* 236–248.

Huttenlocher, J., Vasilyeva, M., Cymerman, E., & Levine, S. (2002). Language input at home and at school: Relation to child syntax. *Cognitive Psychology, 45*(3), 337–374.

Kubicek, L. F. (1992). *Organization of parent-child repair and non-repair sequences in routine interactions at 15 and 21 months.* Unpublished doctoral dissertation, University of Chicago.

Kubicek, L. F. (1996). Helping young children become competent communicators: The role of relationships. *Zero to Three, 17*(1), 25–30.

Kubicek, L. F. (2002). Fresh perspectives on young children and family routines. *Zero to Three, 22*(4), 4–9.

Kubicek, L. F., & Emde, R. N. (2004). *Assessing the development of earlier- and later-talking toddlers during the transition from one- to two-word speech: Language, emotion, and temperament.* Manuscript in preparation.

Kubicek, L. F., Riley, K., Miller, G., & Stokka, K. (2003, December). *Enhancing social and emotional development for young children with disabilities: A comparison of direct and indirect approaches.* Poster presented at the 18th National Training Institute of ZERO TO THREE: National Center for Infants, Toddlers, and Families, New Orleans, LA.

Parlakian, R. (2003). *Before the ABCs: Promoting school readiness in infants and toddlers.* Washington, DC: ZERO TO THREE.

Partnership for Reading. (2003, Spring). *A child becomes a reader: Birth through preschool.* (2nd ed.). [Brochure]. Portsmouth, NH: RMC Research Corporation.

Reiss, D. (1981). *The family's construction of reality.* Cambridge, MA: Harvard University Press.

Rogoff, B., Mistry, J., Goncu, A., & Mosier, C. (1993). Guided participation in cultural activity by toddlers and caregivers. *Monographs of the Society for Research in Child Development, 58*(8, Serial No. 236).

Rosenkoetter, S., & Barton, L. R. (2002). Bridges to literacy: Early routines that promote later school success. *Zero to Three, 22*(4), 33–38.

Snow, C. E. (1993). Families as social contexts for literacy development. In C. Daiute (Ed.), *The development of literacy through social interaction.* San Francisco: Jossey-Bass.

Tomasello, M., Mannle, S., & Kruger, A. C. (1986). Linguistic environment of 1- to 2-year-old twins. *Developmental Psychology, 22*, 169–176.

Wolin, S. J., & Bennett, L. A. (1984). Family rituals. *Family Process, 23*, 401–420.

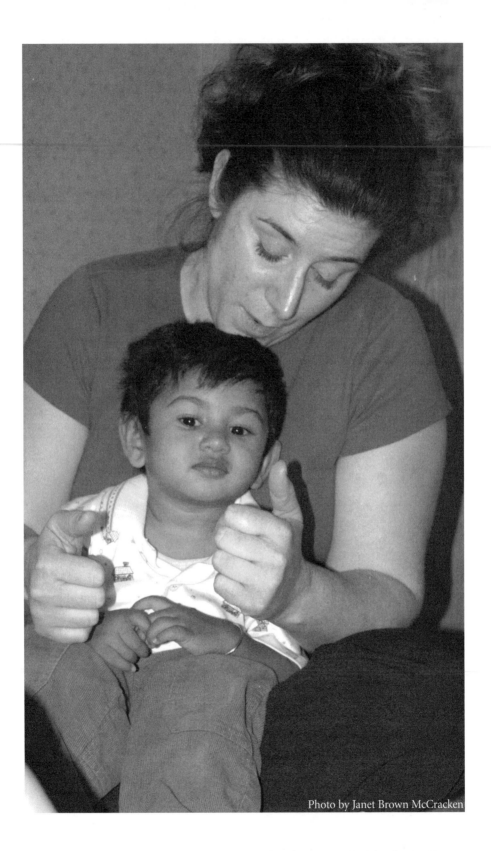

CHAPTER 9

Culture and Parental Expectations for Child Development: Concerns for Language Development and Early Learning

Wendy Jones and Isabella Lorenzo-Hubert

Culture is "an integrated pattern of human behavior which includes but is not limited to thought, communication, languages, beliefs, customs, courtesies, rituals, manners of interacting, roles, relationships, and expected behaviors of racial, ethnic, religious, social and political groups; and the ability to transmit the above to succeeding generations; ... dynamic in nature" (Goode, 2002b, p. 2).

The population of the United States is diverse and rapidly changing. Results of the 2000 U.S. Census revealed that the characteristics of people residing in the United States are more diverse than ever. This diversity in the U.S. population extends to young children. The Children's Defense Fund (2001) states that one in every five children has a foreign-born mother; approximately 1% of the nation's children under age 5 are foreign born. Further, the actual number of children from diverse cultural backgrounds who are under the age of 5 and who are being reared by foreign-born parents is embedded in the number of children born in the U.S. as American citizens. Among families of diverse backgrounds, with longtime U.S. residence, differences in ethnicity, religious beliefs, geographic locale, and worldview may cause families to display cultural attributes that are quite disparate from that of the majority culture. Such diversity has definite implications for early childhood programs and the development of language and literacy.

Early care and education of children outside the home has increased in importance and prominence. West, Wright, and Hausken (1995) estimated that some 60% of children between the ages of birth and 5 years spend time in an early childhood care and education setting. Some care environments reflect the rich racial, ethnic, and cultural groups represented in the United States. However, it is widely recognized that many young children attending early childhood programs are from families that are non-English speaking or for whom English is a second language and who differ from the dominant culture in social customs, perspectives, and expectations with respect to their children's pathways of development, including early language and literacy.

As the population of early childhood programs becomes more diverse and as educators seek to provide all children an optimal start in life, there is a growing recognition of the need for strategies that enhance the learning experiences of children of diverse cultures and languages. It is critical that staff of early childhood programs be aware of how parental perspectives, beliefs, and practices affect children's overall development as well as their adjustment to and success in early childhood settings. In addition, staff should consider their own roles in each child's development and how their own views on development may differ from those of a child's family. When such differences occur, staff should work with families to bridge the cultural gap between home and school expectations to aid children in their transition between settings. Beginning language and literacy is a particularly important area in which families and early childhood providers must work together to enable children to succeed in their families, schools, and communities. This chapter will explore the effect of culture and language on child development, early language development, and learning. The discussion will explore parental beliefs, practices, and expectations for child development and child-rearing practices. Additionally, the chapter will cover the intricate relationship between culture and language learning. Each discussion offers suggestions for bridging gaps between provider and parental expectations.

Harkness and Super's "Developmental Niche"

Children are heavily influenced by the culture, opinions, and attitudes of their families and caregivers as they "are taught to act, believe, and feel in ways that are consistent with the values of their communities" (Bowman, 1989, p. 119). Harkness and Super (1994) developed the *developmental niche*, a theoretical framework for conceptualizing the cultural structuring of a child's daily environment. The niche comprises three components, including (a) the physical and social settings of everyday life, (b) the routine customs of care, and (c) the psychology of the child's caregivers, including the language, thoughts, cultural practices, beliefs, and expectations of the child's parents and other care providers.

A child is affected by his environment and by caregiver belief systems; he also shapes his niche through individual characteristics such as temperament, health status, age, gender, and birth order. Parents and caregivers, too, reflect not only their own family's culture but also the social context or community in which they live.

Members of cultural groups have shared understanding of the nature of children, their development, and the significance of behavior. Such common understandings and perceptions are developed and fostered within the cultural context of life in a given time and place and are linked to one's understanding of experiences and of the meaning of parenthood, self, and family in society. Adults assimilate their culture's key understandings and beliefs about child development and desirable behavior and use these principles to select child-rearing practices.

Culture and Child-Rearing Practices

Child-rearing practices reveal cultural perceptions about young children's development, abilities, and timelines for expected achievement of milestones. Such understandings are based on cultural and familial experiences, often passed down from family member to family member and from generation to generation. Child-rearing practices represent a cultural agreement about young children rooted in cultural values, beliefs, and practices. Some differing cultural perspectives on when and how to encourage communication and language in young children follow.

When Is the Time to Start Talking to Babies?

A society's ideas on children's ability to engage in interactive communication at a given age guide its behaviors related to verbal engagement with infants. There is wide variation in cultural perceptions about infants as possible partners in conversation. In some cultures, infants are viewed as incapable of both talking and understanding speech; therefore, adults in these societies do not converse with them (LeVine, Miller, Richman, & LeVine, 1996). LeVine and colleagues note other examples of variability among cultural groups with respect to beliefs about infant communication in studies conducted in the Pacific Basin. For example, Samoans and the Kaluli people of New Guinea do not engage in conversation with infants whereas the Kwara'ae people of the Solomon Islands routinely participate in interactive speech with 6-month-olds. In addition, LeVine and colleagues (1994) found that among the Gusii of western Kenya, older women who had not attended school viewed communication with children under the age of 2 years to be foolish since they believed the children incapable of understanding speech. Findings such as these provide insight into cultural variation in ideas and practices concerning infant and toddler abilities to participate in interactive communication and in the subsequent way these beliefs guide adults in their interactions with young children.

Does Culture Influence the Perception of What Constitutes the Ideal Child?

Clearly, all parents have preferences, expectations, and goals for their children. Differences in parental goals and expectations may be based on varying cultural values and expectations for members of a society. Many Western cultures, including Euro-American traditions in the United States, emphasize individual achievement, independence, self-reliance, and self-assertiveness. Children are taught to excel and purposefully to stand out from others; hence, the Star Baby is the ideal child. In contrast, many Asian and Latino cultures stress interdependence, cooperation, and collaboration as important values. These community values are typically expressed in parental expectations that children be obedient, act in a friendly manner, share toys, and get along well with others. The ideal child reared in this type of culture is encouraged to fit in and not to stand out or challenge others. These two different cultural orientations—independence versus interdependence—lead to very different approaches to guiding language and literacy development and seeking demonstrations of mastery of concepts. It is important for parents and caregivers to understand how different cultural values are translated into adult expectations and what socializing strategies adults choose to teach children.

Harwood (1992) queried two groups of Puerto Rican mothers and two groups of Euro-American mothers (one group each from lower socioeconomic status and one group each from middle socioeconomic status). The mothers were asked to identify behaviors and qualities that they most liked and disliked for their 12- to 24-month-old children. Thirty-five percent of the responses from both groups of Euro-American mothers indicated traits related to personal development, such as independence, self-control, and self-confidence. In contrast, 40% of the responses of both groups of Puerto Rican mothers identified characteristics that emphasized respectfulness, politeness, obedience, friendliness, and getting along with others. Less than 3% of the responses of the Euro-American mothers fell into the cooperative category. The differences seen in this study suggest clear cultural orientations toward individuals and relationships that carry over into the uses of language and literacy in home and community life.

Okagaki and Sternberg (1993) found that parents from four immigrant groups—Filipino, Cambodian, Vietnamese, and Mexican—rated developing obedience and conformity to outside standards as more important to children's development than developing problem-solving and independent thinking skills. American-born parents of European and Mexican ancestry rated the development of independent behaviors and creative thinking as more important than developing conforming behaviors. Okagaki and Sternberg's work points out the contrast between an individualistic cultural orientation and a mutual interdependence or collective orientation and suggests that acculturation may shape parental perceptions of desirable characteristics for their children.

What Does It Mean for a Child to Be Intelligent?

In their study of immigrant and nonimmigrant families, Okagaki and Diamond (2000) found differences in parental opinions as to what constitutes intelligence. Western families favored verbal expression and creativity as primary indicators of intelligence. Latino and Asian parents held a broader view, that intelligence represented a blending of attributes, including motivation and social skills. In sharp contrast to the Western model of intelligence that emphasizes inherent cognitive abilities, Latino and Asian parents felt that "to be intelligent is to work hard at achieving one's goals" (Okagaki & Diamond, 2000, p. 76).

The above examples of differing cultural beliefs regarding communication, desired behaviors, and intelligence indicate that early childhood personnel must not presume that all families have the same ideas about either the characteristics of the ideal child or the nature of exemplary developmental support. When family expectations for behavior and development agree with those of the educator, the child may have a relatively easy transition between home and center settings. However, when family and teacher expectations differ, children may experience difficulty in discerning the cultural rules of the two environments.

Bridging the Gaps: Differing Views of Development

How are children affected when their daily routine is divided between home and center caregivers who may have divergent beliefs, practices, goals, and expectations? How are conflicts in values and beliefs resolved? How is agreement achieved regarding goals, methods, and beliefs? The responsibility of translating values and goals into child-rearing and child development practices should be shared among parents, extended family members, and knowledgeable providers. By working together, the adults in a child's life can address the numerous questions that arise when a child experiences different developmental expectations at home and in an early childhood setting.

Following are some suggestions to assist early childhood staff members in their joint efforts with families:

- Be aware of one's own cultural biases and expectations and their implications for child-rearing practices.

- Consider each child and family's cultural background, but avoid assumptions about a family's practices.

- Ask the family about their preferences, expectations, and goals for their child—including those about language and literacy—and learn the ways in which families assist their child in achieving important goals.

- Demonstrate the program's methods and how staff interact with infants and toddlers, but avoid telling family members what they should or should not do.

- Explain clearly the program's goals, methods, and practices to encourage emerging language and literacy, and seek suggestions from the family about how these practices fit with their views on development.

- Seek suggestions from the family about how the early childhood program can support their efforts.

- Reflect with a cultural mentor (see Rosenkoetter, this volume, p. 369) regarding staff comfort in making accommodations that reflect the values of each family.

- Learn how the family regards talking to young children, who in the family typically does that talking (e.g., mother or father, sibling, older relative, community member), and what forms and content describe the language that occurs.

- When differences arise between the home and care environments, negotiate with family members to resolve the differences.

By exploring and comparing their individual perspectives, families and educators will formulate a basis for working together and support each child's individual development.

Family Choices and Preferences: What to Adopt and What to Keep

All families are faced with making decisions regarding what they perceive to be best for their child or children's overall emotional, social, and educational well-being. Families from diverse cultural backgrounds face the additional dilemma of deciding the extent to which they *assimilate* ("assuming the cultural traditions of a given people or group" [Goode, 2002a, p. 1]) and embrace the values and practices of the United States while maintaining their own. Over time, many families experience some degree of *acculturation* or "cultural modification by adapting to or borrowing traits from another culture" (Goode, 2002a, p. 1). Indeed, it is important to be aware that "individuals from culturally diverse groups might desire varying degrees of acculturation into the dominant culture" (Goode, 2002a, p. 1). A key concern for many newcomers to this country is whether they will accept, learn, and use English as their exclusive language at home, school, and in the community or whether they will accept and acquire two languages and two cultures at the same time (Pham, 1994). For caregivers and teachers, the challenge of meeting the children's linguistic needs is heightened when most classroom instruction occurs in English. The following scenario underscores the importance of understanding, supporting, and partnering with families regarding their preferences around acculturation and assimilation.

> Leo was born in Samoa, lived the first year of his life in Hawaii, and moved into a community on the U.S. mainland 6 months ago. His mother, father, and grandparents share a small, cramped apartment. Leo is 19 months old. His parents and grandparents are raising him because the family views child rearing as a responsibility for all family members. Major family decisions are made as a unit, not just by Leo's parents. Leo's parents would like for him to attend the child-care center, where they feel that he will be exposed to "American ways." They also want him to know and keep the Samoan customs such as speaking the Samoan language, respecting the land, and honoring one's ancestors.

In the above scenario, the family, including both parents and grandparents, has expressed a desire to maintain aspects of their culture of origin while supporting Leo's acquisition of U.S. customs and language. Leo's parents are bilingual, speaking both Samoan and English, but his grandparents seem to understand English better than they speak it. Early care and education staff need to learn from the family and identify their preferences, child-rearing practices, and expectations for Leo's language development and literacy. It is important to engage the family in conversation, inquiring about the primary caregivers, sharing which languages are used by the caregivers interacting with Leo, asking which languages they speak in the home and community, noting how language is incorporated into daily activities, and inquiring about how Leo expresses his wants and needs. Be sure to include questions that will provide information about the family's language goals for Leo, such as naming objects and persons, recognizing pictures, pointing to objects on request, pointing to desired objects and people, and following directions. Engaging in this type of conversation is an initial step in the process of communicating with Leo's family. It is important to speak with families on a regular basis to foster a trusting, collaborative relationship. Such partnerships afford many opportunities for ongoing dialog about progress, expectations, goals, and the child's future development.

Parenting Roles Differ Across Cultures

Culture influences the roles of parents and extended family members in child-rearing practices as well as the ways that parents and other adults interact with children. Various cultural groups understand parenting differently. In some cultures, there is the expectation that the mother is primarily responsible for all aspects of an infant or toddler's care. In many cultures, families such as Leo's share the care and nurturing of children among mother, father, and extended family, including aunts, uncles, grandparents, and godparents. This wide circle of caregivers may also have responsibility for disciplining and other decision making about a child's upbringing.

Parenting roles vary based on culture, and those outside that culture may view these familial roles in childrearing as "unusual." For example, Okagaki and Diamond (2000) point out that in some Asian communities, child-care responsibilities are shared between the mother and other family members. The mother's role focuses on training and teaching children. Asian mothers participating in this study reported that being a good mother meant discerning when a child is ready to be trained and then teaching him. These mothers stated that they display love for their children by helping them succeed, especially in educational situations. Understanding cultural practices can help child-care providers approach language and literacy learning in culturally appropriate ways that will be successful for the child, family, and staff.

Caregivers can apply the following practices to demonstrate respect for families and their culture-specific child-rearing practices:

- Talk with family members and identify the primary and secondary caretakers for each infant or toddler.

- Freely discuss practices of child rearing while seeking to understand common practices.

- When the family determines it is appropriate, include extended family members in meetings where decisions will be made about the child and when teaching the family, the child, or both a new task or technique.

- Demonstrate understanding and respect for requests for additional time for decisions so families can seek and include the opinions of elders or other family members.

The Relationship Between Language and Culture

Four key constructs underlie the integral relationship between culture and language: (a) Culture defines language, and language is shaped by culture; (b) language is a symbol of cultural and personal identity; (c) cultural groups have different worldviews based on the shared experiences that influence their various languages; (d) language is the medium by which culture is transmitted from generation to generation (Alverez et al., 1992).

Culture defines language, and language shapes culture. Just as, by definition, culture is dynamic and always changing, so also does language evolve and change. In the child-care arena, the words to describe the individual who provides care for an infant or toddler have evolved from *babysitter* to *caregiver*. It is the writers' opinion that this development is, in part, because of changes in cultural perception from the notion that "all an infant or toddler requires is someone to sit with her" to the idea that the individual who provides protection for an infant or toddler is helping to form the child's developing brain and, therefore, requires specialized knowledge and skills. The writers feel that it is likely that the terms *caregiver* and *teacher* guide the society to offer greater respect than the term *babysitter*.

Language is a symbol of cultural and personal identity. People hold on strongly to their language as a sign of who they are. Language contains embedded cultural concepts that influence the way that children understand their world. "Families and other caregivers provide learning experiences and furnish language labels as children demonstrate culturally acceptable roles, behaviors, and practices. These practices and behaviors contribute to the child's definition of self" (Jones, 2000, p. 6).

Cultural groups have different worldviews based on their own culture's shared experiences. Culture is the lens through which group members view the world. Because each cultural group has unique experiences, environments, objects, histories, and practices that influence their language, each culture has its own special worldview. Children learning language are affected by the cultural nuances inherent in language including the way that they see and experience the world.

Language is the medium through which individuals transmit culture from generation to generation. Whether a language is spoken, written, or both, it conveys the history and values of the group. In every culture, adults play key roles in teaching children the roles, norms, and language of their culture. They are likely to use *language codes* (such as pacing, turntaking, and dialects), *nonverbal communication* (such as gestures, proximity, eye contact), and cultural *communication styles* (customs regarding the use of language and communication, such as length of utterances, duration of silences, use or absence of humor, and story formats, blessings or prayers).

Personal history, style, and perceptions about language and culture contribute to *individual differences* in communicative style. Styles of expression, pronunciation, pacing, and approaches to learning language vary from child to child even within the same culture. It is said that children of similar age and in the same family develop language differently, especially in the earliest years of life. Thus, no two members of a cultural group are alike in their communication or literacy patterns.

Regardless of culture, the functions of language are the same: to communicate information, build and maintain relationships, and develop the self through the expression of new thoughts and ideas and the identification of acceptable cultural symbols of one's family of origin. Beginning at birth, infants build connections between sounds, gestures, and meaning. As they develop and grow, each child's family, culture, and linguistic background give rise to the child's development of language and communication. "Many cultural factors influence language development in young children, including their exposure to different quantities and styles in language usage, child-rearing practices, the cultural and linguistic backgrounds of parents and other caregivers, the presence of siblings and other extended family members, and individual child differences" (Jones, 2000, p. 5).

Bridging the Gap: Language, Communication, and Culture

Early childhood providers can enhance their understanding of the nuances of language across cultures by being aware that there are differences in verbal and nonverbal communication styles among different cultural groups. Other strategies to facilitate communication among those from different cultures follow:

- Be aware that body language such as gestures, facial expressions, and eye contact differ among cultures.

- Understand that some cultures rely on nonverbal cues to provide meaning for exchanges while others rely more on verbal exchanges.

- Remember that it is appropriate to inquire about the communication style of a culture that is different from one's own.

- Ask about appropriate ways to communicate with families and community leaders to nurture language and literacy learning among children.

Supporting the Native Language When Children Are Learning More Than One Language

Across the country, programs serving infants, toddlers, and their families are experiencing increasing diversity. Program administrators and staff members may wonder when to introduce English and how best to support children's home culture. Research supports the fact that children who are able to develop their native or home language while acquiring English experience positive long-term academic outcomes (Pham, 1994; Sanchez & Thorp, 1998). In contrast, studies indicate that learning English at an early age "in the absence of support for the home language can negatively effect future academic achievement" (Cummins, 1984, p. 89).

Early childhood programs that foster linguistic diversity provide a good foundation for the development of young children's early literacy. Such programs have relevance that extends beyond future academic success. Sanchez and Thorp (1998) identify profound cultural and social consequences of environments that emphasize the sole use of English with young children from diverse linguistic and cultural backgrounds. Underemphasis of a child's native language can contribute to the breakdown of intergenerational bonds by creating linguistic barriers, leading to loss of family connections and cultural heritage.

The use of the home or native language can have a critical effect on infants' and toddlers' adjustment to early child-care environments. "Continuity between the home and child care setting can benefit young children's sense of self" (Lorenzo-Hubert, 2004, p. 17). "A sharp linguistic or cultural divide can cause confusion and inadvertently lead to the assignment of positive or negative values to one language or culture over the other" (ZERO TO THREE, 2003). The development of partnerships among families, program leaders, and staff members are critical to ensure that children are exposed to both English and their home languages in natural, everyday situations in which they experience words and concepts normally.

Bridging the Gaps: Supporting the Native Language

Language and culture have an important and reciprocal relationship. As children are showered with language throughout the day, they are receiving information about culture, including ways of communicating ideas, feelings, and opinions; clarifying wants and needs; and resolving conflict. Caregivers simultaneously model language and convey important cultural values and beliefs. Consequently, these shared experiences and interactions have significant influence on the development of infants and toddlers. Because infants and toddlers learn through daily rituals and routines, it is important for early education and care staff members to partner with families to support each child's development of the native language.

Following are suggestions to consider when families speak a language different from that of the caregivers:

- Encourage parents to share aspects of their language and culture that they would like to see present in the program.

- Engage family members to share common words and longer utterances in the language that the family uses with the child. Examples could include words such as *please, thank you, diaper,* or *bottle,* and longer expressions such as *Would you like a bottle?*

- Invite parents to share songs, poems, drawings, music, and stories from their cultural backgrounds, and introduce these items into the daily routines.

- Enlarge and display photographs of children and their families, neighborhood landmarks, and community activities such as street fairs.

- Ensure that dolls for the housekeeping area represent a variety of cultures.

- Invite parents to donate empty boxes of common foods for housekeeping play with older toddlers.

When program leaders, staff, and families come together in these ways, the result is the creation of a nurturing environment that supports language development and literacy for all children.

Acquiring a Second Language

"Infants are quite capable of learning two languages from birth. They begin life with the ability to hear the differences among the sounds of many languages" (ZERO TO THREE, 2003). When infants regularly hear sounds that are not of their native language, the brain connections used to process these sounds are reinforced, and the child retains capacity to perceive and reproduce them. Infants and toddlers can be exposed to a second language in a variety of ways. Some children experience simultaneous exposure to two languages in the home from birth. This simultaneous acquisition can be the result of (a) each parent speaking a separate language with the child or (b) both parents speaking one language and a caregiver speaking another as well as (c) the child being exposed to English by means of television or the community. Other young children encounter a second language in a sequential format after the first language is partially established. For some, exposure to a second language occurs on entering a child-care situation.

Children follow different paths to become bilingual, and the stages that they pass through can be quite varied. McLaughlin, Blanchard, and Osanai (1995) report that "young children learning a native language and a second language simultaneously make unequal progress in the languages" (p. 2) and that one language from time to time is more prominent than the other. This unequal progress may be, in part, because of the amount of input that the young child receives from various speakers or because of greater opportunities to use one language more than the other. By the age of 2 to 3 years, toddlers become able to use each language with different people in different contexts. One example might be speaking Farsi with the mother or father and English with the care provider; another might be speaking English with the mother and Farsi with the grandmother. Some children discern the separateness of such contexts without difficulty.

It is important to understand that although "the [toddler] brain is especially open to different languages at this age, it is not necessarily easy to learn more than one language, nor does it mean that the learning will take place overnight" (ZERO TO THREE, 2003). Research supports the idea that young children sometimes acquire both languages at a slower rate than their peers who learn only one language. "Multiple factors influence how well and how quickly a toddler will become bilingual, including parental motivation to make the child bilingual, the amount of time the child spends in the care of each language partner, the toddler's degree of security in having his/her needs met in either language, and the quality of communication of the care provider and the toddler in a given language" (Lorenzo-Hubert, 2004, p. 10). Switching between English and a child's native language (also known as code switching) is normal for young children learning two languages simultaneously. It is vital to remember that a toddler exposed to two languages is navigating between two very different systems of communication.

For sequential second-language learners, the developmental progression is somewhat different from simultaneous second-language learners. The four stages in the process of sequential second-language acquisition for bilingual preschoolers are presented in Table 9.1.

It is important for caregivers to know and understand these stages of language acquisition for young children who are in the process of learning a new language. Awareness of the stages and the related behaviors can assist the caregiver in providing the appropriate support that the child needs to acquire a second language.

The following scenario offers an example of some of the challenges that a caregiver may face in attempting to design a program that meets the linguistic needs of a child and family.

> *Vigor was recently adopted from Croatia. He lived in an orphanage from the time he was born until his recent adoption at age 2. Vigor is 27 months old. He has lived with his American parents and Croatian nanny for 3 months. While the nanny*

Table 9.1. Stages in Sequential Language Acquisition

Stages of Sequential Language Development	Characteristics
Use of the home language: A child who speaks a different language is introduced into an environment in which another language is spoken.	The child speaks in his native language, until she recognizes that she is unable to communicate within the environment. Many children stop talking during this period and frustration increases.
Nonverbal period: The child elects not to talk in the native language.	The child uses nonverbal communication (such as pointing, whining, crying) to get his needs met. The child begins to rehearse some of the sounds and words of the new language.
Telegraphic and Formulaic Language: Telegraphic language involves the use of one word to convey a meaning; formulaic language involves the use of two-word, routinely heard phrases to get needs met.	Telegraphic Language: The child uses one word to name people or objects. Formulaic Language: The child memorizes, recalls, and uses two-word phrases to communicate an idea or thought.
Productive Language Use: Language becomes more useful.	The child is able to go beyond the use of telegraphic patterns and memorized chunks to express personal meaning.

speaks to Vigor in Croatian, he has only recently been exposed to English. He does not communicate verbally in English, though he does use a few phrases in his native language to express most of his needs. Vigor has been in a child-care program for 1 week. Both his parents and caregivers have noted that when people do not understand him or when his needs are not met, Vigor tends to remove himself from class and home activities. His parents fear that he is depressed, and they are seeking professional advice.

This scenario presents a variety of challenges. Vigor is new to his family and the United States. He also has experienced some of the hardships of living in an orphanage, including possibly limited attachment, attention, and stimulation. His American family does not speak his native language, but his nanny does. Vigor is facing the challenge of trying to learn a new language. Vigor's child-care provider is attempting to meet both the child's needs and those of the family. The caregiver's primary goal at this time is to provide a comfortable, secure, and stable environment with few language demands on Vigor. The caregiver should invite Vigor's parents to include the nanny in a conference. During the conversation, the caregiver should try to identify the activities, toys, and any other items that will support Vigor's transition from home to the classroom. The caregiver should ask the nanny to teach a few key phrases in Croatian and discuss the benefits of having the nanny participate within the classroom for a short time until Vigor is more comfortable there. By participating, the nanny will provide stability, speak Vigor's native language, and facilitate his transition to his second language and to literacy. The family and caregiver should establish a communication book that will travel back and forth from home to school, keeping all parties informed of Vigor's adjustment and progress.

Bridging the Gap: When a Child Is Learning More Than One Language

When a child's family speaks a language other than English, the questions for early childhood professionals become how much English to present during the early years and how best to support bilingual language development. Decisions regarding that question should be based on each family's preferences and needs, the language or languages of the child's home and community, the child's own progress in initial language acquisition, and the effect of second-language learning on the child's first language.

Following are some strategies that child-care providers can use to support children and families and foster language development:

- Involve family members in discussions about communicating with their infant or toddler, with understanding and respect for the variety of beliefs that families hold.

- Provide opportunities for children to hear and use their home language in natural interactions.

- Model responsive strategies for infant–toddler communications for family members.

- Discuss the family's goals related to English and home language usage, share the program's goals, and develop a personalized approach for each child.

- Remember that culture and language are intertwined and have a strong effect on the way that a toddler experiences and understands his world.

- Communicate with the toddler during nurturing activities such as diaper changes and dressing.

- Share with the toddler the caregiver's culture and language while embracing and supporting the culture of her native language.

- Allow time for the toddler to practice communicating.

Ensuring Adequate Communication With Families From Diverse Linguistic Backgrounds

In a society as diverse as that of the United States, it is probable that early childhood providers will not have the capacity to speak the language of every family. Child-care settings that receive federal funding have an obligation under Title VI (Nondiscrimination in Federally Assisted Programs) of the Civil Rights Act of 1964 (Pub. L. 88-352) not to exclude, deny, or subject to discrimination any individual on the basis of race, religion, gender, or national origin. In 2000, the U.S. Department of Health and Human Services (DHHS) issued a *Guidance to Federal Financial Assistance Recipients Regarding Title VI Prohibition Against National Origin Discrimination Affecting Limited English Proficient Persons* (U.S. Department of Health and Human Services, Office for Civil Rights, 2000). The guidance mandates agencies that receive federal funds from DHHS to take reasonable steps to ensure meaningful access to programs, services, and activities for persons with limited English proficiency (U.S. Department of Health and Human Services, Office of Civil Rights, 2000). This document provides guidance to agencies, programs, and organizations with respect to their obligation to provide language assistance to those for whom English is not a primary language. The Office for Civil Rights, Department of Health and Human Services Web site (http://www.hhs.gov/ocr/lep/revisedlep.html) provides valuable information about ways of ensuring language access for individuals and families with limited English proficiency, including the use of qualified interpreters and translators, qualified bilingual staff, language banks, language lines, and trained community volunteers.

Bridging the Gaps: Ensuring Adequate Communication With Families From Diverse Linguistic Backgrounds

It is critical for early childhood programs serving infants and toddlers to develop strategies to foster communication with all families:

- Whenever possible ensure that signs, memos, announcements, or materials are translated into the families' preferred languages.

- Use interpreters or bilingual staff trained in interpretation when conveying information orally, and use translators or qualified bilingual staff to provide information in written formats.

- Encourage bilingual staff and families to assist staff members who are not bilingual to learn and use basic phrases (hello, good-bye, thank you) in the languages of the families that participate in the program.

Building partnerships with formal and informal community resources is an important way to reach out to other community agencies and organizations. Such agencies may include, but are not limited to, ethnic-specific community groups, faith-based organizations, community health centers, other children's agencies, and other community-based organizations. These entities can often provide the bridge between care providers and families for whom English is not a primary language. They may also offer cultural brokering services. A cultural broker is a "liaison, cultural guide, mediator and catalyst for change" (National Center for Cultural Competence, 2004, p. 3). As such, the person understands the strengths and needs of the individual or community and the particular systems, agencies, or organizations with which it seeks to engage. "Almost anyone can act as a cultural broker" (p. 5), including but not limited to family members, child-care providers, administrators, nurses, office assistants, etc. Some cultural brokers also act as interpreters. One strategy is to cultivate and support family mentors from diverse language backgrounds, individuals who are current or former parents of children enrolled in the program. Such families can provide the vehicle for interpretation as well as welcome and involve families in the group care of their children. Whenever possible, link families to bilingual-bicultural staff who are able to communicate with them. Such a linkage affords families the opportunity to make their beliefs and values known, helps staff to gain a better understanding of the child, and may contribute to more individualized services. Making families from diverse linguistic backgrounds feel welcome and able to participate in program activities is key to forming partnerships.

When working with culturally and linguistically diverse families, it is important to understand and learn about the context of each family and each infant's or toddler's language development. However, it is essential that this information be gathered in a way that feels safe and assuring, an interaction that is not threatening or intrusive to families. The following two sections suggest two types of questions to use for obtaining information: (1) questions about the family and (2) questions about language.

Obtaining Family Information

The first set of questions is designed to elicit information with respect to family constellation, the infant's or toddler's primary caregivers, the number of languages spoken by the family and by whom, and family literacy. The answers to these questions can assist with (a) determining the most appropriate ways and languages to use to convey information to the family in oral and written formats, (b) identifying the individuals who interact with the infant or toddler, and (c) learning the extent of the child's exposure to and use of English.

- Who are the important individuals in the infant or toddler's life?

- What languages do they speak? Understand? Read? Write?

- What languages are spoken in the home? By the parents or caregivers?

- Is there another person who provides care for the infant or toddler? If so, what language or languages does he or she speak?

- What languages are spoken in the neighborhood or community?

- What language (or languages) is spoken on the family's television or radio?

- How are these languages viewed in the community at large?

Obtaining Information About Language Usage

The second set of questions can provide information with respect to (a) how language is included in the child's daily routine, (b) key words or phrases that staff should learn in the child's native language, and (c) the circumstances under which the first, second, or other language is used with the infant or toddler.

- If there are siblings, cousins, aunts, uncles, or other individuals living in the household, how old are they? What language or languages do they use to speak to one another? What language or languages do they use to speak to the infant or toddler?

- What are recurring topics of conversation with the infant or toddler? How long are conversations with the infant or toddler? What key words should both the child and the center's caregivers master in the child's non-English language?

- Does turntaking occur? How long do people wait for a response from the infant or toddler?

- When the infant or toddler is being fed, is language used? How? Which language is used?

- Does the person who is feeding the infant or toddler make eye contact with him or her during feeding?

Responses to these questions can assist in developing plans and activities that will meet the individual linguistic and social needs of each child and family. Additionally, the questions can provide valuable information to guide program planning and ensure the access and participation of all families from diverse cultural and linguistic backgrounds.

Family–Professional Partnerships Across Cultures

The numbers of children in early care and education programs continue to grow. Although families place their children in group settings for a wide range of reasons, the decision to place an infant or toddler in an early childhood program reflects trust, respect, and a reverence for education as well as for the persons who interact with the children. Many families have had no previous experience with very young children in care outside the family structure, and therefore, they may have a variety of expectations and assumptions that may differ from those of the caregivers and the program. Some families may expect that the early childhood setting will provide for all of the child's needs: physical, emotional, social, and educational. It is not unusual for family members to view the caregiver or early childhood educator as someone who will act in the role of a surrogate parent. Collaborative partnerships between family members and staff provide a safe haven for information sharing and the clarification of issues and concerns.

Partnerships between families and the staff members who provide care for their children support reciprocal learning and cooperation. Families can provide a wealth of information regarding the settlement history of their cultural group, which can, in turn, provide caregivers and program staff members with invaluable insights into the behaviors and needs of a young child and his family. The toddler's family who recently emigrated to the United States as refugees has completely different needs from a family with an extensive history in the community and a well-established network of social supports. Additionally, acquainting family members with the culture of the early childhood program is essential to the development of partnerships for learning. This exchange can help bridge differences in expectations of the program and the families it serves, thereby minimizing conflicts for the child.

Parents from diverse cultural and linguistic backgrounds can be vital to curriculum enhancement as they offer suggestions for adaptations that honor their cultures in meaningful ways. Soliciting the ideas and contributions of parents regarding their culture is an important aspect of establishing partnerships. Such engagement with families enriches the curriculum, but it also includes parents as meaningful partners in the literacy development of their young children.

Another facet of family and program collaboration involves inviting families to assist in the planning of all aspects of the program, including attending and participating in meetings, celebrations, and family events. "Respecting and including families in the daily life of the program shows families that they are valued and respected" (York, 1991, p. 114). Complex schedules and the demands of multiple responsibilities may hinder the participation of some families in such events, but activity announcements and newsletters (in various languages) can serve as a way to keep the lines of communication open and the partnership thriving. It is as important to create, support, and sustain positive experiences for families of infants and toddlers involved in early childhood programs as it is to make children's learning experiences rewarding. Parent involvement is essential to ensuring successful early learning experiences.

Bridging the Gap: Family–Professional Partnerships Across Cultures

Child-care providers can consider the following suggestions to enhance parent involvement in program activities:

- Recognize that it takes time to establish rapport with parents or family members.

- Provide a safe environment for the sharing of information.

- Seek assistance with communication if a family's preferred language is not English. Bilingual staff, adult family members, or both can provide this assistance.

- Whenever possible, provide information to families in easily understandable ways such as pictures or symbols, verbal messages if literacy is an issue, and translated fliers and announcements.

- Enlist the help of a veteran parent from the program to act as a cultural broker or liaison. Choose an individual who has not only knowledge of the program but also the experience of parenting an infant or toddler who is in the program.

- Invite parents and family members to visit or participate in program activities and to share stories, customs, food, and songs.

- Establish a lending library of toys, books, videos, manipulatives, and homemade materials such as touch-and-feel books or homemade play dough.

With interpreters, remember the following:

- Speak with the interpreter before conversation with a family to familiarize the interpreter with the family and the information to be shared or obtained from the family.

- Underscore the need for the interpreter to maintain confidentiality regarding information shared by the family. It is okay for the interpreter to share the information with you, but not with others.

- Debrief to ensure that both the family and staff understood all that was communicated.

- Look directly at the family and not the interpreter when speaking.

- Ensure that the interpreter does not respond for the family without **first** conveying information that staff requested or provided.

- Use gestures such as head nods to demonstrate understanding.

- Ask family members to repeat information to be sure of their understanding.

Conclusion

The nation is moving toward a majority population of diverse cultural and linguistic backgrounds. At the same time, the nation struggles to enhance the educational system to assure that every child reaches her full potential. The need for understanding and accepting differences among people is an important part of this effort. Any effective educational foundation must respect and honor cultural beliefs, practices, preferences, and traditions as it nurtures the individual abilities and learning needs of each child. It is not an easy task, but through professional–family partnerships and the use of the approaches listed above, a balance between program goals and parental expectations can be achieved. When these partnerships are forged around early language and literacy, young children will thrive personally and educationally, and families will begin to walk a path of positive collaboration with educators.

References

Alverez, R., Barton, A., Clark, G., Keenan, J. F., Lalyre, Y., et al. (1992). *Young lives: Many languages, many cultures.* Malden: Massachusetts Department of Education.

Bowman, B. T. (1989). Educating language minority children: Challenges and opportunities. *Phi Delta Kappan, 71*(2), 118–221.

Children's Defense Fund. (2001). 25 key facts about American children. In *The state of America's children: Yearbook 2001* (p. 1). Washington, DC: Author.

Civil Rights Act of 1964, Pub. L. No. 88-352, §601 [Electronic Version] 241–268. Retrieved January 15, 2004, from http://usinfo.state.gov/usa/infousa/laws/majorlaw/civilr19.htm

Cummins, J. (1984). Minority students and learning difficulties: Issues in assessment and placement. In M. Pardis & Y. Lebrun (Eds.), *Early bilingualism and child development* (pp. 47–68). Lisse, Netherlands: Swets & Zeitlinger.

Goode, T. D. (2002a). *Key definitions.* Washington, DC: Georgetown University Center for Child and Human Development, National Center for Cultural Competence.

Goode, T. D. (2002b). *What is cultural competence?* Washington, DC: Georgetown University Center for Child and Human Development, National Center for Cultural Competence.

Harkness, S., & Super, C. (1994). The developmental niche: Implications for children's literacy development. In L. Eldering & P. Leseman (Eds.), *Early intervention and culture: The interface between theory and practice* (pp. 115–132). Paris: UNESCO Publishing.

Harwood, R. L. (1992). The influence of culturally derived values on Anglo and Puerto Rican mothers' perceptions of attachment behavior. *Child Development, 63,* 822–839.

Jones, W. A. (2000). *Linguistic competence in early intervention and early childhood settings.* Paper presented at regional meeting on Cultural Competence in Early Intervention and Early Childhood Settings, Albany, NY.

LeVine, R., Dixon, S., LeVine, S., Richman, A., Keefer, C., Leiderman, P. H., & Brazelton, T. (1994). *Childcare and culture: Lessons from Africa.* New York: Cambridge University Press.

LeVine, R., Miller, P., Richman, A., & LeVine, S. (1996). Education and mother-infant interaction: A Mexican case study. In S. Harkness & C. Super (Eds.), *Parents' cultural belief systems: Their origins, expressions, and consequences.* New York: Guilford.

Lorenzo-Hubert, I. (2004). *Linguistic competence in early intervention & early childhood settings: What do you need to know about second language learning?* Paper presented at the Training Institutes 2004, Developing Local Systems of Care for Children and Adolescents with Emotional Disturbances and their Families—Early Intervention, San Francisco, CA.

McLaughlin, B. G., Blanchard, A., & Osanai, Y. (1995). *Assessing language development in bilingual preschool children.* NCBE Program Information Guide Series No. 22. [Electronic Version] Retrieved November 30, 2003, from http://www.ncela.gwu.edu/pubs/pigs/pig22.htm

National Center for Cultural Competence. (2004). *Bridging the cultural divide in health care settings: The essential role of cultural broker programs.* Washington, DC: Georgetown University Center for Child and Human Development.

Okagaki, L., & Diamond, K. E. (2000). Responding to cultural and linguistic differences in the beliefs and practices of families with young children. *Young Children, 55*(3), 74–79.

Okagaki, L., & Sternberg, R. (1993). Perspectives of kindergarten: Rafael, Vanessa, and Jamell go to school. *Childhood Education, 71*(1), 14–19.

Pham, L. (1994, Winter). Infant dual language acquisition revisited. *The Journal of Educational Issues of Language Minority Students, 14,* 185–210.

Rosenkoetter, S. E. (2006). Mentoring: Together we're better. In S. E. Rosenkoetter & J. Knapp-Philo (Eds.), *Learning to read the world: Language and literacy in the first three years* (pp. 369–394). Washington, DC: ZERO TO THREE Press.

Sanchez, S., & Thorp, E. (1998). Discovering the meaning of continuity: Implications for the infant/family field. *Zero to Three, 18*(6), 1–6.

U.S. Department of Health and Human Services, Office for Civil Rights. (2000). *Guidance to federal financial assistance recipients regarding Title VI Prohibition Against National Origin Discrimination Affecting Limited English Proficient Persons.* [Electronic Version] Retrieved January 15, 2004, from http://www.hhs.gov/ocr/lep/revisedlep.html

West, J., Wright, D., & Hausken, E. G. (1995). *Childcare and early education program participation of infants, toddlers and preschoolers.* National Household Education Survey No. 95-824. Washington, DC: U.S. Department of Education, Office of Educational Research and Improvement, National Center for Education Statistics.

York, S. (1991). *Roots and wings: Affirming culture in early childhood programs.* St. Paul, MN: Red Leaf Press.

ZERO TO THREE. (2003). *Tips for practitioners: Supporting a linguistically diverse environment in infant/family programs.* [Electronic version]. Retrieved December 17, 2003, from http://www.zerotothree.org/search/index2.cfm

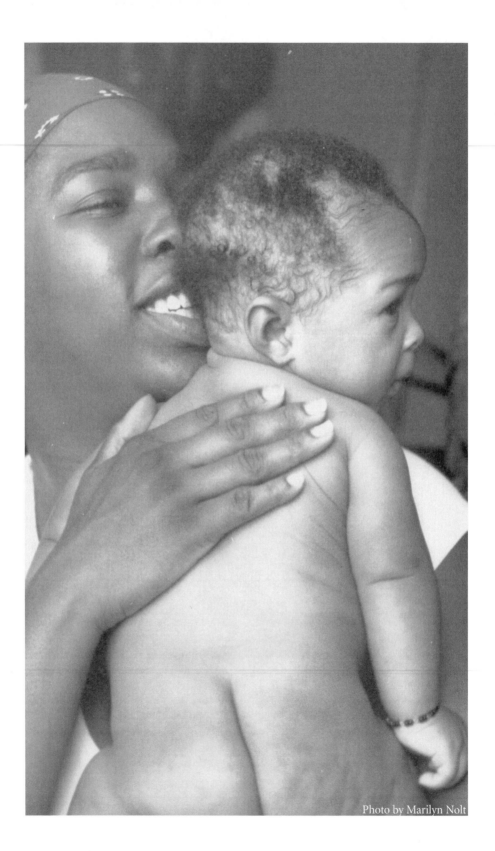

CHAPTER 10

Family Literacy

Michael Gramling and Sharon E. Rosenkoetter ·

The encouragement of family literacy has support all the way from the White House (n.d.) to the local library ("Creating Welcoming Library Environments," 2001). The discipline of family literacy is a relatively new field, synthesizing research from traditional disciplines of early childhood education, elementary education, adult education, parent education, and family studies, with an emphasis on how each discipline works together to support literacy development in family settings (Goodling Institute for Family Literacy Research, 2004).

In practice, family literacy is a complex concept with at least five components:

1. The first component is **families talking and using print with their young children**. Based on the assumption that children's development of language and literacy skills is critically affected by the people closest to the infant or toddler, this view appears to be simple and almost self-evident, but it also has a research base (Gregory, 2001; Heath, 1983; Snow, Burns, & Griffin, 1998). Much of this volume supports this element of family literacy.

2. The second component of family literacy is **families as environmental arrangers**. The world that the baby comes to know is the environment inside the home plus outside places where the infant or toddler is taken. These environments include both the social interactions discussed above and the physical setting (Fabes & Martin, 2000; Heath, 1983). Key features of any environment are the diverse ways that it supports or fails to support early language and literacy. Every day, the family makes 1,001+ decisions that establish the baby's early language and literacy environment—for example, whether to eat together or independently, whether to buy a mag-

azine or a six-pack, whether to take time to talk and listen to one another or rush off to some other activity, and whether to have a bedtime routine or simply go to sleep whenever exhaustion comes.

3. The third component of family literacy is **families as readers**. Without conscious effort, parents use language and print in their own individually and culturally driven ways and model those uses for their infants and toddlers (Heath, 1983). They may—or may not—have a variety of purposes for talking and reading: to have fun, to establish and maintain connections with others, to accomplish tasks, to earn a living, and to learn new ideas and skills. Young children imitate what they see; that is, they use language and print in the ways they observe their siblings and parents using them (Burns, Griffin, & Snow, 1999; Hart & Risley, 1999).

4. The fourth component of family literacy is **families as students**. Some parents view life as an ongoing adventure to gain novel ideas and master new skills; others do not. Family members may be students enrolled in General Educational Development (GED; high school equivalency) or PhD programs. They may be eager learners who informally consume whatever new information they can gain access to on a host of topics apart from formal degree programs. Or they may demonstrate neither of these student-like behaviors. In any case, the significant adults model their attitudes toward lifelong learning for their offspring to imitate.

5. The fifth component of family literacy is **parents[1] as community mobilizers for early language and literacy**. When a community organizes to include infants and toddlers in its literacy efforts (see Zukoski & Luluquisen, this volume p. 429), parents can be key players, telling their own stories, motivating civic action, and providing volunteer services, perhaps with their children in tow. In addition to mobilizing the community, such efforts model for young children the citizen role and the power of personal action to improve one's milieu.

This chapter will discuss each of these five components of family literacy as well as the supports that can be offered to enhance their effects. Because understanding of family literacy is mediated by the personal experience of

---

[1] *Parents* here means the individual or individuals in the primary nurturing and caregiving roles in the home and may include foster parents, partners, grandparents, older siblings, live-in members of the extended family, and friends.

each reader, the chapter will also illustrate the key concepts through the sharing of several family stories. We believe that families—all families—are an extraordinary resource for every community, celebrating its present and creating its future.

Families Talking and Using Print With Their Young Children

A major contribution of family literacy to young children's future success is the act of talking with infants and toddlers. After studying 42 children and their families in depth for 2+ years beginning with the children's first speech, Hart and Risley (1995, 1999) noted incredible disparities in the amount of language that infants and toddlers hear in their homes. Over the course of their study, the authors noted that the children in the lowest group heard, on average, 616 words per hour, those in the middle group heard 1,251 words per hour, and those in the highest group heard 2,153 words per hour. This pattern was repeated hour by hour, day by day, year by year, so by the time these children were 4 years old, the ones in the lowest group would have heard 13 million fewer words than those in the middle group and 32 million words fewer than those in the highest group. Hart and Risley noted that these relative amounts of speech that were heard were directly related to the amounts and types of language the children produced as they moved on into preschool and elementary school. Oral language is a major predictor of school readiness and later school success (Snow et al., 1998). In commenting on these data, Bloom (1995) noted that the finding is "heartbreaking" (pp. xii–xiii) in that by the time the children in the study were 3 years old, the parents in the least talkative group had used fewer different words in their cumulative monthly vocabularies than had the children in the most talkative families. Hart and Risley emphasize that language acquisition is influenced to a large degree by the sheer volume of words heard in the home during the early years.

The richness of interaction in the home has a strong influence on early language development and acquisition of literacy that lasts throughout the school years. Vocabulary, in particular, was found to be directly related to the total number of words heard in the home (Hart & Risley, 1995, 1999). According to the National Early Literacy Panel, richness of vocabulary is tied to later school success (*National Early Literacy Panel Report*, in press). The authors also noted tremendous variability in the words that families use when they talk to their infants and toddlers. Of the many thousands of words that families used over the 2+ years of the study, only 94 words were used by all 42 of the families in the investigation. This finding is certainly a demonstration of the rich diversity in culture, interests, and lifeways that American families represent.

The development of language and emergence of literacy are inextricably intertwined. A second major contribution of family literacy is the act of sharing symbols and print experiences with infants and toddlers (see, in this volume, Anderson, p. 553; Cole, & Lim, p. 537; and Notari-Syverson, p. 61; see also Schickedanz, 1999; Snow et al., 1998). From cereal boxes to T-shirt messages, TV commercials to name stickers, storybooks to stop signs, infants and toddlers grow up in a world of print. They learn to gain meaning from that print through the interpretations of their families (Butler, 1998) and usually first experiment with the writing of symbols in the context of the family (Taylor, 1983).

When family members call attention to the printed word during daily routines, they contribute significantly to literacy development (Snow et al., 1998). For example, the father who runs errands with his child learns through printed words that the convenience store does not take checks, that the laundromat closed at 6 o'clock, and that a particular street is closed to through traffic today. The parent may or may not realize, however, that all of these messages affect the child strapped in the car seat or the stroller just as much as they do the adult. Perhaps the parent provides numerous interactions with print for the young child simply by pointing out these printed messages to the child, reading the words aloud, and stating the consequence of a particular message: "We won't do the laundry today after all."

Interactions of this sort not only provide opportunities for conversation and add to the total number of words heard but also begin to show the child from the earliest age that printed words convey messages that are personally meaningful and that influence, and sometimes direct, daily activities. Through hundreds of such focused daily interactions with print, children begin to see that written language is used to communicate, to remember important information, to find missing objects, to cook, and to find out what is on television, among other important functions.

Parents as Environmental Arrangers

As described above, families set the social scene for early language and literacy. Families also set the physical environment with interesting objects (Schatz, 1994); accessible catalogs or storybooks (Neuman, 1999); and explorations of the unknown in the yard, the neighborhood, or beyond (Gopnik, Meltzoff, & Kuhl, 2001).

A literacy-rich household contains many tools of literacy (see Notari-Syverson, this volume, p. 61), symbols, and print that families can label and interpret. Special tools include markers, crayons, paper, chalk, books, magazines, and computers. The child who "helps" while her father reads a bill, who climbs onto her mother's lap while Mom types her research paper, or who recognizes the sign for the women's restroom in Kmart becomes familiar with the everyday importance of literacy and gains confidence in the ability to manipulate literacy's tools.

Parents as Readers

Seeing parents reading sends a strong message to a child (Heath, 1983). Observing adults reading recipes, directions for assembling toys, TV guides, warranties, maps, religious materials, hunting magazines, or whatever else is important to the child's family communicates the message that reading is a useful skill. Writing shopping lists, checks, or cards to Grandma indicates that print helps organize lives and allows people to reach out to others. Many parents, of course, expand their own literacy activities beyond making grocery lists and following directions to make microwave popcorn. Many adults also read for enjoyment or because they want to gain information about a hobby, a job skill, or a legal right. Perhaps they are enrolled in formal course work. When parents model literacy in daily life, the effect on infants and toddlers can be immediate. One sees the toddler climb into the small easy chair with book in hand or observes the preschooler write a list while "playing house." Just as there are individual, socioeconomic, and cultural variations in what adults do with reading, there are also individual, socioeconomic, and cultural variations in what their children do in imitation (Heath, 1983).

However, one worries when the role model of the literate adult is absent from young children's lives. For example, during early childhood, children are guided to read, but they are also encouraged to engage in activities such as dramatic play and finger painting. When children mature and come to understand that these latter activities are not much pursued in the adult world, finger painting and dress-up may be dropped from the older child's repertoire. It is quite possible, then, that in the absence of the adult role model, reading itself could be discarded for the same reasons. It may be, then, that providing books and other interesting reading materials for adults is just as important as encouraging the reading of children's books (Gramling, 2002).

Parents as Students

The presence of adults in the home who are committed to lifelong learning not only provides positive role models but also establishes expectations that support the child's ongoing use of literacy and anticipation of academic success. Such continuing learning may occur in a formal degree program, in classes pertaining to a hobby or vocation, or in independent pursuit of improved knowledge through sustained efforts to acquire new knowledge or valued skills. The critical element that children observe is ongoing adult effort to learn. Picture Miguel who works hard in the fields all day and then attends English classes in the evening. His children know that their dad values learning! Or consider Cassandra who finished high school by earning a GED (high school equivalency) degree and now is attending community college to hone her computer skills. Cassandra's daughter knows that her mother is thrilled when she deciphers a new software package. Damien's grandfather went to work rather than to high school in Ecuador, the land of his birth, and Damien's grandmother has spent her life as a housewife without any degrees, but they both read books in Spanish every day; they talk about interesting words, ideas, and newspaper articles with their grandchildren; and they study books on plant propagation and insect pests to improve their large vegetable garden. Damien, even at age 3, knows that learning and literacy matter to his grandparents.

Ongoing adult participation in education sends the message that in this household, literacy is a family value, perhaps like respecting elders or not wasting food. Seen in the family literacy context, recruitment to and retention in adult education are no longer about passing or failing a test, earning a degree, or receiving some distant and unlikely economic payoff. Instead, education is pursued for its own sake, and for the sake of one's child. Enrollment in a basic literacy class or in a doctoral program are of equal value in demonstrating desire for self-improvement. No content is too basic, nor is there a stopping place that says "now I've finally done enough."

Because there is a significant correlation between the parent's educational level and the child's success in school (Benjamin, 1993), there has been ongoing interest among the early childhood community in enrolling parents with limited education in formal adult education classes such as GED, basic literacy, and English as a Second or Other Language (ESOL) classes, primarily to enhance the adult's economic status and employability. This motivation is stated explicitly, for example, in the federal definition of *family literacy* that drives the adult education activities of Even Start, Head Start, and the Department of Education Office of Vocational and Adult Education (The Head Start Act, 1998).

If earning a GED certificate and subsequently achieving economic self-sufficiency are the yardsticks for success for adult literacy efforts, however, this approach to adult education has proven to be less than effective. A very small percentage of those who enroll in GED classes actually earn a GED diploma (Abt Associates, 2004). Likewise, in Head Start–Early Head Start, where data annually indicate high numbers of parents referred to adult education, there is no mechanism in place to track actual enrollment and retention in adult education classes (*ACF Child Outcomes and Evaluation*, 2002). Anecdotal data, however, gathered by the first author from Head Start–Early Head Start managers attending the training of the Head Start Family Literacy Project in spring–summer 2003, overwhelmingly report high dropout rates among parents referred to GED classes. Further, because of limited employment opportunities in many areas, there is no guarantee that education itself, particularly at the GED level, will actually produce the economic outcomes that might motivate parents to expend the sustained effort necessary to achieve success (Baker, Scher, & Mackler, 1997).

A more meaningful view of adult education is a process-oriented approach that measures success, not in terms of the parent's economic status or attainment of credentials, but in enhanced outcomes for children. Children's success in school is a nearly universal goal of parents, as is the desire that their children "have a better life" (Strickland, 1996). While many parents identify their child's education as a means to a better life and make necessary sacrifices to provide it, very few parents would identify their own role as lifelong learner to be critical. It is noteworthy that the parent's own pursuit of education does, in fact, have a positive influence on the child's success in school (Snow & Tabors, 1996). Convincing parents of this argument is a key task of effective family literacy services.

Parents as Community Mobilizers for Early Language and Literacy

Children, families, and practitioners do not exist in vacuums, nor do language and literacy develop in isolation. To bring about sustainable change in current family literacy practices, an ecological approach considers the role of agencies, neighborhoods, and communities in supporting families and helping to nurture early literacy and language development (Knapp-Philo & Stice, 2004). Family members can be effective advocates in telling their own stories and in convincing fellow citizens to include infants and toddlers in developmentally appropriate literacy education activities. Family literacy programs such as Even Start focus on family educational needs, establish community collaborations that build on existing resources, and offer instruction that provides families with tools and support (Goodling Institute, 2004). Given the five family literacy roles outlined above—roles that parents can provide better than any other agent—it is important for community infant–toddler programs to work closely with community partners as well as with parents to achieve family literacy outcomes.

Ways to Support Family Literacy

Given that family–child relationships are central to language and literacy development (see Bus & DeJong, this volume, p. 123, and Rosenkoetter & Wanless, this volume, p. 81), it follows, then, that intervention strategies that bypass or marginalize the parent will not be productive. The most effective strategy for encouraging facilitative home environments emphasizes the development of reciprocal relationships with parents in which the values, goals, and practices of families are honored. Of course, this process is much easier said than done, especially when practices differ from what research with certain populations shows to be efficacious for school readiness (Cummins, 1981).

Strategies for Encouraging Family Literacy

The importance of parent participation in program-based strategies is widely acknowledged and enshrined in practice. The extent and content of such participation, however, varies considerably. One familiar approach to family literacy has been to provide parents with specific activities that supplement classroom experiences. For example, when Head Start and Early Head Start programs were asked to list specific family literacy services provided by their agencies, sending books into homes for parents to read to children was the most common response (Abt Associates, 2004). A second strategy for parent involvement focuses not only on the content of parent–child activities but also on the manner in which the activity is carried out by the parent. In this approach, the program not only provides an at-home activity to supplement the child's classroom experiences but also provides fairly prescriptive parent training on how best to implement these activities (*Head Start Family Literacy Project,* 2003).

A third and more developmental model for family literacy emphasizes the importance of the overall home environment as well as the primary nature of the parent–child relationship (*Head Start Family Literacy Project,* 2003). Exposure to language and print in the context of day-in and day-out parent–child interactions is seen as having a far greater effect than exposure to language in classroom settings or during the few moments of daily parent–child interaction suggested by a program (e.g., PACT—Parents And Children Together—in Even Start). In this model, the widely practiced strategy described earlier of sending books home for parents to read to children is quite appropriate and consistent with enriching interaction, particularly because shared story reading is an activity that fits neatly into daily routines like bedtime and nap time.

Providing children's books for families, however, also raises more issues about parent education than previously discussed approaches. Some in the early literacy community, for example, maintain that (a) parenting education on how to read books to children is a necessary component of any efforts to encourage reading to children in the home and (b) parenting education on how to be the child's teacher is an essential component of family literacy services in general (The Head Start Act, 1998). On the other hand, parent training continues to be a very sensitive topic within the field of family literacy. For many, questions about which practices are best and therefore ought to be taught dwarf in comparison to concerns about professionals' sensitivity to family culture, the dignity of the family, and respect for the competence of parents as well as the propriety of institutions intruding into family practices. For example, the National Center for Family Literacy (NCFL), although a strong advocate for parenting education, cautions that the desire to have parents do activities better (or do activities "right") can easily turn to frustration and blame when parents fail to attend training, fail to follow through on program recommendations, or produce outcomes for children that are below expectations (*Head Start Family Literacy Project*, 2003).

The NCFL therefore recommends that parent education be seen broadly, not as a requirement for parental participation but as an ongoing dialogue between programs and parents. Such a dialogue might include formal classes but would also include parent–teacher conferences, informal conversations, modeling, exchanges of information, sharing of strategies at home and at the center, and mutual goal setting. In this light, the practice of providing books to families can be seen as a training strategy in itself. Agencies that provide families with books that are thoughtfully and intentionally chosen to be appropiate for the child's age, provided in the home language, and sensitive to the family's culture send messages to parents and pregnant women that reading to children is valuable, it cannot start too early, and it cannot happen too often. Program-provided books also offer concrete models of the kinds of books that are appropriate for the age of the particular child or children in the home, enabling parents to make better choices when they select books for their family.

Certainly, there are some ways of reading books to children that are shown to be better than others (Baker et al., 1997; Cole & Lim, this volume, p. 537), especially approaches that emphasize enriched interaction. Evidence-based information of this sort can be provided to parents through an ongoing dialogue that honors parent practices and provides a wide variety of options from which parents may choose.

Although sharing books with children is important, discussion of the printed words that parents and young children encounter in routines throughout the day is also valuable. Parents who may not have the time or opportunity to read a book to their child more than once a day can, nevertheless, interact more frequently around print.

Encouraging Language at Home

In the Hart and Risley (1995) study in which vocabulary development was found to be a direct function of words heard, *words heard* meant exactly that: words spoken by family members and heard by children, not necessarily words spoken to the child or words intended to elicit a response or engage children in conversation. This finding suggests strongly that parents' verbal behaviors during the child's early years affect language development 24 hours a day, 7 days a week. Consider the toddler who spills his milk when his grandparents are visiting for dinner and then unleashes the exact same four-letter epithet with the exact same intonation that his mother used when she spilled the spaghetti sauce on the new tablecloth earlier in the day. Children, it seems, use vocabulary that we have no intention of teaching. If Mama talks on the phone while Junior plays in an adjoining room, then he is likely to inform Daddy later that Mama is overdrawn at the bank again. If parents talk privately in the front seat of the car while the 2-year-old daughter entertains herself on the back seat, she will undoubtedly announce at the destination that Mommy is still not pregnant. Evidently, some vocabulary words need a lot less work than others!

In terms of intervention strategies, then, the key is not purposefully to introduce new vocabulary or concepts one at a time or to seek parental assistance in supporting these words and concepts through planned activities (e.g., the word of the day or the color of the week drill), but instead to enrich the interaction in the home so children's language and vocabulary development are stimulated during the unplanned moments that constitute most of everyday home life. One implication of this approach is that in homes in which vocabulary is extensive and the quantity of words spoken is large, families can prepare children for school and support language development almost effortlessly. As the saying goes, "Children learn what they live."

Parents who speak little and whose usual vocabulary is limited, on the other hand, may wish to be more intentional in supporting the language development of their children. Being more intentional in this respect is no small task, but new resources are available that demystify early literacy and provide activities for families. Some of these suggestions include self-talk in which the parent carries on a monologue describing the immediate surroundings and activity while the child assumes the role of passive listener. Self-talk is a particularly useful strategy because it can occur while the parent and child are driving in the car, running errands, cooking dinner, folding laundry, or replacing the broken belt on the vacuum cleaner. In homes in which an adult spends much of the time accompanied only by an infant or toddler who does not yet converse, generating large numbers of words can sometimes be very difficult for the parent without intentionally planning to do so, as the following story illustrates:

> One-year-old Cotton has yet to say his first word. But from the day Daddy learned from his Early Head Start home visitor that it was very important for his young son to hear lots of words, it seems that Daddy has never stopped talking to Cotton. Because Daddy and Cotton are alone together in their apartment most of the time, and because babies can't talk, the home visitor suggested a technique for Daddy to use known as self-talk. With her encouragement, Daddy talks to Cotton the way a marooned sailor talks to a coconut. Verbal response by Cotton is neither expected nor necessary.
>
> "How about we make pancakes for breakfast?" Daddy asks rhetorically this morning. Cotton turns his sippy cup upside down.
>
> "How about we use flour?" Daddy asks, while Cotton beats the high-chair tray vigorously with the now empty sippy cup.
>
> "How about some wheat germ, some milk, and eggs ... how about a banana this morning?"
>
> "How about pineapple?" the 1-year-old suddenly suggests.
>
> A dozen eggs crash to the floor. For once, Daddy is completely speechless. The baby speaks! Not only that, he has preferences! Interesting preferences!
>
> Daddy on the other hand, has no pineapple (and after the surprise, no eggs). Because these are Cotton's first words, Daddy worries that his inability to provide instant positive reinforcement (pineapple) will mean that Cotton might never speak again. He needn't worry. Cotton already knows that you can't always get what you want, but talking to Daddy definitely gets a reaction!

Encouraging English Language Learners

Because parents and other family members are the chief means by which children acquire language, the most effective strategy for supporting infants and toddlers who are English language learners is to enrich interaction in the home in the primary language (Tabors, 2001). At minimum, this strategy involves offering materials produced in the home language and providing staff capable of supporting parents in the primary language spoken in the home.

During the early years, children are not merely acquiring vocabulary. They are assimilating all of the conventions, grammar, and underlying structure of spoken language. They are also using language as a tool for making sense of their world and for engaging in the entire range of developing cognitive processes. These cognitive and language processes may be delayed when the child's acquisition of the home language is interrupted or when the content and quality of exposure to the home language is diminished (Cummins, 1981). Support for the child's first language must continue even as English is introduced.

Supporting Families With Literacy Needs

English as a Second or Other Language (ESOL) classes are often assigned to the same category of adult education as GED or basic literacy, as if adult participation in ESOL classes carried with it the same benefits for children. Although it is true that role modeling of lifelong learning, the demonstration of education as a family value, and the evidence of literate behavior all occur with ESOL instruction, enriched interaction in the home language does not. Thus, parents who have low literacy or little formal education in their home language can support their very young children's development of language and literacy by enrolling in adult basic education in their home language while simultaneously attending ESOL classes to learn to deal with English speaking society (G. Italiano-Thomas, personal communication, January 15, 2004).

Fostering Adult Education

When benefits to children rather than economic gains are the primary motive for individuals to pursue adult education, then learning activities apart from enrollment in formal classes are recommended for speakers of any language (*Head Start Family Literacy Project*, 2003). Examples of such activities include reading newspapers and magazines and using the library and the Internet to pursue interests or to acquire information. This emphasis suggests one view-point: that family literacy service providers should honor parents' decisions not to participate in formal education while providing support and resources for more individualized, informal pursuits of learning.

Nevertheless, many families are ready for more formal education. It is surprising that, although adult education can be a decisive factor in the success of a child, many early childhood educators tend not to include it in their supposedly comprehensive planning. Adult education may seem to be a foreign discipline, with a separate pedagogy, faculty, and professional organizations housed in a completely different universe of systems and protocols. However, to make sustainable changes in the lives of children, early childhood educators most certainly need to look beyond the familiar and begin to build bridges to the adult education community. Referrals may be acted on if the personnel know and respect one another and smoothly transition families between one agency and another (Knapp-Philo & Stice, 2003). Early childhood professionals must begin with awareness of resources at the local, state, and national levels. However, awareness may still not translate into sustained access of resources by families.

Evidence suggests, however, that a more comprehensive community-building approach can stimulate the recruitment and retention of parents in adult education (Regalado, Goldenberg, & Appel, 2001). Recommended activities include the development of partnerships and interagency systems that provide for frequent formal and informal communication among adult education and early childhood agencies, joint planning, and coordinated case management that provides mechanisms for follow-up and ongoing support for enrolled families (Knapp-Philo & Stice, 2003).

Positive examples of such collaboration abound in Head Start, Early Head Start, and Even Start programs that provide GED and other adult services on site while children attend early childhood education programs. Likewise, many Early Head Start programs that serve a significant population of teenage parents provide infant–toddler classrooms in high schools to enable parents to finish high school while remaining in close contact with their babies. Many secondary schools and colleges provide early childhood services while offering academic credit to parents who volunteer in their own children's classrooms. Some family literacy professionals and parent advocates (*Head Start Family*

Literacy Project, 2003; Knapp-Philo & Stice, 2004), however, recommend improved interagency collaboration in which families experience adult education, early childhood education, and parent training as a seamless and fully integrated package. In this model, adult educators incorporate parenting materials and activities provided by the early childhood programs into adult education curricula.

Conclusion

A family literacy approach to language and early literacy development operates from the premise that experiences in the home during the first 5 years are extremely important. A developmental model of language acquisition suggests that the key to providing optimal home environments is to support and enrich interaction in the home during everyday activities to enable children to hear language and interact with the printed word during everyday routines. Five major roles for family members were explored: (a) families talking and using print with their young children, (b) families as environmental arrangers, (c) parents as readers, (d) parents as students, and (e) parents as community mobilizers for early language and literacy. The most effective strategies for supporting these kinds of parenting roles are grounded in reciprocal relationships with parents in which the values, goals, and practices of families are honored. This grounding is especially important when the family's first language is other than English. The concept of family literacy emphasizes that the pursuit of learning, language, and literacy by significant adults, both informally and formally, is the key to enriching daily interaction and instilling in young children positive attitudes toward education and literacy. Some experts envision the creation of integrated systems of adult education, early childhood education, and parenting education to support families in their important roles in fostering early language and literacy.

References

Abt Associates. (2004). *Family literacy practices identified by Head Start programs, Fall 2003* (Draft summary). Washington, DC: Author.

ACF child outcomes and evaluation. (2002). Washington, DC: U.S. Department of Health and Human Services, Administration for Children and Families. Retrieved June 12, 2004, from http://www.acf.hhs.gov/programs/core/ongoingresearch/faces/faces_pubs_reports.html

Anderson, S. (2006). Books for very young children. In S. E. Rosenkoetter & J. Knapp-Philo (Eds.), *Learning to read the world: Language and literacy in the first three years* (pp. 553–562). Washington, DC: ZERO TO THREE Press.

Baker, L., Scher, D., & Mackler, K. (1997). Home and family influences on motivation for reading. *Educational Psychologist, 32,* 69–82.

Benjamin, L. A. (1993). *Parents; literacy and their children's success in school: Recent research, promising practices, and research implications.* Retrieved September 19, 2002, from http://www.ed.gov/pubs/OR/ResearchRpts/parlit.html

Bloom, L. (1995). Foreword. In B. Hart & T. R. Risley, *Meaningful differences in the everyday experience of young American children* (pp. ix–xiii). Baltimore: Paul H. Brookes.

Burns, M. S., Griffin, P., & Snow, C. E. (Eds.). (1999). *Starting out right: A guide to promoting children's reading success.* Washington, DC: National Academy Press.

Bus, A., & de Jong, M. (2006). Book sharing: A developmentally appropriate way to foster preacademic growth. In S. E. Rosenkoetter & J. Knapp-Philo (Eds.), *Learning to read the world: Language and literacy in the first three years* (pp. 123–144). Washington, DC: ZERO TO THREE Press.

Butler, D. (1998). *Babies need books: Sharing the joy of books with children from birth to six.* Portsmouth, NH: Heinemann.

Cole, K. N., & Lim, Y. S. (2006). Language is the key: A proven approach to early language and literacy. In S. E. Rosenkoetter & J. Knapp-Philo (Eds.), *Learning to read the world: Language and literacy in the first three years* (pp. 537–552). Washington, DC: ZERO TO THREE Press.

Creating welcoming library environments for infants, toddlers and their families. (2001). [Special issue]. *Zero to Three, 21*(3), 4–37.

Cummins, J. (1981). School and language minority students: A theoretical framework. In G. Italiano-Thomas (Ed.), *Identification of promising literacy practices with English language learning populations* (pp. 89–101). Washington, DC: Head Start Bureau; Salt Lake City: Centro de la Familia de Utah.

Fabes, R., & Martin, C. L. (2000). *Exploring child development: Transactions and transformations.* Boston: Allyn and Bacon.

Goodling Institute for Family Literacy Research. (2004). Retrieved on June 5, 2004, from www.ed.psu.edu/goodlinginstitute/about.asp

Gopnik, A., Meltzoff, A. N., & Kuhl, P. K. (2001). *The scientist in the crib: What early learning tells us about the mind.* New York: Perennial/Harper Collins.

Gramling, M. (2002). *Supporting parent child interactions.* Paper presented at Community Action Partners' Annual Conference, New York.

Gregory, E. (2001). Sisters and brothers as language and literacy teachers: Synergy between siblings playing and working together. *Journal of Early Childhood Literacy, 1*(3), 301–322.

Hart, B., & Risley, T. R. (1995). *Meaningful differences in the everyday experience of young American children.* Baltimore: Paul H. Brookes.

Hart, B., & Risley, T. R.. (1999). *The social world of children learning to talk.* Baltimore: Paul H. Brookes.

The Head Start Act. 42 U.S.C. §§ 9831 et seq. (Amended October 27, 1998). Retrieved June 12, 2004, from http://www.acf.hhs.gov/programs/hsb/budget/index.htm#head

Head Start Family Literacy Project. (2003). Paper presented by the National Center for Family Literacy, Louisville, KY.

Heath, S. B. (1983). *Ways with words: Language, life and work in communities and classrooms.* Cambridge: Cambridge University Press.

Knapp-Philo, J., & Stice, K. (Eds.). (2003). *StoryQUEST 2: Celebrating beginning language and literacy.* Rohnert Park, CA: California Institute on Human Services.

Knapp-Philo, J., & Stice, K. (Eds.). (2004). *StoryQUEST 3: Celebrating beginning language and literacy.* Rohnert Park, CA: California Institute on Human Services.

National Early Literacy Panel Report. (2004). Louisville, KY: National Center for Family Literacy. Manuscript in preparation.

Neuman, S. B. (1999). Books make a difference: A study of access to literacy. *Reading Research Quarterly, 34,* 286–312.

Notari-Syverson, A. (2006). Everyday tools of literacy. In S. E. Rosenkoetter & J. Knapp-Philo (Eds.), *Learning to read the world: Language and literacy in the first three years* (pp. 61–80). Washington, DC: ZERO TO THREE Press.

Regalado, M., Goldenberg, C., & Appel, E. (2001). Building community systems for young children: Reading and early literacy. In N. Halfon, E. Shulman, & M. Hochstein (Series Eds.), *Building community systems for young children.* Los Angeles: University of California–Los Angeles Center for Healthier Children, Families, and Communities.

Rosenkoetter, S. E. (2006). Learning to read the world: A beginning. In S. E. Rosenkoetter & J. Knapp-Philo (Eds.), *Learning to read the world: Language and literacy in the first three years* (pp. 1–14). Washington, DC: ZERO TO THREE Press.

Shatz, M. (1994). *A toddler's life: Becoming a person.* New York: Oxford University Press.

Schickedanz, J. A. (1999). *Much more than the ABCs: The early states of reading and writing.* Washington, DC: National Association for the Education of Young Children.

Snow, C. E., Burns, M. S., & Griffin, P. (Eds.). National Research Council, Committee on the Prevention of Reading Difficulties. (1998). *Preventing reading difficulties in young children.* Washington, DC: National Academy Press.

Snow, C., & Tabors, P. (1996, January). *Intergenerational transfer of literacy.* Paper presented at the symposium Family Literacy: Directions in Research and Implications for Practice, Washington, DC. Retrieved September 12, 2002, from http://www.ed.gov/pubs/FamLit/integ.html

Strickland, D. (1996, January). *Meeting the needs of families in family literacy programs.* Paper presented at the symposium Family Literacy: Directions in Research and Implications for Practice, Washington, DC. Retrieved September 10, 2002 from http://www.ed.gov/pubs/FamLit/need.html

Tabors, P. (2001). Talk is cheap—and effective. *Children and Families, 15*(4), 34–43.

Taylor, D. (1983). *Family literacy: Young children learning to read and write.* Portsmouth, NH: Heinemann.

The White House.(n.d.). *Good Start, Grow Smart: The Bush administration's early childhood initiative.* Retrieved June 5, 2004, from http://www.whitehouse.gov/infocus/earlychildhood/sect1.html

Zukoski, A. P., & Luluquisen, E. M. (2006). Building community support for early literacy. In S. E. Rosenkoetter & J. Knapp-Philo (Eds.), *Learning to read the world: Language and literacy in the first three years* (pp. 429–454). Washington, DC: ZERO TO THREE Press.

Photo © Paragons of Nature

CHAPTER 11

Music: The Great Organizer for Early Language and Literacy

Linda Kimura

Not clothes, nor language, nor color, nor nation can change the
soul of the child; in kissing, in crying, and in song, the children
of the world are one.
—Luchi Blanco de Cuzco

Where words fail, music speaks.
—Hans Christian Anderson

Music gives a soul to the universe; wings to the mind; flight to
the imagination ... and life to everything.
—Plato

Music, the great organizer, helps the body and mind work together by combining rhythm, melody, lyrics, motion, and interaction to support early literacy and learning. Music is one of the first and most important modes of communication for infants. For example, parents' lullabies instill in babies a sense of trust and love that helps them learn that their environment is a secure one. Music teaches toddlers that the world is a fun and exciting place to be as it strengthens their foundations of early literacy. Music enhances memory and develops important language skills (C. Palmer & Kelly, 1992). It reinforces basic ideas of logic and perception, such as beginning and end, cause and effect, sequence and balance, and harmony and dissonance, as well as arithmetic concepts such as number, enumeration, and timing (H. Palmer, 2001). Music can be used to teach basic content such as counting, colors, relationships among ideas, social skills, and the wonders of the natural world (Levine-Gelb Communications, Lerner, & Ciervo, 2002). Very young children demonstrate their attraction to musical patterns and structure by smiling, bobbing their heads, clapping, and making hand motions and sounds during songs they like.

Musical From Before Birth

Shellenburg and Trehub (1999; Trehub, 2001) have shown that most babies arrive with built-in musical systems responsive to the music of any culture. This ability seems to be connected to an instinctive push toward language that is characteristic of most human babies. Research demonstrates that before birth, babies hear their mothers' voices and are aware of varying tones of speech (DeCasper, cited by the Associated Press, 1992). What babies hear before birth may resemble what adults hear underwater, yet, somehow, they are able to isolate the tones, pitches, rhythms, and melodies of their own mothers from other sounds. This ability is demonstrated by the universal phenomenon of newborns recognizing mother's voice and distinguishing it from the voices of other women within 24 hours after birth, often even before birth and sometimes by the thirtieth week of gestation (Kisilevsky et al., 2003). Early exposure to their mother's language—not only the words but also the musicality of the words—may explain babies' immediate attraction to their native language. Folk songs and popular music seem to attract babies from the time of birth because they reflect the constraints and capabilities of the human auditory system more closely than other types of music (Beaton, 1995; Shellenburg & Trehub 1999).

Music Communicates Emotion and Strengthens Relationships

Music communicates human emotion in ways appropriate to children's experience. Young children who are not developmentally ready to express their happiness, anger, or sadness through words or sentences can often find an outlet for these feelings in music. Carol Brunson Day, executive director of the Council on Early Childhood Professional Recognition, noted: "The presence of music sends supremely important messages to our youngest children: because you can own your own experience, you are empowered; because you can make music, you are a builder and creator of your own culture, and as such, you are a maker of your own meaning" (MENC, NAEYC, & U.S. Dept. of Education, 2000, p. 4).

Singing and chanting, both infant-friendly communication patterns, are important ways for parents to share emotions with babies because babies are very sensitive to socially significant visual and auditory stimuli (Ecklund-Flores & Turkewitz, 1996). Music itself becomes a source of communication and interaction between children and adults (The Task Force on Children's Learning and the Arts & Goldhawk, 1998).

When infants kick their legs, wave their arms, babble, and smile while parents sing to them, they are signaling important emotional cues to their parents. Adults who respond by smiling back and continuing to sing or chant are telling them, "We understand that you like this, and we are going to do it some more just for you." Historical accounts indicate that mothers, fathers, grandparents, and siblings have always engaged in singing to babies (Shellenberg & Trehub, 1999). Maternal singing to babies tends to differ from typical adult singing because it has greater emotional expressiveness, higher pitch level, and slower tempo (Trainor & Heinmiller, 1998; Trehub et al., 1997). Fathers' singing, although more rare, is also marked by heightened emotionality (O'Neill, Trainor, & Trehub, 2001).

Infant-directed speech is more musical than adult-directed speech, and it captures infants' attention better than adult-directed speech. Caregivers across cultures have been observed using similar intonations in similar contexts, for example, rising contours to attract infants' attention, smooth falling contours to soothe infants, and abrupt flat contours to discourage undesirable behaviors (Fernald & Mazzie, 1991). Parents' singing, whether soothing lullabies or playful songs, helps to regulate their infants' state of awareness. Loving, nurturing care calms an infant's stress responses and helps protect the baby's brain from harm to its emotional regulation (Gunnar, 1998). What could better support the infant's calming than a soothing lullaby? Later on, when toddlers are disorganized or angry, adults can help them "let off steam" by turning a potential tantrum into an "I'm Mad" dance, allowing children to get their feelings out without the exchange turning into an argument (Kimura, 2004).

The national anthem of Venezuela is a "cancione de cuna" (lullaby). "Duérmete mi Niño" ("Sleep My Child") gently tells little ones that it's time to sleep because their parents have to wash their diapers and prepare food for them (Kimura, 2004). Parents across the world and over the centuries have shared family and cultural values with their children by singing their babies to sleep at night, repeating the same song over and over to help toddlers sleep. One of the sweetest moments that a parent and child can share is a lullaby time. The words of a lullaby are intended to have a soothing quality to help baby sleep. Lullabies are songs that say to the sleepy child, "Close your eyes, and go to sleep now. Sleep, sleep, sleep; I am here with you." Lullabies are very similar to baby talk, and infants appear to like the two language forms for the same reasons. Infants' favorite songs and speech patterns have obvious pitch changes, repeating rhythms, a slow beat, and long, soothing vowel sounds (Kimura, 2004).

Calming, nonsense syllables were the earliest lullabies. "Loo loo, la la, lullay, lullye" were the kinds of sounds that became incorporated into songs and that we still hear today in the refrains of many lullabies. Many languages have a sound similar to "lull," and in all the languages, those sounds are associated with peace and calm. It's the repeated sounds, single syllables, and whole words that contribute to the charm of lullabies. So, although one might not think of some songs as lullabies, they certainly can be sung as lullabies, especially if they have softly repetitive refrains.

Shenfield, Trehub, and Nakata (2002) reported that maternal singing is more effective than maternal speech in maintaining attention and reducing infant arousal. For infants, familiar voices, performance styles, and songs provide a source of security. Shenfield et al. found that mothers adjust their musical performances to respond to their infants' states of awareness, producing either playful or soothing renditions as appropriate for the moment. In other words, mothers fine-tune their music to meet the needs of their young audiences. In addition to helping infants with state regulation, adults' singing to babies also tends to regulate the singers' emotional states. This type of regulation is valuable because caring for infants involves not only stress but also pleasure. In many cultures, the privacy of mother–infant interactions and the preverbal status of infants means that sometimes parents can sing in private to their child about things they would not say in public. Thus, singing can calm mothers as well as infants, and playful singing can bring renewed energy to both (Trehub, 2002).

Music Sensitizes Children to the Sounds of Language

Children learn the sounds of language when they are exposed to songs, chants, linguistic awareness games, nursery rhymes, and rhythmic activities. Nursery rhymes are songs that have survived through oral traditions, books, and songs for many generations because children love their humor and rhythm and can easily learn and repeat them. Most nursery rhyme songs have a five- or six-note range. For example, "Rain, Rain Go Away" has a simple three-note range. Why is this limited range important? Phonemic awareness, a powerful predictor of later reading skill, requires conscious awareness of phonemes and the ability to manipulate them (see Griffin, this volume, p. 145). Bryant suggests that the roots of phonemic awareness are found in traditional rhyming, skipping, and word games (Bryant, Bradley, MacLean, & Crossland, 1989). The rhymes, rhythms, and repetition in music such as nursery rhymes enhance children's phonological sensitivity that, in turn, helps them to learn to read (Bryant, MacLean, Bradley, & Crossland, 1990; Neuman, Copple, & Bredekamp, 2000).

For many children, phonemic awareness may begin with their daily use of oral language. They learn how language is structured when adults talk, read, and sing to them. Children instinctively listen to music and try to identify familiar melodies and rhythms, just as early readers look for words that sound alike, have patterns, or rhyme (Jalongo & Ribblett, 1997). Picture books of songs such as *The Ants Go Marching* or *The More We Get Together* support young children's language and literacy development and illustrate how the use of familiar text, predictability, and repetition encourage children to explore the sounds and word associations of print (Woodall & Ziembroski, 2002).

Music Builds Children's Communication and Conversational Skills

Babies recognize familiar melodies before they understand the meanings of words, and they often use their cooing and babbling as a type of musical conversation before they can form and pronounce words (Mangione, 1995a). As children repeat rhymes and rhythms, they begin to associate symbols with the sounds they hear. Younger and older toddlers love to fill in the blanks (e.g., "And on that farm, he had a _____."). Very young children don't understand the concepts of turntaking or cause-and-effect actions and consequences. However, as they grow, children actively explore these concepts and experiment through play and sound making (Mangione, 1995a). They have fun first discovering all the sounds they can make and then using those sounds to represent objects as if the object (e.g., a stuffed animal) were talking. When an adult responds to the sound a child produces for that stuffed animal, the child begins to learn turntaking as well as cause and effect ("I made my little cow say 'moooooo, please.' I think that means 'pet me, please,' and then Mommy came over and petted my little cow."). Toddlers love to create their own music. They can be their own best musical instrument by clapping, stomping their feet, and singing strings of sounds. Singing and reading songs with young children, with the adult using proper inflection, emphasis, and meaning, enriches and expands young children's vocabulary (Beaton 1995).

Music Helps Children Observe, Organize, and Interpret Experiences

Researchers Mason and Sinha (1993) noted that the child is an active constructor of her own learning, aided by the critical role of the supporting, engaged adult who provides scaffolding for the child's development of understanding and greater skill (see also, Cole & Lim, this volume, p. 537; Neuman, this volume, p. 275; Pierce, this volume, p. 335). To put it more concretely, as children sing, chant, play musical instruments, and dance, they observe, organize, and interpret their experiences. They make decisions, take actions, and observe the effect of those actions on others. Adults support their musical explorations by singing along, beginning new verses and allowing the child to complete them, demonstrating new ways to hold or play an instrument, and joining in the dance with joy.

Children Use Music and Movement to Increase Vocabulary and Coordination

Some of the most important early literacy activities with music can be the most fun because they involve moving to a beat. Enhancing movement vocabulary through music is an achievable early step in developing oral and written literacy skills because movement words are critical vocabulary for very young children

(Asher, 1996; Palmer, 2001): (a) vocabulary for body parts such as *head, shoulders, knees, toes, arms, legs, fingers, elbows,* and *wrists;* (b) action words such as *crawl, walk, run, jump, bend, skip, twist, turn,* and *wiggle;* and (c) space words such as *low, medium, high, up, down, big, small, right, left, front, back,* and *beside.* Movement words describe qualities such as slow and fast or loose and tight. They describe relationships between things such as on and off, in and out, or in front of and behind. Music brings elements of early literacy together through patterns and activities that many parents do instinctively: singing, humming, chanting, and talking in infant-directed speech. Infants and toddlers learn with all their senses as music brings experiences and words together in a fun and creative way.

Infants, toddlers, and young children respond to music by listening and moving their heads, arms, and legs. They begin to chant syllables and words and sometimes put new words in familiar songs as well as moving with the music. After a song has been sung, older toddlers can provide narrative and story lines that continue where the song leaves off. Parents and caregivers can support early literacy through music by following singing with other experiences that build on the same concept as the song. For example, children enjoy singing *The Ants Go Marching.* The next time children are outside and see some ants, adults can remind them about the song, talk about where the ants are marching to, sing the song again, and march around. Children's responses to the rhythmic beat of music of moving and singing enhance their coordination and reinforce the vocabulary and concepts. Additionally, finger plays, adding dance to music, and using instruments can support fine and gross motor development.

Music Supports Cultural Values and Helps Young Children Learn About Other Languages

Children first hear music and learn about communication and literacy through their experiences at home and in their cultural and ethnic communities (National Association for the Education of Young Children [NAEYC], 1996). When communication, including music in its various forms, is similar at home and in child care, children's learning is easier and less stressful (NAEYC, 1996). Caregivers' and families' efforts to recognize, respect, and support one another's cultural values and forms helps affirm for children that competence is beyond any particular language, dialect, or culture. Caregivers sharing non-English songs, chants, and other musical materials help support children's first language while they acquire oral proficiency in English. Singing in a second or third language is usually much easier than trying to have a conversation in that language (Kimura, 2004). Families and other caregivers can encourage positive oral communication traditions such as reading and singing to children during lap time, sharing an enjoyment of traditional cultural stories and songs, and generally enjoying music in many forms. Providing a strong foundation in the child's first language promotes literacy in a second language (Cummins, 1979). Children who are learning more than one language are more likely to become readers and writers of English when they are already familiar with the vocabulary and concepts in their first language (International Reading Association [IRA] & NAEYC, 1998), a familiarity that music can help to build.

Children from linguistically and culturally diverse families bring multiple perspectives and impressive skills such as code switching to child care settings. Code switching (i.e., the ability to go back and forth between two languages to deepen conceptual understanding) is often demonstrated through the songs, chants, and rhymes that children who are learning more than one language bring from home. These rich musical gifts should be used as learning resources for all children (IRA & NAEYC, 1998).

Music Helps Children Learn English When Child-Care Workers Speak Another Language

While second language acquisition is enhanced through the use of music, complications may ensue when caregivers also speak English as their second language. Songs, rhymes, and chants that use correct, repeated, and easily pronounced vocabulary can help caregivers and children alike. Although it is critical that children gain a firm foundation in their primary language to build self-esteem and support home culture (Mangione, 1995b), it is also important that children in the United States learn English as part of literacy development and school readiness. The alliteration and rhythm of music activities can help caregivers who speak English as a second language as they share English learning materials with children in their care. Child-care providers who are not completely literate either in their own language or in English can still provide early literacy experiences for infants and toddlers through songs, rhyming and word games, conversations, shared picture books, and storytelling.

Caregivers Partner With Families to Encourage Music as a Literacy Tool

Clearly, partnering between families and caregivers is a key to education (Boyer, 1991), especially when parents and caregivers engage with children in similar, developmentally appropriate activities (Jones & Lorenzo-Hubert, this volume, p. 187). To support young children, particularly children who are learning more than one language and children from low-income environments, it is important to recognize that most families from a variety of socioeconomic and ethnic-linguistic backgrounds provide nurturing environments for their children and will provide more support if given appropriate guidance and opportunities. It is equally important to acknowledge that while many middle-class American families may place a high value on the written word, families from other cultural-ethnic groups and other social classes may place more value on and encourage their children's aesthetic, musical, and kinesthetic development (Delpit, 1995). By sharing songs and encouraging singing at home, caregivers can enhance young children's early literacy and general development without putting an extra burden on families, perhaps otherwise stressed, who may have varied beliefs about learning. Handouts with simple songs written in more than one language and accompanied by illustrations help to promote such musical interactions. Singing songs and chants in multiple languages and including non-English materials as part of the daily schedule helps to ensure that children will maintain their home language while becoming proficient in English (Fillmore, 1991).

Urban Legends About Music and Young Children

Three common "urban legends" (Levine-Gelb et al., 2002) must be dispelled. Child development personnel have a responsibility to understand the concepts, reject the three erroneous notions presented here, and urge others to do so, too.

Legend 1: Mozart's music makes baby geniuses; therefore, only classical music should be played for babies. The so-called Mozart Effect is an example of the confusion and misinterpretation that is possible when science and the media interact. *Mozart Effect* is a term that was coined by Dr. Alfred Tomatis, an ear, nose, and throat specialist, to describe the alleged increase in brain development, including the development of early literacy, that he believed he saw in very young children when they listened to the music of Mozart (Linton, 1999). Look in any children's toy store to see a profusion of toys that specifically incorporate the classical music of Mozart as "brain-builders" for babies. Following the initial claim, a controversial study was conducted at the University of California–Irvine in 1993 to test college students on a specific university-level task while they listened to music by Mozart (Levine-Gelb et al., 2002). Subsequently, Campbell (1997) trademarked the term *Mozart Effect*.

Sharing classical music with babies should certainly be encouraged because such rich, complex music can offer wonderful, relaxing, intimate experiences that expose babies to a variety of forms and patterns. There are, however, no studies on infants that have demonstrated long-term intellectual gains as a result of listening to compositions by Mozart or any other classical composer (Levine-Gelb et al., 2002). In fact, as stated earlier, research shows that both folk and popular music optimally address the capabilities of the human auditory system (Shellenburg & Trehub, 1999). These two types of music seem to connect with the deep roots of many home cultures (Beaton, 1995) and follow musical patterns that coincide well with language learning, using techniques such as stressed and unstressed syllables (Palmer & Kelly, 1992). These types of singing help to increase the toddler's memory for words and phrases. Of course, music in general is a rich encoder of language that supports perception and comprehension, anticipation of new words and text, and memory (Serafine, Crowder, & Repp, 1989, cited in Palmer & Kelly, 1992).

Legend 2: Babies should receive only the best in learning tools; thus, infants and toddlers should be exposed to only good singers. How often does a parent or other caregiver say, "I don't sing" or "You don't want to hear my voice!"? Well, babies do want to hear caregivers' voices! Infants and young children are not music critics. They are music lovers, and there are no voices that young children love more than those of their families and caregivers. Babies prefer their parents' voices, particularly the voices of their mothers (DeCasper & Fifer, 1980). Babies recognize the voices of those who are special to them early in life.

Parents across the world sing, chant, and talk rhythmically to babies, and their infants respond positively to the loving sounds from the earliest days after birth. The adults needn't have training in singing. Rather, familiarity and the adult–child relationship are what counts.

Another popular option for parents and caregivers is to select music recorded specifically for infants and toddlers. Commercial recordings, while often musically proficient, lack the familiar voice and emotional qualities of a person who cares deeply for the young child. So, how can one use commercially produced music to create enjoyable early literacy and learning experiences? Join in the fun with the children. If toddlers watch musical videos or listen to music CDs, stay with them, and dance and sing along to make this activity into a meaningful experience. Add the children's names and activities they like to the words of the songs they are hearing. Whether old songs, new songs, or made-up songs, what counts is that very young children and adults share the musical experience together.

Legend 3: Don't bother using music with children who have disabilities because they can't benefit from it. Most children of all abilities enjoy music and music-related activities. Children with special needs should be provided with appropriate adaptations in the instructional environment and the physical environment to enable them to participate fully (MENC et al., 2000). Children with limited or no hearing can touch instruments to feel the vibrations. They can feel the beat and rhythm and have meaningful participation in music experiences if, for example, they use drums with various degrees of flexibility in their skins (drum heads). Clappers and rhythm sticks are other helpful choices. Children with limited or no vision can sing and can dance to music when caring adults provide a safe environment and direction. Infants and toddlers with sensory disorders may prefer soft music or a generalized chant rather than more complex compositions. Look to them for cues as to what is pleasing or upsetting. Infants and toddlers with motor impairments can feel the beat and rhythm of the music and perhaps be carried as adults move to the music. Drums are wonderful tools for children with movement limitations. Adding their beats or pats to a drum can bring them into a delightful group music experience (Kimura, 2004). To support an inclusive musical environment, make time to give all participating children a chance to explore the adaptive music equipment and devices. Families and caregivers must experiment to find the kind of rhythmic and musical experiences that each child prefers and enjoys.

Just as they share stories and all the other activities that support beginning language and literacy, children with disabilities should be exposed to music that supports their learning.

Music Supports Early Literacy If It Is Tied to Developmentally Appropriate Practice

In our product-rich society, it's not unusual to find potty chairs playing music so toddlers can have their brains stimulated while they are learning to use the toilet. Is this level of support really necessary? Presenting a variety of music, sounds, textures, and colors helps infants and toddlers grow and learn, but including every one of those elements in every activity can be overstimulating to young children. Musical toys designed to support baby's learning blossomed as a result of the reports of brain development research in the 1990s, but simple ideas have sometimes been taken to extremes. As the nation emphasizes literacy acquisition, we see an unfortunate use of inappropriate teaching practices that may work quite well with older children and adults but are inappropriate with infants, toddlers, and preschool-age children (Levine-Gelb et al., 2002). Children should be encouraged to learn in, through, and about music, and they should be supported through a child-centered approach that focuses on each child as a primary learner. Adult facilitation is necessary to set the stage and provide support, encouragement, and challenges to make the most of learning opportunities in the everyday environment (Beaton, 1995).

To use developmentally appropriate music practices with infants and toddlers, one must have realistic expectations. Key music skills are tied to early literacy skills because they are based on the acquisition of language and practiced through play and daily routines. The following is a list of skills connected to music that one can expect to see in the early years (Kimura, 2004; Levine-Gelb et al., 2002; Neuman et al., 2000):

- **Infants From Birth to Approximately 9 Months Old**
  - Recognition of primary caregivers' voices as different from other voices
  - Attention to quiet, rhythmic, high-pitched voices

- Imitation of sounds adults make, such as babbling during or after someone sings

- Eye contact with singers

- Arm and leg wiggling and kicking to show enjoyment or overstimulation

- Use of objects to make sounds, such as banging blocks together, perhaps with a little help

- **Infants Approximately 9–18 Months Old**

  - Use of facial expressions, sound, and movement to encourage singers to continue

  - Recognition of a particular song or sound as denoting a safe, secure place or time, such as a naptime song that is sung every day as the child prepares to sleep

  - Recognition of use of songs or sounds that signal routines

  - Creation of new lyrics for songs, either because the participants don't remember the lyrics or because they want to sing the ideas in their own way

  - Increasingly complex moving and dancing

  - Use of sounds and voices as children play or look at books with adults

- **Toddlers Approximately 18–36 Months Old**

  - Use of singing to themselves for comfort or enjoyment

  - Repetition of the same song over and over and over again

  - Dancing alone and with others

  - Creation of new songs and dances

  - Increased interest in social activities, such as children playing together with musical instruments or dancing in a group to music

  - Ability to change or enhance songs for fun, with encouragement and support from adults

Music as Part of Daily Routines Supports Early Literacy

Music should be embedded in the daily routines of children's relationships with family members, caregivers, and others in the community (Mangione, 1995a). Strategies that support music as part of daily routines include the commonly used techniques of self-talk, lap time, and parallel talk. *Self-talk* involves an adult describing what he or she is doing to help the young child understand daily activities. Adults can enhance diapering by using a self-talk song such as "I'm changing Sue's diaper now; I'm changing your diaper now. Take off the dirty, put on the clean; I'm changing Sue's diaper now." The song can be uncomplicated and unrhymed. The key is a simple description housed in a simple melody. *Lap time* describes the period when an adult has a particular child on his or her lap for individual support, caring, and personalized interactions (Honig & Shin, 2001). Perhaps lap time is a warm and comfortable time to sing favorite songs together. Often, young children ask for the same song over and over. *Parallel talk* differs a bit from self-talk in that it can describe what the adult is doing, what the child is doing, or what the two are doing together. Use musical sounds during parallel talk to describe the everyday sounds connected with actions and events. For example, "Jane's looking out the window at that rain! Swish, swish goes the rain against the window. It's a swish-swish song!"

Songs and Books Help to Scaffold Early Literacy

Music, like art, often arises and repeats through play. It should be used to scaffold more complex and meaningful play experiences for young children wherein they apply vocabulary and familiar concepts to new situations (The Task Force on Children's Learning and the Arts & Goldhawk, 1998). Repeated music activities, including the use of picture books of songs and rhymes, help children reflect on previous learning, develop expanded concepts, and refine their thinking skills. When selecting books that incorporate music, choose those with the best and simplest elements of music. Many wonderful songs have been written as picture books. Examples include *Five Little Ducks* by Raffi (1999) and *The Bear Went Over the Mountain* by Rosemary Wells (1998). Children can explore the books themselves and can sing them with a family member or other caregiver. Placing musical picture books in the same area as children's rhythm instruments adds additional early literacy options to a music center. As children mature, families or caregivers can embellish the language in the books and add additional verses to the songs.

Easily Replicated Music Activities for Families

Families foster the development of early language and literacy through music activities with their infants and toddlers. Families can share music they enjoy with their children's other caregivers. Conversely, an important contribution to home–school partnerships for early literacy occurs when caregivers create and demonstrate enjoyable activities that families can use, including strategies such as (a) singing sounds, nursery rhymes, and songs to promote the awareness of sounds; (b) building on the child's responses by adding new words and sentences to songs (e.g., "And on the farm he had a boy named Sasha"); (c) providing and using picture song books; (d) reading and singing stories to the child while using enthusiasm and facial and body movements; and (e) matching the child's developmental and temperamental pace by watching for his or her cues and then responding to them appropriately. It is valuable for families to imitate the sounds their children babble by singing ("ooh, ooh, ooh!"). If the child changes the sound, the adult can change, too ("ahh, ahh, ahh!"). As children grow, adults can purposefully change the sounds for children to imitate ("ooh, ooh, ooh, ahh, ahh, aah, ohhh, ohhh, ohhh"). Songs such as "Wheels on the Bus," a toddler favorite, can serve as a starting point. Raffi's "Apples and Bananas" is another good choice that can be expanded as the child grows and becomes more reflective about the sounds of the language. Choose songs that encourage children to move, that are interesting to them, and that engage them in more than one way. Repetitive, easy-to-learn phrases often engage children's attention. Rhyme, rhythm, and alliteration make learning fun. Caregivers can encourage families to create rituals and routines with babies and young children by using favorite songs and sounds.

Conclusions

From the moment of birth, infants and toddlers use music to organize their world. When infants successfully achieve mutuality of attention with caregivers—through music and reciprocal sounds as well as through visual and kinesthetic cues—they move toward language (Bruner, 1987). They hear words in lullabies, nursery rhymes, and music in the environment. Increasingly, infants and young children have fun learning through music, with singing, chanting, rapping, or responding to "call-and-response" songs. Many ideas about the value of music in language and literacy learning were offered in this chapter. Music as an early language and literacy enhancer can be a source of communication between families and caregivers to support home–school partnerships across cultures. Music is, indeed, a medium through which children develop beginning language and literacy skills. Music helps children read their world!

References

Asher, J. J. (1996). *Learning another language through actions: The complete teacher's guidebook* (6th ed.). Palo Alto, CA: Sky Oaks.

Associated Press. (1992, October 2). Studies: Speech is heard before birth. *The Oregonian,* C1.

Beaton, P. (1995). The importance of music in the early childhood language curriculum, *International Schools Journal, 15*(1), 28–38.

Boyer, E. L. (1991). *Ready to learn: A mandate for the nation.* Princeton, NJ: The Carnegie Foundation for the Advancement of Teaching.

Bruner, J. (1987). *Making sense: The child's construction of the world.* New York: Methuen.

Bryant, P. E., Bradley, L., MacLean, M., and Crossland, J. (1989). Nursery rhymes, phonological skills, and reading. *Journal of Child Language, 16*(2), 407–428.

Bryant, P. E., MacLean, M., Bradley, L., & Crossland, J. (1990). Rhyme and alliteration: Phoneme detection and learning to read. *Developmental Psychology, 26*(3), 429–438.

Campbell, D. (1997). *The Mozart effect: Tapping the power of music to heal the body, strengthen the mind, and unlock the creative spirit.* New York: Free Press.

Cole, K. N., & Lim, Y. S. (2006). Language is the key: A proven approach to early language and literacy. In S. E. Rosenkoetter & J. Knapp-Philo (Eds.), *Learning to read the world: Language and literacy in the first three years* (pp. 537–552). Washington, DC: ZERO TO THREE Press.

Cummins, J. (1979). Linguistic interdependence and the educational development of bilingual children. *Review of Educational Research, 49*(1), 222–251.

DeCasper, A. J., & Fifer, W. (1980). Of human bonding: Newborns prefer their mothers' voices. *Science 208*(6), 1174–1176.

Delpit, L. (1995). *Other people's children: Cultural conflict in the classroom.* New York: The New Press.

Ecklund-Flores, L., & Turkewitz, G. (1996). Asymmetric head turning to speech and non-speech in human infants, *Developmental Psychology, 29*(3), 205–217.

Fernald, A., & Mazzie, C. (1991). Prosody and focus in speech to adults and infants. *Developmental Psychology, 27*(2), 209–221.

Fillmore, L. W. (1991). When learning a second language means losing the first. *Early Childhood Research Quarterly, 6,* 323–346.

Griffin, P. (2006). Sound steps in phonological form for later literacy. In S. E. Rosenkoetter & J. Knapp-Philo (Eds.), *Learning to read the world: Language and literacy in the first three years* (pp. 145–162). Washington, DC: ZERO TO THREE Press.

Gunnar, M. (1998). Quality of care and the buffering of stress physiology: Its potential role in protecting the developing human brain. *IMPrint: Newsletter of the Infant Mental Health Promotion Project, 21,* 4–7.

Honig, A. S., & Shin, M. (2001). Reading aloud with infants and toddlers in child care settings: An observational study. *Early Childhood Education Journal, 28*(3), 193–197.

International Reading Association (IRA), & National Association for the Education of Young Children (NAEYC). (1998). *Overview of learning to read and write: Developmentally appropriate practice for young children, a joint position of the International Reading Association (IRA) and the National Association for the Education of Young Children (NAEYC).* Washington, DC: NAEYC.

Jalongo, M., & Ribblett, D. (1997). Using song picture books to support emergent literacy. *Childhood Education, 74*(1), 15–22.

Jones, W., & Lorenzo-Hubert, I. (2006). Culture and parental expectations for child development: Concerns for language development and early learning. In S. E. Rosenkoetter & J. Knapp-Philo (Eds.), *Learning to read the world: Language and literacy in the first three years* (pp. 187–214). Washington, DC: ZERO TO THREE Press.

Kimura, L. (2004). *The Ukulele Baby Lady presents: Songs for early childhood folks.* Woodland, CA: Babies Can't Wait Publishing.

Kisilevsky, B., Hains, S., Lee, K., Xie, X., Huan, H., Ye, H., et al., (2003). Effects of experience on fetal voice recognition. *Psychological Science, 14*(3), 220–224.

Levine-Gelb Communications, Lerner, C., & Ciervo, L. (2002). *Getting in tune: The powerful influence of music of young children's behavior.* Washington, DC: ZERO TO THREE.

Linton, M. (1999). The Mozart effect. *First Things, 91,* 10–13.

Mangione, P. (Ed.). (1995a). *Infant toddler caregiving: A guide to cognitive development and learning.* Sacramento: California Department of Education and WestEd/Far West Laboratory Center for Child and Family Studies.

Mangione, P. (Ed.). (1995b). *Infant toddler caregiving: A guide to culturally sensitive care.* Sacramento: California Department of Education and WestEd.

Mason, J., & Sinha, S. (1993). Emerging literacy in the early childhood years: Applying a Vygotskian model of learning and development. In B. Spodek (Ed.), *Handbook of research on the education of young children* (pp. 137–150). New York: Macmillan.

MENC (National Association for Music Education), National Association for the Education of Young Children (NAEYC), & U.S. Department of Education. (2000). *Start the music: A report from the Early Childhood Music Summit.* Washington, DC: Texaco.

National Association for the Education of Young Children (NAEYC). (1996). Responding to linguistic and cultural diversity: Recommendations for effective early childhood education. *Young Children, 51*(2), 412.

Neuman, S. B. (2006). Literacy development for infants and toddlers. In S. E. Rosenkoetter & J. Knapp-Philo (Eds.), *Learning to read the world: Language and literacy in the first three years* (pp. 275–290). Washington, DC: ZERO TO THREE Press.

Neuman, S. B., Copple, C., & Bredekamp, S. (2000). *Learning to read and write: Developmentally appropriate practices for young children.* Washington, DC: National Association for the Education of Young Children.

O'Neill, C., Trainor, L. J., & Trehub, S. E. (2001). Infants' responses to fathers' singing. *Music Perception, 18*(4), 409–425.

Palmer, C., & Kelly, M. (1992). Linguistic prosody and musical meter in song. *Journal of Memory and Language, 31*(4), 525–541.

Palmer, H. (2001). The music, movement, and learning connection. *Young Children, 56*(5), 13–17.

Pierce, P. (2006). High expectations for language and literacy with infants and toddlers who have significant disabilities. In S. E. Rosenkoetter & J. Knapp-Philo (Eds.), *Learning to read the world: Language and literacy in the first three years* (pp. 335–352). Washington, DC: ZERO TO THREE Press.

Raffi. (1999). *Five little ducks.* New York: Crown Books for Children.

Shellenberg, E. G., & Trehub, S. E. (1999). Culture-general and culture-specific factors in the discrimination of melodies. *Journal of Experimental Child Psychology, 74*(2),107–127.

Shenfield, T., Trehub, S. E., & Nakata, T. (2002, April). *Salivary cortisol responses to maternal speech and singing.* Paper presented at the International Conference on Infant Studies, Toronto, CN.

The Task Force on Children's Learning and the Arts: Birth to Age Eight, & Goldhawk. S. (1998). *Making creative connections: A report of the Task Force on Children's Learning and the Arts: Birth to age eight.* Washington, DC: Arts Education Partnership.

Trainor, L. J., & Heinmiller, B. (1998). The development of evaluative responses to music: Infants prefer to listen to consonance over dissonance. *Infant Behavior and Development, 21*(1), 77–88.

Trehub, S. E. (2001). Musical predispositions in infancy. *Annals of the New York Academy of Sciences, 930,* 1–16.

Trehub, S. E. (2002). Mothers are musical mentors. *Zero to Three, 23*(1), 19–22.

Trehub, S. E, Unyk, A. M., Kamenetsky, S. B., Hill, D. S., Trainor, J. L., Henderson, J. L., & Saraza, M. (1997). Mothers and fathers singing to infants. *Developmental Psychology, 33*(3), 500–507.

Wells, R. (1998). *The bear went over the mountain.* New York: Scholastic Press.

Woodall, L., & Ziembroski, B. (2002). Promoting literacy through music. Retrieved May 24, 2004, from http://www.songsforteaching.com/lb/literacymusic.htm

Photo by Eric Mathisen

CHAPTER 12

Caregiving Routines and Literacy

Janet Gonzalez-Mena

*A video clip shows a woman reading a children's book to a baby
who is just a few weeks old. The woman has the baby positioned
to look at the book, but the baby does not want the book. He
wants her. He wiggles in the woman's arms until he is able to
look into her face. She repositions him. He moves again holding
a steady gaze even though his little head keeps wobbling. She
keeps on reading, oblivious to the baby's signals.*

This reader, whoever she is—mother, caregiver, or friend—seems to have something in mind related to early literacy. She has, however, missed the point.
Reading the baby is a lot more important at this age than reading the book.
Adult responsiveness is the set of behaviors that underlies and supports language and literacy development. This chapter is about responsive caregiving
during the essential activities of daily living with infants and toddlers. Paying
attention to babies in responsive ways supports the kinds of communication
that lead to relationships. Relationships are the supports on which literacy skills
depend.

Using Caregiving Routines to Build Relationships

The essential activities of daily living are called caregiving routines. What happens during diapering, feeding, grooming, bathing, and toileting influences a
baby's sense of security, feelings of attachment, and concept of empowerment.
All are supports for positive language and literacy development (Sachs, 1991).

The hours spent in caregiving routines add up to a great deal of time when adults are in close contact with the child. Responsive interactions that include language foster language and literacy learning (Neuman, Copple, & Bredekamp, 2000). For example, examine a routine event, diapering:

> *The infant teacher has lots on her mind, including a potential biting incident in progress in a far corner. She mechanically diapers the baby in front of her, but her attention is elsewhere. She is aware that her co-teacher is busy in the kitchen area getting ready to feed a hungry baby who is screaming in another corner. The co-teacher cannot see what is happening in the other corner. One aide is busy settling a tug of war, and the other is gathering up toys to sanitize them. No adult is paying attention to the potential problem, so the teacher who is diapering calls to one aide to forget cleaning the toys and move over to the corner where a known biter is headed for one of her favorite victims. Because the aide looks helpless, the teacher hurriedly finishes with the child she is diapering and puts him down at her feet. She turns her back on the child without a word and rushes through cleanup to be able to go where she is needed. A smile covers her face when she remembers that tomorrow a substitute will be in, and all the diapering will be assigned to him.*

What is wrong with this picture? Just about everything. For one thing, the teacher does not value the time she spends diapering. For another, the supervision system is not working. Even if the teacher wants to pay close attention to the child on the diapering table, there is too much else to distract her. The child on the diapering counter is certainly not receiving support for his emerging language and literacy. He probably picks up the unspoken message that he and his body processes are a source of annoyance. Several thousand diaperings like this one (possible if this child stays in this program for his first 3 years of life) will do little to contribute to early literacy or to any other developmental outcome except perhaps physical comfort. Even if the teacher finds time to read books to this child regularly, which appears doubtful, she misses out on the intimate moments on the diapering counter when close relationships can grow and contribute to early language and literacy development. Reading books without routine social support for early language is insufficient to nurture literacy's foundations (Snow, Burns, & Griffin, 1998).

Here is what the child being diapered could have gained if his teacher had interacted with him while diapering. He could have learned (a) action words, as the caregiver described what was happening while diapering him; (b) listening skills and social cues, as he listened to the caregiver's tone and began to "read" her feelings; (c) emotion words that accompany feelings; and (d) turntaking through babbling and interacting.

See how the first diapering scene contrasts with this next one:

> The teacher is talking to a baby on the diapering counter. He is lying so his face is just below hers when she leans over. She has the baby's full attention as she tells him that she is going to change his diaper. She waits for the tension to leave his muscles before she begins to remove clothing. She is directive as well as responsive. "Lift your bottom, please." She waits to see what he will do. He is not old enough to understand entirely and comply, but she does see a body response and uses that as her cue to continue. She talks to the child each step of the way, always keeping him focused on not only the task itself but also their interaction. She does not distract the child with endless chatter, and she is not using this time to try to teach him unrelated concepts like colors or shapes. This time together is about diapering and the relationship between the two of them. When she is finished, the caregiver holds out her arms and says, "I'm going to pick you up now." He responds with a slight forward thrusting of his head and body in anticipation and comes willingly into her arms with a smile on his face.

Unrealistic? Certainly the teacher in the first scene could not have pulled off this sequence, but infant teachers across the nation are interacting with babies in warm, responsive ways like this example when they work in programs that support the kind of one-on-one attention required for early learning.

Magda Gerber calls the type of interaction in the second scene "wants-something quality time" (Gerber & Johnson, 1998). The name comes from the fact that the adult initiates and directs the action but at the same time is respectful and responsive. Wants-something quality time is appropriate during diapering, feeding, and other daily routines. Wants-nothing quality time occurs during playtime and puts the child in the position of being the initiator. Instead of directing or initiating, the adult in wants-nothing quality time sits quietly nearby, attentive and responsive.

When adults give toddlers want-nothing quality time, they have multiple opportunities to support language and literacy skills. This kind of interaction is about the adult being close and available but not directive or intrusive. However, wants-nothing quality time requires practice on the part of the adult and a willingness to be comfortable responding to a child rather than "teaching." Adults who perfect wants-nothing quality time observe and follow the child's lead to capture what the child is interested in and motivated to learn. Instead of interrupting infants' play to point out colors or name objects, these caregivers help children learn those concepts through authentic experiences. For example, when offering a choice of cups at snack time, these caregivers ask, "Do you want the red cup or the blue one?" which is more authentic than "What color is this?" and thereby gives children real choices among the concepts in a context. Further, handing the child the chosen cup and adding, "You want the blue one" is both a responsive action and a reinforcement of the color concept. These types of interactions provide multiple opportunities for children to develop language and cognitive skills in a positive environment that encourages and supports their learning (Lally, 1995).

The second diapering might have been completed by an infant teacher who was following Magda Gerber's (1984) Resources for Infant-Educarers (RIE) philosophy. In truth, the second diapering scene is taken from a real-life observation of the changing of an infant in Budapest, Hungary, in 2003. It is similar in tone to a video clip of the diapering of a toddler whose father was following the RIE philosophy (Gonzalez-Mena & Eyer, 2004). Both of these diaperings show the influence of Emmi Pikler, a pediatrician who founded Loczy (now the Pikler Institute), a residential nursery in Budapest that primarily serves infants and toddlers (David & Appell, 2001; Falk, 1994; Pikler, 1971, 1979; Tardos, 1986). The particular approach Pikler created came to the United States in 1956 with Magda Gerber, who incorporated it into her RIE philosophy.

Of course, many infant teachers provide responsive caregiving, not just those who follow Pikler or Gerber. Some use the approach of the WestEd Program for Infant Toddler Caregivers (PITC; see www.pitc.org). Some infant teachers carry out responsive caregiving without following a named philosophy. Working with infants in warm and personal ways comes naturally to many adults, though almost nobody used the word *respect* in relation to infants until Magda Gerber introduced the concept in the 1970s (Gerber, 1984).

Caregiving, Relationships, and Learning

Warm, responsive care is not just about diapering. Feeding, grooming, toileting, and, indeed, any caregiving activity can be carried out in respectful ways that involve the kinds of interactions that create close relationships and secure attachments (Falk, 1979). The child who consistently has the kind of caregiving interactions described by Pikler and Gerber is likely to feel that the world is a safe and interesting place to explore, a place that is free from threats. That security allows the child's attention and energy to be focused on making discoveries in the environment. Such discoveries create a path to learning that will eventually include several components of literacy including (a) attention to detail such as letter shapes and (b) attention to abstract ideas and sequences such as story lines (Hammond, 2001). Hammond notes specific ways that caregiver communication in the context of nurturing relationships is a primary support for language and literacy. Repetition of simple songs, words, and nursery rhymes helps children build vocabulary and identify discrete sounds within words. Speaking to children about what interests and concerns them, listening to their responses, and acting on what they have said support language, social skills, and social–emotional development in young children.

Helping Babies Learn to Use Symbols

Babies learn early to recognize and use symbols during daily routines. Reading and writing depend on sophisticated symbol usage (i.e., connecting visual symbols to representations of the sounds of speech and then clusters of letters to words to word meanings). Although they are not yet ready for this kind of complex process, babies do begin to recognize a wide variety of symbols in daily interactions long before they become aware of letters or words. Miller (2002) named three types of symbols that infants and toddlers learn and use: action symbols, object symbols, and picture symbols.

Action Symbols. The outstretched arms of the caregiver at the end of the second diapering scene provide an example of an action symbol. Every day babies come to understand new action symbols. For example, the sound of the squeaky area of the floor in front of the refrigerator tells a particular baby that an action involving a bottle or food is about to occur. The sound of the door opening is a trigger for babies waiting for a family member to appear and take them home. In fact, one program oiled its door hinges because several children who were experiencing separation loss were continually distracted by the sound the door made. These children were repeatedly disappointed by that particular action symbol. The lights of a car driving up the driveway or the sound of the elevator door opening in the hall communicate to the baby that mommy is about to appear in the doorway and come over for a kiss.

Most infants and toddlers learn action symbols without direct teaching from an adult, just by linking one event or situation with another (Miller, 2002). Infant teachers can expand on the natural link by putting words into the situation. Eventually, the words create the same effect as the earlier action symbol (Sachs, 1991). For example, in the second diapering scene when the caregiver linked the action symbol of stretching out her arms with words, the baby's ability to understand language increased. As babies' receptive language develops, they can be comforted by words even when the action symbol does not produce the expected result. For example, the words of the caregiver soothed the babies who were upset when the door's opening did not produce their mothers.

Object Symbols. Object symbols enhance toddlers' play as the young children use a toy telephone, or perhaps a block, to represent a remote control for a pretend TV. Using object symbols shows that young children are developing what Piaget called *symbolic representation* (Piaget, 1976). *Symbolic representation*, which means that the children are able to hold an image in their minds, is an important step in cognitive development and is vital for literacy. Adults can encourage toddlers to learn to pretend—regularly using object symbols—by setting up a rich environment that lends itself to play and exploration and then by being available to support them in it. Wants-nothing quality time, which is not directive or intrusive, supports and empowers children to explore pretend experiences (Gonzalez-Mena & Eyer, 2004). Adults can also use object symbols to help children through emotionally trying periods. For instance, one girl who cried constantly when her mother went out the door was soothed when her mother left an old purse for the child to hold whenever she wanted. The object stood for the person and the emotional comfort that person provides, just as later squiggles stand for words that represent meaning.

Picture Symbols. A picture symbol has an even more obvious connection to learning to read. Pictures are most useful when they depict something that the toddler can connect to a meaningful real object. A picture of a bowl of baby cereal on the cereal box at mealtime is a more meaningful picture symbol than a zebra in a picture book, unless, of course, the toddler saw a zebra at the zoo that day. Photos or line drawings of familiar people and pets are more readily discerned than representations of strange objects. Picture symbols can have practical uses in daily routines. For example, cleanup time becomes a literacy learning experience when picture symbols mark the place where a toy is to be stored. Matching an object to a picture is interesting to most toddlers, and they may come to find picking up toys to be a game instead of a chore. Separation anxiety can be reduced when pictures of family members are offered as comfort items and are always available to toddlers to view or hold. Of course, pictures in books not only help symbol and vocabulary development but also give infants and toddlers repeated chances to experience word meaning through books as well as learn that books are interesting and enjoyable. After all, when toddlers learn to love books, in the context of a relationship with a warm and caring adult reader, their motivation to learn to read and write increases greatly.

Literacy in Action

Opportunities for infants and toddler learning language and literacy skills appear throughout the day in child-care settings. Imagine that the reader is observing Baby X in a small infant center. She is called Baby X so the reader can imagine her ethnicity, race, and background as well as those characteristics of the adult who brings her to the center and the adults who work in the center. Consider what leads the reader to assign Baby X and the others in this scenario to a particular ethnicity-race-background. What clues, if any, are used?

> *You the reader are seated in a corner near the door, when Uncle arrives at the center with Baby X in his arms. You can tell right away that the two have a close relationship. Teacher approaches smiling. She stops within touching distance but doesn't touch. "Good morning," she says, first to Baby X and then to Uncle. Looking at Baby X, she asks, "Are you ready to come to me?" She holds out her arms. As expected, Baby X turns to Uncle and hides her face in his jacket, snuggling up to his chest. Teacher waits. "Not yet. You want Uncle, don't you?"*

Uncle walks over to a low chair and sits down, still holding Baby X. "I want to take off your coat," he says. He waits to see what Baby X will do. She takes her face out of his jacket and looks at him. "Give me your arm," says Uncle. The arm that had been tucked snuggly between her chest and Uncle's comes out a little way. "Oh, there's your arm," says Uncle. You wonder whether Baby X really understood because she's so young. It's hard to tell whether that movement occurred because she was feeling more secure or whether she really responded to Uncle's words.

Uncle takes hold of Baby X's sleeve. He tugs gently one way while Baby X pulls her arm the other way and it comes out of the sleeve. Uncle moves his attention to the other sleeve and repeats the action, talking to Baby X through the sequence. When the jacket is removed, he says to Baby X, "Teacher is going to hang up your jacket now."

Baby X watches as Teacher, who has been squatting nearby, reaches for the jacket. Teacher notes the frown that flashes across Baby X's face. "You don't like me to take your jacket away. Maybe you want to help me hang it up?" Again, she holds out her arms.

Baby X hides her face in Uncle's chest. "I guess not," says Teacher. She walks over to the cubbies. Baby X immediately turns around to watch Teacher and begins to wiggle in Uncle's arms. Uncle notices too, and he says, "I'm going to put you on the floor." At that, she wiggles more, and he gently puts her on the floor on her back. She immediately flips over and begins to crawl after Teacher, who turns and acknowledges her but does not bend over and pick her up. When Baby X gets to her cubby, she looks up at it, watching each movement Teacher makes as she hangs up the jacket. Uncle follows and puts the diaper bag in the cubby, which is prominently labeled with Baby X's name and beside it, a flower sticker. Baby X pays no attention to either symbol.

Teacher turns from the cubby and goes to sit on the floor near a basket that contains several objects. Curious, Baby X crawls over to her and when she goes by you the reader, she looks up. Teacher introduces you as a visitor. Baby X passes by, headed right for the basket of toys. When she reaches it, she gets into a sitting position. Then she reaches in and pulls out a floppy rag doll. She examines the doll with her fingers before scrutinizing its face. Teacher says, "Oh, you found the doll." Baby X smiles up at her and then turns back to the doll. She pokes an eye with one finger, then puts her mouth on the doll's face (Is she kissing it?), and finally places it on the floor and puts her feet on it. Then she looks in the basket again. Uncle comes over, squats down, and says, "I have to go now."

Baby X looks up, distressed. Did she understand the words? When he says, "Good-bye," it's clear that she knows what is about to happen. As he turns to walk to the door, she crawls after him, whimpering. He stops at the door, waves good-bye, turns, and leaves. She gives a plaintive cry. Once the door shuts, and Uncle is no longer visible, Baby X stops crying and crawls back to Teacher, who is still in the same spot but now has another child on her lap. On her way to Teacher, Baby X spies a book beside her path. She takes a detour and picks up the book. Then she heads straight to Teacher and climbs over the other child, settling herself comfortably on Teacher's other knee. She hands over the book.

Now pause for a moment and examine that scene in terms of early literacy. The most obvious objects related to literacy were the book as well as the name and picture symbol on the cubby. Baby X ignored both her name and the picture, but when she eventually does notice them, she may find the flower more interesting and recognizable than the name. If adults continue to link the same symbol with Baby X's name, she will come to associate them and begin at an earlier point to identify her place or her belongings either by the flower or with both name and flower than by name alone. Nobody is pushing Baby X to recognize these symbols. They are there for whenever the time comes that she shows interest. There is no goal to have her reading before she leaves the infant–toddler program. Baby X is developing a repertoire of symbols, but there is no urgency for her to learn these two particular symbols.

Even more important than the visual symbols was the conversation that Teacher and Uncle had. They spoke to Baby X about what was going on, and both waited for her responses. They moved at a sufficiently slow pace that Baby X could both perceive and respond. The adults told her what was going to happen in advance. Rather than unrelated chatter, talk was used as an early step toward symbolic representation, that is, the spoken word was used here as a symbol for an action or object.

A theme throughout these scenes is how Teacher responds to what interests Baby X. *Responsiveness* helps the child remember the objects and events, linking the words to their meaning with a positive emotional charge. Another theme is *pace.* This program operates at baby pace, not adult efficiency. *Freedom to move* is another theme, which appears in each scene. Freedom to move encourages gross motor development. As the child's hands are free for exploration and manipulation, freedom also supports fine motor development. Baby X is in Piaget's period of sensorimotor development (Piaget, 1976) and needs the freedom to use her body and senses in a variety of ways to form new concepts. Although Baby X is crawling, some infants who have physical or neurological challenges may not gain mobility so readily. Nevertheless, they too pass through this same exploration stage and need freedom to move in whatever ways they can. Positioning may be an important factor in encouraging their whole body movements, the use of the hands, or both during their daily routines. The scene with Baby X continues:

> When an infant cries in another part of the room, Baby X watches that infant and looks a bit distressed herself. She crawls off Teacher's lap and heads for the baby. Teacher gets up and walks over to see what the other baby needs. In the meantime, Baby X notices a toy, stops and turns it over, picks it up, bangs it on the floor, and then abandons it. She moves on once again, following Teacher. But then she spies another baby lying on a rug. She abruptly changes direction and heads over toward that baby.

One might wonder whether Baby X's ability to focus on a goal is a problem. She had no problem focusing on Uncle's leaving, but this time the other baby distracts her from following Teacher. Baby X seems to have one thing in mind and then changes her mind twice on the way to accomplishing it. The ability to focus and concentrate is a key factor in learning to read. Does this incident show that Baby X is distractible? No! It shows she is a baby. One way to look at a child this age is to consider, not how easily distracted she is, but how easily she is satisfied. The whole world is new to Baby X, and she is vitally interested in almost everything that comes into her sensory range. This strong pull of curiosity is a plus for her cognitive development. Another plus is how aware of her senses she is. When she bangs the toy, she is listening closely to the sound it makes. As she leaves the smooth floor and crawls over the edge of the rug, her face shows her awareness of the difference in texture under her knees and hands. Our scene continues to unfold:

> Now Baby X moves near the baby. She comes close and then sits back to stare. The baby makes a noise, and Baby X smiles. She gets up on all fours again, and as she reaches for the baby's face, she looks up and sees that another teacher is settling down on the rug beside her. "Gently," says the teacher and shows her how to stroke the baby lightly. Baby X follows the adult's example and touches a chubby cheek. Then she pats it. She watches the baby for a bit and then crawls off to inspect some nesting cups that are scattered on a different part of the rug. She picks one up, and bangs it on another cup. Baby X seems to like the noise it makes; she bangs it again. She picks up another one, and now she has a cup in each hand. She tries to put a big cup into a smaller one. It doesn't fit. She tosses both cups on the rug and moves on to pick up yet another cup, which she puts up to her mouth.

The reader may wonder why the caregiver nearby isn't helping Baby X learn how to nest the cups, an obvious cognitive task related to ordering objects by size. The caregiver's explanation is that her job is not to teach but to facilitate discoveries by sitting back in a responsive, but not directive, mode. She also adds that it doesn't matter if the baby learns to nest those cups today, next week, or ever. What matters right now is that Baby X is exploring and using all of her senses. She is learning about size, even though she does not "get it" yet. She needs a number of chances to explore the sizes of various objects before she understands the concept of big and small or big and bigger. Observers will know Baby X has "got it"—even if she never nests the cups—when she protests that the child next to her got the big apple slice and all that was left for Baby X was the little one! At that point, she will be demonstrating her conceptual learning from the exploration of objects by using language. Oral language is a significant precursor to literacy (Snow et al., 1998). Thus the ordinary routines of the infant–toddler years evolve into literacy.

Baby X is also experimenting by using many different modalities as she develops "learning schemes" (Mangione, Lally, & Signer, 1992). She manipulates, bangs, and mouths. She uses those actions (or learning schemes) on objects to begin to classify them into categories. For example, this object makes one kind of noise, but this one makes another. This one is hard, but so is this one. Baby X is constructing knowledge. Eventually she will learn that this smaller piece fits inside a bigger one, but not the reverse. She is noticing the details that will lead to differentiation, an important skill for eventually distinguishing one sound from another and one letter from another (Neuman et al., 2000). Our attention returns to the scene:

> *During the observation time, Baby X has been all over the room, busy every minute. She seems to be slowing down now. She sits on her bottom and whimpers. She has begun to slump. She lets out a little moan, straightens up, and then goes on all fours over to a low bulletin board on the wall that has photographs displayed. She reaches up and touches one. She pats it and then gets up on her knees and puts her mouth on it. It is a picture of Uncle and a young woman, presumably Baby X's mother. There is also an older woman with a family resemblance to both Uncle and the young woman. Baby X sits on her bottom and whimpers softly. Then she crawls over to a ball. She reaches out for it, but when she touches it, it rolls away from her. That upsets her and she lays her head down on the rug, her bottom in the air, and cries loudly.*

> *Teacher's voice comes from a comfortable easy chair nearby where she is feeding another infant. "I know, I know. You want to eat!" Baby X stops crying and looks toward her caregiver. Then she rolls over on her back, cries loudly, and kicks her feet. "You really want to eat! You can't wait! I wish I could come*

right now, but I'm feeding Mikey." Baby X stops at first to listen, but when she sees that her caregiver is not getting up, she rolls back over and sobs softly.

Before long, Baby X and Teacher are snuggled together in the chair with a bottle, and Baby X is making contented murmurs and sucking sounds. She stops now and then and gazes up at Teacher. After she has satisfied her first hunger pangs, she stops eating for a minute and relaxes her mouth, which lets the nipple fall out. She gives her caregiver a big smile. Then she starts sucking again. She has a fist locked around one of Teacher's fingers. Both look very relaxed and happy. Baby X has her eyes closed and seems to be almost asleep when the last suck brings nothing but air. She opens her eyes and sits up.

"All gone," says Teacher. You drank it all." Baby X gives her a sleepy smile. She was changed before she started eating, so she's ready for her nap. She gives a big burp as Teacher picks her up in her arms. "I'm going to put you in your crib now," Teacher says. Baby X puts her head on Teacher's shoulder as Teacher walks with the infant to the nap room.

After an hour nap, Baby X is making noises in the nap room. Teacher goes to pick her up and change her diaper. As Teacher lays her on the diapering counter, Baby X begins to make cooing noises. Teacher imitates those noises. Baby X waves her hand in the face of Teacher, who makes the same gesture back. The two appear to be enjoying this little turntaking game. Teacher conducts the diapering much the way Uncle took off Baby X's coat. She says what she will do and waits for Baby X to respond. In between, the game of imitation continues. Although usually it's Baby X who initiates a gesture, on one or two occasions Teacher makes the first sound or movement.

This time, all the vocalizing is not just about the event at hand as it was earlier. Baby X and Teacher have been playing with sounds and gestures. They are taking turns, just as in "real conversations." They are exploring imitation, an important way that babies learn. Just as Baby X now imitates sounds and gestures, one day she will imitate reading and writing. Playful imitation sets the stage for later learning of academic skills. We take one final glimpse of Baby X:

> *Soon almost everyone is outside. Teacher takes Baby X to the*
> *door and puts her down. She immediately crawls outside onto a*
> *big deck and makes a beeline for a toy on wheels that she pushes*
> *back and forth from a kneeling position. Teacher settles down*
> *near Baby X on the deck, and when Baby X pushes the toy over*
> *to her, Teacher says, smiling, "You really like that toy, don't you?"*

One of the many tasks of the early years is for youngsters to discover who they are and what they like (Lally, 1995). By paying attention to what interests Baby X, Teacher facilitates this process. Teacher support also helps some objects or actions stand out in the child's memory, and she is motivated to learn the names of the things she is interested in. Remembering is another foundational skill for literacy as is building vocabulary (Snow, 2002).

The following list outlines a number of elements seen in the above account that foster early language and literacy for Baby X:

- Responsive caregiving in a timely manner
- Relationship building through close, warm, responsive interactions with a primary caregiver
- A slow pace to give Baby X time to perceive and respond
- Encouragement for Baby X to explore and discover
- Freedom of movement (Baby X was restricted only by the edges of the diapering counter and the sides of the crib. Even while eating she was free to make her own decision about when to leave.)
- A safe, rich environment in which to discover what interested her
- Attention to symbol use, including examples of action symbols, object symbols, and picture symbols
- Rhythm, rhyme, and repetition
- Books to choose from
- Environmental print

Parent Education and Early Literacy

Using caregiving routines as a way to promote the foundations of literacy has relevance for parent education. One strength many families have, including those with low income, is their ability to relate to their children in predictable, positive, close, and personal ways during daily routines such as dressing, play time, dinner, and bedtime (Kubicek, 2002, and this volume, p. 163). Parent education can take a strength-based approach. The first step lies in finding out not only what parents want for their children but also what they are already doing. By discussing these questions, teachers and parents engage in mutual education. Parents teach teachers so teachers can support families in what they are already doing, help them expand on it, and fill in gaps. As a result of this mutual exchange about daily routines, teachers expand their ideas about how to meet each child's needs in accordance with child development principles as well as family goals, values, and priorities. When teachers and families partner around literacy development, teachers learn about the symbols children bring from home and share with the families the ones that children experience in the infant–toddler program.

Different Daily Routines—Different Paths

The program that Baby X attends, described above, works to promote literacy skills based on a philosophy that empowers infants and toddlers by helping them see themselves as capable individuals with choices within the daily routines. Some families do not highly value these characteristics because they have a strong priority of creating tight, long-lasting bonds that come from focusing on interdependence instead of independence (Greenfield, 1994; see also Jones & Lorenzo-Hubert, this volume, p. 187). The philosophy shown here might not be comfortable for families who want their child to learn interdependence. Depending on what ethnicity the reader assigned to Baby X's family, the program may or may not have been a good match. Rogoff (2003) explained:

> *There is not likely to be one best way. Understanding different cultural practices does not require determining which one way is "right" (which does not mean that all ways are fine). With an understanding of what is done in different circumstances, we can be open to possibilities that do not necessarily exclude each other. Learning from other communities does not require giving*

*up one's own ways. It does require suspending one's own
assumptions temporarily to consider others and carefully sepa-
rating efforts to understand cultural phenomena from efforts to
judge their value. (p. 12)*

There can be rich opportunities for language and symbol use in programs with
guiding philosophies other than the one seen here—but their approaches
would be different. It is important to recognize that the example given here is
not the only way to promote literacy in the early years. Further, the field of
early childhood–early intervention has great influence on whether or not cultural diversity is preserved because this discipline is the first educational system
with which families come into contact. In the varied routines and divergent
philosophies of diverse cultures, we are beginning to discover a variety of paths
to literacy—and everything else! We need to continue to strive to assure that as
we give infants and toddlers the best experience possible as well as support their
literacy development, we are doing so in a way that also honors the values and
priorities of their families.

References

David, M., & Appell, G. (2001). *Loczy: An unusual approach to mothering.* (J. M. Clark & J. Falk, Trans.). Budapest, Hungary: Association Pikler-Loczy for Young Children. (Original work published 1973, 1996)

Falk, J. (1979). The importance of person-oriented adult-child relationships and basic conditions thereto. In M. Gerber (Ed.), *Resources for infant educarers* (pp. 29–39). Los Angeles: Resources for Infant Educarers.

Falk, J. (1994). Forty years of Loczy. *Sensory Awareness Foundation Bulletin, 14*(Winter), 38–44.

Gerber, M. (1984). Caring for infants with respect: The RIE approach. *Zero to Three Bulletin, 4*(3), 1–3.

Gerber, M., & Johnson, A. (1998). *Your self-confident baby.* New York: Wiley.

Gonzalez-Mena, J. (2004). Observing infants toddlers and caregivers: A video to accompany J. Gonzalez-Mena & D. Eyer, *Infants, toddlers, and caregivers,* [Videotape]. New York: McGraw-Hill.

Gonzalez-Mena, J., & Eyer, D. (2004) *Infants, toddlers, and caregivers* (6th ed.) New York: McGraw-Hill.

Greenfield, P. M. (1994). Independence and interdependence as developmental scripts: Implications for theory, research, and practice. In P. M. Greenfield & R. Cocking (Eds.), *Cross-cultural roots of minority child development* (pp. 1–37). Mahwah, NJ: Erlbaum.

Hammond, R. A. (2001). Preparing for literacy: Communication comes first. *Educaring, 22*(4), 1–5.

Jones, W., & Lorenzo-Hubert, I. (2006). Culture and parental expectations for child development: Concerns for language development and early learning. In S. E. Rosenkoetter & J. Knapp-Philo (Eds.), *Learning to read the world: Language and literacy in the first three years* (pp. 187–214). Washington, DC: ZERO TO THREE Press.

Kubicek, L. F. (2002). Fresh perspectives on young children and family routines. *Zero to Three 22*(4), 4–9.

Kubicek, L. F. (2006). Encouraging language and literacy through family routines. In S. E. Rosenkoetter & J. Knapp-Philo (Eds.), *Learning to read the world: Language and literacy in the first three years* (pp. 163–186). Washington, DC: ZERO TO THREE Press.

Lally, J. R. (1995). The impact of childcare policies and practices on infant-toddler identity formation. *Young Children, 51* (1), 58–67.

Mangione, P., Lally, J. R., & Signer, S. (1992). Discoveries of infancy: Cognitive development and learning. *Child Care Video Magazine* (publication of Far West Laboratory, Sausalito, CA).

Miller, K. (2002). How infants and toddlers use symbols. *Child Care Information Exchange, 145*(May), 80–82.

Neuman, S. B., Copple, C., & Bredekamp S. (2000). *Learning to read and write: Developmentally appropriate practice for young children.* Washington, DC: National Association for the Education of Young Children.

Piaget, J. (1976). *The child and reality.* New York: Penguin Books.

Pikler, E. (1971). Learning of motor skills on the basis of self-induced movements. In J. Helmuth (Ed.), *Exceptional infant* (Vol. 2, pp. 54–89). New York: Bruner/Mazel.

Pikler, E. (1979). A quarter century of observing infants in a residential center. Can infant-child care centers promote optimal development? In M. Gerber (Ed.), *Resources for infant educarers* (pp. 1–7). Los Angeles: Resources for Infant Educarers.

Rogoff, B. (2003). *The cultural nature of human development.* New York: Oxford University Press.

Sachs, J. (1991). Emergence of communication: Earliest signs. In J. R. Lally, P. L. Mangione, & C. L. Young-Holt (Eds.), *A guide to language development and communication* (pp. 3–11). Sacramento: California Department of Education and the Far West Laboratory for Educational Research and Development.

Snow, C. E. (2002). Ensuring reading success for African American children. In B. Bowman (Ed.), *Love to read* (pp. 17–30). Washington DC: National Black Child Development Institute.

Snow, C. E., Burns, M. S., & Griffin, P. (Eds.). (1998). *Preventing reading difficulties in young children.* Washington, DC: National Academy Press.

Tardos, A. (1986). The Pikler/Loczy philosophy. Loczy research and current popular views. *Educating, 7*(2), 1–7.

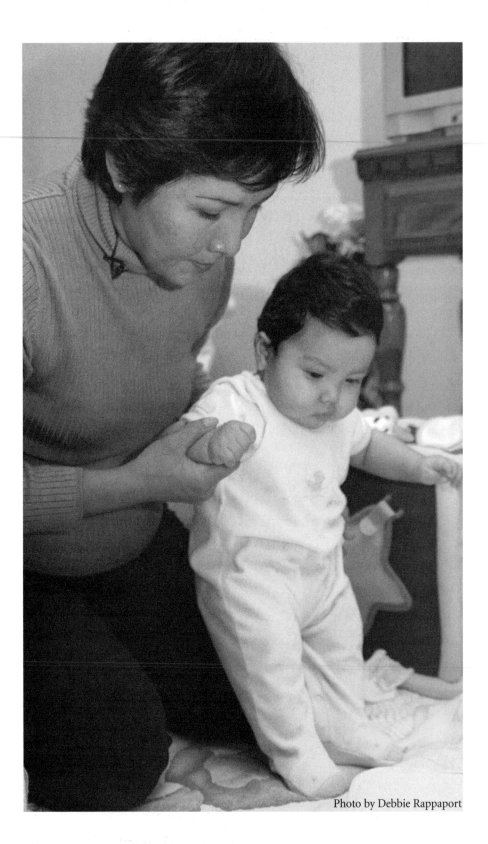

Photo by Debbie Rappaport

CHAPTER 13

Literacy Development for Infants and Toddlers

Susan B. Neuman

Scientific evidence from recent groundbreaking syntheses (Bowman, Donovan, & Burns, 2001; National Research Council & Institute of Medicine, 2000; Snow, Burns, & Griffin, 1998) now provides incontrovertible evidence. Over the last few years, there has been an explosion of knowledge about how infants and toddlers develop, leading to a whole new appreciation of ways in which a baby's earliest experiences set the stage for later learning and social–emotional development. Today, we recognize that the first 5 years of a child's life is a time of enormous growth in linguistic, conceptual, and social competence. Right from birth, healthy infants use all their senses to explore, try to control their environments, and master their universe.

These early years have tremendous consequences, not only because this period of development provides an indelible blueprint for learning, success, and well-being, but also because it sets the foundation for what will follow. From birth through age 5, children develop the foundational capabilities upon which their linguistic, cognitive, social, and emotional development builds (National Research Council & Institute of Medicine, 2000). And in these early years, all of these critical dimensions of early development are interrelated. Each requires a great deal of attention.

This chapter describes the beginnings of literacy development for infants and toddlers. It argues that literacy in these early years is more than the development of cognitive skills such as decoding, rhyming, or handwriting. To the contrary, literacy consists of mastering a complex set of attitudes, expectations, behaviors, knowledge, and skills (Neuman, Copple, & Bredekamp, 2000). But children do not learn these behaviors as if by magic nor do these behaviors naturally unfold with age. Rather, early literacy development takes place in the context of children's interactions with others and with supportive relationships with their immediate caregivers, first at home, then in the neighborhood, and eventually in other care settings.

Bridges to Literacy

For infants and toddlers, the beginnings of literacy may not look much like reading or writing. Instead, beginning literacy appears in activities such as pretend play, drawing, and conversations about books with their closest personal relations, their family (McLane & McNamee, 1990). During these years, children learn to use these multiple symbol systems in increasingly defined ways to create and communicate meaning. These symbols may include words, gestures, pictures, numbers, and objects, all wonderfully configured into a mixed medium to represent their imaginative ideas and creative thinking. Children use these early symbolic activities to build bridges to literacy (Dyson, 1988).

Babies who grow up experiencing reading and writing in many facets of their everyday lives begin to understand the purposes that literacy serves. As children encounter written language, they try to figure out how it works. They form hypotheses, play with ideas, and sort out relationships. It is important, then, to recognize that children are not passive receptacles for the knowledge delivered by others. Rather, they follow a logic of their own (which may look very different from adult convention; Gibson, 1979) and are active constructors of understandings about written language.

In 1998, the International Reading Association (IRA) and the National Association for the Education of Young Children (NAEYC) developed a joint position paper on developmentally appropriate practices in learning to read and write (IRA & NAEYC, 1998). The document describes a portrait of a young literacy learner and the various milestones that children pass in the early years along the path to literacy (see Table 13.1).

The following sections describe some of the unique characteristics of infants' and toddlers' developing awareness of writing and reading as well as recommendations for how families and caregivers can support these discoveries on the road to conventional understandings of writing and reading.

Table 13.1. Literacy Learning in the Early Years

Babies can

- Enjoy listening to books with familiar objects.
- Point and look intently at pictures and identify objects.
- Hold a book right side up and turn the pages.
- Play with language, rhymes, and songs.
- Write scribbles and lines on paper.

Toddlers can

- Enjoy listening to and talking about storybooks.
- Begin to understand that print carries a message.
- Engage in early writing attempts.
- Identify signs in their environment.
- Participate in rhyming games.
- Use approximations of letters to represent written language (especially meaningful words like their name and phrases such as "I love you").

To help literacy learning, caregivers can

- Share books with children from the very beginning of life.
- Establish a literacy-rich environment.
- Re-read favorite stories.
- Engage children in language games.
- Talk with children.
- Encourage children to recount experiences and describe ideas and events that are important to them.
- Visit the library regularly.
- Write with children.

Adapted from IRA & NAEYC (1998).

The Early Stages of Writing Development

Beginning about the ages of 18 months to 2 years, most children begin to be fascinated with writing objects. They are able to hold a large pencil and, if offered paper, will begin to scribble. Scribbling first appears to be rather random. Toddlers love to explore the movement of pencils, crayons, and markers on paper. But as they gain greater control and coordination, what soon emerges from this scribbling are recognizable shapes, lines, and patterns (Clay, 1991).

Our youngest writers tend to experiment with the visual features of writing, exploring the distinctive features of shapes or letter-like forms. Distinctive features of the English alphabet, for example, include straight and curved lines; open and closed curves; and diagonal, horizontal, and vertical lines. Some letters are closed (*D, O*) while others are open (*C, L*). Some have curvy lines (*S*), while others are straight (*T*), and some are diagonal (*K*). In a fascinating series of experiments, Eleanor Gibson (1979), found that very young children tended to group letters together on the basis of their perceptual characteristics (e.g., whether or not letters were closed or open). She found that to distinguish one letter from another, children needed to pay attention to what makes them different rather than what makes them similar. Generally this insight begins at approximately age 2½ and develops as children have encounters with print in their environment.

At these young ages, children often begin to display their understanding of what writing is all about (Neuman & Roskos, 1992). They begin to use their writing in pretend play. They write orders, pay checks, and make lists, all to embellish their dramatic play. Although "just play," these early activities indicate that children are beginning to understand the functions and purposes of print. They are also beginning to recognize that writing is an activity worth knowing and that it can be manipulated to suit their needs. These beginning adventures with writing provide a powerful motivation for children to learn to write to communicate with others.

For many young children, drawing and writing are closely linked in these early years (Dyson, 1988). Sometimes children draw pictures, write random letters, and scribble all over the page, playfully manipulating shapes and experimenting with different forms. But at other times, young children begin to combine drawing and writing to convey a message, which may be interpretable only when it is explained to an adult or an older peer. At this point, children do not recognize that writing is meant to stand on its own and can substitute for talking. Rather, all of these mixed media—talking, writing, drawing—are forms of expression for young children.

Children's emerging word creation strategies are fascinating in these beginning years. For example, a toddler might use two "marks" to write her own name, but four "marks" to write her mother's name, explaining that mother is bigger and older (Schickedanz, 1998). Or, given a choice between two pictures and their corresponding two words, for example, *mosquito* and *cow*, a child might say that the shorter word *cow* is longer because a cow is bigger than a mosquito. Children also develop a visual design strategy, assuming that each word has its own special "design." Because they do not yet attend to all the distinctive features of a word, such as different letter forms, they rely on the special design to differentiate one word from another. Another strategy that some children use is to assume that any word beginning with the same letter as their name *is* their name.

Even in the first 3 years, it is important not to be guided by strict developmental timetables when caring for children. Although many children begin to show an interest in writing at age 2, some do not. Individuals vary considerably in early writing development (Read, 1971), depending on children's exposure to print and opportunities to observe and engage in writing activities. Some children may have difficulty grasping objects, showing minor delays in fine-motor control. In addition, an individual child's "writing" may vary in different contexts. For example, when pretending to write a message in the kitchen play center, Rachel may use scribble, which may approximate cursory writing. At other times, when writing a valentine, she may write real letters if it suits her purpose. All of this variation implies that the course of writing development is not always linear, nor does it occur in fixed sequences. In fact, there are no reliable developmental milestones tied to specific ages and stages of writing.

Although the process of learning to write differs among children, it is not totally random. As children progress and are exposed to print, usually at least by age 3, their more controlled scribbling begins to acquire some of the characteristics of print. Marie Clay (1975), a New Zealand educator who studied children's early writing, found that children begin to notice the visual features of print. They notice its linearity, its horizontal orientation, and the arrangement of letter-like forms. For example, a child begins to recognize (a) that letters consist of a limited number of shapes that can be put together in various ways and (b) that the shapes can be used to generate numbers as well as letters and words. Sometimes this realization leads a child to write "strings of letters," writing the same letters many different ways, in many different arrangements or positions, or reproducing letters in long strings that are more or less in random order.

Between the ages of 4 and 7, children begin to try to translate the words they hear and can say into the letters that spell them. This effort is the beginning of the development of an alphabetic principle (Adams, 1990), the understanding of the match between letters and their sounds. Not surprisingly, the first word most children learn to spell is their name. This accomplishment places them on the road to learning many different things about print. They learn about beginning sounds. They learn that a name starts with a capital letter that is followed by lowercase letters. And most important, they learn that there is a set order to the letters in their name and that order never varies. This insight marks an important transition to conventional reading and writing.

Children's development in writing, therefore, depends on a number of factors: interest, opportunities to write, and the amount of informal feedback from a caring adult. When young children have lots of opportunities to observe, engage, and interact around writing, they develop and refine their initial hypotheses about how writing works. With adult involvement, they begin to make active comparisons between their writing and "the adult way." In these playful contrasts and comparisons, children begin to use writing to communicate with others.

The Early Development of Reading

Two-year-old Christopher can't read yet, and he hasn't shown much interest in letters. But he is always eager to listen to books. When he and two friends at his child-care center listen to *The Three Little Pigs*, they shout, "And I'll huff, and I'll puff, and I'll blow your house in." As Ms. Helen reads on, they wait for the next episode, only to repeat the lines even louder this time. While they are enjoying the story, these children are probably not aware that the little black squiggles on the page are telling a story and that the words in the book are always the same. Nevertheless, they are learning important features of written knowledge, its rhythms and cadences, and they are displaying their knowledge of language structure. They are learning to participate in book reading activities and to "talk like a book" which will have important consequences in successful reading later on (Snow, Tabors, Nicholson, & Kurland, 1995).

Storybook reading to children is the single best predictor of their success in learning to read. Even though children's attention spans may be short, studies (Sénéchal, LeFevre, Thomas, & Daley, 1998; Whitehurst et al., 1988) indicate that babies and toddlers benefit significantly from listening to stories. They learn to focus their attention on the words and the pictures. Storybook reading between caregivers and children at early ages is highly social. Interactions are playful or game-like while they are also instructional. Many caregivers do not just show the pictures to children but, instead, talk about them, asking questions like "What's that?" or making comments like "That's a lion. Remember when we went to the zoo?" Ms. Darlene, for example, finds that the clear photos of everyday objects and animals in Tana Hoban's (2003a, 2003b) board book series (e.g., *Black on White, White on Black*) fascinate 10-month-old Devon for about 5 minutes as he focuses all of his attention on one particular page. Later on, Ms. Darlene finds him intently looking at the pictures by himself, holding the book and turning the pages.

Even if babies and toddlers don't seem to be attending carefully, they are absorbing the sounds and rhythms of their caregivers' voice (Friedberg, 1995). An 8-month-old, for example, listens to the words from a short book, especially one with pictures of familiar objects. A 1-year-old baby who has been read to may already know how to hold a book right side up and turn the pages from front to back.

Certain types of books are especially intriguing to babies and toddlers (Neuman, 1999). Books with photographs or drawings of animals, people, and single brightly colored objects draw children's attention and interest. Easy-to-hold board books that can stand lots of hard wear enable young toddlers to "read" by themselves. Interactive books such as the Spot lift-the-flap stories by Eric Hill, provided in Spanish and English, playfully reinforce children's efforts to master the basics of book handling. Book care is an important lesson even though adults know that books are not to likely last long in the hands of toddlers. Books that take children though familiar routines or repeated phrases ("Marvin K. Mooney, will you please go now!"; Seuss, 1972) help young children become part of the story due to its predictable patterns and repetitive language. Teachers find that children like Devon have a tendency to chime in, saying the last words of the phrase "will you please go now!" Such chiming is a positive feature of early engagement. It provides for all sorts of language play, allowing the young child to say and use words that might be new and unfamiliar, and it keeps the child's attention from wandering. And of course, nursery rhymes are well-loved at this early age.

After hearing books several times, toddlers begin to pick out their favorite books by seeing the covers or even just the spine that runs down the side of a book. They are learning to "read" the landmarks and signs on a book, much as they are beginning to read familiar signs in their environment, such as the "stop" or "exit" signs. Toddlers are not really reading the words yet, but they are beginning to get the book's message from the arrangement of pictures, letters, colors, and patterns, reminders that symbols carry important messages. They are also learning how to figure out sequences of events from looking at the pictures.

Children at this age, and sometimes even younger, can begin to tell a story from a familiar book (Friedberg, 1995). Most adults have seen a child hold a book facing out, the way an adult would read in front of a group, and "read" it to a pretend audience of friends or stuffed animals. Some toddlers hold the book in their laps and quietly tell the story to themselves. They are practicing learning to be readers just as when they were babies they practiced their intriguing language sounds until they mastered the art of speaking.

For children at these young ages, story times work best when they are relatively brief (about 5 to 10 minutes) and conversational (Neuman, 1999). Sitting side by side with one or two children has its special advantages. Children nestled close can follow the text and pictures, ask questions, and point to their favorite characters. In some cases, adults might go with one child to a cozy spot away from the others to help the child concentrate on a book for brief, highly interactive readings. If the story is not completed, that doesn't matter. Rather, the point of these beginning storybook times is for the interaction to be enjoyable and to be filled with language. Caregivers can choose among many "readable moments" throughout the day: time between activities, quiet times, or moments when stories can bring the day to a fulfilling close.

The Importance of Assisted Instruction

It is the end of the day at Tiny Tots, a busy time when parents are picking up their children and gathering their many things. Three-and-a-half-year-old Edward and his cousin, 2-year-old Kalief, have their attention riveted not on the door, however, but on the short book *Houses* being read by Ms. Kimberly:

Ms. Kimberly: *Do you see the plumber Kalief?*

Edward: *I see the plumber.*

Kalief: *He's working on the pipes. I bet he's working on the pipes.*

Edward: *Here go the ladder.*

Kalief: *There go the lights.*

Edward: *Who's in the house?*

Kalief: *A worker man?*

Ms. Kimberly: *The workers are painting and putting up the doors and the windows.*

Edward: *Turn it [the page] back, turn it back, turn it back, I want to see the worker man.*

Ms. Kimberly: *(turns back the page). Here's the workers. The workers leave. That means they go home. You know like when you leave here with your mommy. They go home.*

No doubt, Ms. Kimberly would consider this informal conversation rather typical and uneventful. But there are a number of striking features in this book-reading activity. For one, Ms. Kimberly has selected a book that is challenging, but understandable (Lidz, 1991; Rogoff, Mosier, Mistry, & Goncu, 1993) for the children (IRA & NAEYC, 1998). Although it contains many new words, the topic is highly familiar and interesting to the boys. Here, the children are labeling words that are related to their everyday lives.

Notice that Ms. Kimberly begins by recruiting their attention and asking the children to focus on a page. Once they become involved, she steps back a bit, as they give meaning to the pictures. She then helps the children define "workers" and extends the description beyond the printed page, bridging what is seen in the picture to what they can relate to in their own lives. In this respect, Ms. Kimberly provides some level of metacognitive support, controlling and taking primary responsibility for higher-level goals while the children engage at a level in which they are capable at the time (Diaz, Neal, & Vachio, 1991).

Within the context of a book-reading activity, caregivers may accentuate certain features as being more relevant and meaningful than others. Through this process, children learn the labels of common objects as well as the relationships among objects and events. Once the context and meaningfulness of an activity are conveyed, caregivers may extend children's understanding by linking the activity to something that is either within or slightly beyond the children's own experiences. For example, Ms. Kimberly defines what it means for the workers to leave, then compares their movement with the children's own activity of leaving for the day. This task of connecting concepts is seen as essential for intellectual growth, helping children make sense of present experiences by relating these issues to the past. This task also may facilitate children's understanding of events that cannot be actually be perceived, by encouraging them to employ their imagination to anticipate further activities. Sigel and his colleagues (McGillicuddy-De Lisi, Sigel, & Johnson, 1979; Sigel & McGillicuddy-De Lisi, 1984) have described this concept as "distancing," and have documented the association of these behaviors to the cognitive development of preschoolers.

Not seen in this particular interaction but a critical feature of assisted instruction is the transfer of responsibility from caregiver to child (Rogoff, 1990; Tharp & Gallimore, 1988). Caregivers need to carefully gauge their support to see when children are able move ahead or beyond their current level of ability. Caregivers may encourage and prompt the children to turn the pages, to ask questions, and to predict what may come next so the children can work toward independence and self-regulation. For example, the next day, Ms. Kimberly places the now-familiar and well-loved book *Houses* in the block area or the classroom library so Edward and Kalief can "read" it by themselves. They may sit in the corner and re-read the story. Or they may use blocks in the block corner to construct a house, with ladders, pipes, and lights, and then pretend to be "worker men." By doing so, they will be making the book their own, retelling parts of the book in their own language. In the course of their pretend play, they will engage in "decontextualized language," that is, specialized uses of language that arise in response to the need to communicate apart from the actual context in which it was crafted (Snow, Tabors, Nicholson, & Kurland, 1995)—a predictor of academic success.

This chapter has defined the following as critical steps in assisted instruction: (a) get set, (b) give meaning, (c) build bridges, and (d) step back (Neuman, 1995). *Get set* focuses on the importance of attention getting and recruiting children's interest by asking predictive questions as well as structuring the physical setting (e.g., sitting in comfortable chairs or the floor in a way that allows children to point to the pictures) so the children can effectively participate. *Give meaning* helps children understand the story by focusing on the illustrations, describing new words, adding affect to voice ("meeeow") to make the words or pictures more understandable to them, and talking about and elaborating on the actions in a story. *Build bridges* highlights the importance of extending children's understanding by linking what is read to something that is either within or beyond their own experiences. Caregivers might build connections between what is going on now in the classroom and other experiences either past or present to move the story experience beyond the pages. And finally, *step back* encourages caregivers to give children increasing responsibility, letting children take a turn and ask questions, and providing them with elaborated feedback to encourage their strategic thinking.

Essentially, these steps remind all caregivers that high-quality reading to children is sensitive to development. Interaction plays an important role in helping children develop higher order thinking. Edward and Kalief's conversational turns, for example, would not have been as rich if Ms. Kimberly had simply placed the book in the play centers without first reading and discussing it. It was her sensitivity to careful book selection and interaction that supported the children's language and thinking.

The Importance of the Library

Informal libraries at homes or in child-care settings complement and extend children's learning from books (Neuman, 1999), but they need not be large or fancy. Rather, a library needs to feel cozy and inviting to children. A library should include attractive books that are not tattered and worn. Familiar titles and other books that have been recently read by a caregiver will draw children's attention. Multiple copies of these favorite books will encourage children to read to one another. The following list outlines critical features of design for infant–toddler reading centers:

- Books need to be accessible on open-faced shelves that allow children to look at the pictures and titles at their own eye level.

- Various materials, including magazines, information, alphabet, counting and wordless books, attract attention.

- Stuffed animals and comfortable seating such as bean bag chairs, mattresses, and pillows invite children to come in and read.

- Good lighting highlights the setting.

- Lively displays, book covers, posters and a catchy name like "Cozy Corner Library" add color and dimension to the walls of the library.

Caregivers must help children learn how to care for books in their library. Ms. Fernanda, for example, gives several children lessons on turning pages. Giving them each a book, she guides their hands to go "across the top, down to the corner, and flip over." Ms. Fernanda also makes sure that the library includes a "book hospital" (an old dairy box "where books go to get better"). The book hospital contains torn books and invisible tape, eraser, scissors, and glue. On regular occasions, Ms. Fernanda invites children to a fix-it lesson. They watch while she repairs a well-loved book.

The library is not the only area to include books, however. Some caregivers "decentralize" parts of their library by placing books about fish near the fish tank, books about cooking in the play kitchen, and books and magazines in the doctor's office dramatic-play center. Caregivers commonly observe children referring to these materials not only during their play but also during project activities. In addition, decentralization of the library sends the important message that books are useful sources of information that can enhance children's imagination and learning.

The design of physical spaces and materials within them is important (Neuman, 1999), but equally critical is scheduling time for children to use these resources. Infants and toddlers need time throughout the day to browse; read alone; read with a parent, caregiver, or aide one-on-one; or read with their friend or teddy bear. Sometimes children pretend to read, like Clarissa, who opens a book and says, "Once apon a time, once apon a time, once apon a time. There…I readed it." Although Clarissa's behavior might be amusing to observers, what she is demonstrating is important: her motivation and interest in reading. In fact, when observing this kind of behavior, the thoughtful caregiver might wisely ask a key question, "Would you like me to read the words to you?"

Conclusions

Early literacy development does not merely happen. Rather, it is a social process that is nurtured through meaningful relationships with parents, caregivers, friends, and siblings. These caregivers play critical roles in children's motivation and knowledge about literacy by serving as models, providing necessary resources, and conveying their hopes and expectations to children. It is these interactions that shape how children come to see literacy in their daily lives.

References

Adams, M. (1990). *Beginning to read*. Cambridge, MA: MIT Press.

Bowman, B., Donovan, M. S., & Burns, M. S. (Eds.). (2001). *Eager to learn: Educating our preschoolers*. Washington, D.C.: National Academy Press.

Clay, M. (1975). *What did I write?* London: Heinemann.

Clay, M. (1991). *Becoming literate*. Portsmouth, NH: Heinemann.

Diaz, R., Neal, C., & Vachio, A. (1991). Maternal teaching in the zone of proximal development: A comparison of low- and high-risk dyads. *Merrill-Palmer Quarterly, 37*, 83–108.

Dyson, A. H. (1988). Appreciate the drawings and dictating of young children. *Young Children, 43*, 25–32.

Friedberg, J. (1995). *Super storytimes: A guide for caregivers*. Pittsburgh, PA: Beginning With Books.

Gibson, E. (1979). *The ecological approach to visual perception*. Boston, MA: Houghton-Mifflin.

Hoban, T. (2003a). *Black on white*. New York: Greenwillow Books.

Hoban, T. (2003b). *White on black*. New York: Greenwillow Books.

IRA (International Reading Association), & NAEYC (National Association for the Education of Young Children). (1998). *Learning to read and write: Developmentally appropriate practices for young children*. A joint position statement of the IRA and NAEYC. Newark, DE: IRA; and Washington, DC: NAEYC.

Lidz, C. (1991). *Practitioner's guide to dynamic assessment*. New York: Guilford.

McGillicuddy-De Lisi, A., Sigel, I., & Johnson, J. (1979). The family as a system of mutual influences: Parental beliefs, distancing behaviors, and children's representational thinking. In M. Lewis & L. A. Rosenblum (Eds.), *The child and its family* (pp. 91–106). New York: Plenum.

McLane, J. B., & McNamee, J. (1990). *Early literacy*. Cambridge, MA: Harvard University Press.

National Research Council & Institute of Medicine. (2000). *From neurons to neighborhoods*. J. P. Shonkoff & D. Phillips (Eds.). Committee on Integrating the Science of Early Childhood Development. Board on Children, Youth, and Families, Commission on Behavioral and Social Sciences and Education. Washington, DC: National Academy Press.

Neuman, S. B. (1995). Enhancing adolescent mothers' guided participation in literacy. In L. M. Morrow (Ed.), *Family literacy* (pp. 104–114). Newark, DE: International Reading Association.

Neuman, S. B. (1999). Books make a difference: A study of access to literacy. *Reading Research Quarterly, 34*, 286–312.

Neuman, S. B., Copple, C., & Bredekamp, S. (2000). *Learning to read and write: Developmentally appropriate practice*. Washington, DC: National Association for the Education of Young Children.

Neuman, S. B., & Roskos, K. (1992). Literacy objects as cultural tools: Effects of literacy related activity in play. *Reading Research Quarterly, 27*, 202–225.

Read, C. (1971). Preschool children's knowledge of English phonology. *Harvard Educational Review, 41*, 1–34.

Rogoff, B. (1990). *Apprenticeship in thinking: Cognitive development in social context.* New York: Oxford University Press.

Rogoff, B., Mosier, C., Mistry, J., & Goncu, A. (1993). Toddlers' guided participation with their caregivers in cultural activity. In E. Forman, N. Minick, & A. Stone (Eds.), *Contexts for learning: Sociocultural dynamics in children's development* (pp. 230–253). New York: Oxford University Press.

Schickedanz, J. (1998). What is developmentally appropriate practice in early literacy?: Considering the alphabet. In S. B. Neuman & K. Roskos, *Children achieving* (pp. 20–37). Newark, DE: International Reading Association.

Sénéchal, M., LeFevre, J., Thomas, E., & Daley, K. (1998). Differential effects of home literacy experiences on the development of oral and written language. *Reading Research Quarterly, 33*, 96–116.

Seuss, D. (1972.) *Marvin K. Mooney, will you please go now!* New York: Random House.

Sigel, I. E., & McGillicuddy-De Lisi, A. (1984). Parents as teachers of their children: A distancing behavior model. In A. Pellegrini & T. Yawkey (Eds.), *The development of oral and written language in social contexts* (pp. 71–92). Norwood, NJ: Ablex.

Snow, C., Burns, M. S., & Griffin, P. (Eds.). National Research Council, Committee on the Prevention of Reading Difficulties. (1998). *Preventing reading difficulties in young children.* Washington, DC: National Academy Press.

Snow, C., Tabors, P., Nicholson, P., & Kurland, B. (1995). SHELL: Oral language and early literacy skills in kindergarten and first-grade children. *Journal of Research in Childhood Education, 10*, 37–48.

Tharp, R., & Gallimore, R. (1988). *Rousing minds to life.* Cambridge, UK: Cambridge University Press.

Whitehurst, G. J., Falco, F. L., Lonigan, C. J., Fischel, J. E., DeBaryshe, B. D., Valdez-Menchaca, M. C., et al. (1988). Accelerating language development through picture book reading. *Developmental Psychology, 24*, 552–559.

CHAPTER 14

Promoting Language and Literacy in Child Care

C. Chris Payne and Marion O'Brien

Many infants and toddlers spend large portions of their waking hours in child-care settings while their parents work. Child-care providers, therefore, play a key role in promoting all aspects of children's development. When care providers create child-care environments that emphasize language and emergent literacy with all children, including the youngest babies, they have the opportunity to leave a legacy of learning that can truly make a difference in children's lives.

This chapter will focus on ways in which child-care providers may enrich early language and literacy opportunities by

- understanding that the strongest foundation for early learning is through an emotionally supportive relationship with a caregiver,
- creating a language-rich environment throughout the day,
- including literacy in the curriculum for infants and toddlers,
- utilizing teaching strategies that are highly effective in promoting early language and literacy learning, and
- forming partnerships with parents.

Importance of Child-Care Environments

Child care is an important context for children's development, and caregivers play a critical role in this development. Research in the areas of early intervention and child care consistently find that the combination of direct child and family interventions is what best promotes early learning and later readiness skills related to early school performance. This critical partnership of parents and child-care providers is particularly important when working with young children with disabilities and those from disadvantaged circumstances (NICHD Early Child Care Research Network, 2003; Ramey & Campbell, 1984).

Research evidence strongly supports an important role of the quality of child-care environments in children's development of school readiness skills. For example, the results of the NICHD Study of Early Child Care (NICHD Early Child Care Research Network, 2002a) clearly link both the influence of parents and the quality of early caregiving relationships to children's skills in language and literacy. This long-term, 10-site study is among the very few longitudinal investigations that have followed a large sample of children from birth through the school entry years and into elementary school with multiple, rigorously conducted observations of children and their caregivers. The study was designed to examine both children's child-care environments and their family environments, and it provides extensive information on the ways in which experiences of children in child care contribute to the development of their school readiness. In this respect, this study has confirmed what others have suggested: (a) academic and social skills that define readiness for school begin developing long before children enter school; (b) these early foundations of school readiness can be assessed as early as age 2 or 3; (c) readiness is affected by children's experiences in their families; and (d) readiness is affected by children's experiences in child care. After controlling for multiple child and family characteristics, children in higher quality care were found to score higher on measures of cognitive and language development at 24, 36, and 54 months. In particular, they scored higher on standardized measures of pre-academic skills at 54 months: they were more likely to know more words, correctly identify the letters of the alphabet, count, and understand language (NICHD Early Child Care Research Network, 2002b). Largely, the "quality factor" was based on warm, responsive, language-supportive interactions from care providers. In addition, when child-care providers talked and read more to children, the children's language development was enhanced.

Quality child care is especially important for children whose families are living in poverty. Extensive research has shown the value of early intervention programs in promoting the overall development of children at risk (Shonkoff &

Meisels, 2000). Perhaps the most widely implemented early intervention program for economically disadvantaged U.S. children is Head Start. Approximately 1 million children are now being served in Head Start and Early Head Start programs nationwide. The magnitude of these programs, combined with their support for teacher training and curriculum development, creates an opportunity to enhance school readiness for a large number of children by strengthening the foundation for early learning—the child's relationships with caregivers and exposure to early and consistent literacy experiences. Evaluations of Head Start and other intervention programs support the importance of (a) early caregiver–child relationships, (b) language-rich child-care environments, and (c) the provision of literacy experiences in child care as the foundation for later school readiness (Gilliam & Zigler, 2000; Warr-Leeper, 2001). The following sections of this chapter describe ways in which child-care environments can effectively implement these three important components of quality care. This chapter also suggests teaching strategies for language and literacy learning as well as emphasizes the importance of forming strong partnerships with parents.

Relationships Are the Key

Young children's early learning takes place within their social relationships. When interactions with other people are emotionally positive and supportive, babies and toddlers are motivated to seek out opportunities to share their experiences with others. By responding to infants' signals about their internal states and by meeting their physical needs, caregivers teach babies one of the most important lessons they will ever learn—that good things happen when you communicate with other people.

Although children's first and most emotionally intense relationships are formed with parents and family members, other caregivers also play an important role (Ashiabi, 2000). Within child-care environments, teachers and caregivers who invest their own emotional energy in their relationships with children contribute in immeasurable ways to children's social development. Infants and toddlers are particularly sensitive to the emotional states of people around them. When caregivers are fully attentive and truly enjoy the children they care for, then infants and toddlers will respond with affection and contentment. Caregivers whose minds are elsewhere or who show boredom or irritation on the job make children wary and cautious, contributing to children's stress and negative moods. Consistency and predictability are important to infants and toddlers who are just beginning to be able to anticipate events and other people's reactions. There is security in knowing that another person can be counted on to smile back and share one's good feelings. That sense of security contributes to children's confidence in themselves as they seek to understand their social worlds.

The sensitive and predictable responses of caregivers also build young children's ability to regulate their own emotions and behavior (Crockenberg & Leerkes, 2003). When children are distressed or in a state of heightened arousal, intervention by a caring adult not only helps the child through that particular situation but also teaches the child strategies for maintaining him- or herself in a more calm and controlled state. With increased self-regulation comes increased ability to focus attention, higher levels of engagement with the social and physical environment, and a sense of efficacy that contributes to an intrinsic motivation to learn.

Young children whose social experiences are supportive, emotionally positive, and consistent tend to develop a positive and energetic approach to life and learning. This characteristic has been termed *emotional vitality* by Robinson and Acevedo (2001). Children who show this temperamental characteristic are more confident and effective in their interactions with others, both adults and peers. Further, studies of children who exhibit such a profile have been found to be more competent in language and cognitive skills by age 2 (Olds et al., 2002; Robinson & Acevedo, 2001). Thus, the quality of early relationships contributes to a positive approach to life and learning that, in turn, supports the development of language and literacy skills.

Creating a Language-Rich Environment in Child Care

Language and literacy begin with babies' first nonverbal cues—gestures, facial expressions, and body language—that convey needs and feelings to sensitive caregivers. When caregivers also *talk* about the messages they are receiving and what they are doing in response, they help babies link vocal sounds with events and emotions. Babies attend to and imitate adults' vocalizations in patterned ways that form the basis for what has been termed the *rhythm of dialog* (Jaffe, Beebe, Feldstein, Crown, & Jasnow, 2001), the start of true conversation.

Some adults do not talk to children very much until children begin to say intelligible words, perhaps because they think that one-sided conversation is not really communication. But infants participate in conversations long before they can talk. Caregivers who respond consistently to nonverbal signals and early vocalizations with language that describes the child's experience let children know they are being "listened" to and create a desire to become an effective communicator. By being attentive to an infant's facial expressions and gestures, caregivers can respond sensitively to the child's nonverbal conversations and encourage babies to continue and expand their communicative efforts.

A language-rich child-care environment is one in which adults talk about everything they do and everything the children are doing. By surrounding the child with language, caregivers encourage and support communication. Children come to understand that objects, people, and events have unique labels; they learn to segment the stream of sound into meaningful chunks; and they are encouraged to experiment with their own lips and tongue. The descriptive use of language is more important to children's language development than its directive use. That is, caregivers who simply talk about things and events that the child can see promote communication more effectively than those who use language primarily to give directions or to quiz the child. When children are just beginning to learn language, questions and directions are demand situations that can be stressful and discourage children's continued participation in interaction (O'Brien & Bi, 1995). Once children are able to respond reliably to verbal requests and to participate actively in verbal exchanges, open-ended questions and verbal suggestions work effectively to build language skills. But for preverbal children and in the very early stages of language acquisition, caregivers should be happy to be the only one talking. It is certain that the children are listening and learning.

Young children are particularly attracted to speech that consists of simple, short sentences spoken in melodic tones that vary in pitch. They also love repetition of sounds, words, and phrases. One type of speech that includes all of these characteristics is singing. Babies and toddlers are drawn to songs and rhymes and appear to be entranced by anyone who will sing their favorite songs. And they will never criticize the performance! All the speech children hear doesn't have to be intelligent, either; babbling, oohing, and making mouth noises that would be rude in adult company are wonderful ways to interest babies in making their own unique and fascinating sounds (for more information on the important role of music in early language and literacy, see Kimura, this volume p. 235).

In addition to an enriched spoken-language environment, child-care settings can offer children extensive exposure to the written word. This statement is not a recommendation to teach toddlers to read or write. But just as babies and toddlers begin to recognize people and objects that have significance to them, they can begin to recognize important letters and words: their name, for example, or the label on their favorite cereal package. Success at reading and writing involves the acquisition of many small skills—holding the book right side up, turning one page at a time, keeping the paper still while making marks on it—and toddlers learn these skills by watching others and by experimenting for themselves. When a child-care environment includes lots of books—ones that children can handle and explore as well as ones that are used by teachers and children together—and lots of activities with paper and crayons, children have opportunities to practice and master the many preliteracy tasks that will provide the building blocks for later reading and writing. Learning to read and write has much in common with learning to speak, and children build emergent literacy skills during infancy through exposure to environments rich in oral language and filled with opportunities to share reading and writing experiences with adults.

Including Literacy in the Curriculum for Infants and Toddlers

A language-rich environment in child care is one in which language is a part of everything that children do, at diaper changing time and during outdoor play as well as at story time. More focused efforts to encourage the development of language and literacy skills and to guide children's growing communicative abilities are also needed. The inclusion of language and literacy objectives in the curriculum plan for infant and toddler care helps caregivers identify children's strengths and challenges as well as provides a range of experiences to foster communication and language learning. A curriculum that uses both incidental and planned learning activities is most effective in promoting language development (Payne-Donnelly, 1992).

Published curriculum models for infant–toddler care offer ideas for age-appropriate, language-focused activities that can be used in one-to-one and group situations. Use of a specific curriculum approach helps to ensure consistency across caregivers. When the approach is also shared with parents who can implement its design at home, too, then children can benefit even more. One example of this type of approach that has been used by child-care programs such as Early Head Start that have a parent visitation or family advocacy component is Partners in Parenting Education (PIPE; Butterfield, 1996) and its companion curriculum, Emotional Beginnings (EB). PIPE is a set of relationship regulation principles that have been translated into concrete strategies for use by high-risk parents of infants and toddlers, and EB offers a similar approach for child-care providers. In both these curricula, the adult–child relationship and its effect on the child's emotional development is a central focus; a secondary focus is on the promotion of the child's language development. These models have been shown to have significant effects on both mothers' sensitivity and children's cognitive and language development.

Whether a child-care setting uses an existing curriculum model or encourages caregivers to develop their own lesson plans and learning activities, one important component is the organization of caregiver responsibilities to assure adequate time for a variety of different types of play activities. Infants and toddlers require a lot of physical care and individual attention; without a plan for the day's activities that anticipates children's needs, caregivers can find themselves moving from crisis to crisis and coming to the end of the day without having arranged any individually meaningful materials or activities to entice the children. Thus, it is critical to the implementation of *any* infant–toddler curriculum that careful attention is paid to advance planning and division of caregiving responsibilities (O'Brien, 1997).

All the activities in an infant–toddler curriculum lend themselves to promoting communication and language skills. Some types of activities, however, are more logically tied to language and literacy objectives and provide not only clear opportunities for alert and knowledgeable caregivers to identify children's individual levels of competence but also experiences that build new skills just beyond the child's current level of performance. One obvious area for language and literacy learning is book reading (Honig & Shin, 2001). Infants and tod-dlers love books. They love to look at the pictures, point to interesting shapes and colors, taste the cardboard cover, and feel what the pages are like when crumpled. In other words, infants and toddlers truly want to experience books and explore all their properties. Although making inexpensive cloth and card-board books available for children's exploratory play is a good thing, it is not enough. Children also need to learn that there are "rules" about how books are handled and that books offer new worlds of ideas and imagination. Caregivers who value books, who love to read aloud, who are skilled at elaborating on sto-ries and pictures as well as eliciting responses give children a lifelong gift. Another way to incorporate literacy skills into the curriculum is to have chil-dren "help" caregivers make their own books, incorporating photographs, children's artwork, and stories told by children.

A second necessary part of a literacy curriculum is rhyme, rhythm, and song (Suthers, 2001). Infants and toddlers need live music—songs and chants per-formed by the caregivers they know and love, not canned music, the background noise of the radio, or video programming. Only the live perform-ance is responsive to children's level of understanding and participation; only the live performance can be flexible enough to incorporate children's names and familiar events and objects into its tunes. No audio- or videotape presents songs or rhymes at the slow speed that fledgling language users can follow or captivates the young child's attention the way caregivers' songs and rhymes do. Children learn the finger motions of songs and rhymes with astonishing speed and use them as communicative symbols to request an encore. Songs capture so much attention from infants and toddlers that creative caregivers can make up songs to teach new words and encourage children to practice speech sounds. Songs also can help children and caregivers through rough spots in the day—transitions, cleanup times, and unavoidable waits for something to happen. Songs and rhymes that are interactive help children learn the pragmatics of conversational speech—the turntaking, the links between what one person says and does and how the other responds, the body language that shows one is involved and attentive. In short, songs and rhymes offer caregivers unlimited possibilities to teach language and literacy skills.

As children become more socially aware, caregivers can add curriculum com-ponents focusing on promoting communication with peers. Conversations are difficult when both partners in an interaction are just learning the basics of communication. With caregiver help, however, toddler peers can practice communicative exchanges that will ultimately develop into cooperative play. Much of toddlers' play occurs in parallel with another toddler; that is, two or more toddlers may do similar things with similar toys and be in proximity to one another, but they will not actually appear to communicate. However, these types of episodes—called parallel play—commonly involve imitation (see also Barton & Brophy-Herb, this volume, p. 15). One toddler, while seeming to be unaware of another, gradually begins to incorporate the actions of the other into his or her own play. Shared laughter also happens frequently during parallel play. This early imitation and sharing of experience is thought to mark the beginnings of communication and cooperation among toddlers (Didow & Eckerman, 2001; Eckerman & Stein, 1990). Alert caregivers can use parallel play situations, which are common especially when children are playing with construction toys or vehicles, to encourage children to notice one another's actions and recognize shared experience.

Peer interaction and communication can also be fostered in the context of early pretend play with dolls and household materials. Caregivers can help promote role taking by labeling familiar roles for the children and making simple suggestions for joint play. Repetition is the key to fostering elaboration of early role playing. When the same materials are available over a period of time, toddlers are able to replay the same situation day after day, gradually incorporating more complex play themes and extending their engagement. An ideal curriculum plan for infants and toddlers includes both repetition and variety—repetition to allow practice as well as consolidation of skills and variety to encourage development of new skills and interests.

Teaching Strategies for Language and Literacy Learning

Research has clearly shown that environments in which children hear a lot of language promote growth in both receptive and expressive language as well as cognitive skills (Hart & Risley, 1995; NICHD Early Child Care Research Network, 2000). In addition to making language a constant part of their work with children, skilled caregivers also know and use specific, time-tested techniques for promoting children's use and understanding of language and communication. Most of these techniques, which are discussed in the following subsections, have been developed by specialists in communication disorders, but they are useful for promoting the communicative development of all children.

Self-talk. Self-talk involves caregivers' talking in descriptive terms about what they themselves are doing. "I'm getting out the dress-up clothes. First I'll open the closet door. I see all kinds of dress-up clothes! Scarves and hats and high-heeled shoes! Dress-up is so much fun!" These simple, slow-paced descriptions, using the same words repeated several times, give children a chance to associate sounds and words with actions and objects, to repeat or imitate sounds or words, and eventually to respond and participate in the conversation. Thus, self-talk is appropriate for all infants and toddlers, from the youngest baby to the already verbal almost-preschooler.

Parallel talk. Parallel talk is similar to self-talk except that caregivers describe what *children* are doing instead of what they themselves are doing. In parallel talk, the focus is on labeling objects that a child is looking at or using, express-ing a descriptive verb that fits what a child is doing at that moment, and naming people as they come near. Although caregivers using parallel talk describe what children are doing, they do not give children directions or ask them questions. Thus, parallel talk is narration, rather like that of a color announcer at a sports event or of the stage manager character in *Our Town*. Parallel talk is particularly effective at getting children's attention when care-givers make creative use of language, for example, by inserting sound effects to accompany children's activity ("The tower is falling ... KEEErash!"). Parallel talk also helps children identify abstractions such as feelings ("You're angry!") and sensations such as smells and textures ("The grass tickles your feet."). By labeling children's experience, caregivers not only help to link words with their referents but also convey that the child's experiences are shared and are the basis of communication.

Expansion and continuation. As children begin to make sounds that resemble words and then move to recognizable words and sentences, caregivers can pro-mote language learning by responding to children's talk in a way that both acknowledges understanding (the sign of successful communication) and adds new information. *Expansions* allow caregivers to model pronunciation and grammar without obviously correcting children who are, after all, doing their best. Any partial word or communicative attempt can be responded to with an expansion. A child reaching for a doll that is firmly grasped by another toddler says "Baba me." A nearby caregiver who quickly brings to the situation another doll responds with, "A baby doll for Derek." As children's speech becomes more competent and clear, caregivers can follow children's sentences with *continuations* that are similar to the kinds of conversations adults have with one another. Continuations are closely tied to the child's words but provide more information or help the child's understanding. For example, if a toddler getting ready to go outside in the winter says, "Boot shoe," a caregiver might respond, "That is your boot. It's a kind of shoe."

Open-ended questions. Adults' conversational turns when talking with children tend to be dominated by questions (O'Brien & Bi, 1995; see also Neuman, this volume, p. 275; Notari-Syverson, this volume, p. 61; Pierce & Profio, this volume, p. 103). Many of these questions can be answered with a simple nod or shake of the head, a pointing gesture, or a single word. Questions can be effective ways to engage children in conversation (especially if adults take turns asking and answering) once children have acquired a reasonable vocabulary and are using at least two-word sentences. However, to encourage more complex use of language, caregivers need to become skilled at asking open-ended questions that require more than a one-word answer. Instead of asking "Are you looking at a book?" the caregiver using an open-ended question might ask, "That book is about fish. What is the fish doing in that picture?" This type of question-asking does not come naturally to most of us and therefore is a skill that must be practiced and mastered.

Dialogic reading. An approach to reading books with children known as dialogic reading has recently been extended from home to child-care contexts (Lonigan & Whitehurst, 1998; Valdez-Menchaca & Whitehurst, 1992; Whitehurst et al., 1988, 1994; see also Cole & Lim, this volume, p. 537). Dialogic reading encompasses all of the language-teaching techniques described previously within the context of adult–child reading. Children are encouraged to be active participants in telling the story, setting the occasion for the adult reader to provide labels and add descriptive details, to use expansions and continuations, and to ask open-ended questions.

Dialogic reading is particularly appropriate during a child's third year (age 2), when children's vocabularies are expanding and their abilities to express their thoughts are blossoming. The approach of dialogic reading offers systematic instruction for adults in reading with young children in ways that specifically encourage children's early language development during the time of the young child's rapid acquisition of expressive vocabulary. In dialogic reading, adults use evocative techniques—specifically questions, prompts, elaboration, and praise—to draw the child into conversation about the story depicted in the book. The techniques of dialogic reading are based on the kinds of adult behaviors many parents and caregivers use naturally but do not think about, such as the use of what- and where-questions, labels, requests to imitate, repetition, expansion, and praise. Becoming aware of effective reading approaches makes it more likely that caregivers will use them regularly.

Initially developed in a one-to-one parent-child reading context, the dialogic reading approach has also been used with small groups in child-care settings and has been shown to promote language learning, especially when implemented both at home and in child care (Lonigan & Whitehurst, 1998; Whitehurst et al., 1994).

Forming Partnerships With Parents

The results of studies examining the effectiveness of intervention programs that combine home- and center-based programs and of the dialogic reading approach when implemented at home and in child care emphasize the importance of collaborative efforts between parents and child-care providers. Preliminary findings from the Early Head Start Research and Evaluation Project suggest that Early Head Start is an effective method of involving low-income families in support of their children's school readiness (Administration for Children, Youth, and Families, 2001). It appears that Early Head Start mixed-model programs that combine both home- and center-based services are especially effective. Programs that offered mixed services provided the broadest positive effects not only on children's relational skills, behavior-attention regulation, and language development but also on their parents' efforts to support their children's readiness to learn (Administration for Children, Youth, and Families, 2001). Children show the greatest gains when similar teaching approaches are used both at home and in child care. Young children thrive on consistency and learn through repetition. When language and literacy are encouraged and supported in similar ways across children's environments, the opportunities for learning and practice of skills are multiplied.

Most parents are fascinated and thrilled by their children's acquisition of communication and language. Babies' early gestures and babbling sounds elicit parents' rapt attention. The vocabulary explosion that typically occurs in children's second year is a source of great delight to parents, and the insights they get into their children's thinking once the child can talk contributes to the development of the parent–child relationship. Unless parents have taken courses in child development or read widely about language learning, however, they are not likely to be knowledgeable about environmental contributions to children's language competence. Caregivers can build on parents' inherent interest in early infant communication and in toddler language by exposing families to the language and literacy approaches used in the child-care setting. Parents can be invited to visit the care setting at times other than open house or parent meeting days and participate actively in play, book reading, and other activities with a language or literacy focus. If paired with a compatible caregiver who is able to describe the language facilitation approaches as they come up, a parent can pick up and begin to use many of the same techniques.

Parent–caregiver partnerships are effective and helpful to the child only when they are true partnerships. Parents are individuals, with varying interests, skills, and demands on their time and energy. Caregivers can offer opportunities for involvement but must respect the parent's right to make decisions about the use of their time.

Caregivers do not replace parents in the child's life, even when children spend more waking hours in child care than at home. The parent–child relationship is unique and takes primacy over other relationships. But the relationships that caregivers have with children are also important. Children develop their ideas about themselves and about how others will respond to them through all the day-to-day experiences they have with many different people. When caregivers put their emotional energy into developing affectionate and stable relationships with children, when they provide an environment that is rich with language and literacy learning opportunities, and when they support children's families in their important work, they are making an investment in the future of our children that will return benefits to everyone in society.

References

Administration for Children, Youth, and Families (2001). *Building their futures: How Early Head Start programs are enhancing the lives of infants and toddlers in low-income families.* Summary Report. Washington, DC: Department of Health and Human Services.

Ashiabi, G. S. (2000). Promoting the emotional development of preschoolers. *Early Childhood Education Journal, 28,* 79–84.

Barton, L. R., & Brophy-Herb, H. E. (2006). Developmental foundations for language and literacy from birth to 3 years. In S. E. Rosenkoetter & J. Knapp-Philo (Eds.), *Learning to read the world: Language and literacy in the first three years* (pp. 15–60). Washington, DC: ZERO TO THREE Press

Butterfield, P. (1996). The Partners in Parenting Education Program: A new option in parent education. *Zero to Three, 17*(1), 3–10.

Cole, K. N., & Lim, Y. S. (2006). Language is the key: A proven approach to early language and literacy. In S. E. Rosenkoetter & J. Knapp-Philo (Eds.), *Learning to read the world: Language and literacy in the first three years* (pp. 537–552). Washington, DC: ZERO TO THREE Press.

Crockenberg, S., & Leerkes, E. (2003). Infant negative emotionality, caregiving, and family relationships. In A. C. Crouter & A. Booth (Eds.), *Children's influence on family dynamics: The neglected side of family relationships* (pp. 57–78). Mahwah, NJ: Erlbaum.

Didow, S. M., & Eckerman, C. O. (2001). Toddler peers: From nonverbal coordinated action to verbal discourse. *Social Development, 10,* 170–188.

Eckerman, C., & Stein, M. (1990). How imitation begets imitation and toddlers' generation of games. *Developmental Psychology, 26,* 370–378.

Gilliam, W. S., & Zigler, E. F. (2000). A critical meta-analysis of all evaluations of state-funded preschool from 1977 to 1998: Implications for policy, service delivery and program evaluation. *Early Childhood Research Quarterly, 15,* 441–473.

Hart, B., & Risley, T. R. (1995). *Meaningful differences in the everyday experiences of young American children.* Baltimore: Paul H. Brookes.

Honig, A. S., & Shin, M. (2001). Reading aloud with infants and toddlers in child care settings: An observational study. *Early Childhood Education Journal, 28,* 193–197.

Jaffe, J., Beebe, B., Feldstein, S., Crown, C. L., & Jasnow, M. D. (2001). Rhythms of dialogue in infancy. *Monographs of the Society for Research in Child Development, 66*(2, Serial No. 265).

Kimura, L. (2006). Music: The great organizer for early language and literacy. In S. E. Rosenkoetter & J. Knapp-Philo (Eds.), *Learning to read the world: Language and literacy in the first three years* (pp. 235–254). Washington, DC: ZERO TO THREE Press

Lonigan, C. J., & Whitehurst, G. J. (1998). Relative efficacy of parent and teacher involvement in a shared reading program for preschool children from low-income backgrounds. *Early Childhood Research Quarterly, 13,* 263–290.

Neuman, S. B. (2006). Literacy development for infants and toddlers. In S. E. Rosenkoetter & J. Knapp-Philo (Eds.), *Learning to read the world: Language and literacy in the first three years* (pp. 275–290). Washington, DC: ZERO TO THREE Press.

NICHD Early Child Care Research Network. (2000). The relation of child care to cognitive and language development. *Child Development, 71,* 958–978.

NICHD Early Child Care Research Network. (2002a, March). *Child care and school readiness.* Congressional Briefing Presentation, Washington, DC.

NICHD Early Child Care Research Network. (2002b, March). *Child care, family, and children's lives.* Congressional Briefing Presentation, Washington, DC.

NICHD Early Child Care Research Network. (2003). Does quality of child care affect child outcomes at age 4? *Developmental Psychology, 39,* 451–469.

Notari-Syverson, A. (2006). Everyday tools of literacy. In S. E. Rosenkoetter & J. Knapp-Philo (Eds.), *Learning to read the world: Language and literacy in the first three years* (pp. 61–80). Washington, DC: ZERO TO THREE Press.

O'Brien, M. (1997). *Inclusive child care for infants and toddlers: Meeting individual and special needs.* Baltimore: Paul H. Brookes.

O'Brien, M., & Bi, X. (1995). Language learning in context: Teacher and toddler speech in three classroom play contexts. *Topics in Early Childhood Special Education, 15,* 148–163.

Olds, D., Robinson, J., O'Brien, R., Luckey, D., Pettit, L., Ng, R., et al. (2002, September). Comparison of pregnancy and infancy home visitation by nurses and paraprofessionals: A randomized controlled trial. *Pediatrics, 110,* 486–496.

Payne-Donnelly, C. (1992). High quality early childhood curriculum. In B. Day (Ed.), *North Carolina public school early childhood programs: A call for leadership* (pp. 7–18). Greensboro: North Carolina Association for Supervision and Curriculum Development.

Pierce, P., & Profio, A. (2006). From cooing to conversation to *The Carrot Seed:* Oral and written language connections. In S. E. Rosenkoetter & J. Knapp-Philo (Eds.), *Learning to read the world: Language and literacy in the first three years* (pp. 103–122). Washington, DC: ZERO TO THREE Press.

Ramey, C. T., & Campbell, F. A. (1984). Preventive education for high-risk children: Cognitive sequences of the Carolina Abecedarian Project. *American Journal of Mental Deficiency, 88*(55), 515–523.

Robinson, J. L., & Acevedo, M. C. (2001). Infant reactivity and regulation during emotion challenges: Prediction of cognition and language skills in a low income sample. *Child Development, 72,* 402–416.

Shonkoff, J. P., & Meisels, S. J. (Eds.). (2000). *Handbook of early childhood intervention* (2nd ed.). New York: Cambridge University Press.

Suthers, L. (2001). Toddler diary: A study of development and learning through music in the second year of life. *Early Childhood Development and Care, 171,* 21–32.

Valdez-Menchaca, M. C., & Whitehurst, G. J. (1992). Accelerating language development through picture book reading: A systematic extension to day-care. *Developmental Psychology, 28,* 1106–1114.

Warr-Leeper, G. A. (2001). A review of early intervention programs and effectiveness research for environmentally disadvantaged children. *Journal of Speech-Language Pathology and Audiology, 25,* 89–102.

Whitehurst, G. J., Epstein, J. N., Angell, A. C., Payne, A. C., Crone, D. A., & Fischel, J. E. (1994). Outcomes of an emergent literacy intervention in Head Start. *Journal of Educational Psychology, 86*, 542–555.

Whitehurst, G. J., Falco, F. L., Lonigan, C. J., Fischel, J. E., DeBaryshe, B. D., Valdez-Menchaca, M. C., & Caulfield, M. (1988). Accelerating language development through picture book reading. *Developmental Psychology, 24*, 552–559.

CHAPTER 15

Group Environments That Foster Language and Literacy

Terry DeMartini

Each one of us tends to imprint specific places in our memories. If we reflect on where we have been happiest or most content, we realize that an environment is much more than a physical location; it is a powerful influence that encompasses many spheres of human connection. Its imprint affects our emotional linkages, our physical experiences, our social networks, and our cognitive accomplishments. At its best, an environment is a place in which we feel completely "at home," accepted for who we are in the company of people who care about us—a place in which we move through the day with consummate ease and pleasure.

Infants and toddlers, too, are strongly influenced by the routines of the environments they experience every day (Lally, 2000). Beneficial outcomes for children in child care are associated with settings that provide both nurturance and support for early learning and language development (National Research Council & Institute of Medicine, 2000). It is widely recognized that infants and toddlers learn almost everything through their interactions with those who care for them. From their first days at their mothers' breasts or being nestled in their fathers' hands, babies reach out to connect—with their eyes and voices and, later, with their hands, arms, and whole bodies. They listen carefully to sounds, wanting to decipher them, building meaning during every waking moment, and integrating those meanings during sleep (Mangione, 2004). The caregiver's everyday face-to-face contact and conversational interactions include imitating an infant's cooing and babbling, self-talk (i.e., describing to the infant what is happening; see Payne and

O'Brien, this volume, p. 291, for a more detailed discussion on self-talk), naming objects for the inquisitive young toddler, and asking and answering questions of the older toddler. Indeed, beginning on their first day of life, infants develop communication skills, language, and literacy (National Research Council & Institute of Medicine, 2000).

Because the social–emotional foundations of learning are well documented and covered elsewhere in this book, this chapter will focus specifically on three aspects of the child-care environment that affect beginning language and literacy: (a) a program's values, including its philosophy of child development, (b) the physical environment that children experience each day, and (c) the interpersonal environment in the program. Although these three elements are interconnected in the experiences of the adults and children in any type of caregiving setting, we separate them here to offer clarity.

Child Development Values and Philosophies Set the Environment

Each caregiving environment is based on what the adults want for children, how they believe children learn, and what kinds of activities and experiences they believe support that learning. Environmental decisions that adults make based on their beliefs directly affect what and how children learn because as children engage their environments, they adapt their intellectual tools to meet new situations and they integrate thought and action in response to what they experience (Roskos & Neuman, 2002).

For example, the Reggio Emilia Schools in Italy operate from the philosophy that a child has enormous potential. The mission of Reggio Emilia is to promote children's education through the development of all their "languages": expressive, communicative, symbolic, cognitive, ethical, metaphorical, logical, imaginative, and relational (Municipal Infant–Toddler Centers & Preschools of Reggio Emilia, 2000). Given this philosophy, a Reggio Emilia infant–toddler care setting provides—in its *atelier* (or workshop area)—multiple opportunities for children to interact and use all their "languages." A key element in the environment is light. Natural light streams in through the windows between the atelier and the patio or garden, which is open to the sky. The setting may include the following components:

- A tile floor

- A low sink with workspace alongside

- A light table with various colored segments of rice paper strewn on it

- Child-sized worktables and chairs

- Various sized blocks of clay (some of which have natural materials such as stones pressed into them)

- An overhead projector on the floor

- Shelves, boxes, bowls, and baskets containing items such as flashlights, pebbles, rocks, sticks, branches, all types and colors of paper, seashells, wire pipe cleaners, various types of wire, rolls of bark, pinecones, varieties of recycled materials (cardboard, packing materials, plastic bottles and containers)

- Child-created constructions hanging from the ceiling

- Easels, paints, markers, pencils, and crayons

- Plastic safety mirrors

- Small boxes containing cornmeal, with dishes of small objects such as popcorn, lentils of different colors, dried peas, and beans

- A lamp on a table, which casts shadows of toys onto a wall

- Towers of blocks

- A magnifying glass

- Shadow puppets

- Rope lights

Caregivers might encourage a group of toddlers to explore the materials together by asking them to "put together the materials that would be *friends*," or to "create a composition on the light table using the color blue." The children usually engage in animated discussions about how to proceed. Then they discuss what they are doing as they are doing it. Finally, when they are finished, they admire one another's products. The children learn and expand their vocabularies by communicating, expressing theories and concepts, listening to one another, cooperating, compromising, investigating, experimenting, analyzing, and explaining. Sometimes, the caregiver asks the children to draw pictures of their results; children might also record the entire process with a videocamera or tape recorder. Clearly, this environment is the actualization of the Reggio Emilia value that children need multiple opportunities to develop all of their languages through interacting with a variety of materials in a variety of ways.

Programs that support the inclusion of children with disabilities provide another example of how environment animates philosophy. Programs that embrace inclusion as a core value provide dolls with disabilities, display posters of active toddlers with disabilities playing happily among their typically developing peers, and make available books about children with disabilities—regardless of whether a child with a disability is enrolled in the setting at any given time (Petersen, 1990).

A child-care program that values beginning language and literacy as a part of a young child's overall development reflects this value by infusing developmentally appropriate elements of language and literacy into the physical environment. These elements include

- An intimate physical setting that fosters adult–child interactions

- Structures and furniture that encourage caregivers to create nurturing relationships with each child

- A warm, interesting, joyful, and cognitively challenging atmosphere that is comfortable for children and families

- Indoor and outdoor settings that are developmentally appropriate for all the children and that offer creative, open-ended activities—for example, providing special activities for the infants who do not move about and other activities for the older children who do

- Spaces and adaptations that enable children with disabilities to fully participate in all activities

- A setting that reflects the languages and cultures of enrolled children and their families

- Support for each family's literacy needs and practices

- Activities and values that promote the health and well-being of caregivers, children, and family members

Program Policies and Practices

Program values and philosophy manifest themselves in the policies and practices that programs adopt—which then lead to the creation of environments. For example, the philosophy of the Program for Infant–Toddler Caregivers (PITC; Lally, Mangione, & Signer, 2002), asserts that infants and toddlers learn from their interactions with their key adults and with the environment. PITC holds that very young children develop a sense of safety as responsive, loving adults repeatedly and regularly meet their needs. This secure base enables the young child to interact comfortably with people and objects in the environment and to learn from the interactions. This understanding of child development naturally leads programs to develop policies and practices that include (a) primary caregiving, (b) small group sizes, and (c) continuity of care (see Lally & Mangione, this volume, p. 499).

Each of these practices plays an important role in supporting beginning language and literacy. Programs that adopt primary caregiving assign each child to one primary caregiver who is principally responsible for that child's care. In this way, primary caregivers are uniquely positioned to understand each child's own special language, temperament, and routines as well as to read and respond to each child's cues. This regular, ongoing relationship with a caregiver enables children to increase their language and communication skills because they feel safe to experiment and explore and are motivated to communicate with familiar, nurturing people.

Key studies, including that of the Cost, Quality, and Child Outcomes Study Team (1995), have noted that small group size and good ratios are key components of good-quality care. Small groups of 3–4 infants or 4–5 toddlers with one primary caregiver ensure that the caregiver can respond promptly to each child, thereby facilitating intimacy between caregiver and children. In addition, small groups create a small "family" in which each child can become comfortable while chatting freely, playing, and sharing early literacy experiences.

Continuity of care ensures that the same caregivers and children are together for as long as possible, optimally for the child's first 3 years. This continuity enables their relationships to deepen over time. Continuity of care supports literacy development because the child's learning is not interrupted by an emotional challenge of needing to get to know a new caregiver (Mangione, Lally, & Signer, 1992b). Continuity of care also supports opportunities for literacy development in partnership with families because, as parents and staff members get to know one another better over time, they can easily share literacy ideas and information between home and child care.

The Physical Environment

First and foremost, every child-care environment must be clean and safe. Although a discussion of health and safety is beyond the realm of this chapter, it is essential to note that the health and safety of children and caregivers must be subject to constant vigilance.

In addition to the program's philosophy and understanding of child development, the physical layout of each room and the choice of learning materials and equipment should be based on an understanding of the ages and learning needs of the children who spend time there. Environments should support exploration while giving the children the sense of control that enables them to engage in focused, self-directed play. Infants and toddlers have three basic needs; however, each stage of development requires a different emphasis. Young infants need security, slightly older infants who are beginning to move about need opportunities to explore, and older infants need autonomy (Mangione et al., 1992b).

Young infants require safe spaces that are away from the more active toddlers and that have appropriate toys within reach. Caregivers should attend to ways to entice mobile infants to practice their emerging mobility skills while still ensuring that the environment is safe. For example, a caregiver might create an environment in which a mobile infant is encouraged to creep toward a favored toy or to reach up for an interesting object. Caregivers of older infants should place creative art and manipulative materials on a worktable to encourage exploration. Toddlers need their materials to be in places where they can choose them so they can practice their developing sense of autonomy. Well-designed environments are engaging and thereby minimize aggressiveness, aimless wandering, and other problematic behaviors (Roskos & Neuman, 2002). High-quality environments also encourage teachers to observe and foster each child's learning and development. Low walls, risers, platforms, and strategically placed lofts divide the space while allowing the teachers to observe the children. Infant–toddler classrooms can be "sculpted" to support small groups and early learning (Torelli, 2002). Environments that support optimum learning provide enough space to comfortably accommodate all the functional areas in a classroom (such as eating, napping, diaper changing), open-ended play with toys and manipulatives, and large-muscle play opportunities. Caregivers who work in environments such as these are more relaxed than in crowded spaces and are better able to maintain nurturing relationships and promote language development (Torelli, 2002).

Specific aspects of the physical makeup of the room have a direct effect on children's ability to engage in positive experiences that develop language and literacy. The minimum space guidelines for same-age groups include the following:

- Ages birth–8 months: 6 children, 350 square feet

- Ages 8–18 months: 9 children, 500 square feet

- Ages 18–36 months: 12 children, 600 square feet (Mangione et al., 1992b)

Space for children from birth to 16 months should be designed for no more than 6–8 children and two caregivers.

An environment that supports a group of children and caregivers should be arranged for comfort and convenience as well as to support learning. Small activity centers, laid out around the perimeter of the room, invite children to congregate in groups of two or three to explore. Furniture such as low book-cases or risers separate activity centers and groups of children, allowing the children to concentrate on their learning and to interact verbally with one another and with their caregiver (Torelli & Durrett, 1996). Adult-sized furniture such as an easy chair or a hammock enables caregivers to sit with two or more children. Risers around the classroom and multilevel activity areas help care-givers ensure that they position themselves at the children's eye level where it is easier to read their cues and engage in interactions. These areas also protect caregivers from the wear and tear of constantly getting up and down from the floor. "This position makes it possible for all the channels for human communication to connect easily. I believe the greatest gift I can conceive of having from anyone is to be seen by them, to be understood, and [to be] touched by them" (Satir, 1976). (Note, however, that caregivers must adapt for children who come from cultures in which direct eye contact with adults is not appropriate.)

Furniture, too, can support or discourage developing language and literacy interactions. When children are positioned comfortably, they can focus on learning, attending to others, listening, talking, and exploring. Child-size furniture should fit the children in each classroom. For example, when toddlers sit at a table, their feet should rest on the floor and they should be able to move themselves into and out of their chairs safely. The table should stop at the children's waists so when they are seated, they can easily see and manipulate a glass of milk, puzzle pieces, play dough, or other objects on the table. All furniture and equipment should support the child's natural movement. Adaptive equipment for children with disabilities should be as similar as possible to the furniture used by the other children and should support full participation in all classroom activities. For example, children with adaptive seating should sit at the same table as their peers. If this kind of accommodation is absolutely not possible, then the specialized chair should be at the same level as the other children's chairs and located next to the table where the rest of the group is sitting so all the children can engage in the conversation that accompanies the activity.

Carpeting, walls, and floor coverings should be in muted, pastel colors, and furniture should be made from natural wood to create a peaceful setting for the young children and adults who will spend many hours there. "The only bright colors in the [infant–toddler caregiving] environment should come from the toys and the children" (Torelli, 2004). Rich, uncluttered environments without a large number of toys support children's ability to concentrate (Mangione, Lally, & Signer, 1992a). In addition, a safe, uncluttered environment dramatically reduces the number of times a caregiver needs to say no to a child and significantly increases the number of times a caregiver smiles (Lally, Mangione, & Signer, 2002). Caregivers maintain the balance between providing new, interesting, and novel items and keeping the environment comfortable by rotating some of toys while also retaining familiar ones. This variety gives children opportunities to broaden their experiences and provides new objects to talk about while maintaining the security that familiar toys provide.

Because children learn through play (Lally et al., 2002), the physical environment should support play interactions between adults and children. A caregiver who feels relaxed and energetic can be more playful with children. A well-planned physical environment enables adults to be available for children in a variety of ways. How many times do we see a caregiver lying on her back with children swarming all over her, everyone giggling and squealing—or a caregiver sitting quietly in a soft space with a few children, singing together or looking through a book with them? Witnessing these interactions, one sees that both caregivers and children revel in one another's presence, appreciate one another, and find life, at that present moment, to be quite pleasant. Careful planning for the soft spaces, comfortable seating for adults and children, and easy ways for adults to rise from the floor all increase the probability that scenes such as these will occur more frequently.

Family child care and kith-and-kin child-care settings must also consider the same principles. Family-centered spaces with ordinary rooms and furniture also can provide opportunities for growth and learning. For example, activity areas can include

- the couch for large-muscle climbing,
- the kitchen for messy play,
- the coffee table for small-muscle activities,
- a sheet over a table or two chairs for a private, quiet space, and
- a comfortable easy chair for book reading (Lally & Stewart, 1990).

The Importance of a Calm, Quiet Atmosphere

Babies hold important concepts about language literally from the time they are born, and they learn a great deal about language before they say even a word. Most of what infants learn in the earliest months involves the sound system of language (Gopnik, Meltzoff, & Kuhl, 1999). Therefore, child-care programs must provide a calm, quiet environment in which the sounds come primarily from the children's play and from the verbal interactions between the caregivers and the children. Sound-absorbent material and quiet areas (also known as *stimulus shelters*) help to keep spaces quieter (Mangione, Lally, & Signer, 1998). Soft, natural fabrics that cover private spaces and quilts or other fabrics that hang on the walls or ceiling soften the environment and control the noise level.

Caregivers must avoid large groups, constant music, and television (Mangione et al., 1998). They should play music only for a particular purpose such as movement, group singing, or sharing with a child when the mood or moment seems right. Background music that caregivers play for the enjoyment of the staff members interferes with the child's ability to listen carefully to conversations, to overhear her peers' use of language, and to hear herself as she attempts to use language to communicate with her peers and caregiver.

Physical Environments That Foster Beginning Language and Literacy

The key to early literacy is to link language development and literacy to all of the interests of the child. The more that teachers are inventive about what they put in an environment, the more the environment stimulates a child's vocabulary and learning. Objects offer experiences for verbal and nonverbal exchanges that are the foundation for literacy. Items from nature—such as leaves, stones, and seashells—can be used safely in an environment designed to support a primary caregiver and small groups. Of course, an attentive caregiver watches that no child puts potentially harmful objects in his mouth and that these objects are available only with supervision. Baskets that are made of natural materials, available at reasonable cost, not only are aesthetically pleasing but also present the child with many shapes, scents, and textures not found in commonly used plastic cartons and boxes. Even in the hands of very young infants, objects such as colorful scarves or sheets of colored cellophane provoke tactile understandings and communication as well as stimulate new vocabulary. The more that teachers are intentional about what they put into an environment, the more a child's emerging language and beginning literacy can be expanded. For example, the following activities enrich language and literacy:

- Sorting blocks and shapes (and, later, distinguishing letters and other symbols from one another)

- Rolling a ball back and forth with an adult (a turn-taking skill that is an important component of conversations)

- Dumping pop beads into and out of a basket (and developing the vocabulary to describe the activity)

- Matching puzzle pieces (and, later, differentiating the differing shapes of letters of the alphabet)

- Using a peg board (developing the small hand muscles needed for writing)

- Listening to a song sung by a caregiver (discovering that words can be used to communicate in many different ways)

- Looking at a board book with pictures of balls, blocks, and shapes (discovering that books can tell about familiar things in life and that books can be fun)

- Listening to a caregiver name the object and what she is doing with it (learning that words can describe an interesting activity)

- Listening to peers imitate the caregiver (learning to practice what she hears)

A very young infant in a sensory perception area is developing skills that will eventually be useful for talking, reading, and writing—skills such as

- Running her hand over carpet samples (stimulating hand muscles needed for grasping and writing)

- Lying on a quilt made of various fabrics (and distinguishing shapes and colors, later useful in identifying letters)

- Playing with small texture boards (coordinating touch and shape with the hand as well as color and texture with the eyes, skills used later in identifying letters of the alphabet and in writing)

- Listening to wind chimes (refining a skill used extensively in learning to read)

- Looking at a mobile (practicing the ability to focus, used later in reading) or

- Playing with colored cellophane (linking movement of the hands, the sound of the paper, and the changing shape of the paper, all supporting the coordination needed to read and write)

Every activity corner provides opportunities for language and literacy development. The block corner encourages vocabulary development and communication with respect to size, shape, weight, color, distance, planning, conjecturing, experimenting, fantasizing, explaining, labeling, and balancing. The manipulative play and indoor equipment areas provoke language that refers to pulling, pushing, crawling, climbing, sliding, and jumping; language that is connected to recognizing and labeling sizes and shapes; and language that is involved with developing negotiation skills and relationships. The dramatic play area provides opportunities for expanding vocabulary related to places and occupations; labeling items; describing their uses; exploring relationships; imitating verbal interchanges; describing textures, sizes, and colors; and role playing. The caregiver's role in these environments is to facilitate language learning, be responsive, ask questions, make commentary, and allow the creativity of the moment to flourish.

Space for Books and Storytelling

A quiet corner enhances the use of books, allowing children and their caregivers to explore pictures and stories in a calm and peaceful environment. Away from the eating, the messy play, and the large-muscle activities, this spot can provide the perfect setting for the thoughtful exploration of books. Age-appropriate books allow for many types of book-related interactions. Infants might pick up and bang board books, chew on them, and even allow their caregiver to sit with them and turn the pages while describing the toys, animals, or activities portrayed on the pages. Toddlers prefer picture books, flipping them from front to back or back to front, upside-down or right-side-up, or they may go through the book with a caregiver and discuss the pictures and the story. Toddlers often just sit quietly by themselves with a book, "telling" themselves the story or commenting quietly on the pictures.

Although a quality program has dozens of books available, only a few books should be displayed at a time, either on a small slanted book shelf or in hanging pockets that allow young children to see, take out, and return the books. Teachers should be sure that a toddler's favorite book remains available during the stage in which she is especially attached to it—even though it seems to have been read already 5,000 times. The toddler is learning to master concepts, enjoy language, and understand the world around him by repeatedly returning to the same book. Pillows, a hammock, and an easy chair in the book area not only encourage cuddling up with a good book but also provide comfort to the adult while he shares books and stories with the children.

Placement of Books Throughout the Environment

Most readers place books in many areas throughout their homes. They may have cookbooks in the kitchen; books on the bedside table; magazines next to a living room chair; and phone books, catalogs, and instruction manuals on the desk. We take books about plants and flowers out into the yard and magazines onto the patio in nice weather. Many homes even have a collection of magazines in the bathroom. Readers have books in the workshop or the garage and songbooks on the piano or near the guitar.

An infant–toddler classroom should similarly reflect the presence of books. The block area can contain books about cars, fire trucks, construction and construction vehicles, cities and towns, roads, as well as hills and rivers. The manipulative area can contain books about animals, farms, as well as city and country life. The dramatic play area can contain books about foods, fruits and vegetables, family life in many cultures, as well as homes and houses from various communities and cultures.

The Interpersonal Language and Literacy Environment

Quality of care—in particular, the quality of daily interactions between child-care providers and children—carries the weight of the influence of child care on children's development (National Research Council & Institute of Medicine, 2000). Daily nurturing interactions with caregivers; program policies and practices that underpin these interactions; and partnerships among families, child-care staff members, and programs are key aspects of the social environment in early care and education settings (Mangione, Lally, & Signer, 2001).

High-Quality Relationships and Interactions With Caregivers

The more children are talked to and the more they talk, the more elaborate their talk becomes (Hart & Risley, 1995). Thus, environmental input plays a key role in determining the rate at which children acquire and use language. The amount of language stimulation that caregivers provide is one of the features that distinguish higher quality from lower quality care (NICHD Early Child Care Research Network, 2000). Indeed, Harwood, Miller, and Irizarry (1995) noted that children's rate of language acquisition and use is likely an important factor in cognitive growth and functioning.

Infants and toddlers need caregivers who not only talk with them but also listen to them, thereby truly fostering communication (Mangione et al., 1998). Adults should not engage in rapid-fire speaking but, rather, in quiet exchanges and explanations as opportunities present themselves. Adults need to notice and respond to nonverbal communications such as facial expressions and smiles. These kinds of responses from adults enable children to learn that communication is reciprocal and that learning is exciting. In high-quality interactions, caregivers reflect the child's communication and expand on it. This responsiveness conveys a positive regard for children as well as respect for and acceptance of individual ideas and feelings. It encourages verbal give-and-take and independent thought, implies alternatives and choices, and includes "other-oriented induction" in which caregivers provide reasons and explanations. Responsive language ensures that teachers express their requests and necessary commands in nurturing ways. Age-appropriate supportive strategies that caregivers can use to facilitate children's development of beginning language and literacy skills are listed in Table 15.1.

Routines—An Important Part of the Environment

Routines provide the day-to-day activities during which young children learn about their world and the people and places in it. In particular, routines that are connected with play schedules, community environments, and outdoor environments are important to the young child's language and literacy development.

Play Schedules

Play and active exploration are important vehicles for facilitating learning in babies (Lally, 1993; McMullen, 1999). Many varied opportunities for playful activity ensure that, through their daily activities, young children can exercise curiosity, interest, and drive as well as sustain their inborn eagerness to learn. Children must be given long, uninterrupted times to play. If play periods are too short, children will have barely gotten into their play when it is time to stop and put the toys away (Zigler, 2003; Zigler, Singer, & Bishop-Josef, 2004). Routine play times provide almost limitless opportunities to promote language and literacy by introducing new vocabulary, extending utterances, and developing stories that they can tell and retell.

Community Environments

Children see language displayed in everyday activities through their communities (Lally, 2004). After an excursion into the community, the caregiver can present books related to what the children saw and expressed interest in. For example, after a trip to the park, caregivers can make a book about the park

Table 15.1. Adult Supportive Techniques

Birth–6 Months

• Take the baby on looking and listening tours, naming interesting items.

• Position the baby so she can watch and hear the flow of language at conversation times.

• Expose the baby to a variety of pleasant sounds—music, bells, music boxes, ticking, rattles, and chimes—while preventing overstimulation.

• Provide the baby with toys that he can manipulate to produce various sounds.

• Talk through simple books with the baby; reread favorites regularly.

• Include sturdy board books among baby's playthings.

6–12 Months

• Integrate language into baby's playtime in a way that involves more than just naming objects (e.g., "Teddy *fell down*").

• Show the baby hand and finger rhymes.

• Read a simple-concepts book to the baby, one that labels an object on each page.

• Encourage the baby to point to a particular item that she enjoys.

• Ensure that cardboard, cloth, and fabric books are among the playthings that the infant can carry about.

• Respond with "Shall I read?" to a child who brings a book to an adult, then talk about the pictures in the book.

• Place books on furniture edges so baby will discover them while cruising.

• Use hand puppets for storytelling.

12–18 Months

• Encourage dramatic play by acting out situations such as going to the grocery store.

• Provide large paper, crayons, paintbrushes, chalk, finger paint, and play dough for developing eye–hand coordination and exposing the child to prewriting experiences.

• Choose storybooks with simple language that the child understands as well as books with rhymes and songs.

• Provide toys that the child can use for imaginative play.

• Ensure that the child has durable books so he can "read" and turn pages independently.

• Ask the child to find familiar items in pictures when reading a book.

• Share storybooks as a part of the daily routine.

• Set aside a space or shelf that the child can reach, so she can select books and put them away.

19–36 Months

• Spend significant time every day with stories, songs, and rhymes.

• Hold conversations with children, filling in bits now and then.

• Use new words daily in conversations.

• Accept the child's speech rather than correct her mistakes.

• Sprinkle the environment with good reading material.

• Use directional words and prepositions when playing together.

• Provide the child with materials for "writing" and "drawing."

• Take cues from child about how he likes to be read to.

Source: From *Using Children's Books in Preschool Settings: A How-to-Do-It Manual* by S. Herb and S. Willoughby-Herb, 1994. Copyright 1994 by Neal-Schuman Publishers. Adapted with permission of the author. All rights reserved.

that contains the children's own pictures. These books provide rich opportunities for discussions about what the children saw or did, what happened when they went into the community, and sequences of events. Later, the caregivers can extend the children's learning with books that contain pictures of other parks and different children.

Outdoor Environments

An outdoor environment for infants and toddlers can be a simple area with grass, trees, flowers, sand, benches, and pathways. It does not need to have all the aspects of playgrounds as we think of them for older children. The outdoors should offer children concepts that are new and different, including climate, landscape, openness, messiness, and wildlife. Going outside adds variety and provides a place for motor and sensory exploration, nurturing interactions, and adult–child conversations (Greenman & Stonehouse, 1996). To take advantage of these environments to optimally support language and literacy, adults should engage with children frequently, consciously provide new and novel words to describe the new experiences, and regularly refer to these experiences when they are in different environments.

Environments That Promote Positive Relationships With Families

Programs must ensure that the physical environment welcomes families as well as children and that it provides daily opportunities for connections and story sharing. This type of environment honors each family's cultural, linguistic, and literacy approaches and supports information sharing (see Jones & Lorenzo-Hubert, this volume, p. 187). A warm, welcoming space for arrivals and departures has

- A place to rest a diaper bag or backpack and celebrate the good-bye moment

- A convenient location for signing in and out

- A place for conversation among parents or between a caregiver and family member that does not interfere with those who may be signing in or out

- A place for leaving special instructions

- A box or cubby in which each child can store coats and other personal items

- A bulletin board or wall displaying photos of the families in the program

- A bookshelf at adult height with a lending library of adults' and children's books

- A notice board for announcements and other important communications in the preferred languages of the families in the program

It is also valuable to provide a small space in home- or center-based child care with adult-sized furniture where family members can sit, if for only a moment. This adult sitting area minimizes the rush and encourages communication between the caregiver and the family. In this area, caregivers might also consider placing journals or binders of children's artwork on nearby tables or hanging up photos of the children at play.

These small additions to the physical environment provide routine opportunities to support each child's language and literacy development. As children witness an exchange of greeting or collaborative problem solving between their parent and caregiver, they learn that language can express connection and emotion. The photos on the wall give parents a chance to name people, objects, and relationships and give the child an opportunity to respond to questions or imitate the parent's words. These experiences enable the child to connect words to images, symbols, and time sequences—skills that he will later use to read. These environmental opportunities not only welcome families but also teach them important ways to support beginning language and literacy.

Support for each family's own literacy skills and activities occurs when programs provide interesting books and articles on child development and children's activities—and when programs take care to match the literacy levels and language of the materials to those of the families enrolled in the program. In addition, caregivers promote the children's language and literacy development by sharing research findings with families so the families come to understand their own importance to children's developing language and literacy (Mathews & Roman, 2002).

Routine meetings with families can also provide environmental opportunities for literacy development. In these meetings, parents can create posters or journals or contribute family photographs to be displayed in the setting. These materials can introduce new vocabulary, support word–image connection, build a child's positive affect toward words and images, and foster a stronger bond between the family and the caregivers.

Examples of Language Learning and Story Making

The following three vignettes illustrate ways in which the interpersonal environment promotes language learning and literacy development for children from birth to age 3 years.

> Bessie, age 6 months, arrives at the program in her mother's arms. The room is warm, with lots of light flooding in from the windows and skylights. The children who have already arrived are playing quietly at an activity center or having breakfast with one of the caregivers. Bessie notices how her mother smiles when she greets Bessie's primary caregiver and how her caregiver smiles back at Bessie and her mom. Bessie hears her name and her mother's name coming from her caregiver, and hears her caregiver's name in her mother's voice. Her caregiver, Veronica, smiles into Bessie's eyes. As Bessie continues to rest in her mother's arms, she listens to the quiet conversation between her mother and Veronica, hearing them laugh quietly.

> Then she finds herself going into Veronica's arms, with Mom giving her a hug and kiss as she goes. Veronica looks Bessie in the eyes and soothingly explains, "We're going to take off your jacket and hat and put them in your cubby. We'll put your diaper bag there, too." Then Veronica takes her to a soft quiet area, talking to Bessie about the day's activities and about where Bessie is going at that present moment. "I'm going to put you down here where you can play with your toys. Don't worry, these pillows will keep the other kids from running into you!"

> Bessie is now sitting in a place where she can watch and hear the other children when she is not exploring the interesting toys that Veronica has put in front of her—including a brightly colored

toy that is soft and squishy and a fuzzy ball that tinkles when she moves it. She listens to the caregivers greet the other families and hears the other children near her chattering to one another as they play with the blocks. Soon, one of the caregivers places another child in the play space with Bessie, so Bessie begins to practice with her the sounds that she heard her mother and her caregiver make earlier, while still playing with her toys and listening to what is going on around her.

After some time, Veronica comes over and tells Bessie that she is going to pick Bessie up and take her to the changing area so her diaper can be changed. Veronica asks Bessie, "Did you like your new toys? What did you think of that one that tinkles when you move it? (Bessie responds by smiling and babbling.) Did that surprise you? Did you show your friend Riccardo how to make it tinkle? (Bessie responds with a smile and waves her arms.) I'm going to change your diaper now. I'll just lay you down here and take out a clean diaper. You have such a cute outfit on today! Such pretty flowers on your shirt! Can you help me by lifting your legs? (Bessie responds with "words" and actions). Thanks! You're getting to be such a big girl!" Veronica continues to describe her actions to Bessie. "All finished now! Let's go over to where the other kids are playing. You can sit on my lap and watch, or you can lay on your tummy and practice rolling over!"

Bessie was just exposed to many varied uses of language in terms of both context and vocabulary development. She heard the give-and-take between her mother and caregiver, their different tones of voice, the role of laughter in a conversation, the reassuring tone of voice when Veronica took her from her mother, the description of what was going on, the encouraging tone when she was left for a quiet time, the conversational back-and-forth, and questions and answers during her diaper change. She was exposed to dozens of words, vocal inflections, interactions, relationship building, and empowering language. She will likely begin to look forward to her many upcoming interactions with her loving caregiver and will be eager to play her role as a participant in the conversations with other caregivers and children that she encounters throughout the day. She will practice the sounds that she has heard, coordinating them with movements of her arms, legs, and head. She will practice shaping her mouth, her tongue, and her jaw in certain ways. She will seem to have pleasant conversations with herself as she falls asleep at naptime or as she waits for her infant-care teacher to pick her up after her nap. She will initiate conversations while at the changing table, while she pauses in her feeding time, and as she is being carried outside. She will greet each new situation, such as looking at the flowers in the infant garden or seeing a loud truck go by, with verbal interactions.

As children engage in their environments, they adapt their intellectual tools to meet new situations or challenges, integrating thought and action. Both their mental and their physical processes are the means by which children achieve new understandings and developing skills (Roskos & Neuman, 2002). Bessie has demonstrated ways in which she is doing exactly that.

In the second vignette, four older babies experience interpersonal environments that foster their language and literacy development in ways that are similar to but more advanced than what 6-month-old Bessie experienced.

> *Three 20–24 month olds, Ana, Patrick, and Russell, are sitting on the floor near Diego, their caregiver. Diego is sitting on some pillows, holding on his lap 2-year-old Peter. Each child is looking at a small book of home and program photographs that parents made at a family meeting. The children are "discussing" what and whom they see in the photos, identifying people and objects, and voicing one- or two-word statements or questions about the pictures. They are most excited about the pictures showing the puppy that belongs to the next-door neighbor of their family child-care provider. The neighbor recently brought the puppy over to visit. The children call out the names of people and places they recognize. "Mommy!" "Daddy!" "Puppy here?" "Blocks!" "Dress-up!" "Eating lunch!" "Riding!" At one point, Ana jumps up to go over to the family picture wall near the cubbies to point to another photograph, this one of her grandmother.*
>
> *Diego is propping up Peter's book for him. This book has popsicle sticks glued to the outside corner of each page to make it easier for him to turn the pages. Peter's speech pathologist pro-*

vided the adapted books for Peter, who does not yet communicate with words. Peter says "Uh, uh!" as he sees photos of people he knows and places he recognizes. As Peter says "Uh, uh!" Diego says, "Yes, Peter, that's your mommy!" "That's the puppy that came to visit us!" "Look, there you are having your snack!" Diego responds to the other children in the same way. "Look, Ana, there you are all dressed up!" "Yes, Russell, that's you on the tricycle!"

Peter comes to a photograph showing him in the swing in the child-care program's backyard. He exclaims, "Uh! Uh!" Diego responds, "Look at Peter in the swing!" Patrick gets up to look at Peter's book, and then he begins to turn the pages using the popsicle sticks. Peter wriggles in Diego's lap, raising his voice a little and saying "Uh! Uh! Uh!" Diego looks and him and asks, "Do you want to look at a different picture?" Peter reaches out and flips back to the picture of himself in the swing. He becomes animated, taps the photo over and over again, and repeats "Uh! Uh! Uh!" "Oh!" Diego says, "You want to go outside and swing!" Peter wriggles again, with a pleased expression on his face. "Uh! Uh!" he exclaims. "What a good idea!" says Diego. "We've all been inside for awhile; let's go outside." The photo books are gathered up and put on a nearby shelf. Diego lifts Peter into his adapted stroller and the group goes outside.

These cheerful interactions with the books of photographs evidence a multitude of language learning and early literacy opportunities in this environment. Diego's comments offer the children an expansion on their one- or two-word utterances, giving them the chance to hear their ideas fully stated. The children's comments indicate memory of previous actions and anticipation of future activities. Diego interprets for Peter and gives language to his thoughts and desires just as he does for the other children. Obviously, Peter knows that sound has some meaning. He is making his "uh uh" sound to indicate his choices. Diego's interpretations not only keep Peter an active participant in the conversation but also help all of the children by enhancing their understanding of the possibilities of language and the role that language plays in interpersonal relationships. In addition, Diego takes advantage of the opportunity to use new words such as *inside, outside, up,* and *down.* Many small environmental adaptations such as the popsicle stick book, the adapted stroller for outside play, and Peter's communication board (not seen in this vignette) do not require any specialized skill or training to allow Peter or other children with disabilities to have access to meaningful literacy activities with peers (see Pierce, this volume, p. 335).

Children who have disabilities are entitled to participate in child-care settings with children who do not have disabilities (Americans With Disabilities Act, 1990). Recommended practice indicates they should also receive their special education services in the caregiving environments so the child's caregivers and family members can continue the specialized interventions throughout the child's day (Sandall, McLean, & Smith, 2000). This practice requires close collaboration among the child's family, the child-care staff members, and the early intervention program to ensure that the physical and social environments and the schedule of the day work for all the children, surrounding every child with language and literacy opportunities.

The third vignette illustrates how interpersonal environments can foster language and literacy development for older toddlers.

> *Two-and-a-half-year-old Ilena enters the housekeeping area and begins to take dishes, cutlery, and pots out of the cupboards. Mark comes in and sits at the table. Ilena turns to him and says, "I'm making some Chinese. I need to give you a spoon. Want some pepper on it?" Mark nods. Ilena hands him a small container. She says, "This is pepper. Want to put some pepper on it?" Mark says "Yeah." Ilena asks, "Can I do it?" Mark responds "Yeah." Ilena picks up a toy telephone and says to Mark, "This is your daddy. Talk to your daddy." She shows him a face that is on the earpiece of the phone and says, "See, that's your daddy." Mark leaves the area. After some unsuccessful attempts to get other children in the area to talk on the phone, Ilena returns to the housekeeping area, puts down the phone, and picks up a tablet and a crayon. She says to herself, "I need to make a list." She scribbles on the tablet, saying "Bread, pepper, chips."*
>
> *After a few minutes, she joins a group of children listening to a storybook being read by a teacher. The teacher then opens the*

door to the outdoor play area, and Ilena goes out. She spots
Nathan on a bicycle and cries "There's a monster!" She turns to
Wilma and cries again, "There's a monster!" Ilena and Wilma
begin to run away from Nathan. Then they turn and begin to
chase him.

Ilena has discovered the interactive value of language. She is creating relationships with her peers through invitation, questioning, and demands. She is using language to sustain a relationship. Ilena is inventive, using props such as the telephone to vary the interaction. By making her grocery list, she shows she understands that written symbols refer to everyday items that are in her life and that she can use to communicate a message—in this case, a message to herself. She uses the language of fantasy to engage others in her play. Children's easy access to richly varied and sufficiently abundant materials appears to increase their behavioral repertoire, which in turn creates more opportunities to learn through interactions with objects (Roskos & Neuman, 2002). These settings also provide adults the opportunity to introduce new words and richer vocabulary, extend the length of sentences, and share new ideas.

Conclusion

This chapter has discussed how spaces used for child care should be designed to encourage language, learning, and literacy development in infants and toddlers while also supporting adult caregivers to facilitate these processes. Program philosophies, values, and understanding of development—combined with the everyday wisdom of families—guide caregivers to establish physical and interpersonal environments that are uniquely suitable for our youngest children. Environments such as these stimulate new learning by engaging young children's curiosity, eagerness to learn, and sense of wonder—as well as their need for nurturance and love in the first 3 years of life. These environments also promote infants' and toddlers' growing physical, emotional, social, and cognitive capacities (Dickinson & Sprague, 2002) and support children to flourish and develop strong foundations for learning and life.

References

Americans With Disabilities Act of 1990, 42 U.S.C.A. §§ 12101–12213. (West 1993).

Cost, Quality, and Child Outcomes Study Team. (1995). *Cost, quality, and child outcomes in child care centers.* Denver: University of Colorado at Denver, Department of Economics.

Dickinson, D., & Sprague, K. (2002). The nature and impact of early childhood environments on the language and early literacy development of children from low-income families. In S. B. Neuman & D. K. Dickinson (Eds.), *Handbook of early literacy research* (pp. 263–280). New York: Guilford Press.

Gopnik, A., Meltzoff, A., & Kuhl, P. (1999). *The scientist in the crib.* New York: HarperCollins.

Greenman, J., & Stonehouse, A. (1996). *Prime times.* St. Paul, MN: Redleaf Press.

Hart, B., & Risley, T. R. (1995). *Meaningful experiences in the everyday experiences of young American children.* Baltimore: Paul H. Brookes.

Harwood, R. L., Miller, J. G., Irizarry, N. L. (1995). *Culture and attachment: Perception of the child in context.* New York: Guilford Press.

Herb, S., & Willoughby-Herb, S. (1994). *Using children's books in preschool settings; A how-to-do-it manual.* New York: Neal-Schuman.

Jones, W., & Lorenzo-Hubert, I. (2006). Culture and parental expectations for child development: Concerns for language development and early learning. In S. E. Rosenkoetter & J. Knapp-Philo (Eds.), *Learning to read the world: Language and literacy in the first three years* (pp. 187–214). Washington, DC: ZERO TO THREE Press.

Lally, J. R. (1993). Play. In A. Gordon & K. Williams Brown (Eds.), *Beginnings and beyond* (3rd ed., p. 364). Albany, NY: Delmar Learning.

Lally, J. R. (2000). Infants have their own curriculum: A responsive approach to curriculum planning for infants and toddlers. *National Head Start Bulletin, 67,* 6–7.

Lally, J. R. (2004, April). *Introduction to Module III of The Program for Infant/Toddler Caregivers.* Presentation made at the program event for the Infant–Toddler Caregivers' Institute, San Diego, CA.

Lally, J. R., & Mangione, P. L. (2006). Policy recommendations to support early language and literacy experiences in the home and in child care. In S. E. Rosenkoetter & J. Knapp-Philo (Eds.), *Learning to read the world: Language and literacy in the first three years* (pp. 499–514). Washington, DC: ZERO TO THREE Press.

Lally, J. R., Mangione, P., & Signer, S. (2002, November). *The importance of intimacy in infant/toddler care.* Paper delivered to the preconference session of the National Association for the Education of Young Children Annual Conference, New York.

Lally, J. R., & Stewart, J. (1990). *A guide to setting up environments.* Sacramento: California Department of Education.

Mangione, P. L. (2004, April). *Language, culture, and communication.* Presentation made at the program event for the Infant–Toddler Caregivers' Institute, San Diego, CA.

Mangione, P. L., Lally, J. R., & Signer, S. (1988). *Space to grow: Creating a child care environment for infants and toddlers* [Video magazine]. Sacramento, CA: CDE Press.

Mangione, P. L., Lally, J. R., & Signer, S. (1992a). *Discoveries of infancy: Cognitive development and learning* [Video magazine]. Sacramento, CA: CDE Press.

Mangione, P. L., Lally, J. R., & Signer, S. (1992b). *Together in care: Meeting the intimacy needs of infants and toddler in groups* [Video magazine]. Sacramento, CA: CDE Press.

Mangione, P. L., Lally, J. R., & Signer, S. (1998). *Early messages: Facilitating language development and communication* [Video magazine]. Sacramento, CA: CDE Press.

Mangione, P. L., Lally, J. R., & Signer, S. (2001). *The next step: Including the infant in the curriculum* [Video magazine]. Sacramento, CA: CDE Press.

Mathews, V., & Roman, S. (2002). *The library-museum Head Start Partnership.* Alexandria, VA: Department of Health and Human Services.

McMullen M. B. (1999). Achieving best practices in infant and toddler care and education. *Young Children, 54*(4), 69–76.

Municipal Infant–Toddler Centers and Preschools of Reggio Emilia (3rd ed.). (2000). Reggio Emilia, Italy: Municipality of Reggio Emilia, Italy.

National Research Council, & Institute of Medicine. (2000). *From neurons to neighborhoods: The science of early childhood development* (J. P. Shonkoff & D. A. Phillips, Eds.), Committee on Integrating the Science of Early Childhood Development; Board on Children, Youth, and Families; Commission on Behavioral and Social Sciences and Education. Washington DC: National Academy Press.

NICHD Early Child Care Research Network. (2000). The relation of child care to cognitive and language development. *Child Development, 71*(4), 958–978.

Payne, C. C., & O'Brien, M. (2006). Promoting language and literacy in child care. In S. E. Rosenkoetter & J. Knapp-Philo (Eds.), *Learning to read the world: Language and literacy in the first three years* (pp. 291–308). Washington, DC: ZERO TO THREE Press.

Petersen, S. (1990). *When children soar with the wind.* Unpublished manuscript. Denver, CO.

Pierce, P. (2006). High expectations for language and literacy with infants and toddlers who have significant disabilities. In S. E. Rosenkoetter & J. Knapp-Philo (Eds.), *Learning to read the world: Language and literacy in the first three years* (pp. 335–352). Washington, DC: ZERO TO THREE Press.

Roskos, K., & Neuman, S. (2002). Environment and its influences for early literacy and learning. In S. B. Neuman and D. K. Dickinson (Eds.), *Handbook of early literacy research* (pp. 281–292). New York: Guilford Press.

Sandall, S., McLean, M., & Smith, B. (2000). *DEC recommended practices in early intervention/early childhood special education.* Denver, CO: Council for Exceptional Children, Division for Early Childhood; and Longmont, CO: Sopris West.

Satir, V. (1976). *Making contact.* Millbrae, CA: Celestial Art.

Torelli, L. (2002). Enhancing development through classroom design in Early Head Start. *Children and Families, 16*(2), 44–52.

Torelli, L. (2004, January). *Space to grow: An infant–toddler environment.* Presentation made at the program event for the Infant–Toddler Caregivers' Institute, Rockville, MD.

Torelli, L., & Durrett, C. (1996). Landscape for learning. *Early Childhood News,* March/April, n.p.

Zigler, E. F. (2003). *Concept paper: Play and its relationship to pre-literacy for infant/toddler development and learning guidelines.* Sacramento: California Department of Education.

Zigler, E. F., Singer, D. G., & Bishop-Josef, S. J. (2004). *Children's play: The roots of reading.* Washington, DC: ZERO TO THREE Press.

CHAPTER 16

High Expectations for Language and Literacy With Infants and Toddlers Who Have Significant Disabilities

Patsy Pierce

Nigel, age 20 months, has severe cerebral palsy. He has beautiful, big brown eyes, and sometimes his voice makes melodic sounds. Unless he is placed in a special chair, Nigel cannot sit or hold his head upright. His hands are constantly closed into tight fists. His child-care provider wonders whether Nigel understands anything other than his name. She thinks he knows his name because he turns his head the best that he can and smiles when she says, "Nigel." The child-care providers worry about whether the other toddlers in their room understand storybooks and are very concerned whether or not Nigel will "get anything out of it" if they read to him along with the other children. The caregivers read with him anyway.

One in particular notices that when she reads the repeated line "How about a hug?" from the book of this same name by Nan Holcomb (1992) and then reaches out and hugs Nigel that he always smiles and makes his musical sounds. One day, after she has read this book several times, she pauses after reading the line "How about a hug?" to see what Nigel will do. Even before she hugs him, he smiles and vocalizes. The caregiver begins to take note of Nigel's vocalizations, and every time she hears them, she goes over and gives him a hug. The other teachers and children begin to do the same. Everyone, including Nigel's family members, think that he is making so many more sounds. His mother says one of the sounds even sounds like the word hug.

Nigel, like many children who have significant disabilities, is at great risk for having difficulty in learning to read and write. Significant disability is defined by the Hilton–Early Head Start Project—SpecialQUEST—as "any disability requiring adaptations in the environment" (Hilton–Early Head Start Training Program, 2002, p. 4). Disabilities such as severe cerebral palsy, autism, and sensory impairment often result in the need for environmental adaptations. Approximately 90% of children with severe speech and physical impairments have significant literacy learning difficulties (Koppenhaver, Evans, & Yoder, 1991). Approximately 40% of preschool children with moderate–severe language impairments develop significant reading and writing problems, even if their delays appear to have been resolved by age 5 (Scarborough, 2002).

Challenges in Becoming Literate

What is the connection between communication disorders and later literacy learning difficulties, even for infants and toddlers? The connection lies in the term *communication*. All four of the primary methods of communicating— listening, speaking, reading and writing—share the same basic phonemic or sound base, the same rule system for combining the sounds into words (morphology) as well as combining words into phrases and sentences (syntax). Spoken and written language share much of the same vocabulary for communicating meaning for a variety of purposes. Therefore, if a child early in life has difficulty hearing, understanding, or using the words of the spoken language (or languages) in his or her environment, then the child is at risk for problems with reading and writing these same words, phrases, or sentences (Butler, 1998; Hart & Risley, 2003 ; Koppenhaver, Coleman-Pierce, Kalman, & Yoder, 1991; Kupetz & Green, 1997; Morrow, 1997).

In addition to having difficulty hearing, understanding, and using words, young children with significant disabilities face other challenges that may influence their later literacy learning. Often, the facial expressions and movements of children with significant disabilities are harder to recognize;

consequently, caregivers have a more difficult time identifying appropriate responses. Because of limited muscle tone or control, a child with a significant disability may, in fact, be smiling, but caregivers may respond as if the child were grimacing and therefore discontinue a pleasurable activity such as shared book reading. Caregivers may also talk and read less frequently to a child who is not as noticeably responsive as other children. Children with significant disabilities may be more difficult to position to experience the pleasure of sitting on the caregiver's lap or to see or turn book pages. When the author was working at the Center for Literacy and Disability Studies, one child with cerebral palsy would become so excited at hearing a favorite story that his stiffened body literally slid off his mother's lap. The need for body positioning supports sometimes make it difficult for a caregiver to hold a child with significant disabilities and a storybook as well as use communication techniques such as picture communication displays or sign language, all at the same time.

In addition to these positioning and response challenges, it may be difficult for a child with significant disabilities to reach out, grab, hold, and use books, story props, and drawing and writing instruments. The child with significant disabilities may have extreme problems in indicating that he or she would like to participate in early literacy-related activities, making comments, labeling objects or actions, asking questions, or even telling caregivers when he or she would like to continue or finish the activity. Some studies indicate that typically developing infants and toddlers rarely hear books and stories because other caregiving demands preempt that activity (Kupetz & Green, 1997; Soundy, 1997), so one can imagine the limited amount of interaction with early literacy activities that children with significant disabilities commonly have because of the increased caregiving demands they bring to the learning situation (Coleman-Pierce, 1991; Light & Kelford-Smith, 1993).

Attitudinal Barriers

The attitudes and expectations of family members and other caregivers may also affect the early literacy opportunities of young children with significant disabilities. Light and Kelford-Smith (1993) found that families of young children with significant motor and speech impairments were more concerned with their children's abilities to learn to talk and take care of self-help needs (e.g., using the toilet, feeding themselves) than they were worried about their children learning to read and write. Coleman-Pierce (1991) found that preschool teachers believed that 2- and 3-year-olds with significant disabilities were "not ready" to be given books or crayons or to hear storybooks read to them. Children with significant disabilities in this and other similar studies were offered few literacy-related opportunities in their early childhood classrooms or home situations (Marvin, 1994; Marvin & Mirenda, 1993).

The Ecological Approach

Because of the multiple child, family, and community factors that may influence literacy growth, many programs serving young children and their families use an ecological approach to emergent literacy development. The ecological model, developed by Bronfenbrenner (1989), recognizes the importance of community, family, and environmental influences on a young child's development. Several factors such as community and familial understanding and valuing of early literacy help to determine a child's successful understanding and use of print for meaningful purposes (International Reading Association [IRA] & National Association for the Education of Young Children [NAEYC], 1998; Koppenhaver, Coleman-Pierce, et al., 1991). When working with a child with significant disabilities, several other elements must also be considered: text, reader, writer, and technology. Figure 16.1 depicts a literacy-enhanced version of the ecological model.

Classrooms serving any and all infants and toddlers more commonly use an activity-based versus a direct approach to fostering emergent literacy. An activity-based approach encourages children's energetic and meaningful engagement within a literacy-rich environment, including purposeful interaction with literate role models (Smith, 2000). Teaching in an activity-based program is accomplished through prompting, modeling, and purposeful environmental arrangement of meaningful and accessible literacy-related materials and activities (Conzenio & French, 2002). The Division for Early Childhood (DEC) of the Council for Exceptional Children and the National Association for the Education of Young Children (NAEYC) support an activity-based approach for all young children (Hendrix, 2003). High-quality programs serving infants and toddlers with or without significant disabilities should offer activity-based emergent literacy instruction through an ecological approach involving children, their families, and other members of their communities.

Figure 16.1 Ecological Model

Bronfenbrenner and Literacy

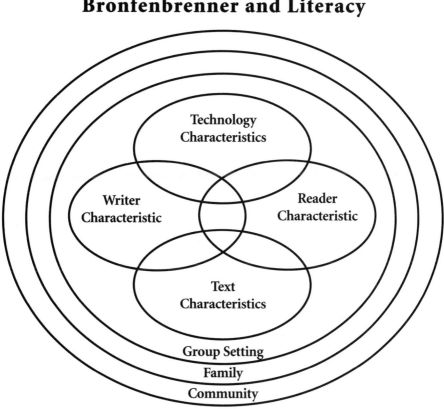

Within an infant–toddler program serving children with and without significant disabilities, caregivers and family members should make literacy-related
activities accessible to all and interactive in delivery. Literate role models using
written language for functional purposes (e.g., cooking, shopping) should also
be accessible and interactive.

Specific Examples of AIMing for Literacy

Pierce (1994) described an approach to working with infants and toddlers with
significant disabilities as AIMing for Literacy: *Accessible, Interactive Materials,*
and *Models.* The remainder of this chapter describes examples of how families
and care providers of infants and toddlers with and without significant disabilities can work within the ecological model through activities that AIM for
literacy.

Community Aspects

Two examples demonstrate community support for including very young children with disabilities in every daily activity. One community advertised that it highly valued *all* young children's and their families' participation in literacy-related activities such as story hours at local libraries, book mobiles, and literacy–council trainings. This public position was found to have a significant positive effect on literacy development and use in the community (Fader, 2002; Meyers & Henderson, 2002). Another example of community-wide literacy support including all infants and toddlers and their families is found in collaborative work among community-based programs for children and parents. For example, Early Intervention programs can work closely with the Parents As Teachers programs, Early Head Start, and Even Start to provide training and materials for families and community members with respect to the importance of reading with all children. Rosenkoetter (2003) has compiled a comprehensive list of community-based emergent literacy supports, including activities such as placing children's books on public buses and developing parks with storybook themes. One of the most helpful things a community can do is have high expectations for all of its children to become readers and writers.

Family Aspects

Family members' attitudes toward the perceived literacy abilities and learning potential of young children with disabilities greatly influence these children's early exposure to literacy, which subsequently influences their understanding and use of print (Light & Kelford-Smith, 1993; Marvin & Mirenda, 1993; McConnell & Rabe, 1999). Similarly, family members' modeling of engagement in literacy-related activities and use of literacy for accomplishing real purposes significantly affects their child's understanding of the functions of print. This finding is true for young children with disabilities as well as for typically developing infants and toddlers (Brooks, 2000; Dickinson & Tabors, 2001; Teale & Sulzby, 1989). One of the most helpful things a family can do is have high expectations for all of its children to become readers and writers.

Program Leadership

Infant–toddler programs can provide family members of young children with disabilities with written information regarding oral and written language development in the family's native language. Such information may include examples of children with disabilities who are learning to talk and to read, perhaps with the use of assistive technology. Language stimulation materials such as books on audiotape, books with raised pictures or textured shapes, and descriptions of related activities can be sent home to family members on an ongoing basis. Infant–toddler programs may also provide workshops for families and send home to families progress reports that reflect their child's interests and progress. For example, literacy kits containing board books, puppets, and songs can be sent home with children on a weekly basis. Programs serving infants and toddlers with and without significant disabilities can also offer home visits to assist families in meeting family identified literacy goals for both children and adults.

Programs serving all infants and toddlers might also wish to take advantage of Motheread's Books for Babies program (Motheread, 2001), which offers a list of excellent multicultural books appropriate for children functioning within the birth-to-3 age range and teaches approaches to engaging and maintaining interest and interaction while reading books with distractible infants and toddlers. A helpful resource for family literacy involvement ideas is the book *Developing Partnerships With Families Through Children's Literature* (Lilly & Green, 2004). One of the most helpful things a program can do is have high expectations for all of its children to become readers and writers.

Environmental Considerations

Accessibility of reading and writing activities for every infant and toddler positively influences early literacy development, regardless of physical, linguistic, cognitive, or sensory abilities; socioeconomic status; or any combination of these characteristics. So does sustained interaction with responsive adults and modeling by the child's important people of the significance of literacy in everyday life. One of the most important things that all can do is have high expectations that every child will become a reader and writer (Bus & van IJzendoorn, 1995; Justice & Kaderavek, 2002; McCathren & Allor, 2002; Musselwhite & King-DeBaun, 1997; Schickedanz, 1999).

Access. Currently, many early childhood programs are serving children with a range of cognitive, linguistic, motoric, and sensory abilities. Many infant–toddler programs also serve children for whom English is their second language; whose families have varying degrees of literacy ability, especially in English; and who come from a range of socioeconomic levels. It is important to make books abundantly accessible to this variety of children and families. In addition to simply providing lots of books, program leaders may arrange for pages to be laminated, placed in baggies (watch out for children who may chew the plastic), separated more easily by adding page "fluffers," and turned more easily by adding "page tabs" (see Figure 16.2). Illustrations may be seen more easily if they are enlarged or enhanced with nontoxic fabric or "puffy paint" (Pierce & McWilliam, 1993). Note, however, that program leaders and caregivers must ensure that all page separators and extenders are securely fastened and checked frequently because they may become a choking hazard if they come loose. Roten (as cited in Lilly & Green, 2004) offers several suggestions for making print more accessible to children with visual impairments. These include choosing books with simple yet colorful illustrations, outlining illustrations with a black marker, and enhancing illustrations with textures and associated objects. Books may also be made more accessible by stabilizing them with nonslip placements, available in a camping store, or securing them with male (scratchy) hook and loop fabric placed on the back cover and affixed to a surface with female (fluffy) fabric.

Figure 16.2. Book With Page Turners

Either books propped on a slanted surface or accordion books (Albrecht & Miller, 2000a, 2000b; see also Figure 16.3) that are made of cardboard to allow the book to stand upright may also help children with significant motor or visual impairments to be able to participate in story reading and to turn pages.

Figure 16.3. Example of an Accordion Book

Most infants and toddlers, including those with special needs, appear to enjoy interacting with books made from discontinued upholstery fabric and wallpaper samples (see Figure 16.4). The variety of colors and textures capture the young child's attention. These fabrics are thicker than ordinary paper and therefore easy to manipulate. They also better survive being chewed. Care providers and families can sew favorite objects and laminated pictures onto the fabric, leather, or wallpaper pages. Peekaboo books (Albrecht & Miller, 2000a, 2000b) can also be made with these upholstery and wallpaper samples. An infant or toddler's photograph, family photos, and pictures of favorite objects can be partially hidden by preceding pages in a peekaboo book.

Figure 16.4. Example of Book With Varied Textures

Program leaders should also have some children's books printed with larger pictures and type and others audiotaped in languages represented in the community. Infant–toddler classrooms should have a wide range of books available that reflect different types of genre, children's interests, cultures, and cognitive–linguistic levels (Roskos, Christie, & Richgels, 2003).

Infants and toddlers with and without significant disabilities also need opportunities to scribble, draw, and experiment with a variety of coloring, painting, drawing, and writing tools. The handles of large crayons, markers, and paint brushes may be made even larger if needed by children with motor impairments by placing the grip surface through a tennis ball or sponge roller. Hook-and-loop fabric attached to a coloring–writing tool may be more easily picked up by a child wearing a terry-cloth sweatband on his or her hand. A variety of special grips, holders, and orthopedic splints may be personalized to help a child be able to use these types of tools to participate in literacy activities with classmates (see Figure 16.5). For some children with significant disabilities, technology may be their only access to turning book pages or to coloring and scribbling.

Figure 16.5. Adapted Writing Tools

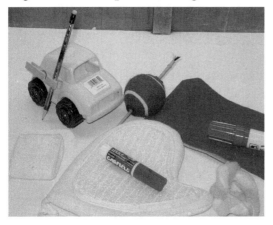

Interaction. Classrooms serving infants and toddlers with significant disabilities may wish to use Board Maker software (Mayer-Johnson, 2002) to make communication boards that offer children a means of communicating. Both speaking and nonspeaking children should be given opportunities and ways to label pictures and actions as well as to make comments and ask questions in conversations and while stories are read. Figure 16.6 shows samples of simple communication boards that may be used with infants and toddlers with significant disabilities.

Figure 16.6. Examples of Simple Communication Boards

Programs may make story sharing more interactive for all infants and toddlers by using and making predictable books, repeated-line books, and stories based on everyday personal experiences and children's interests. Caregivers may routinely conduct repeated readings, paraphrasing text to meet children's developmental needs and cultural backgrounds. They can choose and use appropriate vocabulary to stimulate children's interest as well as their language growth.

Infants and toddlers, both with and without disabilities, appear to be more engaged with action-filled books that allow the readers to open paper doors to find hidden pictures, stick their fingers through holes in the book, touch different textures, smell various odors, hear unusual sounds, and see shiny objects (Albrecht & Miller, 2000a, 2000b). These interactive books often interest children with significant disabilities because of their need for multisensory stimulation. Enhancing and adapting books with these attractive factors will help to gain and maintain the interest of a variety of children. Figure 16.7 shows examples of action books adapted for infants and toddlers with significant disabilities. Some infants and toddlers with disabilities may experience tactile defensiveness and be hesitant to interact with books or other materials of varying textures. "Squishy" books (Albrecht & Miller, 2000a) made with plastic sandwich bags that are filled with different textures such as hair gel and plastic animals may foster acceptance for these children. Another way to increase interaction during story time with infants and toddlers is to let them choose their own books from selections with fewer than three lines of print per page.

Figure 16.7. Adapted Action Books

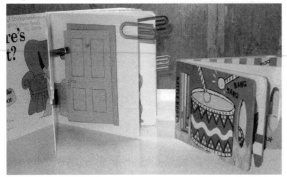

Modeling. Modeling the use of print to accomplish real purposes and modeling the reading of letters and words is important for all children to build early literacy abilities such as concepts of print, phonological awareness, and letter–name knowledge (Burns, Griffin, & Snow, 1999; Roskos, et al., 2003; Teale & Sulzby, 1989). These actions and accompanying descriptions are important for infants and toddlers with significant disabilities as for other children (Owocki, 1999; Roskos, Vukelich, Christie, Enz, & Neuman, 1995). For example, empty baby cereal boxes and diaper boxes can be stuffed with paper and sealed with tape to be used as building blocks. Adults can talk about these labels as they play "stack and knock over" with infants and toddlers (Albrecht & Miller, 2000a, 2000b). It is important for adults to have the same high expectations for young children with disabilities to participate in these types of games as they do for other infants and toddlers.

Summary

Infants and toddlers with significant disabilities are at risk for reading and writing difficulties because of the challenges they face in communicating and physically interacting with literacy materials. Another challenge confronting them is low expectations, when family members or caregivers do not expose these young children with special needs to literacy opportunities. However, given appropriate access to early literacy opportunities and means to communicate about these experiences, children with significant disabilities can and do become literate. All children need adults in their lives who cherish their strengths, who value literacy, and who therefore read to them and model the power of using print.

As Christy Brown, the late Irish poet who had severe cerebral palsy, commented, "What had I to look forward to? What prospect had I of being anything other than a cripple who painted with his toes?… Then suddenly one day I had an idea. I had been fond of writing letters, but now I decided to try something more ambitious, not just letters, but stories. The idea grew and grew till it invaded my mind" (1971, p. 64). Believing that all children can learn and offering them language and literacy-rich opportunities to do so from birth can become a self-fulfilling prophecy.

References

Albrecht, K., & Miller, L. (2000a). *The comprehensive infant curriculum.* Beltsville, MD: Gryphon House.

Albrecht, K., & Miller, L. (2000b). *The comprehensive toddler curriculum.* Beltsville, MD: Gryphon House.

Bronfenbrenner, U. (1989). Ecological systems theory. *Annals of Child Development, 6,* 187–249.

Brooks, G. (2000, November). *The influence of preschool literacy experiences on early literacy attainment: The research evidence.* National Literacy Trust Occasional Papers. Paper presented at the second annual conference, Early Years: Building the Foundations for Literacy, London, England.

Brown, C. (1971). *The childhood story of Christy Brown* (previously titled *My left foot*). New York: Pocket Books.

Burns, S., Griffin, P., & Snow, C. (1999). *Starting out right: A guide to promoting children's reading success.* Washington, DC: National Academy Press.

Bus, A., & van IJzendoorn, M. (1995). Mothers reading to their 3-year-olds: The role of mother-child attachment security in becoming literate. *Reading Research Quarterly, 30,* 998–1015.

Butler, D. (1998). *Babies need books.* Portsmouth, NH: Heinemann.

Coleman- Pierce, P. (1991). *Literacy lost: A qualitative analysis of early literacy opportunities for children with severe speech and physical impairments.* Unpublished doctoral dissertation, Chapel Hill: University of North Carolina.

Conzenio, K., & French, L. (2002). Science in the preschool classroom: Capitalizing on children's fascination with the everyday world to foster language and literacy development. *Young Children, 57*(5), 12–18.

Dickinson, D., & Tabors, P. (Eds.). (2001). *Beginning literacy with language: Young children learning at home and school.* Baltimore: Paul H. Brookes.

Fader, E. (2002). *How story times for preschool children can incorporate current research.* Chicago: Public Library Association.

Hart, B., & Risley, T. (2003, Spring). The early catastrophe: The 30 million word gap by age 3 [Electronic version]. *American Educator.* Retrieved July 16, 2004 from http://www.aft.org/pubs-reports/american_educator/spring2003/catastrophe.html

Hendrix, J. (2003). *Total learning: Developmental curriculum for the young child* (6th ed.). Upper Saddle River, NJ: Merrill-Prentice Hall.

Hilton–Early Head Start Training Program. (2002). *SpecialQUEST3 Training Manual (Session 5D).* Rohnert Park, CA: Sonoma State University, California Institute on Human Services.

Holcomb, N. (1992). *How about a hug?* Hollisday, PA: Jason & Nordic.

International Reading Association (IRA), & National Association for the Education of Young Children (NAEYC). (1998). Joint Position Statement: Learning to read and write: Developmentally appropriate practices for young children. *Young Children, 54,* 30–46.

Justice, L., & Kaderavek, J. (2002). Using shared storybook experiences to promote emergent literacy. *Teaching Exceptional Children, 34*(4), 8–14.

Koppenhaver, D., Coleman-Pierce, P., Kalman, S., & Yoder, D. (1991). The implications of emergent literacy research for children with developmental disabilities. *American Journal of Speech-Language Pathology, 1*(1), 10–25.

Koppenhaver, D., Evans, D., & Yoder, D. (1991). Childhood reading and writing experiences of literate adults with severe speech and motor impairments. *Augmentative and Alternative Communication, 7*(1), 20–33.

Kupetz, B., & Green, E. (1997). Sharing books with infants and toddlers: Facing the challenges. *Young Children, 52*(2), 22–27.

Light, J., & Kelford-Smith, A. (1993). The home literacy experiences of preschoolers who use augmentative and alternative communication systems and their peers. *Augmentative and Alternative Communication, 9*(1), 10–25.

Lilly, E., & Green, C. (2004). *Developing partnerships with families through children's literature.* Upper Saddle River, NJ: Pearson/Prentice-Hall.

Marvin, C. (1994). Home literacy experiences of children with single and multiple disabilities. *Topics in Early Childhood Special Education, 14,* 436–454.

Marvin, C., & Mirenda, P. (1993). Home literacy experiences of preschoolers enrolled in Head Start and in special education programs. *Journal of Early Intervention, 17,* 351–367.

Mayer-Johnson, (2002). *Board Maker* (Version 4.0) [Computer software]. Modesto Beach, CA: Author.

McCathren, R., & Allor, J. (2002). Using storybooks with preschool children: Enhancing language and emergent literacy. *Young Exceptional Children, 5*(4), 3–10.

McConnell, S., & Rabe, H. (1999). Home and community factors that promote early literacy development in preschool-aged children. *Just in Time Research: Children, Youth, and Families, 1,* 39-46.

Meyers, E., & Henderson, H. (2002). Overview of emergent literacy project. Chicago: Public Library Association.

Morrow, L. M. (1997). *Literacy development in the early years* (3rd ed.). Boston: Allyn & Bacon.

Motheread. (2001). *Books for babies.* Raleigh, NC: Author.

Musselwhite, C., & King-DeBaun, P. (1997). *Emergent literacy success: Merging technology and whole language for students with disabilities.* Park City, UT: Creative Communicating.

Owocki, G. (1999). *Literacy through play.* Portsmouth, NH: Heinemann.

Pierce, P. (Ed.). (1994). *Baby power: A guide for families for using assistive technology with infants and toddlers.* Raleigh: North Carolina Department of Health and Human Services.

Pierce, P., & McWilliam, P. (1993). Emerging literacy and young children with severe speech and physical impairments: Issues and possible intervention strategies. *Topics in Language Disorders, 13*(2), 47–57.

Pratt, C. C., & Hernandez, R. (2006). Early literacy communications campaigns: The important role of social marketing. In S. E. Rosenkoetter & J. Knapp-Philo (Eds.), *Learning to read the world: Language and literacy in the first three years* (pp. 455–476). Washington, DC: ZERO TO THREE Press.

Rosenkoetter, S. (2003). *70+ ideas for communities related to emergent literacy*. Corvallis: Oregon State University.

Roskos, K., Christie, J., & Richgels, D. (March, 2003). The essentials of early literacy instruction. *Young Children, 58*(2), 52–60.

Roskos, K., Vukelich, C., Christie, J., Enz, B., & Neuman, S. (1995). *Linking literacy and play*. Newark, DE: International Reading Association.

Scarborough, H. (2002). Connecting early language and literacy to later language reading (dis)abilities: Evidence, theory, and practice. In S. Neuman & D. Dickinson (Eds.), *The handbook of early literacy research* (pp. 97–111). New York: Guilford Press.

Schickedanz, J. (1999). *Much more than the ABCs*. Washington, DC: National Association for the Education of Young Children.

Smith, P. (2000). *Talking classrooms: Shaping children's learning through oral and language instruction*. Newark, DE: International Reading Association.

Soundy, C. (1997). Nurturing literacy with infants and toddlers in group settings. *Childhood Education, 73*, 149–153.

Teale, W., & Sulzby, E. (1989). *Emergent literacy: Young children learn to read and write* (pp. 1–16). Newark, DE: International Reading Association.

CHAPTER 17

Leading the Way to Quality: The Importance of Supervisory Support

Joanne Knapp-Philo and Amy Flynn[1]

If your actions inspire others to dream more, learn more, do
more, and become more, you are a leader.
—John Quincy Adams

High-quality leadership is necessary for an excellent infant–toddler program, and it is certainly necessary if staff members, families, and children are going to develop their potentials related to early language and literacy. Indeed, Sergiovanni and Starratt (1979) suggest that supervisors need to generate a curriculum that provides experiences to foster growth in adults and children. Supervisors often face significant challenges such as lack of preparation, competing responsibilities, staff turnover, and inappropriate societal pressure toward early reading. Given those obstacles, supervisors become effective leaders when, as the quote above implies, they help others to dream more, learn more, do more, and become more. This chapter will discuss the characteristics of effective supervision and share practical supervisory strategies that support staff to provide appropriate language- and literacy-rich experiences for young children. The chapter also will provide an introduction to supportive supervision, an overarching strategy for creating a culture of caring and continuous improvement, and will offer two scenarios that exemplify supervisory support for beginning language and literacy. The principles discussed here apply to all kinds of early care and education settings.

[1] The authors appreciate the contributions of Dena Davis.

The world of early education and care is grounded in human development. Children are entitled to a nurturing environment featuring interactions with adults that foster children's optimal development. As infants and toddlers grow, learn, and change, adults must modify the environment and the specific patterns of adult–child interactions to acknowledge each child's development and encourage continuing developmental progress. Similarly, leaders of adults in early care and education settings should view their work through the lens of human development. Like the teacher in a caregiving situation, the supervisor of adults is responsible for individually appropriate support for the ongoing development of each staff member, and the nature of this support changes over time as the colleague grows in knowledge and skill. As teachers do with children, supervisors may need to ensure that staff members comply with the rules that have been developed to promote the smooth functioning of the organization, but this management role is but one aspect of a supervisor's job. Effective supervisors are mindful of the importance of early language and literacy development skills when they hire new teachers, evaluate them, develop organizational policies, and plan professional development opportunities. Supervisors are called to lead in developing activities and curricula that support a literacy-rich environment. Supervisors must also help staff members understand new language and literacy information as well as translate it into practice.

In addition, staff members will likely need assistance from their supervisor as they develop skills in articulating how and why specific activities, interactions, and daily routines are related to language and literacy development (Knapp-Philo & Stice, 2003). Families and staff members are regularly inundated with information and materials intended to help children learn to read. They confront a plethora of toys, videos, and CDs marketed to teach reading skills to children from birth onward. Unfortunately, the push for early academic learning may be the impetus for parents and teachers to suggest a literacy curriculum for infants and toddlers that looks more like a diminished preschool curriculum. Only leaders with a firm knowledge of child development, learning theory, early childhood curriculum, and infant–toddler pedagogy as well as a solid relationship with their staff members can effectively guide colleagues to make wise choices from among the available array (Carter & Curtis, 1998; Yelland, 2000). Effective supervisors clearly and repeatedly articulate that young children develop literacy skills through open-ended interactions with people and materials in their environments.

These leadership activities must occur within a climate of caring for children, families, and staff members. Indeed, Caruso and Fawcett (1999) suggest that

> supervision is a caring process. Supervisors as caregivers strive to develop in programs a culture of caring, a place where staff members and children grow in their capacity to care. Supervisors are also advocates for policies based on attitudes of caring. (p. 45)

Typically, supervisors in early care and education settings are successful teachers or caregivers who move up the ranks to become directors. Many have had little training in supervision when they first take on their responsibilities. New supervisors soon learn that the skills that enabled them to be successful with children are not sufficient for work in complex situations with adults. There are numerous levels of responsibility in supervising early care and education programs and a myriad of licensing requirements to address. In addition, early care and education supervisors often fulfill roles beyond those of supervision, such as teaching part-time in classrooms, substituting when a caregiver is absent, and performing extra responsibilities that might include payroll, accounting, and preparing for state or federal audits or reviews. Within this array of responsibilities, supervisors must ensure that time is given to supporting each staff member's contributions to early language and literacy skills for children and their families.

The Timing of High-Quality Supervision

Ralph Waldo Emerson said, "What you do speaks so loudly that I cannot hear what you say." Early care and education leaders have the responsibility to personify their organization's mission and vision as well as to help others reach upward. As leaders conduct the day-to-day administrative tasks, they also set the organization's tone and ensure that the values of the program are lived out in daily interactions with children, families, and staff members. The values of an organization are conveyed in numerous ways as they are infused throughout all levels of activity (Fullan, 1999; Sergiovanni & Starratt, 1979). For example, if beginning language and literacy are valued in an early care and education program, then questions about promoting them are part of the interview process, a component of the regular formal evaluation process, elements of conversations and training with parents and staff members, and part of "water-cooler" conversations among colleagues. Early language and literacy are featured at staff meetings. Indeed, they permeate the consciousness of all the adults in the program every day. Following a recent training on beginning language and literacy, a group of administrators made the following comments:

> *I realized I had to lead this program to foster beginning language and literacy.*

> * * *

> *If the message is good and you deliver it with enthusiasm and walk the walk, that will make all the difference. The administrator is a role model for the rest of the staff.*

> * * *

> *In my role as administrator and team leader … my mission is to ensure that the staff … get to participate,… not isolating staff, but making them part of the process.*

> * * *

> *[I need to] make sure there is enough time—make an effort that there is time for people to [work on beginning language and literacy]. As an administrator, I must be a leader.*

> * * *

> *I must be as articulate as staff must be present. [I] feel like a cheerleader most of the time.*

> * * *

> *Staff needs to understand why, not just because they were told. That's my job—to help them understand!*

In early childhood programs, it is often difficult to find time for ongoing staff supervision and training. Yet it is widely recognized that a trained professional staff is a key predictor of high-quality child care and education (Peisner-Feinberg et al., 1999; Ruopp, Travers, Glantz, & Coelen, 1979; Whitebook,

Howes, & Phillips, 1989) and that good supervision is a critical factor in keeping staff motivated and reflective about their practice (Caruso & Fawcett, 1999). Indeed, because many child-care providers have limited education and training, on-the-job training is often the main opportunity for staff development. Therefore, supervisors in early care and education have a critical role in daily promoting staff growth and development.

Characteristics of High-Quality Supervision

Kloosterman (2001, 2003) studied the professional relationships of 7 supervisors and 10 preschool teachers who participated together in a longitudinal training program. She found 12 markers of successful supervisory behaviors:

- Working collaboratively toward a shared goal
- Promoting confidence and trust in the supervisor–teacher interaction
- Listening carefully to teachers' needs and concerns
- Creating a safe environment
- Being accessible to teachers throughout the day
- Making teachers aware of their observation schedule
- Including teachers in the evaluation process
- Allowing teachers to reflect on and self-evaluate their practice before sharing their evaluations
- Expressing appreciation for teachers' effort and work
- Emphasizing and acknowledging teachers' strengths
- Getting to know staff members as individuals
- Making the time for supervision, even when there are competing priorities

Given the myriad demands on early care and education leaders, it may be challenging to find the time to spend on the above supervisory behaviors, yet supervisors have no alternative but to take on the task of fostering staff growth much as they expect caregivers to nurture children's development. Factors of low morale (Willis & Ricciuti, 1975), low status and low pay (Jones, 1994), limited participation in decision making (Whitebook, Howes, Darrah, & Friedman, 1982), a prevailing feeling of a "treadmill of activity" (Bloom, 1995), stress and burnout (Boyd & Schneider, 1997), and the potential for resultant high turnover are all reasons that early care and education supervisors must develop their leadership skills. If children are to be properly cared for and their developing language and literacy supported, it is essential that supervisors ensure that early care and education staff members have the information, materials, skills, attitudes, and guidance they need to do their jobs. Clearly, supervisors must "nurture the nurturers." Stice and Levine (this volume, p. 395) discuss staff development as an essential component of developing the human resources of early care and education and provide strategies for developing and implementing an ongoing staff development program to promote beginning language and literacy. Pawl and St. John (1998) suggest that self-awareness, good observation skills, and flexible responses plus a tone of collegiality are important characteristics for supervisors to develop in themselves and their staff members.

Another aspect of staff development, known as clinical, reflective, or supportive supervision, is an additional supervisory strategy that has been shown to improve program quality and support staff learning and growth (Fenichel, 1992). By combining an ongoing, well-planned, and well-executed staff development effort with a supportive, responsive, formal evaluation system plus the regular practice of supportive supervision, a supervisor can indeed integrate Kloosterman's (2003) 12 principles into a pattern of outstanding leadership.

Supportive Supervision Promotes Beginning Language and Literacy

Patton defined a leadership style that draws on the wisdom of the staff member: "Never tell people how to do things. Tell them what to do and they will surprise you with their ingenuity." Supportive supervision, also called reflective, individual, or clinical supervision, has been discussed in education circles for decades as a way to promote teacher skill in a relationship-based context (Sergiovanni & Starratt, 1979). It is now used in early education and care settings, particularly those serving infants and toddlers (Fenichel, 1992).

Supportive supervision is based on the following principles (Norman-Murch, 1996):

1. Everyone deserves the opportunity to be supported in a collaborative relationship.

2. Learning takes place in the context of relationships and is affected by the quality of those relationships.

3. We all bring our past experiences, values, and expectations to every situation. How we (and others) respond is based on these experiences, values, and expectations.

It is essential that supervisors create an environment where staff members reflect on their work and share ideas with others. Indeed, it is the mark of a dynamic community of learners (Carter & Curtis, 1998), and such a collective environment begins with individual supervision. Once a supervisor embraces the basic responsibility to support and supervise staff members and selects supportive supervision as an effective approach, then finding the time and the resources for ongoing supervision becomes built in to the expectations of the program. For example, budgeting for and ensuring staff time for supervision sessions becomes an essential part of daily practice.

Several tenets of supportive supervision, described further in the following sections, make it a positive experience for the supervisor and supervisee and help to promote a community that continually reflects on its work with children and families.

Supportive supervision is a joint effort between the supervisor and supervisee. Collaboration is essential. Supervision begins with the development of goals. The supervisee develops goals as she reflects on her work and decides on the areas of focus. Adults learn best when the learning is connected to something that is meaningful to them (McCollum & Catlett, 1997). This relevance keeps them motivated and willing both to try new ideas and to share concerns with their supervisor. Often it is helpful to keep supervision journals. Supervisees should come to the session prepared to discuss their experiences, concerns, and successes since they last met with their supervisor. Supervisors should also be prepared to discuss what they have observed since the last meeting.

Supportive supervision is different from job performance discussions and reviews. The purpose of supportive supervision is the supervisee's professional growth and development. This meeting is an opportunity to reflect on one's work with children and families and to consider alternative strategies. Thus, this opportunity is a perfect venue to support ongoing skill development related to beginning language and literacy. However, there are times when a supervisor must set down basic rules about job expectation and performance. Although having a supportive supervisory relationship can be helpful in discussing basic work performance issues, the supportive supervision session is not the appropriate venue for such discussions.

Supportive supervision supports the teacher's skills where they are and moves them forward. Supervisors must have direct knowledge of the supervisee's skills and experience. It is essential that supervisors observe the supervisees' work on a regular basis. Often the most useful observations are informal and done in the natural course of the supervisor's day. In addition, the supervisee may request a more formal observation so the supervisor can provide input on a particular activity or time of day. It is often challenging for supervisors with many other job responsibilities to spend this kind of formal plus informal time observing staff, but being around and part of the life of the classroom is critical not only to good supervision but also to effective program administration.

Supportive supervision creates a safe and supportive environment for learning and trying new ideas. Supervisors must create a place of safety and support for supervisees so they feel secure in exploring new ideas and various ways of approaching curriculum, working with parents, and collaborating with team members. Many skilled teachers often have at least 20 ways to encourage a child to try a new experience because they know that at any given time what worked previously may not work again. In a parallel fashion, this ability to try out new ideas, get feedback, revise the plan, and try again is at the heart of supportive supervision and should be nurtured and modeled by the supervisor.

Supportive supervision must be regularly scheduled, ideally at least twice a month. Naptime is often the best time for teachers and their supervisors to meet. Home visitors may have a different schedule. Conscientious planning, scheduling, and commitment to appointments clearly communicate the value and importance that the leader gives to supervision. Indeed, when supportive supervision is not scheduled, it tends to be overlooked and just drifts away. The supervision schedule should also include time for teams to meet regularly and times for the entire staff to discuss important issues.

Supportive supervision is a reflective process that takes time. Supervisees need time to think about their practice and to ponder future directions. For instance, a teacher may want to consider why a strategy works for one child and not another. Supervisees need time to talk with a mentor who will listen carefully to their concerns and questions and then join them in finding a solution.

Supportive supervision must include a time for both supervisor and teacher to reflect on and evaluate the process. How do the participants know whether the supervision and support being provided is working for the supervisor and for the teacher? It is important to set out written goals and expectations. These goals should be reviewed periodically to see whether they have been met or need to be revised or, perhaps, whether new goals should be added. Supervisors should work with supervisees to establish dates and timelines for goals. Moreover, it is critical that both the teacher and the supervisor regularly engage in a reflective review of the supervision process to ensure that it is meeting their expectations and needs (Fenichel, 1992).

With a supportive supervision approach, both parties are expected to be active participants. Supervisees participate by developing their own goals and reflecting on their practice. The supervisor facilitates the professional growth and development by asking open-ended questions and making comments to enable the supervisee to develop her own insights. Open-ended questions and comments assist staff to be more open and regularly practice problem-solving processes. Supervisors should resist the temptation to add ideas quickly, encouraging staff to work through problems on their own initially and to reflect on their practice outside the supervisory session. Over time, as staff members participate in ongoing reflection, they become better able to refine their practice not only on their own but also within the supportive supervision relationship.

Following are some effective open-ended comments and questions (Klein, 1999):

- What I heard you say was …

- How did you think that activity (parent conference, conversation) went?

- What did you think worked best?

- How might you handle it differently next time?

- How do you think everyone else feels about it?

- What led you to handle the situation this way?

- How do you think this worked for the other person?

- Were there any surprises?

- Let's reconstruct what happened …

- It sounds as if you were feeling very frustrated.

- You seem to be very pleased with how that turned out. Tell me more about it.

- Have you asked the other person what would work best for him?

What Supervision That Supports Beginning Language and Literacy Looks Like

The following scenario is an example of how supportive supervision was used to facilitate teacher professional development, reflection, and problem solving to ensure that the infants and toddlers in care have high-quality language and literary experiences. Note how it also supported staff competence and sense of accomplishment. The session exemplifies a comment by Harold S. Geneen: "Leadership is practiced not so much in words as in attitude and in actions."

> A supervisor was observing a classroom of children ranging in age from 12 months to 34 months. The teacher, Anna, was trying to read a story to eight children who were sitting on the rug. This effort proved a frustrating task because some toddlers were coming up to the book and pointing at the pictures while others complained because they couldn't see. The youngest children were wandering away. Other teachers in the room were scrambling to pull everyone together to hear the story.

> Later that day, when they had a chance to talk, Anna's supervisor asked her, "How did you feel it went when you were reading to the group of children this morning?" Anna said that it was frustrating. The book chosen was one that she knew all the chil-

dren liked. She had thought it would be good for some of the older children to sit in a group and hear a story. After all, they would soon be going to a preschool classroom, and Anna wanted to make sure they were "ready" for the transition. Her supervisor asked Anna what she thought was the goal of reading a story to young children. Anna clearly explained the importance of children enjoying reading, attending to the story, asking questions, and making connections. The supervisor then asked Anna whether she had achieved those goals at the group story reading. Anna was sure she hadn't! The supervisor drew on a time recently when she had observed Anna reading with two toddlers cuddled on her lap. Anna described the richness of that interaction and how she was able to support the children to expand their language, ask questions, and attend to the story.

The supervisor suggested that Anna visit the preschool classroom and talk with the preschool teacher about her experiences with group story time, her expectations for children, and the difference between this group reading and reading to children either individually or in a small, intimate group. Anna found that, in fact, the preschool teacher's expectations for 3-year-olds were not different from her own and that many preschoolers continue to struggle with the reality of group story times. Anna no longer felt obliged to ensure that the children were "ready" to move to preschool. She decided that in the future she would not try to read books to more than two or three children at a time. Rather, she would find time every day to read individually to each of the children in her primary care.

Throughout this example, the supervisor asked many open-ended questions to lead Anna to talk about her experience and reflect on her work. In addition, the supervisor suggested that Anna talk with another teacher to get a clearer picture of what future expectations would be for the children. The preschool teacher was happy to share her own experience, and the conversation served to open important lines of communication between the two. The supervisor's suggestion also served to build Anna's confidence in her own ability to solve her problems and to work with peers to resolves issues. This outcome enhances the team as a whole and supports an atmosphere of collegiality in the program.

Another example shows how supportive supervision can help a caregiver deal with a challenging situation in a way that enlightens all involved.

> Sally is an infant–toddler caregiver in a child-care program in a large city. A parent of one of the children she works with is concerned that the classroom curriculum is not preparing her child for preschool. The child will be moving to preschool in 6 months, and her parents are desperate to get her into a "good" preschool program. The child has already been scheduled for interviews at a number of preschools. The parent also has talked with other parents, who then came to Sally with their concerns. Sally feels pressure to "step up" her curriculum and has begun to drill the children on letters and words.
>
> Sally's supervisor asked her why she felt the parents were so concerned. Sally talked a bit about the pressures parents were feeling related to finding a good preschool in their community. She understood the concerns of the parents, but she was worried that the parents felt she wasn't doing a good job.
>
> Her supervisor encouraged Sally to talk about what was happening in the classroom that supported the children's language and literacy development. Sally made a long list of language- and literacy-rich experiences that she brought to the children each day.
>
> As Sally named all the wonderful language and literacy experiences that were taking place in her classroom, she felt more comfortable and confident in her work. She began to think about additional ways that she and other teachers could support the children's language and literacy learning and involve the parents in supporting and complementing these efforts. She asked the parents to participate in more reading activities with their children by making audiotapes of themselves reading books that they shared regularly with their children at home. Sally provided tapes and a tape recorder for them to use. Some par-

*ents chose to tell a story rather than read one. These tapes were
then used throughout the day in the classroom. They not only
supported parents' and children's literacy activities but also
brought parents into the classroom throughout the day, building
essential bridges between home and school.*

*Sally, reassured about the work she was doing in her classroom,
was able to use what she knew was developmentally appropriate
for the children to create a richer environment and still address
the parents' concerns. Later, she developed a presentation for all
the parents that addressed their issues, educated them about
beginning language and literacy development for toddlers, and
illustrated how the literacy-rich classroom environment stimulated the children's growth and development.*

The well-placed questions that Sally's supervisor asked enabled Sally to see that
she was on the right path. This insight engendered her confidence and enabled
her to have a broader perspective, appreciate the parents' concerns, and avoid
acting from defensiveness or hurt feelings. Bolstered by these new realizations,
Sally was able to work constructively with the families and educate them. As she
respected their concerns, she found a productive solution to what could have
been a divisive and contentious situation.

Conclusion

High-quality supervision is essential for high quality early education and care
programs. As society learns more about beginning language and literacy
for infants and toddlers, it is important for staff members to have current
information about evidence-based strategies to support children's growth and
development and to inform families about the variety of ways that they can
contribute to a child's foundation for lifelong learning. This chapter has
described the need for leaders to provide planned and effective staff supervision
using an approach such as that suggested by Kloosterman (2003) and incorporating supportive supervision into the practices in their programs. These
approaches will enable them to "grow" staff, support families, and ensure
that children receive optimal opportunities for learning.

References

Bloom, P. J. (1995). The quality of worklife in early childhood programs. In S. Bredekamp & B. Willer (Eds.), *NAEYC accreditation: A decade of learning and the years ahead* (pp. 13–24). Washington, DC: National Association for the Education of Young Children.

Boyd, B. J., & Schneider, N. I. (1997). Perceptions of the work environment and burnout in Canadian child care providers. *Journal of Research in Childhood Education, 11,* 171–180.

Carter, M., & Curtis, D. (1998). *The visionary director: A handbook for dreaming, organizing, and improvising in your center.* St. Paul, MN: Redleaf Press.

Caruso, J. J., & Fawcett, M. T. (1999). *Supervision in early childhood education: A developmental perspective* (2nd ed.). New York: Teachers College Press.

Fenichel, E. (Ed.). (1992). *Learning through supervision and mentorship to support the development of infants, toddlers, and their families: A sourcebook.* Washington, DC: ZERO TO THREE.

Fullan, M. (1999). *Change forces: The sequel.* Philadelphia: Falmer Press.

Jones, E. (1994). Breaking the ice: Confronting status differences among professionals. In J. Johnson & J. B. McCracken (Eds.), *The early childhood career lattice: Perspectives on professional development* (pp. 27–30). Washington, DC: National Association for the Education of Young Children.

Klein, C. (1999, April). *Tips on reflective supervision.* Presentation at SpecialQUEST Learning Coach Training, Washington, DC.

Kloosterman, V. I. (2001). *A qualitative examination of the impact of the Literacy Enrichment Project on preschool teachers and supervisors' practices.* Paper presented at the Conference on Ethnographic and Qualitative Research in Education, Albany, NY.

Kloosterman, V. I. (2003). A partnership approach for supervisors and teachers. *Young Children. 58*(6), 12–19.

Knapp-Philo, J., & Stice, K. (Eds.). (2003). *StoryQUEST 1 Training Guide.* Unpublished training manual, Sonoma State University, California Institute on Human Services, Rohnert Park, CA.

McCollum, J. A., & Catlett, C. (1997). Designing effective personnel preparation for early intervention: Theoretical frameworks. In P. J. Winton, J. A. McCollum, & C. Catlett (Eds.), *Reforming personnel preparation in early intervention* (pp. 105–125). Baltimore: Paul H. Brookes.

Norman-Murch, T. (1996). Reflective supervision as a vehicle for individual and organizational development. *Zero to Three, 17*(2), 16–20

Pawl, J., & St. John, M. (1998). *How you are is as important as what you do.* Washington, DC: ZERO TO THREE Press.

Peisner-Feinberg, E. S., Burchinal, M. R., Clifford, R. M., Culkin, M. L., Howes, C., Kagan, S. L., et al. (1999). *The children of the cost, quality, and outcomes study go to school: Executive summary.* Chapel Hill: University of North Carolina at Chapel Hill, Frank Porter Graham Child Development Center.

Ruopp, R. J., Travers, F., Glantz, F., & Coelen, C. (1979). *Children at the center: Final results of the National Day Care Study.* Cambridge, MA: Abt Associates.

Sergiovanni, T. J., & Starratt, R. J. (1979). *Supervision: Human perspectives* (2nd ed.). New York: McGraw-Hill.

Stice, K., & Levine, T. (2006). Resources to promote early language and literacy. In S. E. Rosenkoetter & J. Knapp-Philo (Eds.), *Learning to read the world: Language and literacy in the first three years* (pp. 395–412). Washington, DC: ZERO TO THREE Press.

Whitebook, M., Howes, C., Darrah, R., & Friedman, J. (1982). *Caring for the caregivers: Staff burnout in child care.* New York: Teachers College Press.

Whitebook, M., Howes, C., & Phillips, D. (1989). *Who cares? Child care teachers and the quality of care in America: Executive summary of the National Child Care Staffing Study.* Oakland, CA: Child Care Employee Project.

Willis, A., & Ricciuti, H. (1975). *A good beginning for babies: Guidelines for group care.* Washington, DC: National Association for the Education of Young Children.

Yelland, N. J. (2000). *Promoting meaningful learning: Innovations in education for early childhood professionals.* Washington, DC: National Association for the Education of Young Children.

CHAPTER 18

Mentoring: Together We're Better

Sharon E. Rosenkoetter

Watching others is a great way to learn. We can discover a great deal from observing infants, toddlers, and their families and then reflecting with others about the developing early language and literacy. We can learn what infants and toddlers like and dislike and what overstimulates or bores them. We can learn which adult actions encourage young children to venture out and which cause them to withdraw. By observing other parents or caregivers and discussing their interaction styles with them, we can learn how to hold a child on our lap or encircled in our arms to make special times together warm and cuddly. We can learn how to choose books that maintain a young child's attention and how to use vocal inflection and facial expressions to sustain an infant's or toddler's interest in an interaction. We can learn to expand on the text and follow the child's lead, rather than just read words. Adults and adolescents can learn from mentors how to bring the riches of language to bear on routine times with infants and toddlers (Kubicek, 2002; also see Kubicek, this volume, p. 163) and how to deal wisely with difficult dilemmas as young children struggle to learn self-regulation (Bronson, 2000; National Research Council & Institute of Medicine, 2000).

Communicating with infants and toddlers and reading to them require skills that some adults learned in childhood. If our parents and grandparents interacted with us around language, then we "absorbed" strategies from their modeling. But some individuals never had the benefit of such modeling, and most of us could learn some new ways to "connect" with infants and toddlers in ways that foster early language and literacy. A variety of supports are available to help family members and staff colleagues interact in more effective ways. Mentoring is one of those supports. Individuals who have mastered some of the lifeways that promote early language and literacy can nurture infants and toddlers by sharing their wisdom, even as they enjoy learning from the reactions of a young child and the child's caregiver, both of whom are relating in new ways around language and literacy.

This chapter will describe mentoring, an important vehicle for sharing emergent language and literacy strategies family-to-family and care provider-to-care provider. It will describe different types of mentoring, including a section on cultural mentoring, an approach that helps service providers or family members understand an unfamiliar culture in ways that allow them to navigate more effectively with people who live within it. This chapter will also describe the qualities of effective mentors, ways to set up mentoring programs around early language and literacy, and several mentoring programs that are in use across the country, including one for Early Head Start communities that focuses on fostering language and literacy for infants and toddlers. The author has guided mentoring partnerships related to early language and literacy and believes strongly in mentoring as a component of family support, comprehensive staff development, and community mobilization to enrich the language and literacy development experiences of very young children and their families.

Definition

Mentoring is a particularly strong reciprocal relationship that embodies ongoing interactions for learning between two people. Traditionally, the mentoring partners consisted of a novice and "a wise and trusted counselor"(*Random House Dictionary*, 1980, p. 549), but more recently they may be peers who share their differing expertise (Knapp-Philo & Stice, 2003a, 2003b). Mentoring is intended to provide new ideas, skills, and encouragement for a less knowledgeable or experienced partner. "Mentors are guides. They lead us along the journey of our lives" (Daloz, 1999, p. 18). In some cases, mentoring leads to entirely new ways of thinking about self and world (White, 2001). Moreover, both individuals in a mentoring partnership are learners, as the more confident or knowledgeable partner frequently is challenged to justify and rethink familiar positions, reflect on personal practices, and explore how to improve the application or practice (Delgado, 1999; Head Start Bureau, 2001). As French moralist Joseph Joubert stated, "To teach is to learn twice." Both partners in a mentoring relationship develop skills in communication and joint problem solving. They are likely to appreciate any recognition that comes for their commitment to improving skills and services, and they typically will enjoy the social aspects of their experience as well as feel pride in contributing to others (Bellm, Whitebook, & Hnatiuk, 1997).

Abundant evidence proves that mentorship is especially important at critical turning points in people's lives (Daloz, 1999; Head Start Bureau, 2001). Either parenting as the infant or toddler enters a new stage of development or caregiving as the professional takes on a new role is certainly a turning point where mentoring may be especially appreciated. Early childhood program directors who aim to enhance their parent education program, their staff's skills, or both with a focus on beginning language and literacy might choose to initiate a mentoring program because this strategy can expand the influence of early language and literacy efforts to more families and caregivers, fostering their positive early literacy efforts for years to come.

Two Types of Mentoring

Two types of mentoring relationships will be described. Each of these relationships may be encouraged by an organization or a campaign to promote early language and literacy with infants and toddlers.

Informal Mentoring

The first approach, informal mentoring, occurs when a more experienced family member or early childhood professional takes "under wing" a less experienced person. Interactions typically develop from a one-time conversation and progress to periodic reflections on related topics of mutual interest. Unstructured and spontaneous rather than planned or structured, informal mentoring may focus wherever the less knowledgeable partner has questions—for example, how to choose a book, how to get a toddler to sit still for a book, or how to engage a baby in interactions during a routine such as feeding or diapering. Informal mentoring relationships may last for short periods of time until a specific skill is learned, or they may be long term, continuing across decades—as in the case of a mentor who teaches a young mother to breast-feed her child and later guides the mother in managing challenging adolescent behavior.

Often in informal mentoring, meaningful conversations begin from something that one of the partners notices, and the partners proceed to reflect together on the elements of an incident, strategies that were followed, and ways that those actions might have been improved. For example, White's (2001) ethnographic study described a mother in Head Start who was mentored with respect to both family and teaching matters by other Head Start parent volunteers whom she met at the center and by a Head Start teacher. Each of the three relationships in White's account, plus the interplay among them, was transformative for the mother's interactions with children. Each relationship developed spontaneously, and each one was based on caring and mutual respect. As seen in this account, informal mentoring relationships require responsiveness, tact, and time commitment on the part of both participants.

An agency or community early literacy campaign may encourage informal mentoring by sharing extensively about the importance of talking and reading with infants and toddlers, seeking suggestions about how to make this literacy support happen in homes and group settings, and encouraging individuals to share with one another about their daily early language and literacy interactions with infants and toddlers. As interest grows among families and caregivers, informal mentoring may arise and may generate worthwhile outcomes, but because informal mentoring is not planned or systematic, its breadth of coverage is probably limited and its outcomes are uncertain.

Formal Mentoring

The second approach, formal mentoring, is organized and framed by ground rules or specific operating procedures. Carried out by pairs of family members or professionals, formal mentoring may be conducted by voluntary participants or by supervisors with their supervisees. Formal mentoring is maintained by a regular schedule of conferences with defined goals. As a result, definite outcomes are anticipated. Internships and apprenticeships of all types involve formal mentoring. Many governing boards assign formal mentors when a new member joins their group, and employers commonly establish formal mentoring relationships when a new teacher, caseworker, or nurse enters an employment situation that has many written and unwritten rules and procedures. Formal mentoring may be useful when an agency or community is trying to help its infant–toddler staff or its families become intentional and accomplished in sharing language and literacy with young children throughout daily routines. Administrators and family support groups may find that establishing formal mentoring is effective and economical because it reinforces recommended practices as they are shared and perhaps modeled in individually appropriate ways. Formal mentoring supports through mutual dedication and effort the partners' growing competence in applying concepts of emergent literacy facilitation. Moreover, it conveys emphatically the importance for *everyone*—not only family members but also professionals—to (a) talk responsively with babies during daily routines, (b) develop young children's symbolic understandings, (c) share books with infants and toddlers in the adults' care, and (d) continue to learn new ways to support early language and literacy more effectively. Participant pairs in formal mentoring programs plan desired outcomes, observe adult interactions with children, collect data, reflect on performance, solve problems, answer questions, and evaluate progress (Zachary, 2000). They may or may not report to a supervisor about the progress of their mutual effort.

Two Types of Formal Mentoring

Two arrangements for formal mentoring are typical: peer mentoring and expert–novice mentoring. Each arrangement, discussed in the paragraphs that follow, features a specific type of relationship.

Peer Mentoring

In the peer mentoring approach, both participants are eager to learn and are willing to share with one another. Both partners in peer mentoring wish to explore new ways and develop new ideas and skills. As with any two people, peer mentors have different sets of information, attitudes, and personal and professional traits, and each has much to give the other. The peers are equal in authority. Together, they shape the process, guide the outcomes, and celebrate the individual and mutual successes of their collaboration. The role of the sponsoring group or agency is to bring together the mentoring partners initially, provide a framework within which they can develop their mutual expectations, provide tangible and ongoing support as needed, help to resolve issues, and publicize individual and partnered achievements when it is appropriate to do so. Several examples illustrate the concept of peer mentoring.

The Best Practice in Integration—Outreach project (Tertell, Klein, & Jewett, 1998) paired early childhood teachers who wished to learn about serving children with disabilities and early childhood special educators who wanted to learn about general early childhood practice. When individuals in the two groups mentored one another over time, learning resulted. The early childhood teachers became more skillful at including young children with disabilities in their classrooms, and the special educators developed strategies for addressing individualized education program (IEP) goals within general education classrooms. The mentoring partnerships led to ongoing mutual assistance in making early education work well not only for the children involved but also for their teachers.

The Second Year Teachers' Project, a similar approach, was instituted in McPherson County, Kansas, to help new elementary teachers support one another in using evidence-based teaching practices (John Black, personal communication, May, 13, 2003). After an in-depth study of effective practices, the participants were given release time to mentor one another. One teacher recorded data on the teaching behavior requested by her peer mentor and then summarized the results and shared them with the peer. The two then discussed ways to improve, devised ways to apply the improved strategies to their own settings, and developed indicators and timelines for implementing the plans. A few days later, they reversed the observation process, with the observer now becoming the one who received guided observations. Administrators established the system but were not party to the data collected, the partners' discussions, or their planning for behavior change. Participants expressed appreciation for the process, and the district's director of professional development has continued using it for nearly 10 years.

StoryQUEST (Knapp-Philo & Stice, 2003a, 2003b), an emergent language and literacy program for Early Head Start (EHS) communities nationwide, used peer mentoring to share and apply practices emphasized in training. Participating teams consisted of a parent, an EHS administrator, an EHS caregiver, an EHS coordinator, the Head Start literacy coordinator, and a community member interested in encouraging early language and literacy. After the teams returned home from the 3-day trainings, each team member shared information from the training with his or her peer mentor, a colleague who had a comparable role but who did not attend the training. The "nontraveling" peer was knowledgeable about his or her own setting plus children and families in the community, and the team member who attended the training brought the StoryQUEST concepts, skills, attitudes, and ideas for application back to the work site. Thus, StoryQUEST views peer mentoring as a relationship among equals who bring different competencies and contributions to the learning task. Comments from participants in the peer mentoring process indicate that it contributed significantly to their learning:

> *Peer mentoring helps me internalize what I learned. It helps me to plan what the next steps are.* (Home Visitor)

* * *

> *It's great to have support and get feedback from someone just like you in your job.* (Infant–Toddler Caregiver)

* * *

> *[StoryQUEST is] a great strategy for increasing the effectiveness of training beyond the scope of the attendees … a tangible method of developing and strengthening professional relation-ships.* (EHS Education Coordinator)

* * *

> *It makes me clear in my understanding of information.… It's a chance to share, to plan together, and to divide the load.* (Head Start Literacy Specialist)

Together, the peer mentors developed and followed a plan for their work (see Appendix at end of this chapter), met regularly, and evaluated the outcomes. Every other month, StoryQUEST consultants held regularly scheduled meetings with each dyad of peer mentors to provide support, help solve problems as needed, and aid reviews of progress. They also celebrated successes! Some peer mentors were so enthusiastic about their process and the resulting early literacy outcomes that they have developed peer mentoring relationships with more than one partner.

Expert–Novice Mentoring

Expert–novice mentoring, a type of formal mentoring, occurs when an individual with knowledge and skill in a certain area such as emergent literacy works with a novice to provide encouragement, expertise, and effective problem solving (Zachary, 2000). Many terms exist for each of the mentoring roles: *guide, tutor, coach, counselor,* and *mentor* for the more experienced partner and *student, apprentice, protégé, mentoree, learner,* and *mentee* for the individual whose developmental needs set the agenda for the mentoring interaction. As Zachary (2000) and the Head Start Bureau (2001) explained, the facilitative mentoring interactions are scheduled to occur at certain times, continue over a defined period, and conclude by a specified date. Sometimes expert–novice mentoring is a part of the formal employment supervision process, but at other times it is a stand-alone program of support to early childhood personnel. Because this type of expert–novice collaboration is a formal mentoring system, the organizer of the mentoring system provides (a) the process that mentors and mentees must follow and (b) the forms that they must use to structure their interactions (Eaton & Johnson, 2001). The organizer draws up a contract with objectives, role expectations for each member, and a requirement for measurable outcomes. Either the mentor and mentee or the supervisor of the mentoring system or both typically evaluate these contracts and the related achievements (see also Zachary, 2000). In a formal mentoring system, organizers often ask participants to report to supervisors about their progress in attaining specified goals (see also Knapp-Philo & Flynn, this volume, p. 353). When the mentoring plan becomes part of an individual's professional development plan, mentorship partners typically use work time to confer together.

Organizations that institute a formal mentoring system need to establish clearly stated procedures and processes (Zachary, 2000). Organizations could adapt the sample goal sheet in this chapter's appendix for this purpose. In addition, agencies must provide instruction and technical assistance about mentoring. All participants should be aware of technical assistance and have access to it if their mentoring relationships encounter challenges that the dyad cannot resolve.

The use of formal mentoring appears to be increasing. The Association for Supervision and Curriculum Development (2004) has set up a formal mentoring system for new school principals. Spencer and Logan (2003) used a similar mentoring process to help general educators implement strategic approaches to teaching. These authors found that teachers who used mentoring accomplished their objectives better than those who merely attended training. The California Early Childhood Mentoring Program and the HUGS (Homes Uniquely Giving Support) Program in Northwest Arkansas, among others, have developed formal mentor–protégé programs to guide the professional development of novice child-care providers (Head Start Bureau, 2001). ZERO TO THREE's widely used reflective supervision approach (Fenichel, 1992) incorporates many principles of formal mentoring.

Cultural Mentoring

Cultural mentoring, similar to other types of mentoring, involves communication between partners with differing expertise. One partner has expert family or professional knowledge; the other understands at a deep level the philosophy and lifeways of a particular culture (see Jones & Lorenzo-Hubert, this volume, p. 187). A variety of professional groups have used cultural mentoring, including the following:

- physicians who are beginning work with indigenous families in Australia (Alberts & McKenzie, 2001a);

- speech-language pathologists in the United States who are attempting to serve a multicultural caseload (Green & Vann, 2003);

- child-care providers in the United Kingdom who are guiding inclusive play for young children of diverse faiths, cultures, and communities (Cultural Mentor Service, 2004);

- Anglo physical therapists who are addressing the health needs of older Hispanic adults (Strong, Lusardi, Emery, & Tallant, 2000);

- artists and scholars who are starting work in countries with unfamiliar cultures (Irish Museum of Modern Art, 2004; Lyon, 2000); and

- teachers who are seeking to be more responsive to children from non-dominant cultures (Boreen & Niday, 2003).

In each case, a reflective member of the cultural group becomes an advisor to the professional about how to deliver resources in a respectful, culturally appropriate manner.

Cultural mentors may be formally hired and paid for their services (Alberts & McKenzie, 2001b), but often they are informally accessed and serve without pay. According to Boreen and Niday (2003), four qualities are imperative for individuals to be effective as either mentors or mentees in cultural mentoring situations: (a) a willingness to work with members of another culture or ethnicity, (b) an eagerness to learn about the culture of another person or family, (c) an appreciation that knowledge and the ways of transmitting it or withholding it may be culturally conditioned, and (d) candor in talking with one's mentoring partner about cultural issues and practices.

As described by Jones and Lorenzo-Hubert (this volume, p. 187), numerous beliefs and practices with respect to communication, child development, family structure, and infant learning are guided by culture and could be illuminated by an in-depth cultural mentoring conversation stemming from a respectful relationship. The authors believe that the cultural mentoring role could well be expanded, formally or informally, in many programs that serve infants and toddlers and their families. Views of language and literacy should become a part of the conversations in cultural mentoring programs.

A related type of cultural mentoring may occur with parents who represent a cultural group different from the one providing professional services. Some communities establish parent-to-parent programs to support families in dealing with a "system" that is different from those in their native lands. For example, You, Rosenkoetter, and Zvonkovic (2006) described Korean–American mothers in California and Oregon who were required to deal with the special education system for their young children with disabilities. These women were supported and greatly aided by other Korean–American women who had faced similar language, culture, and system challenges in their own lives. Again, cultural mentorship of this sort may be formal or informal.

Shared Purpose

The common link among all of the varied approaches to mentoring is the purpose of the mentoring relationship: to enhance individuals' knowledge, skills, and commitment to action through a positive, supportive relationship. This purpose can certainly be adapted for both family and professional development to support more intentional and reflective use of early language and literacy strategies. When one stops to consider carefully the nature of one particular interaction with an infant or toddler, or the selection of an appropriate book, or a way to increase language use in a particular setting, the result for both partners can be increased understanding and new ideas about future actions. As stated by a StoryQUEST mentoring participant, "Having a dedicated peer mentor means growing and learning together, supporting and encouraging one another, and finding new ways to do things. It's about being better together than you could each be alone."

Characteristics of Effective Mentoring

The effect of any mentoring relationship is significantly enhanced by having a defined goal (Zachary, 2000). In the case of informal mentoring, this goal may come in the form of a statement of the purpose for a conversation; for example, "I need help in figuring out how to display books for my socialization group because others also use this room." In the case of peer mentoring or novice–expert formal mentoring, this goal may come in the form of a verbalized statement of the purpose for a planned session; for example, "Today we're going to talk about how to use a turn-taking strategy that I learned and practice doing it." The goal statement may also involve a written goal that is included in a plan or contract for one or more mentoring sessions (see above and Appendix).

Several authors have described qualities in a mentoring partnership that help it to be effective in accomplishing its goal or goals. ZERO TO THREE, one of the earliest proponents of mentoring as an approach to both family support and reflective supervision of staff, says that the essential elements for mentoring partnerships include reflection, collaboration, and regularity (Fenichel, 1992). Mink, Owen, and Mink (1993) stressed the primary characteristics of effective mentoring interactions: clarity, coherence, and openness. Head Start (Head Start Bureau, 2001) proposed five adjectives that describe a mentoring relationship that works to accomplish its goals: ongoing, individualized, developmental, reciprocal (mutual), and nonevaluative. Mentoring is a learning relationship— not a therapeutic or counseling one—and a ground rule for its success must be to maintain focus on the desired outcomes (Zachary, 2000). Another emphasis is provided by Lasley (1996): "The crucial characteristic of mentors is the ability to communicate their belief that a person is capable of transcending present challenges and of accomplishing great things in the future" (p. 66).

Berl (1997), who works with corporate child-care centers, says that the ingredients of success in mentoring partnerships include trust, autonomy, time, mutual affinity, descriptive feedback, risk taking (i.e., encouragement to explore alternative ways of achieving goals), two-way communication, and life cycle. The last point emphasizes the mentoring sequence over time, a sequence that includes introductions, trust building, skill development, problem solving, and eventual conclusion: "The long range goal ... is for the [partner] to acquire the skills of analysis and goal setting and, ultimately, the capability of independent reflection and self-evaluation" (p. 38).

In its training meetings, StoryQUEST (Knapp-Philo & Stice, 2003a) asked peer mentors what makes a good mentor. Their answers included the following statements:

- "The mentor really listened."
- "The mentor did not express judgment."
- "The mentor had plenty of time for us to talk."
- "The mentor really cared whether or not I learned the new thing."
- "The mentor expressed pride in my achievements and confidence in my ability to grow."
- "The mentor and I developed a positive working relationship."
- "The mentor didn't let anything, such as gender or previous education or cultural difference, get in the way."
- "The mentor and I had agreed on what we would do together so we had common expectations for how to spend our time."

Rowley (1999) developed a related list based on his research:

- A good mentor is committed to the role of mentoring.
- A good mentor is accepting of a beginner's effort.
- A good mentor is skilled at providing instructional support.
- A good mentor is effective in different interpersonal contexts.
- A good mentor is a model of continuous learning.
- A good mentor communicates hope and optimism.

One way to personalize this discussion is to reflect on mentors who have encouraged the reader to adopt new ideas and ways of acting. What type of mentoring relationship occurred: informal mentoring or formal mentoring (the latter of which involves either peer mentoring or expert–novice mentoring)? What qualities characterize the individual who provided the mentoring? How did that individual cause the reader to feel during the process? How did the mentor explain or demonstrate new skills? What actions helped or harmed the relationship and the learning? How much support and which kinds of support were provided by an outside entity such as an employer, family support group, or professional organization? The next section will describe various ways to individualize a mentoring relationship.

This Partnership Is Special!

Every mentoring dyad is unique, based on the individual characteristics of the partners, the setting, the scheduled duration, the issues undertaken, and the external supports provided. However, several factors—including the motivation, skills, and relative ages and roles of the partners—call for certain mentoring strategies. These factors will be discussed below.

Issues of Dependency and Skill Level

Fostering confidence in one's own ability to encourage early language and literacy through proven strategies must be a goal of the mentorship for both partners. The dependency of one on the other is not a desired outcome of the process! Nevertheless, people who are accustomed to receiving "the right answers" or acting in ways discredited by research will need to gradually learn to voice more effective, evidence-based strategies. They will want to reflect on critical events, develop more appropriate responses, and trust their own more facilitative actions.

Needless to say, a competent mentor adjusts mentoring style to the motivation and skill level of the partner and changes in response to the partner's ongoing growth. Eaton and Johnson (2001) divided mentees into four groups and provided suggestions for mentors who have mentees with different levels of motivation and skill. These four groups are discussed below.

Low will–low skill. Try to learn why the individual entered into this mentoring relationship around early language and literacy. Most likely, the motivation will be voiced as a desire to help children develop in positive ways, perhaps, for them eventually to become ready for success in kindergarten. Build on this motivation, and begin the relationship with the goal of satisfying that desire. Determine obstacles to progress toward the agreed-on goal and address them. Plan to commit considerable time and support in this effort, and provide clear directions. Tout and celebrate even the smallest accomplishments.

High will–low skill. Guide the partner specifically to build new skills and set achievable goals to build confidence and then gradually encourage the individual to offer greater self-guidance. Celebrate small successes.

Low will–high skill. Affirm the importance of the partner's actions to developing language and literacy in the infants and toddlers in his care. Be sure to sufficiently challenge him with new ideas, strategies, or skills. Seek to connect with the mentee's personal goals, and determine ways to excite the individual about new challenges. Focus on building a personal relationship of optimism and trust, especially related to the importance of early language and literacy.

High will–high skill. Encourage the mentoring partner by mutually identifying challenges and opportunities that, for the mentee, can apply in the future— either personally or professionally. Spend time listening to the partner's ideas, reflections, opinions, and expansions on familiar applications of early language and literacy opportunities, and ask probing questions to take the application to a higher level of skill. Sometimes it is sufficient to appreciate and get out of the way as the mentee soars to unforeseen heights.

Effect of Previous Professional Experience

Lilian Katz (1972) proposed four stages of preschool teacher development:

- Stage 1—the survival stage, when a new teacher is struggling with pressures of time, inadequacy, and the conflict between idealism and the pressures of reality.

- Stage 2—the consolidation stage, when a reflective person combines learnings from the first year and begins to differentiate skills to learn and tasks to master.

- Stage 3—the renewal stage, when the professional may begin to tire of repeating the same activities and seek innovations.

- Stage 4—the maturity stage, when the professional has come to terms with the job and asks deeper and more abstract questions.

Based on the author's experience, mentoring to encourage beginning language and literacy with infants and toddlers in diverse settings can be effective at any one of these levels and with family mentoring as well as professional mentoring. However, the content and style of the mentoring always need to be adapted to the people, situation, and participants' personal goals.

Issues of Life Events

In professional mentorship (as opposed to parent-to-parent relationships), Cohen (2001) pointed to life stage—another element that often affects the individualization of mentoring. (By life stage, we mean the family and other external responsibilities of a mentoring partner that may hinder or enhance motivation for developmental opportunities). Especially vulnerable to life stage influences, according to Cohen, are professionals in their late 20s and 30s who have young children and those in their 50s who are beginning to anticipate retirement and are expanding their nonprofessional interests. Additionally, individuals who are "mellow" in their profession may be slower to adopt new ideas and strategies. Cohen suggests pairing persons for mentoring who can empathize with one another in terms of personal and professional life stage.

Similar challenges may arise in family-to-family mentoring in which family members support others to develop high-quality beginning language and literacy skills to use with their children. The family-to-family relationship and enjoyable incidents that result from their partnership can motivate family participants to continue working together and trying new early literacy strategies with their infants and toddlers. Evidence of success with the new strategies is a powerful motivator of behavior change when mentees see progress that they admire. Enhancing motivation is yet another reason to celebrate accomplishments.

Developing a Formal Mentoring System

Formal mentoring systems can contribute significantly to efforts by a family support group, agency, or community to enhance among family members, seasoned professionals, and "new hires" the attitudes and skills for fostering beginning language and literacy. In a peer mentoring model, families can mentor other families, caregivers can mentor their peers, and administrators can mentor administrators. In an expert–novice model, formal mentoring can be reserved for people coming to new positions, roles, or services; it can be expanded to include anyone who wants to acquire and systematically practice new skills with critical support from a colleague; or it can become part of an agency's comprehensive staff development and evaluation plan. Only a few people may be involved, or many may participate. In formal mentoring, the commitment of the mentoring partners is usually for a significant period of time—often 6 to12 months or even more. This degree of commitment required, in addition to agency policies, is likely to influence the number of individuals who choose to become involved. Formal mentoring implies a system wherein all parties share similar expectations for process and desired outcomes. The degree of specificity to be provided by the agency depends on the size, history, and potential outcomes of the mentoring relationships (for more information, see Zachary, 2000, or Head Start Bureau, 2001).

Matching of Mentoring Partners

Pairs of mentors who are working in a formal mentoring system to enhance early language and literacy outcomes may come from within an agency or family group or from outside of it. Organizations choose mentoring partners in various ways (Head Start Bureau, 2001):

- Pairs volunteer together.

- Individuals who volunteer are subsequently matched with mentoring partners by administrators or group leaders.

- Individuals are invited to participate because of particular competencies or a potential learning style match with specific potential partners.

- Supervisors decide or are assigned to mentor their supervisees (see Knapp-Philo & Flynn, this volume, p. 353).

When mentoring partners choose one another, there is likely to be a personal affinity, though not necessarily an ability to address professional development needs. When partners are assigned, an administrator can match strengths with needs but may not anticipate differences in attitudes or working styles (Zachary, 2000).

Planning by Mentorship Pairs

In some agencies, including most mental health settings and many home visiting programs, employees participate in formal mentoring relationships as a condition of their employment that needs to support continuous professional growth. In other settings, the duration of the mentoring relationship is time limited. Whichever is the case, proponents of formal mentoring systems unanimously and firmly endorse the importance of a contract, plan, or agreement that defines goals and activities for the partners (Eaton & Johnson, 2001; Head

Start Bureau, 2001; Zachary, 2000). Together, the partners create an overall plan for the duration of the mentorship and for flexible goals related to each session. Repeated clarification of *flexibility* reiterates that formal mentorship is not a counseling session but, rather, an ongoing professional development experience in which both partners are accountable for achieving specified outcomes (Zachary, 2000). The paragraphs below describe the importance of each stage of the mentoring process.

Planning. Setting, monitoring, and maintaining timelines for the long-term plan and individual mentoring sessions are important for the success of a formal mentorship. Otherwise, meetings can be readily postponed, and interactions can wander off track and miss their essential purposes. In non-supervisory mentoring, both partners need to be continually aware that their learning relationship has a start and a finish and defined work for which they will be accountable to one another and perhaps to others. In supervisory mentoring, the mentoring plan and timelines will typically be written into the employee's annual plan.

Measuring progress. The mentoring partners should be expected to conduct each scheduled session with an agenda of what is to be discussed and to end it with a review of what has been accomplished, future actions to be taken, and responsibilities for next steps. Achievements related to mentoring goals are noted regularly, perhaps in a portfolio. In addition, the employer or mentoring facilitator may request periodic reports or evaluations that may concern either process or outcomes or both. Both participants in a mentoring relationship need to be intentional in monitoring their own changes in attitudes and skills and incorporating their observations about progress into the reflection process (Eaton & Johnson, 2001; Fenichel, 1992; Zachary, 2000).

Coming to closure. The facilitator of the mentoring system can support participants by insisting on a stop date as part of the agreed-on timeline for developing language and literacy facilitation skills. The process of bringing a relationship to closure can evoke a variety of emotions: discomfort, anxiety, fear, disappointment, relief, grief, fear of separation, joy, or excitement (Zachary, 2000). Usually some issues remain as the mentoring partners move toward ending their formal relationship. Some partners avoid closure because they fear to hurt or offend the other, they fear inadequacy apart from the mentoring relationship, or they just plain enjoy the learning relationship and want it to continue. System administrators can assist the concluding session or sessions by emphasizing that a personal relationship can continue even after the professional mentoring relationship ends.

In ongoing, supervisory mentoring partnerships, the system should require a date when each goal will be achieved and when the mentoring relationship will move on to another goal. Following this process of results-oriented planning will visibly support the agency's emphasis on continuous improvement.

On occasion, mentoring partnerships end unexpectedly because one of the party is transferred or becomes ill or because the institution is realigned. Even in situations of this nature, it is helpful to plan at least one concluding session to honor the effort of the participants, reflect on accomplishments, express mutual appreciation, plan the next steps that each individual will take independently, and celebrate achievements (Eaton & Johnson, 2001; Zachary, 2000).

Sometimes, a mentoring relationship ends awkwardly because of a breach of confidence, the feeling of one party that "this isn't working," or time pressures. Nevertheless, Zachary (2000) encourages partners to meet, review achievements, and wish each other future success. Closure brings the opportunity for both mentoring partners to move on.

Evaluating the Mentorship System

Developing and maintaining a formal mentoring system for a specific purpose such as increasing the commitment and competence of families or staff in encouraging early literacy practices has its costs. Thus, the facilitators of the system must periodically determine whether this approach is accomplishing its goals (Head Start Bureau, 2001). Brief surveys of participants and—in the case of staff, surveys of their supervisors—can yield general information. Anecdotal logs and participant evaluations can provide clues en route. Interviews or focus groups with representative participants can reveal outcomes. Reflective use of evaluation results can be used to take local emergent literacy practices to a higher level. In addition to providing the information that the program or early literacy campaign needs to make decisions about future policies, this type of deliberative evaluation models the reflective practice required of the participants in the mentoring program.

Conclusion

Mentoring—informal or formal, peer or expert–novice, professional or cultural—provides a valuable way for family members, care providers, administrators, and community members to develop, reflect on, and practice new ideas and skills related to language and literacy with infants and toddlers and their families. Mentoring fosters the development of new understandings, skills, and confidence, and it enables mentoring partners to observe children closely as well as delight in enhanced early learning as result of improved caregiving practices. Mentoring fosters the application of critical skills, including those presented in more traditional pedagogical settings (Knapp-Philo & Stice, 2003a; Spencer & Logan, 2003). As a result of these potential benefits, mentoring offers an individualized adult learning tool that helps participants shape a positive social and physical learning context for infants' and toddlers' language and literacy development.

Appendix

Planning Peer Mentoring

Signatures of peers   Date signed

_____   _____

_____   _____

_____   _____

_____   _____

Purpose for peer mentoring:_____

_____

_____

Schedule for peer mentoring meetings:

Issues we will work on together	Steps we will take	Start date	Completion date

Peer-Mentoring: Building and Maintaining Your Partnership

Agree on the goals of your partnership.

1. Be sure that you both understand what the other expects.

2. Talk about your goals and expectations for peer-mentoring in the beginning and revisit them often.

3. Agree on how you will know when you have succeeded.

Communicate openly and often.

1. Determine a schedule for communicating and meeting and stick to it!

2. Be specific in your requests of one another.

3. Address and solve problems directly when they arise.

4. Identify who is responsible for what.

Make a commitment to peer-mentoring and honor it.

1. Honor the times you have set to meet.

2. Be persistent, but not annoying, in following up on unfulfilled commitments by your partner.

3. Be flexible, but fulfill your commitments.

4. Set clear timelines and meet them.

Ask for support and help when you need it.

1. When challenges arise and you are stuck, ask for help.

2. Recognize that someone else can provide new insight or suggestions.

3. Take the initiative to move forward.

Parts of this appendix were adapted from Knapp-Philo & Stice (2003b) and National Mentoring Center (n.d.).

References

Alberts, V., & McKenzie, A. (2001a). *Cultural mentor handbook.* Developed from a workshop conducted in Townsland, North Queensland, Australia. Retrieved August 14, 2004, from www.racgp.au/downloads/pdf/20030115nationalguidelines.pdf

Alberts, V., & McKenzie, A. (2001b). *National guidelines for the development of indigenous cultural mentors.* Developed from a workshop conducted in Townsland, North Queensland, Australia. Retrieved July 10, 2004, from www.weftweb.net/naccho/Files/Guidelines_for_the_development_of_Cultural_Mentors_-_Sarah_A_version.doc

Association for Supervision and Curriculum Development. (2004). *Exploring mentoring.* Retrieved August 10, 2004, from http://www.ascd.org/cms/index.cfm?TheViewID=867&topnav=1

Bellm, D., Whitebook, M., & Hnatiuk, P. (1997). *The early childhood mentoring curriculum: A handbook for mentors.* Washington, DC: Center for the Child Care Workforce.

Berl, P. (1997). Teachers coaching teachers: Development from within. In R. Neugebauer and B. Neugebauer (Eds.), *Does your team work? Ideas for bringing your staff together* (pp. 36–39). Redmond, WA: Child Care Information Exchange Press.

Boreen, J., & Niday, D. (2003). *Mentoring across boundaries: Helping beginning teachers succeed in challenging situations.* Portland, ME: Stenhouse.

Bronson, M. B. (2000). *Self-regulation in early childhood: Nature and nurture.* New York: Guilford.

Cohen, L. A. (2001). *Supporting teachers – nourishing inexperienced teachers to reach maturity.* Workshop presented at National Association for the Education of Young Children, Anaheim, CA.

Cultural Mentor Service [Electronic Version]. (2004). South Yorkshire, UK: Development Education Centre. Retrieved July 14, 2004, from http://www.decsy.org.uk/culturalmentor.asp

Daloz, L. A. (1999). *Mentor: Guiding the journey of adult learners.* San Francisco: Jossey-Bass.

Delgado, M. (1999). Lifesaving 101: How a veteran teacher can help a new beginner. *Educational Leadership, 56*(8), 27–29.

Eaton, J., & Johnson, R. (2001). *Coaching successfully.* London: Dorling Kindersley.

Fenichel, E. (1992). *Learning through supervision and mentorship to support the development of infants, toddlers, and their families: A sourcebook.* Arlington, VA: ZERO TO THREE National Center for Clinical Infant Programs.

Green, B., & Vann, B. (2003, November). *Developing culturally competent SLPs.* Paper presented at the conference of the American Speech Language Association, Chicago, IL. Retrieved August 16, 2004, from www.asha.org/NR/rdonlyres/8845CA38-F0FS-4361-9043-52E3DAC10/0/36

Head Start Bureau (Developed by American Institutes for Research). (2001). *Putting the PRO in protégé: A guide to mentoring in Head Start and Early Head Start.* Washington, DC: Department of Health and Human Services, Administration for Children and Families, Administration on Children, Youth, and Families.

Irish Museum of Modern Art. (2004). *Exhibition of 20th century European painting at the Irish Museum of Modern Art.* Retrieved July 10, 2004, from http://www.modernart.ie/News/PressOffice.asp?id=117

Jones, W., & Lorenzo-Hubert, I. (2006). Culture and parental expectations for child development: Concerns for language development and early learning. In S. E. Rosenkoetter & J. Knapp-Philo (Eds.), *Learning to read the world: Language and literacy in the first three years* (pp. 187–214). Washington, DC: ZERO TO THREE Press.

Katz, L. G. (1972). Developmental stages of preschool teachers. *Elementary School Journal, 73*(1), 50–54.

Knapp-Philo, J., & Flynn, A. (2006). Leading the way to quality: The importance of supervisory support. In S. E. Rosenkoetter & J. Knapp-Philo (Eds.), *Learning to read the world: Language and literacy in the first three years* (pp. 353–368). Washington, DC: ZERO TO THREE Press.

Knapp-Philo, J., & Stice, K. (2003a). *StoryQUEST 1: Celebrating beginning language and literacy.* Rohnert Park: California Institute on Human Services at Sonoma State University.

Knapp-Philo, J., & Stice, K. (2003b). *StoryQUEST 2: Celebrating beginning language and literacy.* Rohnert Park: California Institute on Human Services at Sonoma State University.

Kubicek, L. F. (2002). Fresh perspectives on young children and family routines. *Zero to Three, 22*(4), 4–9.

Kubicek, L. F. (2006). Encouraging language and literacy through family routines. In S. E. Rosenkoetter & J. Knapp-Philo (Eds.), *Learning to read the world: Language and literacy in the first three years* (pp. 163–186). Washington, DC: ZERO TO THREE Press.

Lasley, T. (1996). Mentors: They simply believe. *Peabody Journal of Education, 71*(1), 64–70.

Lyon, C. R. (2000). *Cultural mentors: Using transformative learning theory to examine adaptation and supporting relationships of women educators in cross-cultural settings.* Paper presented at the Adult Education Research Conference, Vancouver, BC. Retrieved August 27, 2004, from http://www.edst.educ.ubc.ca/aerc/2000/ab2000.htm

Mink, O. G., Owen, K. Q., & Mink, B. P. (1993). *Developing high performance people: The art of coaching.* Reading, MA: Addison Wesley.

National Mentoring Center. (n.d.). Good practices in building and maintaining partnerships. In *Strengthening mentoring programs training curriculum. Module 4: Forming and maintaining partnerships* (pp. 27–30). Retrieved August 14, 2004, from http://www.nwrel.org/mentoring/pdf/Mod4.PDF

National Research Council, & Institute of Medicine. (2000). *From neurons to neighborhoods: The science of early childhood development* (J. P. Shonkoff & D. A. Phillips, Eds.). Committee on Integrating the Science of Early Childhood Development; Board on Children, Youth, and Families; Commission on Behavioral and Social Sciences and Education. Washington, DC: National Academy Press.

Random House Dictionary, The. (1980). New York: Ballantine Books.

Rowley, J. B. (1999). The good mentor. *Educational Leadership, 56*(8), 20–22.

Spencer, S. S., & Logan, K. R. (2003). Bridging the gap: A school-based staff development model that bridges the gap from research to practice. *Teacher Education and Special Education, 26*(1), 51–62.

Strong, L. L., Lusardi, M., Emery, M., & Tallant, B. (2000, June). Decreasing health disparities of older Hispanic populations: An interdisciplinary service learning course on Spanish language, culture, and health concepts. Paper presented at the conference of the American Physical Therapy Association, Indianapolis, IN. Retrieved August 14, 2004, from http://apta.confex.com/apha/128a.m./techprogram/paper_8217.htm/

Tertell, E. A., Klein, S. M., & Jewett, J. L. (1998). *When teachers reflect: Journeys toward effective, inclusive practice.* Washington, DC: National Association for the Education of Young Children.

White, L. E. (2001). Raced histories, mother friendships, and the power of care: Conversations with women in project Head Start. *Chicago-Kent Law Review, 76*(3), 1569–1603.

You, H. K., Rosenkoetter, S. E., & Zvonkovic, A. (2006). *The more the wheat ripens, the lower it hangs its head: Korean American mothers' humbling experiences related to their children's disabilities.* Manuscript submitted for publication.

Zachary, L. J. (2000). *The mentor's guide: Facilitating effective learning relationships.* San Francisco: Jossey-Bass.

CHAPTER 19

Resources to Promote Early Language and Literacy

Kimberly Stice and Tarima Levine

Resource: Something that can be used for support or help and drawn upon when needed.
—The American Heritage Dictionary of the English Language (2000)

Resource: The finances, personnel, time, and other considerations necessary to carry out a program.
—Stephen L. Walter (1999)

Where do we get the resources? is one of the first questions that early education and care program leaders ask as they plan to expand or improve infant–toddler services. Finding extra resources to enhance programs and achieve new outcomes often seems overwhelming for programs that already have tight budgets.

The good news is that programs can expand early language and literacy opportunities with little or no financial cost. Indeed, because early language and literacy experiences occur within high-quality adult–child relationships, most resources can come from families and staff members within the program rather than from additional external resources. Community partners and the Internet provide additional resources at limited cost.

Because early language and literacy fundamentally develop through children's nurturing relationships and interactions with family members and caregivers, the primary resource in any infant–toddler program is caring staff members who are intentional and strategic about fostering early language and literacy.

Other resources for programs include the families of enrolled children, community members, children's books and other classroom materials, and informational material for adults such as books, journals, scientific reports, and the Internet. This chapter will discuss ways that early education and care programs can use each of these kinds of resources to enhance their beginning language and literacy efforts for infants and toddlers.

Staff as a Resource

The human mind is our fundamental resource.
—President John F. Kennedy

Because adults play the integral role in a child's language development, it is vital that their language strategies be optimal. In a caregiving or home visiting program, management and supervisory staff members have the responsibility to support direct-service providers to provide quality experiences that foster language and early literacy skills and that help family members do the same.

When seeking to enhance beginning language and literacy efforts, administrators should first assess the current practices and values in use by the children's families, their caregivers, and their community at large and then build on the existing attitudes, knowledge, and skills with additional information, supportive supervision, and a sustained emphasis on early language and literacy throughout the program. Ask: Do caregivers and home visitors know how to encourage give-and-take within interactions? Are they expanding on an infant's or toddler's verbal and nonverbal communications to continue each conversation? Do the children feel heard and valued when they speak? Are the babies and young children in the care of caregivers and home visitors learning the dynamics of interaction? Are the adults using and practicing purposeful language as well as providing rich experiences with words to build a foundation for literacy for the children? Are staff members repeating a baby's sounds, asking questions about objects or the child's environment, and raising voice pitch to catch a young child's interest and encourage interaction? Are staff members using strategies regularly and intentionally to expand each child's exposure to language? Once the assessment of current practices and skills is complete, a training plan should be developed and implemented.

Because staff skills are vital to effectively fostering beginning language and literacy, staff development should be ongoing. It must include both new and experienced staff members so all can learn new skills, refresh old ideas, and practice and master them with the support of their colleagues and supervisors (Knapp-Philo & Stice, 2003a, 2003b). Make staff development an opportunity for caregivers to learn about a variety of research-based language and literacy topics, reflect on their practice, and make improvements in their interactions with children and families. This kind of approach sets a tone of continuous improvement throughout the program.

Staff development should be thoughtful, strategic, and delivered according to a specific training plan (Sparks & Hirsh, 1997). Whether comprehensive or specific, the plan should grow from a multifaceted statement of individual staff members' needs. When planning staff development, consider three aspects of a training plan: the content, the learning outcomes, and the design of the training itself. In our experience, a not uncommon approach is to focus staff development planning on only content and avoid how that content is to be taught or what specific results are expected. All three elements are equally important and should be given equal weight in the planning process (Sparks & Hirsh, 1997). For example, by clearly stating the learning outcomes for each training session and how those fit together, planners can ensure they achieve what they are setting out to accomplish. In addition, when the outcomes are clearly stated, both those initiating the training and those attending know what to expect, can contribute to the learning process, and can evaluate and intentionally apply what they have learned (Sexton et al., 1996). In addition, clear learning outcomes connect to the needs assessment and help to justify costs associated with staff development experiences.

Teaching staff members how to use everyday language and literacy from the "tools of literacy" found in the environment can occur in informal settings. These new skills will encourage meaningful adult–child interactions and language growth at no extra cost to the program (see Notari-Syverson, this volume, p. 61). For example, in preparing a child to go outside, the caregiver can talk about the child's fluffy coat, how her shoes are red just like the child's shirt, what the weather will be like outside, what to take outside, and what the child might do with the toy she is taking. These examples from an everyday activity promote language and literacy at no extra cost to the program. Although modeling by an administrator can contribute to the training effort, there are times when formal education needs to be part of a staff development program.

When planning formal training, whether day long or brief as during naptime, consider how to use the strategies that support adults to learn (Brookfield, 1986), appeal to their diverse learning styles, and use a variety of approaches such as reading, viewing audiovisual presentations, demonstrations, minilectures, discussions, observations, applications, mentoring, and reflective supervision (Fenichel, 1992; Knapp-Philo, Corso, Brekken, & Bair Heale, 2004). Senge et al. (1999) note the need to tie professional development to everyday issues and needs with the attending staff members, especially when seeking to promote behavior change.

Professional education with respect to early language and literacy can be implemented in a variety of formats. A *text-based study group* is a form of staff development where participants meet in small or large groups based on topics or work assignments while a facilitator leads a discussion of a chapter, article, or newspaper story. A facilitator, who may be a member of the group, offers questions to help participants extract main ideas, connect the material to past experiences, and consider ways to apply the concepts to members' work with infants, toddlers, and families. In a Connecticut Head Start program, staff members developed written action plans based on their readings, which then served as a concrete way to process new knowledge and apply it to their practice. Follow-up, including class observations, feedback, and individual meetings, carried principles from the group work into the classroom.

Another form of staff development includes *large group sessions.* In large group training, the facilitator must ensure that the various experience levels among the staff members are accommodated. One strategy is to use multiple methods to help a diverse group apply the information. For example, while new staff members are practicing ways to incorporate new practices into their repertoires, experienced staff members might work on explaining the strategies and giving examples to parents or volunteers. Key themes might include literacy skills developed in the first 3 years of life (Snow, Burns, & Griffin, 1998), strategies for turntaking (MacDonald, 2001), ways that infants and toddlers communicate their preferences, the use of the tools of literacy to support beginning language and literacy (Knapp-Philo & Stice, 2003a), dialogic reading strategies (Knapp-Philo & Stice, 2003b), language- and literacy-rich environments (Hart & Risley, 1995), positive versus commanding language (Hart & Risley, 1995), and opportunities for practice in varied settings (Knapp-Philo et al., 2004; Winton, 1990).

Caregivers can also learn a great deal about fostering early language and literacy from one another. During meetings, lunch breaks, or at the beginning or end of the day, caregivers can exchange ideas and materials with their colleagues. For example, at the Bank Street Family Center in New York City, caregivers frequently visit one another's classrooms for 5 minutes in the morning to see what activities are available for the day. During this calm time before the children arrive, caregivers can share literacy ideas and materials such as books, soft blocks with pictures, homemade instruments, felt board stories, multicultural songs, recipes for sensory experiences, and accommodations for children who speak a second language or those with special needs. Administrators have a key role in supporting and nurturing this kind of exchange in which all staff members are joined in an effort to improve continuously.

Visits to neighboring infant–toddler programs can be another effective method of staff development. At the Bank Street Family Center, teachers go in small groups to observe various child-care programs in the morning. Before the visit, caregivers are briefed on areas to notice during the visit, such as adult–child interactions or environmental design. In the afternoon, the caregivers come together, share their observations and reflections, and make suggestions for improvement in their own settings. Organizing such efforts requires a commitment on the part of the program. There are ways of cutting costs, such as having administrators cover for staff members while they are out of the classroom for short periods. In addition, interactive training approaches such as program visits are beneficial because they are a forum for dialogue and team building (Thorp & McCollum, 1988).

Regardless of format, an integral component of staff development is follow-up after the training. Staff members need time to practice new strategies learned during trainings and reflect on their experiences during discussions with supervisors. As discussed in Knapp-Philo and Flynn (this volume, p. 353), reflective supervision (Fenichel, 1992) provides the opportunity to support a culture of continuous improvement in encouraging language and literacy. It also allows caregivers to customize their learning opportunities. It is essential for administrators to observe regularly, support, and provide feedback to staff members on new or expanded skills.

Systems whereby staff members provide ongoing coaching to one another as they strive to master and incorporate new skills into their repertoire can also be highly productive and fun. Staff members who work with young children and families in their homes may be particularly challenged to find time to exchange resources and information with their colleagues. Team meetings, scheduled phone calls, and activity logs are avenues to bridging potential communication gaps among home-based staff members.

Families as a Resource

Family members are invaluable resources as they share with caregivers their children's interests, learning styles, preferences, temperaments, and language and literacy milestones. By initiating conversation and seeking information about families' and children's interests, caregivers simultaneously build relationships and gather useful learning resources. The goals offered by families provide caregivers with topics for meaningful, individualized literacy opportunities for infants and toddlers. For example, a caregiver in a child-care center learned that the mother of a newly enrolled child with Down syndrome was especially concerned about the child's drooling and her future ability to speak. This mother wanted the caregiver to attend to her daughter's oral-motor skills during the period that the speech therapist was primarily working with the child's expressive language. The caregiver gathered suggestions from the speech therapist and implemented oral-motor experiences within the daily routines. She introduced crunchy foods and straws at snack time, offered tooth brushing after meals, invited all the children to blow bubbles, and sang nursery songs that required various mouth movements. In addition, all the adults in the setting consistently matched their vocabulary to their actions, promoting the child's language and literacy development. As time passed and the child became a full participant in group play, she learned to control her drooling, and she shared her newly acquired signs (which she had learned from the speech therapist) with all the other children. By the end of her time in the classroom, she was making verbal approximations as she signed and sang, and all the children could sign their names, the names of common animals, and words in their daily routines. Without using the mother as a resource, the staff members of this program would have been less effective in serving this child, and the other children in her group would have missed out on rich learning experiences about communication.

In addition to sharing information about their own children, families can also be a tremendous resource about a variety of other topics and ideas. Families can share information about their culture and cultural activities that they enjoy as well as suggest resources for materials, books in a variety of languages, and community agencies or individuals who can support children's efforts in beginning language and literacy. Families are often willing to offer materials for use in their children's program. For example, many infant–toddler centers place a drop box where parents can donate books, magazines, catalogs, and circulars, which are later used to make picture books, collages, environmental print displays, and games.

Another way to gather family literacy resources is to have a "family share night," where family members have the opportunity to talk about the games and sing the songs of their childhoods. Family members may be asked to complete simple surveys about their hobbies, skills, and interests, including questions like "Do you play an instrument? If so, would you be willing to play it at school?" or "Are you artistic? Would you be willing to create puppets or felt board stories?" A parent in an Early Head Start in New Jersey created a colorful mural in a basement room to create a bright, appealing space for children, families, and staff members.

Many families may wish to hear suggestions of how to incorporate more early language and literacy ideas at home. Identify the strategies that families are already using (such as responding to a baby's communication cues, reading bedtime stories, looking at magazines on the bus), and determine how parents and siblings are already helping their youngest children learn. Building on these ideas from families, home visitors, caregivers, and family advocates can explain how to use the same strategies in other settings and give families more ideas to use with their children as well as demonstrate how to use the tools of language and literacy in the family's everyday environments.

Community as a Resource

In addition to the resources in an infant–toddler program, numerous language and literacy resources are available throughout local communities. One important partner is the local library, which may host special child and family literacy programs that include or can be expanded to include activities for infants and toddlers. Often, communities have literacy programs for preschool children, school-age children, and adults but no literacy activities for infants and toddlers (see Deerr et al., this volume, p. 477). In these instances, develop a collaboration and support ways to include literacy information, activities, and ideas for infants and toddlers in the current efforts (see also Zukoski & Luluquisen, this volume, p. 429). Supplementing a current program enables growth in the existing community programs, which often have the ability to reach a larger target audience, and provides early care and education with a needed resource.

Begin locating additional community resources by talking to families and friends, looking through the telephone book's yellow pages, perusing Head Start's community services directory, or exploring the neighborhood with early literacy opportunities in mind. Community partners can provide volunteers, donations, or both and can help expand the opportunities available to the children and staff members to participate in new experiences that will foster vocabulary growth. Some potential resources include (a) health offices and clinics, (b) fraternal and civic organizations, (c) museums, (d) colleges and universities, (e) family literacy programs such as Even Start or those offered at the public library, (f) Head Start, (g) elementary, middle, and high schools, (h) local businesses, (i) social service agencies, (j) faith-based groups, and (k) community literacy efforts such as Read to Me, Raising a Reader, and Everyone's a Reader. Before visiting community resources to recruit collaboration, it may be helpful to know what the organization provides, how the infant–toddler program might assist, and what the specific needs are of the early care and education community.

Resources for Children

We have described people as the primary resource in developing early language and literacy, but materials are also valuable. Books and classroom materials help children make the print–idea connection. Scholarly reports, chapters, position papers, and books offer guidance to adults and pique their thinking about creative ways to reach infants and toddlers with language and literacy concepts. Examples from the wealth of good materials available appear below.

Children's Books

Books are an essential component of an infant–toddler literacy program. Books should be varied in content (e.g., families, animals, everyday activities), design (e.g., homemade, textured, board, cloth), and style (e.g., real pictures, rhymes, story plot), and they should reflect the various cultural and linguistic groups in the community. Programs working with babies and families should remember to include books for adults as well as those appropriate for infants and toddlers, so both adults and children see that reading for pleasure is something that people can do at any age.

There are various inexpensive ways to collect books for an infant–toddler program.

1. Donations can come from a variety of places and people, including contributions from families of enrolled children or alumni; faith-based organizations; local businesses; local schools and universities; community book drives; charitable organizations such as First Book, Inc.; fraternal organizations such as Delta Sigma Theta and Omega Psi Phi; and civic organizations such as the Association of Bilingual Educators, Kiwanis, and Volunteers for Literacy.

2. Discounts are often available to early care and education programs from local or large-chain new and used bookstores. Used but attractive books can often be obtained inexpensively from library sales and garage sales.

3. Grants from local, state, and national funders are available to support early language and literacy. More information about these types of resources can be found on the Internet. One example is Books for Kids. In New York, Books for Kids donated high quality books and organized the entire children's library collection.

Classroom Materials for Children

"You don't have to go out and buy anything special. It's just what is around in the environment," said Deb Obermiller (quoted in Porter & Christian, 2004),

Education Coordinator of Central Nebraska Early Head Start. Although early care and education programs must consciously plan to provide literacy-rich opportunities for infants and toddlers (see DeMartini, this volume, p. 309), they do not necessarily have to acquire many expensive or special materials. Infants and toddlers learn language and literacy when adults provide words to accompany daily experiences, when children are given the time to think about and label these varied experiences, and when infants and toddlers regularly enjoy stories, songs, and books. Expenditures on extensive early literacy curricula or equipment are unnecessary.

Sources of Information for Adults

Recent years have seen a proliferation of useful resources to help caregivers (a) understand the developmental process for early language and literacy, (b) learn developmentally appropriate approaches to use with infants and toddlers, and (c) help family members and caregivers grow in confidence and competence in their literacy interactions with very young children. Federal and state governments, foundations, professional organizations, and programs of all sorts have produced valuable materials. A few of the most noteworthy are listed in the sections that follow,[1] and many are available at no or little cost.

Reports and Position Papers

During the past 5 years, several blue ribbon panels of scientists, early childhood leaders, or both have summarized research findings with respect to the development of early language and literacy and the impediments to its success. Other panels have synthesized validated practices that support young children in their progress to become joyous learners and effective readers. These resources are valuable for understanding why implementing recommended practices is so significant for children's development.

The following list includes a helpful basic selection.

National Early Literacy Panel. (2004). *National Early Literacy Panel report.* Washington, DC: National Institute for Literacy.

---

[1] Contributors to these lists include Tarima Levine, Susan B. Neuman, Chris Payne, Marion O'Brien, Sharon Rosenkoetter, and Kimberly Stice.

National Research Council. (2001). *Eager to learn: Educating our preschoolers* (B. Bowman, M. Donovan, & M. Burns, Eds.). Committee on Early Childhood Pedagogy. Commission on Behavioral and Social Sciences and Education. Washington, DC: National Academy Press.

National Research Council, & Institute of Medicine. (2000). *From neurons to neighborhoods: The science of early childhood development* (J. P. Shonkoff & D. A. Phillips, Eds.). Committee on Integrating the Science of Early Childhood Development; Board on Children, Youth, and Families; Commission on Behavioral and Social Sciences and Education. Washington, DC: National Academy Press.

Neuman, S., Copple, C., & Bredekamp, S. (2000). Learning to read and write: Developmentally appropriate practices for young children [Expanded version of the Joint Position Statement of the International Reading Association and the National Association for the Education of Young Children]. Washington, DC: National Association for the Education of Young Children.

Snow, D. E., Burns, M. S., & Griffin, P. (Eds.), National Research Council, Committee on the Prevention of Reading Difficulties. (1998). *Preventing reading difficulties in young children.* Washington, DC: National Academies Press.

Articles and Chapters

A few significant research articles are cited again and again to inform practice. The following list includes some of them.

Britto, P. R., & Brooks-Gunn, J. (Eds.) (2001). The role of family literacy environments in promoting young children's emerging literacy skills. *New directions for child and adolescent development* (Vol. 92). San Francisco: Jossey-Bass.

Hirsch-Pasek, K., & Golinkoff, R. (with Eyer, D.). (2003). Language: The power of babble. *Einstein never used flash cards: How our children really learn— and why they need to play more and memorize less* (pp. 60–96). Emmaus, PA: Rodale.

Neuman, S. B. (1999). Books made a difference: A study of access to literacy. *Reading Research Quarterly, 34,* 286–311.

Regalado, M., Goldenberg, C., & Appel, E. (2001). Building community systems for young children: Reading and early literacy. In N. Halfon, E. Shulman, & M. Hochstein (Series Eds.), *Building community systems for young children*. Los Angeles: University of California–Los Angeles Center for Healthier Children, Families, and Communities.

Rosenkoetter, S. E., & Barton, L. R. (2002). Babies, young children, families, and literacy: Important routines that tie them together. *Zero to Three, 22*(4), 33–38.

Sexton, D., Snyder, P., Wolfe, B., Lobman, M., Stricklin, S., & Akers, P. (1996). Early intervention inservice training strategies: Perceptions and suggestions from the field. *Exceptional Children, 62*, 485–495.

Whitehurst, G. J., & Lonigan, C. J. (1998). Child development and emergent literacy. *Child Development, 69*, 848–872.

Books Exploring the Development of Language and Literacy

Understanding the research on effective language and literacy strategies can reinforce high-quality practices and provide a foundation for productive innovation. These books, some of which are presented in the following list, explore the basis of early learning and, especially, early language and literacy development.

deBoysson-Bardies, B. (1999). *How language comes to children: From birth to two years.* Cambridge, MA: MIT Press.

Gopnik, A., Meltzoff, A. N., & Kuhl, P. K. (1999). *The scientist in the crib: What early learning tells us about the mind.* New York: Perennial/HarperCollins.

Neuman, S. B., & Dickinson, D. (Eds.). (2001). *Handbook of early literacy research.* New York: Guilford.

Shatz, M. (1994). *A toddler's life: Becoming a person.* New York: Oxford University Press.

Van Kleeck, A., Stahl, S. A., & Bauer, E. B. (2003). *On reading books to children: Parents and teachers.* Mahwah, NJ: Erlbaum.

Zigler, E. F., Singer, D. G., & Bishop-Josef, S. J. (Eds.). (2004). *Children's play: The roots of reading.* Washington, DC: ZERO TO THREE Press.

Books Providing Guidance for Families and Caregivers

This list identifies books that present sound guidance for parents and other caregivers on supporting early literacy development.

Bardige, B., & Segal, M. (2004). *Building literacy with love: A guide for teachers and caregivers of children from birth through age 5.* Washington, DC: ZERO TO THREE Press.

Burns, M. S., Griffin, P., & Snow, C. E. (Eds.). (1999). *Starting out right: A guide to promoting children's reading success.* Washington, DC: National Academy Press.

Dickinson, D. K., & Tabors, P. O. (Eds.). (2001). *Beginning literacy with language: Young children learning at home and in school.* Baltimore: Paul H. Brookes.

Notari-Syverson, A., O'Connor, R. E., & Vadasy, P. F. (1998). *Ladders to literacy.* Baltimore: Paul H. Brookes.

Owocki, G. (1999). *Literacy through play.* Portsmouth, NH: Heinemann.

Owocki, G. (2001). *Make way for literacy! Teaching the way young children learn.* Portsmouth, NH: Heinemann; and Washington, DC: National Association for the Education of Young Children.

Schickedanz, J. A. (1999). *Much more than the ABCs: The early stages of reading and writing.* Washington, DC: National Association for the Education of Young Children.

The Internet as a Resource

The World Wide Web provides countless ideas to help families or caregivers enhance early language and literacy efforts, learn what other communities and programs are doing, and locate grants that might assist local efforts. Search engines such as Google, AltaVista, Ask Jeeves, and Yahoo, provide links to Web sites that match relevant key words and phrases. Users need to learn how to search by single words and multiple words to find resources. Any librarian can provide directions. Web users must realize that these search engines do not screen for quality or accuracy for entries on the Web; rather, anyone can post any commentary at will, regardless of how preposterous or inflated the claims may be. Given this lack of preposting review, the user must maintain skepticism about every entry and seek evidence of validation from a reputable organization or from additional research data.

In reviewing ideas presented on Web sites, consider the following questions:

- What is the evidence that this idea works and actually accomplishes the outcomes claimed?

- Is this activity one that our staff members or families would do or enjoy?

- Is this activity one that our agency or program could do?

- Does this idea or activity fit with the mission of our agency?

- What additional resources would it take to do this project?

- How much would this effort cost? Do we have the funding? If not, where could we get additional funds to support it?

- How long has this group been conducting the activity that is described?

- What evidence is there that it has made a difference for families or children? What evidence is there that the costs and claims are realistic?

- How could we adapt this resource to fit the needs of our community?

Remember that it may be easier to duplicate or adapt a program from another community or expand existing services within the community rather than to create something completely new. The keys to developing a successful early language and literacy program for infants and toddlers, regardless of sponsorship, lie in determining outcomes for the program's efforts, finding appropriate strategies that appeal to local families, formulating a plan, and arranging resources to help achieve the program goals.

Conclusion

Building resources for early language and literacy is an ongoing process integral to working with young children and their families. It is critical to focus on human resources as the most important part of any building of resources. Training, supervision, and support for early care and education staff members should be an ongoing process that supports the continuous improvement of individual staff members and the program as a whole. Families and communities are also essential resources for developing and enhancing beginning language and literacy opportunities. Finally, materials in the form of books for the children and updated research and professional information for staff members can be obtained from a variety of sources, including the World Wide Web. Early care and education programs should call on a variety of available resources to ensure that they are providing optimal opportunities for learning for infants, toddlers, and their families.

References

American Heritage dictionary of the English language, The (4th ed.). (2000). Boston: Houghton Mifflin. Retrieved March 6, 2004, from http://www.bartleby.com/61

Brookfield, S. (1986). *Understanding and facilitating adult learning: A comprehensive analysis of principles and effective practices.* San Francisco: Jossey-Bass.

Deerr, K., Feinberg, S., Gordon, E., & Schull, D. (2005). Libraries are family places for literacy and learning. In S. E. Rosenkoetter & J. Knapp-Philo (Eds.), *Learning to read the world: Language and literacy in the first three years* (pp. 477–498). Washington, DC: ZERO TO THREE Press.

DeMartini, T. (2006). Group environments that foster language and literacy. In S. E. Rosenkoetter & J. Knapp-Philo (Eds.), *Learning to read the world: Language and literacy in the first three years* (pp. 309–334). Washington, DC: ZERO TO THREE Press.

Fenichel, E. (1992). *Learning through supervision and mentorship.* Washington, DC: ZERO TO THREE National Center for Clinical Infant Programs.

Hart, B., & Risley, T. (1995). *Meaningful differences in the everyday experiences of young American children.* Baltimore: Paul H. Brookes.

Knapp-Philo, J., Corso, R. M., Brekken, L., & Bair Heale, H. (2004). Training to make and sustain change: The Hilton/Early Head Start Program. *Infants and Young Children, 17*(2), 171–183.

Knapp-Philo, J., & Flynn, A. (2006). Leading the way to quality: The importance of supervisory support. In S. E. Rosenkoetter & J. Knapp-Philo (Eds.), *Learning to read the world: Language and literacy in the first three years* (pp. 353–368). Washington, DC: ZERO TO THREE Press.

Knapp-Philo, J., & Stice, K. (Eds.). (2003a). *StoryQUEST 1: Celebrating beginning language and literacy* [Unpublished training manual]. Rohnert Park: California Institute on Human Services at Sonoma State University.

Knapp-Philo, J., & Stice, K. (Eds.).(2003b). *StoryQUEST 2: Celebrating beginning language and literacy* [Unpublished training manual]. Rohnert Park: California Institute on Human Services at Sonoma State University.

MacDonald, J. D. (2001). *Before your child talks.* Columbus, OH: Communication Partners.

Notari-Syverson, A. (2006). Everyday tools of literacy. In S. E. Rosenkoetter & J. Knapp-Philo (Eds.), *Learning to read the world: Language and literacy in the first three years* (pp. 61–80). Washington, DC: ZERO TO THREE Press.

Porter, J., & Christian, G. (Producers). (2004). *StoryQUEST: Tools of Literacy for Infants and Toddlers* [Videotape]. Rohnert Park: California Institute on Human Services at Sonoma State University.

Senge, P. M., Kleiner, A., Roberts, C., Ross, R., Roth, G., & Smith, B. (1999). *The dance of change: The challenges of sustaining momentum in learning organizations.* New York: Doubleday.

Sexton, D., Snyder, P., Wolfe, B., Lobman, M., Stricklin, S., & Akers, P. (1996). Early intervention inservice training strategies: Perceptions and suggestions from the field. *Exceptional Children, 62,* 485–495.

Snow, C., Burns, S., & Griffin, P. (Eds.). (1998). *Preventing reading difficulties in young children.* Washington, DC: National Academy Press.

Sparks, D., & Hirsh, S. (1997). *A new vision for staff development.* Alexandria, VA: Association for Supervision and Curriculum Development.

Thorp, E., & McCollum, J. (1988). Defining the infancy specialization in early childhood special education. In J. J. Gallagher, P. L. Hutinger, & M. B. Karnes (Eds.), *Early childhood special education: Birth to three* (pp. 147–162). Reston, VA: Council for Exceptional Children and the Division for Early Childhood.

Walter, S. (1999). Identifying resources needed for a literacy program. Retrieved April 2, 2004, from http://www.sil.org/lingualinks/literacy/planaliteracyprogram/identifyingresourcesneededfora.htm

Winton, P. (1990). A systematic approach for planning inservice training related to Public Law 99-457. *Infants and Young Children, 3,* 51–60.

Zukoski, A. P., & Luluquisen, E. M. (2006). Building community support for early literacy. In S. E. Rosenkoetter & J. Knapp-Philo (Eds.), *Learning to read the world: Language and literacy in the first three years* (pp. 429–454). Washington, DC: ZERO TO THREE Press.

CHAPTER 20

Continuing the Story: Sustaining Innovations

Joanne Knapp-Philo, Jerry Hindman, Kimberly Stice, and
Vicki L. Turbiville

*Our program had a 5-year grant, and we did some really great
work, but when the grant ended and we had no money to continue it, it all just went away. We did not know how to keep it
going. We had no strategies.*

—Early Childhood Program Administrator

All too often, innovative ideas and practices are introduced into early care and
education programs only to drift away after a key proponent leaves, the funding
ends, or the next good idea comes along. Making constructive change in organizations and sustaining the change have long been topics of discussion and
research in industry, education, government, and early childhood fields (Senge
et al., 1999).

Currently, we see a major focus on beginning language and literacy (Dickinson
& Tabors, 2001; Snow, Burns, & Griffin, 1998), a tremendous push to improve
literacy throughout the educational systems in this country (National Institute
of Child Health and Human Development, 2000; Whitehurst, 2001), and a
special emphasis on those serving our youngest children (Knapp-Philo &
Stice, 2004; Rosenkoetter & Barton, 2002). To ensure that the best of the new,
research-based language and literacy strategies are not abandoned, to be
replaced by another new initiative, leaders and staff members must make
explicit efforts to nurture the approaches that are working and to improve
them over time. This chapter presents a framework that can be used not only

to sustain innovative practice such as strategies for beginning language and literacy but also to develop, update, and modify an effective program in light of lessons learned from the past and new information that becomes available from research and practice. This chapter discusses six principles found to characterize organizations that have sustained change:

- Shared ownership and active involvement from all levels of the organization

- Understanding that a culture of continuous improvement leads to excellence

- Significant, reciprocal community collaborations and productive partnerships

- Time to plan and implement, to develop new skills and strategies, to practice, and to follow up

- Administrative support

- Idea of a clear purpose and direction

The authors will offer strategies that early care and education programs can use to implement each of the principles to sustain a focus on beginning language and literacy for infants and toddlers.

Six Principles of Sustainability

The nature of successful organizational change and the sustainability of innovations have been studied for decades (Buysse & Wesley, 1993; Fullan, 1993, 1999; Kanter, 1983; Senge, 1990; Senge et al., 1999; Vaughn, Klinger, & Hughes, 2000). Amid organizational differences and unique organizational cultures, common approaches have successfully maintained changed practices across many organizations. The authors of this chapter have identified six principles (listed above) noted in numerous studies of a variety of organizations, including schools, businesses, and human service agencies, that have institutionalized and sustained innovative practices. Although not exhaustive, these six research-based principles provide a solid framework for programs as they plan to sustain innovations in early language and literacy efforts.

All six principles of sustainability must be part of any effort to sustain innovation. There is no one right place to begin working on sustainability; no one

principle is more fundamental than another. What is critical is that every program develops a plan for sustaining an innovation and implement that plan in
a deliberate way, evaluating and adapting the plan as needed. Groups developing a sustainability plan should first select a principle they appreciate, introduce
strategies that put that principle into action, and then build gradually until various strategies address each of the six principles. The "wheel of sustainability"
(see Figure 20.1) visualizes the six principles. Each principle is part of the rim
of the wheel, and all are essential to ensure that the innovation "keeps on
rolling." Each principle will be discussed in turn.

Figure 20.1. StoryQUEST Sustainability

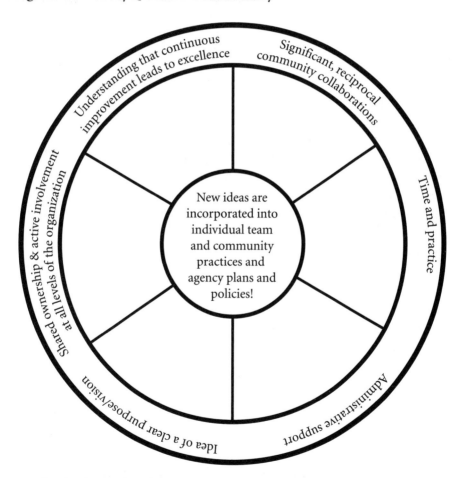

Reproduced with permission from StoryQUEST

Shared Ownership and Active Involvement From All Levels of the Organization

When all levels of the organization are actively involved in understanding the need for a change and then in planning and implementing it, the new practice is more likely to last (Buysse & Wesley, 1993; Fullan, 1999; *Hilton/Early Head Start Training Program, Five Year Summary Report*, 2002; Vaughan et al., 2000). Leaders must plan to ensure that each individual and group affected by a change are part of the innovation process. Such specific planning enables perspectives from all vantage points to guide the change and helps staff members understand the new practice and increase their commitment to it.

The levels of early childhood organization include families, direct caregivers, support staff members, leadership staff members, governing boards, and community partners (indeed, all the levels of the ecological model discussed in Rosenkoetter, this volume, p. 1). All of these groups need to be involved as any substantive change is planned, implemented, and sustained. When an early childhood program begins an initiative to focus on early language and literacy for infants and toddlers, it is necessary to involve families in understanding how children acquire language and literacy skills in the first 3 years of life, in supporting their children's development, in integrating this new focus into the program's existing curriculum and practices, and in reaping the benefits for themselves and their children. Families are also likely to want training about specific strategies that they can use at home. At the same time, staff members will need to

- be assured that the new effort is not a reflection on any weakness in their previous work,

- appreciate that much of what they are already doing is consistent with recommended practice,

- embrace the idea that the new focus will enable them to do better work with children without adding extra burdens,

- realize the power of intentionality as they plan consciously to support children's language and literacy development,

- learn new strategies and techniques,

- practice to develop new skills, and

- integrate the new ideas and practices into their daily routines.

Families and staff members who are part of the planning process, understand the justification for the innovations, and support the change are more apt to be ready to do the work that the new approach entails.

What does it look like when beginning language and literacy innovations have been sustained in an early care and education program that has shared ownership and active involvement for all levels of the organization? Knapp-Philo and Stice (2004) noted the following observations:

- Beginning language and literacy are reflected throughout the agency's systems, including hiring (interview questions and hiring preferences), new employee training, and staff evaluations.

- All staff members can clearly explain their unique roles in supporting a new initiative and can demonstrate exactly what it is they do.

- Families talk about new innovations such as the beginning language and literacy strategies they are using with their children and about books and stories their children enjoy.

- "Water cooler" discussions reflect staff members' interest in promoting new innovations.

- Classrooms and buildings are models of language- and literacy-rich environments.

- Adults consciously model literacy activities in front of children (taking notes during observations and reading aloud the menu at lunch).

- Administrators and supervisors regularly comment on the ways staff members and families are using specific techniques with children.

Understanding That a Culture of Continuous Improvement Leads to Excellence

Organizations that are open to new learning and possible changes are best positioned to sustain innovations (Kanter, 1983; Sprinthall & Sprinthall, 1980). In such organizations, lifelong learning is not only an individual experience but also a collective and culturally valued one that permeates the organization at all levels. Decisions are made after reflection, and actions are based on that reflection. In organizations that embrace a philosophy of continual improvement, leaders introduce and nurture new ideas, support an environment in which new ideas can grow and be refined by group thinking, and empower groups to take action (Knapp-Philo, 2001). Such organizations welcome new approaches, adopt appropriate change, and transform their operations as they assimilate new ideas and practices.

However, no innovation can, or should, be considered as state of the art forever. Learning is an ongoing process in which new information and ongoing experiences require individuals and organizations to reevaluate current practices continuously and initiate improvements as necessary (Fullan, 1993, 1999). As programs strive to sustain innovations in beginning language and literacy for infants and toddlers, they must also consider new ways, evaluate their impact on current practices, and make changes accordingly.

What does it look like when innovations in beginning language and literacy have been sustained in an infant–toddler program that embraces a culture of continuous improvement leading to excellence? Knapp-Philo and Stice (2004) noted the following observations:

- All families, staff members, and leaders are excited by new beginning language and literacy ideas and practices.

- Staff members at all levels of the program work purposefully and publicly to acquire new knowledge and skills to support beginning language and literacy.

- Staff members and administrators regularly talk about the new strategies they are learning, and they share their expertise daily.

- The program and its leaders have specific expectations, procedures, and supervisory practices that encourage people to develop, evaluate, and implement new ideas.

- There is an agency-wide, systematic approach to implementation, reflection, and evaluation of new ideas and practices for language and literacy with infants and toddlers and their families.

- Staff members throughout the organization regularly discuss problems about issues, curricular strategies, and ideas and then work together to solve them as they are implementing beginning language and literacy efforts.

- There is planned time for staff members to discuss new approaches and ideas.

Significant, Reciprocal Community Collaborations and Productive Partnerships

Community input, interaction, and support are essential components of organizational change (Buysse & Wesley, 1993). Fullan (1999) suggested that community collaboration encourages community-wide commitment to an organization's purposes and makes community support more likely in a time of need. Therefore, community collaboration is not only an intrinsic organizational need but also a political reality for early care and education programs, regardless of their source of funding. Organizations that wish to grow and change through their collaborations with "the outside world" must realize that their collaborators "are not in the business of doing them favors" (Fullan, 1999, p. 69). Indeed, collaborative relationships must involve mutual respect and influence and provide a win–win relationship for all. As in any relationship, one partner occasionally gives more than the other, but over time, each gets as much as it gives. Both parties should enter the collaboration prepared both to give and to receive.

Nevertheless, the concept of maintaining genuinely reciprocal relationships throughout their communities may be a paradigm shift for some infant–toddler programs that have traditionally viewed community collaborations as unidirectional, namely, as a way to receive services, materials, or other resources they do not have themselves. Knapp-Philo (2001) found that although some early childhood leaders approached potential collaborative relationships with a "what's-in-this-for-us?" attitude, others approached new opportunities prepared to give first and receive over time. Those administrators who entered relationships with a mindset to give first developed multiple, thriving collaborations of long standing that contributed in many planned and unplanned ways to each partner's work. On the other hand, those agencies that entered partnerships either primarily expecting to have their own needs met or notably feeling superior to others often reported that collaboration was difficult:

> [S]o I have to monitor what they are doing to make sure they understand what they have to do…so it's very challenging to get our partners to understand and communicate. (quoted in Knapp-Philo, 2001, p. 111)

Fullan (1999) observed that program leaders should reflect on their personal and organizational attitudes and avoid any tendency toward "self-sealing," which inhibits an agency's ability to grow and change and interferes with its ability to develop much-needed, productive partnerships.

What does it look like when innovations related to beginning language and literacy for infants and toddlers have been sustained in an early care and education program characterized by significant, reciprocal community collaborations and productive partnerships? Knapp-Philo and Stice (2004) noted the following observations:

- Collaborative partners share the responsibility for successes and failures.

- Day-to-day interactions reflect respect for fellow collaborators and a commitment to collaboration.

- Partner agencies publicly support one another's fundraising and other efforts to promote beginning language and literacy in their programs and community.

- Agency representatives go into collaboration prepared to share leadership and credit with all partners.

- Written policies reflect the vision and philosophy of reciprocal collaboration and commitment to beginning language and literacy.

- Memoranda of understanding that are written between organizations specifically describe their exchange of resources and a shared collaborative vision and philosophy that includes

    - staff input that is gathered from all relevant organizations when the agreement is being developed, revised, or both, and

    - training for staff members from each participating agency that addresses collaborative agreements and the specific procedures that affect them.

- Interagency relationships are maintained at all levels of each agency.

- Families and staff members at all levels of each agency embrace interagency efforts as well as welcome and benefit from the cross-pollination of ideas.

- Staff members meet for both social and professional purposes.

- Funding is shared to achieve shared visions and goals.

Time to Plan and Implement, to Develop New Skills and Strategies, to Practice, and to Follow Up

A new practice can often be put into action relatively quickly, but incorporating it throughout an organization takes much longer. It is well documented, though rarely acknowledged, that a major time commitment (usually 3 to 5 years) is required to institute and sustain substantive change (Fullan, 1993, 1999). Organizations that succeed in institutionalizing change efforts focus on mastery and allow enough time for skills to be developed and integrated (Kanter, 1983). Vaughn et al. (2000) noted that time constraints are an impediment when educational organizations try to sustain innovations.

Time must be considered whenever leaders attempt to institute new practices. Individuals require time to understand the need for change, to comprehend what they are implementing, to practice and master the new skills entailed, and to integrate the new skills into daily routines. Organizations need time to reframe their structures and processes to facilitate and support the change. They also must commit time to accommodate any unanticipated effects of the change (Deming, 1986). Finally, there must be time to evaluate the change, to make needed adaptations, and to evaluate the results.

Nonetheless, educational change efforts (including those in early care and education) often consist of a rapid succession of innovations. One new idea or practice follows another so quickly that none ever becomes institutionalized. Each one is simply replaced by the next "great idea" (Knapp-Philo, 2001). Adult educators and learners each commonly underestimate the amount of time required to master a task. Although talent may enable one learner to reach a higher level of expertise than a less capable person, even talented learners require a significant investment of time to develop a skill (Ericcson, Krampe, & Tesch-Romer, 1993). A training session in which information is explained is not enough. For innovation to be successfully sustained, staff members must have the time to acquire, practice, and master new skills.

What does it look like when beginning language and literacy innovations have been sustained in an early care and education program that takes time to plan and implement, to develop new skills and strategies, to practice, and to follow-up? Knapp-Philo and Stice (2004) observed the following:

- Leaders plan sufficient time for each innovation to support beginning language and literacy to be fully integrated into the organization before new concepts are presented.

- There is widespread recognition throughout the organization that mastering new skills requires practice, support, and time.

- A written philosophy, policy, or both states that mastering new skills to support beginning language and literacy requires practice, support, and time.

- *All* training includes follow-up and ongoing support over time.

- Professional development strategies include reflective supervision, observation, the sharing of ideas and strategies with peers, planning to identify ways to use the new strategies, and onsite follow-up.

Administrative Support

Change requires leadership in the person of a "prime mover to push for implementation of strategic decisions" (Kanter, 1983, p. 125). Administrative support is essential if innovations at the organizational level are to be sustained. Individuals can do a great deal to sustain new practices by their personal behavior; however, administrative support powerfully aids individuals in sustaining new practices. Administrators play a key role in all aspects of a change process. Even if they do not initiate the change, administrators must be holders of the vision and contributors to the impetus and planning processes. According to Kanter (1983),

> *Leadership consists in part of keeping everyone's mind on the shared vision, being explicit about "fixed" areas not up for discussion and the constraints on decisions, watching for uneven participation or group pressure, and keeping time bounded and managed. Then as events move toward accomplishments, leaders can provide rewards and feedback, tangible signs that the participation mattered.* (p. 275)

Administrators hold decision-making responsibility for implementing a new initiative and for assuring that necessary training is provided. Finally, and perhaps most important, administrators play a key role in cheerleading for the practice and problem solving when dilemmas arise. They also facilitate structural adjustments and readjustments. In addition, cross-departmental changes and resource allocations or reallocations require the commitment and consent of those with the authority to authorize them (Alper, 1995). Administrators also are in position to design and carry out systematic evaluation to monitor the change process and to ensure that it is implemented (Katsiyannis, Condevese, & Franks, 1996).

What does it look like when beginning language and literacy innovations have been sustained in an early care and education program that has administrative support? Expect to observe the following:

- Members of the governing board and advisory committees reflect a philosophy of valuing language and literacy.

- Policies and priorities reflect language and literacy as a core value.

- Policies and practices respond to family needs related to a new innovation(e.g., adult literacy and book distributions).

- Budgets reflect a valuing of language and literacy.

- All new hires receive training about language and literacy.

- Leaders model and reward recommended practice behaviors related to language and literacy.

- High-quality, responsive professional development to expand skills is readily available.

- Job descriptions, interview questions, and evaluation forms and procedures explicitly address beginning language and literacy.

Idea of a Clear Purpose and Direction

Blanchard (1996) suggested that the "ultimate organization" is one in which all its members know where they are going, are committed, and are organized and ready to implement new ideas. Undoubtedly, a clear vision, or a focus on a mutual purpose, is not only an essential first step but also part of every phase of the change process (Senge, 1990). When a group has shared images of the future, it is able to build a sense of commitment (Senge, 1990). Without a clear, mutual understanding of what the change will be, the leader cannot gather widespread commitment, move an organization forward, solve problems that arise, or make necessary adaptations.

By explicitly connecting an innovation to an ongoing organizational vision, leaders renew the focus on the vision and work to ensure that the innovation will be sustained as part of attaining it. A vision, then, provides direction to day-to-day decisions, and it motivates and encourages staff members to keep reaching toward each next step.

What does it look like when beginning language and literacy innovations have been sustained in an early care and education program that has a widely accepted clear purpose and direction? One could expect to see the following:

- A written agency vision, mission, policy, or some combination of these clearly describes beginning language and literacy and how the agency supports their development. This document is frequently used by staff members and is often shared with families and community partners.

- All staff members articulate what beginning language and literacy mean and why they matter.

- Families value beginning language and literacy and use strategies that promote them with their children.

- Staff members eagerly embrace the use of strategies related to the new innovation.

- Beginning language and literacy practices are part of every adult–child interaction, classroom and socialization environment, and home visit routine.

- Materials and resources support the core value of early language and literacy.

Conclusion

"To keep a lamp burning, we have to keep putting oil in it," said Mother Teresa. Programs typically look to training to disseminate new ideas and teach new skills, but if the learning is not ongoing and if the new ways do not become part of the vision, systems, policies, and daily life of the organization, then innovations are likely over time to fade and be forgotten. Organizations that wish to adopt and use evidence-based, developmentally appropriate strategies that support beginning language and literacy must consider not only the nature of the new strategies but also how the organization will incorporate new information over time and how it will sustain its language and literacy focus for years to come. By planning how to incorporate a new idea into the systems and daily practices of the organization, leaders will ensure that innovations will be sustained. Children, families, staff members, and organizations will benefit.

> *With ordinary talents and extraordinary perseverance, all things are attainable.*
> —Sir Thomas Fowell Buxton

References

Alper, S. (1995). *Inclusion: Are we abandoning or helping students?* Thousand Oaks, CA: Corwin Press.

Blanchard, K. (1996). Turning the organizational pyramid upside down. In F. Hesselbein, M. Goldsmith, & R. Beckhard (Eds.), *The leader of the future* (pp. 81–88). San Francisco: Jossey-Bass.

Buysse, V., & Wesley, P. (1993). The identity crisis in early childhood special education: A call for professional role clarification. *Topics in Early Childhood Special Education, 13,* 418–429.

Deming, W. E. (1986). *Out of the crisis.* Cambridge: Massachusetts Institute of Technology.

Dickinson, D. K., & Tabors, P. O. (2001). *Beginning literacy with language.* Baltimore: Paul H. Brookes.

Ericcson, K. A., Krampe, R. T., & Tesch-Romer, C. (1993). The role of deliberate practice in the acquisition of expert performance. *Psychological Reviews, 100,* 363–406.

Fullan, M. (1993). *Changing forces: Probing the depths of educational reform.* London: Falmer Press.

Fullan, M. (1999). *Change forces: The sequel.* Philadelphia: Falmer Press.

Hilton/Early Head Start Training Program, Five Year Summary Report. (2002). Unpublished report, California Institute on Human Services, Sonoma State University, Rohnert Park, CA.

Kanter, R. M. (1983). *The change masters: Innovation and entrepreneurship in the American corporation.* New York: Simon & Schuster.

Katsiyannis, A., Condevese, G., Franks, D. J. (1996). Students with disabilities: Inclusionary programming and the school principal. *NASSP Bulletin, 80*(578), 81–86.

Knapp-Philo, J. (2001). *An exploration of training and change in practice in infant/toddler programs.* Unpublished doctoral dissertation, University of Connecticut, Storrs, CT.

Knapp-Philo, J., & Stice, K. (Eds.). (2004). *StoryQUEST 3: Celebrating beginning language and literacy* [Unpublished training manual]. Rohnert Park: California Institute on Human Services at Sonoma State University.

National Institute of Child Health and Human Development. (2000). *Report of the National Reading Panel. Teaching children to read: An evidence-based assessment of the scientific research literature on reading and its implications for reading instruction* (NIH Publication No. 00-4769). Washington, DC: U.S. Government Printing Office.

Rosenkoetter, S. E., & Barton, L. R. (2002). Babies, young children, families, and literacy: Important routines that tie them together. *Zero to Three, 22*(4), 33–38.

Rosenkoetter, S. E. (2006). Learning to read the world: A beginning. In S. E. Rosenkoetter & J. Knapp-Philo (Eds.), *Learning to read the world: Language and literacy in the first three years* (pp. 1–14). Washington, DC: ZERO TO THREE Press.

Senge, P. M. (1990). *The fifth discipline: The art and practice of the learning organization.* NY: Currency Doubleday.

Senge, P. M., Kleiner, A., Roberts, C., Ross, R., Roth, G., & Smith, B. (1999). *The dance of change: The challenges of sustaining momentum in learning organizations.* New York: Doubleday.

Snow, D. E., Burns, M. S., & Griffin, P. (Eds.). National Research Council, Committee on the Prevention of Reading Difficulties. (1998). *Preventing reading difficulties in young children.* Washington, DC: National Academy Press.

Sprinthall, N., & Sprinthall, L. (1980). Adult development and leadership training for mainstream education. In D. Corrigan & K. Howey (Eds.), *Concepts to guide the training of teachers of teachers.* Reston, VA: Council for Exceptional Children.

Vaughn, S., Klinger, J., & Hughes, M. (2000). Sustainability of research-based practices. *Exceptional Children, 66*(2), 163–171.

Whitehurst, G. J. (2001, July 26). *Address to the White House Summit on Early Childhood Cognitive Development,* Washington, DC.

CHAPTER 21

Building Community Support for Early Literacy

Ann P. Zukoski and Esminia M. Luluquisen

It is a beautiful spring day at the park. Lots of people, especially families with children, seem to be heading down a particular path. Posts about 3-feet high with some signs attached to the tops are seen about every 10 feet along the path. As we approach, we observe that each sign is actually a page from a children's book that has been glued to the wood and lacquered. We realize that all the pages of Miss Spider's Tea Party *(Kirk, 1994) have been put onto these signs. Groups of adults and children are moving down the path, scanning each sign, and hustling along to see what will happen at the next sign. Children of elementary-school age read the words of the story. Preschoolers point out the numbers, name the animals, and discuss the story's events with those who are reading to them. Toddlers listen as the adults tell them about the pictures, imitate animal sounds, enjoy the rhymes, point out colors, and count their steps down the path to the next sign. Parents and grandparents enjoy watching the children's delight as the story unfolds. At the end, the last sign invites families to come to a free book distribution. We realize that we have stumbled onto a community literacy event.*

Every community has enormous assets to support early literacy efforts. Individuals, organizations, and agencies concerned about the well-being of children can play important roles to ensure that infants and toddlers and their caregivers—both in and out of the home—gain the knowledge, skills, material resources, and opportunities to provide young children with rich experiences tied to early language development and early literacy skill building. Families, relatives, and friends have a large role to play, as do members of the social and health services, cultural and civic groups, the business community, and citizens who interact with children on a regular basis. The challenge that communities face, however, is in mobilizing these diverse resources to achieve the shared goals they set out to accomplish. Getting early literacy onto the community's agenda and keeping it there requires the contributions of diverse stakeholders, the creation of a shared vision and clear outcomes, and the development of a clear and flexible action plan to move forward.

This chapter guides early childhood leaders in making community mobilization happen. It discusses the role that local communities can play in building broad-based support for emergent literacy. It introduces readers to the rationale and research that support the use of community development practices and to the theory and principles that underlie participatory approaches. The chapter outlines practical steps to launch a community mobilization process. Finally, it includes examples of a range of approaches that communities are adopting with the hope of stimulating more innovation and community action to support early language and literacy for infants and toddlers.

An Ecological Approach to Infant–Toddler Literacy Development: The Role of Community Support

> *Children and families living in communities where the political, economic, health care, and educational infrastructures have joined together to fundamentally support more families are most likely to benefit from targeted efforts to enhance early literacy experiences. Those professionals with routine and frequent contact with families during early childhood—health care workers, day care workers, and preschool teachers—are in the best position to influence children and families in ways that will make a difference in their literacy.* (Regalado, Goldenberg, & Appel, 2001, p. 11)

Building infant and toddler literacy skills will be best accomplished by improving the contexts in which our infants and toddlers grow and learn. Creating environments that support this growth will require efforts to build awareness, knowledge, and skills in families, in the child-care community, and among health and social caregivers. It will require effecting change in all the social and physical environments in which young children interact.

Urie Bronfenbrenner (1977, 1979) defined the importance of *context* to a child's well-being. His research suggested that children's behavior and development are influenced by their interactions with the social systems surrounding them. These systems include their families, caregiving and educational circumstances, their neighborhood's conventions, sociocultural practices that surround them, and larger community factors (Connell & Kubisch, 2001). Public health researchers have combined Bronfenbrenner's ecological model with theories of individual development to account for the ways that individual characteristics, family patterns, social networks, and culture influence health outcomes such as child abuse, smoking, and teenage pregnancy (Glantz, Lewis, & Rimer, 1997; McLeroy, Bibeau, Steckler, & Glantz, 1988). The resulting theory proposes that behavior is influenced by interactions between individual and environmental determinants. For example, a toddler is affected by multiple spheres of influence (see Figure 21.1):

- Intrapersonal factors—child characteristics such temperament and personality traits

- Interpersonal processes—reciprocal support resulting from trust-based interactions that communicate families' culture, values, and expectations, which are most often shared though a child's interactions with adults such as family members and caregivers

- Institutional factors—characteristics and services provided by social and health agencies such as libraries and health care providers

- Community factors—formal and informal relationships among organizations and agencies as well as physical or built environments, for example, relationships among organizations such as Head Start and Early Intervention services, libraries and schools, as well as hospitals and social service agencies

- Public policies—local, state, and national laws and regulations

Figure 21.1.   Ecological Context Influencing Infant–Toddler Development

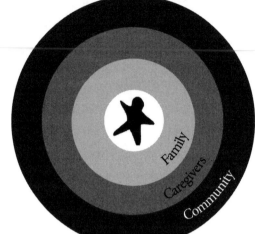

Family:
- Mothers
- Fathers
- Guardians
- Siblings
- Extended family
- Close family friends

Caregivers:
- Child-care providers
- Health-care professionals
- Social service providers
- Early childhood educators

Community
Social Environment
- Relationships between agencies, organizations, and local residents
- Opportunities for public to interact and play with books and language

Physical Environment
- Parks
- Libraries
- Public spaces

Interventions that apply ecological theory are designed to target multiple spheres of a child's context and thus have the potential to positively influence a child's growth and development in multiple ways. Individuals and institutions within the community that have routine and frequent contact with families during the early childhood period are in an optimal position to enhance the early literacy experiences of infants and toddlers. In the earliest stages of life, for example, families come into contact with hospitals and pediatricians. Professionals working in these arenas are in optimal places to influence how families interact and care for their children. More broadly, community members and institutions with the appropriate knowledge, skills, and basic material resources can promote early literacy for infants and toddlers by laying the foundation for their healthy development and literacy success in elementary school and thereafter. For example, community institutions such as child-care organizations and libraries can provide families with opportunities to expose their children to books and stories.

Communities consist of (a) people organized into social units and (b) the physical areas where the people live (Walter, 1997). The place includes the physical neighborhood, city, county, and country that people occupy. The interdependent relationships that result from location may include shared identity, memberships, values, needs, and history, among other common characteristics. As individuals live, engage in civic activities, and work and learn together, they forge social networks based on trust, tolerance, and a common community identity—characteristics found to be associated with improved mortality, health, and well-being (Kawachi, Kennedy, Lochner, & Prothrow-Smith, 1997; Miller, 1997; Yen & Kaplan, 1999). These social networks can mobilize the community's resources toward achieving goals (Kreuter & Lezin, 2002) such as an emphasis on language and literacy experiences for all children from birth onward.

In addition to individuals and groups supporting early literacy, the ecological context includes a built environment—that is, the human-made physical components that provide the infrastructure within which people live, work, play, and learn. Recent research has shown the relationship between the design of physical environments and the quality of life (Jackson & Kochtizky, 2001). In a recent study, Morrow found that children's well-being and health were directly affected by the availability, accessibility, and perceptions of safety in their physical environments (Morrow, 1999). Although little is known about the impact of physical environments on early childhood literacy, communities across the country are beginning to create physical spaces for enjoyable learning by providing opportunities for infants and toddlers and their families to use books and interact with other language and literacy materials. The *Miss Spider* Walk described at the beginning of this chapter is one example of such a physical space.

Social, economic, cultural, and community-level factors interact and influence child development outcomes. This fact is critical to consider for children who are growing up in poverty. These children are at risk for developmental delays in intellectual development and school achievement. Compared to their more affluent peers, children who live in poverty tend to have lower average levels of school-related skills, and their progress through school is slower and more subject to termination from dropout. Children who grow up in poverty often live in families with limited literacy and limited exposure to language and literacy. In a landmark study, Hart and Risley studied 42 families with children who were between 7 and 9 months old and continued the study until those children were 3 years old. They conducted monthly hourly observations for 2 ½ years. By the time the children reached the age of 3, the researchers had found clear trends in the amount of talk, vocabulary growth, and style of interaction for children living in low-, middle-, and high-income families. Children who were living in families that received welfare had smaller vocabularies and added words more slowly than did children of the same age in professional families. In a follow-up study of 29 of the families, the rate of vocabulary growth at age 3 was strongly associated with vocabulary scores at ages 9 and 10. Vocabulary at age 3 was equally predictive of measures of language skill at ages 9 and 10 (Hart & Risley, 2003). This study indicates the importance of reaching families in poverty to encourage language and literacy development. Community-based approaches can be especially powerful and effective in designing strategies that are culturally appropriate and community-specific.

Community Organizing and Community Building: Theory and Principles

Community organizing is a process through which communities identify common problems, set goals, mobilize resources, and develop and implement strategies for reaching the goals they have collectively set (Minkler & Wallerstein, 1997). A community-building orientation requires conceptualizing the community as an inclusive, complex, and dynamic system of which all individuals are a part. The goal of a community organizing process is to build a community's capacity to

- take action on its own behalf or induce outsiders to take action on its behalf;
- link with outside sources of information, power, or financing;
- undertake neighborhood-wide planning or agenda setting;
- engage in collective problem solving and decision making;
- generate local leadership that is effective and has legitimacy; and
- carry out the work of community revitalization effectively (Maker, 2002).

The collective voice and actions of local residents and their leaders can lead to a number of positive outcomes, including the following (World Health Organization, 2002):

- Creation of inclusive communities that support diverse cultural knowledge, skills, and attitudes

- Empowered individuals and communities who understand local conditions and gain control over factors affecting people's lives

- Achievement of better decisions and development of more responsive and effective services

- Creation of holistic and integrated cross-cutting approaches that meaningfully address the complexity of early childhood development

- Ownership and sustainability of programs

All community-organizing techniques are based on four principles:

1. *Community participation.* Community participation requires going beyond consultation or assessment of people's needs; a participatory process enables local residents to become an integral part of the decision-making and action process. Community participation draws on the energy and enthusiasm that exists within communities to define community priorities and take action (World Health Organization, 2002).

2. *Empowerment.* Empowerment encompasses the process through which "individuals and communities gain the confidence, self-esteem, understanding and power necessary to articulate concerns, ensure that action is taken to address them and, more broadly, gain control over their lives" (World Health Organization, 2002, p. 10).

3. *Mobilization of local resources and energy.* Community-building approaches rely on a strengths-based approach rather than a needs-based understanding of social issues. This approach stresses the identification, nurturing, and celebration of local community assets (Minkler, 1997).

4. *Capacity building.* Community-organizing approaches adopt learning processes through which community members, organizations, and groups build skills, systems, and structures that give members the opportunity to gain new skills and effectively use them to achieve collective goals (Kubisch et al., 2002).

Applying the Theory: What Does Community Support of Early Literacy Look Like?

Communities support early literacy development through creating opportunities for children, families, and professionals to interact and play with language, pictures, and written words. These experiences happen in a multitude of ways and places. Activities can be single community-wide events, ongoing activities, or campaigns that build over time. Interventions can target change on the family, caregiver, or organizational or community level.

Coordinated, community-wide strategies are needed to raise knowledge about early literacy development and to improve skill levels. Policymakers, families, community leaders, and child-care providers can become more aware of the importance of this topic. Social marketing—a set of strategies for expanding support (see Pratt & Hernandez, this volume, p. 455)—is one approach for accomplishing this goal.[1] Activities targeted to reach families and caregivers can involve events such as book-making workshops or social activities focused on babbling with infants. Organizational change projects can seek to alter how agencies manage operations, train staff members, and serve children and families by intentionally promoting early language and literacy. Interagency collaboration and care coordination projects can revisit the ways in which foundational language and reading development are addressed for infants and toddlers, including children with special needs and families whose first language is other than English. Early literacy approaches can be integrated within and across organizations and applied to Early Intervention, Early Head Start, Even Start, child care, library offerings, and home visiting programs. Other sectors such as health and social services can examine ways to integrate literacy activities within their own work. For example, health screening for infants and toddlers can be expanded to include a preliteracy screen to assess language development (Regalado et al., 2001).

Community interventions are also needed that address social and built environments. Following are examples of how several communities are supporting the development of early literacy for children and families.

---

[1] Regalado and colleagues present recommendations for policy and practice changes to support early literacy in professional communities (see Regalado et al., 2001).

Books on Buses—Rochester, New York

Children on all 250 of the city's public buses now have access to books. Officials at the Rochester-Genessee Regional Transportation Authority (R-GTA) generated the idea as a way to encourage families to read. "We have hundreds of kids who ride buses every day on the way to day care, grocery shopping, or out seeing family, and there's really nothing for them to do," reported Mark Aesch, chief of staff for the Transportation Authority. "We said, why don't we come up with something informative for kids to do, and create some decent family time" (Stern, 2002). More than 100 area schools, libraries, and national publishers donated books for the project. A class at Fairbanks Elementary School in Churchville, for example, donated 1,400 books to Books on Buses. Each night the books are replenished. The Transit Authority reports that since the start of this program, riders have caught on to the idea of leaving the books for the next rider. However, program leaders are not concerned if a book is taken. Mark Aesch has been quoted as saying, "There are a lot worse things to happen than a family taking a book home." Rochester started its program in 2001. Three other cities are in the process of starting books on buses programs: Anchorage, Alaska; San Diego, California; and Washington, D.C. (Center for Governmental Programs, 2002). For more information, contact the R-GTA (http://www.rgrta.org).

Storybook Land—Albany, Oregon

It takes six trucks and trailers, 100-plus volunteers, and nearly 5,000 hours to plan and set up Storybook Land. Most of the volunteers are regulars. Fueled by doughnuts, hot drinks, and a steady stream of carols blasting from speakers, volunteers come each year to set up 65 scenes from literary favorites such as "Jack and Jill," "Jack and the Beanstalk," and "Little Miss Spider." Every year, 20,000 people visit Christmas Storybook Land, a whimsical walk through a "forest" of lighted trees featuring scenes from children's nursery rhymes and books. Each scene consists of stuffed figures and papier maché creations depicting favorite parts of stories. Families and children stroll from storybook scene to storybook scene, reading rhymes and pointing at favorite characters. Children of all ages call out "Pooh Bear," point at teddy bears, and look for the trolls under the Billy Goats Gruff's bridge. In 1978, volunteers created Storybook Land as a noncommercial, free alternative for families to share during the holiday season. It has become a great tradition in the area, with families returning year after year to share with their children and grandchildren the fun of stories. Admission is free, but families are asked to donate food items. In 2003, 16,000 food items were donated. For more information, contact the Albany Chamber of Commerce by calling (541) 926-1517 or by e-mailing info@albanychamber.com.

Let's Talk ... It Makes a Difference—Boston, Massachusetts

The "Let's Talk ... It Makes a Difference" campaign was created by a city collaborative to help all children and families read. The goal of the collaborative is to bring together city departments, businesses, foundations, community-based organizations, and residents to improve the lives of Cambridge children and families. The "Let's Talk" campaign is aimed at raising awareness about the positive effect that "talking" has on the oral language, vocabulary, and literacy development of children from birth to age 5. The campaign has three components: (a) parent–child activities and community events, (b) professional workshops, and (c) Let's Talk materials. Each component stresses that the quality, not the quantity, of conversation counts. Each component also provides parents with opportunities to learn techniques that enrich everyday conversations with their children. For parents and caregivers of infants and preschool children, educational activities focus on increasing the quality of verbal interaction among adults and children. Events include small groups, community events, and city-wide fairs. For professionals, workshops are offered to help family child-care providers see how they can use talk and reading. Tutors of children in schools, after-school programs, and churches also attend workshops to learn to promote literacy development. The purpose of the Let's Talk materials is to get adults from all cultural, linguistic, economic, and educational backgrounds to realize talking as a way to develop young children's oral language, vocabulary, and literacy skills. Free materials remind parents to talk to their children while doing everyday activities with them. For example, "Let's Talk It Makes a Difference" bibs and washcloths remind parents to talk with their children during meal and bath time. Since its inception in 2002, the "Let's Talk ... It Makes a Difference" campaign has garnered national attention from many who hope to launch similar initiatives in their own communities. For more information, visit the Cambridge Public Health Web site (www.cambridgepublichealth.org/prog_serv/agenda_children/literacy.html).

Reach out and Read—Pediatricians' Offices Across the Country

In 1989, physicians, nurses, and educators at Boston City Hospital started bringing books from home to the clinic waiting room so children could read while they were waiting for their appointments. When they discovered how quickly the books disappeared, the clinic physicians and staff members developed the Reach Out and Read (ROR) concept. ROR is based on the powerful premise that medical practitioners can encourage families to read to young children and give them the tools to do so. During well-child visits for children between the ages of 6 months and 5 years, doctors and nurses in ROR programs provide information about the importance of reading aloud. They offer new, developmentally appropriate books to families to take home. In the waiting rooms, volunteers read to children, modeling techniques for parents.

ROR programs—which serve more than 1.5 million families nationwide—focus on reaching children who are growing up in poverty. These programs exist in a variety of clinical settings, including urban community health clinics, large hospital outpatient clinics, small rural family practices, Indian Health Service medical facilities, and clinics that serve migrant families. Coalitions made up of community members support ROR programs by donating time to read to children in waiting rooms, raising funds to purchase and distribute books, and educating policymakers and legislators about the importance of the program. For more information, see the ROR Web Site (http://www.reachoutandread.org/index.html).

Steps for Building Community Support for Early Literacy

How do these community activities start? Who plans them and makes them happen? The beginning stages of such activities may involve the work of a small group of dedicated people or a broad coalition of agencies and community residents that together capitalize on local resources and take action. Successful groups find unique ways to fit together local assets, needs, resources, passions, and priorities into purposeful plans and actions. The challenge is to create a process of working together that is flexible enough to meet the needs of the program's partners (Melaville, Blank, & Asayeh, 1993).

Many techniques and methods have been developed to assist groups and communities to engage in this process (Dombro, O'Donnell, Galinsky, Melcher, & Farber, 1996; Marois, 2002; Melaville et al., 1993; World Health Organization, 2002). We present here suggestions for initial steps that groups have found to be effective in launching a collaborative effort (see Figure 21.2). Groups might find themselves starting in different places, tackling steps individually or simultaneously, and moving forward and backward through a dynamic process that will, program leaders hope, lead to positive outcomes for infants and toddlers.

Figure 21.2. Steps for Community Mobilization

Source: Adapted with permission from *Together We Can: A Guide for Crafting a Profamily System of Education and Human Services* by I. Melaville, M. Blank, & G. Asayeh, 1993.

Step 1: Bring People Together

Community mobilization efforts typically begin by assembling many people who have the energy, skills, and knowledge to accomplish action in a community. Who are kindred spirits in the community? Who cares deeply for children? Who are "unsuspecting partners"—that is, people or agencies not usually considered to be interested in infants and toddlers? Are there local artists, grandmothers, or business owners who might like to support children's activities?

Try starting by thinking big and identifying ways to bring together a broad range of people. Kretzmann and McKnight (1993), of the Asset Based Community Development Institute at Northwestern University, suggest thinking of the community as being made up of individuals (e.g., residents, families, informal community leaders), associations (e.g., churches, sororities and fraternities, cultural groups) and local institutions (e.g., local government, businesses, schools, libraries, parks, hospitals, community colleges). See also Samuels (1995). Communities' assets are located within these sectors, and their representatives can make valuable contributions to an early language and literacy effort.

Families and agency volunteers are very important partners to include. First, they care deeply about children. They have skills, expertise, and active ties to the community, including its various cultural and ethnic gathering points. They have imagination and can make the planning process fun. By including families and other community residents, projects are more likely to meet the local needs (Samuels, 1995). "As both agents and beneficiaries of community change, [residents] can play a central role in shaping, implementing, and sustaining the change agenda" (Kubisch et al., 2002, p. 35) By involving families, projects and activities are more likely to reflect cultural values, local practices, and beliefs unique to each community.

The goal of Step 1 is to bring people together who will make a decision to act, make a commitment to collaborate, and determine to engage in a planning process (Melaville et al., 1993). The group needs to identify ways to create shared leadership, set ground rules for meetings, decide how to communicate and share governance responsibilities, and establish ways to meet challenges and celebrate success. All these steps are essential for feeding and sustaining a collaborative effort over time (Dombro et al., 1996; Kaye & Wolff, 1995;

Kubisch et al., 2002; Melaville et al., 1993; Shortell et al., 2002; World Health Organization, 2002).

Step 2: Build Trust and Mutual Respect

Studies of community collaboration demonstrate that mutual respect among members is a key element of a group's success (Kubisch et al., 2002). Developing social connections and relationships among participants can build the sense of community identity, commitment, and pride that crosses boundaries of age, race, and economic class (Kubisch et al., 2002). Practical approaches to building relationships include creating opportunities for members to learn about one another's dreams, resources, and daily activities. Strategies to achieve trust and mutual respect include allowing time on meeting agendas for long introductions, incorporating breaks during meetings to allow members to chat informally, and encouraging members to bring food to share (Zukoski, Casey, Sarnoff, Luluquisen, & Prentice, 2003). The following sections share additional ideas for cultivating trust and mutual respect.

Identify Ways to Value Each Member's Contributions

Facilitators should try to recognize people's contributions, express thanks, and acknowledge new ideas. Welcome a diversity of experience. Make new members feel welcome at meetings. Choose meeting times and locations that work for families from the community being served. Allow time, space, and interpretation for contributions from people whose second language is English. This support includes allowing time for people to translate meetings into multiple languages to meet participants' needs. Find opportunities for participants to share personal experiences and share stories (Zukoski et al., 2003).

Create a Way to Communicate Between Meetings

Communication is an important way of helping members feel part of an ongoing process. Groups can create telephone trees where 10 members each volunteer to call 3 others to remind them of meetings and pass on information. Some communities use e-mail or identify creative ways to start each meeting by reminding participants of progress and decisions made to date.

Celebrate a Shared Purpose

Research shows that members participate in groups for a variety of reasons, but celebrations and fun are one approach to building a sense of belonging and strengthened commitment. For example, bring a cake to celebrate the success of a first meeting, arrange a potluck meal, share stories of success, and submit photos to the local newspaper.

Step 3: Develop a Plan

In *Alice's Adventures in Wonderland*, Alice asked the Cheshire cat:

> "Would you tell me, please, which way I ought to go from here?"

> "That depends a good deal on where you want to go," replied the Cat.

> "I don't much care where—" said Alice.

> "Then it doesn't matter which way you go," said the Cat.

> "—so long as I get somewhere," Alice added.

> "Oh you're sure to do that," said the Cat, "If you only walk long enough." (Carroll, 1960, p. 88)

Create a Shared Vision

The first step in a strategic planning process is to create a shared vision. A visioning process seeks to answer the question, What do we want in the future? A vision is a broad statement capturing what a group wants to create and is committed to make happen. It is expressed in the present tense, as if it were already achieved or taking place. Visions are statements such as, "Every child is safe, secure, healthy, nurtured, and educated in home, child care, and community"; "Our community sees our children growing into responsible, productive, and contributing members"; or "Our community provides parents and families opportunities to play and interact with language and books."

The act of creating a shared vision allows a group to establish common ground, begin to build consensus about short- and long-term goals, and develop relationships among the participants. A shared vision serves as the foundation for a group's actions (Center for Collaborative Planning, 2000; Marois, 2002). A wide range of techniques and approaches can be used to develop a vision, including having groups use art supplies to draw dreams of what the envisioned community will look like and then asking children, families, and community members to map a journey to these outcomes (for additional suggestions, see Center for Collaborative Planning, 2000; World Health Organization, 2002).

Identify Outcomes

Groups need to establish ways to know that they are moving toward their visions. The establishment of outcomes is one approach for identifying the steps toward a vision. If an outcome is clear, then it is easier to identify strategies or activities that will lead to the outcome. Outcome statements are usually phrased as positive declarations about changes that the group expects to see in the future for children, families, or the community (SRI International, 2000). Examples include the following:

- "Infants and toddlers will be increasingly attracted to books."

- "Families will increasingly play with books with their children."

- "Our community will offer more affordable, family friendly events to build infants' and toddlers' love for books."

Figure 21.3 provides a sample process for selecting a vision and identifying outcomes. Outcomes are a way to more clearly identify the steps toward achieving a vision. Once groups identify local assets and needs, brainstorm about strategies that match local assets, set priorities, and create an action plan, they can work on how to assess and measure progress toward reaching the vision and outcomes. The following paragraphs discuss these next steps.

Identify local assets and needs. An important component of creating an action plan is to identify both the assets and the needs of the community. One adage states, "You don't know what you need until you know what you have" (Pratt & Hernandez, 2003). Research is required to uncover what exists, what is working, what is not working, what is missing, and what the community wants. Simultaneously, the group needs to discover its existing community assets. What gifts, talents, and resources can local families and people contribute? What are the assets of local associations such as cultural groups, faith communities, and civic groups? What can local institutions such as government agencies, public libraries, and community colleges do to support this cause?

Figure 21.3. Creating a Shared Vision and Outcomes

Developing this level of community understanding requires reaching out and asking people who live in the community what they see as local assets and resources. Professional reports or formal needs assessment will lack the desired level of detail and information.

Potential methods for conducting this research include a formal needs assessment process or a scan of the environment. The identification of assets can occur through interviews with individuals, focus groups where 6–10 people meet and respond to questions, or reviews of existing reports. Kretzmann and McKnight (1993) have developed methods for mapping community assets that have been used extensively in community-building efforts across the United States. The depth of the assessment phase will depend on the time available and the resources of the group. It is important to not get bogged down in a lengthy process of research but, rather, to gather essential information and move forward.

Brainstorm about strategies and match local assets. With information about their assets and needs, communities can begin to brainstorm about ideas for activities and actions. Effective strategies will meet the needs of the community, build on community assets, and lead to the achievement of the group's identified outcomes. In other words, strategies that "fit" or match local assets will most probably be "doable" and lead to success.

Prioritize strategies. Groups will develop many ideas. It is important to look at the ideas and assess the plausibility, feasibility, and potential effect of each approach. Will the strategy lead to accomplishing the desired outcome? Will it work? Have local resources been identified? Will the strategy have an effect? Will it touch the people in the community for whom it is intended? How many people will it touch? Based on answers to these questions, groups should be able to arrive at a decision about the most promising actions to take (Marois, 2002).

Step 4: Take Action

Creating an action plan answers the key questions of who will do what and by when. It provides a blueprint for achieving goals, creates accountability among partners, and sustains the momentum of the planning process (Nagy & Fawcett, 2003). In its simplest form, an action plan consists of taking all the steps completed in Step 3 and organizing them into a written document so everyone in the group knows what is planned, when it is going to happen, and who is responsible. Most participants in community planning for early language and literacy have had experience with action plans in some form or another. Look within the planning group for participants' experience with good action plans, and model from what those members are already comfortable using.

We included four examples earlier in this chapter of groups of people who have come together, built working relationships, developed a plan, and taken action. We hope that these projects, some simple and some more complex, inspire others to take stock of their local assets and create new and more innovative approaches to promoting early language and literacy development for infants and toddlers, ages birth to 3 years.

Step 5: Evaluate and Plan the Next Steps

Participants will want to see how they are making progress. Evaluation data can also help to attract additional resources to the community's early literacy effort. Evaluations answer questions such as How can we improve on what we are doing? or How will we know that we have been successful? Evaluation can be simple or very complex, depending on the group's resources and skills. An outside evaluator can be hired to collect information or to facilitate a participatory evaluation process through which members collect and analyze information to answer the group's questions (Zukoski & Luluquisen, 2002). Various tools such as the following can be used to assess progress in the early literacy campaign:

- A survey of families to determine whether they have increased their use of a new library program

- Focus groups to obtain families' and caregivers' opinions about whether the action plan meets their ongoing needs related to early childhood literacy

- Descriptive stories that relate a successful activity and offer beneficial lessons

- Photographs of the physical environment of libraries, classrooms, and book fairs before the action plan and 1 year after the plan

The goal of collecting information about a group's activities is to reflect on the actions taken, results obtained, and lessons learned so the group can start planning new actions. In this way, groups learn from their past and create more promising futures.

Conclusion

This chapter has provided readers with a theoretical understanding of why community support and promotion of early literacy is important to infants, toddlers, and their families. Interventions targeted to improve early language and literacy development are likely to be more effective in improving young children's development and well-being if they are targeted at multiple spheres of influence, including the community's social and physical environments. Community supports reinforce and validate family, child care, library social service, and health-care efforts. Several communities' approaches to this work were highlighted in the hope that they will stimulate interest and inspire action. Community development strategies are important tools for building broad-based efforts to support emergent literacy. Emphasizing local community involvement ensures that strategies are effective and sustainable because they have broad-based ownership. Basic steps to launching community efforts can be adapted to a variety of settings. The Appendix to this chapter highlights some excellent resources to assist community planners in mobilizing communities to support beginning language and literacy.

Appendix

Community Mobilization Resources

Together We Can. The Together We Can Initiative has developed the Community Collaborative Wellness Tool: Improving Results for Children, Youth, Families, and Neighborhoods. The goal of this tool is to strengthen the capacity of reform initiatives involving collaborative systems to change how public, private, and community institutions work together to support children, youth, and families. The tool reflects the experiences of many community collaboratives in working toward comprehensive reforms. It raises issues that collaboratives must address in accomplishing their ultimate goals of improved results for children, youth, families, and neighborhoods. Summaries of the steps are included in the organization's Web site, or a guidebook can be ordered from the site (http://www.togetherwecan.org/ccwtrationale-s.html).

We Did It Ourselves: Guidelines for Successful Community Collaboration. The Sierra Health Foundation funded a 10-year initiative to promote the health and well-being of children from birth though age 8 and their families through the support of community-level collaboratives operating in 26 counties in California. A three-volume guidebook provides describes step-by-step processes that communities followed to develop a vision, identify and mobilize local assets, engage broad-based support to reach their goals, and learn from their successes and challenges. To order the three-volume set from the Sierra Health Foundation, call (916) 922-4755.

World Health Organization: *Community Participation in Local Health and Sustainable Development. Approaches and Techniques.* This document explores in detail the techniques and methods frequently used in an action planning process. It includes methods such as creating shared visions and identifying community assets. This document can be downloaded from the Web site of the World Health Organization (www.who.dk/document/e78652.pdf).

Community Toolbox. This Web site is committed to promoting community health and development by connecting people, ideas, and resources. Users can download more than 3,000 pages of specific, skill-building information on more than 150 community topics, including community building tools, newsletters, tools for program evaluation, forums, and chat rooms on learning communities (http://ctb.ku.edu/).

Sustainable Communities Network. This site has recommended links on many subjects, including community visioning, asset mapping, partnership building, conflict resolution and mediation, culture, heritage, and celebrations. Visit the Web site (www.sustainable.org).

References

Bronfenbrenner, U. (1977). Toward an experimental ecology of human development. *American Psychologist, 32,* 513–531.

Bronfenbrenner, U. (1979). *The ecology of human development: Experiments by nature and design.* Cambridge, MA: Harvard University Press.

Carroll, L. (1960). *The annotated Alice: Alice's adventures in Wonderland and through the looking glass.* New York: Bramhall House.

Center for Collaborative Planning. (2000). *We did it ourselves: A guidebook to improve the well-being of children through community development.* Sacramento, CA: Sierra Health Foundation.

Center for Governmental Programs. (2002). A simple idea that benefits children and the community receives the award. *Common Accord, 4(2),* 6–7.

Connell, J., & Kubisch, A. (2001). Community approaches to improving outcomes for urban children, youth, and families: Current trends and future directors. In A. Booth & A. Crouter (Eds.), *Does it take a village? Community effects on children, adolescents, and families* (pp. 177–202). Mahwah, NJ: Erlbaum.

Dombro, A., O'Donnell, N. S., Galinsky, E., Melcher, S., & Farber, A. (1996). *Community mobilization: Strategies to support young children and their families.* New York: Families and Work Institute.

Glantz, K., Lewis, F., & Rimer, B. (Eds.). (1997). *Health behavior and health education. Theory, research and practice.* San Francisco: Jossey-Bass.

Hart, B., & Risley, R. (2003). The early catastrophe: The 30 million word gap by age 3. *American Educator,* Spring. Retrieved November 1, 2003, from http://www.aft.org/pubs-reports/american_educator/spring2003/catastrophe.html

Jackson, R., & Kochtizky, C. (2001). *Creating a healthy environment: Impact of the built environment on public health.* Retrieved November 1, 2003, from http://www.sprawlwatch.org/health.pdf

Kawachi, I., Kennedy, B., Lochner, K., & Prothrow-Smith, D. (1997). Social capital, income inequality and mortality. *American Journal of Public Health, 87,* 1491–1498.

Kaye, G., & Wolff, T. (Eds.). (1995). *From the ground up: A workbook on coalition building and community development.* Amherst, MA: AHEC/Community Partners.

Kirk, D. (1994). *Miss Spider's tea party.* New York: Scholastic.

Kretzmann, J., & McKnight, J. (1993). *Building communities from the inside out: A path toward finding and mobilizing a community's assets.* Evanston, IL: Northwestern University Institute for Policy Research.

Kreuter, M., & Lezin, N. (2002). Social capital theory. Implications for community-based health promotion. In R. DiClemente, R. Crosby, & M. Kegler (Eds.), *Emerging theories in health promotion, practice, and research* (pp. 228–254). San Francisco: Jossey-Bass.

Kubisch, A., Auspos, P., Brown, P., Chaskin, R., Fulbright-Anderson, K., & Hamilton, K. (2002). *Voices from the field II: Reflections on comprehensive community change.* Washington, DC: The Aspen Institute.

Maker, L. (2002). *Rebuilding the trust to ensure public safety and health: An exploratory case study of the Alameda Public Health Department's Community Health Teams Initiative.* Unpublished manuscript.

Marois, D. (2002). *Making the path: A guidebook to collaboration for school readiness.* Los Angeles: University of California–Los Angeles Center for Healthier Children, Families, and Communities in partnership with Center for Collaborative Planning, Public Health Institute.

McLeroy, K., Bibeau, D., Steckler, A., & Glantz, K. (1988). An ecological perspective on health promotion programs. *Health Education Quarterly, 15*(4), 351–377.

Melaville, I., Blank, M., & Asayeh, G. (1993). *Together we can: A guide for crafting a profamily system of education and human services.* Washington, DC: U.S. Department of Education and U.S. Department of Health and Human Services, Office of the Assistant Secretary for Planning and Evaluation.

Miller, R. (1997). Healthy Boston and social capital: Application, dynamics, and limitations. *National Civic Review, 86*(2), 157.

Minkler, M. (1997). Introduction and overview. In M. Minkler (Ed.), *Community organizing and community building for health* (pp. 3–19). Piscataway, NJ: Rutgers University Press.

Minkler, M., & Wallerstein, N. (1997). Improving health through community organization and community building: A health education perspective. In M. Minkler (Ed.), *Community organizing and community building for health* (pp. 30–52). Piscataway, NJ: Rutgers University Press.

Morrow, V. (1999). *Searching for social capital in children's accounts of neighborhood and networks: A preliminary analysis* (Vol. 7.) [Electronic version]. London: LSD Gender Institute Discussion Series. Retrieved December 1, 2003, from http://www.lse.ac.uk/Depts/GENDER/morrowpap.htm

Nagy, J., & Fawcett, S. (2003). *Section 5. Developing an action plan.* Retrieved December 1, 2003, from http://ctb.ku.edu/tools/en/section_1089.htm

Pratt, C., & Hernandez, R. (2003). *Community mobilization: From wellness goals to positive outcomes for Oregon's children, youth and families.* Salem: Oregon Commission on Children and Families; Corvallis: Oregon State University Family Policy Program.

Pratt, C. C., & Hernandez, R. (2006). Early literacy communications campaigns: The important role of social marketing. In S. E. Rosenkoetter & J. Knapp-Philo (Eds.), *Learning to read the world: Language and literacy in the first three years* (pp. 455–476). Washington, DC: ZERO TO THREE Press.

Regalado, M., Goldenberg, C., & Appel, E. (2001). Building community systems for young children: Reading and early literacy. In N. Halfon, E. Shulman, & M. Hochstein (Series Eds.), *Building community systems for young children.* Los Angeles: University of California–Los Angeles Center for Healthier Children, Families, and Communities.

Samuels, B. (1995). *Know your community: A step-by-step guide to community needs and resources assessment.* Chicago: Family Resource Coalition.

Shortell, S. M., Zukoski, A. P., Alexander, J. A., Bazzoli, G. J., Conrad, D. A., Hasnain-Wynia, R., et al. (2002). Evaluating partnerships for community health improvement: Tracking the footprints. *Journal of Health Politics, Policy and Law, 27*(1), 49–91.

SRI International. (2000). *We did it ourselves. An evaluation guidebook.* Sacramento, CA: Sierra Health Foundation.

Stern, S. (2002, October 22). Pay your fare and grab a book on Rochester's public buses. *Christian Science Monitor*. [Retrieved August 15, 2004 from http://www.csmonitor.com/2002/1022/p12s01-lecs.html

Walter, C. L. (1997). Community building practice. In M. Minkler (Ed.), *Community organizing and community building for health* (pp. 68–86). New Brunswick, NJ: Rutgers University Press.

World Health Organization. (2002). *Community participation in local health and sustainable development. Approaches and techniques*. Retrieved August 1, 2003, from http://www.who.dk/document/e78652.pdf

Yen, I., & Kaplan, G. (1999). Neighborhood social environment and risk of death: Multilevel evidence from the Alameda County study. *American Journal of Epidemiology, 149*(10), 898–907.

Zukoski, A., Casey, M., Sarnoff, R., Luluquisen, M., & Prentice, B. (2003). *Building local community-based public health systems*. Oakland, CA: Partnership for the Public's Health.

Zukoski, A. P., & Luluquisen, M. (2002, April). Participatory evaluation: Promoting collective knowledge and action. *Community Based Public Health: Policy and Practice, 5*, 1–7.

Photo by Kristen Mathisen

CHAPTER 22

Early Literacy Communications Campaigns: The Important Role of Social Marketing

Clara C. Pratt and Rebecca Hernandez

Effective communication is an essential element of improving the community's and the nation's attention to early language and literacy. A major 2001 report (Regalado, Goldenberg, & Appel, 2001) on building community systems for young children recommended the application of social marketing techniques to increase public awareness and understanding of early literacy development. Specifically, the report stated the following:

> *Illiteracy and low levels of literacy attainment deserve focused and sustained attention comparable to [social marketing] campaigns aimed at encouraging people to stop smoking. These campaigns would be aimed at informing … preschool teachers, physicians, and other health professionals, social workers, and child care workers…and the general public on what can be done to promote language and literacy development in the first 5 years of life and the specific roles they can play.*
> (Regalado, Goldenberg, & Appel, 2001, pp. 20–21)

Social marketing is the application and adaptation of commercial marketing concepts to the planning, development, implementation, and evaluation of communications campaigns that are designed to help bring about behavioral, environmental, or policy changes that will improve the welfare of individuals or society (U.S. DHHS, 1992). Social marketing uses marketing techniques to (a) identify the intended audiences and to understand what is preventing that audience from adopting a desired behavior and (b) develop, monitor, and adjust communications campaigns to stimulate the desired behavior change.

In applying commercial marketing techniques, human and health services programs have most often sought to promote behavior that improves individual health or well-being, such as stopping smoking or encouraging breast-feeding. Social marketing has also been applied to improve social conditions or public policies that enhance general health or well-being, such as discouraging driving while intoxicated or smoking in public places. Clarifying the desired outcome—individual behavior change versus policy change—is the critical first step in social marketing (Coffman, 2003).

Social marketing initiatives are frequently referred to as "strategic communications campaigns," with *strategic* implying that there is a clear goal to which the campaign is targeted. Social marketing initiatives have grown in recent years, particularly in the field of public health, as advocates, educators, and policymakers have recognized the potential value of effective public communications. Too often, however, social marketing initiatives are ineffective because of the failure to carefully apply proven marketing techniques (U.S. DHHS, 1992). Further, the evaluation of social marketing initiatives or communications campaigns has often failed to track both implementation and outcomes (Coffman, 2003).

This chapter will summarize the principles of social marketing and suggest how social marketing can be used to promote individual behaviors, system changes, and new policies that enhance early development and literacy. Evaluation strategies will also be briefly discussed.

A Communications Campaign—One Element of Early Literacy Initiatives

No matter how well social marketing is conducted, communications campaigns alone will not improve early literacy. Even the best designed communications campaign cannot compensate for a lack of early childhood services or supportive parenting education opportunities. A powerful communications campaign, however, can support and enhance other community strategies that support early literacy, strategies such as parent and caregiver education that is focused on language and literacy, teacher training and resources, early intervention services, community literacy mentoring and volunteer programs, dissemination of books and other language resources to families of young children in their preferred languages, and creation of accessible, literacy-rich community environments and events. When combined with other strategies such as these, effective communications campaigns can help to increase and sustain the positive, literacy-enhancing behaviors of parents and other caregivers. Effective communications campaigns can increase and sustain public awareness and support, promote greater investment of private and public resources, and lead to more productive public policies on behalf of the language and literacy development of infants, toddlers, and young children.

Effective communications campaigns include three coordinated strategic activities: media coverage, referral and linkages, and targeted educational events and resources. Each activity is intended to achieve specific outcomes. When applied to early language and literacy initiatives, communications campaigns can contribute to the following three general outcomes:

- **Widespread, strategic media coverage can increase community awareness** of (a) the importance of literacy environments and practices to the well-being of children and families, (b) the availability of local programs and resources, and perhaps most important, (c) specific actions that individuals (parents, caregivers, volunteers, political leaders) can take to help build the foundations for language and literacy with infants and toddlers.

- **Follow-up referral and linkage of services can increase participation in education, volunteer, advocacy, and other opportunities** among people who are committed to act on this issue.

- **Follow-up educational events and resources can enhance knowledge and effective behavior among targeted audience members.**

Communities may want to develop their own follow-up opportunities and materials. On the other hand, communities may increase knowledge by building on their existing education programs for parents or caregivers (such as those sponsored by Even Start or Early Head Start) and distributing extant high-quality materials (such as the National Institute for Literacy's *A Child Becomes a Reader: Proven Ideas for Parents From Research—Birth to Preschool;* Armbruster, Lehr, & Osborn, 2001). Targeting parents and other caregivers of children from birth to age 3, this booklet offers advice on how to support early language and literacy development and how to take advantage of community infant–toddler activities that start children on the road to becoming readers.

The Characteristics of Effective Communications Campaigns

An effective social marketing or communications campaign is not a brochure, a public service announcement (PSA), or a newspaper article. It is not a poster or a poster contest. A social marketing campaign is not a referral hotline for volunteers or a presentation on literacy development for the local Chamber of Commerce or Kiwanis. Rather, an effective communications campaign, though possibly including all these elements, involves much more. Guided by the proven principles of marketing, effective communications campaigns demonstrate the following qualities:

- **Strategic**—venturing to achieve clearly defined desired outcomes, as described earlier

- **Comprehensive**—aligning diverse activities, from paid television advertising to Web sites and brochures, to achieve the desired outcomes

- **Inclusive**—addressing multiple, relevant audiences, such as parents, neighbors, and employers, across diverse sectors and populations in a community

- **Focused**—addressing each audience's unique needs, motivators, and skills

- **Action-oriented**—moving the audience to take specific actions that contribute to achieving the desired outcome

In summary, an effective communications campaign is a strategic, comprehensive, and inclusive initiative that is designed to enhance knowledge and increase specific, positive actions relative to a social issue. Communications campaigns utilize diverse media venues to reach relevant and often diverse audiences that range from the general public to parents to policymakers and officials.

It is critical for a social marketing campaign first to define the behaviors or community conditions that it intends to change and then to provide the appropriate target audience with ideas, resources, and opportunities to act in the desired manner. The specific desired actions will vary across diverse audiences.

For example, for parents or care providers, the desired action may be more frequent interactive reading with young children. For community members, the desired action may involve volunteering in an adult or child literacy program or family mentoring program. For businesses and employers, the desired action may be donating money, merchandise, or services to support literacy programs or giving release time to employees to volunteer as reading partners for young children. Community grocers or fruit stand owners may contribute to early language and literacy by posting signs in the vegetable aisle with simple suggestions (e.g., Ask your child to point to vegetables that are yellow.) to guide rich parent–child interactions involving language and literacy.

To overcome two of the most common barriers to change (cost and time), it is important to identify actions that have minimal costs and that take advantage of already existing opportunities. For example, to address the time and cost barriers faced by many young families, a communications campaign can suggest actions that are free and that can be embedded in existing activities such as singing while driving with children, reading traffic signs to toddlers, or talking with children about colors they see in a grocery store.

Effective marketing campaigns must be planned carefully (U.S. DHHS, 1992; Wallack, Dorfman, Jernignan, & Themba, 1993; Wallack, Woodruff, Dorfman, & Diaz, 1999). Among the most comprehensive of the applied guidebooks is *Hands-On Social Marketing* by Nedra Weinreich (1999). Using a step-by-step workbook approach, Weinreich guides planners through the nine Ps of social marketing. The following paragraphs present these Ps with examples from early literacy.

Product. Product is the desired outcome, that is, the behaviors and actions that planners want an audience to adopt. Planners should identify the product (behavior and action) and how this product benefits the audience by fulfilling their particular needs and desires. For parents, regular reading and singing with young children (the product) can contribute not only several quickly achieved benefits (pleasant interactions, physical closeness, fun) but also important benefits that do not necessarily become apparent right away (a child's success in reading in school, pride in the child and self as parent). In contrast, educational policymakers are more likely to be persuaded to invest in early literacy programs (the product) because these programs show promise to increase school readiness and reduce the costs of later intervention. As planners consider a product's benefits, it is important to remember that benefits may be only indirectly tied to the product itself (e.g., increased sex appeal is the benefit that is often used to sell toothpaste, a product). Similarly, parent education (a product) may be "sold" to parents who seek the benefits of fewer temper tantrums and less sibling fighting.

Price. The element of price asks planners to consider the costs and barriers associated with adopting the product. Obviously, the costs and barriers vary among products and with different audiences. For example, the cost of reading with a child may be that a parent foregoes watching TV. Barriers to action may include a perceived lack of time or opportunity or the lack of confidence in one's ability to sing or read. Some parents may feel they failed in earlier attempts to engage a child in shared reading or storytelling. This previous failure is now a barrier that must be overcome by helping parents understand the great benefit of singing as a way to build language and the love children have of their parent's voices, even voices that would not fare well on *Star Search.*

The desired product (increased reading and singing with young children) will be adopted only when members of the target audience believe that the benefits of that action will be greater than the costs they incur. Effective social marketing reduces both costs and barriers, perhaps by providing free books, or distributing tapes or CDs of young children's songs, or by placing free DVDs in video stores to provide young families with guidelines and models of effective interactive storytelling and reading with young children.

Place. The element of place takes into consideration where the social marketing message can best access or reach audiences. For young families, accessible places may be in Laundromats, workplaces, video stores, grocery stores, doctors' offices, fast food outlets, child-care centers, automobiles, and public transit.

Promotion. The concept of promotion requires considering which media channels will best reach and engage the intended audience. What media channels (specific radio or TV stations and time slots, newspapers, Web sites, DVDs, brochures, transit ads, banners, refrigerator magnets, t-shirts) can reach the audience in the places they are most likely to be? What messages, spokespeople, and images will be most believable and engaging for this audience? For example, many young adults are likely to listen to other young people and celebrities with whom they identify; public officials, on the other hand, are generally more persuaded by facts, experts, and the constituents who elected them. To reach the individuals in a minority community, planners must include influential members of that community in the planning process; must use minority community newspapers, radio, and television stations, festivals, and other favored venues; and must engage spokespeople or performers who are credible to each audience.

Publics. Consideration of publics defines the groups and individuals whose support, internal and external to the sponsoring organization, is essential for marketing success. For language and literacy initiatives, important publics may include civic groups with literacy and education goals, schools and community colleges, libraries, video stores and book stores, elected officials including the mayor and city council, physicians and health services such as WIC, local child-care providers, and faith-based organizations. Such groups may be valuable allies because they applaud the message that the campaign is delivering.

Partnerships. Planners think of partners and partnerships as the people and organizations who should be included on the social marketing team. Partners may be campaign cosponsors who are actively engaged in "getting the word out." Partners may include groups with similar concerns, or they may have the resources (including marketing or other skills) and the political power needed for the communications campaign to succeed. Similarly, key individuals—a storyteller, a "mover and shaker" from the business community, a librarian, or a much-loved teacher—might be instrumental partners in shaping literacy campaigns.

Purse strings. Consideration of purse strings requires planners to consider realistically the financial resources that are available and what will be needed. A specific plan for obtaining required resources should be established before the campaign begins.

Priorities. Priorities is the eighth P of planning and challenges planners to set realistic priorities given the level of purse strings, partnerships, and publics, as well as the anticipated challenges that will arise from price and promotion. When a community's plan exceeds the available resources, Weinreich suggests one of two approaches: (a) trim the plan to fit the resources, or (b) raise additional resources through volunteerism, in-kind matches, donations, grant writing, partnering, or some combination of these strategies.

Policy. The element of policy reminds planners to consider the public policies that affect the desired behavior and consider targeting policymakers to create more supportive policies. For example, motivating a Community Recreation Board to insert literacy activities for infants and toddlers and their families into its strategic plan may provide important new opportunities for young families. A more radical policy target would be a campaign to change welfare policies that require young infants to be placed in poor quality, but available, child-care settings to enable their young mothers to enter the labor market. Given the evidence that many of the child-care arrangements for infants and toddlers in the United States are inadequate (Helburn, 1995; Kontos, Howes, Shinn, & Galinsky, 1995; Vandell & Wolfe, 2000; Whitebook, Howes, & Phillips, 1990), desirable policies would either reduce the demand for infant–toddler care or increase the quality of early childhood care. Obviously, both of these policy targets are exquisitely challenging. Nevertheless, communications campaign planners may identify expanded investments in child-care quality as an appropriate target for an initiative that seeks to promote early language and literacy development.

The Techniques of Social Marketing

Social marketing uses established marketing research techniques to gather information on a target audience's perceptions of a product and its benefits and price as well as information on place and promotion. Useful research techniques include focus group interviews, key informant interviews, and surveys with representative audience members. Pilot testing of proposed promotion plans, including messages, people, and images, is the only way to know how a target audience is likely to respond to the planned promotion strategy. What may motivate a harried young parent to attend parent education classes (fun, prizes, a simple meal, adult social interaction, a break from child care) may differ significantly from what an early childhood professional perceives as the benefits of attendance. No matter what the budget level of the effort, it is essential to learn how the target audience perceives the product as well as its costs and benefits and to pretest promotional plans. Not doing so limits a communications campaign's effectiveness before it ever begins.

Follow-up referral activities and educational opportunities and resources are essential to harness the interest and momentum created by public media. It is important to be prepared to support *immediately* the people who, as a result of their new awareness, want to act to learn more or to help address the issue targeted by the campaign. It is critical to have these appropriate activities and resources, including Web sites and educational events, in place before the communications campaign begins.

In addition to careful research and planning, effective social marketing builds on several simple communications guidelines that are proven to be effective in moving people to action. First, positive messages should be used to communicate benefits and attract people to action. Simply highlighting problems (such as the number of children living in poverty or the number who are not ready for school at age 5) is not likely to lead to more positive individual or public action. Second, audiences are more likely to remember and respond to messages that are high quality, consistent, and recognizable over time—which is why commercial marketers select simple, catchy slogans or taglines. Finally, to move people to action, such as volunteering, it is helpful to reduce problems to a human scale that one person can do something about (Wallack et al., 1999).

Third, social marketing must "frame" social issues so people gain a better understanding of context and effective actions. Framing is particularly important in longer news stories and news releases as well as letters to the editor that can be important parts of most communications campaigns. Media research (see review in Wallack et al., 1993) has demonstrated that most news stories are episodic reports that provide facts on social problems, often highlighting the facts with a specific person or incident. When viewers watch or read such stories, they are more likely to attribute success or failure to individual behavior. In contrast, thematic reports provide contextual information on the factors and conditions that contribute to a social situation and on the actions, policies, and programs that can effectively improve that issue. Often, thematic reports use interviews both with the people in the story and with "experts" who explain the context and possible solutions to a social challenge. For example, thematic stories on early literacy and language might connect these variables to later school readiness and life success, helping audiences understand how language, literacy, and school readiness can be improved through individual actions and social and educational policies and programs.

By investing media time in thematic stories that present problems in context and offer viable solutions, communications campaigns can best motivate actions to improve early language and literacy development. Unfortunately, a recent national forum on communicating children's issues (Human Services Policy Center, 1999) noted that most news and entertainment media frame stories about children in ways that fail to increase public understanding of the economic and social forces underlying children's issues or public understanding of civic and institutional solutions. In this failure, media contribute to the public perception that the solutions to challenges such as school readiness are primarily individual rather than public or civic. Through more conscious use of thematic reporting, communications campaigns can better educate the public and policymakers about the context of, and solutions to, child and family issues such as early literacy. Several examples of successful marketing practices are summarized in Table 22.1.

Look for examples of marketing research techniques and the nine Ps of social marketing in the following description of a media campaign created in Lane County, Oregon.

> In 1997, Lane County, OR, began a comprehensive, multiyear initiative "to mobilize Lane County families, organizations, and communities in a unified effort to assure that all our children are safe, healthy, cherished, and enter school ready to learn." Convened by United Way of Lane County (UWLC), the initiative sought to create a countywide, comprehensive system to promote the health and well-being of young children and their families. Countywide prevention services included parenting education, a telephone and Internet-based Parenting Help Line, and universal risk screening and home visits for all births. Services for higher risk families included longer term home visitation, therapeutic preschools and crisis nurseries, and respite care. From the beginning, the initiative included a vigorous, high-quality media campaign to (a) increase public awareness of the importance of the first years, (b) increase public awareness of positive actions that all people—from parents and child-care providers to citizens and volunteers—could take to promote young children's development and to support young families, and (c) attract people and resources to the initiative.

Table 22.1.
Guidelines for Creating Successful Communications Campaigns

Recommended Practice	Examples Related to Early Literacy
1. **Create a focused, strategic, high quality campaign with a positive theme.** Tie it to a professionally developed campaign, if possible.	• Cherish Every Child—Every Moment Matters; www.cherisheverychild.org • Success by Six (United Way) • Be Part of the Solution
2. **Tell thematic stories that demonstrate context and show how actions promote development.**	• Good stories are personalized, dramatic, visual thematic reports. Localize the issue with data and stories.
3. **Focus on positive solutions. State a positive goal and positive actions.** People are drawn to positive visions and actions, not to problems and guilt.	• Success for All Foundation; www.successforall.org • DEAR: Drop Everything and Read • Each One Teach One • Volunteer—Only YOU Can
4. **Identify specific actions that one can take to contribute to the desired outcome.**	• SMART—Start Making A Reader Today; http://www.getsmartoregon.org/ • Children First: Even a Small Thing Makes a Difference
5. **Use social math.** Translate large impersonal numbers into visions that people can imagine.	• For the price of your daily cup of coffee, you will improve a young child's life. • Reading with a child for 10 minutes a day will improve her life.
6. **Identify knowledgeable, articulate people from diverse communities to advance your message.** Engage and prepare real people to be effective spokespersons.	• Dads are impressed when other dads say "this program made a difference for me and my child." • Policymakers are most likely to listen to their constituents or established experts.
7. **Think long term.** Use media releases to report progress over time; keep your issue in front of people over time with a weekly "letters to the editor."	• Dear Editor, ... (5/1/02) • Dear Editor, ... (5/8/02) • Dear Editor, ... (5/15/02) • Dear Editor, ... (5/22/02)
8. **Track successes and challenges. Revise activities as progress occurs. Change as the audience changes.**	• As time passes, new generations of parents will be reached only if the message remains relevant to their lives.

Source: Adapted with permission from *Building Results Through Community Mobilization* by C. Pratt & R. Hernandez, 2003.

> *The professionally developed campaign was delivered county-wide through multiple media venues (TV, radio, print, outdoor, and transit advertising). Because media research indicates that greater exposure to a media message results in greater recall and*

more influence on behavior, the campaign goal was to reach 95% of Lane County households at least 28 times over 3 years through the combination of broadcast and print media as well as editorial press. Because paid media in prime time reaches people more often and reliably than do PSAs, campaign leaders invested in prime-time paid television ads that reached people during the dinner hour and evening.

During the first year, the media campaign theme evolved to "Cherish Every Child." As the campaign tagline, Cherish Every Child was prominent in all media messages including three 30-second TV and radio ads, seven posters and newspaper ads, and printed Parent Guides. Specific messages described parenting as "one's most important job" and suggested ideas for ways that parents could support early development. For example, one ad promoted the value of repetition and asked parents to "talk, sing, and read with your baby everyday" (see http://cherisheverychild.org/pdf/sb6_every_moment_matters.pdf). Other media messages suggested ways that people could help parents be successful. A Web site for the initiative (www.cherisheverychild.org) provided access to a parent guide and printed resources on early development and school readiness as well as links to parenting education and opportunities to volunteer, donate support, and take other actions.

After 7 months of the Cherish Every Child campaign, 985 parents were surveyed to assess their awareness of the Cherish Every Child messages. Forty percent had heard and remembered the messages. Of the surveyed parents, 10% reported that they had changed their behavior as a result of the Cherish Every Child messages. Many parents, however, related that they did not have enough time to spend with their children and didn't have enough money to purchase the toys and books for their children. Armed with this information from parents, Phase 2 of the campaign sought to provide more specific ideas on how to support young children's development without demanding more time or money. The Cherish Every Child tagline was expanded to "Cherish Every Child—Every Moment Matters." Messages featured the importance of talking, singing, and playing with young children during everyday interactions such as meal time, walks, shopping, and bathing. Early feedback on the Cherish Every Child—Every Moment Matters campaign indicates that these more specific messages have significantly increased parents' awareness of the importance of positive everyday interactions in their children's lives.

Funding for this initiative included significant time and support plus cash commitments from numerous health and human service organizations and media outlets as well as local, regional, and national foundations and businesses. In addition to funds to enhance family and child supports and services, almost $600,000 was invested in the 3-year Cherish Every Child—Every Moment Matters communications campaign. More information on the Cherish Every Child initiative and its media resources is available at its Web site (http://cherisheverychild.org).

Clearly, the creation of powerful communications campaigns is not simple. On the other hand, when organizations attempt a communications campaign without adequately addressing the nine Ps of social marketing, resources are wasted, and the outcomes are often disappointing.

Results From a Social Marketing Campaign for Beginning Literacy

A campaign developed using proven social marketing and communications principles can achieve several measurable outcomes, including increasing the target audience's

- Awareness of early literacy issues and solutions

- Knowledge of and commitment to individual and civic actions and policies that support infants and toddlers and their families

- Participation by family members or caregivers in early literacy events or education workshops and classes

- Routine use of positive literacy practices among parents and other caregivers (will likely have to supplement the communications program with education and training initiatives to achieve outcome)

- Demand for policies and programs that support early development and early literacy

Advertisers know that media also can help to sustain desired behavior. To this end, a communications campaign might reinforce and encourage families and caregivers who are already actively supporting young children's beginning language and literacy.

Social Marketing for Behavior Change

Practical experience and social science research demonstrate that behavior does not change (i.e., people do not act differently) solely because of increased knowledge. If we did, we would all exercise daily, eat right, and not smoke or drink alcohol. Along with basic knowledge, other factors that have been shown to influence behavior are (a) self-efficacy, that is, the perception of capability to perform the behavior; (b) social norms, or the impressions about what friends and family are doing; and (c) subjective norms, namely, awareness of what these significant people want us to do (Coffman, 2003).

Recognizing this gap between knowledge and practice, successful communications campaigns seek to influence how people think about other behavior-shaping forces related to a campaign's issue. For example, by suggesting simple, positive actions that a parent can take during routine daily care of children, a communications campaign is addressing the issue of self-efficacy. Because the desired action (talking) is simple and occurs during routine care, it will not be too hard to do and will not take up more time during a time-starved young parent's life (see *Cherish Every Child*, 2001).

Assessing a Communications Campaign

The outcomes of an early literacy campaign must be assessed. As the first step in planning an evaluation, most experts recommend developing a logic model for the social marketing intervention. A logic model is a road map. This road map describes how an initiative is supposed to work and where it is supposed to go. As a road map, a logic model visually presents the relationships among needs, resources, planned strategies and activities, and the intended outputs and outcomes. Figure 22.1 shows what the framework of a simple logic model looks like.

Figure 22.1.
Framework of a Logic Model

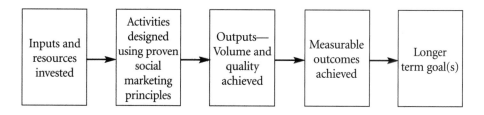

In a logic model, outcomes are the measurable results of strategic activities. Outcomes describe the characteristics such as improved knowledge, skills, attitudes, behaviors, and circumstances that will result if the strategic activities are successful. Outcomes should

- Be observable and measurable,

- Be achievable given the type and duration of the activities undertaken, and

- Contribute to the accomplishment of important higher level goals such as increased school success for children.

Complex behaviors are not likely to change as a result of simple media communications alone. Thus, the outcomes expected for a communications campaign should be realistic. Some possible outcomes for communications campaigns were outlined earlier in this chapter. Figure 22.2 provides a sample logic model for a communications campaign for early literacy. In this figure, inputs at the beginning and goals at the end are omitted. Of course, in real-life situations, the outcomes selected would be locally appropriate.

In her recent paper on evaluation of communications campaigns, Coffman (2003) noted that careful assessments of how well a communications campaign is working are of greater value than are experimental designs that use random assignment to control and experimental conditions. Knowing how well a communications campaigns is working requires thoughtful, rigorous designs for performance measurement that track planned activities as they are carried out as well as output and outcome targets as they are achieved (Pratt, Katzev, Ozretich, Henderson, & McGuigan, 1997; Pratt & Hernandez, 2003).

Figure 22.2.
A Simple Logic Model for a Literacy Communications Campaign
(Inputs and longer term goals omitted)

To track how well the message is getting out, count volume outputs, such as lines of news coverage or minutes of media time. In addition, assess the quality of outputs to answer these questions: How well is the intended message being disseminated? Are media sources using press releases? Is the information correct? Does the coverage accurately highlight key points and provide a *thematic*

view of the issue, not only episodic reports? How likely is it that the target audience is being reached, given the location and timing of coverage?

To track outcomes related to awareness, commitment, and behavior, communications campaigns often rely on telephone surveys of randomly selected members of the target audience. A survey to assess awareness should address three questions:

- Was the message seen or heard?
- Did awareness of the issue grow or change?
- Did people take any action as a result of the message?

For example, the Sample 1-Minute Interview in Figure 22.3 shows a brief survey to evaluate the effectiveness of a community-wide initiative called "Every Child a Success." This sample also could be used or adapted to evaluate the effectiveness of other initiatives.

Figure 22.3.
Sample 1-Minute Interview

The following survey can be conducted through a written, telephone, or face-to-face format with a randomly selected sample of intended audience members.

INTRODUCTION: The goal of *Every Child a Success* is to make sure that all children in our community are ready for school at age 5.

Do you recall ever hearing about *Every Child a Success* before?
YES [go to question 2] NO [go to question 4]

Do you recall where you saw or heard about *Every Child a Success*?
RECORD _____

The *Every Child a Success* campaign suggests everyday actions that parents, grandparents, and others can take to help children be ready for school. Do you recall any of the actions suggested?
NO [Go to question 5]
YES: What actions do you recall? RECORD _____

Have you taken these or other actions to help encourage young children?
YES: What action have you taken? RECORD _____
NO [Go to question 5]

Would you like some more information on *Every Child a Success* and the everyday things you can do to help all children be ready for school?

Thanks!

Another approach to assessing the outcomes of a communications campaign or education program uses a technique called a *retrospective pretest* (Pratt, McGuigan, & Katzev, 2000). Respondents are asked to assess their current knowledge and behavior relative to what they were before participation in the message. Traditional initial and subsequent self-assessments that involve taking the same test before and after information is presented show changes in knowledge. One difficulty is that on traditional pretests, respondents do not know what they do not know and often overestimate their knowledge. After an educational experience, however, respondents have often learned the extent of what they did not previously know and often report lower scores. Consequently, campaign evaluators can underestimate program effects because the higher pretest scores and lower posttest scores create a response shift bias (Pratt et al., 2000). The retrospective method accounts for this bias and offers a convenient and expeditious method for measuring self-reported change that is more accurate than a traditional pre- and posttest design. The sample retrospective pre- and posttest shown in Figure 22.4 addresses awareness and knowledge of specific information (items 1 through 4), and commitment to action (item 5). This sample instrument could easily be expanded by asking about specific actions that would promote early literacy for infants or toddlers.

Figure 22.4. Sample Retrospective Pretest

This retrospective pretest can be used to assess self-reported change in knowledge and skills after a workshop, conference, or other educational session on early literacy and language development.

For each of the items, FIRST, rate yourself **NOW after you saw this communication.** THEN, rate how you were **BEFORE today.**		
I Know	**NOW** Low High	**BEFORE** Low High
1: The percentage of children who live below the poverty line	0 1 2 3 4 5 6	0 1 2 3 4 5 6
2: The percentage of local children who are NOT fully ready for school at age 5.	0 1 2 3 4 5 6	0 1 2 3 4 5 6
3: Three actions that I can take to support early literacy and language development among infants and toddlers.	0 1 2 3 4 5 6	0 1 2 3 4 5 6
4: Three community groups or agencies that work to improve early literacy and language development among infants and toddlers.	0 1 2 3 4 5 6	0 1 2 3 4 5 6
5: How likely it is that I would volunteer to support early literacy development.	0 1 2 3 4 5 6	0 1 2 3 4 5 6

Records are also valuable data sources for assessing communications campaigns. Records can document the ways individuals say they learned about the issue, the dollar amounts of donations, the number of requests for information, the number of new volunteers or number of parents enrolling in workshops, and the number of groups that "adopt" an issue for volunteer work or fundraising. These types of information provide insight into how well a communications campaign moves people to action.

Conclusions

Communications campaigns are important components of initiatives to improve individual and community conditions that foster beginning language and literacy in infants and toddlers. The success of communications campaigns is enhanced by the use of social marketing principles and by strategic planning and evaluation. Examples of social marketing methods, the logic model approach, and simple evaluation tools were provided.

References

Armbruster, B. B., Lehr, R., & Osborn, J. (2001). *A child becomes a reader: Proven ideas for parents from research—Birth to preschool.* Retrieved October 21, 2003, from www.nifl.gov/partnershipforreading

Cherish Every Child. (2001). Sponsored by United Way of Lane County, Eugene, OR. Retrieved January, 2004, from www.cherisheverychild.org

Coffman, J. (2003). *Lessons in evaluating communications campaigns: Five case studies.* Retrieved November 6, 2003, from the Harvard Family Research Project Web site: www.hfrp.org

Helburn, S. W. (Ed.). (1995). *Cost, quality, and child outcomes in child care centers: Technical report.* Denver: Department of Economics, Center for Research in Economic and Social Policy, University of Colorado at Denver.

Human Services Policy Center. (1999). *How should we communicate about children's issues? A report from the Effective Language for Communicating Children's Issues Forum, August 6, 1999.* Retrieved June 16, 2003, from www.hspc.org

Kontos, S., Howes, C., Shinn, M., & Galinsky, E. (1995). *Quality in family child care and relative care.* New York: Teacher's College Press.

Pratt, C., & Hernandez, R. (2003). *Building results through community mobilization.* Salem: Oregon Commission on Children and Families; Corvallis: Oregon State University, Family Policy Center.

Pratt, C., Katzev, A., Ozretich, R., Henderson, T., & McGuigan, W. (1997). *Building results III: Measuring outcomes for Oregon's children, youth, and families.* Salem: Oregon Commission on Children and Families.

Pratt, C., McGuigan, W., & Katzev, A. (2000). Measuring program outcomes: Using retrospective pre-test methodology. *American Journal of Evaluation, 21*(3), 341–349.

Regalado, M., Goldenberg, C., & Appel, E. (2001). Building community systems for young children: Reading and early literacy. In N. Halfon, E. Shulman, & M. Hochstein (Series Eds.), *Building community systems for young children.* Los Angeles: University of California–Los Angeles Center for Healthier Children, Families, and Communities. Retrieved October 21, 2003, from http://www.healthychild.ucla.edu/Publications/ Documents/Readingand%20Early%20Literacy0601.pdf

U.S. DHHS (U.S. Department of Health and Human Services). (1992). *Making health communication programs work: A planner's guide.* Retrieved June 6, 2003, from http://rex.nci.nih.gov/NCI_Pub_Interface/HCPW/HOME.HTM

Vandell, D., & Wolfe, B. (2000). *Child care quality: Does it matter and does it need to be improved?* Retrieved June 6, 2001, from the Office of the Assistant Secretary for Planning and Evaluation, U.S. Department of Health and Human Services Web site: http://aspe.hhs.gov/hsp/ccquality00/index.htm

Wallack, L. Dorfman, L., Jernignan, D., & Themba, M. (1993). *Media advocacy and public health: Power for prevention.* Thousand Oaks, CA: Sage.

Wallack, L., Woodruff, K., Dorfman, L., & Diaz, I. (1999). *News for a change: An advocate's guide to working with the media.* Thousand Oaks, CA: Sage.

Weinreich, N. (1999). *Hands-on social marketing.* Thousand Oaks, CA: Sage.
Whitebook, M., Howes, C., & Phillips, D. (1990). *Who cares? Child care teachers and the quality of care in America.* Final Report of the National Child Care Staffing Study. Oakland, CA: Child Care Employee Project.

CHAPTER 23

Libraries Are Family Places for Literacy and Learning

Kathleen Deerr, Sandra Feinberg, Elizabeth Gordon, and Diantha Schull

On a large multicolored carpet at the center of the meeting room, a group of 20 adults and children are playing, some with play dough and some with educational toys. Parents are sharing board books and toys with their infants and toddlers, exchanging ideas about parenting issues, or talking with a resource professional about the importance of play and language experiences for the development of reading skills.

This scene is repeated in public libraries across the country nearly every day of every week. Libraries are reassessing their roles with respect to emergent literacy and are providing increasing numbers of programs and materials to support literacy at all ages. Librarians are now reaching out to very young children and those who care for them. Libraries across the country are seeking to address critical national needs for literacy and healthy development in the early years (Birckmayer, 2001).

Why Libraries?

Among the current blitz of headlines about the poor reading test scores of American children and the fierce debate about the best methods of teaching reading, [it is important to remember] that there are many ways that children acquire literacy, but to become lifelong readers, they really need to be invested in the

> *power of books within a community of others that love reading.*
> *(Kiefer, 2001, p. 48)*

What better place to find a community of adults and children who love words and reading than the public library? Libraries not only are present in almost all American communities but also are accessible, neutral meeting places where people of all cultural and economic backgrounds are welcome. The public library is a locus for lifelong learning. Specialized services for children and youth are nearly universal in public libraries. Libraries offer language-rich environments in which to nurture children's natural curiosity, responsiveness to stories, and interest in books. They are places of informal and formal education that provide parents and caregivers with the information and assistance they need to take full advantage of educational opportunities and services in their communities. Libraries can provide links to jobs and careers, health information, community services, and a host of other resources, including programs for adult literacy. Libraries are also less intimidating than more formal educational centers, and they provide a socially supportive environment for parents and caregivers with very young children. According to Kiefer (2001), librarians themselves are

> *...most concerned with creating a place and providing time for*
> *children to come to love books and to value learning. Librarians*
> *have the power to give children a rich experience with literature,*
> *to share their enthusiasm for fine books, and to develop readers*
> *who will find a lifetime of pleasure in the reading of good books.*
> *In the end, that is the most precious reading lesson that librari-*
> *ans can teach (p. 52).*

Beyond these obvious characteristics that make libraries ideal settings for nurturing emergent literacy, the position of the library at the intersection of scholarship, human services, and individual families makes the library a natural bridge between theory and practice, research and application. The present chapter examines The Family Place Library Model—one approach to bringing infants and toddlers into the culture of reading and learning—and includes a description of the key components of the model, an examination of how these components contribute to services, and a discussion of efforts to evaluate these components. This chapter also provides a sampling of some specialized programs developed by Family Place Libraries throughout the country to meet the particular needs of the families within their own local communities.

The Context

The importance of early childhood development and emergent literacy as national concerns was underscored some years ago when First Lady Laura Bush convened a Summit at the White House titled "Ready to Read, Ready to Learn." The summit was hosted by Mrs. Bush, a former teacher and school librarian, to highlight the early learning activities that parents and educators can use to prepare young children for school.

> *"We all have a duty to call attention to the science and serious-*
> *ness of early childhood cognitive development," said Mrs. Bush.*
> *"The years from the crib to the classroom represent a period of*
> *intense language and cognitive growth. Armed with the right*
> *information, we can make sure every child learns to read and*
> *reads to learn" (Bush, 2001).*

Given this heightened awareness of early literacy as an issue of national importance and the inherent potential of public libraries as levers for literacy, there is an urgent need to reconsider traditional children's services and to develop a common vision for early literacy services that can inform training and practice. There is a parallel need for benchmarks for such services and for opportunities and incentives to develop communities of practice. Unfortunately, at the current time, individual librarians who have developed service models that include this broader mission are isolated and typically focused on the needs of their particular communities. Advocates, funders, trustees, and government leaders are only beginning to understand the need for more strategic work in this area. Research to evaluate and guide practice has been minimal. Herein lies the current challenge to the library community—namely, to develop, demonstrate, evaluate, and disseminate "best practices" that can help libraries fulfill their potential to promote emergent literacy.

The Family Place Library Model

In this context, the emergence of the Family Place Library Model and its adoption in libraries across the country has implications for the increasing importance of libraries as powerful centers for early language and literacy. Each of the more than 200 Family Place Libraries in 22 states offers Parent–Child Workshops, providing parents of diverse cultural, educational, and socioeconomic backgrounds a series of opportunities to come together to gain the confidence, insights, and skills required to help their children develop the cognition they need to enter school ready to learn. Through activities, information exchange, books, other print and audiovisual materials, and one-to-one interaction, the Family Place Library Model supports parents as first teachers, empowers children's librarians as resources to parents, and positions the public library as a center for services and information with respect to the healthy development of children.

The Family Place Library, which began in 1979 at the Middle Country Public Library (MCPL) in Centereach, New York, has as its fundamental goal to

> *define and disseminate a holistic and developmentally appropriate approach to promoting emergent literacy and healthy child development by addressing the needs of children at the earliest ages, and supporting the role of parent as the child's first and foremost teacher (Feinberg & Rogoff, 1998, p. 50).*

Early childhood information, parent education, emergent literacy, socialization, community services, and family support are shared in a specially designed public place for caregivers with young children. Library staff members who have been trained in developmentally appropriate and family-centered practices work with infants and toddlers and their parents, caregivers, and family service providers, both within the library and in the community. This perspective, based on a commitment to promote early development and literacy by helping parents and other caregivers to build on their strengths as teachers of very young children, is a change from the historical library approach. "In order to be successful, the implementing library must have considered a change in role for the institution" (CDAC, 2000, p. 3). This shift is fundamental, with consequences for the day-to-day activities of children's librarians.

*We really worked over the last two years to refocus our whole
effort with preschoolers ... to say, "Okay, we really need to work
with the parents together with the children in order to promote
language development."... I see this as a part of our mission and
within the context of my commitment to the library contributing to the solutions of the city's issues and problems. (library
director quoted in CDAC, 2000, p. 4).*

The Family Place Library Model has been successful in the local communities
and in the library systems where it has been replicated and has served as a
galvanizing model for systemic change. This success is a result of both the
changes in approach to children's services and the Family Place Library's
comprehensiveness as a model.

Characteristics and Core Concepts of the Model

Characteristics of the Family Place Library Model include the following:

- The infusion into the training and practice of Family Place Library
  librarians of core concepts with respect to child development, emergent
  literacy, and family support

- Redefinition of the librarian's role, from a focus on providing services to
  a focus on empowering parents and caregivers

- An emphasis on collaboration with other community agencies

- Recognition that the library is a place for infants and toddlers and their
  caregivers

- The formation of a professional cadre of Family Place Library practitioners, each of whom takes part in a 3-day Institute and participates in a
  national network

- Integration of new research on early brain development and successful
  approaches to literacy preparation into the training curriculum

- Ongoing summative and formative evaluation

Early work on the Family Place Library curriculum identified four research-
based core concepts that were essential for a new systems-oriented perspective

on library services for families and caregivers of young children. The Family Place Library librarian—when armed with these concepts, examples of how they can be translated into the library setting, and assistance in the form of a supportive network of colleagues—becomes a powerful instigator of emergent literacy practices in the home, the library, and the community.

These four concepts, described further in the following paragraphs, provide the pedagogical and theoretical framework for an approach to children's services that is based on research, that reflects the realities of today's economic and family structures, and that builds on libraries' traditional resources to create a comprehensive model for serving parents, caregivers, and very young children.

Core Concept 1: Emergent literacy is a core component of healthy early childhood development. The Family Place Library Model reflects an understanding with respect to the critical connections between child development and literacy development. Studies indicate that reading to children, even as infants, improves their language skills, strengthens their families, and enables them to perform better in school. Additional findings show that early reading is the key to school success and a precursor to lifelong learning. It is known that the "wiring" of a child's brain begins at birth and that the first 3 years are instrumental in future cognitive and emotional development (Snow, Burns, & Griffin, 1998). Family Place Library librarians are trained to help parents understand the importance of the early years in child development. Family Place Libraries offer specially designed programs and materials, resource specialists, welcoming spaces, and relevant information that help to ensure that the young children of participating families are given a range of opportunities and tools with which to develop their early literacy skills.

Core Concept 2: Parents and caregivers, as a child's first teachers, are essential to the process of literacy development. Family Place Libraries reflect awareness that all families who are trying to raise healthy and productive children, particularly during the early, most formative years of a child's life, need access to resources and information as well as support from knowledgeable and welcoming individuals. Family Place Libraries provide spaces where parents can go to interact and play with their young children and, at the same time, get information and support in their parenting role. The Family Place Library librarian helps parents and caregivers to become knowledgeable about child-rearing practices that support early development, including information about fostering emergent literacy, and to gain a better understanding of their role as their child's first teacher.

> *This program has been very helpful since I got to know a lot about bringing up children. (Parent participant, Arizona, 2003)*

> *Some parents don't always have a support system. Child development, nutrition, play, speech and language development, and reading are all things that parents wonder whether or not they and their children are doing well. (Librarian, Branford, Connecticut)*

Core Concept 3: Play is important in early literacy. Another concept that is embedded in the Family Place Library Model is the understanding that play experiences and supportive parent–child interactions as well as access to books, print materials, and writing tools are critical for the emergence of reading and writing skills in young children. Research studies have demonstrated repeatedly that children develop their physical, mental, sensory, social, and other learning skills through play (Byrne, Deerr, & Kropp, 2003). Parents and caregivers who participate in Family Place Library activities are encouraged not only to create opportunities for children to play but also to engage in play with them as often as possible. Through modeling that occurs in the programs, through interaction with other parents, and through information and conversations with librarians and resource professionals, parents can broaden their views with respect to play.

> *What may seem to the uninformed observer to be an entertaining hour of play for families is actually much more.… Children need time, space, and interaction with other children and adults to use toys effectively and to lay the foundation for future learning. (Librarian, Cleveland, Ohio)*

Core Concept 4: Development of language skills is important in early literacy. Birckmayer (2001) wrote: "In order for emergent literacy skills to develop, children need to explore language that is sung, spoken, recited and written. It is available, knowledgeable, and willing adults who provide babies and toddlers with the experiences that encourage emergent literacy" (p. 26). This statement expresses one of the core concepts embedded in the Family Place Library approach—that is, providing "available, knowledgeable, and willing adults" to encourage young children's language development and to help parents and caregivers create language-rich environments.

> *Kids need lots of experiences in hearing language before speaking that first word.... [Family Place Library] is an opportunity for parents to reach out and get the assistance they need. (Child Care/Library Resource Specialist, Saginaw, Michigan)*

> *I understand how much my child could learn. Without the program I may not have offered him all the opportunities he needs. (Parent, 1999)*

Components of the Model

The characteristics and concepts described above are reflected in the core program components, which are explained below. Each of these components strengthens the value of the library as a lever for literacy.

The Parent–Child Workshop

The Parent–Child Workshop serves as the signature program at each Family Place Library. All participating libraries offer a 5- to 6-week series of sessions, each of which "looks like a toddler playground, and functions simultaneously as a library orientation, parent education class, early intervention screening, parent support group and cooperative program" (Feinberg & Rogoff, 1998, p. 51). The Parent–Child Workshop brings together toddlers from ages 1 to 3 and their parents in an early childhood setting filled with toys, art activities, and books. It encourages parents to play with their children, meet other parents or caregivers, and become familiar with library and community resources. Each week, a different child development professional from a local agency such as a hospital, speech clinic, university, or health or social service agency moves casually about the room and chats informally with participating family members about issues pertinent to their children. The librarian facilitates the smooth flow among the children, parents and caregivers, resource professionals, and library staff members and closes the workshop with a simple circle game, song, or finger play. The librarian's most important role is to get to know each family and promote the many resources that the library and other community agencies have to offer.

The Parent–Child Workshop provides a respite for parents who are raising a toddler and offers a comfortable meeting place for parents, many of whom are isolated and lack peer support. Parents often comment that the workshop provides them with an opportunity to meet other parents in the community with children around the same age as their own child. Some create follow-up playgroups or rearrange their own homes, using the workshop as a model layout. Many sign up for other library programs for themselves as well as their children and continue to use the library on a drop-in basis. They regularly check out age-appropriate materials to use at home and often consult with the librarian when they have child development issues and need information.

The workshop makes an immediate impression on families' perception of what the library has to offer. The program design emphasizes that families can come and leave as they choose, toddlers can select the activity they want to do, young siblings are invited to participate, and the focus is on play and verbal interaction between the caregiver and the child. These features help parents understand that what toddlers need most is autonomy, flexibility, mobility, and adult–child interactions within an appropriately structured environment. The availability of parent materials and community resource professionals—along with interaction with the librarian and other parents—promotes the library as a place to visit for information and support. Community resource professionals often help parents assess their children's development and regularly assist worried parents who are concerned that their children need intervention or evaluation services. The workshop changes the perception that libraries are no place for very young children.

> *The workshop is designed to detect any developmental problems the child may be having prior to entering preschool. That way the child reaches preschool reading ready. It is also designed to bring families together and build a relationship with the library. (Library Manager, South Carolina)*

A Welcoming Space for Infants, Young Children, and Families

Ensuring the right kind of space for families is a primary goal for the Family Place Library. Librarians recognize that the behavior of parents and caregivers within the library setting influences how children feel and act when they use the library and, therefore, influences their cognitive development. By placing comfortable furniture for caregivers in the children's room with parenting materials for them to read while the children play and interact with toys, games, and art materials, librarians create the ideal setting for learning and encourage families to use the library whenever it is convenient for them, not just when the library is offering a program (Feinberg & Schull, 2001). Some of the interesting items found in Family Place Library spaces include a fish tank, dollhouse, wooden train, plastic building blocks and table, and puppet stage. These spaces also might contain art materials that are interspersed with board, cloth, and picture books; puzzles; and multihued blocks spread out on a colorful rug. Many libraries also offer a computer station loaded with early childhood software just for preschool children and their caregivers.

> *Since literacy starts at day one, with the Family Place, children have a literate environment from the start. We do this with nursery rhymes, music, pictures on the wall, comfortable spaces that promote parent-child interaction, and lots of books. It serves as a model for parents of how to create a literate environment in their homes. (Library Director, New York)*

Special Collections for Parents, Caregivers, and Young Children

Public libraries have traditionally offered a wide range of materials targeted to specific audiences. Family Place Libraries emphasize collections that are designed to meet the informational needs of parents and caregivers as well as the developmental needs of very young children. These collections nurture various styles and modes of learning, respond to individual needs and preferences, and are appropriate for children and parents with a range of abilities and learning styles. The following paragraphs describe some of these collections in more detail.

Early Childhood Books and Audiovisual Materials. Infants and toddlers are especially attracted to cloth and board books, oversized picture books, and books with moving parts. A good collection of nursery rhyme, song, and finger-play books located within the Family Place section of the library encourages parents and caregivers to relearn rhymes and songs from their past. Many libraries circulate book–cassette or book–CD packets, CDs and tapes of popular music for infants and toddlers, and videos and DVDs of favorite picture books.

Toys. Establishing a toy lending collection at the library not only provides appropriate toys for use at home but also emphasizes the central importance of play in a young child's development and that libraries are fun and welcoming places. A recent search on the USA Toy Library Association Web site (http://usatla.deltacollege.org/) revealed that of 281 registered toy libraries, 56 are housed in public libraries. Still other public libraries circulate toys without being members of the association. Toy libraries are committed to the philosophy that play is a learning experience and toys are valuable learning tools as they nurture prereading and prewriting skills (Ponish, 1987).

Although a toy collection is an important resource for all families, access to toys with accommodations for various disabilities is a special value for families and children with special needs. A toy collection that integrates commercial toys and ideas for adapting them with specially designed adaptive toys and switches entices participants with a wide range of disabilities to come to the library and use its resources. For a child with a significant disability, one that limits his or her ability to move, communicate, or manipulate a toy, the availability of adapted toys can determine whether the child can experience the learning afforded by play. If children with disabilities are to develop into readers and writers, they must have similar opportunities to participate in literacy-building play experiences during their early childhood years as their peers without disabilities have. Providing these opportunities is the responsibility of libraries dedicated to the development and promotion of literacy. Reaching out in nontraditional ways to children with special needs and providing access to adapted play materials, equipment, and books encourages these children to reach their potential as readers and writers (Feinberg, Jordan, Deerr, & Langa, 1999).

Story Kits. Cleverly packaged kits allow libraries to preselect their materials for specific groups and settings. Story kits are typically designed for use by childcare providers and early childhood teachers, but families may use them also. Story kits include thematic collections of books, puppets, toys, activity guides, media, flannel board stories, and a copy of the book or books that can be enacted with the props provided.

Parenting Resources. Integral to the Family Place Library is the availability of a parents' collection, including books, videos, audiotapes, magazines, and pamphlets as well as access to electronic resources. Family Place Library librarians encourage parents to seek the assistance of all those staffing the Parent–Child Workshop or other library staff members when they have a question concerning their child. Often, while spending time in the early childhood space, parents may observe that their child may be delayed or exhibit a problem in one area of development. They may want to seek the advice of a resource professional and might ask the librarian for assistance in locating help. The additional value of the library, of course, is that information within the library can be readily gathered using a vast array of resources.

Coalition Building and Networking

The Family Place Library approach transforms the usual scenario in which children's librarians work in isolation from other family service providers and restrict their services to families who already visit the library or know about its existence. Creating a new scenario through networking with educators, social service workers, and health and human service providers, Family Place Library librarians reach out to others, reposition the library within the broader community, and become involved in local emergent literacy initiatives and other community issues affecting families of infants and toddlers. Librarians may find themselves sitting on local committees or commissions on children and families, writing joint grant proposals, or developing cooperative programs and services as a result of their coalition building activities (Feinberg & Schull, 2001). This networking is another example of a shift in perspective within the library system.

In addition to enabling collaborative thinking and synergy, coalition building and networking provide the librarian with knowledge about local services. As an information specialist, the librarian often provides referrals to local agency professionals. Being familiar with who and what is available in the community is essential to providing these referrals.

Outreach

Most Family Place Library librarians target families who are in need, traditionally would not use the library, and do not participate in regular language and literacy programming. Through training and technical assistance, Family Place Library librarians learn how to carry out a needs assessment in their communities and identify user groups and families with very young children who may be at risk. By redesigning the environment to be welcoming and appropriate for young children, Family Place Library librarians ensure that even those families who are new to the library can feel comfortable accessing the public resources that help them to be good parents. By reaching out to nontraditional library users and reinventing the image of the public library, librarians expand their constituencies, increase their value to the public they serve, and make the library a more vital influence in the lives of families and in the communities where those families reside.

Outreach strategies vary considerably from community to community, depending on the target population and the community's overall needs and assets. One of the best strategies for identifying and contacting hard-to-reach families and bringing them into the library is to conduct outreach through coalition partners. All across the Family Place Library network, this strategy has helped to draw new users into the library. Consider the following example:

> *The Freeport Library on Long Island has tried to encourage new Spanish-speaking residents to use the library and participate in Family Place Library. To reach these families, librarians worked with a local church that offered a Spanish-speaking mass. Bilingual library staff met with parishioners after a number of masses, established relationships with these families, and eventually accompanied them into the library for a Parent–Child Workshop, which was offered immediately after mass.*

Adaptation and Extension

One of the distinguishing features of a strong model is its capacity to retain its core principles and components while adapting to local circumstances and needs. As the national network of Family Place Libraries has grown, so too have the local variations, many of which have implications for libraries and literacy. Variations and enrichments in local settings are documented by national Family Place Library coordinators who provide a unique inventory of the ways in which a strong program can be replicated with adaptations for the local setting. At the same time, the original Family Place Library—MCPL—continues to experiment with new approaches to applying the core concepts that inform the model. The following sections present a sampling of ways in which the Family Place Library Model has been adapted through the creativity of Family Place Library coordinators working in scores of communities across the country.

Parent–Child Workshop at the Escalante Community Center

Although the Tempe, Arizona, public library successfully offered the Parent–Child Workshop to their middle-class urban families, they were not able to attract the large Spanish-speaking population. The solution was to bring the workshop to a place that the Spanish-speaking families were already frequenting—the Escalante Community Center—and to conduct intensive outreach in the immediate neighborhood. Bilingual library staff members host the workshop one morning per week at the Escalante Center. The center houses a small depository library where parenting materials and children's books not provided directly at the workshop can be ordered from the main library for reference and circulation. The Escalante Center staff members have been successful in getting the center's workshop participants to visit them at the main library where they are subsequently introduced to all the programs and services the library offers.

Portable Preschool for Family Home Child-Care Providers

The Patchogue-Medford, New York, public library offers its Portable Preschool program for registered family home child-care providers. Once a month, a librarian visits a home care site to read stories to the children. During the same visit, the librarian leaves a story kit containing books, finger plays, videos, and props for the home provider to use with the children during the next 4–6 weeks. The program follows the local school district's calendar, operating continually from September to June.

Project Link: The Library, Family Child Care, Parent–Child Connection

This project, designed to reach children and parents through family child care providers and funded initially through a New York State Parent–Child grant, is an ongoing service of the MCPL. Forty-five story time kits emphasizing 15 themes have been designed to enhance reading readiness activities in the family through the child's care environment and at home. The kits include books, audiovisual materials, puzzles, games, flannel board materials, and activity folders. A collaborative composed of the library, the Child Care Council, and Cornell University Cooperative Extension Service conducts programs for the providers and parents on how children learn and how to guide positive behavior. Library staff members conduct home visits to instruct the providers on the use of the kits.

Connect to America @ Your Library

Recognizing the large unmet need for immigrant and refugee families to make connections with educational and community resources and to gain assistance in preparing their very young children for school, the Yucca, Cholla, and Saguaro Branches of the Phoenix, Arizona, public library developed a partnership with the Valley of the Sun Refugee and Immigrant Serving Agencies (VISA) and the Arizona Refugee Community Center, the local office of the International Rescue Committee. The partners developed a multifaceted service program for families that incorporated the Family Place Library Model along with special programs for youth, workshops on economic self-sufficiency and microenterprise for mothers, and systematic work with the City of Phoenix to improve refugee families' access to local libraries. A needs assessment carried out at the outset of the project confirmed that few of the local refugee families had awareness of a public library, and many had low levels of literacy in their own language as well as limited English. The agencies involved undertook multiple simultaneous translations to carry out the Family Place Parent–Child Workshops. Parenting and child resource collections were redeveloped to accommodate languages such as Arabic, Somali, Farsi, and Vietnamese. The coalition that the library had created was critical to the success of the Family Place Library program, particularly with respect to the recruitment of volunteer translators and outreach to potential family participants.

Family Resource Coalition

The Grand Island, Nebraska, public library has organized a coalition of community organizations such as the Literacy Council, Red Cross, Crisis Center, and St. Francis Medical Center with the goal of "working together as a community on literacy and family support." Through involvement of coalition members, the library is able to offer the Parent–Child Workshop year round.

Involving Next Generation Professionals: Saint Paul Public Library, the College of St. Catherine, and the Family Place Library Program

Collaboration between public libraries and academic institutions is rare, especially in relation to literacy programming. A collaboration between the St. Paul, Minnesota, public library and three departments at the College of Saint Catherine demonstrates the benefits of involving students in library-based literacy programs. Through joint development of a service learning project, faculty, students, and librarians worked together to implement Family Place Libraries in a number of branches and to study the impact of Family Place Libraries on early child development and family literacy among immigrant mothers in a community setting. Through the involvement of students and faculty, the library was able to extend its strong commitment to outreach, engaging Hmong, Somali, and Vietnamese families who might otherwise not have known about or participated in the program. The partners were also able to carry out action research that has informed ongoing implementation of the program.

Learning Is a Family Affair

When Family Place Library librarians at the Mastics-Moriches-Shirley Community Library realized that immigrant parents of young children could not participate in ongoing English for Speakers of Other Languages (ESOL) classes or one-on-one tutoring or small-group classes offered through the library's literacy center because they had no child care, the librarians created a program to address the needs of both the parents and their children. Learning English: A Family Affair provided parents of young children instruction in ESOL while their toddlers and preschoolers engaged in a variety of emergent literacy activities in another room. Infants remained with parents. Incorporated into ESOL sessions was instruction on reading a very simple board book such as *I Went Walking* (Williams, 1996). A copy of the selected book was given to each family at the end of each program session. The child component in Learning English: A Family Affair is based on the Parent–Child Workshop model. Various interactive stations are set up throughout the room, including puzzles; plastic building blocks and train tables; art activities; and block, toy, and book areas. Library staff members, following the children's lead, describe in English all the activities that the child engages in and the materials being used. They share age-appropriate books and lead finger-play and song activities one-on-one and in small groups. At the end of the program, parents join their children and share a snack, and then everyone participates in a circle time of nursery rhymes, songs, and finger plays. Each family is then given the gift book, which is read aloud with each parent repeating the text in English. Parents and children are then encouraged to borrow educational toys and bilingual children's books, as well as those in their native language, to share with their toddlers at home.

Emergent Literacy in the Home Setting: The Parent–Child Home Program

This effort is a unique partnership between the Parent–Child Home Program (PCHP), a national home visiting program for toddlers of families with limited access to educational opportunities and public libraries. It provides home visits that offer literacy and school readiness assistance to families for whom libraries are inaccessible or may be intimidating. The partnership between PCHP and four library systems has created a library-sponsored home-visiting model that provides twice weekly home visits by paraprofessionals to support parents' efforts to develop their young children's language and literacy skills and to connect families to the library.

From Family Place to Family Center

This innovative collaboration with the Family Service League of Suffolk County, New York, enables the library to provide support to families, especially those who may benefit from other community programs. Staffed by a part-time family outreach worker, the library's Family Center offers a drop-in space available for parents and young children during all hours that the library is open. The space is complete with bilingual and multilingual materials for parents and children as well as bilingual promotional materials about the Family Center, the library's GED program, adult literacy opportunities, and citizenship programs. A librarian works closely with the family outreach worker to connect families in need of assistance to the services of the program's social worker and to ensure that the social worker is aware of all of the library's services. The family outreach worker conducts weekly parent support and discussion groups, initiates outreach into the community to encourage families not using the library to participate in library activities, meets one-on-one with families to assist them with referrals to community agencies and programs, provides initial family intervention, and helps families determine what resources might be available to address specific needs.

Reaching Teen Parents

The Mastics-Moriches-Shirley Community Library on Long Island has sponsored a Teen Parent–Child Workshop since 1984. Composed of teenage mothers and their children as well as pregnant adolescents, this program rests on the partnership that developed between the Teen Parent Program at the local youth center and the library. Some changes to the traditional Parent–Child Workshop were required to make this program work. For example, adaptations to the workshop were made to account for the developmental stages of the teens as they related to the needs of their babies.

Evaluation

The Family Place Evaluation Plan (Nagle & Gagliano, 2003) provides the framework for considering progress toward achieving goals. It includes surveys, interviews, focus groups, observations, and materials review to answer the following three questions:

- Did the Family Place Library encourage parents and caregivers to use books with children, read aloud to their children, or both?

- Did the Family Place Library encourage parents and caregivers to play and do creative activities with their children?

- Did the Family Place Library support the "parent as teacher" role by stressing parent and caregiver involvement in the child's early education?

Through the accumulating evidence from the ongoing evaluations, Family Place Libraries project organizers are able to continuously refine the program to strengthen its value as a bridge to literacy for infants and toddlers and their families.

Conclusion

Although the Family Place Library Model is not the only service model that advances libraries' inherent value as a bridge to literacy, this model offers a useful example of how a comprehensive approach can help reshape library practice, redefine the role of the librarian, influence parents' understanding of the library and their relationship to the librarian, foster collaboration with community agencies, and above all, provide a language-rich environment and developmentally appropriate activities to foster the formation of emergent literacy skills in the program's infant–toddler and family participants.

References

Birckmayer, J. (2001). The role of public libraries in emergent and family literacy. *Zero to Three, 21*(3), 24–29.

Bush, L. (2001). *Remarks of Laura Bush at the White House Summit on Early Childhood Cognitive Development.* Retrieved August 1, 2004, from http://www.whitehouse.gov/firstlady/news-speeches/speeches/fl20010726.html

Byrne, M., Deerr, K., & Kropp, L. (2003). "Book" a play date: Promoting emergent literacy through play. *American Libraries, 34,* 42–44.

CDAC (Capitol District Answers Corporation). (2000). *Final report on the Family Place/Creating Readers Program.* Unpublished report.

Feinberg, S., Jordan, B., Deerr, K., & Langa, M. (1999). *Including families and children with special needs.* New York: Neal-Schuman.

Feinberg, S., & Rogoff, C. (1998). Diversity takes children to a friendly Family Place. *American Libraries, 29*(7), 50–52

Feinberg, S., & Schull, D. D. (2001). Family Place Libraries: Transforming public libraries to serve very young children and their families. *Zero to Three, 21*(8), 4–10.

Kiefer, B. (2001). Understanding reading. *School Library Journal, 47*(2), 48–52.

Nagle, A., & Gagliano, C. (2003). *Family Place Libraries documentation and evaluation interim report.* Unpublished report.

Ponish, K. (1987). Babywise and toys develop literacy skills. *American Libraries, 18*(8), 709.

Snow, C. E., Burns, S., & Griffin, P. (Eds.). National Research Council, Committee on the Prevention of Reading Difficulties. (1998). *Preventing reading difficulties in young children.* Washington, DC: National Academy Press.

Williams, S. (with Vivas, J., Illustrator). (1996). *I went walking.* Orlando, FL: Red Wagon Books, Harcourt.

CHAPTER 24

Policy Recommendations to Support Early Language and Literacy Experiences in the Home and in Child Care

J. Ronald Lally and Peter L. Mangione

Almost all language and literacy experiences for children under age 3 happen in relationships with those who care for them. When conditions allow attentive care and responsive interactions, relationships between adults and infants blossom. Family support and child-care policies can foster the development of relationships that are full of rich nonverbal and verbal communications between young children and the adults who are important to them. This chapter describes five policy directions that local, state, and federal government agencies can adopt to ensure that parents and caregivers have the time, motivation, knowledge, and skill to engage in warm, caring language and literacy interactions with young children. Some policies affect families directly; others target programs that serve infants, toddlers, and their families. We also recommend a number of strategies for implementing these policies.

Policy Recommendation 1: Adopt and Fund Policies That Provide Newborns and Their Parents Time Together to Build Strong Relationships

The earliest bond between an adult and a child begins in the infant's first days and leads to an attachment that continues throughout life (DeWolff & van Ijzendoorn, 1997). From birth, infants are "genetically wired" to form a primary bond with one or two people whom they can recognize, trust, communicate with, and learn from (Broberg, 2000). Babies, for example, recognize their mother's smell soon after birth and seek her out for closeness and care (Barton & Brophy-Herb, this volume, p. 15; Cernoch & Porter, 1985). The parent–child attachment grows through repeated interactions during simple day-to-day experiences such as feeding, diaper changing, carrying, singing, reading, and simply gazing into one another's eyes. When the adult is physically and emotionally available in times of need, the baby experiences a feeling of security and trust. This trust marks the beginning of healthy social and emotional development for the child and of communicative exchanges between the young child and family members. As securely attached young children mature, they have an easier time developing positive relationships with others than do children whose relationships with parents and other adults are not as satisfying (Belsky & Cassidy, 1994; Sroufe, 1996). Studies show that infants with secure attachments to their mothers and fathers are at an advantage for acquiring competence in language, cognitive, social, and emotional skills (Belsky, Spritz, & Crnic, 1996). To form this vital attachment, babies need to have frequent time with and close proximity to their parents (Lally, 2002).

Paid leave for parents during the first 10 months of a baby's life gives the parent the opportunity to be fully present to build trust and shape crucial early parent–child communications. The United States is one of only a few industrialized nations that do not offer paid parental leave to parents of newborns (Kamerman & Kahn, 1994). Most industrialized countries offer leave with full or 80% salary reimbursement for the first 3 months of life; some provide it for the first 6 months. European nations provide anywhere from 6 months to 3 years of parental leave with some form of salary compensation. Since 1992, member countries in the Organization for Economic Cooperation and Development

(OECD)[1] provide, on average, 10 months of parental leave during the postnatal period, 36 weeks of which are funded (Oser & Cohen, 2003).

Although many U.S. policymakers recognize the importance of the early formation of strong relationships between young children and their parents—as well as the link between the quality of these relationships and children's future performance—only California policymakers have moved to give families comprehensive supported time to develop critical early relationships with their infants. California policymakers have legislated paid parental leave for the birth, adoption, or foster-care placement of a child (California S.B. 1661, 2002). Five other states and Puerto Rico provide paid maternity leave, however, only to parents of newborns (Larner, Behrman, Young, & Reich, 2001).

To enable all infants to have the early relationship experiences necessary for optimal communicative development, we recommend that federal policymakers expand the coverage that is currently available under the Family and Medical Leave Act (FMLA). We recommend that the FMLA

- cover all working mothers and fathers,
- provide 9 months of leave (instead of the current 3 months), and
- provide 80% of the income of the parent who is on leave.

In addition, federal and state policymakers should excuse families with children under the age of 3 from meeting the work requirements of the Temporary Assistance for Needy Families (TANF) program.

Policy Recommendation 2: Adopt and Fund Policies That Provide Adequate Training and Supervision to Family Support Specialists to Help Them Serve Families by Fostering Healthy Child Development and Dealing With Serious Challenges to Children's Well-Being

Many parents lack information about the ways in which talking, singing, reading, and playing with babies and toddlers can encourage their intellectual curiosity and prepare them for success in school. Some families face multiple

[1] OECD is the organization that develops labor practices for the European Union.

risks to their children's well-being, including economic hardship, racial discrimination, domestic or community violence (or both), and the stresses associated with immigration. Serious family problems such as substance abuse, maternal depression, and family violence often go hand in hand with children's communication and learning problems (National Research Council & Institute of Medicine, 2000). For example, a depressed mother may not have the emotional resources to pay attention, read cues, and give responsive messages to her baby, yet her infant needs this kind of attention from a caregiver to gain skills such as self-regulation and turn taking (Lally, Mangione, & Young-Holt, 1991).

We recommend that training programs be launched or expanded in child development, early care and education, child welfare, special education, family support, and infant mental health. The goals of this initiative would be (a) to increase the expertise and number of professional home visitors, child-care providers, and family support staff members who are professionally prepared to provide emotional support and information to young or stressed families and (b) to deal with serious concerns about developmental progress.[2] Practitioners need to know how to help parents develop safe, secure, and loving family relationships; engage in the give-and-take of communication; and create encouraging learning environments. They also need to learn the special skills required to treat parental substance abuse, child abuse and neglect, and prolonged depression.

Policy Recommendation 3: Adopt and Fund Policies That Encourage Opportunities for Children Whose Home Language Is Not English to Continue Developing Their Home Languages as Part of Their Care and Education Experiences

Across the United States, new educational programs are striving to ensure that American children learn a language other than English (August & Hakuta, 1998; Thomas & Collier, 1998). Thus, it is both ironic and unfortunate that

---

[2] This recommendation is similar to a recommendation made in *From Neurons to Neighborhoods*, the groundbreaking report from the National Research Council and Institute of Medicine of the National Academy of Sciences (2000).

children who do speak a language other than English in their early years often abandon that language by the time they reach middle school. In some parts of the country, a stigma is attached to speaking a language other than English. Obvious communication and social advantages result from using English as the primary language. As a result, many children learn English but leave their home language behind (Cummins, 1979; Lopez, 1978; Veltman, 1988; Wong Fillmore, 1991). When the home language is abandoned, children become unable to communicate with family members who speak only the home language.

We recommend that school systems launch public education efforts to alert parents whose first language is not English to the possibility that their children may abandon their home language as they learn English. Outreach to parents should include practical advice on strategies that encourage children to become bilingual (Winsler & Espinosa, 1999), including information about the types of child-care arrangements and early school experiences that parents should seek (or continue) to develop the child's home language in all the communication modes: listening, speaking, reading, and writing. We also recommend that all state and federal performance standards and guidelines for early care and education programs include standards designed to ensure that children whose home language is not English continue to develop proficiency in their home language while they are in care.

Policy Recommendation 4: Adopt and Fund Policies That Ensure That All Children, From Birth and Regardless of Income, Have Access to Positive Early Learning Experiences, Including Opportunities to Develop Language and Early Literacy Skills

High-quality child-care settings foster responsive, effective interactions between adults and young children and positive outcomes for children and their families. Well-trained teachers who are working in a supportive environment can engage infants and toddlers in the communicative exchanges that promote language and literacy (Cost, Quality, and Child Outcomes Study Team, 1995). We have identified six components of infant–toddler child care that, together, ensure high quality:

- A primary caregiver for each child,

- A small group size,

- Continuity of care,

- Individualized care,

- Cultural continuity between home and care environments, and

- Inclusion of children with special needs (see sidebar).

Six Components of Child-Care Quality

The following quality assurance practices, developed by WestEd's Program for Infant–Toddler Care (PITC), increase the chances that adult–child interactions that promote language development and early literacy will occur in the infant–toddler child-care setting (Lally & Mangione, 2002).

1. Primary Care

In a primary care system, each child is assigned to one special caregiver who is principally responsible for that child. When children spend a longer day in care than their primary caregiver, a second caregiver is assigned to also have a primary relationship with the child. Each child should have a special caregiver assigned to him or her at all times during the day. Primary care works best when caregivers team up to support one another and provide a backup for security for every child. Primary care does not mean exclusive care; however, it does mean that all parties know who has primary responsibility for each child (Bernhardt, 2000; Gonzalez-Mena, 2002; Raikes, 1996). New communication skills are likely to develop first with the primary caregiver and then with others in the child-care setting.

2. Small Groups

Every major research study on infant and toddler care has shown that small group size and good ratios are key components of good-quality care (Cost, Quality, and Child Outcomes Study Team, 1995; Kagan & Cohen, 1996). PITC in California recommends primary-care ratios of 1:3 or 1:4 in groups of 6–12 children, depending on their age (Lally, 1992; WestEd, 2000). The guiding principle is the younger the children, the smaller the group. Small groups enable caregivers to provide the personalized care that infants and toddlers need. These groups also support peaceful exchanges, freedom, and safety to move and explore, as well as the development of intimate relationships.

3. Continuity

Continuity of care is the third key to providing the deep connections that infants and toddlers need for high-quality child care. Programs that incorporate the concept of continuity of care continue to pair primary caregivers and children together throughout the 3 years of the infant–toddler period or for the entire time during that period of the child's enrollment in care (Lally, 1992). Again, this approach fosters the development of early language and literacy.

continued

4. Individualized Care

Following children's unique rhythms, styles, and communication patterns promotes well-being and a healthy sense of self. It is important to avoid making a child feel embarrassed because of biological rhythms or needs that are different from those of other children. Responding promptly to children's individual needs supports their growing ability to self-regulate—that is, to function competently in personal and social contexts (Bronson, 2000). The program adapts to the child rather than vice versa, and the child receives the message that she is important, that her needs will be met, and that her choices, preferences, and impulses are respected (PITC, 2004).

5. Cultural Continuity

Children develop a sense of who they are and what is important within the context of culture. Traditionally, during the early years of life, the child's family and cultural community have been responsible for transmitting values, expectations, ways of acting, and communication styles. As more children enter child care during infancy, questions increase about their cultural identities and sense of belonging. Consistency of care between home and child care, always important for the very young, becomes even more so when the infant or toddler is cared for in the context of cultural practices different from those of the child's own family (Mangione, 1995). Because of the important role of culture in development, caregivers who serve families from diverse backgrounds need to (a) heighten their understanding of the importance of culture in the lives of infants; (b) develop cultural competencies; (c) acknowledge and respect cultural differences; and (d) learn to be open, responsive to, and willing to negotiate with families about child-rearing practices. In this way, families and caregivers, working together, can facilitate the optimal development of each child.

6. Inclusion of Children With Special Needs

Inclusion means making the benefits of high-quality care available to all infants and toddlers through appropriate accommodations so each child—including those with disabilities—will have full, active program participation (Sandall & Ostrosky, 2000). Strategies already embraced above—that is, a relationship-based approach to the provision of care that is responsive to the individual child's cues and desires to learn—are as important for children with disabilities or other special needs as for children without these challenges. Infants who have responsive, enduring relationships develop emotional security (National Research Council & Institute of Medicine, 2000). This security gives them the foundation for becoming socially competent and resilient. Infants who have individualized care are allowed to learn and grow in their own way and at their own pace (WestEd, 2000).

Early care and education programs that include these six quality assurance elements have the capacity to structure settings for optimum language and literacy development as well as overall high-quality care. We recommend that implementation of these practices be a condition of governmental support for early care and education settings.

We also recommend three specific strategies for moving toward the goal of positive early learning experiences for every young child. First, we recommend investing public funds in high-quality early care and education for young children in families with low income. Research studies show a strong correlation between children who live in poverty and children who fail in school (Barnett, 1995; Barnett & Boocock, 1998; National Research Council & Institute of Medicine, 2000). Young children in families with low income are the least likely among all children to develop proficiency in language and literacy. They are also least likely to have the early learning experiences that promote later school success (National Research Council & Institute of Medicine, 2000; Snow, Burns, & Griffin, 1998). Currently, children in families with low income receive child care of the lowest quality, delivered by staff members with the least amount of training. This situation is true both for child-care homes and center-based programs (Shonkoff, 1995)—and despite evidence that investments in high-quality services for children in families with low income have a great long-term economic payoff (Lynch, 2004) and long-term benefits to society, including the development of a populace with literate citizens (National Research Council & Institute of Medicine, 2000). Currently, state and local spending for child care for infants and toddlers is so limited that low quality is almost inevitable. We recommend, in contrast to the present policies, the investment of public funds to ensure that all children from birth to age 3 in families with low income have access to comprehensive early care and education services that are comparable in quality to Early Head Start (Head Start Bureau, 1996).

Second, we also recommend investing in early care and education facilities to provide well-designed, aesthetically pleasing spaces and materials that promote exchanges between very young children and caregivers. Minimizing background noise, for example, is critical in a child-care setting for infants and toddlers because they cannot filter out noise as well as adults can (Mangione, 1995). Both infants and adults need places in the classroom where they can easily engage in uninterrupted communication, without distractions caused by traffic flow or other children's noisy play. The physical environment of the infant–toddler child-care setting can support caregivers' promotion of early language and literacy. Supportive environments "minimize management and custodial activities, allowing caregivers more time for interaction, observation, and facilitation of children's development" (Torelli & Durrett, 1996, p. 15). Visually pleasing, acoustically controlled, and efficient work spaces are pleasant for caregivers and allow them to focus on children's needs because their own personal and professional needs are met. Quiet nooks, comfortably furnished with soft objects that absorb sound, make it easy for caregivers and infants to enjoy a book or conversation together. Even the placement of plumbing may influence the quality of an infant's experience with language. A diaper-changing area that is strategically located to minimize disruptions will encourage sustained, one-on-one interaction between the caregiver and child during diapering—which, in turn, will aid rich experiences with language (Gonzalez-Mena, 2002; see also DeMartini, this volume, p. 309; Payne & O'Brien, this volume, p. 291).

Third, and finally, we recommend that all universal preschool and school readiness initiatives provide adequate funding for high-quality services to infants and toddlers beginning at birth, ideally by setting aside for infants and toddlers a percentage of the budget allocated to the overall early childhood initiative. As the universal preschool movement gains momentum (Jacobson, 2004) in the context of existing school readiness initiatives (The White House, n.d.), policymakers should remember that success in school builds on experiences during the infant–toddler period. The child's earliest learning experiences help the child not only to maintain inborn motivation to learn but also to develop a rich, useful vocabulary and a delight in books.

Policy Recommendation 5: Adopt and Fund Policies That Ensure a Well-Educated, Well-Compensated Workforce to Offer Every Infant and Toddler Rich Language and Literacy Experiences in the Child-Care Setting

Research has demonstrated that well-trained and well-compensated staff members promote stability and quality in child care (Johnson, Pai, & Bridges, 2004; Kagan & Cohen, 1997). Yet in 2003, the average wage of a center-based child-care worker was $8.91 per hour (Oser & Cohen, 2003). Policymakers in the United States must come to understand—as leaders of other industrialized nations have—that the market cannot afford the true costs of quality infant–toddler care (Cost, Quality, and Child Outcomes Study Team, 1995; Kagan & Cohen, 1996). Subsidies from sources other than parent fees are needed to ensure the availability of adult–infant ratios in which early language and literacy flourish.

We recommend that compensation for child-care providers be linked to professional development and credentials (Cost, Quality, and Outcomes Child Study Team, 1995). We suggest that the United States follow the lead of many European countries and credential infant-care teachers (European Commission, 1994; Kagan & Cohen, 1996; Kamerman & Kahn, 1994, 1995). We recommend requiring an associate of arts or sciences degree in early childhood education or child development for all infant–toddler teachers and a bachelor's degree for directors of programs that serve infants and toddlers. Pay increases should favor individuals who obtain additional schooling and advanced credentials.

We recommend the use of greater wages and benefits to attract well-qualified caregivers to infant–toddler early care and education settings and to reward them for continued service. For example, we recommend one-time stipends to draw people to work in infant–toddler services, along with higher compensation for caregivers who are fluent in both English and another major language of the community. To encourage continuity of care for infants and toddlers, we recommend access to adequate health insurance and other employee benefits for all infant-care teachers.

We recommend continuing education for all infant–toddler child-care providers, sufficient time to participate in training, and regularly scheduled reflective supervision. To provide individualized language and literacy experiences in a group setting, infant–toddler caregivers need time for training and reflection. They must have time to plan adaptations in practice so they can offer learning experiences to match each child's interests, skill levels, and thinking processes. Teachers need time—individually and with peers, mentors, and supervisors—to review their own efforts and the children's progress. In addition to onsite learning, all staff members should have regular access to outside professional development opportunities.

Conclusion

It may seem that the policy recommendations of this chapter range far from the specific task of supporting the development of language and literacy in infants and toddlers; however, a closer look at the experiences that support early language and literacy in child-care settings shows that core components of quality make meaningful communicative exchanges possible. Very young children need unhurried time with knowledgeable, responsive adults with whom they feel at ease and engaged. Adults need time to spend with individual children and to take responsibility for a small enough group of infants or toddlers that they can read the children's cues and engage them in meaningful, ongoing interactions. Professional caregivers also need supportive physical environments, training in the skills that foster early language and literacy, time for contemplation, appropriate compensation, supportive supervision, and professional recognition to draw them to—and keep them in—the vocation of infant–toddler care. Wise public policy and skilled, sensitive practice mark the path to school readiness.

References

August, D., & Hakuta, K. (1998). *Educating language minority children.* Washington, DC: National Academies Press.

Barnett, W. S. (1995). Long-term effects of early childhood programs on cognitive and school outcomes. *The Future of Children, 5*(3), 25–50.

Barnett, W. S., & Boocock, S. S. (Eds.). (1998). *Early care and education for children in poverty: Promises, programs, and long-term results.* Albany: State University of New York Press.

Barton, L. R., & Brophy-Herb, H. E. (2006). Developmental foundations for language and literacy from birth to 3 years. In S. E. Rosenkoetter & J. Knapp-Philo (Eds.), *Learning to read the world: Language and literacy in the first three years* (pp. 15–60). Washington, DC: ZERO TO THREE Press.

Belsky, J., & Cassidy, J. (1994). Attachment: Theory and evidence. In M. Rutter & D. Hay (Eds.), *Development through life* (pp. 373–402). Oxford, U.K.: Blackwell.

Belsky, J., Spritz, B., & Crnic, K. (1996). Infant attachment security and affective–cognitive information processing at age 3. *Psychological Science, 7,* 111–114.

Bernhardt, J. L. (2000). A primary caregiving system for infants and toddlers: Best for everyone involved. *Young Children, 55*(2), 74–80.

Broberg, A. G. (2000). A review of interventions in the parent–child relationship informed by attachment theory. *Acta Paediatrica Supplement, 434,* 37–42.

Bronson, M. B. (2000). *Self-regulation in early childhood: Nature and nurture.* New York: Guilford.

California Senate Bill 1661, 2002.

Cernoch, J. M., & Porter, R. H. (1985). Recognition of maternal axillary odors by infants. *Child Development, 56,* 1593–1598.

Cost, Quality, and Child Outcomes Study Team. (1995). *Cost, quality, and child outcomes in child care centers.* Denver: University of Colorado at Denver, Department of Economics.

Cummins, J. (1979). *Empowering minority students.* Sacramento: California Association for Bilingual Education.

DeMartini, T. (2006). Group environments that foster language and literacy. In S. E. Rosenkoetter & J. Knapp-Philo (Eds.), *Learning to read the world: Language and literacy in the first three years* (pp. 309–334). Washington, DC: ZERO TO THREE Press.

DeWolff, M. S., & van IJzendoorn, M. H. (1997). Sensitive and attachment: A meta-analysis on parental antecedents of infant attachment. *Child Development, 68,* 571–591.

European Commission. (1994). *Leave arrangements for workers with children: A review of leave arrangements in the member states of the European Community and Austria, Finland, Norway, and Sweden.* Brussels, Belgium: European Commission Network on Child Care and Other Measures to Reconcile Employment and Family Responsibilities for Women and Men.

Gonzalez-Mena, J. (2002). *Infant/toddler caregiving: A guide to routines* (2nd ed.). Sacramento: California Department of Education and WestEd.

Head Start Bureau. (1996). *Head Start performance standard and program guidance: Code of Federal Regulations, Title 45, Parts 1301–1311.* Washington, DC: U.S. Department of Health and Human Services, Administration for Youth and Families.

Jacobson, L. (2004). Early childhood education—States moving toward universal coverage. *Educational Reform Backgrounder, 24.*

Johnson, L. R., Pai, S. A., & Bridges, M. (2004). *Policy Brief 04–1: Advancing the early childhood workforce: Implementation of training and retention initiatives in the Bay Area.* Berkeley: Policy Analysis for California Education.

Kagan, S. L., & Cohen, N. E. (Eds.). (1996). *Reinventing early care and education: A vision for a quality system.* San Francisco: Jossey-Bass.

Kagan, S. L., & Cohen, N. E. (1997). *Not by chance: Creating an early care and education system for America's children.* New Haven, CT: The Yale Bush Center in Child Development and Social Policy.

Kamerman, S. B., & Kahn, A. J. (1994). *A welcome for every child: Care, education, and family support for infants and toddlers in Europe.* Washington, DC: ZERO TO THREE.

Kamerman, S., & Kahn, A. (1995). *Starting right: How America neglects its youngest children and what we can do about it.* New York: Oxford University Press.

Lally, J. R. (1992). *Together in care: Meeting the intimacy needs of infants and toddlers in groups* [Videotape]. Sacramento: California Department of Education and WestEd.

Lally, J. R. (2002, May 8). *Importance of parent/child attachment and how it affects child and adult functioning.* Testimony before California Senate Labor and Industrial Relations Committee, Sacramento.

Lally, J. R., & Mangione, P. L. (2002). *The PITC philosophy.* Sausalito, CA: WestEd.

Lally, J. R., Mangione, P. L., & Young-Holt, C. L. (1991). *Infant/toddler caregiving: A guide to language development and communication.* Sacramento: California Department of Education and WestEd/Far West Laboratory for Educational Research and Development.

Larner, M. B., Behrman, R. E., Young, M., & Reich, K. (2001). Caring for infants and toddlers: Analysis and recommendations. Retrieved June 16, 2004, from www.futureofchildren.org/information2826/information_show.htm?doc_id=79326

Lopez, D. E. (1978). Chicano language loyalty in an urban setting. *Sociology and Social Research, 62,* 267–278.

Lynch, R. G. (2004). *Exceptional returns: Economic, fiscal, and social benefits of investment in early childhood development.* Washington, DC: Economic Policy Institute.

Mangione, P. L. (1995). *Infant/toddler caregiving: A guide to culturally sensitive care.* Sacramento: California Department of Education.

National Research Council & Institute of Medicine. (2000). *From neurons to neighborhoods: The science of early childhood development* (J. P. Shonkoff & D. A. Phillips, Eds.). Committee on Integrating the Science of Early Childhood Development; Board on Children, Youth, and Families; Commission on Behavioral and Social Sciences and Education. Washington, DC: National Academy Press.

Oser, C., & Cohen, J. (2003). *America's babies: The ZERO TO THREE Policy Center data book.* Washington, DC: ZERO TO THREE Press.

Payne, C. C., & O'Brien, M. (2006). Promoting language and literacy in child care. In S. E. Rosenkoetter & J. Knapp-Philo (Eds.), *Learning to read the world: Language and literacy in the first three years* (pp. 291–308). Washington, DC: ZERO TO THREE Press.

Program for Infant/Toddler Caregivers (PITC). (2004). Retrieved June 7, 2004, from www.pitc.org

Raikes, H. (1996). A secure base for babies: Applying attachment concepts to the infant care setting. *Young Children, 51*(5), 59–67.

Sandall, S., & Ostrosky, M. (2000). *Natural environments and inclusion* (Young Exceptional Children Monograph Series No. 2). Longmont, CO: Sopris West and the Division for Early Childhood.

Shonkoff, J. P. (1995). Child care for low-income families. *Young Children, 50*(6), 63–65.

Snow, C. E., Burns, M. S., & Griffin, P. (Eds.). National Research Council, Committee on the Prevention of Reading Difficulties. (1998). *Preventing reading difficulties in young children.* Washington, DC: National Academy Press.

Sroufe, L. A. (1996). *Emotional development.* Cambridge, U.K.: Cambridge University Press.

Thomas, W. P., & Collier, V. P. (1998). Two languages are better than one. *Educational Leadership, 55*(4), 23–27.

Torelli, L., & Durrett, C. (1996). Landscapes for learning: The impact of classroom design on infants and toddlers. *Early Childhood News, 8*(2), 12–15.

Veltman, C. (1988). *The future of the Spanish language in the United States.* New York: Hispanic Policy Development Project.

WestEd. (2000). *The program for infant/toddler caregivers: Group care* (2nd ed.). Sacramento: California Department of Education.

The White House. (n.d.). *Good Start, Grow Smart: The Bush Administration's early childhood initiative.* Retrieved June 4, 2004, from www.whitehouse.gov/infocus/earlychildhood/toc.html

Winsler, A., & Espinosa, L. (1999). When learning a second language does not mean losing the first: Bilingual language development in low-income, Spanish-speaking children attending bilingual preschool. *Child Development, 70*(2), 349–353.

Wong Fillmore, L. (1991). When learning a second language means losing the first. *Early Childhood Research Quarterly, 6*, 322–346.

Photo by Raymond Ching

CHAPTER 25

StoryQUEST: An Ecological Training Model for Beginning Language and Literacy

Joanne Knapp-Philo and Linda Brekken

I want to do all the things that my parents did not know to do for me. I want to absorb the new information like a sponge and do it for my children, so they can have opportunities that were not available for me.
—Parent

Many of us take reading for granted. It is part of our daily lives. We read street signs and construction detours. We read the newspaper. We discuss the latest books that we have read or plan to read. We read and write as we work on computers. We read billboards and signs without awareness of our actions. We read to our children and assume that they, too, will become readers. We value academic achievement and stress how important school performance will be to our children's future professional accomplishments. Reading opens doors to opportunities and success in the mainstream culture. How can we ensure that these opportunities are available for everyone?

Not all American families share the same literacy experience. Because of economics, lack of opportunity, language barriers, or other life circumstances, reading may not be part of their lives. The doors to opportunity that reading can open remain closed for many families and their children.

*I didn't have the opportunity to get an education. Now I want
my children to have those opportunities to study so that their
lives won't be as hard as mine is.* (Parent)

Recent research stresses the importance of the first 3 years in laying a foundation for later skills and in preparing children for successful school experiences. Many studies have focused on effective strategies for promoting language and literacy skills within these critical early years (National Research Council & Institute of Medicine, 2000; Snow, Burns, & Griffin, 1998). Hart and Risley (1995, 1999) suggested that language experiences in the first 3 years of life have a direct and potent influence on a child's ability to succeed in school.

There is also a growing knowledge base about what promotes language and literacy from the first days of life. Researchers such as Bus and de Jong (see this volume, p. 123), Hart and Risley (1995, 1999), Lim and Cole (2000), MacDonald (2001), van Kleeck and Beckley-McCall (2002), and many others continue to document specific experiences and strategies that foster a strong foundation in beginning language and literacy. However, this information is not widely known by families or by practitioners. StoryQUEST, the ecological training approach described in this chapter, synthesizes and shares evidence-based practices for promoting early language and literacy with families and service providers.

Families provide the fertile soil where the seeds of literacy are planted. Children absorb the values of their family and community. They imitate what they see modeled. Yet many families do not understand their important role in promoting literacy, and they may not understand and celebrate what they already do to help their children build a strong foundation for learning. Families want the best for their children, but they may not be familiar with the research-based strategies that can promote their children's future success. Families need access to the specific strategies that support beginning language and literacy to develop within the context of their family's values, beliefs, and lifeways.

Early care and education programs serve as the water that enables the seeds sown by families to grow. To nurture each child's development, programs must increasingly focus on developing staff commitment and skills in this area as well as supporting families to promote beginning language and literacy at home. Early care and education caregivers have the opportunity to provide enriched environments that encourage the overall development of infants and toddlers as well as to model literacy skills with the goal of helping children and their families experience literacy-rich practices. Yet program staff members do not always understand the implications of the newest research for their day-to-day interactions with young children and their families. Direct service providers—indeed, many supervisors and administrators, too—may not be familiar with the strategies that support beginning language and literacy for infants and toddlers. They often cannot explain how their daily activities support literacy development. Similar to families, professionals also need opportunities for new learning.

Communities within which children, families, and programs live provide the nutrients that nurture the development of beginning language and literacy. Community support for the seeds of learning that families plant—and that early education staff members water—may take many forms. Libraries, community centers, early childhood programs, fast food restaurants, waiting rooms, public transportation, parks, and other features of community life can provide rich early literacy experiences. However, most professionals and community leaders lack up-to-date information on beginning language and literacy as well as the most developmentally appropriate, evidence-based strategies for infants and toddlers. Community-level partners need to be educated about research and effective practices just as families and programs do.

Where Do We Start?

How do we provide all families with the necessary sunshine to make the seeds they have planted grow and prosper? Clearly, there is a widespread need for new learning opportunities focused on early language and literacy for families, early care and education staff, programs, and community leaders. How do we begin to address these needs in a comprehensive and cohesive way while honoring the developmental characteristics of infants and toddlers and their families? This chapter describes a training approach that was specifically designed to shine the light of information and action on families, teachers, early care and education programs, and communities. StoryQUEST: Celebrating Beginning Language and Literacy was funded by the United States Department of Education[1] to provide timely, evidence-based information and

[1] This model was developed in part under Early Childhood Educator Professional Development grant #S349A020002 to the California Institute on Human Services at Sonoma State University.

action strategies to stimulate beginning language and literacy. Designed for families, programs, and communities with the highest developmental risk (National Research Council & Institute of Medicine, 2000), StoryQUEST served Early Head Start, but can be adapted to serve child care and Early Intervention as well.

This chapter will discuss the StoryQUEST model of training that provides state-of-the-art strategies to promote beginning language and literacy in infants and toddlers; supports participants to transfer attitudes, knowledge, and skills from the continuing education setting into their daily lives; and presents a framework for sustaining the innovations after the training has ended. This training approach addresses the issues of beginning language and literacy at multiple levels and creates substantive and sustainable change in the formative experiences of many of this nation's most vulnerable infants and toddlers, enabling them to develop a strong foundation for lifelong learning. A discussion of key elements of the training model will be followed by an overview of the cumulative curriculum that builds from session to session, weaving intensive training with application, coaching, feedback, and continuing implementation over a period of years.

The StoryQUEST Training Model

"Be the change you want to see," (Mahatma Gandhi). This spirit of personal responsibility and leadership permeates this model. StoryQUEST aims at changing both individual and system behaviors. The training considers both content and process. The design of a learning opportunity, the ways that information is conveyed, the expectations of the participants and their trainers, and the overall learning environment all profoundly influence adult learners and affect the ways they act on the material presented (Knowles, 1980). The StoryQUEST training model builds on the Hilton–Early Head Start Training Program (for more information about this program, see Knapp-Philo, Corso, Brekken, & Bair Heal, 2004). In addition to multiple, intensive, 3-day training events, the model includes follow-up in the form of frequent on-site visits by learning coaches, online learning opportunities, and conference calls. All initial training and the follow-up efforts are designed to ensure that participants transfer what they have learned in training to use in their daily lives. In addition to supporting change among those who participate, StoryQUEST is designed to alter the cultures and structures of the organizations in which the participants work and, thus, support long-term, organizational change (Sparks & Hirsh, 1997).

Six critical components of the StoryQUEST model address change in the entire ecological system and promote transfer from training to practice. The six components include (a) team training, (b) a variety of milieus through which to foster skill acquisition and teaming, (c) a focus on the needs of learners with diverse experiences and backgrounds, (d) opportunities for participants to incorporate the StoryQUEST philosophy and strategies into their personal systems of beliefs and practices, (e) follow-up after training to ensure carryover to the workplace, and (f) peer mentoring to spread the effect of training. These key concepts not only are integrated into the design of the training but also are discussed directly throughout the curriculum.

Component 1: Team Training

Beginning language and literacy for young children develops through consistent, responsive interactions with families, caregivers, and early care and education programs. Communities can inform, support, and reinforce the strategies used by families and programs as well as endorse and encourage the value of early language and literacy in powerful ways (see Zukoski & Luluquisen, this volume, p. 429). All parts of the ecological system in which a young child lives and grows interact and affect one another (Bronfenbrenner, 1979). It seems only logical, then, that teams of individuals who support young children's language and literacy should be trained together (Bailey, 1989; Garland & Frank, 1997; Winton, 1990). Beam, Ford, and Laurel (1993) found that simply training interdisciplinary groups was not as effective as training specific teams that regularly work together. Team training provides the opportunity for learning to occur in the context in which new knowledge, skills, and attitudes will be used. In addition to providing opportunities for team members to gain specific information, process it together, and develop teaming skills, team training models the outcome that families, programs, and communities will then work together to achieve, producing the desired results.

StoryQUEST teams are drawn from early care and education programs across the country and consist of six members, including the following:

- A parent whose child is enrolled in the program

- A direct-service provider from the program

- A supervisor who works with the direct-service provider, if such a role exists in the program

- The program administrator

- A community partner who has an interest in beginning language and literacy (e.g., the local children's librarian)

- A representative from a preschool program that receives 3-year-olds who transition from the infant–toddler program

The StoryQUEST training schedule includes time to ensure that all team members not only understand their own unique role in the ecological process but also appreciate one another's roles. Participants from the very beginning follow a conscious process of working as a team, and this emphasis continues throughout the training. Focus on teamwork is especially important because some team members know one another and have worked together before the training, whereas others may be new acquaintances. In addition, some participants may be unfamiliar with the reasons for including a parent and a community member on the team. They come to realize that parent members are key participants who are in the unique position to "keep the discussion real" and provide critical guidance to professionals about what families need; they also serve as liaisons to other families in the program and community (Buysse & Wesley, 1993). Likewise, community members offer a broader perspective that can expand the thinking of the program staff members as the team learns about beginning language and literacy, considers how to incorporate the ideas into their own work, and forges new collaborations with community agencies and early care and education programs. Each team member brings a unique set of knowledge, skills, and perspectives that enhance the team's performance. The StoryQUEST model provides ongoing opportunities for role clarification and other teaming activities throughout each training event and on-site follow-up because one intended outcome of the overall experience is to build interdisciplinary teams.

The team is the focal point of the training. Although it is important for each individual team member to learn and grow optimally from the training experience, it is critical that the team as a whole learns and grows. Thus, the structure of the training is designed to support teaming and team development. For the most part, team members participate in the training as a group. No more than six teams, each having six participants, learn together in a training room, called a *cluster.* The cluster's six teams work together with the same two trainers throughout a StoryQUEST event. The cluster serves as a homeroom, and although participants come and go from time to time, this grouping provides a secure base to which they return. Ground rules are established to ensure a safe and productive learning environment. The seating is arranged to facilitate exchange among team members as they work to understand the new information and consider how to apply it with their own family, program, and community (see Figure 25.1). A large training event could have several clusters of six teams, each cluster with its own facilitators and each group learning the same information at the same time.

Figure 25.1. StoryQUEST Training Room Design

Source: Reprinted with permission from StoryQUEST.

Component 2: A Variety of Milieus Through Which to Promote Skill Acquisition and Teaming

The cluster provides the primary setting for learning at a StoryQUEST training event. Trainers present state-of-the-art information and synthesize relevant research findings, which teams then discuss and apply, with the support of a learning coach, to their own setting. Participants often work on ideas and activities in their own team and then share their ideas with other teams in the cluster. This approach provides practice in teamwork and supports the application of key research to the unique local reality while it also ensures cross-pollination of ideas, ongoing sharing, and relationship building with colleagues from other programs. Teams also develop new group norms as they participate in this process (McCollum & Catlett, 1997).

At certain points during each training event, team members disperse into Role-Alike and Breakout sessions. The Role-Alike sessions provide the opportunity for those in similar roles (e.g., parent, administrator) to network, share ideas, support one another, and consider new information in the context of their own unique role. Team members separate to attend Breakout sessions individually or in pairs. The Breakout sessions allow StoryQUEST to deliver more information on more topics during a training event, thereby ensuring each team access to a greater amount of information. Following each Role-Alike or Breakout session, participants return to their clusters to rejoin their teammates and share their experiences with the team. Participants follow a prescribed "share back" process to ensure that all team members have equal opportunities to contribute. Each team member discusses the content of the session that she attended and makes suggestions for how this information might apply to their team, program, and community. Share back involves reviewing material from the session (thereby reinforcing one's own learning), sharing information, making judgments about the material, suggesting ways it applies to the team's work, and practicing listening and teaming skills. Teammates integrate their new learning and discuss what new strategies they will incorporate into program practices. The intention is that each team grows stronger as a result of shared knowledge and commitment.

Component 3: A Focus on the Needs of Learners With Diverse Experiences and Backgrounds

Each team member makes a commitment to learn new concepts; explore ways to implement new ideas into the daily routine; and share the training attitudes, ideas, and skills with others at home. Training participants have widely varied backgrounds, educational experiences, and worldviews. Therefore, the StoryQUEST training model demonstrates ways to ensure that learning is applicable for diverse groups by using multiple modalities for presentation and processing. For example, translated materials and interpretation are available when English is not a participant's preferred language for learning. PowerPoint slides and handouts support those who learn visually. Videos provide pictures of complex actions and ideas in application. Trainers explain the concepts for auditory learners.

A wide variety of activities, including large group discussions, team discussions, role plays, problem-solving scenarios, dyad sharing, and creative group tasks (e.g., the team creates a poster, song, or advertisement about its approach to promoting beginning language and literacy) address the diverse learning styles and backgrounds of the participants. The share back opportunities discussed above allow participants to teach one another. When participants attend break-out sessions in pairs, they are able to confer and support one another as they share back with their entire team.

StoryQUEST encourages reflection to support learning and provides structured time each day to allow participants to reflect on what has been discussed. There are individual, team, and cluster reflection activities. Guidance is provided for those for whom this kind of training is a new experience. Participants may reflect by journaling, dictating into a tape recorder, painting, drawing, writing, or creating constructions. Despite the fact that StoryQUEST focuses on beginning language and literacy, there is recognition that participants have varied reading levels. Thus, the training model provides a variety of ways for participating and responding.

Component 4: Opportunities for Participants to Incorporate the StoryQUEST Philosophy and Strategies Into Their Personal Systems of Beliefs and Practices

Virtually every session in every StoryQUEST training event involves the trainers sharing information followed by an activity in which participants consider ways to apply the concepts in their own lives. All the reflection activities discussed above support participants to move the training ideas, skills, and attitudes into their own practice, that is, to make it their own. Teams are required to develop a vision for their work and to review and celebrate their accomplishments. In addition, the final activity of each training event requires teams to work through a prescribed process, called a Culminating Activity, that brings together all the key attitudes, knowledge, and skills discussed during the training event and asks each team to apply these in a scenario that relates to its own community. This experience provides further opportunity for active involvement in and ownership by the participants (Sparks & Hirsh, 1997).

Finally, teams develop four to six goals, listing actions they wish to take from the training and implement at home (McCollum & Catlett, 1997). They implement the chosen practices between training events and report back on their progress and challenges at the subsequent training event. StoryQUEST's expectation is that after repeating this process several times, the teams will continue the process of goal setting, implementation, evaluation, and new planning after their formal participation in StoryQUEST ends. Participants frequently comment on the effectiveness of the goal-setting process. The model enables teams to develop goals that address the unique assets and needs in their programs and communities. This process has been highly valued by team members and has been seen to result in improved follow-through and accountability.

Component 5: Follow-Up After Training to Ensure Carryover to the Workplace

In their new paradigm for staff development for educators, Sparks and Hirsh (1997) noted that job-embedded training that features follow-up coaching at the worksite helps trainees change their practice. To master skills and move up the continuum from novice learner to expert (Kim, 1999), trainees need opportunities to practice new skills, consider and discuss challenges with their colleagues, and participate in follow-up (Joyce & Showers, 1988). On-site follow-up provides participants with the opportunity to engage with new topics over time and results in sustained, changed behaviors. Trainees who do not have follow-up usually do not continue implementing new knowledge and skills (Joyce & Showers, 1988).

The StoryQUEST model for learning coaches is built on that of the Hilton–Early Head Start Training Program. These highly skilled consultants have

- Strong skills in facilitating team process and organizational change
- Comfort with and skill in adapting to a variety of adult learning styles, personal characteristics, and organizational dynamics
- Experience with data collection for research and accountability purposes
- Willingness to maintain the integrity of a research design
- Experience with and commitment to continuous improvement
- Strong interpersonal and communication skills
- Experience working with infants and toddlers
- Experience working with families of very young children to promote family involvement and leadership
- Experience with infant–toddler programs
- Experience and comfort with diverse cultures, languages, and abilities
- Ability to mentor, support, and supervise others as they assume a mentoring role
- Proficiency in technology and personal access to technology
- Strong knowledge of recommended practices in early literacy for infants and toddlers

Learning coaches (one for each team) participate in the training events with the team; facilitate processing of information and goal development; make on-site visits for 2 entire and consecutive days every other month; and provide phone, fax, and e-mail consultation as needed. During on-site visits, learning coaches meet with their teams to review progress on their goals and plan next steps, work with dyads of peer mentors (see component 6), and observe and provide feedback to staff members about specific strategies under development and application.

Learning coaches receive 2 days of training before each StoryQUEST training event, ongoing supportive supervision from StoryQUEST staff members, and bimonthly conference calls for training, problem solving, and group support. The mantra that defines the learning coach position is "Be the guide by the side, not the sage on the stage." Because the emphasis is on the teams making the learning their own, reflective guidance and facilitation are used to support the team as a whole and individual team members as they come to their own resolution. Following are some comments about learning coaches in action:

> *"Our learning coach is the reason we've accomplished so much."*

* * *

> *"Our learning coach keeps us excited and makes [beginning language and literacy] even more important than we first thought."*

* * *

> *"[She] ... is very supportive, our table's guide. She continues to be a resource to our 'quest' and an asset to our team."*

* * *

> *"[He] ... keeps us focused and on track and reminds us of our next steps."*

Component 6: Peer Mentoring to Spread the Effects of Training

It is often lamented that training rarely changes organizations or even individual practice. One frequently cited reason is that when only part of the staff participates in the training, some staff members have neither the "buy-in" nor the information to create and sustain new approaches (Sparks & Hirsh, 1997). Another challenge in spreading the effect of training in early care and education has been the high turnover rate that permeates the early childhood profession. StoryQUEST uses peer mentoring as a planned way to spread the effect of the training. (See Rosenkoetter, this volume, p. 369, for a detailed description of peer mentoring.)

Each of the six StoryQUEST team members has a peer, an individual with a similar role (e.g., another parent, another supervisor), with whom the training participants share information and materials from the training. In addition, the full team of 12 (training participants plus their peer mentors) meets with the learning coach on a bimonthly basis. At the training event, the team members who travel to training select topics for goals that will be the focus of the full team's work until the next training event. It is the full team of 12, however, that determines the steps to be taken to complete each goal, sets the timelines, assigns responsibilities for each of the activities, and evaluates its results.

A key premise of peer mentoring is that this association is an equal relationship. Each party brings skills, ideas, and challenges to the relationship. Peer mentoring is a journey of learning that both partners travel together, and they support each other along the way. Each dyad of StoryQUEST peer mentors meets bimonthly with the learning coach. Other meetings are strongly encouraged and determined by the pair of peer mentors. The pairs develop specific goals in which they are both interested. Dyads work on these goals, in addition to the team goal. An additional outcome of the peer mentoring approach is that if the traveling team member must resign from participation for any reason, the peer mentor is a knowledgeable and motivated alternate ready to step in.

The StoryQUEST Curriculum

The StoryQUEST language and literacy components of the curriculum are based on the three pillars of beginning language and literacy for infants and toddlers: (a) relationships; (b) opportunities to listen, talk, and communicate; and (c) tools of literacy. Each training event has a cohesive curriculum that focuses on specific, evidence-based strategies that adults can use to promote beginning language and literacy in each of these three areas. The other two pervasive emphases of the curriculum are (a) peer mentoring and (b) developing and involving community-wide support for beginning language and literacy. Individual StoryQUEST sessions focus on broadening a specific information base, developing skills, supporting new attitudes and understandings to move participants in a clearly stated direction, or some combination of these efforts (Havelock & Havelock, 1973).

Participants are presented first with research findings about how infants and toddlers learn and then with specific strategies they can use to support young children's development. For example, dialogic reading is widely recognized as a strategy that promotes language in young children (Whitehurst & Lonigan, 1998; Zevenbergen & Whitehurst, 2003). The *Language Is the Key* video program[2], developed by the Washington Research Institute, has been adapted by StoryQUEST for use with infants and toddlers. The videos are used at training sessions and are also supplemented with several video-clip examples of adults using dialogic reading strategies with infants. StoryQUEST has adapted the training manual to contain examples of appropriate strategies for young infants, children 8–24 months old, and toddlers. The entire strategy was renamed "Follow the CAR" to stress following the child's lead, a critical requirement to engage infants and toddlers. Finally, Follow the CAR materials are designed to attract attention and remind participants to wait at least 5 seconds to allow children to respond (see Figure 25.2).

Figure 25.2. Language Is the Key: Follow the CAR

StoryQUEST

LIK

Talking and Reading With Infants and Toddlers

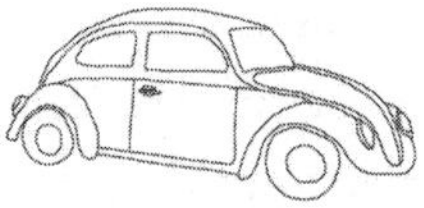

Follow the child's lead!

C   Comment and Wait so the child has time to respond

A   Ask Questions and Wait so the child has time to respond

R   Respond by adding a little more

Waiting gives the child time to respond

Source: Reprinted with permission from StoryQUEST.

[2] *Language Is the Key* videos are available from Washington Learning Systems, 2212 Queen Anne Avenue North, Box 726, Seattle, WA 98109; Web site www.walearning.com; phone (206) 310-7401; fax: (206) 283-9243.

The StoryQUEST curriculum is sequential and builds over the successive training events. For example, peer mentoring is introduced in the 3 days of the first training event when trainers define the concept, share the anticipated outcomes of peer mentoring, explicitly discuss the expectations for participation (including providing peer mentor dyad agreement forms), and teach several strategies for developing a peer mentoring relationship. Learning coaches follow up with each dyad, assisting members to begin this unique kind of relationship, supporting them to develop and work on a goal, and ensuring that they sign the agreement and understand their commitment over the course of the year. The second 3-day training event provides a review of the participants' initial experiences with peer mentoring before moving to a higher level of discussion. Topics covered include strategies for maintaining the peer mentoring relationship and ways to handle challenges such as scheduling, distance, and competing priorities. Every level of the training contains an element of inspiration that is provided through a fable about peer mentoring, through inspirational quotes, by means of success stories from within the group, or by using some combination of these methods. The final 3-day training event weaves peer mentoring into the rest of the curriculum. Throughout all StoryQUEST activities, participants are expected to consider the effect of each training topic on their peer mentor and to plan how they will share the information with their peer mentor. From the first meeting, teams are expected to ensure that their peer mentors as a group are fully included in all aspects of the process to carry out the goals. Finally, over time, more and more responsibility is shifted to the full 12-member team to infuse beginning language and literacy throughout the program.

Another example of the curriculum's sequencing is the focus on specific, research-based strategies that adults can use to promote beginning language and literacy. The first training event introduces a few simple strategies that adults can easily learn and master—for example, turntaking (MacDonald, 2001) and "observe, wait, and listen" (OWL; Manolson, 1983). It also presents the *tools of literacy* concept, which views everyday objects and ordinary routines as the means by which infants, toddlers, and young children come to literacy. The second training event features many more strategies and adds discussions of the research about young children who are learning more than one language. Participants also consider the effect that family literacy behaviors have on young children and the implications for their work with families. A Mastery

Checklist is introduced, listing all the strategies that have been taught and suggesting a framework for skill mastery that can be used by individuals and programs to support staff development. Learning coaches observe team members during on-site follow-up to help them determine which skills they are using and at what level of proficiency. At the final training event, participants are introduced to key principles in the literature that support sustaining innovations. Teams then plan ways to sustain their individual, family, team, program, and community work on beginning language and literacy.

The community mobilization component of the curriculum builds over time. Initially, the curriculum introduces the concept, provides a variety of examples, suggests a process for reviewing community assets and needs, and structures a planning process that community groups can use to plan an initiative to support beginning language and literacy for infants and toddlers. The second session provides participants with specific social marketing strategies to use in "selling" their effort to engage their community in beginning language and literacy for infants and toddlers. The final training event provides participants with a method for examining the strategies currently in use, evaluating their success, adapting them as necessary, and considering other approaches that would extend and sustain a community focus on supporting infants and toddlers to experience optimal language and literacy opportunities.

Potential Contributions of the StoryQUEST Approach

School readiness and performance are matters of grave national concern (National Research Council & Institute of Medicine, 2000). A major emphasis has been placed on promoting school readiness, particularly for preschoolers from high-risk environments (No Child Left Behind Act of 2001). Also generally accepted is the importance of providing appropriate environments and supports for very young children, starting with prenatal care (Advisory Committee on Services for Families With Infants and Toddlers, 1994). The StoryQUEST model provides the structure and process for addressing school readiness from the beginning of life in a comprehensive way and for enhancing the foundational skills that enable young children to become effective learners. StoryQUEST has also proven its success. Preliminary quantitative and qualitative data clearly indicate significant changes in the knowledge base, skill level, and in commitment to beginning language and literacy of families, staff members, and programs who participated in StoryQUEST (*StoryQUEST Final Report to the U.S. Department of Education*, 2004).

This nation must adopt new and effective strategies to ensure that the next generation develops much-needed literacy competencies. StoryQUEST has shown that it is possible to (a) empower families to plant the seeds of beginning language and literacy through nurturing relationships, (b) support early care and education staff members and programs to stimulate its growth, and (c) inspire communities to greater efforts to nurture a love of reading in infants and toddlers. Children, families, caregivers, programs, and communities across this nation are engaged in beginning language and literacy in new and exciting ways. The voices of StoryQUEST participants attest to the changes that have been made as a result of participating in StoryQUEST training:

> *"I used to think that the literacy stuff was someone else's responsibility. Parents are important for kids. A more important thing is giving the knowledge to the parents, which makes them self-confident."* (Parent)

* * *

> *"I used Follow the CAR with my children when I got off the plane after training and it works!!!! If you just wait they will answer you!"* (Parent)

* * *

> *"Parents [in our program] go back to school so they can learn to read. Now they volunteer in classroom story times. Parents are reading more to their children. Teachers have created richer literacy environments."* (Direct-Service Staff Member)

* * *

> *"[Peer mentoring] has helped me improve my teaching and be able to impart information."* (Direct-Service Staff Member)

* * *

"It's so exciting to see the staff and parents using the strategies. They just do it all the time, it's automatic!" (Supervisor)

* * *

"We have trained our staff. We validated what people are doing and now they are able to explain why they are doing what they are doing—and the research behind these practices!" (Administrator)

* * *

"We have been training our home visitors and community teachers at the library. We are locating literacy resources in the community and making sure that staff have the information. We also created a budget—early literacy and language is our focus for the year." (Administrator)

* * *

"I trained all the librarians in our county to understand how to use the tools of literacy in the library and to wait 5 seconds when they spoke to children. They were so excited that it worked and the children responded—even the little babies gave a response when they were given the extra time!" (Community Partner)

* * *

"Our local Read to Me program has never included children younger than 3. Our team worked with them and now they are providing books for babies and all the ads include children from birth to 3 as well as older children." (Community Partner)

* * *

"This [using Follow the CAR strategies to support children's development] will go on and on forever! I'll use it with my daughter and she'll use it with hers and it will go on and on!" (Parent)

References

Advisory Committee on Services for Families With Infants and Toddlers. (1994). *The statement of the Advisory Committee on Services for Families With Infants and Toddlers.* Washington, DC: Department of Health and Human Services.

Bailey, D. B. (1989). Issues and directions in preparing professionals to work with young handicapped children and their families. In J. J. Gallagher, P. L. Trohanis, & R. M. Clifford (Eds.), *Policy implementation and PL 99-457* (pp. 97–132). Baltimore: Paul H. Brookes.

Beam, G. C., Ford, V. L., & Laurel, M. (1993). *Project TIE: Inservice training program for related services personnel final report.* Albuquerque, NM: University of New Mexico School of Medicine.

Bronfenbrenner, U. (1979). *The ecology of human development: Experiments by nature and design.* Cambridge: Harvard University Press.

Bus, A., & de Jong, M. (2006). Book sharing: A developmentally appropriate way to foster preacademic growth. In S. E. Rosenkoetter & J. Knapp-Philo (Eds.), *Learning to read the world: Language and literacy in the first three years* (pp. 123–144). Washington, DC: ZERO TO THREE Press.

Buysse, V., & Wesley, P. (1993). The identity crisis in early childhood special education: A call for professional role clarification. *Topics in Early Childhood Special Education, 13,* 418–429.

Garland, C. W., & Frank, A. (1997). Preparing practitioners to provide early intervention services in inclusive settings. In P. J. Winton & C. Catlett (Eds.), *Reforming personnel preparation in early intervention: Issues, models, and practical strategies* (pp. 363–392). Baltimore: Paul H. Brookes.

Hart, B., & Risley, T. (1995). *Meaningful differences in the everyday experiences of young American children.* Baltimore: Paul H. Brookes.

Hart, B., & Risley, T. (1999). *The social world of children learning to talk.* Baltimore: Paul H. Brookes.

Havelock, R. G., & Havelock, M. C. (1973). *Training for change agents: A guide to the design of training programs in education and other fields.* Ann Arbor, MI: The University of Michigan, Institute for Social Research.

Joyce, B., & Showers, B. (1988). *Power in staff development through research on training.* Alexandria, VA: Association for Supervision and Curriculum Development.

Kim, D. H. (1999). A strategy for building competence. In P. M. Senge, A. Kleiner, C. Roberts, R. Ross, G. Roth, & B. Smith (Eds.), *The dance of change* (pp. 133–136). New York: Doubleday.

Knapp-Philo, J., Corso, R., Brekken, L., & Bair Heal, H. (2004). Training to make and sustain change: The Hilton/Early Head Start Program. *Infants and Young Children, 17*(2), 171–183.

Knowles, M. S. (1980). *The modern practice of adult education: From pedagogy to andragogy.* Chicago: Follett.

Lim, Y. S., & Cole, K. N. (2000). *Follow-up of facilitating first language development in young Korean children through parent training in picture book interactions.* Seattle, WA: Washington Research Institute.

MacDonald, J. D. (2001). *Before your child talks.* Columbus, OH: Communicating Partners.

Manolson, A. (1983). *It takes two to talk.* Toronto: Hanen Early Language.

McCollum, J. A., & Catlett, C. (1997). Designing effective personnel preparation for early intervention: Theoretical frameworks. In P. J. Winton, J. A. McCollum, & C. Catlett (Eds.), *Reforming personnel preparation in early intervention* (pp. 105–125). Baltimore: Paul H. Brookes.

National Research Council, & Institute of Medicine. (2000). *From neurons to neighborhoods: The science of early childhood development* (J. P. Shonkoff, & D. A. Phillips, Eds.). Committee on Integrating the Science of Early Childhood Development; Board on Children, Youth, and Families; Commission on Behavioral and Social Sciences and Education. Washington DC. National Academy Press.

No Child Left Behind Act of 2001. Pub. L. No. 107-110. 20 USC 6301 (2001).

Rosenkoetter, S. E. (2006). Mentoring: Together we're better. In S. E. Rosenkoetter & J. Knapp-Philo (Eds.), *Learning to read the world: Language and literacy in the first three years* (pp. 369–394). Washington, DC: ZERO TO THREE Press.

Snow, C., Burns, S., & Griffin, P. (Eds.). National Research Council, Committee on the Prevention of Reading Difficulties. (1998). *Preventing reading difficulties in young children.* Washington, DC: National Academy Press.

Sparks, D., & Hirsh, S. (1997). *A new vision for staff development.* Alexandria, VA: Association for Supervision and Curriculum Development.

StoryQUEST final report to the U.S. Department of Education. (November, 2004). Sonoma Park, CA: Author.

van Kleeck, A., & Beckley-McCall, A. (2002). A comparison of mothers' individual and simultaneous book sharing with preschool siblings: An exploratory study of five families. *American Journal of Speech-Language Pathology, 11,* 175–189.

Whitehurst, G. J., & Lonigan, C. J. (1998). Child development and emergent literacy. *Child Development, 69*(3), 848–872.

Winton, P. J. (1990). A systematic approach for planning inservice training related to Public Law 99-457. *Infants and Young Children, 3,* 51–60.

Zevenbergen, A. A., & Whitehurst, G. J. (2003). Dialogic reading: A shared picture book reading intervention for preschoolers. In A. van Kleeck & S. A. Stahl (Eds.), *On reading books to children: Parents and teachers* (pp. 177–200). Mahwah, NJ: Erlbaum.

Zukoski, A. P., & Luluquisen, E. M. (2006). Building community support for early literacy. In S. E. Rosenkoetter & J. Knapp-Philo (Eds.), *Learning to read the world: Language and literacy in the first three years* (pp. 429–454). Washington, DC: ZERO TO THREE Press.

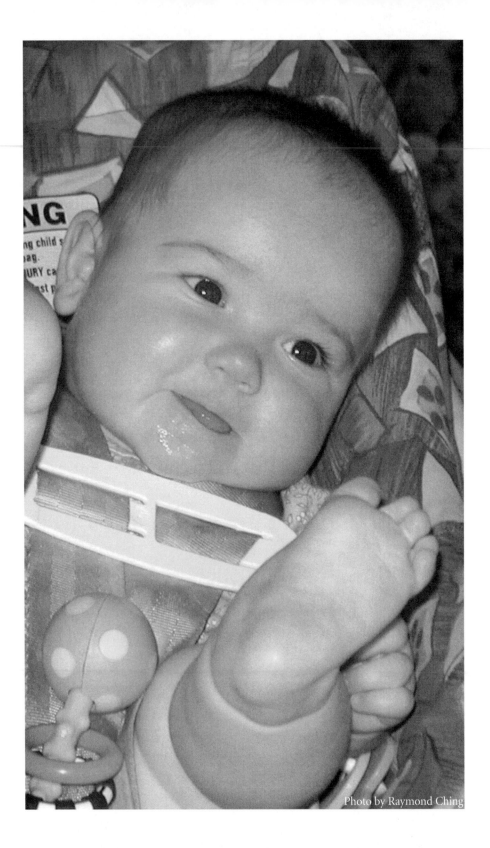

CHAPTER 26

Language Is the Key: A Proven Approach to Early Language and Literacy

Kevin N. Cole and Young Sook Lim

Perhaps the most important academic challenge children face in the early years of school is learning to read (Burns, Griffin, & Snow, 1999; Snow, Burns, & Griffin, 1998). Children with less well-developed language skills in kindergarten are at high risk for reading disabilities (Catts, Fey, Tomblin, & Zhang, 2002). Children often lack the language competence that they need for school literacy instruction (Larney, 2002; Notari-Syverson, O'Connor, & Vadasy, 1998). By the end of first grade, children who have delayed language development usually score in the bottom quartile on reading assessment measures. More than 8 out of 10 children who read poorly at the end of first grade will still read poorly at the end of fourth grade (Juel, 1988). Children who receive early language support and improve their language skills are significantly less likely to experience later reading difficulties (Catts et al., 2002; Dickinson & McCabe, 2001). Thus, it is clear that early language development sets the foundation for reading ability. In *Beginning to Read: Thinking and Learning About Print*, Adams (1990) recognized the critical relationship between early language and reading:

> *Skillful reading is not a unitary skill. It is a whole complex system of skills and knowledge. Within this system, the individual printed words are useless in and of themselves. They are valuable and, in a strong sense, possible only as they are guided and received by complementary knowledge and activities of language comprehension.* (p. 3)

This chapter will discuss (a) the nature of the relationship between early oral language development and subsequent reading ability; (b) evidence-based ways of helping children interweave their knowledge of language with their ability to move successfully into print, especially through one particular approach called *dialogic reading*; and (c) a strategy based on that approach—*Language Is the Key*[1]—an exemplary approach that is easy for families and caregivers to implement and that has been proven to enhance language and literacy. Experience of the authors and others shows that families who adopt Language Is the Key after brief training and then incorporate it in their daily interactions with their young children enhance their children's language skills that foster school success.

Exploring the Relationship Between Early Language Development and Reading Success

Early research on the relationship between language and reading focused on how language boosted a very narrow set of skills important to reading: phonological sensitivity (e.g., Bryant, Bradley, MacLean, & Crossland, 1989; Wagner & Torgesen, 1987). Within this framework, the key contributions of language experience to later reading ability were thought to be the growing awareness of a relationship between phonemes and graphemes (for a discussion of phonemes and graphemes, see Griffin, this volume, p. 145) and how each can be manipulated to convey meaning. Early work clearly established the importance of sound awareness and the nature of sounds as discreet units that individuals can arrange, rearrange, separate, and blend to form spoken and written words.

Although this early model of the language–literacy relationship provided important information, later research (e.g., Roth, Speece, & Cooper, 2002; Nagy, Berninger, Abbott, Vaughan, & Vermeulen, 2003) indicated that early language skills actually played a much larger role in subsequent reading ability. In addition to the phonological awareness abilities acquired through early lan-

---

[1] *Language Is the Key* is an educational program that shows parents and teachers how to promote children's language development during the preschool years. For more information on the program and materials, please contact Washington Learning Systems, 2212 Queen Anne Avenue North, Box 726, Seattle, WA, by phone (206-310-7401) or through their Web site (www.walearning.com).

guage development that were key to learning to read, researchers also found that skill with the core components of language were also key to success in reading (e.g., Catts, Fey, Zhang, and Tomblin, 1999). These core components include semantics (word meanings), morphosyntax (the rules for putting words and sentences together), and pragmatic and discourse skills (how people use language in a flowing, social context).

Researchers have long correlated vocabulary development and morphosyntactic skills with later reading success (e.g., Butler, Marsh, Sheppard, & Sheppard, 1985; Hart & Risley, 1995; Nagy et al., 2003; Scarborough, 1990). However, more recent research has indicated that these skills actually play a stronger and more independent role in predicting reading ability (Roth et al., 2002). For example, Roth et al. (2002) noted that vocabulary development strongly predicts reading comprehension, indicating that specific aspects of language development may influence specific aspects of reading ability. Catts and colleagues (1999) also suggested this idea, noting that oral language skills and phonological processing abilities account for unique variance in reading ability, with each of these skills and abilities influencing literacy development in different ways. Thus, the role of different aspects of oral language appears to be greater than simply having a positive effect on phonemic awareness skills. Oral language skills appear to affect reading performance in a much more direct fashion.

From these studies with respect to the importance of oral language development in subsequent reading success, we can conclude that scientists are now documenting what providers of early childhood services have known intuitively for decades. Beyond serving as simply a catalyst for developing phonological awareness, language skills function as indispensable strands in a braid of skills woven to create the complex ability to derive meaning from print.

As we become more sophisticated in our understanding of the components and the developmental sequencing of skills that lead to reading success, we look to younger and younger ages of childhood to begin facilitating literacy. In the past, efforts to foster reading were thought to be most appropriate near the end of kindergarten or during first grade. Now, however, because we know that semantic, morphosyntactic, and pragmatic skills significantly develop by the time a child reaches kindergarten and because society recognizes these skills as integral aspects of successful reading ability, we look to the home environment to promote reading. Not surprisingly, researchers see strong correlations between the presence of language and literacy activities in the home environment and positive literacy outcomes (Burgess, 2002; Burgess, Hecht, & Lonigan, 2002).

Using Picture Books to Foster Language and Literacy Skills in the Home

One promising approach to weaving language facilitation and emergent literacy skills in the home environment is to encourage parents to use books with young children in ways that emphasize talking and listening as well as reading. Interactions between adults and children around picture books provide a rich opportunity for young children to learn language and preliteracy skills (Ninio & Bruner, 1978; Wells, 1985). Picture-book interactions may not involve reading at all. In terms of promoting language development in very young children, it may be more beneficial for adults *not* to read but, rather, to use books as points of departure for talking and listening. Thus, appropriate books for this model might include picture books with no text at all as well as books with both text and pictures that one would share by focusing more on the pictures.

In a key study involving preschoolers with typical language development (described in greater detail later in this chapter), Whitehurst et al. (1988) demonstrated that specific techniques that caregivers used during picture-book sharing can positively affect language development. Researchers found significant differences in children's grammatical complexity and verbal description of objects between experimental and control groups after only two 30-minute training sessions provided to parents. Although these effects were somewhat diminished later, researchers still observed them at a 9-month follow-up. Perhaps the most convincing argument for the use of the picture-book interaction techniques described above is the cost:benefit ratio of the intervention. Two brief parent trainings led to meaningful gains in the children's language performance.

The rationale for the success of picture-book interactions is more practical than theoretical. Books provide a specific shared context for interactions, and children often associate them with undivided adult attention and comfort. In addition, a well-chosen picture book is developmentally appropriate and, thus, interesting to the child. Book interactions may also reinforce adults in using books as mood regulators for the child (e.g., a calming activity before bedtime) and as positive social routines with the child that are inherently enjoyable.

Maintaining Sustainable Routines

For a language intervention method to work, it must not only be effective it must actually get used. This rather fundamental notion may be especially relevant for parents and child-care staff members. Odom (1988) used the term *impact* to describe the relationship between an intervention's effectiveness and its likelihood of being implemented. Thus, Impact = Effectiveness x Likelihood of Implementation (Odom, McConnell, & McEvoy, 1992). If we ask parents to attend evening workshops over the course of 6 weeks to learn how to work with their children and then ask them to rearrange their schedules to build new activities into their daily routines, we might actually reduce rather than increase the likelihood of implementation. Even a remarkably powerful intervention cannot be effective if trainees do not use that intervention. Interactions around picture books typically are enjoyable and "dovetail" into existing family, school, and child-care facility routines; thus, they are likely to be used.

The Effectiveness of Picture-Book Routines

Researchers have examined the effectiveness of language facilitation in the context of picture-book interactions with children who were developing typically, with children who had delayed language development, with children who came from middle- and lower-class environments, and with children who spoke languages other than English as their first language. We describe some of the key studies below.

One of the seminal studies (Whitehurst et al., 1988) included parents and typically developing 2-year-old children from middle- to high-socioeconomic-status families. After random assignment, parents in the intervention group received a home-based intervention of two half-hour sessions. The control group received no training but read to their children as often as did the intervention group.

Researchers analyzed audiotapes of parent–child interactions at home. The mothers in the intervention group performed significantly better at using the target language facilitation techniques. The target behaviors included asking "wh" questions and open-ended questions, following answers by the child with a question, repeating what the child says, praising the child, helping the child as needed, following the child's interests, expanding what the child says, and having fun. Whitehurst et al. (1988) referred to this model as *dialogic reading* to differentiate between this language facilitation focus and simply reading a body of text to the child.

After approximately 6 weeks, posttests consisting of grammatical complexity and expressive language measures revealed significant gains for the intervention children relative to the control group, with changes from pretest to posttest of at least 6 months in skill development. Researchers observed that children retained these effects, only slightly diminished, at a 9-month follow-up. These results were especially striking because the children were already functioning at an advanced level in language ability when they began the program, and parents were already reading to their children frequently. The rather simple change that dialogic reading promoted in parents' reading with their children had very strong effects. Researchers found these results promising, and they began examining the use of the methods with other target groups, including children from low socioeconomic backgrounds, children with disabilities, and children who spoke languages other than English.

For example, Whitehurst et al. (1994) as well as Lonigan and Whitehurst (1998) examined the use of these picture-book interaction methods with typically developing preschoolers from low socioeconomic families. Whitehurst et al. (1994) randomly assigned 3-year-old children to one of three conditions: (a) Exposure to dialogic reading from child-care staff members and parents, (b) exposure to dialogic reading from child-care staff members only, and (c) exposure to play activities rather than book interaction. Researchers found significant differences favoring the intervention groups, and they noticed that children again maintained these effects at a 6-month follow-up. The combined child-care and home condition produced greater gains than did the child-care-only condition. Lonigan and Whitehurst (1998) conducted a replication of this study and included one additional condition: picture-book interactions with parents only. Again, researchers found significant gains for the school–home intervention groups and no significant difference between the school-only and control groups. Thus, the greatest gains in both studies occurred in groups that involved parents.

Building on the work of Whitehurst and colleagues, we explored whether this same type of approach also would be effective with children who have language delays and the parents of those children (Dale, Crain-Thoreson, Notari-Syverson, & Cole, 1996). We were also interested in the relative efficacy of the picture-book interaction in evoking language compared with the more traditional training around conversational use of language facilitation techniques during play.

In Dale et al. (1996), we randomly assigned parent–child dyads to either the dialogic reading training or a conversational training. Children in the study ranged in age from 3 to 7 years. They exhibited language delays in the mild to moderate range. The dialogic reading training consisted of having mothers view a videotape developed by Whitehurst and then participate in a brief group discussion. The conversational training consisted of mothers' viewing a videotape that described and modeled the use of informational talk (i.e., describing what the child is doing or seeing), using expansions of child utterances, encouraging open-ended questions, and showing interest in the child's activities. In other words, the two conditions involved the same procedures but researchers varied the context—either book reading or conversation.

Researchers gathered and analyzed pretest and posttest language samples for both parent and child behaviors. Parent behaviors included asking yes–no questions and open-ended questions as well as producing expansions, information talk, and imitations. Child behaviors included making statements, asking questions, imitating adult utterances, and attending nonverbally. Parents in the picture-book intervention produced significantly more what and who questions, open-ended questions, and imitations than did the conversational intervention. Children in the picture-book intervention also produced significantly more different words than did the children in the conversational intervention. We found that a correlation between parents' use of the techniques and child gains, supporting the interpretation that the intervention resulted in child change.

Hargrave and Senechal (2000) also examined the efficacy of picture-book interactions with children exhibiting language delays. They compared two types of book interactions—dialogic reading and traditional book reading—with preschool children who were delayed in expressive vocabulary only. The traditional book-reading situation involved parents reading to their children with no emphasis on interacting with the child about the contents of the book. This condition is opposite the characteristics of dialogic reading. Both the traditional book-reading condition and the interactive book use (dialogic reading) resulted in vocabulary gains from pretest to posttest, but the interactive method resulted in significantly more gains than the traditional reading method. Crain-Thoreson and Dale (1999) found similar results. They trained parents and early childhood special education staff members in interactive reading methods and examined language development during an 8-week period for children with mild to moderate language delays across a range of developmental levels. Delays included both isolated language delays and delays occurring as one aspect of overall developmental delay. They found that both the parent and the staff instruction resulted in longer utterances by children, more diverse vocabulary use, and more frequent utterances during book interactions. Again, researchers correlated the magnitude of change in children's language performance with the frequency of use of the techniques presented in the training.

These findings indicate that children with disabilities benefit from parent training in specific picture-book interaction methods. In fact, comparisons of book interaction and play as contexts for the use of language intervention have indicated that where differences exist, book reading produces more significant gains. Available studies also suggest that information presented to parents in videotape format can be an effective component of intervention. A study by Arnold, Lonigan, Whitehurst, and Epstein (1994) also supported the efficacy of using a videotape format with parents of typically developing children. The researchers randomly assigned parent–child dyads to three conditions:

1. A direct-training group received instruction by a trainer in dialogic reading during two sessions; participants also received written descriptions of the intervention components.

2. The video-training group received training by means of videotape; participants also received the written instructions.

3. The group in the control condition received no training.

All groups looked at approximately the same number of books per week during the 4 weeks of intervention.

Researchers administered posttests to children, including the Expressive One Word Picture Vocabulary Test (EOWPVT), the Peabody Picture Vocabulary Test–Revised (PPVT–R), and the Illinois Test of Pyscholinguistic Abilities–Verbal Expression subtest (ITPA–VE). The video group performed significantly higher than the control group on each of these measures. The direct-training group outperformed the control group on the ITPA–VE, but not on the other measures. The video condition also was compared with the direct-training condition. The video group scored significantly higher on the EOWPVT and the PPVT-R. The authors suggested that the video training may have been more effective because it consisted of a more standardized presentation. They also postulated that the videotape's inclusion of mothers modeling desired behaviors may have been more effective than modeling by professionals because it allowed those mothers participating in the study to see more clearly the effect of the methods on children.

In addition to evidence of general efficacy with typically developing and language-delayed children, several studies have indicated that specific language facilitation methods used in the context of picture-book reading are effective with adult–child dyads who speak a language other than English. Valdez-Menchaca and Whitehurst (1992) trained staff members in a Mexican child-care program to use picture books to facilitate language with typically developing 2-year-old children from lower socioeconomic backgrounds. A control group of children received arts and crafts training from the same teacher. The intervention group scored significantly higher both on standardized language measures and on measures of language production.

We wondered whether the picture-book interaction methods might also be appropriate and useful for Asian families. To explore this possibility, we conducted a study with Korean families (Lim & Cole, 2002). Twenty-one children, ages 2–4 years, and their mothers participated. The children were considered by their parents to be developing typically. The mean length of utterances in words (MLU-W) for the total group was 2.28. Korean was the parents' first language, and it was spoken in the home. Dyads were assigned randomly to a treatment or control condition. The treatment group received approximately 1 hour of instruction in specific language facilitation techniques around picture-book interactions. The control group received approximately 1 hour of instruction in general emergent literacy development and the importance of first-language acquisition. The parent intervention then lasted approximately 6 weeks. Results from pretest–posttest language samples indicated significant between-group differences in parents' use of methods as well as in children's language production, with both samples favoring the treatment group. Specifically, the treatment group of parents made significantly more gains in asking questions to children, responding to children's talking, and providing time for children to respond. The children in the treatment group had significantly longer MLU–W, produced more utterances, and used a greater variety of vocabulary than did the children in the control group. The mean effect size in this study was 1.8 for the treatment group, indicating that changes were large enough to be educationally meaningful.

We then conducted a follow-up of the treatment and control groups 1 year after the initial study (Lim & Cole, 2006). The children in the treatment group still produced significantly more utterances (effect size = 1.82) and significantly more diverse vocabulary during picture-book interactions with their parents (effect size = 1.53), and the parents were still asking questions (effect size = 1.82) and making comments (effect size = 1.50) more often than parents in the control condition. Many of the parents in the treatment group, when contacted to participate in the follow-up study, apologized because they felt they were no longer using the methods (when, in fact, they *were* still using them). They apparently had internalized the use of the techniques to the degree that it had become second nature.

In addition to conducting research in school and clinical settings, researchers also have examined the efficacy of picture-book interactions in a broad dissemination through a city library system (Heubner, 2000). Librarians were trained to teach picture-book interaction methods, which they then taught parents during two 1-hour sessions. Parents were assigned randomly to the intervention group or to a group that received only information about general library services. After 6 weeks, pretest–posttest comparisons indicated a significant advantage for the interactive picture-book group in terms of expressive vocabulary development.

In summary, research with respect to specific methods of interaction around picture books by parents and teachers indicates both short-term and longer term gains in language production and development for children with delayed language and children who are developing typically. In addition, the methods appear to be culturally appropriate for families who speak a language other than English at home.

Taking Dialogic Reading From Research to Practice: The *Language Is the Key* Model

In response to research about the efficacy of using picture-book interactions to facilitate language and early literacy development, the authors developed a video-based program, *Language Is the Key* (see, e.g., Cole, Maddox, Lim, & Notair-Syverson, 2000a; Cole, Maddox, Lim, & Notari-Syverson, 2000b; Notari-Syverson, Maddox, & Cole, 1998) to foster the use of specific language facilitation methods by parents and early childhood service providers. The *Language Is the Key* program consists of videotapes in a variety of languages (English, Spanish, Vietnamese, Korean, Mandarin Chinese, Mandarin Chinese with Chinese subtitles, and Philipino–Tagalog). Each language set features parents, children, and narrators who represent the target linguistic or cultural group. We designed the accompanying written training materials to guide parents and other caregivers in using language facilitation techniques with children when they look at books together. In addition, we also developed a videotape in each language that models the use of language facilitation in the context of play. This videotape encourages families and other caregivers to generalize language use throughout the child's day. The materials focus on the following target behaviors: (a) following the child's lead, (b) making comments about what the child is interested in, (c) asking questions related to the child's interests, and (d) responding to child utterances by adding a little more information. The training content also includes providing wait time for the child to respond after an adult talks. The phrase used to represent this wait-time strategy is "Follow the CAR," that is, **Follow** (the child's lead), then **C** (comment and wait), **A** (ask a question and wait), and **R** (respond with a bit more information and wait). Figure 25.1 in chapter 25 of this volume presents the Follow the CAR model. Across the nation, people have demonstrated and used the phrase and acronym, have displayed it on refrigerator magnets and bookmarks, and have shared it with other families and caregivers (see Knapp-Philo & Brekken, this volume, p. 515). We designed *Language Is the Key* to allow teachers to present the materials to parents in approximately 1 hour. They can easily teach this strategy for fostering early language and literacy in a group setting.

Our goal in developing *Language Is the Key* was to give parents tools that work and tools that fit into their daily routines. We now know that early language development is critical to later reading success, and we know specific ways that picture books can be used with young children to increase their language and emergent literacy skills. Children deserve to succeed. New research knowledge and strategies that prepare children to read show significant promise toward meeting this challenge.

References

Adams, M. (1990). *Beginning to read: Thinking and learning about print.* Cambridge, MA: MIT Press.

Arnold, D., Lonigan, C. J., Whitehurst, G. J., & Epstein, J. N. (1994). Accelerating language development through picture book reading: Replication and extension to a videotape training format. *Journal of Educational Psychology, 86,* 235–243.

Bryant, P., Bradley, L., MacLean, M., & Crossland, J. (1989). Nursery rhymes, phonological skills, and reading. *Journal of Child Language, 16,* 407–428.

Burgess, S. R. (2002). The influence of speech perception, oral language ability, the home literacy environment, and pre-reading knowledge on the growth of phonological sensitivity: A one-year longitudinal investigation. *Reading and Writing, 15,* 709–737.

Burgess, S., Hecht, S., & Lonigan, C. (2002). Relations of the home literacy environment (HLE) to the development of reading-related abilities: A one-year longitudinal study. *Reading Research Quarterly, 37,* 408–426.

Burns, S., Griffin, P., & Snow, C. (Eds.). (1999). *Starting out right: A guide to promoting children's reading success.* Washington DC: National Academy Press.

Butler, S., Marsh, H., Sheppard, M., & Sheppard, J. (1985). Seven-year longitudinal study of the early prediction of reading achievement. *Journal of Educational Psychology, 77,* 349–361.

Catts, H., Fey, M., Tomblin, J., & Zhang, X. (2002). A longitudinal investigation of reading outcomes in children with language impairments. *Journal of Speech, Language, and Hearing Research, 45,* 1142–1157.

Catts, H., Fey, M., Zhang, X., & Tomblin, J. (1999). Language basis of reading and reading disabilities: Evidence from a longitudinal investigation. *Scientific Studies of Reading, 3,* 331–361.

Cole, K., Maddox, M., Lim, Y. S., & Notari-Syverson, A. (2000a). *Language is the key: Resource guide.* Seattle: Washington Research Institute.

Cole, K., Maddox, M., Lim, Y. S., & Notari-Syverson, A. (2000b). *Talking and play: Language is the key/Talking and books: Language is the key [Korean][videos and manual].* Seattle: Washington Research Institute.

Crain-Thoreson, C., & Dale, P. (1999). Enhancing linguistic performance: Parents and teachers as book reading partners for children with language delays. *Topics in Early Childhood Special Education, 19,* 28–39.

Dale, P., Crain-Thoreson, C., Notari-Syverson, A., & Cole, K. (1996). Parent-child storybook reading as an intervention technique for young children with language delays. *Topics in Early Childhood Special Education, 16,* 213–235.

Dickinson, D., & McCabe, A. (2001). Bringing it all together: The multiple origins, skills, and environmental supports of early literacy. *Learning Disabilities Research and Practice, 16,* 186–202.

Griffin, P. (2006). Sound steps in phonological form for later literacy. In S. E. Rosenkoetter & J. Knapp-Philo (Eds.), *Learning to read the world: Language and literacy in the first three years* (pp. 145–162). Washington, DC: ZERO TO THREE Press.

Hargrave, A., & Senechal, M. (2000). Book reading intervention with preschool children who have limited vocabularies: The benefits of regular reading and dialogic reading. *Early Childhood Research Quarterly, 15*, 75–90.

Hart, B., & Risley, T. (1995). *Meaningful differences in the everyday lives of American children.* Baltimore: Paul H. Brookes.

Heubner, C. (2000). Promoting toddlers language development through community-based intervention. *Journal of Applied Developmental Psychology, 21*, 513–535.

Juel, C. (1988). Learning to read and write: A longitudinal study of 54 children from first through fourth grades. *Journal of Educational Psychology, 4*, 437–447.

Knapp-Philo, J., & Brekken, L. StoryQUEST: An ecological training model for beginning language and literacy. In S. E. Rosenkoetter & J. Knapp-Philo (Eds.), *Learning to read the world: Language and literacy in the first three years* (pp. 515–536). Washington, DC: ZERO TO THREE Press.

Larney, R. (2002). The relationship between early language delay and later difficulties in literacy. *Early Child Development and Care, 172*, 183–193.

Lim, Y. S., & Cole, K. N. (2006). Facilitating first language development in young Korean children through parent training in picture book interactions. *Bilingual Research Journal, 26*, 367–381.

Lim, Y. S., & Cole, K. N. (2004). One-year follow-up of Korean parent training in picture book interactions. Manuscript submitted for publication.

Lonigan, C., & Whitehurst, G. (1998). Relative efficacy of parent and teacher involvement in a shared-reading intervention for preschool children from low-income backgrounds. *Early Childhood Research Quarterly, 13*, 263–290.

Nagy, W., Berninger, V., Abbott, R., Vaughn, K., Vermeulen, K. (2003). Relationship of morphology and other language skills to literacy skills in at-risk second-grade readers and at-risk fourth-grade writers. *Journal of Educational Psychology, 95*, 730–742.

Ninio, A., & Bruner, J. S. (1978). The achievement and antecedents of labeling. *Journal of Child Language, 5*, 1–15.

Notari-Syverson, A., Maddox, M., & Cole. K. (1998). *Language is the key: A multilingual language building program for young children.* Seattle: Washington Research Institute.

Notari-Syverson, A., O'Connor, R., & Vadasy, P. (1998). *Ladders to literacy.* Baltimore: Paul H. Brookes.

Odom, S. (1988). Research in early childhood special education. In S. Odom & M. Karnes (Eds.), *Early intervention for infants and children with handicaps: An empirical base* (pp. 1–21). Baltimore: Paul H. Brookes.

Odom, S., McConnell, S., & McEvoy, M. (1992). Implementation of social competence interventions in early childhood special education classes: Current practices and future directions. In S. Odom, S. McConnell, & M. McEvoy (Eds.), *Social competence of young children with disabilities* (pp. 277–306). Baltimore: Paul H. Brookes.

Roth, F., Speece, D., & Cooper, D. (2002). A longitudinal analysis of the connection between oral language and early reading. *Journal of Educational Research, 95*, 259–272.

Scarborough, H. (1990). Very early language deficits in dyslexic children. *Child Development, 61*, 1728–1734.

Snow, C., Burns, S., & Griffin, P. (Eds.). National Research Council, Committee on the Prevention of Reading Difficulties. (1998). *Preventing reading difficulties in children.* Washington, DC: National Academy Press.

Valdez-Menchaca, M. C., & Whitehurst, G. J. (1992). Accelerating language development through picture book reading: A systematic extension to Mexican daycare. *Developmental Psychology, 28,* 1106–1114.

Wagner, R., & Torgesen, J. (1987). The nature of phonological processing and its causal role in the acquisition of reading skills. *Psychological Bulletin, 101,* 192–212.

Wells, G. (1985). Preschool literacy-related activities and success in school. In D. R. Olson, N. Torrance, & A. Hildyard (Eds.), *Literacy, language and learning: The nature and consequences of reading and writing* (pp. 229–255). Cambridge England: Cambridge University Press.

Whitehurst, G. J., Arnold, D., Epstein, J., Angell, A., Smith, M., & Fischel, J. (1994). A picture book reading intervention in day care and home for children from low-income families. *Developmental Psychology, 30,* 679–689.

Whitehurst, G. J., Falco, F. L., Lonigan, C. J., Fischel, J. E., DeFarshe, B. D., Valdez-Menchaca, M. C., et al. (1988). Accelerating language development through picture book reading. *Developmental Psychology, 24,* 552–558.

CHAPTER 27

Books for Very Young Children

Sally Anderson

Some parents and professionals may see reading books to babies as an exercise in futility. Can infants really hear what is being read to them? Can they even tell whether the book is right side up? Aren't babies more interested in chewing the corners of a good board book than hearing the words and looking at the images? Why should we bother? These are common questions among young parents and some caregivers.

Although research began in the early 1900s, it wasn't until the last three decades that scientists and educators began to understand the vast capacity of infants and toddlers to learn and grow (Gopnik, Meltzoff, & Kuhl, 1999). Since then, researchers have confirmed that talking and reading with very young children have a profound effect on their ability to develop language, literacy, and critical thinking skills (Brazelton, 1992; Kuhl & Meltzoff, 1996; Mason & Allen, 1986; Snow, Burns, & Griffin, 1998).

The author is a librarian, children's literature specialist, and founder of Mother Goose Programs in Vermont and has long been active in creating book-based programs that actively involve families in their young children's learning. Over the past 20 years, Mother Goose Programs have created and developed for families and educators successful, research-based, award-winning early literacy programs based on picture books. The programs have been introduced through workshops that prepare librarians, Head Start teachers, social service workers, and educators to recruit and engage families in participatory, multisession, hands-on activities. These professionals have worked with tens of thousands of parents nationwide in public libraries, Head Start centers, and other community settings. Mother Goose Programs are based on research that supports the positive effect that early reading and conversation have on children's learning (Bruner, 1996; Bus, van Ijzendoorn, & Pellegrini, 1995; Hart & Risley, 1995; Snow et al., 1998). It is never too early to talk and read with young children.

This chapter discusses the importance of talking and reading with infants and toddlers. It also includes information about how to find and select age-appropriate, diverse books, and how to collaborate with other community partners, advocate for support for literacy, find funding, and recruit families to programs.

Babies Love Books

Babies and toddlers most certainly need books; moreover, they *love* books. They respond to the colorful pictures, the sounds of words, and the music of a trusted voice. Providing books and the know-how to read and talk about them are among the most important tasks of an early childhood professional. See, for example, how one early literacy consultant helped a young family:

> *Maria, a young mother from Lynn, Massachusetts, was unsure why her WIC program suggested she attend a Mother Goose Program. After all, her baby, Brianna, was only 4 months old. "Shouldn't I wait until she's old enough to hold the books and understand the words?" she asked. Over the course of the program, Maria learned that Brianna was able to focus on the pictures and became very interested in them. Brianna showed her interest by opening her eyes wide, lifting her head to look at the book, and moving her arms and legs. Maria also learned that Brianna signals that she is tired of reading a book by looking away or starting to fuss. Maria became quite fond of Helen Oxenbury's* Clap Hands *when she saw how much Brianna enjoyed it. "This book is just right for a baby," she enthused. "The pictures are big enough for Brianna to focus on—and they're faces, which my baby loves to look at!" Maria showed a visitor how she props the book open so her baby can look at it on the changing table or when she is on the floor. She added, "I don't mind if she pulls the book to her mouth and starts chewing it. I know that is how she is exploring the book, and besides, it's a board book. It's designed for that."*

Shared book reading has emerged as a key component to facilitating early literacy. Infants and toddlers are not only beginning to make connections between sound and meaning but also are beginning to make connections between sound and print. Reading out loud with infants and toddlers helps them to more readily acquire concepts about the functions of written language in books (Hiebert, 1986; Mason & Allen, 1986). Toddlers learn that print differs from speech (Morrow, 1990) and that print, not pictures, contains the story that is being read.

The more fun an adult and infant have together while reading and talking, the more powerful the learning will be and the more likely both participants will want to engage in reading more often. Lancy and Bergin (1992) found that children who were more fluent and positive about reading came from parent–child pairs who viewed reading as fun, kept stories moving with a semantic rather than a decoding orientation, and encouraged questions and humor while reading. Author Mem Fox (2001) summed it up eloquently: "The fire of literacy is created by the emotional sparks between a child, a book, and the person reading. It isn't achieved by the book alone, nor by the child alone, nor by the adult who's reading aloud—it's the relationship winding between the three, bringing them together in easy harmony" (p. 10).

Choosing the Best Books for Infants and Toddlers

How does one find good books? Which books are appropriate for an infant or toddler? How do adults read books that have very few words?

Picture books are a visual art form. They provide infants and toddlers with their first experiences in art and literature. Our first criterion in selecting a book is that it be a good story well told, not just a story that the child will like but one the adult will enjoy, too. When the parent or caregiver takes an interest in a book, delights in reading it, and, better yet, has fun and laughs, then the child is more likely to enjoy reading and continue reading later (Snow et al., 1998).

Some general guidelines for finding the best books for infants and toddlers have been identified by literacy specialists such as Mem Fox (2001), Dorothy Butler (1995), Bernice E. Cullinan (2000), and Jim Trelease (1995). For infants, these authors suggest books with clearly defined, uncluttered pictures. Faces (especially baby faces), infants' first point of focus, are very appealing. The following anecdote shows how one caregiver introduced a picture book to infants in his care:

> *Gabriel, an infant caregiver in Columbus, Ohio, reads* Peek-A-Boo *by Roberta Intrater to the infants in his care. He holds the book so the baby can see each page. While he reads, he talks about the pictures. "Look, Amber! This baby is laughing! This is just how you look when you're laughing." He shows the laughing face to all the other babies. Then he shows the next page. Gabriel reads the book several times, talking to the baby about each page. He will probably read the same book again tomorrow, too.*
>
> *Gabriel notices that the babies love to look at pictures of baby faces, so he follows up by photographing each child's face. He mounts the pictures where the children can see them, above the changing table and on top of a low activity table. As the babies recognize the faces, he reminds them of each child's name and pronounces it clearly for them.*

Toddlers enjoy many of the same books that infants enjoy. But they also are ready for more complex texts and pictures, for example, of animals and familiar household objects. Toddlers often delight in taking part in the reading process by repeating special words or mimicking funny sounds. They appreciate humor in a story or picture and may want to imitate certain movements or act out an idea or event.

> *Katherine, a home child-care provider in Centralia, Washington, reads* Ten, Nine, Eight *by Molly Bang every morning. During the day, she very naturally integrates the element of counting into her activities with the toddlers; for example, while diapering each child, she counts feet, toes, eyes, and nose and encourages the toddlers to count with her. But Katherine makes more connections to the story than just counting. She talks with the children about who puts them to bed at home. She asks questions such as, "Who has a nightgown like the one in the story? Does it have buttons? What other clothes have buttons?" She continues to connect everyday objects from the story with everyday objects the children*

see in their homes or in her center. Later in the week, Katherine reads the classic Goodnight, Moon *by Margaret Wise Brown, and other bedtime stories, and talks about all the different ways children and animals get ready for bed.*

All of these interactions help the very youngest child experience a sense of mastery over language and more fully participate in the reading experience. Concepts expand as children see the elements of the book also in their everyday environments.

The Importance of a Diverse Collection

A collection of picture books should reflect the diversity of the world, which means that the collection strikes a balance in gender, ethnicity, lifestyle, and place. Children and adults from many different backgrounds are drawn to and inspired by literature that mirrors their unique cultural heritage (Walters, 2002). For example, an African-American professional attending a training session in Florida admired the Bruce McMillan edition of *Mary Had a Little Lamb*:

The families I work with are really going to enjoy this book. I always thought Mary was a little White girl—but this little girl, with her glasses, she looks just like the girls in the families I work with," the educator told us. *"They're not used to seeing books where people in the pictures look just like us. I'm* not *used to it!"*

Diversity plays an important role in choosing and reading picture books, but it is important not to isolate these books or categorize them according to the demographic they may reflect. Nor should books be chosen simply because they represent a particular culture, even if there are few books from that culture. Story, art, and publishing excellence are always the primary criteria in book selection. In all the books choosen, the characters share the same needs and desires: They want to be loved, and they want to feel safe, but they want to have adventures, too.

Suggested Books for Infants and Toddlers

Books and stories do not simply build a language and knowledge base. They help us understand who we are, where we come from, and what our possibilities are (Im et al., 2004). Telling family stories, retelling stories read in books, and making up stories together are all activities that help children make sense of their world.

The following list of recommended titles for reading with infants and toddlers is by no means comprehensive. It does not include many classic titles because these can usually be found through local libraries and in many homes. The following books, however, cover the spectrum of genres, styles, and levels of complexity from the very simple (*Clap Hands*) to the sophisticated (*Max Found Two Sticks*). The list has not been subdivided into separate sections for infants and toddlers because any such division is arbitrary. Toddlers often want to hear again and again the books they heard as babies, and sometimes infants prefer books that parents think are too long, too wordy, or too sophisticated for them.

Uncluttered Pictures

Clap Hands by Helen Oxenbury

Baby Says by John Steptoe

Where's Spot? by Eric Hill

Faces

The Big Book of Beautiful Babies by David Ellwand

Peek-A-Boo by Roberta Intrater

Guess Who? by Margaret Miller

Animals

I Went Walking by Sue Miller

Mary Had a Little Lamb with photographs by Bruce McMillan

Sam Who Never Forgets by Eve Rice

Sounds

One Afternoon by Yumi Heo

Max Found Two Sticks by Brian Pinkney

The Baby Goes Beep by Rebecca O'Connell

Rhymes

Baby Dance by Ann Taylor

The Eensy Weensy Spider: Finger Plays and Action Rhymes by Joanna Cole

My Very First Mother Goose by Iona Opie, illustrated by Rosemary Wells

Las Nanas de Abuelita (Grandmother's Nursery Rhymes) by Nancy Palacio Jaramillo

¡Pío Peep! Traditional Spanish Nursery Rhymes selected by Alma Flor Ada and F. Isabel Campoy

Familiar Things

Everywhere Babies by Susan Meyers

Ten, Nine, Eight by Molly Bang

Mama Zooms by Jane Cowen-Fletcher

On Mother's Lap by Ann Herbert Scott

Repeating Words

So Much by Trish Cooke

Caps for Sale by Esphyr Slobodkina

The Little Red Hen by Margot Zemach

Humor

Moo, Baa, La, La, La by Sandra Boynton

Ten Minutes Till Bedtime by Peggy Rathmann

Eat Up Gemma by Sarah Hayes

Movement and Dramatic Play

Pretend You're a Cat by Jean Marzollo

"More, More, More," Said the Baby by Vera B. Williams

We're Going On a Lion Hunt by David Axtell

Making Choices

There are several strategies for finding the best picture books for infants and toddlers. First of all, become familiar with the books on the list included in this chapter. Learn to recognize the qualities that make these books first-rate: appealing contents, succinct text, and distinctive artwork. Regularly browse book review magazines such as *Horn Book, Booklist,* and the *New York Times Book Review.* We also recommend consulting local or regional resources, including children's literature experts at the state department of libraries and the state department of education, early childhood educators at colleges and universities, and experts in bookstores' children's sections. Internet sites can be helpful, but the reader must ascertain that the webmaster is not simply trying to sell products. In addition, resources such as a Mother Goose Program can provide valuable information and support:

> *Randy is a single father who has never read to his children. He recently moved to Rutland, Vermont, where he was invited to attend Especially for Dads, a Mother Goose Program. The three-session program emphasized the importance of his role as a father. It also gave him books and strategies to help him get into the habit of reading and talking with his three children. After*

attending the first session, Randy practiced what he had learned
about reading aloud and using books as springboards for conver-
sations with his children. At the second session Randy told the
group that Ten Minutes till Bedtime *by Peggy Rathmann had*
become the bedtime favorite with his 2-year-old son. "Every
night he wants to hear it before he goes to sleep," Randy said.
"The first time I read it, I made up different things for the little
hamsters to say. He loves that and thinks it's so funny."

Conclusions

Good books and stimulating conversation do make a difference in the lives of
very young children. Choosing high-quality books and reading them in a conversational way maintains the child's interest, nurtures the parent–child bond,
and teaches early literacy skills (Schickedanz, 1999).

References

Brazelton, T. B. (1992). *Touchpoints: Your child's emotional and behavioral development.* Reading, MA: Perseus.

Bruner, J. (1996). *The culture of education.* Cambridge, MA: Harvard University Press.

Bus, A. G., van Ijzendoorn, M. H., & Pellegrini, A.D. (1995). Joint book reading makes for success in learning to read: A meta-analysis on intergenerational transmission of literacy. *Review of Educational Research, 65,* 1–21.

Butler, D. (1995). *Babies need books: Sharing the joy of books with your child from birth to six.* New York: Penguin.

Cullinan, B. E. (2000). *Read to me: Raising kids who love to read.* New York: Scholastic.

Fox, M. (2001). *Reading magic: Why reading aloud to our children will change their lives forever.* New York: Harcourt.

Gopnik, A. G., Meltzoff, A. N., & Kuhl, P. K. (1999). *The scientist in the crib: Minds, brains, and how children learn.* New York: William Morrow.

Hart, B., & Risley, T. R. (1995). *Meaningful differences in the everyday experiences of young children.* Baltimore: Paul H. Brookes.

Hiebert, E. H. (1986). Issues related to home influences in young children's print-related development. In D. B. Yaden & S. Templeton (Eds.), *Metalinguistic awareness and beginning literacy* (pp. 145–158). Portsmouth, NH: Heinemann.

Im, J., Merrill, S., Osborn, C., Martens, J., Striniste, N., Sanchez, S., & Thorp, E. (2004). Stories change a person's heart: Zero to Three's literacy, learning, and life initiative. *Zero to Three, 25*(1), 23–28.

Kuhl, P. K., & Meltzoff, A. N. (1996). Infant vocalizations in response to speech: Vocal imitation and developmental change. *Journal of the Acoustical Society of America, 100,* 2425–2438.

Lancy, D. F., & Bergin, C. (1992, April). *The role of parents in supporting beginning reading.* Paper presented at the annual meeting of the American Educational Research Association, San Francisco, CA.

Mason, J. M., & Allen, J. B. (1986). *A review of emergent literacy with implications for research and practice in reading.* Technical Report No. 379. Champaign: University of Illinois.

Morrow, L. (1990). Effects of a story reading program on the literacy development of at-risk kindergarten children. *Journal of Reading Behavior, 22*(3), 255–275.

Schickedanz, J. A. (1999). *Much more than the ABCs: The early stages of reading and writing.* Washington, DC: National Association for the Education of Young Children.

Snow, C., Burns, S., & Griffin, P. (Eds.). National Research Council, Committee on the Prevention of Reading Difficulties. (1998). *Preventing reading difficulties in young children.* Washington, DC: National Academy Press.

Trelease, J. (1995). *The read-aloud handbook.* New York: Penguin.

Walters, T. S. (2002). Images, voices, choices: Literature to nurture children's literacy development. In B. Bowman (Ed.), *Love to read* (pp. 73–81). Washington, DC: National Black Child Development Institute, Inc.

CHAPTER 28

Thoughts From a Children's Author (and Jazz Drummer): Going Through the Day With Snap, Crackle, and Jazz

Matthew Gollub

I am a storyteller and a children's author, and much of what I know about sharing stories with children I first discovered by playing jazz drums. In a jazz combo, the musicians follow a song's basic structure but take plenty of opportunities to interact and explore. You play, "Ska-Diddle." I play "Ska-Diddle." But if you play "za-BING," I may play "za-BOING." In other words, at times, I may echo your phrase; at other times, I will respond with a statement of my own.

As musicians, we merrily navigate a theme, entertaining one another by entertaining ourselves. We could make our music more interesting by incorporating unexpected cadences and twists: We might play a swing standard with a bossa nova feel, play a ballad at twice the prescribed tempo, or … take … things … slow. Jazz musicians stimulate and validate one another's creative ideas. The connections they make with one another are unique and many times cannot be reproduced.

Such creative interaction may be applied to language development. Creating rhymes as we go through our day is not only fun but also useful in acquainting a small child with phonemes, the sounds of speech and, later, reading. Reciting *knocks, talks,* and *fox,* for example, invites a child to distinguish the first consonant sounds, *n, t,* and *f.* Moreover, these rhyming words acquaint the child with "ahks," a building block with which she will construct more vocabulary over time. Integrating simple melodies into everyday routines is another fun, easy, and effective way to stimulate a child's linguistic development. Try diapering or dressing a child while singing to the tune of "Bingo." For example, if the child's name is Jacob, sing:

> *There was a boy who had a sock,*
> *And Jacob was his name-o.*
> *Pull, pull, pull it on. Pull, pull, pull it on.*
> *Pull, pull, pull it on, and Jacob pulled his sock on.*

Other verses can focus on shorts, pants, shirts, and shoes. Other songs that most any adult can modify include "Old McDonald," "Row Your Boat," and "Twinkle, Twinkle Little Star."

While you are integrating rhythm into the child's routines, why not also make connections with his visual senses? The bricks of a chimney form a rhythmic pattern, as do the printed swirls on a dress. The lines on the sidewalk can provide focus to walking—step, step, step, *line*, step, step, step, *line*. And the car's windshield wipers on a rainy day keep time like a conductor's baton. As with jazz, the emphasis should be on the joy and fun of creative interaction.

The Jazz of Sharing a Good Book

The experience of reading with an infant or toddler is similar to playing a jazz duet. In fact, the creative interplay—the "jazz"—can begin before we even pick up the book. Gentle hand claps, jiggling key chains, finger plays, and simple rhymes all stimulate the baby's mind. Even games of peekaboo and hide-and-seek help to develop a baby's attention span, encourage thinking about logical sequences, and teach the child that what goes away usually comes back. Often, we can initiate creative play around books through simple questioning or call and response:

> Adult: Here's a book called *Fox in Socks*. Where's the picture of the fox?
>
> Toddler: *(points)*
>
> Adult: Good! And where's the picture of the socks?
>
> Toddler: *(points)*

Adult: That's right. There's the fox, and he's wearing socks. The socks are BIG!

Toddler: BIG!!! Big, big, big, big …

Adult: Excellent! Let's begin.

Reading becomes an extension of this give-and-take interaction, one that uses a book as a focal point. Reading books from start to finish is great. But when babies want to start from the end of the book, indulge them—likewise for when they wish to read the book upside down. Some of the best reactions from infants and toddlers come when we think of the book as a prop, turning the pages with a dramatic flair or occasionally snapping the book shut. Board books and plastic waterproof books stand up well to such antics. My only rule is that the book should not be an impediment to the joyful connection one feels with the child. The following is a list of my favorite guidelines for reading to children from birth to age 3:

- Cuddle while reading to enjoy closeness or, with a toddler, let the child move around the sofa or room while listening.

- Let the child participate in reading by pointing to pictures or by turning the book's pages.

- Speak clearly and with model elocution. Let the child study your mouth as you speak.

- Use lots of expression, altering your voice for different characters. Pretend to be an actor or actress with a captive and enthusiastic audience of one.

- Invite toddlers to complete rhymes and sentences.

- Play up the passages the child enjoys most, even if it means straying from the text, for example,

   Adult: *(reading book)* Grrr. The bear began to growl.

   Toddler: Grrr.

   Adult: *(no longer reading the book)* That's right. It was a BIG bear! GRRR!

   Toddler: GRRR!

- From time to time, hold a familiar book upside down, or try turning the pages and telling the story in reverse. The child will delight in demonstrating how the book "really goes."

- Choose books that appeal to the child's interests, even if they don't necessarily coincide with those of the adult. Avoid gender stereotypes in choosing books.

- The flow is key. Take time to explain a few unfamiliar words, but be sensitive to the child's desire to move on. Because children often hear books 20 times and more, we do not have to explain all the new words at once. Many new words will be learned through context, without explanation.

- Try chanting stories, especially when they rhyme, with a snap, clap, or jazzy bounce. Swing, sway with, or even sing the stories to keep them sounding fresh and lively.

Chanting With Jazz

Chanting a story while snapping your fingers can energize the reader as well as the child and can keep the adult from dozing off in midsentence! For me as an author–storyteller, the bounce is almost as important as the content itself. I have gone so far as to record stories set to music. And I marvel at how quickly children pick up the beat. The following examples compare reading with chanting. First, read the following couplet:

> *Three baby bunnies giggled in the night.*
> *Then Papa Rabbit turned on the light.*

Now try chanting the same couplet while snapping or clapping wherever you see an X.

> *Three baby bunnies giggled in the NIGHT.*
>   X   X   X   X

> *Then Papa Rabbit turned on the LIGHT.*
>   X   X   X   X

Once the reader gets the rhythm and knows where to clap, try reading faster for older toddlers to create more swing and bounce.

When adults read to children, we impart vocabulary, wisdom, and glimpses of the broader world. The following are my favorite ideas for reading to more than one child at a time.

- Try sounding a bell or other simple instrument to add a sense of ceremony. The bell signals to children that something fun is about to begin.

- Make sure that listeners have enough physical space to move around and feel comfortable.

- Try getting listeners focused by inviting them to join in reciting a simple rhyme with gestures, for example,

  Hands high … Hands low … Hands wave … to and fro.

- Allow the children to come and go as they wish.

- Relax, and read slowly with lots of feeling and expression. The adult's enthusiasm and animation will motivate the children to listen.

- Invite toddlers to complete certain rhymes. The more obvious the cues, the better.

  Reader: Way down south where bananas grow,
  a grasshopper stepped on an elephant's …

  Toddlers: Toe!

  This jazzy give and take is a source of great satisfaction for children.

- Invite listeners to further participate by chanting recurring lines, modeling recurring gestures, and of course, chiming in with animal sounds when appropriate.

- Simplify the story by paraphrasing or skipping details. By doing so, readers can use picture books intended for older children while still communicating the gist of the story.

- Read the same story on different days. Children take comfort in knowing what is coming next, and familiarity helps the reader find more opportunities for interaction.

Unique Experiences in Jazz

Considering the profound benefits of reading aloud—cultivating language, knowledge, comfort, trust, and stronger emotional ties between child and reader—it is well worth enhancing opportunities to read aloud by sprinkling some "jazz" throughout the day. Remember, in the spirit of jazz, to be *you*! Sharing language with children in *your* voice, with *your* improvisations, is a gift that only you can provide.

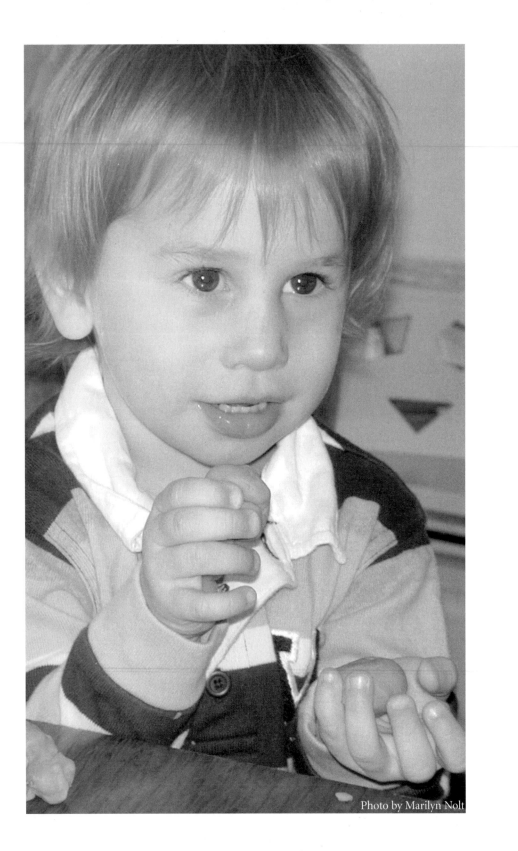

CHAPTER 29

Learning to Read the World: A Celebration!

Sharon E. Rosenkoetter

A familiar person, a well-known voice, a repeated sound, a response, a word, a squiggle, a label, a connection—the first 3 years are times to explore, discover, and celebrate the joyful new world of "me" and the incredible new vistas "out there." Guides on this monumental journey are family members and other special caregivers who delight in adventuring with their newborn or young child in learning to read the world. By enfolding the infant or toddler in love and by helping the young one make meaningful connections, these very special people provide the foundations for language and literacy, which subsequently provide the basis for school success.

The Goal

The goal was stated well by Dr. Seuss (1978):

> The more that you read, the more things you'll know.
> The more that you learn, the more places you'll go.
> (unpaginated)

Our goal—the goal of every parent, caregiver, teacher, administrator, and policymaker—is that the children who are now infants and toddlers will grow to have opportunities and options to contribute to their world in a vast array of ways. Nurturing those opportunities and options requires literacy. Literacy begins soon after birth when infants begin to fathom myriad aspects of their new world.

Key Ingredients

As shown in the previous 28 chapters, learning to read the world requires presence, time, words, print, and intention provided by families, caregivers, programs, and communities.

Presence. Families and caregivers need to be with young children physically, mentally, emotionally, and verbally, seeing the world from their children's vantage point and stimulating the gradual expansion of understanding and communication.

Time. This necessary empathetic presence takes lots of time, time that parents and caregivers must allocate for every child and time that program leaders and policymakers must budget for attention to individual children and responsiveness to their communicative attempts. Further, time must be committed to new, relevant, accessible, and enticing adult learning opportunities for family members and professionals. With adult models, young children observe that learning never ends. When adults' own learning opportunities with respect to child development encompass adult learning strategies (Brookfield, 1986), then parents and caregivers increasingly enjoy words, stories, and songs and build their own competencies in fostering language and literacy with infants, toddlers, and older children.

Words. Infants and toddlers learn language when they hear words—lots of words—spoken and sung in meaningful contexts by people who matter to them. Language develops gradually, as shown by many of the authors in this volume, but it always requires conversational partners who label, query, commiserate, exclaim, and celebrate using words.

Print. Text is omnipresent in our world, but it is meaningless to infants and toddlers unless significant people call it to their attention and interpret its messages. This effort does not mean that we read every sign and newspaper article to the baby. It does mean that we communicate about how important print is to getting along in the world. It means that we share printed symbols, like the logos for Cheerios and Wendy's, with young children. It means that we tell stories, surround young children with developmentally appropriate books, and read books with them several times every day.

Intention. The key to a more literate society, the route to more academically successful elementary school classes, the path to greater family literacy, and the way to help young children feel more competent and confident in talking and responding to print—all these avenues to literacy begin in early infancy with adults' intention to achieve those outcomes. Families, caregivers, programs, and communities must show purposeful attention to nurturing our youngest citizens to become talkers, listeners, readers, and writers. Large public campaigns are important, but so are minute-by-minute, one-to-one interactions throughout every day. What will truly make a difference for every infant and toddler is the comprehensiveness of the intention, the surround of the sound, and the universal cherishing of the value "Words matter; reading matters," even with our youngest citizens.

Changing Identities

A part of every toddler's identity must become "I talk and listen. I am a reader and a writer." This statement must be true even when (perhaps especially when) extensive adult support, assistive technology, and bilingual staff members are necessary to bring the self-fulfilling prophesy into reality. It will become true when every child's inborn drive to read the world is linked to language and literacy by the important people in that world.

A part of every family member's identity must become "I teach my child to talk. I teach my child to read." This statement must be true no matter what language the family speaks and no matter what language the family reads—and no matter whether significant family members do not themselves possess reading skills. With families of infants and toddlers, the intention is paramount; interactions incorporating language and literacy follow.

A part of every caregiver's identity must become "I support families by talking with their child. I support families by reading with their child several times each day." This statement must be true no matter what the caregiver's level of previous formal education or language or literacy skills is. Success in encouraging young children's language and literacy is possible for every caregiver who is provided with the intentional support of program administrators along with ready access to relevant training opportunities.

A part of every program leader's identity must become "I lead my program in fostering early language and literacy." As program leaders apply this intention in hiring, employee evaluations, reflective supervision, budgeting, and family and professional training, the effect on families, staff members, and especially young children will become obvious in the greater numbers of effective talkers, motivated readers, and enthusiastic communicators who develop throughout the program.

Finally, a part of every community's identity must become "We celebrate the beginning of language and literacy in the earliest years. We honor and support families, caregivers, and programs that are teaching our youngest children to talk and read." This progressive identity must become true even if a community has not thought in this way before. It will become true when (a) a small group of people mobilize their community as described in this volume, (b) effective social marketing about early language and literacy conveys strategies for families and caregivers in meaningful, motivational ways, (c) libraries become gathering places and information sources for families of infants and toddlers, and (d) policymakers realize and act on the importance of the earliest years to their vision of a literate, more productive community.

Specific Recommendations

The seven recommendations that follow provide a framework within which to bring about a literate, more productive community.

Families must talk, sing, and read with responsiveness to their babies and young children throughout every day from birth onward. Consider the following examples.

> *Lila sings to Jeremy every time before she breast-feeds him. At the age of 4 months, Jeremy associates the sound of her song with a positive experience and coos when the song begins. If Lila is delayed after singing, Jeremy wails his frustration. These actions show that, already, Jeremy understands the essence of communication.*

* * *

> *Tony has books for his son in every room in the house, in the bathtub (plastic books), in the diaper bag, and in the car. At least 20 times every day, 18-month-old Tony Jr. looks at a book. Doing so is as natural to him as breathing.*

* * *

Carrie takes 6-month-old Tira with her when she cleans houses. Throughout the routines of housecleaning, Carrie describes her actions to Tira who is watching from her infant seat. When Tira babbles, Carrie imitates the baby's vocalizations.

* * *

While sitting in the crowded waiting room of the pediatrician, Lakisha bounces 30-month-old Shawnell on her knees and chants nonsensical but rhythmical jingles. The toddler is entertained during the long wait and enjoys the words she is hearing.

Every caregiver in a home or center-based setting must talk, sing, and read with responsiveness to every baby and young child throughout every day. The following vignettes show examples.

Two-month-old Pauli focuses on Maria's face as she chatters about the festival to come on the weekend, her new costume, and the food she will prepare. Maria intersperses her account with words from Pauli's home language.

* * *

"This is the way we wash our hands, wash our hands, wash our hands. This is the way we wash our hands every day in the morning." Singing of this old, old rhyme during hand washing teaches word–meaning associations, reminds about a health ritual, and teaches a social script for appropriate behavior before eating. Later reading comprehension depends on connecting a series of such scripts together with words and print symbols.

* * *

At Growing Oaks Center, there are books in every area of the infant and toddler rooms, along with beanbag chairs and rockers where adults can share stories with young children and hideaways where children can look at books on their own. Parents and townspeople are invited in to read to children, and posters remind adults that talking and reading with infants and toddlers are among their most important responsibilities.

Program leaders must act in numerous ways to encourage family members and caregivers to talk, sing, and read with responsiveness to babies and young children throughout every day from birth onward. For example, consider the following situations.

Carlos asks job applicants who are applying for home visitor positions to demonstrate how they read to a 2-year-old. He asks them for suggestions about how to integrate language and literacy experiences into every home visit. Their responses are factors in the decision to hire or not to hire.

* * *

Director Penny visits every infant–toddler classroom in her center on a weekly basis to see how language and literacy are being encouraged. She touts as examples those caregivers who are using good practices and quietly works with those who are not using them to foster an improved literacy climate. She has set up a voluntary mentoring program on company time to support new learning among her staff members.

* * *

Nicole sends home a weekly newsletter with language and literacy tips. She has enlisted high school students to make home literacy bags to send to send to children's homes. She has recruited the local Rotary Club to donate books three times a year to share with families and the Extension Homemakers' Club to make cloth books. When several Ukrainian immigrant children arrived in her program, Nicole worked with the state library system to order books in the children's home language, which were then delivered weekly.

* * *

Margaret has established Pizza and Books gatherings for the teen mothers and their babies every two weeks in the summer,

*Lunch and Books gatherings for the parents who work in the
neighborhood, Parenting and Books gatherings for the stay-at-
home parents, and Supper and Books gatherings for young
families who prefer early evening events. A church group and
the local Soroptimists help to pay for the food, which is cooked in
some cases by a high school life skills (special education) class. A
Parent Advisory Committee advises Margaret on these activities,
which have a two-fold purpose: (a) to model and encourage language and literacy and (b) to promote social relationships
among young families. Margaret tries to reach every family in
her program with the "read to your child" message.*

* * *

*Many staff members and families served by one early child-
hood program have significant language and literacy needs
themselves. Brenda has invited the adult basic education–
GED–ESOL program to offer classes on location in her
center, requires the CDA certificate for all new staff members
within 6 months of employment, pays for staff members to
attend community college courses, and provides incremental
salary incentives for staff members' progress toward a BS
degree. Brenda consistently states that everyone—parent or
professional—is a learner throughout life. She requires professional development plans to list activities tied to each staff
member's desired learning outcomes for the year. From these
needs, as well as her own observations of staff members'
performance, Brenda makes the agency staff development
plan, which always has components on relationship-based
language and literacy learning.*

**Communities must develop comprehensive plans to foster early language
and literacy, intentionally including infants and toddlers, and they must
systematically support families, caregivers, and programs in their vital
everyday language and literacy interactions with babies and young children.**
Consider the following examples.

*United Way of Lane County, Oregon, has coordinated a
$600,000+ campaign called Cherish Every Child (see Pratt &*

Hernandez, this volume, p. 455). Key emphases are "talk to your child during family routines" and "read to your child every day." The campaign is backed by public access to information about parenting; welcoming postures on the part of community agencies; high-quality artwork; and pervasive reminders on radio, television, billboards, and bus ads. Carefully planned evaluations have shown increased knowledge and positive behavior change among parents in Lane County.

* * *

Brad, an Early Head Start director, noticed that infants and toddlers were not included in his community's literacy activities. Brad took his concern to a meeting of the local interagency Council on Children and Families, which then formed an Early Literacy Committee to study the matter and make suggestions for the strategic plan. Now infants and toddlers are considered in all community literacy activities, and some events are planned just for this age group.

* * *

Kerry, a Head Start inclusion specialist, realized that some of the child-care centers she visited had a paucity of book and toys. With the help of several civic groups, Kerry developed and maintained a lending library for child-care programs in her community.

* * *

The StoryQUEST team in Logan, Utah, has worked with the city leaders to establish a books on the bus program. Families traveling on the bus can borrow books to read en route.

Policymakers must realize the relationship between language and literacy in the early years and children's later school success. Because relationships are at the heart of early language and literacy and because the tools of early literacy are in children's natural environments (McLane & McNamee, 1990), federal, state, and local policies must stimulate literacy-rich environments and foster positive adult–child relationships that include language. Age 5 is too late. Age 3 is too late. Language and literacy learning must begin soon after birth, and political leaders must act to ensure that every individual in the nation realizes this imperative.

Laws, regulations, appropriations, and visible public support are the means by which policymakers can underscore a focus on early language and literacy. At present, the nation spends least on children during the earliest years, the period when their brain growth is greatest (Karoly et al., 1998), even though studies show that support for quality early experiences pays off in reduced later educational costs and fewer societal problems such as juvenile delinquency, teen pregnancy, and school dropout rates. Programs with strong evaluations, such as the Abecedarian Project, the IHDP Program, and Early Head Start, have shown substantial cost–benefit ratios (Bruner, 2002). Often, political leaders will act on initiatives for infants and toddlers and their families if advocates provide the supportive information, the public backing, and the appreciative acknowledgment that their actions do make a difference in both the beginning language and literacy of young children and the long-term outcomes for schools and society.

Further, policymakers must acknowledge the important influence that family support and education, caregiver support and education, and the development of new or expanded teacher education programs have on the promotion of early language and literacy with infants and toddlers. Given that families and caregivers are the primary instruments for early language and literacy development, families and caregivers must learn effective strategies to enhance infant–toddler growth in these areas. Adults must receive affirmation where their strategies are already salutary but must also continue to have access to learning opportunities to gain more effective practices. In early childhood communities that are committed to ongoing learning, training builds higher and higher levels of challenge and develops greater and greater expertise for families and caregivers beyond initial skill levels. Such training also creates family and caregiver networks of individuals pursuing additional strategies to boost infant–toddler learning about language and literacy. This effective training is tied to the needs, schedules, and learning styles of adults; provides opportunities for immediate application and follow-up feedback; and is evaluated to demonstrate accountability for the resources invested in it. Additional training funds are desperately needed by programs to enhance the competence of families and caregivers related to beginning language and literacy for infants and toddlers. Nevertheless, one of the most significant ways that policymakers can support early language and literacy is to insist on high standards and demonstrated outcomes for the training programs they support. One-shot workshops are not sufficient; rather, sustained attention is necessary to alter the ecology of early language and literacy as described in this volume.

In a similar vein, there currently exists a shortage of teacher education programs that focus on the earliest years. Many excellent early childhood education departments at universities around the nation offer no or limited coursework on children ages birth to 3. Policymakers should consider the expenditure of public funds to address this shortage, much as they have voted appropriations to Early Childhood Special Education to overcome its teacher shortages during the past 15 years.

Finally, policymakers must address the need for new research on effective strategies for early language and literacy learning that include or focus on the infant–toddler years. Especially needed is research on ways to facilitate early language and literacy development for children whose families talk little (Hart & Risley, 1995, 1999), have limited reading skills (Goodling Institute for Family Literacy Research, 2004), or represent a culture other than the one dominant in their children's caregiving setting (Ballenger, 1999; National Research Council & Institute of Medicine, 1998). The development, implementation, and evaluation of effective, affordable training strategies for infant–toddler caregivers make up another area where expenditures on research would lead to notable child outcomes.

Celebration

As we strive to bolster the foundations of language and literacy from birth to age 3, there is already much to celebrate! Most children are born with a natural propensity to make sense of their world and a natural set of abilities with which to begin to acquire language. Recent advances in knowledge, technology, and policy afford ways to intervene with infants and toddlers when their progress in communication is slow or atypical. Many, many family members comfortably interact with their infants and toddlers in ways that foster early language and literacy. Again, science-based strategies exist for supporting all families to grow in competency in parenting for literacy and family literacy when they wish to enhance the skills that foster their children's future success. Across the nation, many caregivers use effective, culturally sensitive practices to nurture early language and literacy. Validated models for training, including several presented in this volume, can be used to increase the capacity of family members and caregivers to stimulate the early language and literacy of the infants and toddlers in their care.

Another cause for celebration is that a growing number of program leaders embrace a relationship-based language and literacy emphasis in setting the direction of their services. The leader's role in these settings is to lead, not just to manage the accounts. Given an administrator's ability to influence many others, the leader's attention to strategies for beginning language and literacy throughout every program is warranted. Surely these areas, along with health and safety, are ones that merit modeling, discussion, and prominence in organizational life.

Finally, we celebrate that a rising number of communities across the nation feature at least one initiative that emphasizes the importance of language and literacy in the earliest years. Program models, social marketing supports, and scattered infant–toddler initiatives are working in many communities to enlarge those efforts, even though some communities still mistakenly start language and literacy efforts at kindergarten age. What appears to be needed in many locales is comprehensive planning to pull together potential participants and resources, plus motivation to deliver strategic programs in accessible ways and messages to their target audiences multiple times each day. These efforts must be followed by careful evaluation to determine the outcomes of community efforts. Means to accomplish these tasks are readily available. Here and there all across the nation, individuals and programs are coming together to share their successes and generate new and more effective ways to help young children learn to read their world. There is much to celebrate!

Presence, time, words, print, and intention by families, caregivers, programs, communities, and policymakers will carry forward this monumentally important effort. Let us continue to work to foster the joy in language and literacy, the foundational skills of language and literacy, and the supports that will make growth in early language and literacy a reality for every infant, toddler, and family.

References

Ballenger, C. (1999). *Teaching other people's children: Literacy and learning in a bilingual classroom.* New York: Teachers College Press.

Brookfield, S. (1986). *Understanding and facilitating adult learning.* San Francisco: Jossey-Bass.

Bruner, C. (2002). *A stitch in time: Calculating the costs of school unreadiness.* Washington, DC: The Finance Project.

Goodling Institute for Family Literacy Research. (2004). Home page of Goodling Institute for Family Literacy Research Web site. Retrieved June 5, 2004, from http://www.ed.psu.edu/goodlinginstitute/about.asp

Hart, B., & Risley, T. R. (1995). *Meaningful differences in the everyday experiences of young American children.* Baltimore: Paul H. Brookes.

Hart, B., & Risley, T. R. (1999). *The social world of children learning to talk.* Baltimore: Paul H. Brookes.

Karoly, L., Greenwood, P., Everingham, S., Hoube, J., Kilbrun, R., Rydell, P., Sanders, M., & Chiesa, J. (1998). *Investing in our children: What we know and don't know about the costs and benefits of early childhood interventions.* Santa Monica, CA: RAND.

McLane, J. B., & McNamee, G. D. (1990). *Early literacy.* Cambridge, MA: Harvard University Press.

National Research Council & Institute of Medicine. (1998). *Educating language-minority children* (D. August & K. Hakuta, Eds.). Report of the Committee on Developing a Research Agenda on the Education of Limited-English-Proficient and Bilingual Students; Board on Children, Youth, and Families; Commission on Behavioral and Social Sciences and Education. Washington, DC: National Academy Press.

Pratt, C. C., & Hernandez, R. (2006). Early literacy communications campaigns: The important role of social marketing. In S. E. Rosenkoetter & J. Knapp-Philo (Eds.), *Learning to read the world: Language and literacy in the first three years* (pp. 455–476). Washington, DC: ZERO TO THREE Press.

Seuss, Dr. (also known as Theodore Geisel). (1978). *I can read with my eyes shut.* New York: Random House.

Editors

Sharon E. Rosenkoetter, PhD, is associate professor in Human Development and Family Sciences at Oregon State University with special interest in young children with disabilities and their families. After 20 years as a teacher educator and outreach provider in numerous U.S. Department of Education and State projects, Dr. Rosenkoetter now studies early communication and literacy and early transitions. A member of the StoryQUEST research team, Dr. Rosenkoetter is also the Director of Early Childhood Leadership Directions for professionals in health, human services, and education and Rural Links, an innovative approach to teacher education for rural communities.

Joanne Knapp-Philo, PhD, is the director of the National Head Start Family Literacy Center at the California Institute on Human Services at Sonoma State University. She was formerly the director of StoryQUEST, an innovative research and training program to support families, early education and care staff, programs, and communities to promote beginning language and literacy in infants and toddlers. Dr. Knapp-Philo served as the SpecialQuest Director of the Hilton/Early Head Start Training Program from 1998 until 2002, and has been a staff developer, principal, university instructor, and classroom teacher in special education and early intervention programs. Her areas of research include staff development approaches and methods of evaluating the effects of staff development approaches.

Contributors

Sally Anderson, MLS, is the executive director of Mother Goose Programs in Vermont. Mother Goose Programs give parents, librarians, child care providers, and other educators picture books, training, and activity guides that transform the act of reading to children into a multidimensional and powerful learning experience.

Lauren R. Barton, PhD, is senior research scientist at the Center for Education and Human Services at SRI International in California. Her work has focused on identifying components that contribute to highly effective preventive intervention programs for low-income families with young children and on supporting programs in their efforts to implement and sustain these practices.

Linda Brekken, PhD, is the director of the Hilton/Early Head Start Training Program at the California Institute on Human Services at Sonoma State University. Dr. Brekken has a laudable history of leadership in Early Childhood Special Education and has directed numerous training programs in California, the western region, and throughout the nation.

Holly E. Brophy-Herb, PhD, is associate professor of Child Development in the Department of Family and Child Ecology at Michigan State University, where she studies the development of infants and toddlers within the context of the family. She is co-author of *Talking With Your Baby: Family as the First School*.

Adriana Bus, PhD, is professor at Leiden University, The Netherlands. She was involved in several Dutch projects to stimulate literacy in home visits, preschool, kindergarten, and first grade and has published articles in leading international journals in the fields of education, educational psychology, and child development.

Kevin N. Cole, PhD, lives in Seattle, where his research foci are the efficacy of diverse language facilitation methods, longitudinal efficacy of preschool curriculum models, and exploration of how children with varied profiles respond differently to aspects of early intervention. Leader of the StoryQUEST Research Partnership, Dr. Cole has developed the *Language Is the Key* approach to language and literacy development.

Kathleen Deerr, MLS, has 30 years experience in bringing innovative, interdisciplinary services to children and families through libraries and is active in the continuing development of librarians through regional and national presentations and published works, including *Running a Parent/Child Workshop* and *Including Families of Children With Special Needs*. She is currently the assistant director and National Family Place Libraries administrator at the Middle Country Public Library in New York State.

Maria de Jong, a former primary school teacher, is now a postdoctoral student at Leiden University, The Netherlands. She studies how new media affect early literacy.

Terry DeMartini, MA, recently retired as director of Training and Technical Assistance at the Center for Child and Family Studies, WestEd, where she was manager and faculty for The Program for Infant/Toddler Caregivers national training institutes. With over 30 years' experience in early childhood education, she has served as adjunct faculty at three California community colleges, consulted for the State of California Commission on Teacher Credentialing and Child Development Division, and directed a California child care resource and referral agency.

Sandra Feinberg, MLS, is the director of the Middle Country Public Library in New York, where she created the Parent Child Workshop, the core program of Family Place Libraries. Author of many books on library transformation and family-centered librarianship, she has spent more than 30 years in community development related to literacy, recently spearheading the Community Resource Database of Long Island, the region's first comprehensive source of programs and services for individuals and families.

Amy Flynn, MA, director of the Bank Street Family Center in New York City, uses her MS in Special Education and MEd in Supervision and Administration to promote the inclusion of children with disabilities into early childhood programs, quality care and education for all children in early childhood programs, and family and teacher support and training. Adjunct faculty for Bank Street College's graduate school and the State University of New York's early childhood video conferences, she has worked as a consultant for projects including SpecialQUEST, Playhouse Disney's *Jo Jo's Circus*, and *Sesame Street Parent Magazine*.

Matthew Gollub, an award-winning author, musician, and storyteller, speaks Spanish and Japanese in addition to English and plays a variety of drums. His popular picture books reflect this background; *The Jazz Fly* and *Gobble, Quack, Moon* even include his musical narrations on audio CD.

Janet Gonzalez-Mena, MA, retired from Napa Valley College in California and became an early childhood consultant. With Dianne Eyer, she wrote *Infants, Toddlers, and Caregivers*, one of the first textbooks focused on that age group and now in its sixth edition.

Elizabeth Gordon, executive director of Libraries for the Future, a nonprofit dedicated to championing the role of libraries in American life, has over 30 years' experience in editing and publishing books for children, in nonprofit management, and in library staff development. She is a former senior vice-president and publisher of children's books at HarperCollins, the founder of Hyperion Books for Children, former director of a school–library collaboration program, and adjunct faculty at New York University.

Michael Gramling, MA, has worked and written in the early childhood field since 1979. The father of five children who taught him all the most important lessons about family literacy, Michael has a masters degree in Human Development from Pacific Oaks College and currently serves as a training specialist for Training and Technical Assistance Services at Western Kentucky University and the National Center for Family Literacy in Louisville, KY.

Peg Griffin, PhD, is affiliated with the Laboratory of Comparative Human Cognition through which she collaborates with cognitive scientists in this country and abroad. Dr. Griffin's recent books include *Preparing Our Teachers: Opportunities for Better Reading Instruction* with D. Strickland, C. Snow, P. McNamara, and M. S. Burns; *Language in Action: New Studies of Language in Society* edited with J. Peyton, W. Wolfram, and R. Fasold; and the National Academy of Sciences committee books with C. Snow and M. S. Burns, *Preventing Reading Difficulties in Young Children* and *Starting Our Right: A Guide to Promoting Children's Success in Reading*.

Rebecca Hernandez, MPA, has extensive experience teaching in both public and private schools and working with not-for-profits on evaluation and cultural competency. The co-author of *Building Results Through Community Mobilization: From Wellness Goals to Community Outcomes for Oregon's Children, Youth and Families*, she is employed by the Center for Health Disparities Research at Oregon Health Sciences Univeristy, where she applies experience in evaluation and cultural competency to improving the service system for the Latino community in Oregon.

Jerry Hindman, MA, has worked in education for over 30 years and has been involved with various programs serving infants, toddlers, and their families. Since 1998, Jerry has served the Hilton/Early Head Start Training Program as Regional Coordinator for Regions V, VII, and XI.

Wendy Alegra Jones, MEd, MSW, is senior policy associate and director of the Children and Youth with Special Health Care Needs Project, National Center for Cultural Competence at the Georgetown University Center for Child & Human Development and also research instructor in the Department of Pediatrics, Georgetown University Medical Center in Washington, DC. She has provided extensive training to families, administrators, teachers, and staff regarding the importance of culture on the development of language and learning, as well as providing strategies for engaging and supporting families in their children's development.

Linda Kimura, MA, who holds a Masters degree in Human Development from Pacific Oaks College, is the director of Babies Can't Wait: International Training and Technical Assistance and the author of *Babies Can't Wait: Relationship-based Home Visiting* and *The Ukulele Baby Lady Presents: Songs for Early Childhood Folks*. Her work and songs focus on learning that occurs in the context of close, caring relationships.

Lorraine F. Kubicek, PhD, is on the research faculty in the Program for Early Developmental Studies, Department of Psychiatry, at the University of Colorado Health Sciences Center, where her interests include the relation between emotion/temperament and early language development, narrative development, parent–child interaction, family routines, and parenting. Dr. Kubicek is a graduate fellow of ZERO TO THREE: National Center for Infants, Toddlers, and Families.

J. Ronald Lally, EdD, codirects the Center for Child and Family Studies at WestEd and the Program for Infant Toddler Caregivers, based in northern California. Dr. Lally's recent publication is "Infant–Toddler Child Care in the United States: Where Has It Been? Where Is It Now? Where Is It Going?" in the 2003 anniversary issue of *Zero to Three*.

Tarima Levine, MA, who holds a master's degree from Bank Street College in Early Childhood Special Education, is a staff developer for her alma mater, working with infant through prekindergarten teachers in Even Start and Head Start programs in New York and Connecticut. She has worked as an early intervention teacher, infant–toddler CDA instructor, and early childhood consultant.

Young Sook Lim, PhD, of Seattle, WA, is a specialist in ESOL/Bilingual Education and has conducted research in parent facilitation of early language development in Asian cultures. Dr. Lim's areas of interest include bilingualism, biliteracy, young children's language development, and curriculum development relating to children from culturally and linguistically diverse backgrounds.

Isabella Lorenzo-Hubert, MA, is a senior policy associate, National Center for Cultural Competence and Bilingual Special Educator and Outreach Coordinator at Georgetown University's Center for Child and Human Development. A native of Uruguay and 20-year resident of the United States, she has worked with Spanish-speaking families in early childhood settings in the areas of language and cognitive development and has learned the importance of honoring each family's cultural, linguistic, and educational values.

Esminia (Mia) M. Luluquisen, DrPh, earned her doctorate from the School of Public Health of the University of California at Berkeley, where she focused on Community Health Education. She has developed numerous curricula and conducted training and university coursework in a variety of community change areas, including maternal–child health, for physicians, nurses, health educators, providers, and community-based groups.

Peter L. Mangione, PhD, codirects the Center for Child & Family Studies at WestEd. One of the principal developers of the *Program for Infant/Toddler Caregivers*, a comprehensive multimedia curriculum, Dr. Mangione has edited publications on language development and communication, culturally responsive care, and cognitive development and learning and has collaborated in the creation of a nationally recognized series of videos on infant–toddler care and development.

Susan B. Neuman, PhD, served as the U.S. Assistant Secretary for Elementary and Secondary Education under President George W. Bush, where she headed the implementation of the No Child Left Behind Act and established the Reading First and Early Reading First programs. Currently Dr. Neuman is Professor in Educational Studies at the University of Michigan, where she previously directed the Center for the Improvement of Early Reading Ability (CIERA) and co-edited the *Handbook of Early Literacy Research.*

Angela Notari-Syverson, PhD, who has degrees in Child Psychology and Communication Disorders from the University of Geneva, Switzerland, and Early Childhod Special Education from the University of Oregon, is senior researcher at the Washington Research Institute in Seattle, where she directs research, model development, and training projects in the area of early literacy and language and assessment for young children. She has authored books and journal publications in those areas and is co-author of *Ladders to Literacy*, an early literacy curriculum developed for use in inclusive settings.

Marion O'Brien, PhD, is professor in the Department of Human Development and Family Studies and director of the Family Research Center at the University of North Carolina–Greensboro. She directed inclusive child care and early intervention programs for infants and toddlers for 20 years, and participates as an investigator in the NICHD Study of Early Child Care and Youth Development, a longitudinal study of more than 1,000 U.S. children focusing on the immediate and long-term effects of child care on children and families.

C. Chris Payne, PhD, is assistant professor of Human Development and Family Studies and director of Birth–Kindergarten Student Teaching at the University of North Carolina–Greensboro, where her research program focuses on the influence of early care and school environments on children's development across early and middle childhood, in particular, parent involvement and teacher preparation in children's early care and schooling. Dr. Payne is co-principal investigator of two collaborative interdisciplinary, longitudinal studies that focus on the influences of family and early child care on children's development and school success: the National Institute of Child Health and Human Development Study of Early Child Care and Enhancing Child Preschool Readiness in Early Head Start.

Patsy Pierce earned her PhD from the University of North Carolina–Chapel Hill where she developed her research interest in literacy for children with disabilities. A frequent national and international speaker and consultant, Dr. Pierce is currently preschool language and literacy consultant in North Carolina's Department of Public Instruction, Division for Exceptional Children.

Clara C. Pratt, PhD, recently retired from the B. E. Knudson Chair in Family Policy at Oregon State University, where she also directed the Family Study Policy Center and conducted research and evaluation to improve the lives of families at all stages of the lifespan. Since 1995, Dr. Pratt and her colleagues have designed outcome accountability systems for community-based prevention programs and, most recently, community mobilization initiatives targeting critical child and family issues.

Andrea Profio, BS, was, at the time of her authorship, a senior and NC Teaching Fellow at Meredith College in Raleigh, NC, majoring in Child Development and also obtaining her Birth–Kindergarten teaching licensure. A portion of her chapter was developed as part of her Honors Thesis.

Diantha D. Schull is president of Libraries for the Future, a national organization recognized by public, corporate, and nonprofit leaders for its role in expanding awareness and support for libraries across the country through its *Equal Access Libraries, Family Place,* and *Reading America* programs. A much sought after trainer in professional staff development, Ms. Schull was the Executive Director of the French-American Foundation, where she directed cross-cultural policy projects including major bilateral studies of Early Childhood Education and Urban Development and currently serves as a member of the Board of the Mid-Hudson Library Foundation and the National Advisory Committee of The Children's Partnership.

Catherine Snow, PhD, is the Henry Lee Shattuck Professor of Education in the Human Development and Psychology Department at the Harvard Graduate School of Education, where her research interests focus on children's language development, including the role of the family and cultural differences in familial roles related to language, literacy development, social and familial influences on literacy development, acquisition of English and bilingualism in language minority children, and literacy acquisition in a second language. The author of numerous journal articles and books, Dr. Snow chaired the National Research Council Committee on Preventing Reading Difficulties in Young Children, which produced two books that have been widely adopted as a basis for reform of reading instruction and professional development related to young children and literacy.

Kimberly Stice, BA, is the director of curriculum for the National Head Start Family Literacy Center. From 2002–2005 she was coordinator for StoryQUEST: Celebrating Beginning Language and Literacy, an Early Childhood Professional Development grant project through the U.S. Department of Education. Her background includes teaching infants, toddlers, and young children with special needs and providing training and technical assistance related to infants and toddlers with disabilities to American Indian and Alaska Native Early Head Start programs.

Vicki L. Turbiville holds a PhD from the University of Kansas in Special Education with a focus on families of children with disabilities. She was a speech-language pathologist in both public and private schools and currently consults nationally from her Texas home.

Shannon B. Wanless, MS, is a doctoral student in Human Development and Family Sciences at Oregon State University. As a result of her experience as a Head Start teacher, Shannon's research interests focus on maintaining emotionally healthy environments for young children, and also on issues of school readiness.

Ann P. Zukoski, PhD, is an assistant professor at Oregon State University, Department of Public Health. With over 15 years' experience in planning, implementing, and evaluating community-based initiatives, Dr. Zukoski studies literacy promotion by individuals, families, and public and private organizations to stimulate public systems and policies to support early childhood development.